THE LDS
MOTHER'S
ALMANAC

THE LDS
MOTHER'S ALMANAC

JANENE W. BAADSGAARD

DESERET
BOOK®
SALT LAKE CITY, UTAH

Visit us at deseretbook.com

Library of Congress Cataloging-in-Publication Data

Baadsgaard, Janene Wolsey.
    The LDS mother's almanac / Janene Wolsey Baadsgaard.
      p.   cm.
    Includes index.
    ISBN 1-57008-907-8 (pbk.)
    1. Mothers—Religious life.   2. Mormon women—Religious life.   3. Motherhood—Religious aspects—Mormon Church.   4. Child rearing—Religious aspects—Mormon Church.   I. Title: Latter-day Saints mother's almanac. II. Title.

    BX8641.B22 2003
    248.8'431'088283—dc21   2003001569

Printed in the United States of America   54459-7026
Malloy Lithographing Incorporated, Ann Arbor, MI

10   9   8   7   6   5   4   3   2   1

for my children

April
Aubrey
Jordan
Arianne
Joseph
Jacob
Amy
Ashley
John
Alisa

CONTENTS

SECTION ONE: BETTER BEGINNINGS

*"We declare that God's commandment for His children to
multiply and replenish the earth remains in force."*
—The Family: A Proclamation to the World

SECTION TWO: UNDERSTANDING THE BASICS

*"Parents have a sacred duty to rear their children in love and righteousness, to provide for their
physical and spiritual needs, to teach them to love and serve one another, to observe the commandments of God and to be law-abiding citizens wherever they live."*
—The Family: A Proclamation to the World

SECTION THREE: CREATING CELEBRATIONS

*"Successful marriages and families are established and maintained on principles of
faith, prayer, repentance, forgiveness, respect, love, compassion, work,
and wholesome recreational activities"*
—The Family: A Proclamation to the World

SECTION FOUR: ENCOURAGING EXPRESSION

"Mothers are primarily responsible for the nurture of their children."
—The Family: A Proclamation to the World

SECTION FIVE: RENEWING THE SPIRIT

*"Happiness in family life is most likely to be achieved when founded
upon the teachings of the Lord Jesus Christ."*

—The Family: A Proclamation to the World

FOREWORD

Mothers are given the greatest task known to man—raising children. Through her children, each mother touches the world and influences the progress of society for good or bad. What an incredible responsibility for mothers at every stage of life: the woman who contemplates future motherhood and becomes overwhelmed at the thought of raising children and the mother at the other end of the spectrum whose children are leaving the nest and who struggles with the conflict of being in control while still encouraging her children to be independent. Both women need guidance. Luckily, encouragement and advice for all Latter-day Saint mothers is here.

The LDS Mother's Almanac is a complete manual for motherhood. Janene Baadsgaard has undertaken the enormous task of sharing in print much of what she has learned while raising her family of ten children. As you read this book, you will learn about family health, child development, nutrition, relationships, spirituality, housework, artwork, and the joy of being a mother, among other things.

When parents arrive at new crossroads or are faced with difficult challenges, they often find themselves struggling to know what to do. Some may rely on their own experience. Others, who are lucky, have trusted friends or family members who can give them advice. Now all LDS parents have *The LDS Mother's Almanac,* a comprehensive parenting book written with the Latter-day Saint family in mind and covering many of the concerns unique to our heritage and culture. The *Almanac* helps parents know what to expect as their children mature and enter Church activity. It provides numerous ideas that will help children grow strong as individuals and in the gospel. Many of society's ills could be solved if parents really knew how to care for their children, not only temporally but

emotionally and spiritually as well. We have frequently been frustrated in our professional careers with not being able to impart completely the great responsibility of parents in the rearing of tender, young children. Janene Baadsgaard understands that responsibility perfectly and presents idea after idea for parents who wish to teach children by example and love and by organizing their families on the same principles.

But don't think this book is only spiritual or emotional in nature! In fact, the first section of *The LDS Mother's Almanac* is full of pertinent and accurate medical information. All parents need sound medical advice to insure the well-being of their children. Sometimes this advice is given in the doctor's office during a routine checkup. But frequently medical advice is needed at inconvenient times, such as the middle of the night while comforting a sick child. *The LDS Mother's Almanac* provides sound medical advice any time, night or day.

The *Almanac's* "medical coursework" begins with early pregnancy. See pages 7 and 23, for instance, for information on what women can do to help prevent birth defects. Pages 161 through 167 make up a primer on basic childhood illnesses and practical tips on dealing with these illnesses at home. One of our favorite sections was the concise presentation of first aid from a mother's point of view. The importance of being a partner with your pediatrician in helping to raise your child is also emphasized. Armed with the pages of this book and information provided by

their pediatricians, mothers should feel confident that they are equipped with the knowledge necessary to best care for the medical and physical needs of their children.

While *The LDS Mother's Almanac* provides a vast amount of information and help for every LDS mother, it is the spirit in which the book is written that captures its readers. We are the parents of eight beautiful children whom we love very dearly. As we read her suggestions and observations, Janene's love of children and of motherhood shone through her writing. This book makes moms feel good about being moms. The importance of having a sense of humor while parenting is also evident. Moms will chuckle as they relate to the funny experiences Janene shares in her mothering stories. It is likely that readers will also shed a tear or two as they are touched by the stories of tenderness and love inherent in raising children.

One of the greatest gifts we can give our children is our love. Every mother is different, just as every child is different. But love is constant. Seeking help and information about mothering is an act of love to our children. In Psalm 113:9 we read, "be a joyful mother of children." *The LDS Mother's Almanac* expresses the joy found in being a mom, while providing everyday, practical advice in all areas of motherhood. *The LDS Mother's Almanac* by Janene Baadsgaard is an invaluable guide for every Latter-day Saint mother.

—*D. Mark Valentine, M.D., pediatrician
Julie Valentine, B.S.N., R.N.*

A NOTE FROM THE AUTHOR

When my publisher called one afternoon and calmly asked me to consider writing a comprehensive book for Latter-day Saint mothers, my first thought was, *I don't have time to write a comprehensive book for mothers. I don't even know how to be one.* I politely told her I'd think about it and, frankly, that's all I planned to do . . . think about it.

Later a string of events followed that changed my mind and gave me new motivation to try. First I witnessed the terrorist attacks of September 11, 2001, and thought of all the children left without a parent for the rest of their lives. I wondered what those mothers would have longed to tell their children had they known they weren't going to be around. Next my oldest married daughter *and* son announced I was going to be a new grandma twice over and wanted recommendations for a good book with solid information *and* down-to-earth advice to help them on their perilous new journey. Then a generous reader sent me a letter thanking me for writing books with helpful ideas for mothers and encouraged me to write more because her own mother had passed away unexpectedly and wasn't around to talk to. That's when it occurred to me that if I had something to share about being a mother, I better share it . . . now.

As a result of all this, I've attempted to compile the wealth of information I wish I'd had when I became a mother 25 years ago. I've snatched short moments to write while my toddler crayoned masterpieces on the living room walls and in the groggy midnight hours waiting for my teenagers to make it home before curfew. I've written about giving birth, toilet training, throwing weddings, and sending children off on missions while I've been experiencing it. I've been distracted, interrupted, and continually humbled and mystified because I've been

writing about and *living* this motherhood business 24/7.

Please forgive my omissions and limitations, for there are many. This book is an attempt to share—not fill the impossible role of know-it-all encyclopedia or perfect example. No one can write a book with everything a mother needs to know because it's not likely that anyone really does know *everything* about motherhood. The suggestions in this book are not the only or even necessarily the right way for *you* to do things. You'll have to figure that out for yourself. My suggestions are intended to give you *ideas* and *support* on your journey through motherhood. This book is my honest and heartfelt attempt to make sense of the jumble of conflicting information available to LDS mothers these days and pass along some *simplifying, restorative,* and *practical* insights based on long years of trial and error that are still in progress.

After 25 years of writing about and raising ten children of my own, I know full well that experts and researchers will always disagree and keep changing their minds. Yet, the truly needful things you learn right in your own home laboratory and in the secret recesses of your heart—those things don't change that much through the years and need to be passed along from one busy mother to another with sweet comradeship, mutual awe, and love.

BETTER BEGINNINGS

BEGINNINGS

Whether you're having your first baby or your last, a positive reading on your pregnancy test is bound to overwhelm you with a flood of concerns. That deluge of emotions will keep you off balance for the next nine months *and quite possibly for the rest of your life.* You may be absolutely ecstatic; you may also be scared or even in a state of denial or complete shock. There is no *right* way to respond to the news that you will soon become someone's mother.

Luckily, nature gives you nine months to adjust. If your pregnancy is planned and eagerly anticipated, you may not be able to quit smiling or crying for days. You may find yourself calling every friend or relative you know to tell. Or you may be quietly reluctant and self-conscious about sharing the news. How you respond to and share the news of imminent motherhood is as individual as you are.

One thing is certain, those anxious nine months of pregnancy and the first year of your child's life will be an adventure you will never forget. Because no two babies are alike, each pregnancy and each first year of life will be a unique experience for both you and your child. You may have the opportunity of encountering baby beginnings only once or many, many times. No matter how

many times you take part in the beginning of life, you will have moments of reverent awe as you realize you are involved in the highest partnership you've ever known. You will also have moments when you are certain you are simply not up to the task.

And, no matter how many times you've done this, you may always feel like a rookie. Sooner or later something like this will dawn on you: "I don't know what *I'm* doing; and the whole world is being run by people just like me." This startling insight can be totally unnerving or the catalyst for a good hearty laugh.

So relax. Don't be overwhelmed with your seeming incompetence. All mothers are rookies whether we're having our first or our last. We're all muddling along day after day trying to do the best we know how. Learning to love someone more than yourself, even once, will not leave you untouched or unchanged. God is working his wonders through you. You are his partner in this, the miracle of life.

When you're a first-time mother it's hard to see the end from the beginning. The ability to conceive and then bear children is often taken casually. Sometimes it's difficult for a mother to understand what she has been given because she's blinded by what she *seems* to be giving up—a trim body, time, sleep, money, freedom. Before we've had one of our own, the vast majority of us do not comprehend what it means to be given a child, let alone think about the fact that how this child is reared will affect hundreds of people for generations. And it's a good thing that most people don't understand this idea before becoming pregnant. Otherwise, no one would ever dare have a child.

Eventually, however, after the peripheral excitement and worry have died down a little and you have had some quiet time to reflect on the new life inside of you, you will begin to experience glimpses of this ultimate truth: your opportunity to bear, raise, and care for children is, without a doubt, God's greatest gift to you.

Once I read about the last hours of a famous author. On his deathbed a reporter asked him if he was content surrounded by all his great works and the prize-winning books he'd written. The author turned to the reporter and replied, "If I had it to do over again, each one of those books would be a dearly loved child or grandchild."

You have the privilege of being someone's mother. There is nothing more important you can do with your life.

PREGNANCY

Planned Pregnancy

If your pregnancy is planned and eagerly anticipated, allow yourself the luxury to celebrate. When, where, and how soon to tell your family and friends is entirely up to you. Some women like to share the good news as soon as they find out. Make sure your husband is the first to know. If you have other children, they should be second in line. Next you can tell your extended family and friends.

Some couples like to wait for a few months to tell their family, friends, and other children about the baby for a variety of reasons. One reason some couples wait is because of the possibility of having a miscarriage. They believe that the fewer people who know, the less disappointment there will be if something goes wrong. In reality, the more people who know about your pregnancy, the more people there will be to offer love and support if something goes wrong. Celebrating the gift of life, when you're ready to share, is always the right thing to do.

If your pregnancy is planned but you've previously experienced a miscarriage or stillbirth, you may find yourself feeling worried about what might happen or trying to hold back your feelings until you know if

things are going to work out this time. Each pregnancy is precarious at best and parents who have lost children know first-hand just how fragile life is. Your apprehensive feelings are normal, but don't let them block your happiness.

Surprise Pregnancy

If the pregnancy is a surprise, you may be caught so off guard that you panic or find yourself swirling into a state of despair. Give yourself all the time you need to adjust to the news. Don't think you're a bad person or will be a bad mother if you feel desperate, scared, or sad for a while. Nature thankfully gives you nine months to prepare yourself for birth. Nine months will either seem like forever or be way too short, depending on your state of mind and body.

Be gentle with yourself and pray for comfort and reassurance. Eliminate any unnecessary stress in your life. Cut back on your workload and responsibilities. Ask your husband or another worthy priesthood holder for a blessing. Be honest about your feelings and allow your spouse to be part of the adjustment period. Given enough time, you'll come to know that *every* baby is a blessing from God. Trust Him. Where he sends his little lambs, green pastures will follow. My doctor told me if every pregnancy were planned, he wouldn't stay very busy.

A Hormonal Roller-Coaster Ride

Pregnancy is bound to strap you into a hormonal/emotional roller-coaster ride . . . so brace yourself. Warn those who love you that you may not be quite yourself occasionally. You may find yourself snapping at people when you're normally mild

mannered. At other times you might find yourself crying at the strangest times for reasons you don't understand yourself. When you're having a dramatic day, chalk it up to hormones and try to keep your perspective by rediscovering your sense of humor. Look in the mirror and chuckle instead of crying. Count your blessings: you don't have to worry about birth control or put up with menstrual cramps, and your doctor will actually advise you *not* to diet.

Trying *not* to feel what you're actually feeling is way too hard. Let yourself run through a list of varied emotions, talk about them, *and then* don't take those feelings too seriously because they will probably change in about two minutes. Hormones will do that to you. If no one will listen to you or feel sorry for you, talk to your Father in Heaven. He always listens and understands. Don't worry. Things usually look better in a day or two.

Living with Pregnancy 24/7

Pregnancy has the tendency to consume your thoughts and actions. Don't be surprised if you bring up the subject in every conversation and annoy your companions with talk of weird aches, pains, and fears all the time.

Your husband will probably consider the fact that you are pregnant once or twice a

day. You, on the other hand, will be aware of your pregnancy 24 hours a day. You might have more trouble focusing on and completing projects or feeling like the things that were once important still are. Or, you may find yourself in a new creative mode. You may be excited, stressed, or bored. In other words, how you feel during your pregnancy will change from moment to moment, week to week, and month to month.

Do keep a journal—one for yourself and one for your child. There will probably be moments when you'll be more emotional and moody than usual and find yourself bothered by things that you can normally take in stride. Be gentle with yourself. Pregnancy is truly a roller-coaster ride of ups and downs, highs and lows, and everything in between. Try to relax and enjoy the ride.

If you just grit your teeth and wait for the big reward at the end of the line, you're bound to miss half the fun. So keep your sense of humor and perspective. My doctor once told me that the hormonal difference between a pregnant woman and a non-pregnant woman is as much as the hormonal difference between a non-pregnant woman and a man. Think of it—you're a whole new hormonal creature for nine months. Enjoy the hills and valleys. What makes nine months of pregnancy so exciting is the same thing that makes a roller-coaster ride fun: the element of surprise . . . you never know what to expect next.

Just imagine, in a mere 266 days, you'll produce a totally new human being who will insist on waking you up in the middle of the night just because he needs to burp.

Now let's talk a bit more about those miraculous nine months.

THE FIRST TRIMESTER

I JUST FOUND OUT I'M PREGNANT. WHAT DO I DO NEXT?

After your drug store pregnancy test reads positive you'll want to make an appointment to see your healthcare professional. And even before your first appointment you should start taking a good prenatal vitamin. When you call for the appointment, the receptionist will tell you when your doctor wants to see you for the first time. It may not be for several weeks, or, if you're bleeding or at a high risk for miscarriage, it may be right away. Many OB/GYNs wait to see patients until the pregnancy is 10 to 12 weeks along.

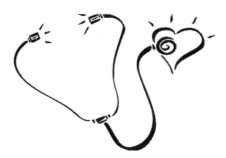

CHOOSING A DOCTOR/MIDWIFE

After you find out you're pregnant, ask friends, family members, neighbors, co-workers, or ward members for their suggestions in selecting a good doctor or nurse-midwife in your area. Having a baby

VITAL PRENATAL VITAMINS

Taking prenatal vitamins is an important and inexpensive nutritional insurance plan for women in their childbearing years. Most doctors advise pregnant and nursing women to take supplemental vitamins in addition to eating a nutritious diet. Prenatal vitamins can be purchased over the counter or by a prescription from your doctor. Here are some important facts about prenatal vitamins:

- Women need essential vitamins in their system *before* they become pregnant.
- Folic acid, an important vitamin every mother should take, is necessary for the proper development of a growing fetus. Insufficient folic acid in the diet increases the risk that a fetus will develop spina bifida or other neural tube defects. Spina bifida can occur in a developing fetus *before* a woman knows she is pregnant.
- All women of childbearing age should consume at least 400 micrograms of folic acid a day.
- Green leafy vegetables and legumes are rich in folic acid.
- Both folic acid and vitamin B_{12} function interdependently in the formation of normal red blood cells and in the production of an essential building block of DNA called thymidine. A deficiency of either of these results in the fetus having a serious anemia where the red blood cells are few in number but large in size.
- While you're pregnant and nursing you have an increased need for all nutrients. This is to prevent malnutrition and other serious conditions in yourself and your baby. Remember to continue eating a nutritious diet and taking prenatal vitamins while you're nursing. When you're not pregnant or nursing, eating a nutritious diet and taking a good prenatal vitamin will give you the peace of mind that you're doing all you can to promote good health for yourself and your future children.
- Taking prenatal vitamins causes an increase in nausea in some women. If this happens to you, try taking your pill with meals or right before going to bed at night. You can also ask your doctor to prescribe a different vitamin to see if it is less likely to cause nausea.

is a normal body function, not a medical procedure. Still, you'll want someone at your birth who knows when things are going well and when emergency help is needed. You need someone with years of training, experience, and a personality that matches your needs. Both doctors and nurse-midwives have their advantages and disadvantages. Mothers who are expecting multiples or whose pregnancies are considered high-risk due to such problems as diabetes, high blood pressure, or babies in a breech or transverse position who won't move, should choose an obstetrician. If a qualified OB/GYN isn't available in your area or through your insurance provider, you may want to select a family practice physician who also delivers babies.

Obstetricians

If you prefer the security of a hospital for your delivery, with all the latest equipment and best-trained professionals on hand in case of an emergency, you'll likely choose an obstetrician to see you throughout your pregnancy.

Obstetricians work in a variety of different office environments. The most common are solo practices (the obstetrician works for himself or herself) and partnerships or group medical practices (several obstetricians work together).

At some group practices, your own doctor will see you personally at each of your appointments as often as possible. Because an obstetrician's job is to deliver babies, however, there will be times when your doctor is away delivering a baby and you'll either have to see another doctor at the clinic or wait until your doctor returns. In these situations, you'll probably be able to develop a good relationship with your doctor and he or she will likely be the doctor who delivers your baby.

At other clinics, the practice is set up so that expectant mothers see each doctor who works in the practice before their delivery. The doctor who is on call when you go into labor will deliver your baby. One advantage of the second type of group clinic is that you seldom wait as long for appointments because the practice has someone delivering babies *and* someone else seeing patients. One disadvantage is that you never know whom you're going to see for an appointment or who will deliver you.

When choosing an OB/GYN, ask enough questions to help you get a feel for his or her philosophy on childbirth and prenatal care. Some doctors are willing to spend extra time at the end of an appointment answering questions. Others may be more rushed. Some doctors are likely to encourage episiotomies during childbirth, while others leave the decision up to the mother. You may want to write down what you would like to happen during your delivery and make sure the OB/GYN you choose is agreeable to your terms.

Nurse-midwives

Most nurse-midwives take only low-risk patients and offer a backup doctor on call along with an operating room nearby. Some mothers prefer a nurse-midwife because they are more likely to offer unhurried appointments and provide more education in pregnancy, nutrition, childbirth, and breastfeeding. Nurse-midwives often give expectant women greater freedom to control their activities during labor. Studies also suggest nurse-midwives offer more help throughout the entire labor and delivery, use fewer painkillers, and don't perform episiotomies as often as doctors do. Your nurse-midwife should be board certified. Lay midwives don't have special education, usually deliver babies at home, and can't prescribe medication. Certified nurse-midwives are legal in all 50 states, are licensed with college degrees, write prescriptions, and deliver babies in hospitals and birthing centers.

At this time, fewer than ten percent of deliveries are assisted by nurse-midwives in the United States. Of these, 96 percent occur in hospitals, 3 percent in birthing centers, and 1 percent at home. If a midwife's patient wants an epidural and is in a hospital, the midwife can have an anethesiologist administer one. If you are interested in a certified midwife, you can contact the women's health office at your local hospital or review your insurance company's list of providers.

I've heard numerous horror stories about both doctors and nurse-midwives over the years. Don't let the stories you've heard color your decision. The whole point of having professional help is to spot and stop potential life-threatening problems in pregnancy and to secure a healthy mother and baby after delivery. In the vast majority of cases nothing goes wrong and everything works out just fine.

Before you make the final decision on what healthcare provider you want to use, you can call or make appointments to interview them. Remember to look for someone who will take the time to talk to you and treat you with respect. You don't want someone who scares, intimidates, or rushes you. Choose someone who will answer your questions without making you feel like an idiot and someone who is gentle, understanding, and discreet. Remember, you are the boss. Your doctor or midwife is hired help. Whatever choice you make, it should be *your* choice based on solid information.

Ask Questions

Once you've chosen a doctor or midwife, don't be afraid to ask questions. Most doctors will gladly discuss weight gain, diet, and embryo growth with pregnant women. But sometimes the information will be given out so quickly it will whiz in one ear and out the other before you hop off the examination table. If you want to know more, purchase a few pregnancy books at your local bookstore—or check them out from the library. Most books will be able to answer all your questions in detail. You can also find a lot of good information on the Internet at a variety of sites designed specifically for expecting parents. You'll have lots of very scientific questions like, "Why is my belly button poking out?" and "Why do they call it morning sickness if I always feel nauseous at night?" No matter your question, remember that the only stupid question is one that never gets asked and causes you a lot of unnecessary worry.

CHOOSING WHERE TO HAVE YOUR BABY

As you choose an obstetrician, nurse-midwife, or family practice doctor to see you throughout your pregnancy, don't forget the important decision of where you actually want to deliver your baby. Obstetricians typically deliver in a hospital. Nurse-midwives may deliver in hospitals or at home but also use birthing centers with a nearby backup hospital. Wherever you have your baby, make sure you'll be within ten minutes of a hospital so you can have an emergency cesarean section or other emergency procedure if necessary. Tour several birthing centers and hospitals before you decide where to deliver. Make sure your insurance will cover expenses at that facility. Most hospitals have you pre-register sometime early in the third trimester to make admitting run smoothly and quickly when the time comes.

Hospital

A hospital is by far the most common choice for delivery because emergency equipment and highly qualified medical teams are present in the event that something goes wrong. Most newly built or remodeled hospitals include a women's center or wing with large birthing rooms and private postpartum suites. Some hospitals even have private rooms where a mother can stay from labor to discharge.

If you have a choice, consider a hospital that will give you a private room and bathroom, a labor nurse who is not spread too thin between too many patients, and a lactation expert on staff to help you start breastfeeding. You'll also want an anesthesiologist who is on duty around the clock

and who won't be tied up in surgery with other patients when you need him most.

If you tour the hospital you'll probably notice that the surgical delivery room (where you would be taken for a cesarean section) looks very sterile, somewhat empty, scary, and awfully bright. It may remind you of the examination room in a B-grade outer-space movie where aliens poke human beings to see what makes them tick. If, in fact, you do use the surgical delivery room for a cesarean section, your medical team and husband will have to put on outer clothing that actually makes them resemble spacemen.

Today the birthing rooms in most hospitals, as well as in birthing centers, are much nicer than the cold and sterile rooms your mothers labored in. These rooms came about because mothers demanded them. We were tired of being forced to lay flat on our backs with our legs in stirrups and our hands strapped down while being told it wouldn't hurt if we'd just breath correctly. So instead of facing a mass retreat to home births, the medical community finally compromised and attempted to give us the best of both worlds: a more relaxed, homelike atmosphere and greater freedom to control the labor and delivery experience. As a result, birthing rooms came into being.

Birthing rooms are designed to resemble your bedroom at home. They usually include nice curtains at the window, a rocking chair for Dad, color-coordinated wallpaper, a nice picture on the wall, and maybe even a flower arrangement—all to convince you that this is *not* where painful things happen. Most birthing rooms hide the scary looking medical equipment behind closet doors and in

POINTS TO CONSIDER

When choosing a facility for your labor and delivery, be sure to ask about the following:
- visiting hours
- restrictions on visitors
- birthing rooms
- the number of people allowed in the room at the time of birth
- nursery and rooming-in rules
- security concerns
- emergency procedures and equipment
- lactation specialists and classes
- pain relief options
- natural childbirth assistance

cabinets. They also have a special bed you can stay in throughout labor, delivery, and recovery. These beds are designed to be adjustable so you can deliver in whatever position you prefer.

Birthing Center

A birthing center is a compromise between a home and hospital birth and is equipped to handle normal, uncomplicated pregnancies. By providing a homelike atmosphere and allowing family and friends to be present, they help women have an informal, personal experience. If complications develop, these centers usually have an arrangement with a nearby hospital to transfer a woman quickly. Birthing centers usually offer amenities like a Jacuzzi to aid women in labor. Most are located near a hospital and stays are typically four to 24 hours.

Birthing centers have become more popular because they encourage natural childbirth and give mothers more control over the birth experience. A birthing center is usually run by a nurse-midwife who has been certified; but you will need to ask if there is a physician overseeing the center. If you're considering a birthing center be sure to ask if they screen mothers for high-risk pregnancies and deliveries. Know what backup arrangements they have for both you and the baby in case of an emergency. Also ask how long you stay after delivery and find out if your insurance will cover the cost.

Home Birth

A home birth is quite economical and can be very meaningful, but should be considered only if you have competent help and no known problems. Home deliveries are more risky because of unexpected complications such as sudden detachment of the placenta, fetal distress (lack of oxygen), unexpected multiples, and complications after delivery, such as excessive bleeding. Home deliveries should be considered only by women who have had at least one uneventful delivery. A home near a hospital should be used along with a plan for rapid transport.

Choosing the Safest Option

My first children were delivered in hospital delivery rooms because there was no other safe choice. My later children were delivered in birthing rooms. My last was delivered in an operating room because of a necessary cesarean section. I've had two miscarriages in hospital emergency rooms and one at home. I'm grateful new mothers have several safe options today. My mother was rendered unconscious with general anesthesia for her deliveries back in the days when that was the norm. My grandma had her children at home because she had no other choice, and six of them died. Whatever you decide, it's always wise to go with a safe choice for your own peace of mind.

YOUR DUE DATE

When you schedule your first doctor's appointment, you'll enter into a world where pregnancy really isn't the nine-month's-long event you always thought it was. Instead, you'll learn all about *gestational age, trimesters,* and a whole new way of looking at the seven days that make up a week—those seven days will seem like seven years as you near the end.

Gestational Age

When you make that first appointment you'll likely discuss your due date briefly with the nurse-midwife or a nurse or medical assistant at the OB/GYN's office. Because most women don't know the exact date of conception but can usually remember the beginning of their last menstrual period, a majority of doctors use the menstruation cycle as a basis for determining a baby's due date. Pregnancy is,

therefore, most often dated from the first day of your last period. The medical term for this type of calculation is the *gestational age.* Using a gestational age gives doctors a standard to follow as they track your baby's development, chart your own progress, and order specific tests and procedures. It is also about two weeks earlier than the day you ovulated and most likely conceived your baby. But who's counting, right?

Calculating the Day

Pregnancy lasts about 280 days, or 40 weeks. To calculate your due date, add 280 days to the first day of bleeding of your last period. If your last period began on February 1, your baby's estimated due date would be 280 days later: November 8.

Trimesters

Once an estimated due date has been established, your doctor or midwife will likely begin referring to your pregnancy in weeks. Those weeks will be grouped into three trimesters. Each trimester lasts approximately 13 weeks and is full of important milestones in your baby's development. During the first trimester, for example, all of your baby's organs will develop.

40 Weeks Is Not the 9 Months I Thought It Would Be

In the past, you probably imagined that babies simply and suddenly appeared as the product of wishful thinking on your mother's part. Your babies, on the other hand, will definitely *not* appear quite so easily. Your medical professional will probably tell you that you'll be pregnant for nine months, but they often leave out the following information on pregnancy stages that you simply need to know.

Stage One: In the early part of stage one, you are either in shock, denial, or a state of joyful bliss about being pregnant. This early stage lasts for about 27 seconds before the "Oh, boy, am I ever pregnant!" segment of your nine-month journey begins. At this stage you may well spend most of your time racing for the toilet, which has suddenly taken on several practical uses these days. Food is not your friend. Even the sight of anything resembling food can make you gag. It isn't just morning sickness but all-day-and-night sickness. You have about as much energy as a hound dog on a hot day in July sunning on the porch.

Stage Two: During stage two you furiously attempt to make up for stage one by answering the question that everyone seems to be asking you: "Where did all the food go?" "I ate it," you answer. "Yes, all of it. I'm hungry. I'm hungry all the time. I have to make up for lost time in stage one." Stage two is also the "take a breather" part of pregnancy. Someone upstairs must have designed it that way so

women would have more than one baby per life span. In this stage you're almost over the complete exhaustion and nausea and you haven't yet reached the huge, clumsy, and uncomfortable stage. You can still do simple necessary tasks like squatting down and getting back up, tying your shoes, and reaching your kitchen sink. Count your blessings. This stage will quickly pass.

Stage Three: Where in stage one you resemble a pear and in stage two you looked like a cantaloupe . . . in stage three you look like you swallowed a watermelon in one bite without even burping up the pits. You bump into everything and fit into nothing. You can't eat, sleep, work, or remain vertical comfortably, and you're tired of having a good attitude. Everything aches or feels like it's falling out. You are sick and tired of all the stares you get in public. You can't reach the steering wheel and the gas pedal at the same time, and your panty hose are always slipping down around your ankles. By the time you go into labor, you don't care what it takes, you just want to get stage three over with. That foolish thought leads to stage four.

Stage Four: Stage four is when you are actually in labor. This is where medical people with smiles on their faces proceed to make small talk, strap all sorts of bands and cords around your protruding middle, invite several total strangers into the room to stare at your private parts, and then tell you it won't hurt if you just breathe correctly. Now, mind you, this is in addition to the actual pain of labor. Labor is definitely when you feel like you are giving birth to that watermelon you swallowed whole in stage three.

Stage Five: Stage five comes when all that labor and delivery stuff is over and you're resting comfortably in your bed. At this point, another foolish thought will probably pass through your brain: "I'm so glad the hard part is over." In stage five you'll feel as relieved and comfortable as you'll ever be. After all, the hard part is just beginning.

WHAT SHOULD I EXPECT AT MY DOCTOR'S APPOINTMENTS?

Your first appointment usually includes an internal exam to confirm the drug store pregnancy test, along with a general physical exam, a chat about any past pregnancies, and a review of your general health history. You may also receive a pap test and have a sample of your blood drawn

DO I REALLY HAVE TO TAKE ALL THOSE TESTS?

Some tests are necessary to ensure a healthy pregnancy. Others are optional and sometimes do nothing more than cause a mother-to-be unnecessary stress and worry.

Tests that all pregnant women should agree to include:

- **A complete blood workup.** This is done at one of your first appointments and includes checking for infections, anemia, and determining your Rh factor. This is routine and includes only the stick of a needle and the drawing of a few vials of blood.
- **Glucose tolerance test.** This test, which tests moms for gestational diabetes, is generally done around 28 weeks. It is very important to screen for gestational diabetes, as it can cause severe problems for the baby. It is also a simple, though sometimes nasty-tasting, test. A mom-to-be drinks a sweet, soda-like drink that contains a large amount of glucose. Her blood is then drawn an hour later, and the glucose levels are tested. Some moms fail this test and must take an additional test. Many times there is nothing wrong. Other times, your doctor will determine that you have or are at risk for gestational diabetes and must go on a prescribed diet.

Tests that are optional but often performed include:

- **Triple-screen blood test.** This test assesses the risk of chromosomal problems through analysis of a blood sample taken at about 16 weeks gestation. Unfortunately, this test has a fairly high percentage of reporting abnormal levels when the fetus is absolutely fine. For this reason, many women choose not to take the test and then be plagued by unnecessary concerns about their fetus's well-being. The only way to absolutely detect chromosomal abnormalities is through amniocentesis, which can be risky to your baby and is not recommended for most women under 35.
- **Ultrasound test.** Most insurance companies will pay for one ultrasound test, typically performed around 18 to 20 weeks gestation. During this test a technician surveys your baby's vital organs and measures the fetus to estimate a delivery date.

for testing. This will be the most thorough visit of your pregnancy. After this appointment, you'll likely have appointments every four weeks until you hit 32 weeks, then every two weeks until you're 36 weeks, and then once a week until delivery.

Tests and Procedures

For each new appointment, you'll probably be given a urine test. Your urine will be tested for sugar, protein, and bacteria. High levels of sugar indicate diabetes, high levels of protein indicate preeclampsia (high blood pressure), and the presence of bacteria indicates an infection. Expect to have your blood pressure checked at each appointment and your expanding uterus measured. Your ankles will be examined for swelling.

The highlight of most appointments will be listening to your baby's heartbeat, which can be heard as early as eight weeks.

At some point in your pregnancy your doctor will probably order a complete blood workup and a glucose test. An ultrasound test might also be ordered to check things like amniotic fluid levels, the baby's due date and position, and whether the baby has any major problems. This test may also tell you whether you're having a girl or boy. Dating of a pregnancy is most accurate at 12 weeks and again at 18 to 20 weeks.

Why Do They Have to Weigh Me?

Expect to participate in the weighing-in ceremony all pregnant women hate. Try not to blow this ritual out of proportion. Most pregnant women hate being weighed at regular monthly appointments. But professionals must chart your weight gain to detect a variety of potential problems. And even though it feels more like you're

TIPPING THE SCALES

Expect to gain about five pounds in the first few months and about a pound or so a week after that. But don't panic if you have a month or two of whopping weight gain especially around the fifth, sixth, or seventh month. Weight gain is highly variable. Some women will gain weight early in their pregnancies and taper off at the end. Others won't gain any weight the first trimester, but will continue to gain weight right up until delivery.

APPROPRIATE PREGNANCY WEIGHT GAIN

Body Type	Appropriate Gain (in pounds)
Underweight	28 to 40
Normal weight	25 to 35
Overweight	15 to 25

taking a test and always failing—because you keep gaining weight—you really are being successful if you gain some weight between each appointment.

If you find yourself anticipating your appointments by suddenly becoming paranoid about everything you eat, or you start dieting, wearing lightweight clothing to your appointment, taking off your shoes at the scale, or fasting before you step on, Stop! Please remember you're *supposed* to be gaining weight.

You can also tell your doctor, "I don't want any unnecessary weight-gain lectures unless there's a serious problem," and he or she will likely honor your request.

What If I'm over 35?

If you're over 35 be prepared to be called "high-risk." That title sounds scary but it's better than being called old and worn out. Most medical professionals are trained to tell women *not* to have any more babies after a certain age. That decision is not the doctor's to make. Each couple can seek more than one professional opinion and always pray and fast about their choice to conceive. When and how many children to conceive is possibly the most important decision you and your husband will ever make together and should be made very carefully.

If you're an older expectant mother, your doctor might also want to order extra tests. Always ask what the test is for and why the test was ordered. If you're not going to terminate the pregnancy based on the results of any test, you might want to think twice before agreeing to it. Many tests are expensive, and the results can create undue concern and worry, while others increase the chance of miscarriage.

FIRST TRIMESTER CONCERNS AND COMPLAINTS

Exhaustion

Most expectant mothers feel a wave of exhaustion hit during the first few months. This is nature's way of making sure you slow down a bit and give your body the extra rest it needs to produce a growing baby. Even though you won't look like you're pregnant for a few months, all kinds of amazing things are happening inside you. Your body is doing a lot of extra work, and it's expected that you'll feel tired. If this is your first baby, take any time you can to nap and put up your feet. If you have other children at home already, find small things they can do to help you out so you can sit for a few minutes during the day and just take a break.

Increased Urination

If you're not already exhausted, you may become that way from getting up so often to go to the bathroom. Most expectant moms feel an increased need to urinate during the first few months of pregnancy because the uterus is pressing against the bladder. Plan ahead to make sure you're near a bathroom during the day and at night or you'll get pretty desperate.

Tender Breasts

You may experience a darkening of your nipples and enlargement and tenderness in your breasts, along with the need to buy a bigger bra. Breast changes occur throughout your pregnancy because of increased amounts of estrogen and progesterone in your body. The tenderness, however, often subsides after your third or fourth month.

TIPS TO HELP WITH QUEASINESS

- If you feel nauseous in the morning, stay in bed for a few extra minutes and try eating something like saltine crackers or a banana *before* getting up. Keep these items at your bedside just in case. And put some in your purse as well to nibble on throughout the day.
- If you feel nauseous at night, go for a walk and get some fresh air or go to bed early, cover your head with your pillow, and bawl. I'm serious here. A nice little crying session can do wonders for your well-being. Trying to act brave and strong when you really feel terrifically crummy makes you, and everybody else around you, crazy because you'll eventually blow your top over something trivial.
- Try eating several mini meals during the day and continue drinking plenty of fluids. It often helps to keep a little something on your stomach all the time, whether you're hungry or not.
- Keep trying to get eight glasses of water down a day.
- Some women find it helpful to fill up on protein-rich foods like poultry, eggs, and yogurt.
- Keep experimenting and don't give up. Make it your goal in life to find things that make you feel better, but don't be surprised if what works one day won't work the next.
- Don't feel guilty if you can only stand to eat certain foods for a while. Eating something is better than not eating anything.
- You may find strong odors will set you off, so steer clear of perfume and strong food odors.
- On the other hand, some smells can actually calm nausea. Try drinking some peppermint tea and breathing in the warm, scented steam as you do.
- Some women find that 50 milligrams of vitamin B_6 by mouth, twice a day, helps reduce nausea.
- Remember to call your doctor if you go more than a day or so without keeping anything down.

Nausea

Some mothers feel queasy throughout the early months, some never have nausea at all, and others barf up their heels so bad they wind up in the hospital dehydrated. Morning sickness occurs in 60 to 80 percent of all pregnancies and is typically caused by increased levels of estrogen and an expanding uterus. The term *morning sickness,* however, is a misnomer, so don't worry if you feel great in the mornings and horrible all night long. Experiment with whatever works to help you feel better. Nausea or a queasy feeling in your stomach, along with a weird off-balanced feeling in your head, is usually a good sign that you're still pregnant and things are going well—for the baby that is.

To keep from getting dehydrated when you're on the nausea roller coaster, it's better to drink small amounts of water (like a sip or a tablespoon at a time) all day long rather than guzzling down a cup or two at one sitting. You can carry a water bottle with you. Each healthcare professional, family member, and friend will have suggestions for what to do to help. Listen to everybody politely, experiment with what they say, then do whatever works for you. If standing on your head while drinking ginger tea laced with vitamin B6 works for you, go for it girl.

Fainting

You may also find you feel light-headed and faint during the first few months of pregnancy. Don't try to be brave and talk yourself out of it. If you feel a blackout coming on, sit down quickly and put your head between your legs or lie down until the feeling passes.

A fainting episode usually proceeds like this: First you'll feel yourself breaking out in a cold sweat. Pretty soon your head will feel like it's whirling, and your legs and arms will start feeling tingly. You might even feel like you're going to lose your lunch or your hearing. Then suddenly everything goes black and you wake up later with a bunch of strangers glaring down at you while you are sprawled very unladylike on the cold tile floor at Wal-Mart. Don't do it that way. You'll hit your head on something hard on the way down and you'll have a goose egg to add to your already long list of body-related complaints. Trust me on this one. It's *less* embarrassing to just lie down for a while *before* you pass out.

Eventually you'll reach your second trimester and the queasy, light-headed feeling will probably go away naturally.

Skin Changes

You may experience the so-called mask of pregnancy, a blotchy brownish pigment that appears on the skin of the forehead and cheeks. This occurs more often in dark-haired women and usually fades with time if you stay out of the sun and use a sunscreen with an SPF of 15 or higher. Another common skin condition is a dark line that appears down the middle of your abdomen. This is called the linea nigra, which means dark line. It is also more common in dark-haired women. It does not always go away after pregnancy but does tend to lighten.

TAKING CARE OF YOURSELF

You're going to feel better while you're pregnant if you eat a healthy diet, sleep when you're tired, take your vitamins, and find a mild form of non-jarring exercise to do every day. Discuss with your doctor an appropriate health regimen and diet. You shouldn't fast while you're pregnant or take medications without checking with your doctor first. Tobacco, alcohol, or caffeine aren't good for you or your baby. The whole Word of Wisdom is worth a second look and a promise of renewed compliance during pregnancy.

Dieting during pregnancy is not recommended, even if you're overweight. Don't take any drugs, including nonprescription drugs such as aspirin, without first checking with your doctor, especially in the first three months.

What's a Healthy Diet When You're Pregnant?

During pregnancy, all the nutrients you eat make their way into your bloodstream; and it is your blood that carries the nutrients to the placenta to feed the baby. If you don't eat right, then your baby won't either. When you're pregnant you'll need about 300 extra calories a day, roughly 2,400 to 2,600 calories altogether. You may need more if you're underweight or if you've had a baby, miscarriage, or stillbirth in the past year. You'll probably gain about 25 to 50 pounds.

You'll need about four servings of milk or milk products, three servings of grains, three servings of fruits or vegetables (emphasis on vitamin C), and two leafy green vegetables, the fresher the better. You also need 75 to 100 grams of protein a day. You can divide this into four servings of things like turkey, beef, fish, cottage cheese, soy products, eggs, and beans. Drink two quarts (that's eight cups) of water a day to help circulate blood, pre-

vent urinary tract infections, and metabolize protein.

One word of caution: 300 extra calories is not a lot. One glass of milk and a couple pieces of fruit quickly adds up to 300 calories, and one candy bar does the same. Of course, with the milk and fruit, you add extra calcium and vitamins.

COMMON WORRIES AND FEARS

When you find out you're pregnant, you're bound to have a million questions, doubts, and fears. Some of your worries will center on your own emotional and spiritual capabilities, others will focus on your own physical condition and your ability to endure nine months—not to mention a lifetime after that—of uncertainty and fear.

I Don't Know What to Do!

Every baby who is born into the universe comes with a brand new personality, destiny, and set of needs. Every mother is

obliged to muddle through making mistakes and trying to figure all of this out with each new child. There is no collective know-it-all wisdom simply because you've

---

KEGEL EXERCISES

One of the physical effects of childbirth that may leave you discouraged is decreased bladder control. Even delivering the smallest of babies stretches out your vaginal muscles and loosens everything up down there. Like many aspects of your physical well-being, however, you do have some control over getting your body back into shape and even overcoming incontinence—if it's been exacerbated by delivering a baby.

No woman should be in the dark about a helpful and easy exercise called a Kegel exercise. A Kegel exercise is the voluntary repeated contraction of your vaginal muscles. The exercises are simple once you know how to control the muscle, and they can be done anywhere at most anytime. If you don't know what muscles these are or how to contract them, imagine that you are trying to stop your urinary flow in midstream. That's a Kegel! You should do Kegel exercises throughout your entire pregnancy to keep your vaginal area in shape and prepared for labor and delivery. After delivery, you should keep doing Kegels to heal and strengthen that area. Start off by doing ten to fifteen Kegel exercises at least three times a day. Doing your Kegel exercises regularly also increases the pleasure of sexual intimacy.

---

had a half dozen children. The minute a mother thinks she knows all the tricks, child number six will send her back to the drawing board. The only expert on your individual child is God; you'll probably have to ask him over and over again to help you figure things out every day, and sometimes several times a day.

Will I Be Permanently Scarred?

Most mothers-to-be worry at some time or another that this pregnancy will permanently change their feminine figure in a negative way; in other words you just know you're probably going to lose total control and get fat. Yes, your present figure will definitely explode all over the place for the next few months; but your body is amazingly adaptable and retractable. Some days you may even feel like your entire body is a science fair project gone mad, assuming a life of its own. You may worry that you've lost any semblance of power over all bodily mechanisms and that you'll never be attractive again.

Yes, your body will have permanent changes. My daughter, an archaeologist who is an expert on bones, can tell if a deceased woman has delivered a baby by inspecting her pelvic bones, which widen during childbirth. After your childbearing years, you may end up with breasts that sag a bit, a cesarean section scar, a hemorrhoid or two, and a number of stretch marks. But look at what you get for your efforts. It's a pretty good trade by any standards. After several months of motherhood, you'll either come to accept your physical deficiencies for what they are or you'll be bound and determined to get yourself in shape. Exercise and good nutrition work wonders for restoring a body—and all its parts—to full strength.

Feeling Self-Conscious in Public

You may also find yourself wondering why women have to carry their unborn children in such an obvious place. When

you're good and pregnant, no one ever notices your face anymore. Family, friends, and the man on the street look straight at that protruding middle and address your belly. I've known pregnant women who have been tempted to glue facial features into their maternity tops. Total strangers pat your expanding waistline and make comments about your appearance that can be annoying and embarrassing. Don't be surprised if you hear comments like these:

"Looks like you're expecting. My friend's behind got really big too, and she's never been able to get back into her pants!"

"Is it a boy or girl?"

"How's the little mother?"

"Haven't you had that baby yet?"

"Pregnant again?"

Pregnant women are often the recipients of unwanted advice and wiser-than-thou personal experience. They are teased, counseled, and constantly told excruciating horror stories about the agonizing process of childbirth awaiting them. They are also bombarded with the world's worst history of old wives' tales—all untrue of course. Try to take all this unwanted atten-

tion in stride. In a few short months, no one will even look at you anymore. Your adorable newborn will become the new family star.

After a time, most pregnant women realize that expecting a baby is a positive event, a time of optimism and hope. Even though the extra public attention you receive is a little much at times, you'll realize that people simply are excited to share this time with you. Like weddings and graduations, babies are a joyful time of life. Even though birth may be the most common human experience, it will always be the most profound and beautiful.

When Do I Start Wearing Maternity Clothes?

If this is your first baby, your expanding body will most likely hold things up and in quite well. You might even be able to wear your normal clothes for months. If this is your umpteenth baby, you'll find you can't hold things in or up at all. You'll start wearing maternity clothes as soon as your regular clothing feels tight, which may be at five weeks instead of five months.

You'll also discover that there is a period of time during which maternity clothes fit you like a tent and your regular clothes are too tight to zip and button. Dressing yourself at this stage can get really depressing. To remedy the misery, be creative: wear your husband's shirts untucked over a pair of stretch pants; invest in a few pairs of inexpensive pants with drawstring waistbands—these also come in handy in the weeks after delivery; loop a rubber band through the buttonhole in your pants and attach it to the button— this gives you an extra inch or two but makes you feel like you've at least attempted to button your pants. And don't worry, in just a matter of months you'll probably start growing out of those huge maternity clothes.

Will My Baby Be Normal?

At some point in your pregnancy, you'll probably worry if your baby will be normal. You'll worry about the medication you took before you knew you were pregnant and what effect it had on your unborn child. Every mother hopes her baby will be normal; but we don't have total control over most things in this life. Rest assured, you will love your baby and take care of your baby even if he or she arrives with some challenges.

What If I Can't Handle Pain?

You'll probably worry about how you'll respond during labor and delivery. Every mother has visions of herself completely losing control in front of total strangers who also happen to be staring at a very private part of her body. In reality, no one cares much about how you react during labor and delivery. Family and medical professionals have seen it all and are more concerned with getting your baby here safely and helping you navigate the experience with as little pain as possible. How you act or what you say during delivery will not be reported on the ten o'clock news or written in gold for your posterity.

MOURNING THE LOSS OF A PERFECT CHILD

All mothers hope for a healthy, normal child. Yet about 3 to 4 percent of newborns are born with a major birth defect. Considering all the millions of complexities involved in a developing baby, it is a wonder that any child is born without some complications. Birth defects may be minor and repairable or major and lifelong. You can avoid some risks, but not all. Even women who do everything that is recommended, such as eating a healthy diet, getting enough rest, and avoiding drugs may still have babies with abnormalities.

It helps to remember that most things in life are out of your control. Birth defects can occur for no known cause. Known causes of birth defects include nutritional deficiencies, radiation, certain drugs, alcohol, certain infections and illnesses—herpes simplex, Rubella (German measles), chicken pox, syphilis, toxoplasmosis, and infections with cytomegalovirus (CMV)—trauma, and hereditary disorders. As you can see, many of these factors come into play through no fault of your own. The one thing you can control in situations as trying and tender as these is your attitude about what happens to you.

If you have a child with a birth defect you will probably go through a grieving period where you mourn the loss of the healthy, normal, or perfect baby you envisioned. It is normal, healthy, and healing to feel loss, anger, and sadness. Rest assured . . . in time you will come to love your baby no matter what package he arrives in. Many times what seems to be a tragedy in the short run is a treasure in the long. You can trust God and know that your life and the life of your child is in his hands. He will not leave you alone or comfortless. He will give you the knowledge, wisdom, and courage to face any challenge.

DRUG USE DURING PREGNANCY

Check with your doctor before using any drug during pregnancy, including over-the-counter remedies such as aspirin. How a drug affects a fetus will depend on your baby's stage of development and the potency and dose. Your growing child is most vulnerable to birth defects during the 17 to 57 days following fertilization. This is when all major organs are developing.

Many women, however, are not aware they are pregnant for all or part of this period. If you've taken any drug during those early weeks before you knew you were pregnant, tell your doctor and discuss all the potential risks. It helps to have an informed sense of perspective by understanding that drugs account for 2 to 3 percent of all birth defects. Others result from heredity, environment, and the vast majority from unknown causes. Smoking cigarettes, drinking alcohol, and abusing drugs during pregnancy are the most common concerns. All these habits cause grave, irreversible health risks for both you and your unborn child.

Drugs known to produce birth defects when taken during pregnancy include: alcohol, isotretinoin (Acutane®), phenytoin (Dilantin®), lithium, triamterene (found in some diuretics), trimethoprim (found in some urinary anti-infectives), the antibiotics streptomycin and tetracycline, and warfarin (Coumadin®).

Most Latter-day Saint mothers who obey the Word of Wisdom and the law of chastity automatically avoid the vast majority of chemicals and illnesses that pose risks to their unborn children.

Do your best to stay healthy during pregnancy. If you do become ill, talk to your doctor about over-the-counter remedies that are considered safe during pregnancy or about the few prescription drugs that can also be taken to relieve severe pain and clear up infections. Among the over-the-counter remedies your doctor might deem safe if taken sparingly are: acetaminophen, some antacids, a few cold remedies—such as Sudafed®—and a small number of cough medications, including Robitussin®.

Can I Still Have Sex with My Husband?

Many women worry about having sex during pregnancy. Sexual relations during pregnancy are perfectly normal and healthy unless you experience spotting and cramping or your doctor recommends restraint for other reasons, such as pre-term labor or placenta previa. Some women experience an increase in desire during pregnancy and some a decrease. Most experience a wide variety of desire depending on the trimester they happen to be in. Nausea and exhaustion during the first few months and a growing belly during the last few months sometimes require couples to be more understanding with each other. Motivated couples learn to be creative and adaptable.

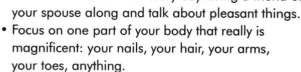

I FEEL HUGE AND UGLY

I've met thousands of people who think pregnant women are beautiful and glow with a special light. I've never met a pregnant woman who felt that way about herself. You're more likely to feel good about the way you look if you learn to look at your expanding body as a miracle. You're offering God a sacred use of your body to bring one of his spirit children to earth. You are in partnership with your Father in Heaven and doing his work. There is simply nothing more important that you could do with your body or your life.

Okay, so you get all of that—and deep down you really believe it—but you *still* feel huge and ugly, that's normal too. Try some of the following to cheer you up and make you look better, too:

- Take a pregnancy yoga class. Staying in shape will help you feel better— and thus look better.
- Take a 30-minute walk every day. Bring a friend or your spouse along and talk about pleasant things.
- Focus on one part of your body that really is magnificent: your nails, your hair, your arms, your toes, anything.
- Get a pedicure, manicure, facial, or new haircut—anything that you think will make you feel pampered and pretty.
- Have someone give you a backrub.
- Go swimming.
- Make a daily ritual of lathering yourself in your favorite scented lotion— at least you'll smell good and your skin will be soft.
- Breathe deeply ten times. This will increase circulation and help you clear your mind of worries.

How Can We Afford a Baby?

Finances often create a bundle of worries for expectant moms. If you are not insured or are underinsured, most states offer medical and nutritional help for expectant mothers. Many hospitals and doctors offer free pregnancy tests. Check the local phone book and hospital for help and direction in signing up for programs as soon as you know you're pregnant. Extended family and friends can also be a great resource. If you are insured, check your policy and find out what it covers and what you need to pay. Then make plans for how you will pay for the rest. Many insurance policies also require you to choose your doctor from a pre-approved list they provide.

COPING WITH THE HEARTACHE OF PREGNANCY LOSS

Not all pregnancies have a happy ending. Every pregnancy is marked with a few problems and worries, and some, unfortunately, end in tragedy. A relatively small number of babies are born with major birth defects and lifelong challenges. Some babies die before they are born. Experiencing a miscarriage or stillbirth is devastating. If this happens to you, please don't think you have to go through this trial alone. Most hospitals or church leaders can direct you to grief support groups where you have the opportunity to talk about your loss with other parents who have gone through a similar trauma. Relatives, friends, and ward members can provide much-needed support. Ultimately, your faith in God and your Savior Jesus Christ will help you find the courage to live with your loss.

What Happens During a Miscarriage?

Statistics show that approximately 10 percent of diagnosed pregnancies end in miscarriage. About 85 percent of miscarriages occur during the first 12 weeks of pregnancy. The remaining 15 percent occur during weeks 13 to 20, with many attributed to physiological problems in the mother. The loss of a baby after the 20th week of pregnancy is defined as a stillbirth. Because miscarriages often occur early on in pregnancy, it is estimated that another 20 to 40 percent of pregnancies end before a pregnancy is even diagnosed. Many of these miscarriages are unnoticed. Most miscarriages in diagnosed pregnancies, however, do not pass by unnoticed. Before

---

I'M BLEEDING. WHAT'S WRONG?

Many women experience spotting or cramping in the early months of pregnancy. This is often normal and is not usually cause for concern. If cramping is mild or accompanied by a pulling sensation on one or both sides of the abdomen, this is probably just the ligaments in your uterus stretching and preparing to support your growing fetus. Lying down and taking it easy usually helps the cramps subside somewhat. Light spotting is also normal very early in pregnancy and usually only occurs briefly.

If, however, you experience any of the following, call your doctor:

- Bleeding as heavy as a menstrual period. Also, when light spotting continues for more than three days.
- Cramping and bleeding occuring together. Also, when the pain occurs in the center of your lower abdomen.
- Pain that is severe and does not subside after a day—even if you are not bleeding.

Obtain medical attention in the following circumstances:

- Bleeding and cramping occuring together and you have a history of miscarriage.
- Bleeding soaking through several pads in an hour, or pain that is unbearable.
- You pass clots or grayish or pink material. This means a miscarriage may have already begun.

---

a miscarriage or stillbirth, a woman typically has some spotting or more obvious bleeding from the vagina. The uterus then begins contracting, which causes cramps. If the miscarriage continues, the bleeding, discharge, and cramping become more severe.

Many women are totally unprepared for the events that surround a miscarriage or stillbirth and do not realize that part of a miscarriage can involve going through a painful labor and delivery. Contractions can be intense, and bleeding often profuse. It's normal to feel terrified, confused, and disoriented.

Eventually part or all the contents of the uterus will be released. No treatment is necessary when all the contents of the uterus are expelled, but suction curettage should be performed if anything is left in the uterus. This prevents complications and infection.

Although many obstetricians can perform a dilation and curettage (D and C) in their offices, a D and C can also be done at an outpatient surgical center or hospital. This allows the woman to be completely sedated during the procedure, which may be easier to cope with when a D and C is needed as a result of the death of the fetus. Discuss these options with your doctor.

After a miscarriage, many women experience months of anger, guilt, and sadness. Miscarriages are often followed by an intense, overwhelming feeling of loss. The mother's arms may ache to hold her baby. Sometimes she may even feel phantom kicks or think she hears a baby crying in the distance. A grieving mother often feels vulnerable and afraid she might lose another child or even her husband. Whether the pregnancy is four weeks or four months along, that pregnancy brought weeks of planning for the baby's future. When the baby dies, that future dies.

Unfortunately, a lot of people don't comprehend the anguish that accompanies

miscarriage. Many people lead the grieving mother to believe that there is no reason to be sad or mourn her loss. Society at large tends to allow parents a month or two to grieve after the death of a newborn, while parents of stillborn children or those who have had miscarriages seem dismissed altogether.

Blaming Yourself

The medical community calls a miscarriage a spontaneous abortion, which sometimes gives a woman the mistaken idea that she caused the problem. This is not true. If you miscarry, the blame is not yours. Most miscarriages occur for no known reason. It has never been proven that physical activity, such as lifting children, carrying groceries, performing moderate exercise, or even moving light furniture causes miscarriage. Even minor injuries and falls have not been shown to cause a miscarriage. About 20 to 30 percent of pregnant women have some bleeding or cramping at least once during the first 20 weeks of pregnancy. About half of these episodes result in a miscarriage. Most of the time, however, there is no known cause.

The Grief Process

Husbands and wives go through the same stages of grief but often express their loss in different ways and at different times. Both mothers and fathers feel the loss deeply. It is a tremendous letdown, and both will be left wondering about the empty space in their family and if there was a spirit involved. But because mothers and fathers often bond differently with their baby before birth, their expressions of grief will be different. Men may feel they are supposed to be brave and strong for their wives. The more a couple can discuss their feelings, the more supported the individual grieving will be.

Each mother who experiences a pregnancy loss needs to experience and express her grief. It hurts to lose a baby no matter how far along you are. Many mothers are surprised by their emotions after a pregnancy loss. Life seems unreal for a time. They express depression, anger (directed at themselves, their mates, a doctor, God, or even life in general), guilt, irritability, lack of interest in normal activities, and sadness. Many experience irregularities in sleeping or eating. Some feel anger or sadness in the presence of babies or pregnant women. Most mothers appreciate anyone who will put their arms around her and tell her they are sorry it happened.

If, after suffering a miscarriage, you have difficulty functioning and doing daily tasks—such as caring for your other children, getting out of bed, and so on—and that depression does not improve, talk to your doctor. At times, miscarriages can trigger severe depression that needs medical attention.

Why Did My Baby Die?

There is really no single answer to the question, *Why?* in most cases. There are cer-

tain specific medical problems that can cause miscarriages and stillbirths. In many cases, especially in the first few months, doctors often attribute the fault to some kind of chromosomal abnormality in the fetus. Those that occur later in the pregnancy, when the baby appears normal, are often attributed to some maternal factor, such as uterine abnormalities. But in the vast majority of cases, there is no obvious reason. Whatever the cause, the end result is the same. Many children who were eagerly expected never make it. Miscarriages, like car accidents, just happen. In the majority of cases, the problem won't recur. In some instances, however, mothers endure multiple miscarriages and years of discouragement.

Unanswered Eternal Questions

As Latter-day Saints, parents have the eternal assurance that children who die after taking even one breath of life will be reunited with their families one day. A baby who takes a spontaneous breath or who registers a heartbeat after birth is considered a live birth at any stage of pregnancy, and can thus be given a name and be listed on family group sheets. Parents who have children die in the womb before birth are left with many unanswered questions and may wonder if their stillborn or miscarried child had a spirit, if that spirit will ever be reunited with them, and whether it would be apropriate to name the child or record his name on a family group record.

Although stillborn children may be given a name and listed on family group sheets, Church policy is that temple ordinances are not performed for stillborn children. The Church Temple Department instructions state, "If a stillbirth takes place after the parents are sealed in the temple, those children can be identified on the record as being born in the covenant. Miscarriages, however, are usually not recorded on family group records."

There are simply some questions that we don't have answers to in this life. Yet the gospel offers all of us great comfort. Many grieving parents find sweet assurances in the words of the Savior: "I will not leave you comfortless. . . . Peace I leave with you, my peace I give unto you: not as the world giveth, give I unto you. Let not your heart be troubled, neither let it be afraid" (John 14:18, 27).

Grieving parents can cast their burden on the Lord and he will sustain them. Believe his promise, "Blessed are they that mourn: for they shall be comforted" (Matthew 5:4; see also 3 Nephi 12:4).

I've had three miscarriages. Though we now have ten living children, my heart still aches as I remember our three babies who never made it. It's hard to say good-bye when you never had the chance to say hello. I may never be able to hold my three babies in my arms, but I will always hold them in my heart.

One night my four-year-old son cried

A MOTHER'S LETTER TO HER UNBORN CHILD

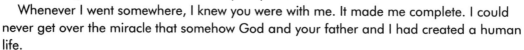

Dear Child,

It's been only a day since I lost you. Yesterday I had such plans for you; now today you are gone and where you are I cannot go.

You were the answer to your parents' prayers. You should have seen the look in your father's eyes when I told him you were coming. We were so happy. We told everyone you were on your way.

Each morning when I woke I would stroke my palm across the place where you were growing. Your father teased me about wearing maternity clothes before I really needed to. But I wanted the whole world to know. Even morning sickness reassured me of your presence.

Whenever I went somewhere, I knew you were with me. It made me complete. I could never get over the miracle that somehow God and your father and I had created a human life.

Then I lost you.

I'll never forget you. You are my child. You have been part of me. But I miss you and when I go out now, I feel alone.

I don't live life in the same way since you went away. I walk softer now. Life is more fragile, more precious. I hope someday I will be able to have another baby. But it will never be the same as it was with you. The feelings I've had with you are separate and unique. It's so hard to say good-bye when I never had the chance to say hello.

I thank God for the time we had together. I love you. I may never be able to hold you in my arms, but I will always hold you in my heart.

Love,
Your Mother

out to me from his room. I quickly crawled from my bed and went to his side.

"What's the matter?" I asked as I entered his dark room.

"I'm so scared," he replied.

I held him in my arms to reassure him, and we talked. Soon he settled back in his bed with his arms around his teddy bear.

"If you need me again, just call me and I'll come," I said as I kissed him on the cheek and stroked his shoulder. He was content.

You too, may cry out on your dark nights, and God will be there. Even without all the answers you can have peace, the peace that someday you will know and understand, the peace that only the Savior can give.

To say that coping with a stillbirth or miscarriage means forgetting would diminish a very real sorrow. Maybe coping with this very real loss doesn't mean forgetting or even having the sorrow lessen with time. Perhaps coping with this sadness means living with it . . . living more gently and fully, allowing this sadness to make the bearer a more Christlike person. The realization of our limited mortality can make our stay here on earth more sweet and meaningful. I've learned that sorrow can harden or soften us, embitter us, or cause us to see more appreciatively, limit our view or widen our horizons.

These gentle words from the Doctrine and Covenants describe the nature of life during the Millennium: "And there shall be no sorrow because there is no death. In that day an infant shall not die until he is old; and his life shall be as the age of a tree" (D&C 101:29–30).

Seasons offer the rebirth of spring after the death of winter. As you observe nature around you, realize life is a process of living, dying, and living again. The whole earth proclaims the miracle of the resurrection. You can find great peace in the knowledge that your family is part of that great plan.

THE SECOND TRIMESTER

The second trimester is the take-a-breather part of pregnancy, so appreciate every day you don't feel queasy or so huge you have a tough time navigating through a crowd without smacking everybody with your belly button. This is the period when you'll probably start wearing maternity clothes. Enjoy them now; by the end of your pregnancy you might be so tired of them you'll want to burn them. Because of all the extra blood circulating around your body, you'll probably feel warmer than usual; purchase clothes that are loose-fitting, comfortable, and cool.

SECOND TRIMESTER CONCERNS AND COMPLAINTS

Even though the second trimester is a breather of sorts, it's not without some discomfort. Your breasts may still be tender as they continue to grow and your body prepares itself to produce milk for your infant. They may feel lumpy and leak a little colostrum. Colostrum is the nutrient-rich liquid that nourishes your baby for a day or two before your milk comes in after delivery. Some women notice they're growing extra moles. Other concerns may include heartburn, hemorrhoids, trapped gas, constipation, leg cramps, and backaches.

Heartburn

Heartburn is a warm, burning sensation that moves from your stomach up into your throat and is often accompanied by a sour taste in your mouth. Heartburn is most often caused by a backup of stomach contents into the esophagus. To avoid heartburn, eat smaller meals and wait a few hours before lying down after you've eaten. Avoid foods that might contribute to the problem, such as chocolate, fatty foods, caffeine, alcohol, onions, mint, tomatoes, and citrus. Also try chewing your food more slowly and thoroughly. Get regular exercise and avoid carbonated drinks and spicy foods. Heartburn is one of the few ailments during pregnancy that can be helped by over-the-counter medications. Ask your doctor about taking small amounts of Maalox, Mylanta, or some other mild antacid.

Muscle or Tendon Strains

The same hormones that run through your body in high levels during pregnancy and help to get your body and baby through the whole nine months also cause muscles, ligaments, and tendons to relax and lengthen. This sets the mother-to-be up for increased likelihood of muscle or ligament strains and sprains. Be particularly careful while exercising not to overdo any one muscle group. As soon as you feel any pain, it's best to stop what you were doing.

Hemorrhoids

Hemorrhoids are varicose veins—swollen tissue containing veins—located in the wall of the rectum and anus. Hemorrhoids sometimes become inflamed, develop a clot, bleed, or become enlarged and protrude. To relieve the pain, avoid things that would strain the rectal area. Sleep on your side, avoid long hours of either standing or sitting—which causes pressure on the rectal veins—drink plenty of fluids, and eat a fiber-rich diet to avoid constipation. Talk to a doctor who knows you are pregnant about taking a stool softener if constipation is a problem; but don't take mineral oil. You can also soak in a warm tub or apply witch hazel pads or ice to the affected area. Avoid straining on the toilet. Get plenty of rest.

Leg Cramps

Many women experience painful leg cramps during pregnancy, especially at night. Leg cramps are likely caused by an excess of phosphorus and a shortage of calcium circulating through the blood. Make sure you are getting plenty of calcium and maintaining a healthy diet. Your doctor may advise you to take a calcium supplement. Stretching and walking also helps legs cramps. When you get a charley horse, lock your knee and slowly point your toes toward your head. A few of these stretches usually takes care of the pain. You may also want to incorporate some stretching into your bedtime routine—this may help to prevent cramps in the first place.

FEELING THE BABY MOVE

There will probably be two major highlights during the second trimester: feeling the baby move and taking a memorable glimpse—via sonogram—of your growing future. Relish and savor both events.

Sometime in the second trimester you'll feel your baby move for the first time. I'm not exaggerating when I say this will be one of the biggest thrills of your life. After spending several months feeling downright crummy, one day you'll be standing or sitting somewhere and suddenly you'll feel something unmistakable . . . another person moving around inside you. This is not the moment when you're wondering if what you just felt was another gas bubble or something you ate for supper. This is the exact moment when you *know*, without a doubt, what just happened.

I was standing in the BYU library the first time this happened to me and I still remember after all these years how it felt. This magic moment generally happens after you've spent several long months continually looking for a place to sleep, racing to the sink just in time, and frantically looking for a bathroom. It's a good thing this monumental event takes place about now, because you've just about had it up to here with being pregnant. All it takes is that magic bloop and then a little bleep-bleep and you're on cloud nine for months. Nausea, light-headedness, continual bathroom emergencies, and extreme exhaustion are suddenly unimportant because *there's a real baby in there!* You're not just tired and miserable, you're going to have a *real* baby.

Although your baby has been moving about freely since the seventh week of pregnancy, it takes some time before the mother can feel the movement. That first wonderful awareness is called "quickening" and can occur anywhere from the 14th to the 26th week. For most women, however, it is generally closer to the 18th to 22nd week.

If you haven't felt your baby move for a while, or you're concerned about his movement at any point in your pregnancy, call your doctor. He may recommend that you count the kicks or come in for a non-stress test just to be safe.

Backache

Most pregnant women have backaches. After all, everything inside of you is being stretched to the limit and forced to fit into increasingly small places. This causes a great deal of strain on your back and skeletal muscles. Try eliminating too much strain on the back by avoiding standing for long periods of time. When you sit, don't cross your legs. This might cause you to tilt your pelvis too far forward and increase back pain; it's also bad for circulation. Use a firm chair with a good back. A lightweight maternity girdle may also help. Wear low, rubber-soled shoes. Avoid lifting anything heavy and sitting straight up from

ULTRASOUND TEST

The second highlight of the middle part of pregnancy is the ultrasound test your doctor may order. My first five children were presents I didn't get to peek at until I'd delivered. I actually lived back in the days when you didn't have the option of knowing if you were having a boy or a girl. My first experience with ultrasound technology was when I was scheduled for an appointment at the hospital to confirm the death of my sixth baby at five months along after the doctor couldn't pick up a heartbeat. I'd prepared myself for the worst when suddenly there was my son Jacob doing somersaults on a small black and white screen in front of me. Talk about a moment. Both the technician and I were in tears.

1. Preparing for the Test

When you receive your ultrasound, you'll likely go to your doctor's office, hospital, or a center that specializes in these kinds of tests. You may be asked to drink a lot of water before you arrive. Then you'll be shown into a private room along with family members you chose to bring along. Wear pants and a shirt that you can pull up and down enough to expose your growing tummy.

2. What to Expect

Someone will drape your clothing with paper sheets, then proceed to spread a cool colorless gel on your tummy. Next someone will place an instrument called a transducer on top of your belly. As the test reader moves the instrument across your belly, you'll be able to look at a monitor that resembles a television screen and see what the reader sees. Sound waves will penetrate your body, reflect off internal structures, and be converted to electric impulses, which will then be processed to form an image displayed on a monitor.

3. Learning the Sex of Your Child

While the reader is measuring the head and femur bone and analyzing dozens of other areas of concern, such as the heart and organs, you'll be holding your breath and hoping and praying your baby is all right. When you receive the assurance that everything looks good, you'll probably be asked if you want to know the sex of your child. This is an individual decision. Some

lying on your back. Sometimes a warm compress applied directly to the back helps to alleviate the pain. Regular exercise also helps relieve some of the strain.

Gas

Pregnant women often have a problem with trapped gas because pregnancy causes your digestive system to slow *way* down. Gas is no laughing matter when you feel like a stuffed turkey ready to explode. Trapped air hurts, big time. Try avoiding anything with the potential to create extra air inside you, such as certain foods, chewing gum, or carbonated drinks. You should also work hard to stay regular, as constipation is a common cause of gas. Eating smaller, more frequent meals also tends to help.

Learn to burp yourself. I know this sounds strange, but burping yourself will be good practice for burping your baby later on. Lay down and sit up while gently pushing in and up on your tummy over and

mothers and fathers want to know and some don't. My husband never wants to know and I always want to know. I think the person who is packing the little bundle should also get to pack the power to make the final decision on whether or not she wants to be told the sex of her unborn child.

4. Asking Questions

Be sure to ask lots of questions during the test. Some readers are better than others at communicating with parents. Many offices will allow you to bring a videotape and record the test to bring home with you and replay over and over again. Ask for a running commentary as the reader proceeds to chart, measure, and observe.

Tell your reader what you're worried about. Ask your reader to explain what you're seeing on the screen and point out details. Seeing your baby before he or she is born will be one of the most exciting and touching moments in your life. Don't be surprised if the medical guys or your spouse don't react with cartwheels and applause. Just go ahead and feel as giddy as you want with laughter and tears—all by yourself if necessary. This is a moment to savor. In many medical offices, the person performing your ultrasound is a technician without authority to *interpret* results. If this is the case, don't worry that the technician can't tell you everything. A radiologist will view the scans and medically interpret the results.

5. When Something Is Wrong

Ocassionally, ultrasound tests are not celebratory events. Sometimes ultrasound tests are ordered during a pregnancy if the doctor suspects problems or needs to monitor the pregnancy closely. You may receive troubling or tragic news at the conclusion of your test. Always make sure you bring along a trusted family member or friend for support.

Medical professionals who work with expectant mothers sometimes seem callous and uncaring, especially if you've just been told your baby is dead or has serious problems. These professionals deal with life-and-death situations every day. Don't expect them to be your support and comfort at difficult times. Do expect them to provide you with names of counselors or support groups you can see later.

over again. It also helps to find a fun way to keep moving like regular swimming or walking.

Constipation

As pregnancy progresses, your growing uterus creates pressure on the rectum and lower intestine, often causing constipation. Constipation is worse in pregnancy because the waves of muscular contractions in the intestine which normally move food along are slowed by high levels of progesterone. To relieve constipation, drink plenty of fluids, eat fiber-rich foods, and get plenty of exercise every day.

Braxton Hicks Contractions

Your twentieth week of pregnancy not only marks the halfway point, but it is also a time for a major growth spurt. You might find that your weight gain and appetite alert you to this news. You might also notice your uterus contracting off and on from time to time. If you're a first-time mom, you might not know what you're feeling. You will probably think your stomach feels unusually tight at times. This is a normal event that some people call false labor.

Doctors, on the other hand, like to give everything an official medical name, so they call this event a Braxton Hicks contraction (intermittent uterine contractions with unpredictable frequency throughout pregnancy). You can call this experience whatever you want, but what's actually happening is pretty simple: your uterus is trying to stay in shape and practice for the big event. This tightening usually starts at the top of your uterus then moves down until your womb forms a hard ball then relaxes. These contractions actually strengthen the uterine muscles and circulate your blood in and near the placenta and help thin the cervix before delivery.

Apparently some guy named Braxton Hicks was the first *man* to identify the uterine tightening so they named these contractions after him. Can you believe that? The guy never had a Braxton Hick in his life and he gets them named after him. No self-respecting female would name that experience "false labor." There is nothing false about it. You're sitting or standing about anywhere, minding your own business, and suddenly your uterus becomes so hard you can launch fireworks off your abdomen.

With all that tightening, your bladder screams, your back aches, and your heart races. This is not false. This is real. The more babies you have, and the older you get, the more Hicks you seem to notice. The last time I got pregnant, my doctor said my uterus was so worn out, just the thought of being pregnant made it start

Hicking. Pregnancy is so filled with aches, pains, and Hicking you'll always be wondering if everything is all right. Whenever you have any question about what's happening to your body, don't be afraid to pick up the phone and call your doctor. No concern is stupid if you're having it at the moment. Ask away and sleep better at night.

Bed Rest

Your pregnancy might not go as planned and you may find yourself ordered home and sent to bed just when you least expect it. Bed rest is a common treatment for a variety of pregnancy concerns. If your doctor tells you to go home and stay in bed except for bathing and trips to the

bathroom, you'll probably laugh and think it's a joke. It's not.

You may be asked to put your life on hold for a while, and a whole army of people will have to step up to the task of filling in for you while you're down. Even if you have 16 preschoolers or a tremendously important career that can't survive without you, you may find that in order to

---

KEEPING BUSY WHILE YOU'RE IN BED

Think of bed rest as a time when you get to do things you never have time for otherwise. You'll be surprised how many things you can do from bed if you have to.
- pay bills
- work on your family history
- organize your recipe box
- catch up on the family photo albums or memory books
- knit and crochet
- fold clothes
- read good books and newspapers
- start or continue a journal for your baby and yourself
- call friends and relatives
- write letters
- study a language
- take a home study class
- write poetry, your life's story, a novel, short stories, or a stage or screenplay
- do your Christmas or birthday shopping on the Internet
- research any topic on the Internet

keep you or your baby healthy, you'll have to stay down. This is a major adjustment for you and all those around you. After you get used to the idea, you'll be amazed at what you're willing to endure to keep yourself and your little one healthy.

You may be asked to lie on your side, day after day . . . week after week . . . or even the whole time you're pregnant. Bed rest is sometimes ordered when you're threatening to miscarry or experiencing early labor or high blood pressure. The times I've been ordered to bed were some of the most challenging and rewarding of my life. If this happens to you, don't fight it.

It helps to get in touch with other people who are also bedridden when you're down. One of the times I was on bed rest I developed the sweetest friendship with a sister in my ward who had been bedridden for three years. I'll never forget her wonderful outlook on life. She was always telling me what she was grateful for and teaching me how to celebrate each day like a holiday. I'll never forget her zest for life and her humble spirit of gratitude.

Taking the time to shower, putting on clean underwear and a nice nightgown, and applying just a touch of makeup and combing your hair will help you feel better about the way you look as the days wear on. Family members can help with childcare and housecleaning. Your husband can perform marvelously well if you don't hold him to your standards.

Bed rest teaches you some things that are hard to learn any other way. For starters, after this confinement is over you will promise your Father in Heaven you'll never, *ever* complain about having too much work to do *ever* again. You will realize that work and the ability to do it, are really blessings. You will even discover that your other children can do much more for themselves than you thought possible and that you can still mother them without doing everything for them.

You will learn that your children and husband can take care of things on their own better than you thought. You'll discover that many people love and care as you become the recipient of countless acts of compassion and kindness. When the time comes and the tables are turned, you'll be eager to return the kindness shown to you as you serve others in the same boat.

THE THIRD TRIMESTER

During the third trimester you'll probably find yourself slowing down. It's hard to lug around that much extra weight and remain light on your feet. The extra not-so-evenly-distributed weight you're packing around makes it harder to do even simple things such as trim your toenails or slip on your socks. You'll feel big, awkward, and clumsy; but don't let that make you so paranoid that you stop eating well.

Your baby gains about an ounce a day in the last two months—close to a half a pound every week—and needs all the nutrients you can provide. Your baby's brain is developing faster during those last few weeks of pregnancy and the first few months after his birth than at any other time in his life. So be sure to get plenty of protein.

Try eating five or six small meals a day because there will be less and less space left over for food in there as the days go by. Don't worry if it seems like this baby has taken over your body and your life. Luckily pregnancy doesn't last forever.

CHILDBIRTH EDUCATION CLASSES

If this is your first baby, don't neglect to attend a childbirth education class. Most classes begin early in the third trimester, when you're about 27 or 28 weeks along. Classes are often held one evening a week for four to six weeks. Many hospitals and clinics offer classes on Saturdays or longer classes that take fewer weeks to complete.

Both you and your husband will have lots of questions and fears that need to be addressed. A good class should help ease your fears. If you understand labor and childbirth you will be more likely to have a satisfying experience when the time comes to deliver your baby.

At most classes, mothers- and fathers-to-be learn about the stages of labor, the options available for managing pain during labor and delivery, and the variety of ways in which your partner can support you through the pain and hard work of labor.

Check with your doctor, hospital, or birthing center to find out when and where these classes are offered. Childbirth classes can be very informative or just plain scary. Make sure you get an instructor who has actually had a few babies and who is able to inspire you with self-confidence, not deathly fear.

Childbirth classes were originally designed to teach mothers how to cope with the pain of labor without fear or medication. Now, however, classes teach a variety of pain management and relaxation techniques but also prepare mothers for the possibility of using any type of medication and undergoing procedures such as an episiotomy or a cesarean section. Remember, no matter what your instructor says, breathing correctly during labor doesn't make the pain go away; it is, however, supposed to distract you from the pain. Relaxation doesn't make the pain go away either, but it does help your muscles go with the flow instead of tensing up and working against you.

You'll probably be shown a film or two that graphically demonstrates the many different ways babies are born: face up, face down, or rear end first. Don't panic. I've had my babies upside down, inside out, and backward; but with good medical help, I always managed to get them out somehow.

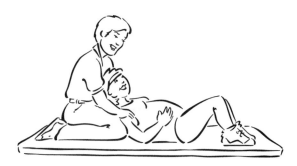

THIRD TRIMESTER CONCERNS AND COMPLAINTS

Last trimester discomforts seem to get worse as the pregnancy progresses. Your growing baby will put pressure on the bladder, making you feel like you have to go to the bathroom all the time. Your expanding waistline will probably produce shortness of breath, backaches, swelling, sciatic nerve problems, round ligament

pain, and a host of other common complaints. Hang in there. You're almost to the finish line.

Toward the end of your pregnancy you will also develop a new goal in life: namely, finding a place to sit down. Getting out of a chair once you sit down will be another fine challenge to conquer. Soon you'll find that you can't fit behind the steering wheel in the car, that your belly gets wedged under the dining room table, and that your panty hose won't stay up. And . . . you'll get very, *very* tired of people asking you when you're due, like you're a ticking bomb waiting to go off.

Shortness of Breath

Your growing uterus is putting a lot of pressure on your internal organs, making it more difficult to breathe. For relief, sit up straight rather than slumping, and be sure to sleep on your side at night, with pillows propped between your legs and behind your back. Slow down. You don't have to be superwoman. If, however, you have extreme difficulty breathing and you experience chest pain or blueness of lips, call the doctor immediately.

Nasal Congestion

When you are pregnant your blood volume increases by about 45 percent. This means that all the membranes in your body, including your nose, receive increased blood flow, which may cause them to swell and soften. To help stave off nasal congestion and a dry nose that is prone to bleeding, increase your fluid intake and try using a cool mist humidifier at night. Your doctor may also suggest that

you take an additional 250 mg of vitamin C to strengthen your capillaries and reduce the chance of bleeding.

Swelling

As the amount of fluids inside your body increases during pregnancy, you will likely notice some swelling of your feet and ankles. This is normal but uncomfortable nonetheless. For relief, try elevating your legs or lying down on your side as often as possible; don't wear anything tight or restrictive, such as uncomfortable dress shoes or elastic-top socks or stockings; avoid standing for long periods of time; drink plenty of water. Sometimes your healthcare provider might recommend wearing support hose. This is particularly true for women who must stand for long periods of time during the day, such as nurses or schoolteachers. Ask your healthcare provider about forms of exercise, such as walking or swimming, that may also bring comfort.

If your swelling is extreme and does not go down after elevating your feet, or if it is accompanied by rapid weight gain, you may be developing preeclampsia (pregnancy-induced hypertension). Call your doctor immediately.

Backache

Backaches seem to get worse as the pregnancy progresses. Try to maintain good posture when standing and sitting by keeping your back straight. Take frequent breaks during the day to sit or rest. Don't lift anything heavy and don't sit up straight in bed without first rolling to your side and pushing yourself up with your arms.

Sciatic Nerve Problems

Your growing uterus will put pressure on a lot of things during this last trimester, and one of those may be the sciatic nerve, which runs down your lower back, buttocks, and legs. This pressure causes tingling, numbness, and pain in your backside, hips, thighs, and feet. Rest, a heating pad, and your baby repositioning herself may relieve the pain.

Round Ligament Pain

You may experience knife-stabbing pain on the sides of your lower abdomen or groin that come quickly and go quickly and make you feel like yelling out loud even if you're out in public. This pain

comes from stretching or spasms of the round ligaments on the sides of the uterus. Sometimes a sudden change in position can cause these ligaments to spasm. About the only thing you can do to help yourself is basically hang in there until the pain passes. It's all right to be dramatic and yell if you feel like it. After all, yelling tends to keep the people around you on their toes.

A Special Consideration for LDS Women

During the third trimester you'll have a progressively hard time finding clothes that fit comfortably. You might want to consider purchasing special temple garments made for LDS women who are pregnant or nursing. These garments should be purchased in your prepregnancy size.

PREPARING FOR BABY

The third trimester is the point in your pregnancy when you actually begin realizing that a new person will be living with you . . . soon. You are not really going to be pregnant forever, even though you will doubt that during the last few weeks of your incubation period. This new person is going to need food to eat, clothes to wear, and a place to snooze.

Don't panic; your new baby won't care whether he sleeps in a bottom dresser drawer, laundry basket, or in a frilly bassinet. You, on the other hand, will probably have a grand vision of some kind of elaborate nursery like the ones you've been staring at for months in the magazines you read while waiting for your doctor appointments. You'll wonder if you're going to be a major disappointment for

---

SERIOUS SYMPTOMS TO WATCH FOR

The last four weeks of pregnancy seem to drag on the longest, and you may be awash with aches and pains that never seem to let up. Hunker down and hang in there; it won't last forever. Most symptoms are normal but there are a few that should be immediately reported to your doctor:
- persistent headaches
- nausea and vomiting
- dizziness
- disturbances of your eyesight
- consistent contractions
- vaginal bleeding
- leakage of amniotic fluid
- unusual swelling of hands and feet
- reduced or increased urine production
- any illness or infection

---

junior because you can't supply all that luminous illusion.

Always remember this: stuff in magazines is not real! Stuff on television and in the movies is not real. The smiling, beautiful skinny new mothers are not real. The grinning, deliriously happy, clean newborn babies are not real. The fancy, color-coordinated nurseries are not real. There is nothing real about magazine layouts; they are all staged. Real life is not the way it appears in movies or magazines. Real new mothers don't have time to comb their hair, let alone get out of their bathrobes. Real newborns cry whenever they're not eating or sleeping. Real nurseries often smell a little stinky. So take a deep breath and relax. There are only a few things you *really* need before you have the baby and a sense of humor is by far the most important.

Shopping for Baby

Sometime near your sixth month of pregnancy, it's wise to start collecting a few baby things—if only to help you feel prepared and less anxious. Shopping for tiny baby things is great fun. Don't be surprised if your husband seems uninterested or less excited than you are when you go shopping for the new baby. My husband always used to say, "Oh honey, you don't need all that stuff. All the baby needs is a box of diapers and a few blankets."

Long ago, I foolishly decided not to go shopping for my first new baby until after a scheduled baby shower so I wouldn't buy anything I'd already received. Big mistake. My first baby was due in June, but she arrived in April, *before* my scheduled shower. The only thing I had on hand was a sample disposable diaper I'd received at a prenatal class. Frankly, I had to use that diaper for myself on the way to the hospital because my water broke in the middle of the night. My husband and I were caught with no insurance and subsequently a short hospital stay, a premature naked baby with absolutely no clothing or diapers to her name, and two very naïve, shell-shocked, unprepared parents.

Not only should you have a few things picked out for baby in the third trimester,

---

THE LAYETTE

- 6 undershirts (if it's cold outside)
- 6 snap-up-the-front pajamas
- 4 other outfits, such as kimonos, dresses, or pant sets, depending on the sex
- 6 receiving blankets
- 2 baby quilts (one for the floor and outings and one for the bed)
- 1 snow suit, sweater, or hat (depending on how cold it is outside)
- 6 bibs
- 1 dozen cloth diapers (for burp cloths and sheet protectors)
- 3 to 4 dozen pre-folded cloth diapers, 2 sets of diaper pins, and a half dozen plastic pants (if using cloth)
- 1 very large box of newborn or small disposable diapers (if using disposable)
- 3 to 6 bassinet sheets (can also substitute flannel blankets or pillow cases)
- 1 Sunday outfit
- 1 blessing outfit
- 2 to 4 pacifiers, if you decide—or if your baby prefers—to use them

For baby's bath you'll need:
- several small soft washcloths
- cotton swabs for cleaning the umbilical cord
- mild baby soap
- lotion
- cotton balls for cleaning the eyes
- baby oil for dry skin and cradle cap
- zinc oxide and petroleum jelly for diaper rash
- soft bristle toothbrush for combing baby's hair

you'll also want to pack your own bag if you're going to a birthing center or hospital. I'd recommend packing a bag at the end of your seventh month, just in case.

The Layette

A layette is just a fancy name for the first set of clothing your new baby will need. If you have access to a washing machine and can launder clothes every few days or so, the list on the previous page page should get you through your baby's first few months. If you're using a Laundromat, the kitchen sink, or a relative's washing machine, you'll want to adjust this list to include more items. Newborns spit up and leak through their diapers several times a day and night, so they'll go through multiple outfits a day. When selecting sizes, be warned that most newborns go through the newborn size in roughly two weeks. You'll want to buy mostly three- to six-month sizes for starters.

Also remember, babies couldn't care less about what they wear as long as they're comfortable, so don't overdo it in the wardrobe department. In the summer months, babies require little more than a clean diaper and an undershirt most of the time. New mothers tend to overdress and overheat their babies, afraid they'll catch a chill or fail in the "looking cute" department when guests come over. Experienced

mothers who know how quickly babies grow up worry less about stains and spend more time simply enjoying their little ones. So don't spend a lot for fancy things. Babies grow so fast, they'll only be able to wear some outfits for a matter of weeks. It's quite likely that you'll never even take the tags off at least one outfit.

CHOOSING A PEDIATRICIAN

Just when you're finally getting comfortable with the doctor you've chosen for yourself, it's time to start thinking about choosing a doctor for your baby. Choosing a good pediatrician will provide you part of the support team you'll need for many years ahead. You'll be meeting with your pediatrician many times for the next few years, so get one you really like. You'll want a doctor who is board-certified and one who has some experience. Choose a doctor who suits your personality and provides what you expect from a medical professional. Your opinion should be respected and you should be treated as an

WHAT TO PACK FOR THE HOSPITAL

For You:
- birth plan aids, such as lip balm, lotion, music, pillow, hard candy, books, videos, etc.
- food for labor coach and perhaps a change of clothes
- insurance card
- warm socks (your feet may get very cold during delivery)
- robe and nightgown (optional, as gown is usually provided by the hospital and you might be wary of staining your own gowns with blood)
- going home outfit (a comfy, loose-fitting dress or pant-set is best. You'll likely not be able to wear any of your prepregnancy button- or zip-up pants for a while, so spare yourself the disappointment and don't even bother packing them.)
- nursing bra and pads
- several underpants and sanitary pads (if not supplied by hospital)
- toiletries (if not supplied by hospital)
- makeup
- phone card and phone number list
- hair dryer/curlers/brush
- something to read
- loaded camera or camcorder
- your journal

For Baby:
- infant car seat
- going home outfit
- diaper
- bunting or blanket if cold outside
- baby's first journal

---

equal when making decisions for your child.

After you have the baby, you'll be asked what doctor you'd like to examine your baby after he's born and before you're discharged. Your pediatrician will usually visit you the day after delivery and on the day you go home. After your doctor examines your baby, he should provide you with a general information booklet addressing common new-parent concerns and a schedule for well-baby visits and immunizations.

What to Look For

Parents should first consult their list of insurance providers to determine what their choices are. Then, look for a doctor who is well organized, who doesn't keep his patients waiting, is proficient at diagnosing, and has a good grasp of what to worry about. You don't need a doctor that worries you about every little thing, especially when you're a first-time mother. You'll also want a doctor who has hired great help in the front office so you can call with questions and get helpful, friendly advice from the nurses when you have questions or concerns. Find out what office hours are, whether they offer weekend and evening hours, and how to contact medical help after hours.

If breastfeeding is important to you, you'll want a doctor who encourages and supports you in that decision. Ask if the office has made arrangements to separate sick and well children during visits and whether there is an inviting play area for your child while you're waiting. You'll need a doctor who takes the time to talk to you and listen to you. Instructions should be simple and clear. You'll want to choose someone who invites you to be honest about your fears, worries, and inadequacies. Before you go for an appointment make it a habit to write down all your questions. It also doesn't hurt to write down the suggestions you get while you're at the office so you won't forget anything after you leave.

It's more than appropriate to interview a number of doctors before deciding on one. This can all be done before your baby's arrival. One valuable but often-not-thought-of resource in picking a pediatrician is the staff at hospital nurseries or your obstetrician's office. These individuals are usually familiar with a number of pediatricians and their practices.

LABOR, DELIVERY, AND RECOVERY

The most difficult thing about being pregnant is there's only one way out of the situation, and that way is definitely no stroll through the daffodils. The last month of confinement is designed to make women forget what it takes to get it over with. By the time you're big enough and miserable enough to do almost anything, almost anything begins and you suddenly don't feel so ready anymore. The problem is there's no turning back. You can't hop off the delivery table, turn to your husband, and say, "I don't want to do this anymore!" It's ready or not, here I come.

You can count on two things with labor and delivery, you will feel pain, and the outcome of all that pain will be worth it. Please don't have a preconceived idea in your head about how things *should* happen. Stay open-minded. All the worst horror stories I've heard have involved women so set on *one way* to have a baby they wouldn't consider other options. Your labor and delivery may not go as you planned, but you and your baby will most likely survive and thrive.

WHAT TO EXPECT

No two childbirth experiences are alike; so don't expect your labor and delivery experience to go by the book. Also, don't believe everything you hear from other mothers before you deliver. Men tend to brag and embellish stories about hunting trophies, paychecks, and sports prowess. Women tend to brag about and embellish their marathon labor and delivery experiences. Take it from me, you can only believe about half of what you hear.

After everything I'd heard and read before I delivered my first child, I was still basically very naïve. I was completely shell-shocked as my husband raced me to the hospital in the middle of the night in April when our baby wasn't due until June . . . because I was leaking . . . heaven knows what. The doctor barely made it to the hospital in time to catch. I'd read that first-time mothers were supposed to have at least a 12-hour delivery and that labor progresses nicely and neatly through specific stages. Instead, my first delivery was my all-time shortest, and I went from first contraction to baby's head crowning in the time it took to get to the hospital ten minutes away. So be prepared to be surprised.

EXPECT THE UNEXPECTED

I didn't have a clue what was happening to me when my amniotic fluid ruptured. I thought I had a very weak bladder. In my defense, we'd only covered breathing exercises in my prenatal class. I had yet to learn that when you start leaking it means the fluid-filled membranes containing the baby have ruptured. The fluid within the membranes (amniotic fluid) leaks from the vagina. I'm glad my husband had the good sense to report this to a doctor and transport me immediately to the hospital. Learn all you can several months before you are due to deliver; this way, you'll have a small idea of what may or may not be happening.

What actually happens to you will be unique. After all is said and done, remember that whatever happens will provide you with great stories to brag about and embellish some day. The point of labor and delivery is the triumphant, miraculous birth of your baby and a healthy, happy you. *How* that happens is less important than the wonderful reality that it does happen.

PAIN RELIEF

Talk to your doctor before you deliver about the various forms of pain relief available to you during your labor and delivery. Some women feel that "natural (unmedicated) childbirth" is best and focus on relaxation and breathing techniques. Others opt for a little or a lot of the modern medical help available.

NATURAL CHILDBIRTH

If you are interested in natural childbirth, be sure to keep up your Kegel exercises and ask your healthcare provider about touch and massage, pressure points, music therapy, meditation/focal point, visualization/guided imagery, warm water, and changing positions.

Kegel exercises help you learn how to relax the pubococcygeal muscle. Touch and massage have proven to be very helpful in pain relief and relaxation during labor. Pressure point techniques include applying pressure to certain areas of the body that are most painful. Music helps you relax because it drowns out other distractions. Meditation or focusing your attention on one thing allows you to block out distracting thoughts and noise. Visualization or guided imagery involves focusing on an image in your mind that is special or peaceful to you. Warm water from a bath or shower and changing positions also help to reduce pain.

Every expectant mother should learn about relaxation and breathing techniques like these but she should never feel like she's failed if she asks for or accepts pain relief during delivery. I don't think any of us would like to go back to natural tooth extraction. I've had half my babies without any pain relief and half with some help. Frankly, those deliveries where I had some form of pain relief were more peaceful and gave me sweeter memories than the ones where I had no help.

MEDICATED CHILDBIRTH

Several different types of medication are often used during childbirth, including analgesics (pain-relieving medicine), narcotics, tranquilizers, and sedatives. Some are given orally and some through an IV. Each type of medication has advantages and disadvantages you should discuss with your doctor. During labor, a woman usually receives fluids through intravenous tubing to prevent dehydration and as a quick way to give drugs immediately if needed.

Local Anesthesia

A local anesthetic can be given at the opening of the vagina to numb the perineum. It can also be given as a pudendal block or as a regional anesthesia.

A pudendal block is a commonly used procedure that involves injecting a local anesthetic through the wall of the vagina and anesthetizing the pudendal nerve, which numbs the entire vaginal area. Local anesthesia is also effective when repairing episiotomies and lacerations after delivery.

Regional Anesthesia

Regional anesthesia is given in the lower back or in the lower birth canal. The anesthetic blocks the nerve impulses that transmit pain from the contracting uterus, the dilating cervix, and the stretching birth canal.

In the most common procedure, a local anesthetic is injected into the space that surrounds the spinal cord in the lower back. A thin, flexible tube inserted in this space—called the epidural space—carries the anesthesia to the nerves. The procedure is commonly called an epidural block and numbs the lower part of the body.

A woman who chooses to have an epidural may need to push longer. The strength of the epidural is dependent on the amount of medication given, and you are in charge of how much you get. Feel free to tell the anesthesiologist to start off with a small dose of medication in the epidural. You can always get more medication later if needed. If the epidural is too strong, it may take a long time to regain normal hip and leg movement and sensation.

INDUCTION OF LABOR

Although doctors agree that it's best for nature to take its course and let labor begin on its own, there are a few selected occasions when labor might be induced. To induce labor, the mother-to-be is usually given Pitocin®, a synthetic oxytocin that makes the uterus contract. Oxytocin is the hormone in a woman's body that contributes to the start of labor and the "let down" response in nursing. The drug is administered intravenously and is gradually increased until contractions begin. During the whole process, your abdomen will be monitored to check your baby's reaction to the contractions, which are known to come on hard and fast with the administration of Pitocin. Mothers who are induced can choose to proceed with a natural or medicated childbirth.

Being sick and tired of pregnancy or having your mother in town are not ample reasons for induction. A doctor may recommend induction for the following circumstances:
- Labor has been stalled.
- The fetus is not thriving (this may be due to problems with the placenta, low levels of amniotic fluid, postmaturity, and so on) and is developed enough to survive well outside the womb.
- The placenta, as shown by the results of a non-stress test, is not functioning properly or is deteriorating.
- Your pregnancy has lasted two or more weeks past a reliable due date.
- The mother has preeclampsia that cannot be controlled by bed rest and medication. (In some cases, this may require an emergency cesarean section instead of normal induction.)

A day before induction, your doctor may choose to ripen the cervix in preparation for the induction. This is usually done with a drug called Prepidil Gel® (dinoprostone cervical gel) or Cervidil™ (dinoprostone). Your doctor may also break your water to move things along a bit faster.

Spinal blocks, which are commonly used in cesareans, and low spinal (or saddle) blocks are administered in one dose just prior to delivery. In this procedure, an anesthetic is injected into the fluid surrounding the spinal cord.

General Anesthesia

General anesthesia renders a woman temporarily unconscious. It isn't used when it can be avoided because it slows the functioning of the baby's heart, lungs, and brain. It may be used for an emergency cesarean section because it's the quickest way to anesthetize a woman.

STAGES OF LABOR

There are two key ways of knowing you are really in labor: (1) your water breaks, or (2) you begin having abdominal contractions (usually accompanied by pain in your lower back) at regular intervals that won't stop when you change positions. The trouble is . . . you've been having abdominal contractions and pain in your lower back for months. This makes it hard for first-time moms—and even a lot of seasoned moms—to know if it's the real thing. If your water breaks, you're definitely in labor and should get to the hospital in a timely fashion (although some women don't experience their first contractions until hours after their water breaks). If the pain is unbearable and consistent, you should also get moving. And, because you've probably been in pain for the past three months and you're not quite sure that this recurring pain is bad enough to be the real thing, it's always better to go and get checked just in case. It's always better to be sent home than have your baby in the car on the way there. The only real difference between what you've already been feeling and the real thing is that the pain (or contractions) become progressively worse and won't go away. The next few pages will help you review the stages of labor and get some idea of what you're feeling and what stage of labor you are in.

EARLY LABOR

Labor is just what it sounds like, work. Early labor is usually the longest and easiest part of that work. This is not the time to panic and time every contraction. Early labor typically lasts from two to ten hours and sometimes longer, especially for first-time mothers. In early labor, the cervix thins out and dilates to about three or four centimeters. Some mothers feel the pains in their lower back, while others experience the uterine contractions as abdominal cramps. Some women will experience a bloody show (a mucousy, blood-tinged discharge), indigestion, or diarrhea. And some women will barely notice this stage at all. The length and frequency of your contractions will vary; but typically your

---

THINGS TO DO
WHILE YOU'RE IN LABOR

- *anything* that makes you feel better
- listen to soothing music
- watch television
- practice meditation
- ask your husband for a back or foot rub
- have someone squeeze your hips together
- munch on ice
- change positions
- make weird sounds to scare people
- practice your breathing exercises

---

pains will last about 30 to 60 seconds and space themselves anywhere from 5 to 20 minutes apart but will be inconsistent and sometimes irregular. When the contractions are consistently 5 minutes apart, or when your water breaks, it's time to go to the hospital.

Pacing Yourself

It helps to remember that having a baby is a lot like running a marathon. You need to pace yourself and reserve your strength because you have a long way to go yet. During the early part of labor it's best to relax and keep busy. You don't need to sit around and time your contractions. If you're in bed, try to catch some extra shut-eye. I promise, you will not sleep through the birth of your baby.

If you're awake, go ahead and shower, take a walk, or clean your house. Do anything to relax yourself and keep busy. It's a good idea to eat light meals and drink lots of fluids because once you get to the hospital or birthing center, your medical support team will probably tell you not to eat anything. Hydrated muscles contract better. This might be a good time to try out positions and techniques with your labor coach to find out what feels the best and helps the most. You can ask your husband for a priesthood blessing.

As the frequency and consistency of the contractions increase, so will the pain. You'll know it's time to go if you can't keep walking, working, or laughing through the contractions.

ACTIVE LABOR

Your contractions during active labor become longer and more frequent. Typically your pains will last from about 45 seconds to a minute and they'll be about two to five minutes apart. They will dilate the cervix from about four to seven centimeters. By the start of active labor, most mothers are in the hospital or birthing center. If you want to request pain relief, now is the time. If you wait until you're really hurting, it will probably be too late.

Some women choose an epidural because it blocks pain sensations from the waist down but keeps the mother fully alert and participating in the delivery. An epidural is an injection of anesthetic into the area outside the spinal cord. Tell your husband not to watch while they do this unless he's very curious and able to handle the sight of a very long needle.

Your water may break at this stage, which means the warm clear amniotic fluid surrounding your baby suddenly flows from your vagina and soaks your bed or clothes. You may think you've wet your pants for a minute before you realize what's really happening. It may leak a bit at a time or come in a big gush. I remember one labor nurse with her mop and bucket next to my bed saying, "This is definitely the most amniotic fluid I've ever seen come out of one woman."

Active labor goes smoother if you have a loving and supportive partner who can coach you and provide mental distractions and reassurance. That basically means you need a husband or mother who doesn't panic easily and can help keep your spirits up.

Hospitals are generally anxious to get you into bed and strap you with all kinds of instruments, charting your labor valleys and peaks and keeping track of your baby's heartbeat. But remember, even if you are in the hospital, you're in charge of how you want to handle this scene.

I've had my babies naturally, with pain relief, and on the operating table. There is no one method that is superior to the another. The point is to have a healthy baby *and* mother at the conclusion of this drama.

Electronic Fetal Monitoring

During active labor in a hospital or birthing center, an electronic fetal monitor with two belts will likely be placed on your abdomen. The monitor records the baby's heartbeat and your uterine contractions. If necessary, a fetal monitor can also be applied to the baby's head through the mother's vagina.

TRANSITION

During transition (a mini-stage at the end of active labor where the cervix becomes fully dilated to ten centimeters), contractions are faster and more intense. You may feel as if one contraction doesn't even end before getting to the next. This is the shortest and most difficult part. During transition you may feel very nauseous and tremble uncontrollably. You may also feel cold or hot or both alternately. This mad mix of sensations as well as exhaustion can be scary and discouraging.

Do anything that will help you move to the next stage.

Some techniques that help during this period are massage, letting gravity aid you, breathing techniques, hot and cold packs, music, meditation, and staying hydrated. If you've had an epidural, the nurse will tell you when you've reached this stage and you'll see your doctor getting ready for the big show.

PUSHING

When you're fully dilated, it's time to push the baby through the birth canal. Don't worry, it's not that far. The baby is basically almost out anyway. As a first-time naïve mother, I remember I had visions of the birth canal going on for miles. Contractions at this point usually last about 60 to 90 seconds and come about every two to five minutes.

Pushing can last ten minutes to three hours. Good pushers usually have their babies faster than lazy pushers. You'll probably feel a lot of rectal pressure during this stage. The best way to describe how to push is a little graphic: imagine that you're having a huge bowel movement, then push as hard as you can. It's not unusual to actually push out a bowel movement. If you're horribly worried about this you can request an enema when you get to the hospital.

Everything I've ever read always says women have an uncontrollable urge to push when they're fully dilated. You may feel this urge or you may not. I *never* felt the urge to push. No matter what you feel, *do* pay attention and cooperate when your birth attendants tell you to push and when not to push. While you're pushing, ask for a mirror to be positioned so you can see what's happening down there. With a mirror you can check your progress and get a better visual understanding of what makes a productive push. There's nothing quite like seeing your newborn's head crowning for the first time to give you new energy to finish the job.

That little head will slip back in and out a few times before it comes through. When the head comes through the doctor will ask you *not* to push while he suctions out the mouth and nose. To prevent a tear of the perineum, listen closely to your doctor as the baby's head and shoulders are delivered.

Forceps or Vacuum Extractor

Your doctor may use forceps to assist in delivery if certain problems exist (fetal distress, maternal distress, prolonged labor). Forceps are medical instruments that roughly resemble metal salad tongs. They are placed around your baby's head and are used to assist in pulling the baby out while you push. Usually, an anesthetic is administered to the mother and the forceps are used to gently deliver the baby.

A vacuum extractor may also be used. This devise has a small cup made of rubber-like material that adheres to the baby's head when the vacuum is started. Then your baby is gently pulled out as the mother pushes.

Both of these methods seem quite scary but are relatively safe. You should discuss with your doctor any fears regarding the use of these procedures and the necessity for doing so.

EPISIOTOMY

An episiotomy is an incision made in the perineum (layers of muscles and tissues between the vagina and rectum) that allows the baby's head to pass through the vagina more easily and keeps you from tearing. This is not a routine procedure,

and your healthcare provider will tell you if he thinks it is necessary. Many mothers prefer to avoid this procedure if necessary. Your doctor or nurse-midwife should be able to instruct you in ways to soften and stretch that area and thus avoid an episiotomy if you desire.

DELIVERING THE PLACENTA

The final stage of labor occurs after delivery of the baby and usually lasts only a few minutes. You may be so excited about seeing your newborn for the first time that you hardly notice what's going on down there. After your baby is delivered, your midwife or doctor will probably place their hand on your abdomen to make sure the uterus is still contracting. The placenta will usually detach from the uterus during the first or second contraction after delivery. You might notice that a big gush of blood will follow. You will most likely be able to push the placenta out on your own; but if you can't, or if you're bleeding excessively, your doctor or midwife may apply very firm downward pressure on your abdomen to make the placenta detach. If the placenta is not complete, your doctor or midwife will be able to remove anything that remains by hand. As soon as the placenta has been delivered, you may be given oxytocin and/or your abdomen may be massaged to help the uterus continue to contract. Don't fight this. You need your uterus to contract to prevent excessive bleeding from the part of the uterus where your placenta was attached. After the delivery of the placenta, your doctor or midwife will stitch the episiotomy incision or any tears in the cervix or vagina if necessary. The first four hours after the delivery of the placenta are when the risk of bleeding is greatest and you should be closely monitored during this time.

CESAREAN

Be prepared for the possibility of a cesarean birth. In the United States, about 22 percent of deliveries are cesarean. Don't let anyone tell you that having a cesarean section is not as fulfilling as a vaginal birth. I was surprised how fast they got my baby out and how long it took them to sew me back up. It takes only ten minutes to get the baby out and about an hour to repair. The healthcare practitioners involved are an obstetrician, an anesthesiologist, nurses, and a specialist such as a neonatologist, if needed. A cesarean is safe but results in more overall pain after the operation than a vaginal delivery and a longer hospital stay.

This is major surgery and shouldn't be done unless it's really necessary. Multiple births, diabetes, heavy bleeding, blood pressure problems, babies in the breech or transverse position, or other pregnancy-related problems may make a cesarean section necessary. Many are performed because the baby is simply too big for the pelvis or because the labor is prolonged and not effective.

THE INCISION

If possible, discuss the type of incision with your doctor. Tell your doctor you want a low, horizontal incision—a bikini cut—so you can have the choice of a vaginal delivery next time. Many women today are offered an opportunity to deliver vaginally

after a cesarean. Vaginal births are less costly and have a shorter and easier recovery. Cesareans have the greater risk of anesthesia and wound complications. The type of incision made is critical in the later delivery options.

Some conditions, such as placenta previa, may require an incision in the upper part of the uterus. Blood loss is greater with an upper incision and the scar is weaker. Not all moms who have cesarean sections can choose what type of incision is done. If an emergency cesarean section is performed to maintain the life of the baby or the mother, sometimes the fastest cut to get the baby out must be done.

MEDICATION

You can request anesthesia to keep you pain free from the waist down but still awake during the procedure. You'll be able to see and touch your baby sooner this way. Your husband can be with you in the operating room if you'd like. They usually seat Dad next to your head so he can talk to you and reassure you. He won't have to watch the operation if he doesn't want to because they'll have a curtain separating your top half from your bottom half.

Before all the anesthetic wears off, make sure you get a chance to hold and nurse your baby. Just because you had to have a cesarean section doesn't mean something is wrong with you or your baby. Your little one will sport a nice round head and your bottom will feel pretty good. Of course you'll have pain and stitches in another area. The first time I saw my cesarean section scar and stitches I thought it looked like a grotesque smiley face. Now I have to look closely to even see the scar.

AFTER SURGERY

After the surgery you'll probably have a nurse monitoring you closely for a few hours. You can expect a hospital stay of three to five days. Those first few days can be tough and you may need to take some painkillers for a while. They'll have you up and out of bed after the first 24 hours. Remember to go to the bathroom often, at least every four hours. Trust me, a full bladder makes your after pains worse.

Gas pains are typical after abdominal surgery. You may be on a liquid diet for a day. You'll be happy to start solid foods again; but while you're waiting, drink yourself silly with lots of water, juice, and broth. Get up and start walking the halls as soon as you can. You have to pass gas before they let you go home. Your gas pains may be more painful than the incision itself. The more you get up and walk around the better it will be. Your nurse will probably have you cough and do some deep breathing as well.

Expect to have vaginal discharge after a cesarean. Remember to keep your incision clean and dry. Tell your healthcare provider if your incision becomes red, swollen, tender, or starts draining.

Some women feel sad after a cesarean section, wondering if they have somehow failed because they didn't have their baby the way they expected. Remember, it's always better to have a cesarean section than to put you or your baby at risk. Your cesarean is a marvelous medical advancement, not a maternal failure. The birth of your baby is always something to celebrate.

AFTER THE BABY IS BORN

After your baby is born the doctor will suction your infant's mouth and nose so he can breathe better. Then your baby takes his first breath. Two clamps will be placed on the umbilical cord side by side. Many times, your husband will be able to cut the cord between the clamps. Your baby will be dried and laid carefully on a sterile warm blanket or on your chest.

BONDING

You may hear or read that it is absolutely necessary for your baby to be placed immediately on your chest for proper bonding to take place. You have a lifetime to bond with your baby. Don't let anyone scare you into thinking that any one moment in life will eternally alter your ability to love your child. If your doctor's first assessment of your baby is good he will probably place the baby on your chest. If, however, your doctor feels your baby should be evaluated by medical experts as quickly as possible, you may not have that option. Your doctor will do what is deemed most necessary and prudent for your baby based on his first evaluation.

EVALUATING THE BABY

While the doctor is busy delivering the placenta and sewing you up if necessary, the nurse or birth attendant will weigh and measure the baby, then check the heart rate, breathing, muscle tone, reflexes, and color. Your child will be scored in each of these categories, receiving 0, 1, or 2 points in each. The highest possible score is 10. A score of 7 is considered good, and many babies with lower scores also turn out to be normal and healthy. Don't worry. This test, called the Apgar test, is just a quick way to assess your baby and see if everything is working properly. A second Apgar test will be done at five minutes of age. As soon as possible your baby will be wrapped in light-weight clothing and his head covered to reduce heat loss. A few antibiotic drops or a silver nitrate solution will be placed into his eyes to prevent infection.

If your baby is doing fine, pretty soon you'll have your little one in your arms. You may be surprised by how alert and calm he is, how loud he cries, or how far he can urinate . . . but the best surprise is how much you love him already. This tiny piece of heaven will change your life for-ever.

SOAKING IN THE MOMENT

Just for now, soak in the whole delicious moment. The first time you touch your baby is a genuine once-in-a-lifetime moment to savor. Take your time getting to know each other. You are allowed to sing, cry, or *whoop* when you hold your baby for the first time. Don't let anyone hurry you. Talk to your baby. Pretend you two are the only ones in the room and in the universe. Say everything you want to say. Kiss and hug and stroke and nuzzle to your heart's content.

You can nurse your baby right there if you'd like, for nursing helps your uterus contract back to its normal size and your baby to bond. This first nursing experience is mostly trial and error so don't worry about how things work out. Your baby may latch right on or act confused. Don't worry. You'll try again later. Then you'll try again and again until you both get the hang of it. You're the mother now, so do it your way and at your own pace. Don't let anyone hurry you. Somewhere amidst all this happiness, Dad gets his turn in this new family circle of love.

IF THERE ARE PROBLEMS WITH THE BABY

If your baby has any problems, she may be taken to the newborn intensive care

unit and stabilized. Don't panic. Your husband can follow your baby and keep you informed about your baby's progress while you recover. It will be scary and disappointing that you won't be able to hold your baby after all you've been through, but you can rest assured that everything that should be done to help your baby will be done.

YOUR REACTION TO DELIVERY

Don't be surprised if you find yourself shaking uncontrollably after delivery. Your body is reacting to the shock, stress, and strain of this monumental event. Ask for extra warmed blankets and give your mind and your body time to adjust to what just happened. You may be given a shot to help relax your muscles and relieve pain.

WHERE ARE THEY TAKING MY BABY?

At some point your nurse or medical attendant will probably want to take the baby and bring him to the nursery for a while. While your baby is away, he'll probably have his heel pricked for a PKU test and be given a vitamin K injection to help with blood clotting and a hepatitis B

vaccination as required by most state laws. He'll also receive a hospital wristband and his first bath. Your husband will be free to go along and help out.

And finally, after all this drama, the spotlight will shift from you to the beautiful new human being you just brought into the world. After you give birth it may feel like everyone leaves your room just when you start feeling the combined effects of exhaustion, after pains, and nausea. Your husband and other family members usually follow the baby to the nursery. Remember, your nurse is always nearby and you can use the call button at your bedside if you need help.

If you had your baby in the delivery room, you'll be moved to the recovery room for a few hours until your anesthetic wears off and you don't feel sick anymore. If you had your baby in a birthing room you'll probably stay there for recovery and then be sent to the maternity ward or your private or semi-private room for the rest of your hospital stay. You'll spend the next few hours or days learning to take care of yourself and your brand new baby. It will be overwhelming and wonderful.

ROOMING IN

During your hospital stay, you can choose whether you want your newborn to stay in the same room with you all the time or part of the time. If it's difficult for you to sleep soundly while your baby is in the room, you might want the nurses to take your baby in the nursery while you get some much-needed sleep; once you're at home, it will probably be a little harder to sleep. The nurse will bring your baby to you right away when she needs nursing.

Of course, you may prefer that your little one be right with you during the stay at the hospital. This is fine, too, and may give you some peace of mind to hear all her new baby sounds through your first night or two together.

GIVING YOUR BABY THE ONCE OVER

As soon as you feel up to it, give your little one a good looking over. Count every finger and toe. Babies love and need to be touched, stroked, and talked to as much as they need to eat. While you do your first inspection, you may be surprised by some of your newborn's characteristics. The head will seem large in comparison to the body. The genitals may seem oversized and swollen. The umbilical cord and clamp might worry you. Your baby's skin will be covered with a whitish greasy material (vernix caseosa). This substance protects your baby's skin against infection. Your baby's head may seem bruised or misshapen from birth. Yet, by in large, you'll think your baby is the most beautiful child who has ever been born. And he is.

NEW MOTHER CARE

After you deliver, you'll be monitored and treated to relieve pain. In the first 24 hours your pulse rate may drop and your temperature may rise slightly. You can expect a bloody vaginal discharge that should gradually change to a pale brown and finally a yellowish-white. Hospitals try to minimize your risk of bleeding, pain, and

infection. After you deliver the placenta you may be given oxytocin to stimulate contractions of the uterus, and your abdomen will be periodically massaged (unless you had a cesarean section) by a nurse to help the uterus contract.

Once the first 24 hours have passed, recovery is rapid. Women who have had vaginal deliveries can resume a regular diet as soon as they'd like.

Before you leave the hospital a complete blood cell count will be performed to make sure you're not anemic. If your blood type is Rh-negative and you have a baby who is Rh-positive, you will be given Rh(D) immune globulin within three days of delivery. This insures that antibodies produced by you against the baby's blood won't endanger future pregnancies.

The most common complications after birth are excessive bleeding, urinary tract infections, and problems with breastfeeding. Bleeding and infection can be treated with counsel from your doctor and medication. Problems with breastfeeding, however, are usually solved more quickly if you have an experienced mother who has breastfed several babies as a mentor or a competent lactation expert to counsel with.

FOR PAIN RELIEF AFTER DELIVERY

- Apply ice packs to the perineum during the first few hours after delivery.
- Use a squeeze bottle of warm water to rinse yourself after using the bathroom.
- Take a warm sitz bath to relieve painful hemorrhoids.
- Shower as soon as permitted. Don't douche for at least six weeks.
- Keep your bladder empty. Go to the bathroom at least every four hours.
- Drink lots of water and juice and take a stool softener to avoid constipation.
- Take pain medication as prescribed by your doctor. Ibuprofen (Advil or Motrin), acetaminophen (Tylenol), and Lortab, a combination of acetaminophen and hydrocodone, are all common postpartum medications that are safe to take while breastfeeding. Avoid aspirin, as it causes increased bleeding and is not recommended for nursing mothers.

THE THREE B'S

During your hospital stay, your thoughts will center largely on the three Bs: your baby, your bottom, and your breasts. After I had my first baby, I was amazed that my bottom half could go through all that trauma without falling off. I was also sure I would be the first woman in history who never produced any milk because my breasts were so small. Thankfully, I discovered the female body is downright amazing. Don't forget to marvel at everything that's happening to your body, no matter how much it hurts. The birth of a baby and the recovery of a new mother is always a miracle of monumental proportions and worth a grateful audience.

Just when your anesthesia or pain pills wear off and you're sure you never want to move again, your nurse will get you up to use the bathroom. Don't resist. A full bladder makes your after pains more painful. If your nurse inserts a catheter, you're more likely to get a urinary tract infection.

If you had stitches, they may hurt as they shrink and begin healing. You may be constipated. Your breasts will swell and may be painful as your milk comes in. You will look at yourself in the mirror and realize you still look pregnant. You might see stretch marks, a bulging belly, or a cesarean section scar. Take heart. Remember the phrase most used in the Book of Mormon . . . "and it came to pass." All these problems will take care of themselves in time.

AFTER PAINS

After birth, your uterus will continue to contract, getting progressively smaller until it returns to normal size. This sounds nice enough, but that means you'll feel like you're still in labor for a few days—and that hurts. It seems like these after pains get longer and harder after each baby. Ask for pain relief before you're so miserable you scare your friends and family. After pains usually last five to seven days and may be intensified by breastfeeding because the hormone oxytocin is released naturally to start the flow of milk. If after pains are a problem take a pain pill 30 minutes *before* you nurse.

BLOOD LOSS

Normally you'll lose about one pint of blood during delivery as blood vessels are opened when the placenta separates from the uterus. The contractions of the uterus will help close these vessels until they can heal. Your blood loss may be greater if the uterus doesn't contract or if a piece of placenta remains inside, preventing the uterus from contracting. A tear in the vagina or cervix can also cause excessive bleeding.

You'll continue to lose blood, mucus, and tissue, called lochia, from your uterus for quite some time. To keep yourself fresh and unstained in the days and weeks following delivery, you'll need to wear a sanitary pad to soak up blood loss. At first, you will likely bleed as much—or more—as you would during the heavy days of your menstrual cycle. You may experience gushing when you get up and will likely pass a number of clots. After the first three or four days, the bleeding will taper off, becoming pink, then brown, then yellowish-white in color. You may have some type of bleeding on and off for the next six weeks. Do not use tampons during this time.

Eventually, the contractions you experience after delivery will return your uterus to its normal size. If contractions do not occur, you may have excessive bleeding. You will be checked several times during your hospital stay for postpartum hemorrhaging.

HELP! I STILL LOOK PREGNANT

Your abdomen won't become as flat as it was before pregnancy for several months, even if you exercise, so don't despair. Stretch marks may take a year to lighten. Don't try to get back into your old clothes too quickly. Plan to have some elastic waist pants, loose-fitting jumpers, and overalls on hand to wear for a while. It took you nine months of pregnancy to get this baby here. Give yourself at least that long to get your strength back and work

POSTPARTUM HEMORRHAGING

Be on the lookout for the following signs of postpartum hemorrhaging:
- bleeding that saturates more than one pad an hour for more than several hours
- bleeding that is bright red any time after the fourth day postpartum
- heavy bleeding like that listed above that does not slow down with rest
- a foul smell
- large clots (larger than the size of your closed fist)
- pain or swelling in the lower abdomen that occurs beyond the first few days postpartum

into a regular exercise program that works for you and your circumstances. I always figured that each baby was a two-year, total-body commitment.

Give yourself time to get back in shape. Start small. Plan to exercise for just a few minutes a day in the beginning. Go for walks or bicycle rides with your baby in a stroller or trailer. Develop an aerobic dance, stretching, and weight bearing workout to your favorite music that you can do inside your home on any day of the year and in any weather. If you can afford it, you might enjoy joining a local gym or workout class.

You might consider enlisting a group of Relief Society sisters to go on morning or evening walks with you. If he's willing, go for runs, walks, or bicycle rides with your husband. Anything you do to keep yourself moving and breaking a sweat every day will improve your emotions and your physical health. Cut yourself some slack.

Be patient and gentle with yourself. You do not have to look like a professional model to be a beautiful healthy woman.

I'M STILL TIRED AND SHAKY

Don't be surprised if you're shaky and very tired for the first few days and weeks after you have a baby. You'll need help when you get home with cooking, laundry, and housework for a while. Your new baby won't know the difference between day and night, so you'll need help with late-night feedings. If you're nursing you can ask your husband to bring the baby to you and put her back to bed when you're through. Your husband can also help burp the baby and change her diapers and get her back to sleep. If you're bottle feeding your husband can take his turn at the late night feedings. If a relative or your husband can't be home to help, consider hired help.

COPING WITH THE BABY BLUES

After you come home from the hospital, you might find yourself crying a lot and feeling blue. If you do, you're not alone. Most women have some form of the after-baby blues. Mild depression is common and usually appears within three days after birth, lasting for about two weeks. Symptoms include a loss of appetite, feelings of hopelessness, over- or under-concern about the baby, fear of your baby, inability to sleep, or a need for excessive sleep. Lots of things contribute to the after-baby blues. You may find yourself deliriously happy one moment and over-whelmed, crying, and depressed the next. After all, your new parental worries have piled up on you: your bottom and breasts

hurt, you don't get enough sleep, and you probably have too little or too much help. Well-meaning visitors and relatives may even keep you from needed rest and relaxation. You may be worried about going back to work or not going back to work. You may be depressed because your appearance and weight don't seem to be improving much.

Good old family and friend support is the best treatment. Cut yourself some slack during the year or two when you're pregnant and nursing each child. Your body, hormones, and emotions are on a roller-coaster ride. Feel free to throw up your arms and scream occasionally so the ride will be more fun.

POSTPARTUM DEPRESSION

Baby blues are normal, common, and shouldn't cause too much concern. Postpartum depression, on the other hand, should be taken very seriously. If you or someone who loves you thinks you might have postpartum depression, don't reach the desperate zone before you ask for help from your husband, relatives, or your doctor. Depression that lasts for more than two weeks and is combined with lack of interest in the baby, sleeplessness, a feeling of helplessness and hopelessness—even suicidal or violent thoughts, hallucinations, or bizarre behavior— is considered abnormal and treatment is necessary. Doctors can prescribe medications that will help to balance the chemicals racing through your system and return you to a sense of well-being. Some of these medications are even safe to take while nursing. Don't be afraid to seek professional help.

OTHER AFTER-PREGNANCY BODY CHANGES

In addition to after pains, bleeding, and one wild emotional roller-coaster ride, you may experience other changes after pregnancy, including:

• hair loss (don't worry, this should return to normal after several months)

• fading of the dark line on your lower abdomen (it will gradually disappear, and your stretch marks will fade to silvery lines)

• achy, weak, or stiff muscles

• more hemorrhoids (taking a stool softener will help to minimize the strain on your rectal area)

LIFE CHANGES

For the first few days or weeks, you'll probably have help from your husband, mother, sister, or friends. Perhaps ward members will even bring in meals for a few days. Then one day you'll look around and everybody will have gone home or back to work and left you *alone*. You will have days when you feel overwhelmed. When your baby cries, you will join in the chorus. You will wonder what in the world you have gotten yourself into and whether you're going to make it.

Please know that feeling overwhelmed and inadequate is perfectly normal. You are adjusting to the biggest life change you will ever experience. Give yourself time. Be patient with yourself and your baby. Pray a lot for health and strength. You will make it; and someday you'll look back at these early weeks with your new baby with humor and tenderness.

When Can I Have Sex Again?

Although the prospect of getting intimate with your husband may sound uncomfortable and painful in the first few days after delivery, you may be surprised that you feel quite up to it after just a few weeks. Or you may be surprised that it's months before you even have the energy to think about it.

Doctors advise that you wait six weeks before resuming sexual relations. It takes at least six weeks for your body to heal after delivery—longer if you've had a cesarean. After you've healed and you are in the mood again, you may experience a little pain. This is normal and should subside after time. You can also expect some vaginal dryness because of the hormones involved in breastfeeding. Try a water soluble cream or jelly to help. If you have any pain during intercourse, talk to your husband about it. If the problem continues, talk about it with your doctor.

And, remember, even though making love is a no-no in the first month and a half, this doesn't mean that you can't spend time cuddling, hugging, and enjoying one another's company as you revel in the new life you created.

BRINGING BABY HOME

If this is your first baby, it's also the first time you've ever been given complete responsibility for another human being—and it will take some getting used to. You may have a hard time relaxing. You may worry about your ability to feed, diaper, bathe, and soothe your baby. If you have other children, you may worry that you won't be able to give them the attention they need because you'll be so busy with the newborn. You may worry about how this new baby will affect your marriage and how you're going to pay for all this. I guarantee you'll do just fine and things will work out eventually if you can hang in there.

Focus on basic human survival for a few weeks after the baby is born, not some kind of super-mother accomplishment.

Being a mother at any age and circumstance means learning to live with lots of worries, mistakes, and inadequacies without letting them consume or overwhelm you. Remember, you have to live just one day at a time and you're permitted to muddle along the best you can. No matter how it appears, that's what the rest of us are doing. You don't have

to figure everything out today. You have tomorrow and the next day and the next.

GETTING STARTED

TRUSTING YOUR INSTINCTS

First-time mothers often feel their doctors, nurses, and parents are the experts. It's difficult to feel adequate at something you've never done before. Don't worry too much. Pretty soon you and your baby will get used to each other and figure out what to do. We're talking basic survival skills here. Don't be afraid to trust your own instincts. By the time you've had several babies, you'll be telling your doctors, nurses, and parents what to do and how to do it.

NEWBORN SOUNDS

New babies tend to cough and sputter and make all kinds of weird noises you're not used to. Sometimes their breathing seems strange too. I used to think my first-born would stop breathing and die if I didn't watch her hawk-like day and night. My older sister's first baby died after 16 days from a heart defect, and I was paranoid something was also wrong with my baby. It's normal to worry about everything when you've just had a baby, even if you've had a dozen. Just don't let all those worries keep you from enjoying your little one. All mothers have to leave their children in God's hands many, many times in life. God never tires or sleeps.

BABY'S FIRST BOWEL MOVEMENTS

Your newborn's first bowel movement will consist of a sticky, greenish black substance, called meconium. Your baby will pass this meconium within the first few days after birth. As your baby eats, he will gradually clear the bowel, and his stools will turn greenish brown and then yellow. Breastfed babies have bright yellow loose stools, and formula-fed babies have more brownish green stools.

You may be worried as you change your new daughter's first diapers when she has some redness and swelling of the external female genitals and a cream colored mucous or vaginal discharge. Some newborn girls will have a bloody vaginal discharge in the first days of life. This is normal and is caused by your hormones. This will go away in a few days or weeks and not return until puberty. Always wipe your baby girl from front to back and keep the opening of the vagina clean.

Your baby's later stools will vary in color and consistency from day to day. All babies have stools that vary in color and consistency. The number of stools your baby produces will vary from six to eight a day to one every other day. Most babies will strain or cry when they pass their stools.

JAUNDICE

About 30 percent of all newborns get jaundice. Jaundice is a newborn condition caused by excess yellow bilirubin pigment. Treatment may be required but is generally not necessary. You should probably place a call to your doctor after noticing any signs of jaundice. He can give you advice on how to proceed at home and let you know if your baby should be seen. To assess the degree of jaundice in a baby, press lightly on the skin to blanche it just a little. If there is a yellow pigment when the skin blanches, your baby has jaundice. The yellow color that indicates jaundice tends to appear first on the forehead, then the chest, then the knee. The whites of the eyes may also become yellow. Mild jaundice can be helped by placing your baby's bed next to a sunny window or by using a special light. If the yellow skin spreads below the level of the chest, your baby will need to have a blood test. If your baby seems hot, sleepy, or lethargic in addition to being jaundiced, it could be a sign of a serious bacterial infection and should be checked out immediately by a doctor. A fever is not a symptom of jaundice and will likely require close observation in a baby under two months of age.

CIRCUMCISION

If you have a son, you'll need to decide whether or not to circumcise him. Circumcision is the removal of the foreskin of the penis. After our first child was born, I heard the nurses asking every new mother in my ward if they wanted their child circumcised. I turned to my husband in a panic. "Ross, we haven't even talked about that. Should we or not?" I asked bewildered. "Jan," Ross replied calmly. "We have a girl." I'm sure you won't be as naïve as I was.

The number of circumcisions is steadily decreasing as more parents learn that it is seldom medically necessary. This is a personal decision a husband and wife make together after educating themselves.

Reasons for choosing circumcision include health and hygiene issues, religious reasons (although the LDS Church neither recommends nor discourages circumcision), whether the father of the baby is circumcised, and personal choice. This may be one parenting issue where the father has a stronger opinion than the mother. If you choose to have your baby circumcised, talk to your doctor to make sure your son is given local anesthetic. Be sure to follow your doctor's instructions for proper care and healing to take place.

NEWBORN SCREENING

Newborn testing varies in requirements from state to state. In Utah, newborn screening is performed for the following: phenylketonuria (PKU)—a congenital metabolic disease that can cause mental retardation if not treated—hypothyroidism, galactosemia, thalassemia, and hearing loss. Before you take your baby home from the hospital a blood sample will be taken and sent to the state laboratory to test for the first four diseases mentioned above. The procedure involved in drawing the blood sample is commonly referred to as the PKU test. While different states have different screening requirements, all test for PKU. Some states test for illnesses such as cystic fibrosis; and medical groups and parents throughout the United States are

constantly lobbying state legislatures to add other required tests to the screenings.

The procedure varies from state to state. In Utah, for example, when you leave the hospital, you will be given a card in an envelope that you should bring to your first office visit with your child's pediatrician. At the office, they will draw a second sample of blood—the drops of blood are squeezed onto the card, which is then placed back in the envelope—and send this second sample to the same lab.

UMBILICAL CORD

Try to keep your baby's umbilical cord site as clean and dry as possible while it heals. Recently, doctors and hospitals stopped recommending that mothers use rubbing alcohol to clean the umbilical cord. Instead, clean the area with a cotton-tip applicator dipped in water. Keep the diaper folded down underneath the umbilical cord so the cord does not become soaked with urine. If the skin around the cord becomes red or inflamed, let your doctor know immediately. The cord usually falls off after one to three weeks. The site may drain a small amount of creamy or bloody mucous for a few days after that.

DIAPERING

When you think it's time to change your baby's diaper, it's wise to wait five minutes—there's almost always more to come. If your baby's diaper is always leaking you probably have a boy. Point his penis downward while changing him. You may also want to cover it with a rag while you're wiping and pulling out the new

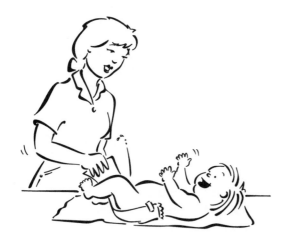

diaper. This will help you avoid a stream right in your face.

Always put a waterproof pad under your baby when you change him on your bed, no matter how fast you think you are. It's easier than changing your sheets. A bathroom counter near a sink makes a great changing table. Keep a stain remover on hand whenever you dress and change your baby. Then treat stains before throwing them in the hamper. There will be a lot of stains.

Once your baby begins to roll over and crawl, be prepared for even more difficulties in this category. When your child is mobile, diaper changing resembles an Olympic event that takes great skill and speed.

Diaper Rash

Every doctor and grandma has their favorite diaper rash remedy. The best remedy for your baby is the one that works for you. Of course, prevention is always best so try to change your baby's diaper as soon as possible after she wets or poops. You can help prevent diaper rash if you wash the diaper area clean each time you change your baby, whether the diaper is wet or soiled. You can also apply petroleum jelly or a diaper rash cream as a preventative.

When the diaper area is red but the skin is not broken, straight zinc oxide from a tube or jar works well. Commercial combination treatments that contain zinc oxide, cod liver oil, petroleum, lanolin, talcum, and purified water may also work for you. Some doctors and pharmacists recommend using a liquid antacid mixed with your favorite cream if the skin is extremely raw. When the skin is broken, straight petroleum jelly or an antibiotic ointment may work well. Some mothers swear by cornstarch or baby powder between changes, although these powders are much less necessary now than in the past because of improvements in disposable diapers that make them superabsorbent.

Ask your doctor for advice, experiment with diet changes and different skin rash remedies. If things get really bad, take the diaper off entirely and place your baby over and under soft cloth diapers while she airs out and heals. Certain rashes may need over-the-counter anti-fungal or hydrocortisone creams, while others may need a prescription. Check with your doctor for advice.

Children with extra-sensitive or dry skin may need to use a moisturizing cream without fragrances or other known irritants. Using straight water and soft paper towels instead of wipes with alcohol can also cut down on irritation. One little-known but highly effective dry-skin remedy is Udder Balm (sometimes called Bag Balm), sold to farmers for their cows. Look for this product at your local farm product store or cooperative.

WHERE IS THAT PERFECT, ROUND, FLAWLESS BABY I WAS EXPECTING?

Your newborn will not look like the babies you've been looking at in magazines. A newborn's skin will be wrinkled and reddish, and his fingers and toes may look blue before circulation improves. Your newborn may also sport a very misshapen head after his trip down the birth canal.

Don't worry; this will only last a few days.

Additionally, your baby may have swelling and bruising on the face and scalp. Dislocated hips are also fairly common in newborns.

Your new baby may display a few spots and blemishes that alarm you. Many newborns have portwine stains (flat, pink, red or purplish discolorations that appear anywhere on the body) or strawberry marks (raised, bright red areas from ½ to 4 inches in diameter). Strawberry marks occur in one out of ten babies and usually fade away by ten years of age. Some babies have "stork bites," salmon-colored patches that appear on the forehead, eyelids, or nape of the neck—where the stork carried your baby to you and dropped him off, of course. These also fade in time.

Your baby's genitals may also appear swollen for the first few weeks because of your hormones.

Don't worry about any of these things; you'll still think your baby is gorgeous. And, in a few weeks, your newborn will lose most of the redness, his head will take on a more round shape, and the swelling and bruising will be gone. He'll look exactly like the babies on the covers of magazines.

SKIN RASHES

Your newborn may have any number of skin rashes, including prickly heat, infant acne, eczema, and a number of other conditions that make you worry and fret. Eventually you'll learn that most skin rashes are normal and fleeting. Your healthcare provider might recommend treatments like less frequent bathing, non-perfumed soaps and lotions, hydrocortisone cream, lighter dressing, patience, or any number of prescription creams or other remedies.

In the first weeks after birth, most babies will have tiny dots on their noses or other areas of the face that look like tiny pimples. These are a result of the hormones that passed by your baby during delivery and are perfectly normal. Don't attempt to pop them, as it may cause scarring.

THRUSH

Thrush is a yeast infection that presents itself in your baby's mouth in the form of white patches on the inside of the cheeks and lips that will not rub off. The patches look something like cottage cheese, and if they do become scraped off, they leave sore red patches. Yeast infections can occur for a number of reasons, including if your baby is on antibiotics, has recently gone off antibiotics, or if her diaper is not changed regularly. Contact your health-care provider for the latest advice and treatment.

BIRTH CERTIFICATES

Soon after your baby is born, you should fill out an information form that includes your newborn's name, among other details, so that your child can receive a legal birth certificate. At most hospitals a nurse or medical assistant will talk to the new mother about these requirements and take care of submitting the form to the county health department. For any number of reasons, however, this may not happen. So, before you leave the hospital, request information about your child's birth certificate if someone has not approached you.

Ultimately, you are responsible to make sure you fill out all the information needed for his birth certificate and submit it in a timely manner even if you don't deliver in a hospital. It helps to have a name selected for your child before you leave the hospital or in the first few weeks.

Each state has different requirements and time limits for turning in information for inclusion on a permanent birth certificate. If you do not submit the necessary informa-tion on time you may not be able to change the original birth certificate document or you may be charged a substantial fee.

SOCIAL SECURITY CARDS

In addition to acquiring a birth certifi-cate, it is highly recommended that you apply for a social security card for your new baby. This can be done in the hospital and will most likely be included with the forms you are given to apply for a birth certificate. If not, be sure to ask about it. The new card will be mailed to your home within a few weeks and should be kept in a safe place. Your pediatrician's office, health insurance company, and any number of other places will be asking for the number as soon as your baby sees the doctor or needs any medical treatment.

BREASTFEEDING

Breastfeeding is one of the best things you can do for you and your baby. It's absolutely amazing that your body is designed to suddenly begin producing the perfect food for your new child. Breast milk is free, convenient, nutritious, prevents a number of childhood illnesses and aller-gies, and has special proteins to promote brain development.

Studies suggest that nursing helps reduce your baby's chance of developing diarrhea, urinary tract infections, respira-tory diseases, ear infections, allergies, pneumonia, and SIDS. Other studies have shown a decrease in obesity in children who have been breastfed. There are many compelling reasons to nurse your baby, and it's worth your best effort and perse-verance. If you can't breastfeed for long, any amount of time is better than no time at all. (See pages 74–76 for information on bottle feeding.)

Most pediatricians recommend that breast milk be a baby's only food for the first four to six months of life and the only milk he gets in the first year.

Breastfeeding is also optimal for you. Weight loss is easier for most nursing mothers because lactation burns 500 extra calories a day. Breastfeeding also produces the hormone oxytocin, which stimulates the uterus to shrink back to normal size more quickly and reduces bleeding. Research has shown that there may be a decrease in uterine and breast cancer for women who have breastfed. Other evidence suggests that breastfeeding may lower the risk of osteoporosis.

Being Comfortable with Your Breasts

If you're a first-time mother, handling your breasts for the first time might seem embarrassing or uncomfortable. You may not have the support of your husband, mother, or friends. Your breasts have previously been a part of your body that you've been taught to keep covered and private. Now you're suddenly expected to discreetly expose this part of your body with skill and produce your new baby's entire diet. That may be a big adjustment at first. Remember, it takes a while to get the hang of anything new. Don't let anyone discourage you. After those first few tough weeks, you'll be glad you hung in there.

The First Try

If you didn't begin nursing in the delivery room, you should try within the first four hours after birth. A full-term newborn should have an active rooting and sucking reflex and be able to start eating almost immediately. It is totally amazing to me that a baby who has been swimming about without eating or breathing on his own can suddenly do things as monumental as eating. It's amazing, magical, and holy. You will often feel nearer heaven in those first few days after birth than at any time in your life.

Not every baby comes with a rooting and sucking reflex, however. My first baby

---

THE ANATOMY OF THE BREAST

Your breasts are made of glandular, connective, and fatty tissues. Though you can't see it, your nipple contains many tiny openings for your milk to flow through. These openings are surrounded by muscular tissue that causes your nipple to protrude or stand erect when stimulated. The darker skin surrounding the nipple is called the areola. The areola contains pimple-like structures called Montgomery glands. These glands secrete a substance that helps lubricate and cleanse the breast.

Your baby's suckling will stimulate the nipples and send a message to the pituitary gland in the brain. This gland produces the hormone prolactin, which stimulates production in the milk glands. The pituitary gland simultaneously releases the hormone oxytocin, which causes the cells around the milk glands to contract and squeeze the milk down the ducts and out the nipples. The milk pools behind the nipple and beneath the areola in the milk sinuses.

Now isn't all that amazing? And you thought all your breasts did was give you a nice figure.

was premature and lacked the normal rooting and sucking reflex. She needed some extra help and patience as I worked with her, encouraging her to latch on and suckle. It takes time for a new mother and baby to get the hang of nursing. Don't expect everything to go smoothly in the beginning. Just keep trying. Pretty soon you'll both figure it out.

Do I Have to Nurse 'Round the Clock?

At first, it will seem like you're nursing all the time. And you may well be. During the first few days of life newborns are worn out from the tiring birth process and don't have much energy to suck for long periods of time. Additionally, newborn babies are so small that their tiny stomachs can't hold a whole lot of breast milk, which digests very quickly. To compensate, most newborns want to eat very often.

Fortunately, it's good for them—and for you—to practice nursing regularly. It will help your uterus contract; and it will help your baby learn to latch on and suck properly.

As the days go on, you'll find that your baby will continue to demand frequent and regular feedings—about 8 to 12 in a 24-hour period. This means you'll be feeding your baby every two to three hours. That is a lot of feeding time. Many mothers, in fact, begin feeling like human-sized walking pacifiers. If you're lucky, your baby will have one long stretch between feedings at night; but don't count on it. And even if your baby does sleep for a long stretch, you will likely want to wake her for a feeding after four or five hours just to keep up your milk supply. At times your baby may want several feedings in a row. As you cope with this new schedule, remember to relax and feed your baby when she shows any signs of hunger. In a short time, you'll recognize the signs that your baby is full, usually when she stops nursing, acts satisfied, or goes to sleep.

Colostrum

During the first few days of nursing, your baby will be fed off a liquid-gold, nutrient-rich substance called colostrum. This early milk is full of antibodies that will help prevent infection in your tiny baby.

When Your Milk Comes In

After a few days your breasts will become engorged—full and hard—indicating that your milk has come in. For many moms, engorgement can be quite painful. It can also be frustrating for baby if it means that the nipple is harder to latch onto. To help, try some of the following:

• Nurse frequently.

• Nurse on both sides at each feeding, starting with the less sore breast first since the baby will be sucking more vigorously then. Keep in mind that the less your baby sucks on a breast, the more engorged you will become.

- Take a hot shower.
- Apply warm compresses to your breasts. Or try an ice pack.
- Pump a little from each breast before beginning a nursing session. This may make it easier for your baby to take hold of the nipple.
- If you're not concerned about leaking, leave the flaps of your nursing bra open to relieve some pressure.

Once your milk is fully established and your soreness goes away, you can nurse from the first breast for as long as you and your baby desire. If your baby seems full and sleepy after the first breast, and you want him to nurse on the other side, try changing his diaper or tickling his feet to wake him up and encourage him to take the other breast. Remember to start your nursing sessions on alternate breasts each time. Babies tend to nurse most vigorously on the first breast offered and you'll want to maintain your supply on each side (this will also help you to keep from looking too lopsided). You can simply feel each breast to see which is the fullest or hardest and start on that one, or you can put a small safety pin on the nursing bra over the breast you started on last time. That way you'll know to start on the other side this time.

Let Down Reflex

When you begin a nursing session, your baby's first few moments of suckling will not produce much milk. The suckling, however, will quickly work to initiate "let down," the release of your milk through the ducts in your breast and out the nipple. The milk your baby receives after let down is called foremilk and is full of protein. Sometimes the amount of milk that is released as your breasts let down is overwhelming for your baby and may cause her to gulp as she works to take in the milk all at once.

You may be able to tell when your milk lets down because you'll feel a tingling sensation and your baby will start to swallow. Some mothers don't feel the let down, however, and only know when they see milk in their baby's mouth. Let down is a good indication that your baby is nursing well and correctly.

Because several things can inhibit the let-down reflex, including fatigue, tension, and pain, it's important to be patient, learn to relax, and make nursing time pleasant for you and your baby.

Hind Milk

If you nurse long enough on one side, you'll notice another let down of milk. This milk is called hind milk, or end milk, and is thicker and fattier. End milk helps make your baby feel full and aids in brain development. When you're trying to increase your milk supply, encourage your baby to nurse as long as possible to promote this second let down. Nursing on a dry breast will send the signal to the brain to produce more milk. If you're trying to discourage your overabundant milk supply, nurse for a shorter period of time.

Is My Baby Getting Enough to Eat?

The average baby usually loses weight in the first few days of life and will likely go home from the hospital weighing less than he did at birth. Your baby will probably regain his birth weight in the first two weeks of life, double it by the sixth month, and triple it in the first year. Don't be surprised if you become as obsessed with your new baby's every ounce as you were with your own weight gain during pregnancy. As a result, one of your biggest worries will be determining whether your child is getting enough to eat.

Over the first few days it will be difficult to know if an infant is getting enough breast milk. Once your milk comes in, however, you will be able to determine if breast milk intake is low by the number of times you change his diaper each day. Five wet-diaper changes or more a day indicates that your baby is, indeed, getting enough to eat. Most breastfed babies have bowel movements every day and sometimes, it seems, in every diaper.

Vitamins and Supplements for the Breastfed Baby

Discuss with your doctor the need to give your breastfed baby vitamin D supplements. Vitamin D helps to prevent rickets and is especially helpful for babies with dark skin pigmentation. Vitamin D is particularly helpful in the winter because humans synthesize vitamin D with the help of sunlight. In northern climates, sunlight during wintertime can be hard to come by. Vitamin D can be purchased over the counter in a variety of ways. Your doctor can best advise you on the proper route to take.

Once your child is around six months of age, when teeth generally start to erupt, many doctors will prescribe fluoride drops.

Overcoming Difficulties

Every mother runs into some problems when breastfeeding. In the first few weeks after birth you and your baby are adjusting to an array of lifestyle changes, as well as aches and pains in intimate places. It takes time to get accustomed to the whole nursing scene. Be patient with yourself and your baby. Many mothers go through the more difficult first few weeks of nursing then give up because they believe they are somehow inadequate to the task. *All* mothers feel inadequate in those early weeks. Give yourself time. Most problems with breastfeeding will be resolved with additional instruction, determination, and—there's that word again—patience.

Nursing your second, third, or later babies. Every mom and nursing baby are a unique "nursing couple." A mom may have nursed one child without any problems but have difficulty with the next child. Don't feel discouraged if you have previously nursed a child with ease but have trouble nursing another child. Persistence and patience are necessary with each child, not just the first.

Sore nipples. Most mothers experience sore, blistered, or cracked nipples for a while. Your nipples may become so sore, in fact, that you'll cry and wonder if you really want to do this anymore. This is normal. There's no getting around it; breastfeeding can be hard at first. Several things can help.

1. Wear a supportive bra.

2. Don't listen to magazine articles and lactation experts who swear that your nipples won't get sore if you're practicing proper latching-on and off techniques. Those kind of claims just make you feel worse. The truth is this: somebody with a very powerful suction device called a newborn mouth is suddenly and continually sucking on a very sensitive part of your body for many hours a day and night. After a while, that hurts . . . even if you *do* know how to get the baby to latch on and off correctly.

NURSING TECHNIQUES

When you begin a nursing session, remember the words *calm, comfortable,* and *close.* Settle into a comfortable, relaxed position. You can either sit up or lie down. Experiment with positions until you find the one that works for you.

Latching on. Support your breast with your free hand, thumb and index finger on top, and other fingers below. Bring your baby's head to the breast and brush your nipple against the baby's lower lip. This stimulates the baby to open his mouth—the rooting reflex—and grasp the breast. Be sure to ease the whole nipple and as much of the areola (colored part) as possible into the baby's mouth. You should also try to center the nipple. Both of your baby's lips should be flared out while nursing.

Cradle hold. Place your baby in the bend of your arm, with his face *and* body turned toward the breast. (If cradling in the right arm, baby's head will be at the right breast). Wrap his arm around your back and snuggle him in. A variation of this position is the cross cradle, in which you cradle your baby with the arm opposite the breast you're using. Support the arm holding the baby with your bent knee, a pillow, or an armrest; your back and arm will tire quickly.

Side-lying position. If you're lying down, use the side-lying position, which is essentially the cradle hold in a prone position. Bring your baby toward the breast as you both recline on your side, facing each other in bed or on the couch.

Football hold. Some mothers prefer the football hold. To get an idea of how this nursing position works, imagine a

---

3. Keeping in mind the advice just mentioned, make sure your baby is taking the entire nipple and areola (the dark area surrounding the nipple) into her mouth. Also, make sure her lips are flared out and that you break the suction (with your fingers) before you take the baby off the breast at the end of the feeding. Then rest assured . . . most women will *still* get sore. I promise the soreness will go away if you hang in there long enough. Your nipples will heal and toughen with time.

4. After nursing, dab some expressed breast milk onto your sore nipples and allow them to air dry. You may need to use a breast shield while nursing or lanolin in the meantime to promote faster healing. Lansinoh® is my favorite sore nipple treatment. It doesn't have to be washed off before you breastfeed. Use this cream several times a day and night.

5. No matter what you read, breastfeeding is not necessarily instinctive. You need someone who has nursed several babies in the recent past to help you figure out how to hold your baby, get the baby to take your nipple, how long to nurse on each side, and how to take the baby off your breast. You'll need someone to tell you how to deal with leaking breasts and how

football player with the ball tucked at his side. Prop a few pillows under your arm for support. Hold the baby's head in the cup of the hand (the right hand if starting with the right breast, the left if starting with the left breast), with his back along your arm. Bring your arm back, so that your elbow is against the back of the chair or sofa. (Your baby's legs will easily bend up into the crook of your arm or wrap back around you slightly). Use your wrist to bring your baby's head up to the breast. Some mothers like to alternate between this position and the cradle hold when their nipples are sore because each position puts a different strain on the nipple. Mothers of multiples use this position so they can nurse two babies at a time.

Breaking suction. Before you remove the breast from your baby's grasp, break the suction by inserting your finger into the baby's mouth and gently pressing the baby's chin down. If you simply pull the baby off or the breast out, it will tug on the nipples and cause a great deal of pain. After the feeding, let your milk dry naturally on the nipples. You don't need to wash them or wipe them off.

Burping. Remember to burp your baby once in the middle of a feeding and again when you're through. You can burp the baby over your shoulder or sit her on your lap, supporting her neck with one hand, and patting her back with the other. You can also lay her on her tummy across your lap and burp her that way. Whichever position you choose, be sure to have a cloth diaper or burping cloth under her mouth to catch any messes.

Timing. To begin, nurse your baby for several minutes at each breast. Gradually increase nursing times until your milk is fully established. When your milk first comes in, try nursing about 10 to 15 minutes at the first breast and until the baby is satisfied on the next breast. Then gradually increase the time spent at each breast to accommodate your baby's desire. Some babies are fast eaters and some like to suckle forever. Don't go by the clock, just use your baby's responses. Your breasts should feel soft after a feeding.

to encourage milk production. Mostly, you'll need someone to tell you to hang in there and that your problems have solutions if you're patient and determined. A quick call to the newborn or maternity ward at your local hospital will connect you with a lactation specialist. You can also look for the local La Leche League in the phone book.

Leaking

You may be surprised at how much you leak and how to handle it. Some women leak breast milk whenever they think about their baby or hear them crying or for no reason at all. Some women don't leak at all. Generally, you'll leak the most during those early weeks and much less as the months go by. Most grocery stores, baby superstores, and discount stores, such as Wal-Mart and Target, carry washable or disposable nursing pads designed to catch leaks. You can also make your own if you want. Nursing pads are made of cloth or paper in the shape of a circle and can fit discreetly into your nursing bra. You can also slip a cloth diaper under your nursing bra at night if you're worried about leaking on night clothes and bed linens. When you are out in public and you feel your breasts leaking, fold your arms tightly across your breasts to stop the flow of milk.

Increasing Your Milk Supply

Almost every mother worries at some point whether she has enough milk for her baby. Perhaps your baby seems unsatisfied or is not gaining weight as expected. Your body is wonderfully designed to adjust to the demand your baby makes on your milk production. If your baby nurses longer on a dry breast (instead of supplementing with formula) and more often (because he isn't satisfied), pretty soon your brain will get the message and send the signal to your breasts to produce more milk. It may take a healthy diet and an increase of fluids on your part, but you will produce more milk as your baby demands it. Never hesitate to have your baby seen by a doctor if you're concerned in any way. A lactation consultant or your baby's pediatrician should be able to give you a number of ways to improve your own diet and help increase the milk supply.

Clogged Milk Ducts

Occasionally, a milk duct will become clogged, causing milk to back up. You can tell a duct is clogged because you'll see—and feel—a small, tender lump on the breast. Clogged milk ducts can lead to infection, so it's best to do whatever you can to remedy the situation. If a duct is clogged, nurse from that breast first and make sure the baby empties the breast. Express any remaining milk by hand. Warm compresses and hand massaging the lump toward the nipple will also relieve pain. If a breast lump does not go away in a day or two, or if you are not sure the lump is caused by a clogged milk duct, see your healthcare provider. Moms can still

get breast cancer while nursing. Any lump or bump that doesn't decrease in size with nursing should be checked out.

Breast Infections

Breast infections, commonly called mastitis, occur due to a combination of factors: the breasts are not fully emptied at each feeding, bacteria invades the breast tissue through cracked skin around the nipple, and the mother is stressed or fatigued and unable to resist infection. Mastitis occasionally develops as a result of a clogged milk duct. If you do have mastitis, rest assured that your milk is not infected. The tissue surrounding the blockage is infected and requires immediate medical assistance.

If you have a breast infection, symptoms may include tenderness and redness, hard and painful breasts, fever, body aches, and chills. It's best to call your doctor right away and get on an antibiotic before you become really sick. Whenever you have a concern about your health, especially if you're running a fever, don't assume it's just the normal after-baby aches and pains. Call your doctor and ask for advice. In very rare cases you might also develop an abscess.

You can continue to nurse without hurting the baby when you have an infection. Don't let an uniformed doctor tell you otherwise. To help speed your recovery, gently rub the hard red place on the breast toward the nipple as you nurse and use hot steamy washcloths on the area between feedings. Always nurse first on the infected breast and make sure it gets emptied, even if you must express the remaining milk after a feeding.

Hang in There

In most cases, you can still successfully nurse your baby if you don't allow yourself to get discouraged and quit. Breastfeeding is a learn-on-the job activity. Almost every mother becomes discouraged and tired of the whole thing during those first few weeks. Your baby will probably want to eat every two to four hours day and night for a while, and that can be exhausting. If you're particularly tired your husband can substitute a water or pumped-breast-milk feeding for you, but don't go more than six hours between feedings during the first few days.

Making Nursing Time Relaxing Time

Take the time to relax when you nurse your baby. If this is your first baby, you can use this time to meditate, read, or listen to soothing and restoring music. If you have other children, make nursing time quiet time or reading time. You can snuggle several children around you and read or sing. I found I could nurse away a headache if I focused on truly relaxing when I nursed my baby. The flushed, satisfied, relaxed look on your baby's face after he nurses is something to notice and appreciate. If you were a baby, wouldn't you want to be fed and snuggled at the same time? How can life get better than that?

Sometimes, most of the time, you'll feel like you didn't get anything done, especially during those hectic early months after you have a new baby. Maybe you didn't finish the wash, vacuum the stairs, or solve the world's hunger problems. Maybe you didn't write the great American novel or even scrub the sinks. But you rocked your baby and told her you loved her. Maybe just maybe, that will be the most important thing you will ever do.

Weaning

Weaning from the breast depends on the needs and desires of both you and your baby. Gradual weaning is much easier than stopping suddenly. Although you may continue to nurse several times a day for well over a year, gradual weaning begins when formula or solids are introduced.

Healthcare professionals recommend introducing solid foods no sooner than four months of age, and usually between four and six months. As you introduce solids or formula, you will likely substitute one nursing session with a bottle session or a baby-sized meal of some simple solid food, such as rice cereal, pureed vegetables, or bananas. Gradually offer formula or solids two times a day, and finally three times a day, conforming with family breakfast, lunch, and dinner times if you'd prefer. You can follow up each solid feeding with breast milk if you'd like. As your baby gets older, he'll probably want a snack or two in between meals.

When you introduce solids, most pediatricians recommend starting with single-grain cereals then adding single-ingredient fruits and vegetables, and finally meats. Your baby will be able to drink from a cup by about ten months but will probably want to nurse or drink from a bottle for another six months. My babies all seemed to wean themselves at about 14 to 18 months. You, your baby, and circumstances will decide what's right for you.

None of the experts will tell you how to handle weaning on an emotional level. The mother-and-baby bond which results

BOTTLE PREPARATION

What size bottles should I use? Most hospitals start bottle-fed babies off with two-ounce bottles. Let your baby drink as much from a two-ounce bottle as she would like. Throw out the remaining formula, which is a potential playground for bacteria. As your baby grows, feedings will increase gradually from one or two ounces to three or four ounces about six times a day. Eventually, your baby will probably drink an entire eight-ounce bottle in one sitting.

How many bottles do I need? If you are bottle feeding, make sure you have plenty of bottles and nipples—four 4-ounce bottles and nipples and eight to ten 8-ounce bottles and nipples. Keep them washed with hot soapy water and rinsed well after each use.

How do I keep the bottles clean and germ free? Generally, you should sterilize the bottles and nipples in boiling water for first use. After that, washing them with hot soapy water and allowing them to air dry completely is an acceptable alternative. Using a dishwasher with hot water and a drying cycle also kills germs. Many items are available to help you keep bottles clean and sterile, including plastic baskets for nipples and caps that can go straight into the top dishwasher rack for cleaning and sterilization.

What type of water should I use? Tap water is usually safe and is the easiest water to use with powdered formula. If, however, you have any concern about the safety of your tap water, you can purchase nursery water or boil your water. Always carefully follow the directions on the container of formula. Powdered formula mixes easier in warm water. But be careful: If you microwave the water to warm it, you might burn your baby's mouth. It's better to simply use warm tap water. If you boil your water, do so all at once at the beginning of the day and allow the water to cool before pouring it into the bottles you will use that day.

When should I prepare the bottles? Preparing a batch of bottles at the beginning of the day will make bottle feeding more convenient. Talk to your baby's pediatrician or a few well-seasoned bottle-feeding moms about the best and easiest ways to keep ready-to-feed bottles at hand.

How do I know if the nipple size is correct? Before using the bottles, check to make sure the nipple hole is the right size. First, tilt the bottle. If the formula comes running out, the hole is too big. If nothing comes out, the hole might not be big enough. Formula should drip from the bottle.

from nursing is hard to adequately describe and hard to give up sometimes. When you are the major food source, you are your baby's first choice. You are the shining star in your little one's life. When you wean your child, either by your choice or your baby's, there is a sort of mourning period that you go through. A special time of your baby's life is past, and sometimes you're not quite ready. This is one of *many* rites of passage you and your child will go through. They are all bittersweet.

BOTTLE FEEDING

If you choose bottle feeding for any reason, you don't have to explain yourself to anyone. Just make sure it's your decision and that you educate yourself before you make it. Discuss the different kinds of formula with your pediatrician and choose one that seems best for your baby. Formula comes in ready-to-feed, liquid, and powder form. Powder is the least expensive.

Baby's First Bottle

A bottle-fed baby may be given sterile water for the first feeding to see if he can swallow and suck and make sure the gag reflex is working. Formula can be given for the next and all subsequent feedings.

Your baby will drink very little formula in the first few days. This is only natural. Your baby is sleepy from the trauma of working his way down the birth canal, and his stomach is still very small. Breastfed babies at this stage need only a teaspoon of colostrum in those early feedings to satisfy. So don't worry if your baby eats only half an ounce in a feeding.

Feeding Basics

To let your little one know it's feeding time, stroke her cheek with your finger or the tip of the nipple. This lets her know that food is on the way, and she'll likely turn to the bottle. Place the nipple between her lips and tilt the bottle up so that the formula fills the nipple. Otherwise, she'll suck in air that might make her gassy and miserable. Don't worry if she doesn't finish off the bottle. If she doesn't act eager to take the last few ounces, she's probably full.

Make Bottle Time Bonding Time

When you feed your baby, hold him in the bend of your arm and snuggle him close. Take that time to relax and unwind. Never prop a bottle in his mouth. Sing lullabies and whisper I love yous into his ears. There is no reason that this time can't be as meaningful to you and your baby as it would be to a breastfed baby and his mother.

Supplemental Bottle Feedings for Breastfed Babies

After your milk supply is established and baby is nursing well—at one to two months of age—you might choose to introduce an occasional supplemental feeding to your child with a bottle of pumped breast milk or formula. Don't overdo the bottle feedings because you don't want your baby to develop a preference for the bottle, which may decrease your milk supply.

You can store pumped breast milk in the refrigerator for five to seven days in the coldest part of the refrigerator (not the door) and for three months in the back of the freezer (not the door). Your thawed breast milk that is unopened or unused is all right in the refrigerator for 24 hours; but don't refreeze breast milk. When you want to freeze your breast milk, chill it first in the refrigerator, then freeze it within 24 hours. Breast milk can be stored in plastic bottles or bags and is easily thawed by placing the bag or bottle in a bowl of warm water. You may have to replace the warm water a few times before the bottle is thawed completely.

Weaning from the Bottle

Weaning from the bottle occurs in much the same way as weaning from the breast. Somewhere between four and six months of age you will likely introduce the first solid foods—probably rice cereal, followed by single-ingredient vegetables and fruit. Substitute one bottle session with a solids session each day, then move up to two sessions, then three. As you're doing so, you can also introduce your baby to a sippy cup of formula and have him drink from the cup with each meal. Eventually your baby will master the sippy cup and may even prefer this. Other babies grow very attached to the bottle. It's important, however, not to use the bottle as a pacifier or to put your baby to bed with a bottle of formula or milk. The milk can pool in your baby's mouth and cause tooth decay. (Tooth decay is especially common in children over one year of age who take a bottle to bed.) If your baby needs a bottle as comfort try tap water right before bedtime, but don't leave the bottle in the crib. Your baby's pediatrician will have helpful information about weaning from the bottle and will be able to advise you on the best route for you and your baby.

SLEEPING

People who claim to sleep like a baby usually don't have one. Sleeping, or more accurately, your lack of it, is usually the number one concern of new parents. Why? Because they never get any. Remember not to take your new baby's sleeping habits personally. Most babies don't sleep through the night for months, although medical experts say they are physically able to miss the middle of the night feeding when they reach 12 pounds.

You have good reason to sleep at night; your baby, on the other hand, does not. Day or night, it's all the same to him.

To encourage your baby to sleep longer at night—or to simply regain some sanity—try the following:

• Wake him up if he's napping too long during the day. Just be sure that your baby doesn't become overtired from lack of sleep in general. This makes it even more difficult to sleep at night.

• Maintain a bedtime routine at the same time each night.

• Try having your baby sleep in a carrier or infant car seat. Some babies prefer sleeping slightly inclined because it helps cut down on reflux problems. The coziness of an infant car seat can also be comforting.

• Try swaddling your infant snugly in a receiving blanket—the snugness is reminiscent of being in the womb.

• Put on some soothing music or quiet background noise. Some babies are even calmed by the hum of the clothes dryer or the dishwasher or a ceiling fan.

PARTY . . . MY CRIB . . . 2 A.M.

I have no teeth, my pants are wet.
I will not sleep, my mind is set.
I cry for Mom, I cry for Dad,
When I'm happy, when I'm sad.
They try to make me sleep, and so
I open my mouth and let it blow.
It's when they tuck me in at night
They think I'm worth that pretty sight—
I smile and coo and wave to them.
But I'm up again at 2 A.M.

• Check the room temperature. Be sure that your baby isn't waking simply because he's too hot or too cold. In warm weather, dress your baby as you would yourself to stay comfortable and not overheat. When it's cold, babies under six months of age need a little more protection than you do. Let your baby sleep in the cap provided by the hospital.

• Don't worry about keeping things quiet so he can sleep during the day. It's best to train your baby to sleep through household noises and disturbances.

• When your baby wakes at night, keep the lights dim and the house quiet.

Hopefully, this will keep your baby from thinking it's play time after he's done nursing.

• Try to sleep when your baby sleeps, even if that means taking several short naps during the day.

SLEEP POSITIONS

Check with your healthcare provider about sleep positions. Recent studies have shown an increase of Sudden Infant Death Syndrome in babies who sleep on their stomachs, so place your little one on her back when putting her to sleep. You will probably be counseled about not placing any pillows, quilts, stuffed animals, comforters, or sheepskins under your baby or in her bed. These items all pose a risk of suffocation.

When your baby is awake, make sure she gets some tummy time so she can learn to lift her head and body and get used to that position as well.

COPING WITH SLEEP DEPRIVATION

I've had some of my most desperate moments—usually due to sheer exhaustion—in the middle of the night, and some of my most heavenly. You and your baby are alone in the universe during this time, or so it seems. It can be horrible or holy and will probably be both. Most newborns wake up for feedings every two to three hours for about two months, sometimes longer. Don't expect your baby to sleep through the night much sooner. You can't really force your baby to change his sleep patterns, but you can encourage him to stay awake during the day as much as possible. When your baby sleeps through a feeding, you want it to be at night, so wake your baby during the day for the usual feedings.

Remember, you can call on help from heaven whenever you need it. You will be blessed and sustained to meet the needs of your baby. Some people will chuckle at your desperate need for sleep and advise you not to become too desperate, for this too will pass. It's difficult to understand or appreciate that kind of advice when you're so exhausted you think you're going to fall

---

GASTROESOPHAGEAL REFLUX

Recently, doctors have determined that some babies who are colicky—they exhibit frequent painful crying, stiffening of the legs and abdomen, writhing as if in pain, fussiness after eating, frequent bouts of spitting up (even regurgitating food) after feedings—actually have gastroesophageal reflux. This causes inflammation of the esophagus, due to contact with stomach acids. Talk to your baby's pediatrician, if your baby seems to have this type of reflux. You can also try the following:

• small, frequent feedings
• keeping your baby's head elevated after a feeding for at least 30 minutes; gravity will help keep stomach contents in the stomach, as well as any antacids or acid blockers your baby might be prescribed
• sleeping in an infant seat or with one end of the crib mattress raised (it's important to do this safely by simply placing one end of the frame on which the mattress rests on a lower rung than the other end)
• letting time take its course; the esophagus gets stronger as your baby grows, which improves reflux

---

apart. If you use these middle-of-the-night feeding sessions to communicate love to your baby and to reconnect with heaven, you'll find that your memories of these moments are both amusing and sweet.

CRYING

All healthy babies cry. In fact, it's quite normal for a baby to cry for 15 minutes to an hour at a time for no reason at all. Most of the time, however, your baby is crying because she's trying to communicate something to you. Don't take your baby's tears as a personal sign of failure in your maternal comforting and nurturing department. Be patient with yourself as you learn to understand this new language and the best way to respond to each of your children. Crying does not mean that you're an incompetent caregiver.

COLIC

Long periods of crying, when your baby seems to be having abdominal pain, are often referred to as colic and are usually blamed on too much gas in the intestine. Sometimes, however, there really is no known cause for colic, which typically begins a few weeks after birth and lasts for three or four months. Much to your dismay, you may even find that your baby's pediatrician labels any long, unexplained bouts of crying colic.

Some breastfed babies become fussy when their mothers eat or drink certain foods. These might include spicy foods, chocolate, or cow's milk. If you think that might be the cause, try going off the suspicious food for a week to see if that helps.

Some formula-fed babies will be fussier on certain formulas and may even be allergic to a type of formula. Allergies typically cause rashes or congestion in addition to fussiness.

I believe unexplained crying probably has more to do with individual differences in babies' abilities to soothe themselves. In other words, your baby may not have figured out how to *stop* crying. Of course, you will want to help.

HOW TO SOOTHE A CRYING BABY

Sucking

Some babies like to suck on something like a pacifier, your finger, a corner of a blanket, or their thumb when they're crying. Your baby can't suckle too much. Do whatever seems to soothe your baby.

Holding

Most babies love to be held . . . whenever they're awake. You may worry that you'll never have your hands free again. Many mothers use a sling or front pack to carry their newborns so they can hold them and still have both hands free. On those days when you can't seem to get anything done but hold your baby, remember that

holding your baby and helping him to feel your love will be perhaps the most important thing you'll ever do. Before you know it, your baby will be too busy and preoccupied to stay in your lap and snuggle. So relish all those hugs while they last.

Movement

Many babies seem to respond well to movement. Activities like rocking in a rocking chair or dancing around the room often get a baby to quit crying. I found that holding my babies tight against my chest while bouncing them on the side of my bed worked wonders. Battery-operated swings are helpful when your arms give out and you actually need to get something done around the house.

Change of Scenery

Many newborns enjoy a change of scenery and will stop crying if you move them around the house with you and give them something new to look at. If the weather's nice, it might help to go outside to the front porch or yard for a few moments.

```
┌─────────────────────────────────────┐
│        TEN THINGS TO CHECK           │
│     IF BABY WON'T QUIT CRYING        │
│                                      │
│  1. Is your baby too warm or too cold? │
│  2. Does her diaper need to be changed? │
│  3. Is your baby hungry?             │
│  4. Does your baby want to be swaddled │
│     (tight blankets) or held snuggly? │
│  5. Is your baby bored?              │
│  6. Does your baby want someone to   │
│     talk to?                         │
│  7. Does your baby want someone to   │
│     play with?                       │
│  8. Does baby want to be held?       │
│  9. Is your baby sick?               │
│ 10. Is your baby tired?              │
└─────────────────────────────────────┘
```

Audio Distraction

Some of my fussiest babies seemed to respond well to audio distraction—loud monotonous noise. Distraction is anything you can do to distract your baby from crying just long enough that they forget they were crying and fall asleep. Some babies seem to need help tuning out noise, lights, and distractions when they're tired. I found that white noise (running a vacuum or even the static on the radio) helped them settle down. Some of my babies liked me to sing lullabies to them and others preferred very loud music on the stereo. Some like the hum of a dryer or dishwasher nearby.

Rides or Walks

Lots of babies will quiet down if you take them for a ride in the car or go for a walk or stroller ride outside.

When You Run Out of Options

There will be times when you simply run out of ideas and energy and begin crying with your baby. At those times consider whispering in your baby's ear, "Mommy's here and she will stay with you until you feel better. I'm sorry I don't know how to help right now. But I'll hold you as long as you need me."

Other times I found that simply laying my baby in the bassinet or crib and walking into the other room for a while seemed the best solution for both of us.

Handling Frustration

Never, ever, shake your baby from frustration or in an attempt to get him to quit crying. You can cause brain damage, blindness, and even death. If you're ever so tired and frustrated that you're thinking about lashing out at your child, simply put your baby to bed and leave him there until you can get control of yourself. Call someone for help. Walk around your house. Your baby is not trying to annoy you or drive you crazy. Your baby will not hurt himself by crying.

Babies cry . . . often. That's how they communicate and relieve stress. Don't hold it against your baby or yourself. If you have a baby who cries a lot, you need to get a break more often. Let your husband watch the baby while you go shopping or for a walk.

A baby who cries for hours is very hard on everyone, especially mom. On the plus side, babies who seem extra fussy are often very healthy and usually thrive. Most new parents have unrealistic expectations of themselves and their baby. Please be gentle with yourself and give yourself and your baby time to adjust to your new life together.

ADJUSTING TO BABY'S TEMPERAMENT

Each baby has her own temperament right from the beginning. And you can't really change her temperament much through the years, but you can help your child learn to develop healthy ways to exhibit her natural disposition. Some babies startle easily and dislike new experiences while others love lots of stimulation. Some babies seem to have a calm, easy-going temperament and adjust well to new situations and sensations, while others are tense and easily upset.

Your baby existed before she was born and came to earth with her own unique personality. You can nurture that personality but you can't create it. Your children come through you but not from you—for they came from your heavenly home. Your Father in Heaven will help you know and love your child, if you ask Him. He will impress you with what you should do to nurture this child if you ask Him. Each of your children will require all your love. If you let him, God will show you your weaknesses and help them to become your strengths. He will never leave you alone or without help in your mothering, for you are also His child, His work, His glory, and His love.

BABY'S FIRST BATH

Your baby's first baths will be sponge baths, until the umbilical cord falls off and you can immerse him in water. That basically means you'll be washing him down with a washcloth for a few weeks.

The first time or two you bathe your newborn it is bound to be a bit frustrating for both of you. Newborns typically don't enjoy being unwrapped and exposed to the air. They also typically spit up and use the bathroom whenever you're trying to give them a bath. Don't be surprised if your newborn screams through his entire bath for a while. Before you know it, your baby will laugh and giggle and love his bath, *I promise.*

You can use cotton tipped swabs to clean around the umbilical cord until it dries up and falls off. Sterile cotton balls dipped in water can be used to clean your baby's eyes, working from the inside corner to the outside. Clean water is all your baby's face needs. A warm, soft washcloth can be used to sponge off your baby's head then neck, torso, arms, and legs. Only uncover the area of the baby you are washing. Make sure you have all your supplies within arm's reach before you start.

Your newborn will probably have dry skin flaking off for a while as he adjusts to life in the dry world outside your uterus. You can use mild lotion and give him a good rubdown in all the cracks and creases. First, however, you may want to test a small patch of skin to make sure your baby is not sensitive to the lotion.

If your baby is a boy it helps to drape a cloth diaper across the penis while bathing and while changing his diaper so you don't get it right in the eye.

If you notice your baby has a crusty looking scalp—doctors call this cradle cap—rub on baby oil and let it soak in for a while before you brush it up with a soft-bristled toothbrush, then shampoo. Another remedy that works quite well is applying a small amount of dandruff shampoo. Just be careful not to get it in the eyes. Some moms think this works better than baby oil.

LATER BATHS

Before you know it, your baby will think taking a bath is the best thing since warm milk and snuggle time with you. The most delightful, delicious piece of little-person magic is a baby just out of the tub, rubbed down with baby lotion, sporting a slicked-back hairdo, and dressed in soft, clean pajamas.

You can collect toys or household items for your baby to play with while she's in the bath. All young children love floating, pouring, diving, and splashing. Don't hurry through bath time. Bath time is always quality time.

Never, ever leave your baby alone in the bathtub, even for a second. It takes only an instant and an inch or two of water for a baby to meet tragedy in a bathtub.

TEETHING

On the average, babies begin teething at six to seven months. But remember, no baby is average. Some begin teething as early as two to four months. Some babies don't seem to notice this rite of passage, while others seem truly troubled by the whole process. Your baby may eat poorly, become fussy, or have sleeping problems. To ease his pain, try teething toys and rubbing his gums with your thumb or a numbing agent.

WHAT TO DO IF BABY GETS SICK

Nothing is quite so troubling for a new mother as a sick baby. And your baby's first cold or other mild illness may well be more difficult for *you* to get through than it is for baby. After the initial alarm sets in and you start worrying about how to treat a feverish or coughing or vomiting baby, you'll realize that it's the middle of the night. Then you'll develop an extreme case of anxiety about whether to call the doctor or an after-hours pediatrics facility or the emergency room. You'll finally figure everything out, get reasonable treatment for your baby, see her through her first cold, and be feeling like a pro . . . when she develops new symptoms in the middle of the night two months later. This scenario will repeat itself several times with each new baby—it's just part of being a mom. But take heart, most babies survive all sorts of colds and viruses and come out just fine. The following will help you keep a little sanity as you do simple self-diagnosis, perform home treatments to make baby more comfortable, and know when to call the doctor or take a trip to the emergency room.

THE COMMON COLD

Although infants are generally healthy—especially if they are breastfed—most will have a cold or two in the first year. Many babies will get a dozen colds a year if they have older siblings in day care or school. Symptoms of a common cold include a runny nose, sneezing, and nasal congestion. At times, your infant may also have a cough or fever and seem lethargic or not as eager to nurse or take a bottle. Colds can linger for quite some time, especially in young babies, and are contagious for several days.

If your baby seems to have a simple cold—runny nose, sneezing, and some congestion but no fever—you can probably treat her at home. If you worry it might be something more, however, or just want some reassurance about treatment procedures, call your pediatrician's office during normal office hours. Antibiotics do not help cold viruses and should not be given to relieve symptoms. Most of what your doctor will tell you to do includes making baby comfortable and using a few home remedies. Try the following to help baby feel better:

• Suction nasal mucus with a bulb syringe. Most hospitals will send you and baby home with a blue bulb syringe. You'll find that this little item comes in handy on many occasions. When suctioning baby's nose, make sure that you work quickly and keep a tight hold on baby. Don't suction the nose too often, however, as this can further inflame the nasal passages.

• Apply a few drops of commercial saline drops in the nose—with doctor's recommendation, of course. This will help baby breathe more easily and may also help you suction her nose if the mucus is hardened at all. You can also make homemade saline drops by mixing one teaspoon of salt with one cup of warm water.

• Run a humidifier—preferably a cool mist one—in baby's room at night.

• Apply petroleum jelly under baby's nose to soothe skin irritation from nasal discharge.

• Keep baby away from crowds or other sick children.

• Elevate your baby's head while sleeping to help the nasal passage drain more easily and to help your baby breathe.

• Use over-the-counter medications, such as nasal decongestants, only at a doctor's recommendation.

Should I Call the Doctor?

A call to the doctor should be placed in the following circumstances:

• Your baby is under four months old and has cold symptoms.

• Your baby is 12 weeks old or younger and has a fever above 100.4° F. (rectally).

• Your baby—or any child—has a fever above 104° F. (this warrants an immediate call).

• Your baby's fever lasts more than two or three days.

• The temperature spikes suddenly.

• Your baby has green or yellow discharge from the eyes.

• Your baby is crying more than normal and seems to be in pain or is inconsolable.

• Your baby has a cough and is under one month old.

• Your baby has a cough that is causing breathing difficulties or sounds like the bark of a seal.

• Your baby is wheezing and having difficulties breathing even after cleaning out the nose or without the presence of a cough.

• The soft spot on the top of baby's head is sunken in or bulging.

• Any other reason that makes you worried. Don't ever discount the validity of a mother's intuition.

If any of the above symptoms are severe or if your child seems to be very sick, go to the emergency room. If possible, take your child to the emergency room of a pediatric hospital, where your child's care will be specialized and where the staff is used to treating young babies.

What to Do about Croup

If your baby develops a cough that sounds very hoarse and sharp—almost like the bark of a seal—chances are he has croup. Croup occurs when the larynx and trachea are inflamed and cause the airways above the vocal cords to narrow. It can be caused by a viral infection or allergies. For babies under one month of age, it's best to call the doctor right away and tell him about your child's symptoms. Croup can cause extreme breathing difficulties and be very uncomfortable for your young baby. In any case, you'll probably want to call the pediatrician to verify treatment. You can try the following at home to open your baby's airways and reduce swelling:

• If it's cool outside, bundle up your little one and take him outside for 15 minutes. The cold air should bring relief to the swollen air passages.

• Turn on the shower (use hot water at full speed) and bring your baby into the steam-filled bathroom until the croupy cough subsides.

• Use a cool mist humidifier in baby's room.

• Keep baby comfortable and minimize crying as much as possible. Crying worsens a croupy cough and makes breathing even more difficult.

If croup symptoms are not relieved by use of a humidifier or cool air, seek medical care.

If you think your child is coughing this way because he inhaled an object, or if his lips are blue, he's having extreme difficulty breathing, he's drooling, or he seems dehydrated, call the doctor immediately. Your doctor may decide to hospitalize your child if his symptoms are severe.

Is It an Ear Infection?

Sometimes a common cold leads to an ear infection, which can be very painful and uncomfortable for a young baby. If you suspect your baby has an ear infection, call your doctor right away. More information about ear infections—including symptoms, home remedies, and other medical advice—is available on pages 127–129. For treatment, ask your doctor about dosage of pain relievers, such as ibuprofen or acetaminophen. Or try applying dry heat to the ear to relieve pain.

DIARRHEA

Diarrhea is a marked increase in the volume, frequency, and wateriness of your baby's bowel movements. In older children, diarrhea can come on after eating any number of foods or drinks: apple juice, pear juice, grapes, soft drinks, dates, nuts, figs, honey, table sugar, milk products, chocolate, magnesium, and caffeine. In young infants, a bacterial or viral infection can cause sudden severe diarrhea.

New babies usually have four to six loose bowel movements a day. Your breastfed baby will have frequent, rather bubbly bowel movements. The consistency of the bowel movements need not worry you unless your baby doesn't act hungry, is vomiting, losing weight, or passing blood in the stool.

In young babies, vomiting, diarrhea, or fever can cause dehydration very quickly. Signs of mild dehydration include:

• a decrease in urination
• dry mouth
• fewer tears

Call your pediatrician if these signs are noticed.

Signs of moderate dehydration include:
• a lack of springiness or elasticity to your child's skin
• dark urine
• no urination for several hours
• sunken eyes
• no tears
• irritability
• rapid heartbeat
• sunken soft spot
• cool hands and feet

If these signs are noticed, your child should be seen immediately. Dehydration in children progresses quickly and can be fatal. The younger the child, the faster the progression.

Your baby may need to be seen or treated at a hospital. Or, your doctor may recommend giving your baby oral rehydration solutions that contain the right mix of salt, sugar, potassium, and other elements needed to help replace lost body fluids. Oral rehydration solutions are sold in liquid or powder form. Powders are easier to store, less expensive, and last longer.

If your child vomits, wait for 30 to 60 minutes after the last time and then give him a few sips of oral rehydration solution with a spoon or a dropper. If that doesn't cause your child to vomit again, you can increase how much you give each time.

If your baby is breastfed you can keep breastfeeding while you're giving an oral dehydration solution. If you're bottle feeding you can switch to oral dehydration solutions for about 12 to 24 hours, then switch back to formula.

CONSTIPATION

Before you worry that your baby's latest cry is a result of terrible pain due to constipation, keep in mind that just because your baby hasn't had a bowel movement in a day or two doesn't mean she is constipated. She may be fussy for other reasons. The normalcy of a baby's bowels ranges from having a messy diaper after every feeding to having one every couple of days. Likewise, some babies have considerable discomfort when passing a large, hard stool and others seem to take it in stride.

If your baby is constipated and it's causing a lot of discomfort, put a call into your doctor. Otherwise, keep nursing or giving formula on a regular basis. Hydration is the best cure for constipation in very young babies. If your older baby has started solids, try giving her some fiber-rich foods: prunes, apple juice, whole wheat breads or cereals, any fresh fruit except bananas. Don't use laxatives. Enemas are discouraged as well, although your doctor may have you try one if everything else is unsuccessful over a longer period of time. The anal sphincter can sometimes be relaxed by taking a rectal temperature and thus stimulating a bowel movement.

Some babies have an anus that is particularly narrow. In this case your child may have bowel movements that tear the lining of the anus, causing pain and maybe a small amount of blood. Most tears heal quickly without treatment.

HERBAL REMEDIES

The use of herbal medications is growing dramatically; and many herbal remedies are marketed as harmless yet effective cures to all sorts of illnesses. Herbal medications do, in fact, work for some people. In others, they seem to have little effect. Before giving any herbal medication to your child, remember that it is still *medication*. Keep the following in mind:

• Some herbal medications can cause adverse reactions when taken with other drugs or herbs.

• The production and manufacturing of herbal medications is not regulated by the federal government. There are no guidelines for labeling or warnings.

• The potency of herbal medications varies from manufacturer to manufacturer, and some herbal medication is purer than others.

• Always research the medication and consult your pediatrician before giving any herbal medication to your child.

A MOTHER'S INTUITION

Even though your newborn is only a few days or weeks or months old, she's yours—and you *know* her. If your mother's intuition tells you that something is wrong with your baby, call the doctor. Sometimes you'll simply be reassured that your baby's okay. Other times, you may be asked to bring your baby in. Doctors and nurses really don't mind the phone call—and your baby is worth any time it takes to make sure that she is healthy and comfortable.

As her mother, you may also know just what she needs to get better and feel loved. Rock her, cuddle with her, put aside chores and housework and errands to just be with her and help her feel well. You'll never regret—and will probably look back fondly on—the extra time you spent nursing a sick child, even if it's in the middle of the night or on the day you planned to run 472 errands.

TAKING YOUR BABY OUT

It's advisable to keep new babies away from large gatherings where there is risk of exposure to communicable diseases. It's also appropriate to avoid visits with anyone who is ill. If friends or family want to hold your baby, make sure they wash their hands first.

TAKING BABY TO CHURCH

Listen to your own common sense and your doctor's advice about when to take your baby to church for the first time. During the early days and weeks of life, newborns shouldn't be exposed to the various communicable illnesses that are rampant in large public gatherings. For the first few weeks, or even months, you and your husband might consider taking turns going to church while one stays home with the baby. The spouse who stays home might even consider attending sacrament meeting in another ward at a later time so you can both partake of the sacrament.

Don't be afraid to ask for a leave of absence from your calling for a few weeks or months. Giving yourself ample time to recuperate and giving your baby ample time to get a good healthy start in life should be your first priority.

When you do feel it's the right time to take your newborn to church, take along anything that will help you keep the baby quiet and happy. You might want to take a pacifier and several quiet toys to entertain and soothe your little one. If your baby cries and you can't soothe him quickly, take the baby out in the hall where you can still hear what is going on. If your baby is still noisy or hungry, take your child to the mother's lounge or nursing room in your church. If your church does not provide one, ask that a room be set aside for this purpose. If that is not possible you may have to take your baby into a nearby classroom. It is quite appropriate for you to nurse your baby on demand during the three-hour block of Sunday meetings, so don't treat this time much differently than you do at home. Just be modest with the careful positioning of a blanket during feedings.

Make sure that you are able to take the sacrament even if you are not in the chapel during the sacrament service. Make sure your ward provides the sacrament for mothers in the foyer or the nursing lounge.

Don't be too self-conscious about the disruption and noise your child makes at church. Don't get discouraged and quit going. Taking your babies and young children to church will always be a challenge,

but is well worth the effort. Don't assume you are annoying people around you; most people are very understanding about the noise young children make in church.

TALKING

Imagine just for a moment that you've been airlifted to a brand new planet where no one speaks your language. Everything that happens to you is strange and new. In order to survive you have to learn how to communicate in a whole new way. The world you previously inhabited was dark, warm, and full of familiar sounds and sensations. In your new world, everything is suddenly full of light, noise, sensations, and experiences you've never had before. Wouldn't you be grateful if two people were assigned as your guides to help you learn the ropes, speak the language, and provide a soft place to land?

Your new baby has likewise been transported to a brand new world. Everything is new and strange. You and your husband have been assigned to be his guides. In those early months, your baby's brain is busily mapping out new connections that will last a lifetime. Every positive nurturing experience you can supply will be to your child's advantage in the years to come.

Language is not learned in silence. Communication skills are better caught than taught. So narrate your life and start talking. You can't talk too much to your baby. Sing to him. Tell him what's on your mind. Tell him what you're doing. Whisper in his ear. Talk face to face. Get in touch with the way your baby communicates.

Learn his language. The sooner your child can talk, the sooner he can tell you what's on his mind, where it hurts, what he wants, and what frightens him. You'll both be happier when your child learns to speak.

Researchers have discovered that babies babble all the sounds of every language during the first year or so. When your baby babbles a sound that fits your language, you respond so positively that he tends to repeat those sounds and forget the rest. That positive attention pattern also tends to promote behavior you want your child to repeat.

In your first conversations with your child make eye contact and respond to each other in any way you feel brings a light to your child's eye. Repeat sounds that your baby responds to and seems to like. During the first months your baby will cry, smile, and coo. Coo, smile, and cry back and forth with each other. Watch your baby for subtle clues that he's had enough verbal interaction and needs to rest or do something else.

Your child will understand many words before he can say them, so don't be self-conscious about keeping a running conversation going. What do you say? Everything and anything. Tell him the name of his body parts when you're diapering or dressing him. Blow on his tummy and kiss his toes while you sing a silly song you make up as you go along. Sing to him when you rock him to sleep. Tell him about the recipe you're using in the kitchen. Discuss world politics and your latest frustration.

Read to your child from the very beginning. Yes, really. Simple board books that your child can chew on are best for the early months. Your child will get a feel for language when you read. He will learn new words and learn to feel that language is something wonderful, warm, and nurturing that people share. Reading to your child helps him build useful language skills. Interacting with your child while you're reading helps build neuron pathways that aid in thinking and analyzing skills. The early years are critical for the wiring of your child's brain. Children need to be thinking, doing, and asking questions. The first five or six years are optimum. After those early years, the brain gets rid of connections it's not using.

When your child tries to talk it will seem like babble, but give him the respect of listening carefully and responding appropriately. When you and your child use a sound to mean a word, it is a word, even if nobody else understands it. As your child gets older he will imitate what you say, so be sure to use language your child can repeat in church without embarrassing you.

Some children are early talkers and some simply are not. It doesn't have as much to do with their intelligence as it does their personality. One of my children refused to imitate typical baby sounds and babble. He waited until he could speak in complete sentences before he'd talk much at all . . . then we couldn't get him to stop talking.

The ability to communicate through language is one of the most satisfying parts of being human. If you think your child may have a speech or hearing problem, don't hesitate to bring it up with your doctor and seek further professional help.

GRANDPARENTS

You will decide what kind of relationship you have with your parents and in-laws after your child is born. Lucky is the child who has both sets of grandparents to love her. Every child should know her grandparents. Every grandparent should know her grandchild. How much contact you have will be pretty much up to you and what you feel is in the best interest of your child.

You can involve your parents and in-laws in your child's life whether they live close by or far away. Phone calls, e-mails, letters, tape recordings, pictures, videos, and packages can be exchanged. If your parents live nearby, consider regular visits and outings, sharing holidays and special celebrations.

Every child deserves as many people in her life who love her as possible. Your job as her mother is not to keep your child to yourself but to share her and surround her with warmth and affection from many sources. You may have different ways of doing things and different rules, but grandparents offer your child something you can't give them. Grandparents offer your

child a link to the past and a new perspective of *you* when you were young. Your children need to know that you were young and full of it when you were their age.

If you ask your parents to baby-sit, be sure not to take advantage of their generosity and time. Occasional baby-sitting may be fine, but daily child care should be provided by you or paid for. You are responsible for your child's care.

BABY-SITTERS

As much as you love your children, you will need a break from them now and then. You should enjoy a weekly evening out and perhaps a few days away each year. Make it a habit to go on a weekly date with your spouse. The best gift you can give your children is a mother who loves their father. If you can't afford a baby-sitter, trade services with another mother.

Your child will learn to accept the fact that Mom and Dad leave sometimes and they always come back. He needs to learn that there are other people who will care for him until you return.

You can make the separation easier by inviting your baby-sitter over to your house before you actually use her services. Or

WHAT TO LOOK FOR IN A BABY-SITTER

- Does this person like and understand children?
- Do your children like and respect this person?
- How much experience does this person have?
- Is this person physically and mentally healthy?
- Does this person keep high standards?
- Does this person have a sense of humor?
- How would this person react in an emergency?
- Do you know this person well or does this person come highly recommended?

you may want to ask your baby-sitter to arrive a half hour before you leave so that your child can get used to the new face. Before you leave, review the following:

- Point out any hazards in your home.
- Show the sitter where to adjust the heating or cooling system.
- Show the sitter where emergency supplies are kept, such as a flashlight, first-aid supplies, telephone numbers where you can be reached, and emergency telephone numbers to a neighbor, doctor, and 911.
- Tell your sitter about your child's eating and sleeping habits and any problems to watch for.
- Tell your sitter how to calm, feed, and put your child to sleep.
- Show your sitter what food is available for her and your child to eat.
- Show your sitter where books, toys, games, music, and the television are kept.
- Let your sitter know if you expect housecleaning service in addition to baby-sitting services.
- Agree on a payment amount.
- Tell your sitter what rules you want your sitter and child to keep while you're away.
- Show your sitter how to operate any equipment that may be needed, such as the stove, oven, microwave, television, telephone, and remote control.
- Tell your sitter when bedtime is and your child's usual bedtime routine.

DEVELOPMENTAL MILESTONES

Your baby's brain grows and develops rapidly during the early years of life. So give your baby all the positive attention, affection, conversation, and interaction you have to offer. Developmental milestones you want to watch for during the first year are: rolling over, sitting up, creeping, crawling, standing, cruising, and walking. There are average times for each milestone; but remember no baby is average. Don't compare your baby's development to others and turn this into a pass/fail test. Regular well-baby visits with your pediatrician should catch any delays or concerns.

ONE MONTH

- Brings hand to eyes and mouth
- Moves head from side to side while lying on stomach
- Follows objects six inches from face
- Responds to noise
- Turns face to sounds and voices
- Focuses on a face
- Looks at objects
- Smiles

THREE MONTHS

- Looks at moving objects
- Raises head 45 to 90 degrees on stomach
- Open and shuts hands
- Reaches for toys
- Smiles at mother and others
- Makes sounds

SIX MONTHS

- Holds head steady
- Rolls over
- Reaches for objects
- Recognizes people
- Smiles spontaneously
- Sits with support
- Transfers objects from hand to hand
- Looks for dropped object
- Plays peek-a-boo

NINE MONTHS

- Sits without support
- Pulls self to standing position

- Can say mama and dada, indiscriminately
- Transfers objects from hand to hand
- May crawl, creep, and stand with support
- Can poke, point, touch, lift, twist, squeeze, pick up, and drop with fingers

TWELVE MONTHS

- Walks while holding a hand
- Goes from stomach to sitting position
- Walks around furniture
- Drinks from a cup
- Waves
- Stands for a few moments

TWELVE TO FIFTEEN MONTHS

- Begins walking alone
- Turns pages and looks at books and magazines
- Knows the meaning of several words
- Tries to help in dressing himself
- Dumps out toys
- Loves the contents of kitchen cabinets

BABY EQUIPMENT

What equipment do you really need for a baby? Not much, but you might want to consider some of the following pieces of baby equipment.

IS YOUR CHILD SAFE IN THE CAR?

Your child will need several different types of car seats as he grows. Whenever you buy a car seat make sure you send in the registration card so you'll be notified of recalls and other safety issues. Contact your local county health department for information on car seat safety classes and car seat checks. If you're a new parent, a safety class and car seat check will be invaluable. Among the things you'll learn at a class are the following:

- *Never* put a child in a front seat with an air bag.
- The back seat is the safest place for your child to ride even if there are no air bags in your car.
- A car seat that has been involved in a crash must be replaced. Sudden, strong impacts can weaken a car seat's design and structure.
- Your vehicle's owners manual contains important information about installing a car seat, including whether or not you will need a locking clip.
- Your vehicle's seat belt should hold the car seat tightly enough so that there is no more than one inch of give from side to side or forward. This tight fit can be achieved by kneeling in the car seat with all your weight while belting in the seat.
- The car seat's harness should be snug against your child; you should not be able to put more than one finger between your child's collarbone and the harness.
- How to correctly route the vehicle seat belt through the car seat.
- Not all car seats fit all cars. The best car seat for your baby will be the one that fits best in your car. Before purchasing a seat, test it out in your car (most stores will allow parents to do this now). Make sure the fit is tight and that the seat is angled correctly. You'd be surprised at how many parents get a seat home only to find out that it doesn't fit in their car. If your seat doesn't fit, don't fudge by not following the instructions provided with the seat. Get a new seat.
- Hand-me-downs are great, but not when it comes to car seats. It's best to purchase a brand new seat that you can register with the company and that fits *your* car, not your sister-in-law's car. It's also difficult to know if used seats have been in a crash or if they are more than five years old, which is the recommended life span of a car seat.
- Reading the installation guidelines that come with your seat is a must. Follow them exactly. For example, if your car seat requires a top tether strap, use it. The seat will not function correctly without it.

Following is an explanation of the types of seats you will need and specific details about their installation.

Rear-Facing Car Seats

Rear-facing seats can be purchased in two forms: an infant car seat and a convertible car seat. An infant car seat can be used for only a few months, but it is ideal for small babies because it reclines enough to keep their heads from wobbling too much. Infant car seats are also portable, meaning you can lift them out of a base that remains in the car and carry a sleeping baby into the house without messing with buckles and straps. Convertible car seats are typically for infants from five pounds to toddlers up to 30 or 40 pounds. A convertible seat faces the rear until baby is one year old *and* at least 20 pounds and then faces forward until your child outgrows it.

- Infants must be in a rear-facing seat until they are at least one year old *and* 20 pounds.
- Keep harness straps snug and fasten the harness clip at armpit level.
- Route harness strap through lower slots.
- Put car seat carrying handle down while driving.
- Recline a rear-facing seat at a 45-degree angle.

Forward-Facing Car Seats

Forward-facing car seats are for children over one year old and between 20 and 40 pounds.

- Route harness straps through upper slots at or above baby's shoulder level.
- Place seat in upright forward-facing position.
- Fasten harness clips at armpit level.
- Keep harness straps snug.

Booster Seats

Booster seats are for children between 40 and 80 pounds and usually between four and eight years old.

- Booster seats should make lap and shoulder belts fit correctly (low over hips and upper thighs and snug over the shoulders).
- Booster seats must be used with both lap and shoulder belts.
- Children this size are too small to fit correctly in the adult belts.
- If your vehicle has a low back seat and your child's ears are above it, you need a high-back booster seat to protect your child's head.

Lap and Shoulder Belts

Children over 80 pounds and eight years old can use lap and shoulder belts.

- To fit correctly in adult belts, your child must be tall enough to sit with knees bent at the edge of the seat without slouching.
- Teach your child to never put shoulder belts under his arms or behind his back.
- Lap and shoulder belts should fit low over hips and upper thighs and snug over the shoulders.

If Your Child Is over 40 Pounds and You Have Only Lap Belts in Your Back Seat

- Buy a special car seat for children over 40 pounds.
- Contact auto dealership about installing shoulder belts.
- Correctly restrain your child in a car booster seat in the front seat using a lap/shoulder belt and move the vehicle seat as far back as possible (do not do this if you have air bags in the front seat.

LATCH System

Beginning in September 2002, the federal government mandated that all new cars (except convertibles) be equipped with the LATCH (Lower Anchors and Tethers for Children) system. This system provides built-in anchors and tethers in cars to secure car seats. All newer car seats are compatible with the LATCH system, which makes installation and achieving a proper fit much easier than before.

Bassinet: A small bassinet is nice to use during the early months after the baby's born because you can usually place the small bed next to yours. This way, you only have to sit up in bed to reach over and grab the baby for middle-of-the-night feedings. Your baby will outgrow a bassinet in a few months, so if finances are tight don't worry about getting one.

Crib: Cribs are beds for babies and toddlers that keep them from falling out on the floor. They generally have sides that raise up and down and a mattress that can be adjusted in height as your baby grows and starts to pull himself up along the side of the bed. Get the best quality you can afford and look for one with slats no more than 2⅜ inches apart and corner posts no more than ⅝ inches high.

Youth Bed: Youth beds are designed for children when they're too big for the crib. Youth beds are usually an unnecessary expense. Since your child will outgrow his youth bed in two years, it's usually better to purchase a regular-sized bed for your child when he outgrows his crib.

Stroller: A stroller is handy baby equipment when you want to leave the house with your baby and you don't want to carry him all the time. Many strollers today come with an attachable car seat/infant carrier. These can be used for the first few months. When your child can sit up unassisted, you can remove the carrier and place your child in the regular part of the stroller. If you're planning to have two or more children spaced closely in age, you might want to buy a double stroller. Always make sure to buckle your child into the stroller to prevent injuries.

Infant seat: Infant seats come in all shapes and sizes. You can buy an infant seat/car seat combination, an infant seat that vibrates, or just a regular carry-around-the house model. A seat that vibrates or bounces lightly with your baby's movement can be very comforting for your little one. It's nice to have a seat you can place your baby in so she can watch you do chores, pay the bills, or cook dinner. She'll be close by if she cries, and she'll be entertained by the action all around her. Once a baby can sit on her own, she shouldn't sit in vibrating or bouncy seats any longer.

Sling: Baby slings come in all shapes and types. Some drape over the mother's shoulder and hold the baby in a nursing position. Some are front-carrying packs that hold your baby turned toward or away from you. Both types are designed to help you hold your baby and still have your hands free to do something else, like fix supper.

Car seat. This is one baby item you must purchase. A car seat must be used every time baby is in the car—even for short distances. See the sidebar on pages 92–93 for specific details on selecting an appropriate car seat.

Swing: Baby swings come in handy during those first few months when your baby wants to be held whenever he is awake. Look for one that is sturdy, lacking a top bar, and battery operated.

Play pen: Play pens aren't used as much today as they were in the past because some experts think they stunt your baby's development by thwarting his natural curiosity and exploration. Play pens are not necessary, but they come in handy as a safe place for your child to play when you're busy.

Portable crib: Portable cribs are handy if you travel frequently. Using them means you don't have to be dependent on the safety and cleanliness of motel cribs. They can also double as an additional crib for your basement or other room in your house; and they're very handy at grandparents' houses.

High chair: High chairs come in a variety of styles, shapes, and sizes. You can buy a freestanding style, one that hooks on to the side of your table, or a booster seat type that straps onto your regular kitchen chair. This last type can also double as a booster seat when your child grows.

Walker/Stationary saucer: Baby walkers can be very dangerous. They have caused many injuries from falling down stairs or by allowing a child to move to a place with hazardous conditions, such as a hot stove. Baby "saucers" or non-mobile walkers are a better option. Most have a variety of activities built into the tray that baby can play with as she turns around in the seat and bounces up and down. Babies should not be put in saucers until about four months of age.

Gate: Baby gates are designed to keep your child from falling down stairs or to keep him confined to a certain room. Look for a gate that is adjustable and easy to use.

Do you really need all this stuff? Not really, except for the law-mandated car seat. Consider your finances and buy only what you can afford. Babies can sleep on a blanket spread on the floor or in a dresser drawer. You can feed your baby from your lap and carry your baby everywhere you go without being deprived. Because most of this equipment is used for such a short time, many extended family members share and pass around baby paraphernalia. Be creative, resourceful, and remember your baby will be happy as long as he has *you* . . . the best baby equipment of all.

BABY PROOFING YOUR HOME

Baby proofing your home doesn't just mean you put your knickknacks away. It means making your child's world as safe and explorer-friendly as possible.

• Set your hot water heater at or below 120° F. to prevent scalding.

• Secure your medicines and cleaning supplies. Childproof locks work well. The safest measure, however, is to place poisons on high shelves out of reach.

• Buy a fire extinguisher and a smoke detector.

• Consider electrical outlet covers.

• Gate your stairs.

• Make sure the crib slats are no more than 2⅜ inches between rails.

• Store toys safely. Don't buy a toy box with a lid on hinges.

• Don't ever leave your child alone in

THE MAKINGS OF A
FAMILY FIRST-AID KIT

- adhesive tape and gauze
- antibiotic ointment
- antihistamines
- bandages (all types and sizes)
- calamine lotion
- consecrated oil
- diarrhea remedy
- dropper
- hydrogen peroxide
- ipecac syrup (call a poison control center before using syrup of ipecac; it can be harmful if misused)
- matches
- measuring spoon and cup
- needles
- pain relievers
- petroleum jelly
- poison control phone number (this national toll-free number will connect you to your local poison control center: 1-800-222-1222)
- rubbing alcohol
- safety pins
- scissors
- soap
- thermometer
- tweezers
- zinc oxide

the bathroom, whether he's a baby or a toddler. Babies can drown in just an inch or two of bath water and a toddler can fall head first into the toilet.

• Always strap your child in place in his car seat, infant seat, swing, high chair, stroller, and even changing table.

• Think ahead about possible accidents and try to prevent them. Check the floor for small items that can be choked on. Make sure space heaters are out of reach. Watch for sharp corners on furniture. Secure any loose rugs. Look for things that can be pulled over or ingested.

The best prevention for accidents is constant supervision. Still, accidents will happen even with the best supervision; so prepare yourself for a visit or two to the doctor's office or the emergency room. Children are so curious and fearless it's an unusual child who makes it through childhood without a few scars.

IMMUNIZATIONS

Most states require that a child receive a number of immunizations before entering public school. The dates of all required immunizations must be reported to your child's school before he can attend. These standards change through the years; but your pediatrician, local school district, or health department should be able to tell you at any time what shots your child will need.

Many shots should be given early in life to protect your child from exposure to serious childhood diseases. Check with your pediatrician for a schedule of immunizations that your child should follow. Most

---

REQUIRED CHILDHOOD IMMUNIZATIONS

Your child may be required to receive immunizations for the following diseases, depending on the state in which you live:

- Chicken pox
- Diphtheria, Tetanus, and Pertussis (tetanus and diphtheria are updated every ten years)
- Hepatitis A (not required in many eastern states)
- Hepatitis B
- Haemophilus Influenzae type b (Hib)
- Influenza (in certain risk groups only)
- Measles
- Mumps
- Pneumococcal Disease
- Polio
- Rubella

shots are given in a series; therefore it's best to start early and be consistent.

Don't overreact to reports or scare stories about adverse reactions to immunizations. Reactions to required immunizations have improved through the years, and your doctor or health department employee can tell you what to watch for. Ask your healthcare provider for the best way to take care of any pain or discomfort your child may experience.

The hardest part about taking your child to get her shots will probably be *your* own pain. It's hard to take your child to a place where you know she will be poked or hurt in any way. Your reaction may be more emotional than your child's. Reassure yourself that you are doing the right thing to protect your child from diseases that have plagued children for generations.

Remind yourself to be grateful that you live in a time when your child can be protected from serious disease and even death.

Most standard health insurance plans pay for all required immunizations. If you don't have insurance to pay for your child's shots, most county health departments subsidize immunizations for children when parents are not able to afford them.

SHOWING AFFECTION

All babies need to be both physically and emotionally nurtured. Babies crave close intimate contact with their mothers and fathers. They need someone to keep them clean and fed; but equally important they need someone who is kind, steady, predictable, patient, and loving. Babies should be hugged, kissed, stroked, held, sung to, snuggled, and encouraged to develop their skills in front of an adoring audience. The way you treat your child will be the mirror he has of himself. If you see a wonderful, beautiful, capable, smart, fun, loving child—he will feel he is in fact . . .

wonderful, beautiful, capable, smart, fun, and loving.

All babies and young children naturally explore and touch all parts of their body. Don't worry about or reprimand your child for exploring his body. Your child should learn that every part of his beautiful body is good and acceptable. Let your child learn the proper name for every body part without embarrassment or self-consciousness.

As your child gets older, your expressions of affection can still include hugs and kisses. You can compliment your child, write him love notes, call him on the phone, perform small favors and acts of service or buy or make gifts that show you know what will please your child.

Children learn to love by being loved. They learn to be affectionate, kind, gentle, and forgiving from parents who demonstrate those same attributes. Every moment you spend loving and caring for your child is worth the effort, time, and energy. The way you treat your child will give him the ability to form close loving relationships later in life. You are filling his bank account with love that he can draw on for the rest of his life. His *head* may not remember all you've done for him during these early years but his *heart* always will.

LULLABIES

The simple words to these lullabies are meant to comfort your baby *and* you. As you sing or even just read these words I hope you feel and pass along your Mother in Heaven's love. Perhaps you could imagine she is holding you as you hold your child.

Use the tunes to familiar lullabies (I've included a handful of traditional lullaby lyrics here) or make up your own tunes to sing to these words as you rock your babies. Join the generations of mothers past and future who have given comfort and love to their babies through the gentle music of a simple lullaby.

Hush, Little Baby

*Hush, little baby, don't say a word,
Mama's going to buy you a mockingbird.*

*And if that mockingbird don't sing,
Mama's going to buy you a diamond ring.*

*And if that diamond ring turns brass,
Mama's going to buy you a looking glass.*

*And if that looking glass gets broke,
Mama's going to buy you a billy goat.*

*And if that billy goat won't pull,
Mama's going to buy you a cart and bull.*

*And if that cart and bull turn over,
Mama's going to buy you a dog named
    Rover.*

*And if that dog named Rover won't bark,
Mama's going to buy you a horse and cart.*

*And if that horse and cart fall down,
You'll still be the sweetest little baby in
    town.*

Bye, Baby Bunting

Bye, O baby bunting
Daddy's gone a hunting
To get a little rabbit skin
To wrap his baby bunting in.

Bye, O baby bunting
Daddy's gone a hunting
To get a little lambie skin
To wrap his baby bunting in.

Bye, O baby bunting
Daddy's gone a hunting
A rosy wisp of cloud to win
To wrap his baby bunting in.

Lullaby, and Good Night
(Brahms' Lullaby)

Lullaby, and good night,
With pink roses bedight,
With lilies o'erspread,
Is my baby's sweet head.
Lay you down now, and rest,
May your slumber be blessed!
Lay you down now, and rest,
May your slumber be blessed!

Lullaby, and good night,
You're your mother's delight,
Shining angels beside
My darling abide.
Soft and warm is your bed,
Close your eyes and rest your head.
Soft and warm is your bed,
Close your eyes and rest your head.

Sleepyhead, close your eyes.
Mother's right here beside you.
I'll protect you from harm,
You will wake in my arms.
Guardian angels are near,
So sleep on, with no fear.
Guardian angels are near,
So sleep on, with no fear.

Lullaby, and sleep tight.
Hush! My darling is sleeping,
On his sheets white as cream,
With his head full of dreams.
When the sky's bright with dawn,
He will wake in the morning.
When noontide warms the world,
He will frolic in the sun.

Rock-a-Bye, Baby

Rock-a-bye, baby,
In the treetop.
When the wind blows
The cradle will rock;
When the bough breaks
The cradle will fall,
And down will come baby,
Cradle and all.

Baby is drowsing,
Cosy and fair.
Mother sits near,
In her rocking chair.
Forward and back
The cradle she swings,
And though baby sleeps,
He hears what she sings.

From the high rooftops
Down to the sea,
No one's as dear
As baby to me.

Wee little fingers,
Eyes wide and bright—
Now sound asleep
Until morning light.

My Mommy Loves Me

My mommy loves me,
My mommy loves me,
My mommy loves me,
Because I am me.

She'll always love me,
She'll always love me,
She'll always love me,
Because I am me.
(Repeat song, replacing "mommy" with
"daddy," "grandma," and so on.)

On the Wings of Angels

On the wings of angels
God sent you to me.
Close your eyes my little one,
I'll watch over thee.

Life comes again, my dear,
After winter's dark night.
Springtime is in my heart,
It opens up to light.

Sleep tight my little babe.
Sleep my little lamb.
Mommy's always here for you,
Whereever I am.

The angels in heaven
Watch over thy head.
Till nighttime is over
Light covers thy head.

Don't Get Big Too Soon

When I was a little girl
I used to dream of you.
Now I am your mommy, so
Don't get big too soon.

I thank my Father every day
For giving you to me.
You're the best baby in the world
It's not hard to see.

Never was a finer child
On the whole big earth.
I hope you know how dear you are
And just what you are worth.

Take my hand and hold it tight,
Never let me go.
I'll love you forever so
You don't have to go.

Close your eyes and dream your dreams.
I'll be here till dawn.
I don't know how to give my thanks,
My account is overdrawn.

So rest your head and go to sleep
I won't forget my lines.
I'll love you forever, dear,
Always you'll be mine.

Hold Back the Dawn

Please forgive, me little one.
I can't let you go.
You were mine such a short time.
Do you have to grow?

It seems as if we barely met
On your birthday yesterday.
And now your dream is far away—
No more time to play.

Tell me that you won't forget
Your funny little mom.
Hold me now as I hold you—
Don't be gone too long

I hope you know I love you so.
You're more precious than gold.
I'll be your friend to the end,
Till both of us grow old.

I'm trying so to let you go.
It's in the Father's plan.
I want to hold you one more hour,
But I don't think I can.

I wish I could follow you out there—
Hold back the dawn.
But in my heart I know the rules
Have already been drawn.

So I sing this little song
And thank God for your birth.
I'll give him back what he gave me
On the day you came to earth.

Grandma's Lullaby

I want to rock my baby
But my baby is all gone.

I want to kiss my baby
But I forgot the song.
I want to teach the world to sing
But the lyrics are not here.
If I forget the lullaby
Who is there to care?

So . . .
I didn't get the washing done
I didn't do the dishes
I didn't vacuum all the rugs
I didn't wish for wishes.
I took my grandchild in my arms
And let the world stand still,
For life is brief and oh so dear
Like birds on the window sill.
For I am learning that windows open,
Then windows quickly close.
Life is full of one-time chances
For those who really know.

So Warm to Hold

Sleep tight my little one.
Momma loves you so.
Take your time getting big.
Take your time to grow.

Just be mine a little while.
You're so warm to hold.
Stay right here in my arms
Till I'm very old.

Yet I know you will grow
And leave my arms some day,
But for now just be mine.
Take your time to play.

The seasons come the seasons go
Like birds upon the wind.
I love to kiss your tiny cheek
And all your tiny things.

Please don't forget these precious hours
When you were mine to love.

Don't forget your father
And mother up above.

But for now I hold you close
And press you near my breast.
Go to sleep my little one.
Close your eyes and rest.

The Seasons Come and Go

It seems my days spin so fast
I can hardly breathe.
When I finally catch my breath
My heart longs to see
Why I can be blinded so
By the cares of this earth,
Why I can't see my children's hearts
And just what they are worth.
If I lose the vision
Of why they came to be
How can my children know?
Will they ever see
They are the wonder of my soul?
I long to hold them close.
They are my jewels and my crown.
They are what matters most.

So today I will slow down
And take them on my knee.
I will kiss their tiny cheeks
And start listening.
Oh, Lord, help me see
The wonder of my child.
Help me see heaven
In my baby's eyes.
The seasons come the seasons go
And soon my child grows old.
Then I'm the grandma on the porch—
My birthright's not been sold

My Little Lamb

Go to sleep my little lamb,
Mommy holds you close.
You're the best baby in the world,
I love you the most.

Let me hold you one more hour
Close here to my heart.
You're the cutest little one.
You're my life's best part.

I wish that I could tell you how
You came to me one day.
Our Father handed you to me
And told me you could stay.

Yet every day you grow so big.
I wish I knew the art,
So that I could keep you small—
Right here by my heart.

Go to sleep my tiny babe,
Rest your weary head.
Know your mother will always be
Right here by your bed

So sleep my little tiny one
Upon the night's full moon.
Close your eyes, dream your dreams,
day will come too soon.

Sleep, Baby, Sleep

Sleep, baby, sleep
The big stars are the sheep.
The little stars are the lambs, I guess.
The big moon is the shepherdess.
Sleep, baby, sleep.

A MOTHER'S DECISIONS

WORKING

Every mother decides if she will go to work outside the home after her children are born. This choice is very personal and never simple. Make sure your choice to work is made in partnership with your husband and Father in Heaven. Don't base your decision purely on money. Ask yourself if you would be working for basic necessities or the extras. In most cases, the extras are not worth it. The decision you make now will likely be addressed again many times as your children grow up.

Perhaps you don't have a choice because you are widowed, separated, divorced, unmarried, or your husband is unemployed, under-employed, or disabled. Do the best you can and don't be afraid to ask your bishop for help. Consider the following options:

• Look for home-based employment. A variety of options exist for home-based employment, including sales jobs, doing medical transcription, running a company Web site or producing a company newsletter, and so on.

If this is your first baby, and you are currently employed full time, you may want to ask your boss if you could do your current job from home. If you work from home, make sure you have the equipment necessary to do a good job. This might include a computer, Internet access, a separate phone line, and a fax machine. Some employers will provide the equipment, others will not.

If you decide to work from home, you'll have to be very diligent to maintain a professional demeanor when working with clients, co-workers, or customers. You'll also have to make sure you can really put in the hours necessary to fulfill your job requirements and earn enough money. This is easier if the job you are doing can be done at any time of day: when your husband comes home from work, for example, or when your children are napping, or after they go to bed. It's also easier if you hire someone to come into your home and care for your children a few hours a day while you are working. Some employers will require that this be the case.

Working from home often sounds like the perfect arrangement, but it can be very difficult if you have deadlines to meet and are forced to choose between completing your work for the day or tending to a fussing baby, a messy house, or any number of other distractions that come from being at home.

• If you work part time outside the home, consider swapping child care with another mother in your ward who also works part time or has other obligations for part of the day. Extended family may be able to help as well. It's wise, however, not to take advantage of the services your family might provide. If you are a single mother, consider sharing living arrangements, meal preparation, and baby-sitting with another single mother. Be creative and ask God to help you make the best of things under your circumstances. If no father is present in the home, do your best to find a loving father substitute for your children.

• If, after sacrificing and weighing all your options, you find that you must temporarily work full time outside the home, it's imperative that you make wise decisions when selecting care for your child.

DAY CARE OPTIONS

Options for care include family care, day care centers, and in-home care.

Many moms are most comfortable with family care, where their children are brought to the home of a nonrelative and receive care in the caregiver's home. This is called family care because the caregiver's home often becomes a second home for the child. One big advantage of this type of care is its consistency. Many family care providers also provide more flexible drop-off and pick-up times than day care centers do. One disadvantage is that the family care provider may not have an organized schedule or curriculum. Some family care providers offer creative learning activities

for children and limit things like TV time, others let children play unsupervised or watch TV for several hours a day.

Day care centers provide reliable routines, structured play and learning, and must be licensed and regulated by the state. Children at day care centers, however, are exposed to more illnesses. Children in day care generally get more ear infections, respiratory infections, and diarrhea than children not in day care.

In-home care is the most expensive option, and is out of reach for many moms who are working just to get by. If you do have a nanny, however, make sure you thoroughly investigate her references and that she maintains the same beliefs and values as you.

Licensing and Regulations

If you are faced with the difficult decision of placing your child in day care, do your best to research all the possibilities. Contact your state's department of health and bureau of licensing to make sure the provider you choose is licensed. Insure that the child to staff ratio is adequate. The suggested ratio for children under two years of age is 3 children to 1 adult; for children two to three, the best ratio is 4 children to 1 adult; for children three to six, the preferred ratio is 8 children to 1 adult. Most states have portions of their Web sites devoted to children's issues, including day care. On these sites you can find important questions to ask of potential providers and other invaluable information.

A WORD OF ADVICE

Don't forget to nourish your own life. All mothers feel frustration, boredom, fatigue, and uncertainty whether they are married or single, full-time homemakers or mothers who work outside the home. You need and deserve time to take care of your needs as well as your child's.

We have been counseled that by divine design, fathers are responsible to provide the necessities of life and protection for their families. We also have been told that disability, death, or other circumstances may necessitate individual adaptation—so *never* think you know enough to judge another woman's situation. Do the best you can to handle your own situation and trust the other women around you to do the same.

Each time you decide whether to work, never underestimate your value in the home. Be creative and consider work at home or part-time work as options. The first few years before a child starts school are so crucial to his sense of security and well-being. Do everything possible to be home when your children are home as often as possible. Any sacrifice is worth it. You'll never regret it.

FAMILY PLANNING

Doctors generally advise women to wait for six weeks after the birth of their baby before resuming sexual relations with their husbands to ensure that complete healing has taken place. Actually, you can resume sexual intercourse as soon as it's comfortable and you want to. Before this point it's time to decide how you want to handle the possibility of *another* pregnancy. If you don't use any birth control, you have a 90 percent chance of conceiving in a year and most likely sooner. Don't assume you can't get pregnant until after

you resume your regular cycle because you ovulate *before* you begin menstruating.

TYPES OF BIRTH CONTROL

Before your six-week postpartum checkup with your doctor, discuss with your husband how you want to handle birth control. Decide together what you feel is best. Types of birth control you might want to discuss are: oral contraceptives, condoms, preparations that kill sperm, diaphragms, cervical caps, withdrawal before ejaculation, rhythm method, contraceptive implants, injectable contraceptives, and intrauterine devices. Your doctor will be happy to discuss the different forms of birth control and answer all your questions from a medical point of view.

How many children you and your husband decide to have and how far to space them, however, is a personal decision you'll have to make through the prayerful use of your individual agency. Church leaders have counseled couples to make this decision together carefully with God's help.

THE *REAL* RULES OF CONTRACEPTION

You may not realize it now, but there are far more reliable rules for contraception than the ones your doctor will discuss with you in his office. If you want to be sure you *don't* get in that delicate condition:

- Announce to your parents, in-laws, friends, neighbors, co-workers, and ward or branch members that you and your husband are going to start your family now.
- Spend your savings redecorating your study into a beautiful, newborn nursery.
- Promise your daughter a baby sister for Christmas.
- Buy a bigger house to accommodate lots of children.
- Quit your well-paying job after announcing to the world you are anxious for motherhood before it's too late.
- Graduate with straight A's in child development and obtain a master's degree in family relations and a Ph.D. in home management.

On the other hand, this is how babies are really made, even when using so-called reliable forms of contraception. Babies are made when:

- A wife finds a fascinating new career she loves, with unlimited possibilities for fame and fortune, and happily assures her new employer that she won't be having any more babies.
- A husband and wife decide they have enough children and proceed to sell or give away all their baby clothes, furniture, and maternity clothes.
- A doctor reassures a woman she doesn't need to worry any longer because she has "gone through the change."
- A woman goes on a diet with her husband in which the first one to lose 20 pounds gets a whole new wardrobe.
- The wife spends a seven-year clothing allowance on one dozen tight, form-fitting dresses.
- A couple finally gives up on the infertility doctors and decides to adopt triplets. This happy pair will promptly become pregnant with twins.
- The couple forgets to keep insurance policy payment current and finds out they have been dropped from coverage, maternity benefits and all.

THE BLESSING OF BROTHERS AND SISTERS

Deciding on how many children you have is an individual choice that husbands and wives make together after prayer and fasting. Yet how many children you have is not always in your total control. You may have one, or several, surprise pregnancies. If you have the privilege of deciding how many children you want to have, I suggest you consider this: In the chaos, clutter, and commotion you call home you will often doubt your ability to give your child everything he or she needs. You will wonder if you should have more children. You will wonder if having more children will negatively or positively affect your child. Then time will pass and you will discover that you have been able to give your child something much more lasting than a room of his own, lots of nice clothes, and your continual undivided attention. You have given your children each other. That constant thing called a brother or sister can't be divorced or lost in a bad financial venture. Your children will always have someone to fight with and someone to laugh with. They will always have someone to slug and someone to hug. They will have someone they're not speaking to and someone to tell all their secrets to. They will have someone to sit next to at family reunions and someone to disown.

Even though your children may have to share the bathroom, hot water, and attention with several other siblings, they will have the privilege of learning that there is such a thing as too much privacy and too many possessions. Yet there is never such a thing as too much family or too much love. Someday your children will thank you for giving them lifelong best friends . . . each other.

FERTILITY

When making plans about when to have your children make sure you are informed about female fertility facts. Statistics say your fertility typically peaks by the time you're 30. Your fertility drops 50 percent by the time you are 35. By your early 40s your chance of carrying a baby to term drops significantly, *even* if you are using fertility techniques. After age 45, the ability to have a baby is rare.

So if you want children, early is better than later. If you put off having children until you're older and can afford them, you may not be able to conceive and you will regret your lost opportunities.

KEEPING THE ROMANCE ALIVE

You may have a much more difficult time finding the time, energy, and privacy for intimacy after your children come. If you're motivated, you'll find ways and times. Remember, physical intimacy in marriage is not solely for the procreation of children. Sexual relations provide not only the means for the creation of physical bodies for God's spirit children, but they are also a deep expression of love between you and your husband. Sexual intimacy will help keep you and your husband emotionally as well as physically close. It is *designed* to be enriching and exciting.

You may feel guilty or confused if you find yourself losing interest in physical intimacy with your husband. Instead, learn to understand the physical changes that pregnancy, nursing, and aging bring to your body and talk freely with your doctor and husband about your lack of desire and what you can do to improve your situation. Your husband will appreciate your ability to discuss this issue with him so that you can both be free from any misunderstandings and work toward gentle solutions.

Misunderstanding is at the heart of most family pain. Most problems in marriages aren't the result of some evil or bad intent at

A MOTHER'S LAMENT

When do you get time to yourself?
When do you finally take a shower?
When do you actually comb your hair?
After you become a mother . . .

I used to think motherhood was all sweet-smelling posies
I'm learning babies are so sweet but they sure don't smell like roses.

When do you get the time to sleep?
When do you finally lose your hips?
When do you actually eat a warm meal
And find your husband's lips?

I used to think motherhood was a dainty walk in the park
But I'm learning the walk's in the hallway with my newborn after dark.

When do you get the time to think straight?
When do you finally stop the worry?
When do you actually feel relaxed?
When do you not have to hurry?

I used to think, as a mother, my dreams
would surely leap
But I'm learning dreams are for people who
actually get some sleep.

When does life get back to normal?
When do you finally wear nice clothes?
Maybe it's when you actually understand
What every grandma knows . . .
Believe it or not, life is best when you're kissing baby toes.

the beginning. These mistakes are usually made later when spouses fail to communicate, understand each other, see clearly into each other's hearts, forgive, and work toward solutions to problems. Your family will usually be about as healthy as your marriage. If your marriage is healthy, loving, and functional, your children have the opportunity to grow and develop in the marinade of unconditional love.

It's vital to make time to keep the romance in your marriage. Romance involves much more than physical intimacy. Make it a habit to go on a weekly date and a yearly getaway. Give your relationship the time and attention it needs to form the heart and soul of a healthy family. A happy mother and father who love each other are the best gifts you can give your children.

THINGS I WISH MY MOTHER HAD TOLD ME

♥ *Children don't see the world as it is. They see the world as they are. So do you.*

♥ *You don't have to be wise or wonderful all the time. You don't have to know all the answers. You don't always have to know the right thing to do. You don't have to be strong all the time. You just have to pray a lot.*

♥ *Learn the difference between what you can actually do something about and everything you are concerned about.*

♥ *People who say they sleep like a baby usually don't have one.*

♥ *Do whatever works.*

♥ *Get a good medical reference book.*

♥ *God will watch over your children while you sleep. Your children are also his children, and so are you. Don't be afraid to leave things in God's hands; that's where everything is anyway.*

♥ *Your children existed before they came to you. They are not lumps of clay for you to mold at will. Try to imagine a wise old grandpa or grandma squished up inside a very tiny infant body looking up at you.*

♥ *Though your child may forget his first estate, God will give you glimpses into your child's soul if you ask. The greatest truths you'll ever receive will be while you are looking into your child's eyes and praying for God to tell you who he is and how to love and lead him.*

♥ *Cut yourself some slack during the year or two you're pregnant and nursing each child. Your body, hormones, and emotions are on a roller-coaster ride. You can throw up your arms and scream occasionally so the ride will be more fun.*

♥ *Don't hurry through bath time. Bath time is always quality time.*

♥ *Going to church with small children is a workout. Remember, little children can't be irreverent; they don't know enough. Little children are supposed to be noisy and wiggle a lot. They aren't trying to drive you crazy. It is their job to explore this big, wide, wonderful world. Your job is to keep them from killing themselves.*

♥ *It is with gratitude that you get a God's-eye view of your life.*

♥ *Refuse to be intimidated by reality.*

♥ *Children grow up.*

♥ *There is nothing more beautiful than a baby just out of the bathtub with a shiny nose.*

♥ *Buy lots of dark blue or black pants with elastic waists. They don't show stains and they are very adaptable to changing waistlines.*

♥ *Disposable diapers and unspillable sippy cups are more important than nuclear fission.*

♥ *You will never get a good night's sleep again. Get over it and get on with your life.*

♥ *Quit wanting your life back. This is your life.*

BETTER BEGINNINGS END NOTES

Having a baby is without a doubt the most life-altering event in a woman's life. No other life circumstance will change the course of your life more. The first year of your child's life will be exhausting and exciting, depressing and exhilarating, terrible and tender. You will find yourself absolutely sure that you are not cut out to be a mother at one moment and absolutely sure that being a mother is all you ever want to do forever. Typically, no other year has quite the roller-coaster ride of ups and downs, changes and chaos, disruption and delight, exhaustion and excitement as the first.

Don't wish away a moment. Though those late-night feedings seem like they'll never end, they will. When you look back on your life you will realize that your child's first year was priceless and fleeting. You will wish you had spent more time in the rocking chair and less time doing absolutely anything else. As the years go by, you will wish you had not taken your opportunity to have children so casually. You will realize how short life really is and how fleeting is the magic of infancy.

There will be days when you never make it out of your nightgown and into the shower. There will be nights when you think you'll die of exhaustion. But there will be other moments too, moments when you check on your sleeping baby and have a wave of warmth so envelope you that you will not be able to hold back tears. While you are caring for your baby, you will often have days when you feel like you don't get anything important done, that all your efforts don't really matter. I promise you that loving and nurturing your child will be the most important thing you will ever do. Your devotion and sacrifice makes your life holy and is irreplaceable in the soul-crafting of your child.

I promise you angels when you need them most. I promise you a life-altering love growing inside you that will continue to expand and increase. I promise you a job title you will never be fired from and a tenderness that will never die. I promise that your life will never matter more than now as you are true to your sacred trust. I promise you payment that is out of this world and meaningful work that never ends. Mostly, I promise you that your choice to be a mother will be, without a doubt, the best decision you ever made.

A number of years ago I was waiting in line for my five-year-old son's evaluation with his new kindergarten teacher. A very stylish young mother and her son sat in the chair closest to the schoolroom door because the teacher was running behind. I was about eight months pregnant at the time and found it hard to walk without waddling.

When this stylish mother saw me lumber down the hall toward her and plop down with a sigh, she stared at my belly and asked, "Why do you want to do *that* again?"

Her question caught me off guard so I just blushed and smiled.

"This is the swan song for me," the stylish mother added. "Boy, am I ever ready to get this last one in school. Now it's my turn to have a little time for me. I finally get my life back." She was wearing beautifully tailored clothes, her hair was elegantly styled, and her long fake fingernails were polished pink with jeweled flowers on the ends. "I just bought that car," the woman added pointing to a shiny red sports car in the parking lot. "Nice, huh."

I looked down at my protruding stomach and silently asked myself, "Why am I doing this again?" My worn maternity clothes were stained orange across the belly with my preschooler's spaghetti from lunch. My fingernails still had dirt under the nails from playing in the sandbox. I could feel several sticky kisses on my cheeks from my toddler. My hair was windblown. The old van I drove was covered with mud and smelled like smoke from our last family camp out.

I cleared my throat several times then turned to this woman and quietly asked, "What if a very important person brought you to the opening of a diamond mine? What if they said you could go inside and gather as many diamonds as you wanted, but there was only one condition? You had only a certain amount of time before your time was up and then you couldn't have any more diamonds. Would you do it?"

"Sure, who wouldn't?" the stylish mother answered.

"But what if some of the diamonds were hidden in the rocks and you had to work really hard to get them?"

"Well, I'm sure I'd be willing to do whatever work it took to get those diamonds because then they'd be mine and I'd be rich forever. Even one diamond is worth a fortune you know."

"That's why I'm doing this again." I answered patting my protruding abdomen.

You too will have people give you a hard time about being pregnant *again*. Don't let their unkind remarks influence the decision you make in partnership with your husband and God to have more children. What those people don't understand is this . . . *If you want to harvest in the fall you have to plant in the spring.*

I had a friend who gave me a hard time about being pregnant *every* time she saw me in the family way. Now that we're both older, she tells me that she envies my wonderful growing posterity and the full rich life I live because of all the people I have to love and be loved by. Don't be distracted by other's comments or society's lack of regard for bearing children. Ultimately, your children will be your finest harvest and make you rich forever.

NOTES

IMPORTANT INFORMATION, FAVORITE WEB SITES, AND GOOD BOOKS ABOUT BETTER BEGINNINGS

UNDERSTANDING THE BASICS

THE BASICS

The basics of being a mother are *not* glamorous. When you're a mom you teach unwilling little people how to use the toilet, fix endless meals that mostly wind up on your floor, wash stained and stinky clothes, pick up an eternally cluttered house, wipe runny noses, bandage bloody knees, change messy diapers, balance the beleaguered budget, and discipline disobedient children. Now, you don't have to do all these things exclusively or without help, mind you. But you do have to do them; otherwise your family will starve, run around naked, or live in a dump.

If Mom doesn't know the basics of handling financial matters, the whole family will soon be in a big pot of trouble. Moms also need to learn coping strategies for living with and providing spiritual nurturing for babies, toddlers, preschoolers, school-

age children, and teenagers . . . sometimes all at the same time. You even need to take good care of yourself as well as the rest of the family through all the bumps and scrapes of life.

Motherhood is a career that seems a lot more glamorous *before* taking it on. Before you're a mother you imagine your picture-perfect self and baby cuddled in the rocking chair while you sing soft, soothing lullabies. What you get in real life is a red-eyed, hasn't-combed–her-hair-for-days self desperately walking the floor with a colicky, screaming newborn. Reality never fits the idealistic visions. Life with children is full of ups and downs and scary turns that leave you wondering why you ever wanted to go on this ride in the first place.

Without a solid understanding of the basics you'll be treading water without knowing how to dog-paddle. But, *and this is important,* you don't have to be an expert and figure all this out by yesterday. Just live one day at a time. The most important basic of mothering, after all, is that you don't have to know, do, or be everything. You just have to wake up, get out of bed, and keep trying.

Though the basics may not seem particularly romantic or charming, they are *real* and they'll keep you afloat until your ship comes in or you learn to dog-paddle, whichever comes first. The following sections will review the basics as they apply to toddlers, preschoolers, school-age children, and teenagers. Then we'll get down to the real nitty-gritty things, like housework, finances, and treating illnesses.

THE TODDLER YEARS

Toddlers are typically given a bum rap. Despite their cherubic faces and disarming ability to make you laugh at any given moment, most toddlers have been called everything from "family terrorist" to "terrible two-year-old" and have—on at least one occasion—been held solely responsible for Mom's trip to the funny farm. It's true that toddlers can be destructive, infuriating, and irrational; but they can also be delightful, enchanting, and full of affection. The same toddler who throws regular fits on the floor at the grocery store can also give the best hugs, the brightest smiles, and the sweetest-sounding I love yous a mother has ever heard. Over the years I've lived with many people—newborns, teenagers, middle-aged adults, and centurions. But toddlers, in my opinion, are right up there on the top of my list as the most exciting and humorous houseguests.

Once your baby starts to toddle, everything in your life will change. Soon he'll start walking, talking, shouting, helping, and getting into a whole barrel full of trouble. For toddlers—who are officially labeled as such from about one to three years of age—life is one big adventure. This is the stage where your "baby" will learn independence, crave freedom, and try his hardest to insist on setting the rules. At the same time, he'll want lots of attention. Most toddlers love affection, being held, and being cuddled. As your toddler grows out of babyhood, you'll likely notice the following behaviors and developments:

- lots of movement
- a short attention span
- a love of simple songs and games (and a desire to sing or play them over and over and over again)
- a fascination with and desire to learn about everything around him
- a concerted effort to control his body and explore his environment
- an awareness of his own wants—and only his wants
- a general inability to foresee the consequences of his actions

Be prepared for one wild ride as you parent your toddler. And don't forget that—just like everything else in life—the tantrums and meltdowns will pass. When they do,

you might even find yourself longing for the days when your 13-year-old was just two and loved to spontaneously throw his arms around you and joyfully exclaim, "I love you, Mommy!"

LOSING THE DARLINGHOOD OF INFANCY

One reason toddlers are given such a bum rap is because they've so recently cast off the darlinghood of infancy. Because they can walk now, they get into *much* more trouble. Toddlers enjoy using the living room walls for artistic easels and toilets for magic, toy-disappearing acts. Food is generally used for dinnertime facials and athletic throwing events. Toddlers typically have more hair than babies; but it's always too long and full of static electricity (from all that movement) to ever look properly combed. Most of the time it will have something sticky in it. Toddlers definitely have a way of shoving their primary caregivers into the anti-sentimental mother period.

Before you actually have one, other people's toddlers seem terrifically funny. They yell embarrassing things at church to entertain you. They show-and-tell you about their new underpants at the grocery store to make you laugh in the check-out line. If you happen to be a bearded man, they think you are Jesus. Before I had toddlers, I used to laugh at my sister's daughter for walking around with her finger up her nose. My sister didn't laugh. She simply said, "You just wait."

By the time your child hits mid-toddlerhood, you will begin to wonder why you ever had a hand in helping this small person learn to walk, talk, and eat on his own. Gone are the quiet moments in the nursery gently nursing your newborn to sleep. In come a bottle of chocolate syrup and a bag of potato chips mashed into the carpet. Gone are the sweet sentimental moments of encouraging your little one to take his first step. In comes the sobbing mother, not because of time hurrying by unappreciated, but because junior can now reach into her makeup drawer. If you are smart, you will teach your little angel to say that most precious of phrases every mother longs to hear in her husband's presence: "I want Daddy to change my pants."

ADVICE FOR THE TODDLER-WEARY

GIVE DAD CENTER STAGE AND YOURSELF A BREAK

Toddlerhood is a great time to let Dad take center stage with your child whenever he's home. If your child can move from

A GLIMPSE INTO THE LIFE OF A TODDLER

People are always telling mothers of toddlers that all they need is a sense of humor. Of course, it's been twenty years since those same people had to pull their children from the garbage can or flour bin. Things like stick figures crayoned all over your new bedspread always seem a lot funnier if they've never happed to you. Other people chuckle when you tell them about your toddler getting into the kitchen cabinets. They can laugh. They didn't have to pick out the 2,364 pieces of elbow macaroni and sort them from the 8,000,000 grains of rice.

Learning to walk, talk, feed yourself, and go to the bathroom are pretty tall orders for someone who's only been on the planet a year. Try to remember this when you realize that your toddler's new desire for independence comes with a one-word vocabulary that pretty much covers everything she'll want to say for two years. That favorite word is, of course, "NO!" She will say this word so often you will want to ban it from the English language. *Don't* take your toddler's negativism personally. *Do* take her wet kisses and bear hugs around the neck personally.

Toddlers are awake a lot more often than babies, which means they are demanding your attention on a nonstop basis all day long. They also have the time and energy to get into everything several times a day. The *third* time my toddler scattered the entire contents of my purse around the house my husband said, "Well, who's the slow learner?" Toddlers usually take a nap in the afternoon; but every other moment of the day, they are rambunctious, curious, climbing, running, falling, and wiping their runny noses on your shoulder or pant leg.

You will find your child insisting on feeding and dressing herself, all to rather humorous conclusions. Your child will probably have bruises and a few stitches, earaches, and a number of high fevers. Your toddler will basically follow you everywhere; and when she's not following you, you can be almost certain that she's into trouble somewhere else.

And even though your toddler's new experimentation with her independence will make her seem hard to get along with, don't forget that you are witnessing a new personality individually unfold right before your eyes. Of course, you'll be doing this awe-inspiring task while preventing your toddler from killing herself every day.

Mom to Dad with total confidence that all her needs will be met, she will be better able to move outside the family circle to the next parent figure, such as a teacher or a favorite baby-sitter. Fathers provide unique bonding experiences and interactions that are crucial at this age.

Plus, you need your spouse to help you *survive* these years. As you will learn quite quickly, having a toddler in the house means you'll constantly be on guard for the next catastrophe. Your toddler's moods will swing wildly from moment to moment; and you'll feel the dizzying

effects of the sudden explosions of emotions. It's okay—and should probably be made medically mandatory—for you to give yourself a break . . . regularly. Pick a day each week where you can have a few hours to yourself; or—and this is even better—pick an hour each day. Your toddler will be in good hands with Dad . . . so you can lock yourself in the bathroom with a warm bath and a good book or go to the mall for some window shopping or take a jog through the park or take a much-deserved nap or visit an old friend or . . .

Gender Security

Children need natural affection, love, and acceptance from both parents to feel good about being a boy or a girl. Children learn to feel good about being male or female from parents who love being a man or a woman and accept their own gender with joy.

If a parent is missing through divorce or death, it's important that your child has access to a role model who will give unconditional love to help compensate for the loss. Extended family members, home teachers, friends, or neighbors can help.

DON'T OVERREACT

Although it may seem like your toddler is often out of control, it's you who will need to work the hardest at maintaining control—of your temper, your anger, your frustration, you name it.

Toddlers respond much better to a calm mother who works hard not to get mad too quickly. Very young children are attracted to low, calm voices and happy faces that are full of tolerance. As a result, the best advice for mothers of toddlers is this: Don't overreact. Let your toddler learn, and therefore make inevitable mistakes, without harsh consequences. Encourage him to be self-sufficient. Let him make choices and explore. You'll soon find that it's easier on you to buy a new tube of lipstick (and begin keeping it out of reach in the future) than it is to be happy with yourself after blowing up at your two-year-old, who used the now-obsolete tube of lipstick to draw a picture on the bedroom wall.

Remember Who's Really in Charge

Living with a toddler sometimes feels like living with a firecracker. Things often blow up in your face. Your toddler will be happier—and you will too—if you remember that *you* run the show. Your toddler really wants you to be in charge and be consistent. If she gets into something she shouldn't, let her know that she shouldn't have. Do it with firmness but gentleness. And then do your best to prevent it from happening again: keep a lock on the toilet, put your favorite earrings up high and out of sight, and so on. If she fights something you need to do for her safety and health, just do it anyway and get it over with as soon as possible. Then get on with life. And always remember, you simply cannot reason with an angry two-year-old.

TOILET TRAINING

The experts will tell you that most children are bowel trained between two and three years of age and bladder trained between three and four years. Most people, expert or not, agree that by the age of five a child should be able to undress and dress himself and go to the bathroom without help. This is specifically so that kindergarten teachers don't get yelled at from across the hall, "Teacher, I need a wipe."

Don't worry too much about all the "averages" you will hear about. No child I've known has ever been average at anything. Your child's move from disposable pants to training pants is simply a process that takes as long as it takes. So relax.

I was so excited to show my first child the joy of a diaperless existence that I began potty patrol before the poor child's second birthday. I made a huge deal out of my toddler's maturity and ability to wear training pants. She, of course, went right along with things and refused to wear a diaper ever again—even when I later regretted my ill-informed and hasty decision. I later found myself longing for those good, old diaper days.

REMEMBERING THE CHILD'S POINT OF VIEW

The older I get the more I'm able to see things from my child's point of view. Just imagine for a minute that you're a very small person—so small, in fact, that your feet never touch the floor when you're seated anywhere. Now imagine that a very large, serious person, three or four times your size, suddenly picks you up, exposes your privacy, plops you on a large, white, gaping porcelain hole, and tells you to relax. I mean, you're no dummy. You've watched that hole before and you're well aware that everything that falls inside suddenly disappears when you pull down on a little silver knob. The way I see it, young children are amazingly patient with their mother's attempts to eliminate diaper duty.

DON'T RUSH THINGS

By the time I'd trained a half-dozen children, I finally learned not to worry about it so much. My later children had to make me wild promises before I'd let them train themselves. I mean, why rush things and ruin your life? I've learned there are worse things than changing a diaper, like making a wild swooping leap for the bathroom every time your toddler gets a concerned look on his face, shampooing the entire living-room carpet and upholstery every week, or washing 47 batches of damp laundry a day.

Things would definitely be much easier if children came housebroken and fully equipped to handle their own bathroom emergencies; but life with children wasn't designed to be easy. Life on planet motherhood takes daring skill and a heck of a lot of wet wipes. So, toilet train your child when you think you and your child are up to it and not before. You can also change your mind and go back to diapers if things are not going well.

POTTY CHAIRS

A lot of young children are afraid of sitting on that big porcelain throne. To help ease your child's worries, you may want to purchase a potty seat that rests on your regular toilet but is small enough to securely hold your child in place. You'll also need a stepping stool to help your child climb up onto the toilet. If you prefer, consider purchasing a sturdy, stand-alone potty chair that can be placed in the bathroom next to the big toilet. These chairs have removable "bowls," from which urine or bowel movements can be dumped into the toilet and flushed away. Some children's stores even sell potty chairs that play music and flash lights when your little one produces something. I've never gone for the expensive models with all the bells and whistles; but hey, if they work for you, go for it. I like to bring out the potty chair months before I want my child to actually start using it because most children are scared of toilets or anything that resembles one. Having the chair around gives young children time to get used to it.

SIGNS OF TOILET TRAINING READINESS

Your toddler may exhibit some of the following behaviors when she's ready to begin toilet training:

- Dry-diaper stretches that last for several hours and occasionally waking from naps dry. Each of these circumstances indicate that your child has developed some ability to control her bladder and may be physiologically ready to start learning.
- Predictable and somewhat regular bowel movements. Having a type of "potty schedule" is helpful when learning to use the toilet.
- Awareness of bodily functions. If your toddler tells you, "Mom, I do a poop" or if she goes to a corner of a room to quietly do the deed, she has become aware of what it *means* to go to the bathroom and will be open to learning more about it.
- The ability to dress herself, albeit in simple things like elastic-waist pants, indicates that she has the physical skills to begin training.
- An understanding of what it means to be dry or wet, and clean or dirty. It's also helpful if she is familiar with the vocabulary needed to express when she needs to go and what she needs to do.
- An interest in your own bathroom habits or those of an older sibling.

METHODS FOR TOILET TRAINING

There are a number of methods moms can employ when toilet training a toddler. Some work well for one child but not for another. By the time your toddler is ready to toilet train, you'll know him well enough that it won't take long for you to figure out which method is best for *your* child. The following are a few of the methods you might try:

Training by Example

Take your child to the bathroom with you every time you go. Have him pull down his pants and sit on his little potty right next to your big one. Explain what you're doing and let him watch how you handle things. You can bring along things like books, treats, or music makers so sitting there together and passing the time of day will seem more fun and interesting.

Timing Method

With the timing method, your child sits (you'll usually have to place her there yourself) on the toilet at set times throughout the day: right when she wakes up, after breakfast, after lunch, before and after naptimes, after dinner, and right before bed. If your child actually produces something, give her a reward.

Reward Method

The reward method is also a winner. With the reward method you place something very attractive to your child—like a gumball machine—in your bathroom. Then tell your child each time he produces something in the potty you will give him a penny and he can retrieve a gumball for a reward. You can do the same thing with stickers and let him put a sticker on a chart or right on the potty every time he goes. You can also invest in a dozen simple surprise treats and allow him to "go fishing" for prizes each time he successfully produces something in the potty.

A Few Simple Helps

Some children seem to take a lot longer to train than others; and boys typically take longer than girls.

Boys can be trained to urinate sitting down or standing up, but they'll probably want to do it like dad does. This will inevitably lead to some messes. If your son has a hard time keeping his stream in the toilet, try throwing a Cheerio or some other kind of target in the toilet bowl and telling him to hit the bull's-eye.

While you're toilet training, and especially until your child quits wetting the bed, you can cover your child's mattress with a water-proof plastic cover. Most children take longer to achieve nighttime dryness than daytime dryness.

TRAINING PANTS

Toilet training pants come in a number of forms: disposable training pants (like Huggies® Pull-Ups®), washable training pants that are thick enough to absorb small accidents, and regular underpants that can be worn with plastic pants over the top for protection. During the training stage, it will help if you let your child wear her training pants around the house without difficult-to-remove pants over them. You don't want to make it too hard to get the underwear off when she needs to hurry. Eventually your child will be able to quickly pull down her pants and go through all the steps of getting to the potty on time. But for now, make it as easy as possible for her to be successful.

Most training pants are designed to catch accidents during the training stage. Disposable training pants, however, are made so well these days that it's hard for your child to tell when she's really wet or dirty. Feeling wet or dirty encourages most children to make an effort to potty train. You may want to reserve disposable training pants like Pull-Ups for nighttime use. This way, your toddler doesn't have to wear a diaper to bed and can still feel like a "big girl." But if she then wears regular training pants during the day, she'll come to recognize what it feels like to have an accident.

TRAINING WHEN THE *CHILD* IS READY

Feeling the urge to go to the bathroom and having the physical ability to hold it until you get to the toilet comes at different ages with different children. It's not possible to force a child who is physically incapable of "holding it" to start doing so.

Likewise, some children are just easier to teach, and others are obstinate and don't adjust well to new ways. You know the temperament of your child better than anyone. Adjust your training methods to suit your particular child.

I often found myself trying to train my child because I was expecting a new baby or because it would be more convenient or less expensive for me. I was always more successful when I waited until my child was *really* ready and willing. Children who are trained when their parents are ready usually relapse because they're simply not ready themselves. All children get to the point when they actually want to use the bathroom and start wearing underpants like their parents or brothers and sisters. So hang in there.

ALLOWING SIBLINGS TO HELP

Siblings can be quite helpful in toilet training their younger brothers and sisters if they also get a reward every time they get the toddler to produce. Small drinks, candies, fruit snacks, or crackers work well as rewards. Siblings can also take the toddler to the bathroom every time they go, and sometimes they're better at communicating to the toddler what he needs to do than you are. If siblings know they get a reward, they'll practically follow your toddler around announcing a play by play of possible opportunities all day.

EARLY OR LATE TRAINING?

You may hear or read of methods where parents trained their children in a day or two at a very early age. These claims are seldom true. These claims usually identify *mothers* who are very well trained, not children. Toilet training is a process and it takes time. If you have a child who was trained at an early age and in only a day or two, for heaven's sake don't brag about it. Being toilet trained is your child's accomplishment, not yours. Some children are more interested and motivated than others. Eventually, I promise, your child will be toilet trained.

REACTING TO ACCIDENTS

If you find yourself overreacting to your child's accidents, remember this is not a toddler plot to stink up your life. Don't get mad or punish your child when she doesn't make it to the bathroom on time. Encourage her when she is successful and don't make a big deal out of it when she isn't. Punishments don't work and aren't appropriate. Do invest in some tools to help get you through this rite of passage with your child. For instance, you might want to invest in a home carpet and upholstery cleaner. Carpet is not a good choice for flooring in the bathroom if you're raising children. You need bathroom flooring that can be wiped up and disinfected easily over and over again.

WETTING THE BED

There is a certain percentage of children who are not able to achieve nighttime dryness for years beyond the expected age. Even when you restrict fluids and make sure they go to the bathroom before bedtime, these children will still wet the bed. If you *and* your child are concerned about this, check with your pediatrician and educate yourself about some of the newest options for treatment.

Medication can be prescribed. There are also belts that can be worn to bed that sound a buzzer when a drop or two of liquid hits them. These are designed to wake the child in time to use the bathroom. Make sure your child is old enough to understand and desires to use medication or some other device before you actually try it.

Don't believe anyone who tells you that punishing or shaming your child will cure him. That's like shaming or punishing a person who snores or grinds his teeth when he's asleep. Never abuse or belittle a child for having an accident. Make sure your child's bed has a plastic waterproof cover and that the bedding is easy to wash and dry. Your child can wear disposable underwear (Pull-Ups) or plastic pants over his underwear if necessary at night.

FEEDING YOUR TODDLER

Your toddler's eating habits may confuse, bewilder, and frustrate you. Just take a deep breath and try to relax. If you're a particularly neat and tidy person, this messy toddler period will give you the opportunity to loosen up, laugh at yourself, and enjoy life more. You may even find yourself squeezing food between your teeth and squirting milk from your nostrils as you momentarily lose total control with your toddler during the family dinner hour.

Toddlers are grazers. That means they like to eat a little all day long. Don't expect your child to eat a lot at each meal. Your toddler will probably eat a bit if she's hungry and then play with her food for the rest of the meal. This is normal and is not the

time to insist that your child clear her plate. Your job is to introduce healthy food and let her experiment.

Don't fall into the trap of preparing a separate meal for your toddler or allowing her to dictate what she will and won't eat. She has a choice. Either she can eat what is put before her or she can wait until the next meal. Just make sure her snacks between meals are healthy.

But because toddlers are famous for being picky eaters, you'll still probably worry about her diet. To ease your anxiety, try to evaluate your toddler's diet over a week's span rather than just a day's time. You will probably be surprised to find that, overall, she eats rather well in a week—some days are just better than others are.

WHAT DOES MY TODDLER NEED TO EAT?

Toddlers are just a few feet tall and certainly don't have stomachs anywhere near the size of yours. This means that toddler portions are relatively small. Three-fourths a cup of milk is considered one serving for a toddler; ½ cup of yogurt is another serving. A serving of fruits or vegetables for a toddler is as small as ½ cup applesauce, ½ of a small orange, or ¼ cup of uncooked broccoli.

Keep these serving sizes in mind and provide a small handful of chopped-up fruits and vegetables with each meal and snack. If you cut up a whole banana into bite-sized pieces, and half of it gets eaten, you've succeeded in providing a complete serving.

Toddlers under two years of age should drink 2 percent or whole milk. Once your toddler is two, however, you can switch to skim milk and other low-fat milk products.

Toddlers need about four servings a day of calcium-rich foods like milk, yogurt, cheese, or broccoli. They also need a few servings of protein, such as milk, yogurt, eggs, or peanut butter. One ounce of meat counts as one protein serving for a toddler, as does one whole egg, 1½ tablespoons peanut butter, and ¾ cup milk. Provide fruits and vegetables five times a day and whole grains or complex carbohydrates six times a day. One carbohydrate serving for a toddler is ½ a slice whole grain bread. This means that a sandwich made with one slice of bread and peanut butter equals two carbohydrates and one protein.

HOW DO I GET MY TODDLER TO EAT?

Once you get over your anxiety and stop worrying that your toddler is eating a diet that consists solely of Cheerios and juice, review some of these ideas:

• A toddler will eat almost anything that he can pick up and dip into a sauce. Ketchup is actually very healthy for your child and some kids think it tastes good on everything.

• Toddlers will eat almost anything that is sprinkled with a colorful topping. Top vegetables and soup with cheese, or applesauce and fruit slices with candy sprinkles.

• Toddlers love food made into shapes, faces, or well-known objects.

• Toddlers will often drink something through a straw that they refuse to drink from a cup, especially if the straw is colorful or shaped in an interesting design.

• Discover the time of day when your child is most hungry, then offer healthy, protein-rich foods, dairy products, and grains, along with fruits and vegetables, at that time.

• Set out small bowls of healthy snacks that your toddler can carry around between breakfast and lunch, when he may seem the hungriest.

• At dinnertime, don't put anything on the family dining table you don't want your toddler to eat first. In other words, leave dessert out of sight and mind until your toddler has a chance to eat his more healthy food. Forcing a toddler to eat something or clear his plate seldom gets you the desired results in the long run . . . a child who enjoys eating healthy food. Your mealtime will end up being a war of wills—and you will lose.

• Toddlers frequently fill up on drinks (juice or milk) and then eat little solid food. If this occurs in your house, you may want to give your toddler a drink later in the meal instead of with it.

• Invite your child to take "just one bite" of a new food, but don't force. Toddlers respond much better to playfulness and silliness than force. If parents and other siblings show excitement and interest in eating healthy food, your toddler will soon follow suit.

• Make dinnertime less of a hassle by using unspillable drinking cups and unbreakable dishes. Spoons and forks that angle in are also helpful for toddlers who have limited movement with their wrists.

• Remember that good eating habits are better "caught" than "taught," so evaluate your own eating habits if you want your child to develop healthy habits that will last a lifetime. If you introduce healthy foods when your child is truly hungry, he will eventually learn to like most foods.

• Don't get too discouraged. You may have to introduce your child to a new food a dozen or more times before he will try it. Just be patient.

• Don't worry about the huge mess your child makes. You can place a plastic tarp under the high chair and remove clothing you don't want stained. Otherwise, just tie a very large wrap-around bib over your child's clothing and get ready for the food party.

• Food for a toddler is much more than nourishment; it is an enjoyable and tactile learning experience. So don't forget to have some fun.

• Since toddlers seem to love doing what you tell them *not* to do, why not try using their obstinate behavior to your advantage. For instance, if you want your toddler to try some nutritious broccoli, don't say, "Child, eat your broccoli." Instead try something more like this: "I don't want any dinosaurs eating these delicious broccoli trees while I have my eyes closed. Hey, are there dinosaurs in this house? Who ate those trees?!" "I hope you don't like these carrots because I love carrots and I want to eat all of them by myself. Don't you dare reach over and sneak one of these carrots." "Here comes the green bean airplane. Buzzzzzzzzzzz! I hope someone doesn't open up his mouth and stick out his tongue so this lean green machine will get sucked in for a crash landing. No . . . No! The green bean plane is getting sucked into the hangar!""Hey, watch this. I'm going to see if I can bite down on this baby tomato inside my mouth until it explodes red stuff all over my teeth. Don't you dare try it."

TODDLER HEALTH ISSUES

EARS, NOSE, AND THROAT

The Toddler Drizzle

Toddlers are famous for getting sick a lot. They do this so they can build up immunities, not so they can drive you crazy by wiping their noses on your shirts and pants. Most moms can expect their toddlers to get seven colds a year, along with an assortment of other illnesses. Most often, you can treat these colds at home.

Sometimes, your child may even be sporting the fashionable toddler drizzle for months at a time. A runny nose is quite normal, especially after playing outside in colder weather, which causes the membranes in the nose to swell slightly. Don't worry too much about the drizzle. Most women who claim they would never let their children run around with a dirty nose have never actually had children. Keep a sense of humor and perspective to help get you through.

Ear Infections

Ear infections are another common problem at this age. A toddler's eustachian tubes are very small and in the just right place for bacteria to sneak in if allergies, a cold, sinusitis, or any number of other conditions are preventing the nose from draining properly. When bacteria is present in the body, pus and mucus are produced to help combat an infection. This pus will sometimes build up behind the ear-drum, causing pain and pressure in your little one's tiny eustachian tubes. Ear infections are normally accompanied by a low-grade fever, a runny nose, and other cold symptoms. Sometimes, however, your child may exhibit no symptoms at all. Other symptoms may include:

• ear pain, which worsens at night and may lessen significantly as the day goes on
  • high fever
  • fatigue
  • irritability
  • loss of appetite
  • muffled hearing
  • occasional nausea, vomiting, or loose stools

If you think your child has an ear infection, it really is best to get her checked out

NON–EAR-INFECTION TRAUMA

There's nothing worse than having a toddler with an ear infection—except having a toddler without an ear infection. The scenario goes something like this:

Your toddler displays all the usual ear infection symptoms, including tugging at ears, loss of appetite, fever, extreme irritability, runny nose, and insomnia. Red-eyed and exhausted, you decide to call the doctor's office for advice. All the receptionists and nurses give the same advice: "I'm sorry, but we can't tell you what to do until the doctor sees your child in the office."

So what does every dedicated mother do? She takes her little less-than-happy bundle to the doctor's office, of course. (When your children are most contagious and susceptible to acquiring other infections, you do what every other crazy mother does . . . you take your child to a place where there are more germs concentrated in one small area than anywhere else on the planet: the pediatrician's waiting room.)

Once there, you quickly assess that every child in the room is either feverish, covered with spots, foaming at the mouth, or coughing up blood. You, therefore, actively prevent your own sweet darling from coming anywhere near all those *other* sick children in the waiting area until you finally hear your name called and you're assigned an examination room. At this point you become ever so hopeful that within another thirty minutes or so you'll be on the way to the pharmacy for some antibiotics and your child will quite possibly sleep through the night

---

by a doctor. Serious infections can lead to other illnesses and even hearing damage.

Usually an ear infection isn't an emergency, so your child may need to wait to be seen until morning or later in the afternoon. If this is the case, try some of the following home treatments:

• acetaminophen or ibuprofen can be given for pain relief or fevers over 102° F. Your pharmacist or pediatrician's office can give you information on proper dosage.

• apply a warm compress to the ear for 20 minutes or, if your child prefers, use a cold pack.

• elevate your child's head while she sleeps or naps. This will relieve the pressure caused by a buildup of fluid in the ear.

If your child exhibits any of the following symptoms in addition to an earache, you should call your doctor immediately:

• severe pain

• pink or red swelling behind the ear

• stiff neck (your child can't touch her chin to her chest)

• fever above 104° F.

• your child looks or acts very sick (listen to your mother's intuition)

• your child's pain is actually caused by sticking a sharp, pointed object into her ear

If an ear infection is diagnosed, your doctor may prescribe immediate treatment with antibiotics or have you treat the symptoms with pain medication for a day or two and see if the infection goes away on its own, which often happens. With antibiotics, your child's pain will typically subside shortly after treatment. It will take longer, however, for the infection to clear because fluid may remain in the ear for

tonight. When the doctor enters the room, you tell him knowingly that junior most definitely has an ear infection. The moment of truth comes as the doctor whips out his eardrum flashlight and carefully looks into both your child's ears.

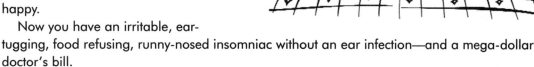

"Your child's ears look fine," the doctor says, smiling, hoping to relieve your nervous suspicions and send you home happy.

Now you have an irritable, ear-tugging, food refusing, runny-nosed insomniac without an ear infection—and a mega-dollar doctor's bill.

One thing you can find some relief in, however, is that your child probably just has a common cold. It should run its course after another week or so, and you do have the assurance from a doctor that your child is not, indeed, suffering from the worst ear infection ever diagnosed—even though you were certain that was the case when you made the appointment.

quite some time. It's important that you continue to give your child antibiotics for the entire time prescribed, even if your child seems better in just a day or so. Recurring ear infections should be given special consideration and may require aggressive antibiotic treatments or tube insertion. These are all matters to discuss with your child's pediatrician.

ORAL HYGIENE

At around six months of age—although it varies widely from child to child—your baby probably started getting teeth. Now that he's a toddler, he has a whole mouthful of those pearly whites. And keeping them clean is not always an easy task.

One simple way to begin is by rubbing his teeth with a wet washcloth each time you clean him up after a meal. Most children this age love to chew on wet washcloths anyway, so he probably won't fight you.

Before bedtime you should also take a few minutes to brush his teeth with a child-size toothbrush (make sure it's one that has soft bristles) and a small amount of toothpaste. This bedtime brushing, however, may not be as easy as getting your child to chew on a wet washcloth. After all, how would you feel if someone else stuck an odd new instrument into your mouth and started moving it around? Even baby teeth, though, can become decayed and damaged, so they must be brushed. To help make things easier for you and more fun for your toddler, try some of the following:

• Let your toddler pick out two or three toothbrushes in different colors. Making

such a "big" decision will help him feel good and encourage him to use his new purchases.

• Let him brush first. Arrange with your toddler for each of you to get a turn to brush: "First, you get to scrub your teeth, then it's Mommy's turn." If he has two brushes, he can hold one while you're using the other for your turn at brushing them.

• Brush your teeth at the same time and then let him inspect them to make sure your teeth are clean enough. After he's inspected your teeth, you get a turn with him.

• Be silly. Toddlers love funny games. Accidentally brush his nose or have his toothbrush fly through the air—do anything that will make him laugh and think this is a fun time.

• If your toddler doesn't always listen to you, try telling him that "the doctor wants you to brush your teeth so they'll be strong and healthy." For many toddlers, a doctor just has more authority than a parent.

Toddlers are prone to swallowing toothpaste instead of spitting it out, so you'll need to make sure the toothpaste you use is safe to swallow. (Read the label on the back of the tube of toothpaste. You may be surprised to find that some toothpastes aren't appropriate for children under six.) Several brands of fluoride-free

paste are available at most stores. If your water is not fluoridated (one-fourth of the United States does not have fluoridated water), your child's pediatrician will likely recommend using fluoride drops or tablets.

Don't make the mistake of thinking you'll start worrying about your child's teeth when he gets his adult ones. Good oral hygiene will save you money and your child lots of pain in the long run.

When Should My Toddler Begin Seeing a Dentist?

Some pediatric dentists will want to see children as early as the eruption of the first tooth at around six months. Usually, however, this is simply to begin a discussion and educational session on proper tooth care. A reasonable recommendation is to have children see the dentist for the first time at around age three as long as (1) there are no obvious concerns earlier, (2) your toddler was weaned from a bottle at about one year of age, and (3) the teeth are brushed regularly. Your child's pediatrician can help you decide what is best for your child and may even be able to recommend dentists who do particularly well with young children.

YOUR TODDLER AND THE GOSPEL

There is no better time to begin teaching your children the gospel—not to mention the routine of the three-hour block—than when she is very, very young. Every trip outside the house is an adventure for a toddler, and every ounce of attention she gets in a family home evening lesson or during a rundown of what everyone learned in church that day is equivalent to a few drops of oil being added to her lamp. It will sometimes be difficult for you to feel successful as you force her to go to nursery with a bunch of strangers for almost two hours or when you are trying to teach her how to pray. But never underestimate your toddler's ability to learn and her amazing skill at throwing you completely off guard by a few words in a simple prayer.

ENCOURAGING YOUR TODDLER TO GO TO NURSERY

When your child turns 18 months old, he is old enough to attend the nursery in your ward. Being old enough and being willing to go, however, are two very different things. Some children love the toys, songs, treats, and interaction with other children. They go to the nursery easily. Others are afraid of being separated from mom and dad and throw a fit every time they enter the nursery room door.

Let your child lead you. If he's ready and willing, give him a kiss and hug and tell him you'll be back soon to get him. If your child is screaming in fear, you might want to spend a few weeks in the nursery with your child until he gets used to the new people and the new situation.

After a few weeks or months, when both you and the nursery leader are ready for the next step, you might have to kiss and hug your child and tell him you will be back, then leave even if he cries. Most nursery leaders will reassure you that it won't last for long. Ask your nursery leader to pick up your child and comfort him as you leave and retrieve you if your child

does not quit crying after a reasonable length of time.

Most children and parents have a hard time separating at this age. But, miracle of miracles, both of you will adjust eventually; and before you know it your child will look forward to his time in the nursery.

The nursery leader in your ward has a most important role in your child's life. This wonderful person is the one who gives your child his first feelings about church outside your arms. Be sure to thank your nursery leaders and appreciate their work. There is no more important calling in the church. Be willing to volunteer and help out in the nursery as needed, especially while your child is there.

TODDLER SPIRITUAL BEGINNINGS

Spiritual experiences for toddlers need not be exclusive to Sunday meetings. Toddlers have a natural sense of wonder and reverence for the natural world and an uncommon excitement for common experiences. You have the privilege of introducing your child to the big, wide world and all its wonders.

If you have the gift of a toddler in your home, you have the perfect opportunity to reawaken *yourself* to the beauties of the

SPIRITUAL AWAKENINGS FOR YOUR TODDLER *AND* YOU

- go on an insect hunt with a mason jar
- start a leaf collection
- dig up worms
- find objects in the clouds
- take a creep (a creep is a very slow walk . . . stopping along the way for discovery of anything interesting)
- let your child finger paint with vanilla pudding (for colors, dye with food coloring)
- run through the sprinklers
- make mud pies
- water the flowers
- swing on swings, slide on slides
- run and shout
- roll down hills
- blow in your milk at dinner
- eat dinner with your fingers
- play hide and seek
- chase monsters with flashlights after dark
- draw lots of pictures with crayons, markers, and paint
- make puppets and perform puppet shows
- sing songs
- dance cheek to cheek
- pray in the garden
- sing in the rain
- Catch a snowflake on your tongue

earth and an opportunity to regain a reverence for all life. Everything you do that promotes light, joy, and liveliness is spiritual in nature. Lucky is the toddler who has a mother who loves life. Relish, don't resent, your baby's transformation into a little boy or girl.

SPIRITUAL FAMILY PATTERNS

Family home evening, family scripture study, and family prayer can be adjusted to meet the needs of your toddler. These three spiritual patterns will help your child develop habits and patterns that will serve her all her life. And while your toddler won't always understand the specific *words* she hears, she will understand the warm, unifying *feelings* that accompany these family worship times. All of the materials mentioned in the following suggestions for involving toddlers in family worship are available at the Church Distribution Center (1-800-537-5971) or online at www.ldscatalog.com.

Involving Toddlers in Family Scripture Study

Just because your toddler can't read or hold still for very long, there's no reason to exclude him from family scripture study. Any of the following suggestions are simple and may be just the trick to capture your tot's attention for a few minutes.

- Display a picture of Jesus when you read scriptures together.
- Use the illustrated scripture books, videos, audiotapes, and CD-ROMs available through Church distribution centers. These include:

Book of Mormon Stories, available as a soft cover book; a set of two audiocassettes; a set of two video-cassettes; or a CD-ROM.

Doctrine and Covenants Stories, available as a soft cover book; a set of three audiocassettes; or a set of two videocassettes.

Scripture Stories, available as a soft cover book.

Old Testament Stories, available as a soft cover book.

New Testament Stories, available as a soft cover book or a set of two audiocassettes.

Bible Stories for Children, Volume 1, available on videocassette.

Bible Stories for Children, Volume 2, available on videocassette.

Bible Stories for Children, Volume 3, available on videocassette.

• Concentrate on storytelling in simple words.

• Use lots of visual aids.

• Sing scripture-related songs from the *Children's Songbook.*

• Borrow pictures from the ward or branch library.

• Experiment with role playing and acting out stories from the scriptures.

• Use the *Gospel Art Kit* (simplified scripture stories and gospel principles can be read off the back of the pictures or you can explain the picture in your own words).

• Purchase a sturdy, picture-filled scripture storybook.

Involving Toddlers in Family Prayer

Just as you work to include your toddler in scripture study, you should also include her in twice-daily family prayer.

• Every morning and evening, kneel right next to her and put your arm around her as someone prays.

• Help your toddler participate in prayers at the table by prompting her with the words to say.

• Allow your toddler to say her own prayer whenever she's ready.

• Assist, prompt, or listen to your toddler as she says her individual prayers at bedside each night.

• Teach your toddler to pray at hard times, such as after a scary dream, when she loses something, when she is sick or sad. Pray with her at these times so she sees your example.

• Teach your toddler to pray in times of joy and happiness, such as after a new sibling is born, after a fun day on vacation, or after she has conquered a fear and learned something new. Set an example by praying at these times yourself.

• Let your toddler see you kneeling in prayer often.

Involving Toddlers in Family Home Evening

Family home evening lessons and activities can be as simple as you'd like. Before preparing a lesson, however, make sure you prepare *yourself* for the awesome task of teaching God's children. Here are some ideas that will help you and your toddler:

• Watch *Teach the Child* (this 24-minute videocassette will inspire you to teach your child the gospel of Jesus Christ).

• Watch and read *Family First* (this booklet and videocassette encourages families to hold family home evening each week and suggests six lessons that families may use to begin).

• Establish a warm relationship with your child during the rest of the week.

• Give your child undivided, unhurried attention and time.

• Sit on the floor next to your child at his eye level.

• Use lots of visual aids of your choosing, including *Visual Aid Cutouts.* These full-color figures come in individual sets or as a complete collection of sets: people, nature, domestic animals, toys, wild animals, insects, people of the scriptures, pioneers, Christmas and Easter figures, foods, buildings, and homes.

• Be animated.

• Include hands-on activities.

• Include treats.

• Play games.

• Use the *Gospel Art Kit* (pictures can illustrate any concept you're trying to teach).

• Use stories, projects, and activities from the *Friend* magazine.

• Sing songs from *Children's Songbook,* which is available in standard size (hard cover or spiral binding); pocket-size paperback; as a set of eight audio-cassettes (music only); or as a set of five compact discs (words and music and music only).

• Use the *Family Home Evening Resource Book* and *Video Supplements I and II.*

A TREASURE HUNT

Life with toddlers is basically like a career in archaeology. Before you've tried it yourself, it sounds fun and idealistic. In reality, both archaeology and rearing toddler require a little lunacy and a great deal of elbow grease. So why do so many women hang in there and survive life with

TODDLERHOOD

Where in the world did my baby go?
There's a monkey here in his place.
I can't keep things picked up anymore,
And there's stuff all over his face.

I'm tired of unplugging the toilet.
I can't take even one more small mess,
I think I should tear out my hair roots.
I don't think I can handle this stress.

He used to sleep in his cradle,
Now he's running all over the house.
My floor's all covered in brown spots.
He thinks we're playing cat and mouse.

He won't eat the good food at supper.
He never feels like taking a bath.
He refuses to keep his shoes on.
He keeps dead bugs in his stash.

He thinks there's a family of monsters
Living under the rug in the hall.
He won't sit still for a moment.
And he always gets lost at the mall.

I've been told I'd have bad days like this.
But no one said they would last for years
I think I'm losing my marbles
Please, God, help me find low gear.

toddlers? Mothers are basically treasure hunters—that's why. You see, it isn't the grit, sun, and sore muscles that brings an archaeologist so much satisfaction at a site. It isn't the toilet training and the temper tantrums that bring you so much satisfaction with your toddler. It is the constant anticipation of finding treasure underneath all that work.

Complete with mops and toilet plungers, mothers are the ultimate keep-the-toddlers-of-the-world-from-killing-themselves volunteers. Somewhere between the muddy shoes and the smeared faces, mothers of toddlers are daily discovering something priceless beneath all that mess. While you dig through large mounds of accumulated childish clutter day after day, you occasionally find a giggling toddler begging to be tickled, hoping to be discovered, longing to be enjoyed. You may not be able to put that in a museum but it's enough for now.

THE PRESCHOOL YEARS

As an infant, your child will learn to trust you. As a toddler, he will gain some independence and feel the desire to self-rule. As a preschooler—aptly named for children who are ages three to five and will be starting school in a year or two—your very own brilliant child will begin to understand some very important principles: taking the initiative to do something for himself, learning to share, and understanding a little bit about fairness. You may even be able to begin reasoning with your preschooler. Of course, this doesn't mean that your child will be reasonable, fair, and generous all the time; it just means he's beginning to understand the idea. He still needs loads of practice.

Thankfully, preschoolers have a better reputation than toddlers. Still, they can be just as disarming and delightful. Your preschooler may show affection at odd times and places. Accept and relish those quick hugs and kisses out of the blue, for they do not last forever. Your preschool child's work will be to conquer his world by doing things, being active, and exploring. He wants to know what his body will do. He may not let you help him, even when he needs help. He may seem selfish, for preschoolers lack the capacity to understand that other people have needs. Preschoolers don't think or act like adults and shouldn't be expected to think or act like them.

Your preschool child needs lots of things to do, draw, cut, run around, jump on, swing in, leap from, listen to, and talk with. Keep your rules simple, easy-to-understand, clear, and direct. Allow your child to make mistakes without harsh judgments and punishments.

ADVICE FOR A PRESCHOOLER'S MOTHER

Preschoolers love to do anything you do—with you. They love to cook when you cook, garden when you garden, and take a bath when you bathe. This can really be annoying at times. And it will often feel like you have no privacy or time to yourself. And you're right, you don't. During a child's early years, most moms start believing that they and their child will be joined at the hip for the rest of their lives.

Actually, there is no need to develop this fear. The preschool years are actually the last time in your child's life when she'll think you're the sun, moon, and stars. Your luster will begin to dim and almost fade away as she grows up. You won't change, but your child's perception of you will change. So *don't* resent these few years when you are everything to your child. *Do* follow some of this advice to help yourself get through it.

GIVE YOURSELF A BREAK

Give yourself a break at least once a day. You need to take a walk, go for a ride, or do something restoring to your soul while your husband or another trusted caregiver takes over for a while.

You can also take a semi-break at home with your child around. Set aside a time of day when you get to do something you want to do while your child learns to entertain himself. If you're consistent about setting aside *your* time, your child will get used to the idea that he can manage himself and his activities for an hour or so a day. This way, you get a break and your child gets to move toward greater independence. Doing this can be as easy as creating "library time," where you curl up on the couch with your favorite book and your child curls up on his bed with a stack of his favorite picture books. Other ideas include:

• "kitchen time," where you get to be in the kitchen baking, straightening cupboards, or sitting at the table with a mug of hot cocoa and a magazine while your child gets to bake a pretend feast with play food and utensils—or the measuring cups, pots and pans, and other unbreakables from your kitchen

• "movie time," where your child gets to watch his favorite short video while you do anything you choose somewhere else in the house

• "art time," where you work on a scrapbook project, a craft, or other fun hobby while your child creates masterpieces on butcher paper taped to the walls or a long table

A Mother and a Father's Roles

Preschool children need an individual relationship with each of their parents. Mothers and fathers provide a preschool child with unique and separate bonding experiences. Each parent has his or her own way of nurturing, playing, working, reading, teaching, disciplining, and living. Don't discount this. Let your spouse spend lots of time with your preschooler. Your three- to five-year-old needs to experience and be comfortable with both of you.

SEPARATE YOURSELF FROM YOUR CHILD'S BEHAVIOR

It's easy to take the blame or the credit for everything your child does at this age because you are *supposed* to be in charge—and your child should know better by now, shouldn't she? Keep reminding yourself that your child is not you and that her mistakes and accomplishments are not yours. If your child misbehaves in public, don't think people are judging your mothering abilities. Don't mistakenly believe that if you were a "good" mother you'd have "good" children. When you see your child as a separate person, you are able to look at things from her perspective as well as your own. If you think it's tough being a mother of a preschooler, try being a preschooler. Motherhood makes more sense if you try to see things from your child's point of view.

WATCH FOR DEVELOPING INTERESTS

If you watch carefully, you may see your preschooler's talents and personality flower and even be able to predict what kind of work he might be interested in later in life. Does your child love to "teach" his younger brothers and sisters? Is your child always "experimenting"? Is your preschooler always "performing"? Does your four-year-old love to "draw pictures" or "sing songs"? Use your child's prompts as a guide when you plan activities, play time, or begin thinking about lessons or classes your child might like. Above all, praise your child often. There's nothing like some good praise and adoration from a smiling mother to get a preschooler really interested in something that could potentially become a lifelong hobby, talent, or pleasure.

BE AWARE OF WHAT YOUR PRESCHOOLER LIKES AND NEEDS

Your preschooler's added confidence with language will often have her saying things that make you laugh out loud or get tears in your eyes. Preschoolers are natural poets—everything that comes from their mouths is original. Preschoolers are generous and love to give presents. They will give you several dozen a day. Nothing in their life or their speech is cliche. Most of what they see and experience is for the first time—so everything is seen with new eyes and uncommon awe. Keep all of this in mind as your care for your preschooler and lead her through a world of adventure, play, work, and learning.

Dress-up and Pretend Play

Preschoolers love to play dress-up and pretend anything. They are the kings and queens of active imaginations. And as such, they don't know the difference between fantasy and reality. Often they combine the two. They may have imaginary friends and are often afraid of the dark. Pretending becomes a way to explore the adult world around them in ways they are comfortable with. All of your child's play is really learning in disguise. At this age, your child might love the following toys and playthings:

• dress-up clothes; Deseret Industries or your own old clothes are the perfect places for starting a "wardrobe" trunk for your budding impressionist
   • toy kitchens and plastic toy food
   • toy tool benches and workshops
   • building blocks and Legos®
   • musical toys: marimbas, small cymbals, drums, and so on
   • dolls
   • toy shopping carts
   • toy gardening tools
   • toy tool sets
   • puppets
   • stick horses

• toy vacuums, brooms, snow shovers, and so on

Quiet Time

Preschoolers do well—and so do their mothers—if they have an hour of quiet time in the afternoon after lunch. They can nap, read books, watch a carefully selected movie or television program, or have snuggle time with mom. (A great deal has been written about the dangers of children watching too much television. I believe that anything that can keep a child entertained and quiet for an hour a day can't be all that bad. Just make sure it's somewhat educational and age appropriate.)

With all the running around, exploring, and playing that your preschooler will do, he needs to take a break during the day. It's good for his mind, body, and spirit to enjoy quiet downtime and restorative rest.

LOSING THE BATTLE, WINNING THE WAR

Preschoolers tend to ask questions even nuclear physicists can't answer. They explore the great unknown inside and outside your home with a magical wonderment that allows you to have a second childhood if you're willing to come along. Preschoolers seldom ask for permission to throw themselves into life.

One morning, when you least expect it, your three-year-old will go outside without you for the first time and you'll be pressing your nose against the pane making sure she's all right. You'll want her to explore and try new things without you, but you'll also want her to live till the ripe old age of four.

One morning my preschooler climbed up on the stove, sat his bottom on the burner,

ON BEING THREE

Being three means buckles that refuse to unhook when you're desperate for the bathroom, towering people who continually rub the top of your head, and five annoying words that are repeated every five minutes: "You'll just have to wait."

It means that every time you really start having a great time, someone walks in and lectures, "Look at this mess! What in the world are you doing? I just washed those clothes, young man!"

It means that every time you proudly dress yourself and walk out into the kitchen for your grand, morning debut, the whole family snickers. Mom looks at your feet and says, "Your shoes are on the wrong feet, dear." You look down and study your feet and proclaim, "But, Mom, these are the only feet I've got."

Being three means that when you go to church, your parents make you sit on a hard bench that is so wide your legs stick straight out from your hips. You can't see a thing except the bench in front of you. You hear voices up front but haven't the foggiest idea what's being said. Every time you pop up to see what's going on, your parents shove you back down. Every time you make weird noises your parents scowl at you and blow air through their teeth like a snake saying, "Shhhhhhhhhhhhhhhhh!"

When you're three, eating can be a real pain. Your wrist tends to lock, your spoon tends to tip in the wrong direction just when you get it to your mouth, and your glass of milk is forever getting in the way of your swinging elbow.

No one takes you seriously when you're three.

When you say, "No, I won't eat it—I hate that," your parents say, "Fine with me, young lady. But just remember—no beets, no apple pie." When you say, "No, I don't want to go to bed," they throw you onto the pillows and promise that if you come out again, you'll be one sorry turkey or that they'll paddle your canoe down the Suwanee River.

When you say, "I don't want to take a bath," they pick you up and stick your soapy head under the running faucet. When you say, "I don't have to go to the bathroom. I already went last week," they push you into the bathroom and hold the door shut until you try one more time. It's humiliating.

You can't see what's going on when you're three. But every time you crawl up onto the kitchen counter, your mother yells, "Now, you get down from there before you fall and break your neck!"

Finding play partners is tough, because your mom won't let you leave the yard, cross the street, or talk to strangers. Sometimes even family members are hard to enlist for buddies because everybody is always too busy working.

Being three is no piece of cake. It takes bravery, skill, and cunning to master the ropes of semi-fearless three-hood.

then proceeded to turn the temperature knob to high. Then he climbed up onto the washing machine, turned it on, lifted the lid and tried to put his foot in the wash cycle. When I asked him why, he responded, "I wanted to see what would happen."

Eating a meal with preschoolers is an adventure in probability. The chance that she will dump an entire bowl of tomato soup down her white shirt, stuff a green pea up her nose, and sit in her mashed potatoes is about 99.999 percent.

Preschoolers like to make miniature villages with their food and start bombing raids. They make a fine art out of elbowing glasses of fruit punch and using their forearms as levers to flip dinner plates onto their mothers' laps. They also create finger paints, fountains, facial masks, and hair conditioner out of common household table food, along with artistic collages on the floor under their chairs.

As you're trying to put up with all of this exploring, just remember what's really important: that your child survive these years knowing she's loved. All spills—even entire gallons of milk—can eventually be wiped, cleaned, or scraped up. The laundry can wait as you watch your child through the window to make sure she's safe by herself in her own backyard. And great talent

can be discovered if you gently redirect her attention from a hot burner and onto some finger paints, coloring pages, playdough, or an extra bowl full of cookie dough right by your side and *your* big cookie bowl.

PLAY GROUPS AND PRESCHOOL

About the time their children turn three or four years old, most mothers wonder if it's time to join a preschool or a play group as preparation for kindergarten. Reasons for joining a preschool or play group vary. Some mothers want their children to attend preschool so they will not be "behind" when kindergarten begins. Others want their children to have a good social experience before kindergarten starts. Others simply want a few hours a week to themselves and see preschool as a great opportunity for both themselves and their child to get away and do something different.

Other moms—and I'm one of them—are content to keep their young ones at home during the preschool years. After all, what's the rush? After you raise a few children, you realize how little time you really have before they start all that school business. I prefer to spend those precious preschool years exposing my child to all the experiences she won't get in school, giving her all the things money can't buy, and providing her with lots of hands-on experiences myself.

This doesn't mean that you have to agree with me. Preschool and play groups can be positive, happy experiences for many children. What follows will help you decide what is best for your child in these "pre-school" years.

PLAY GROUPS

Play groups are less formal than preschools and are typically started by a group of moms that live in the same ward or neighborhood. The best play groups are small (four to six children in a group is ideal) and are held once or twice a week for just an hour or so. Play groups are beneficial for both moms and pre-schoolers: your child has the opportunity to learn and socialize with other children her age, and you have the opportunity to swap war stories with moms of other preschoolers. You can easily start your own play group by simply finding a few moms with preschool-age children and pitching the idea to them. Volunteer your home for the first meeting and have a few simple activities and a snack prepared for the children. If all works out well, the moms can determine a meeting, activity, and snack schedule for the coming month and go from there.

In a play group, children are usually given enriched opportunities to play with other children their age and get involved in learning and sharing experiences that they would not generally have access to at home. Moms take turns planning songs, easy learning games, activities, and show-and-tell type demonstrations. The host of each play-group session typically provides a snack and some juice for the kids as they wind down. Parents should meet together to discuss what types of activities and snacks they feel are appropriate for their children. You can plan activities based on skills that certain children need practice at or based on things that your children simply love to do. Parents should share their children's eating habits and allergies with each other to plan appropriate snacks.

Some play groups find that their children simply need the time to play together and choose not to plan a learning activity for each session. This is fine too. Your child will learn a lot just from playing—and thus having to share, cooperate, take turns with, and be kind to—other children. During the summer months, play groups can meet at the park, the zoo, the pool, or any other fun site for some outdoor fun.

PRESCHOOL

Preschools are designed to help children socialize with other children and to gradually get used to a schoolroom regimen. In this high-tech, competitive day in time, some preschools require that your child be "accepted" through formal testing or screening. You may want to stay away from this type of competitive, almost-too-structured atmosphere. Use the following guidelines when choosing a preschool:

• For three-year-olds, a preschool that meets just twice a week for a few hours is best.

• Four- and five-year-olds do well with a three-day-a-week program.

• The main goal of a preschool should be socialization, not academics. Children should learn about playing in a group, sharing toys, and managing feelings of aggression while away from their parents and home environment.

• Look for a preschool that allows children to learn through play. Basic academics, such as letter and number recognition, should be taught in fun and engaging ways.

• Choose a program for the people that

run it, not for what is taught. Preschool is your child's first school experience and can be positive only if your child and the teacher are a good fit.

• Visit prospective preschools ahead of time and watch what happens. Observe how the children interact with the teachers. Pick a preschool that wants your help and will let you stop in and stay any time.

• Most states provide a list of licensed preschools on the Internet.

INSTILLING A SENSE OF WONDER

Whether you enroll your child in preschool, join a local group of moms at the park each week, or hold daily adventures for your preschooler in his own backyard, you are exposing your child to a world that is still new and fresh. Without the dulling effects of previous experience, young children live in a world of wonder and seem to have a pure instinct for what is beautiful and awe inspiring. Nothing seems common or unimportant to them.

You don't have to teach formal lessons to your preschooler; there will be time for formal lessons later. You can explore the world with him and respond to and encourage his natural sense of wonder and curiosity. Take time out to become more alive and excited about the simple activities in your life. Activities and adventures that promote creativity and feelings of self-expression are appropriate for the child in all of us.

When those school bells do ring, if you are lucky, your child will take with him a curious mind and a hunger for knowledge. This is far more important than a set of expert-reading or -math skills. The child who is curious and eager to learn is far

more likely to emerge from a mountain of drills, papers, and tests with something besides accumulated knowledge. He will emerge with the desire to learn for the rest of his life—and that is what a true education is all about.

PUSHING TOO SOON

Don't fall into the trap of choosing too early for your preschool child what she will excel in. If there is something you presently enjoy and want to share with your child, fine. If, however, there is something you wanted to excel in and never did, please don't make your child achieve your unrealized dreams by pushing her into formal lessons of your choosing early on.

Young children are so eager to please their parents that they may go along with your choice for years, trying to live out your dream and not even realizing they have the right to choose their own dreams. What you *can* do is provide a rich environment and varied kinds of experiences for your child so she has more options to choose from when the time comes to develop a talent or pursue a hobby. Worry less about the rush for early academics and the pressure to pay for formal lessons at an early age and more about spending unhurried time with your child. The best learning takes place in very unstructured, informal ways. If you push too hard for your child to excel, you deprive her of her childhood. Life is more than being good at something or having an expert skill. To have a complete life we need to be complete people.

Let Your Child Teach You

Have you ever thought about your own capacity to be puzzled with the way something works, to wonder and question? Are you observant, spontaneous, playful, and free? Are you open to new experiences? Can you look freshly at common things? If not, become the student of your preschooler: he's the expert at all of these things. Let your child teach you.

KINDERGARTEN READINESS

Before your child starts school, prepare her for the big day. Most states have fairly strict immunization requirements. Check with your child's pediatrician, school, or health department to make sure your child is on a schedule that allows for all shots to be completed before the first day of kindergarten. When you register your child for kindergarten, bring along her birth certificate and proof of immunization.

Before your child starts kindergarten, she ought to know how to do a number of important things, including:
- how to dress herself
- how to go to the bathroom alone
- how to share her toys
- how to wait for her turn
- how to express herself appropriately and feel good about learning

To prepare your preschooler for the things she will learn in the classroom, you should also do the following:
- Give your child simple problems to solve.
- Nurture your child's self-confidence.
- Read to your child every day.
- Allow your child the opportunity to color, draw, cut with scissors, use tape, mold with clay, and paste things together.
- Introduce your child to the alphabet and numbers one through ten, but don't get obsessive about her learning everything right now.
- Teach your child her colors and shapes and perhaps the days of the week.
- Teach your child her full name, address, and phone number. You don't need formal lessons or work sheets. Simply let her practice writing her name with the first letter a capital and the rest lowercase.

Some children are extremely interested in their numbers and letters before starting school and others show little or no interest. Every child learns at his own pace and in his own way. Don't worry about pushing your child to learn. Make learning an

everyday, natural part of her schedule. Let your child learn how to work by helping you around the house and in the yard. Expect her to clean up after herself and take care of daily chores. Most important, don't forget to enjoy your child and love her with all your heart and soul. You will never have this precious time with your child again and you will be glad that you took advantage of every precious day.

BEFORE THE SCHOOL BELLS RING

After my oldest daughter's first week in school, she told me that her favorite subject was recess. I laughed at first; but the more I thought about it, the more I realized that maybe it was recess that had taught me more about life and what is important to know about life than all the classroom studies combined.

In school I was taught to memorize dates, places, names, numbers, and letters. I wasn't taught to feel deeply or to investigate or to question. I was taught to learn the right answers, not to ask the right questions. The awesome magic of things, the sparkle and the terror, the conflicts and the passions—most of these came during recess without adult supervision.

Always realize that the childhood your child is having is not the one you think he is having. Don't worry, he'll tell you about it when he grows up . . . if you ask. But remember, your child sees everything from his unique perspective; and sometimes you can learn more from him than he learns from you.

Recapturing That Recess Feeling

Never forget that children feel everything deeply. Their feelings, dreams, hopes,

and fears are monumental to them even if they seem trivial to you. When children are sad, they literally ache inside. When children are happy, they can literally *almost* fly.

I remember a day in the swings at school during recess when I was young. I leaned back in the swing until the muscles in my neck were tight. Then I put my legs out in front of me. Out and in, out and in, I pumped and stretched until I was almost touching the branches of a tree in front of me. I was breathing with my whole chest, up and down, in a reverie of near flight.

"Look at me!" my mind was screaming to the skies. "I am alive! I am somebody!"

The swing went back and then, with all the energy I possessed, I flew forward toward that tree. At that moment I just knew I could keep flying up into space, up past the tree and over the roof of the schoolhouse, out and beyond the reaches of time and space. Then the bell rang, and I had to drag my feet to stop the swing and jump out. But I've never completely forgotten that feeling I had in the swing, the elation of contemplated possibilities, that exhilaration that *anything* was possible, that my whole body and mind and spirit were alive and free. It was a feeling that I was someone with unlimited possibilities, someone who could soar past the limits of myself.

Your job as a mother is to help your children discover and retain that kind of feeling.

YOUR PRESCHOOLER AND THE GOSPEL

There are few things as sweet as hearing your three-year-old belt out the words to "Jesus Wants Me for a Sunbeam." The preschool years are full of wonderment—the ideal time to solidify habits such as Primary attendance, family home evening, family prayer, and regular scripture study in the hearts of your child.

Your preschool child needs to know she is a child of heavenly and earthly parents who love her unconditionally. She needs to know she is worthy of love. She needs to feel that she belongs and has an important place in your family. She needs to feel competent, secure, and needed. Wise Primary leaders strengthen and reinforce all the good feelings you're working on at home and are invaluable supports for you and your child.

ENCOURAGING YOUR CHILD TO GO TO PRIMARY

Three is the magical age that your child becomes "old" enough and "mature" enough to attend Primary. Of course, your child may not recognize her new stature when the calendar changes to January 1, and he is expected to sit on the front row of a big room full of bigger kids and lots of new things to explore. Your child's move from the nursery to the more formal routine of Primary will take some adjusting time. Sunbeams are full of sunshine *and* wiggles and giggles. Don't expect your child to sit straight in the chair with arms folded without some learning and growing. Look at your child's teacher and Primary leaders as your assistants, not your substitutes, in helping your child learn about the gospel.

Be willing to sit with your child in sharing time if his teacher requests some extra help. Be enthusiastic about attending your own meetings, and emphasize that your "big boy" is just like Mommy, now that he gets to go to a class and participate in sharing time. Most nursery leaders spend a month or two acclimating children who are about to make the move to Primary by bringing them into sharing time or opening exercises and by arranging for them to meet their new teacher.

Primary Talks

Now that your child is in Primary, she will be asked to give talks, prayers, and scriptures during Primary opening or closing exercises on Sundays. Your child's teacher should let you know in advance when your child's turn comes around to participate. Talks for preschoolers should be short, visual, and based on a principle the children are learning in Primary. Practice the talk with your child before she goes to church. If she wants you to, stand next to her in Primary and offer moral support or prompting if she gets stage fright while presenting the talk. Be enthusiastic about your child's chance to participate in the gospel of Jesus Christ and share her testimony.

PRESCHOOL SPIRITUAL BEGINNINGS

Don't limit your preschooler's spiritual awakenings to Sunday meetings. You have the privilege of introducing your child to himself and his unique gifts. It's your job to help your child discover his uniqueness by guiding him to a more creative life and helping him explore many areas of the human experience that promote joyous self-expression. There is a universal divine quality in every preschool child to learn and grow, to create, and be a maker. Your child is more likely to find his own divine potential or his best self if he is allowed to experiment with lots of options.

Invite your child to explore his natural creativity early in life by exposing him to joyful self-expression through uplifting arts such as literature, music, art, and dance. The goal of experiencing creativity through self-expression early in life is to find what each of these areas can do to help your child mature into a whole human being who is truly alive.

Your preschooler truly lives in a world of wonder, in a world of "firsts." Do you remember the first time you saw snow fall, heard ocean waves crash against the rocks, or smelled a hot cinnamon roll? Can you remember what it was like to be very small and learning *everything?*

SPIRITUAL AWAKENINGS FOR YOUR PRESCHOOLER *AND YOU*

- use a hammer
- build with blocks
- draw
- paint
- sing lots of songs
- work with puzzles
- read lots of books
- write in a journal
- cook
- dance
- sew
- use clay
- study nature and people
- use a microscope
- dress up and pretend
- explore nature
- grow something
- help around the house
- make toys
- paste cards and write letters
- watch a thunder and lightning storm
- gaze at the stars
- visit a fire station, post office, airport, bakery, orchard, library, museum

SPIRITUAL FAMILY PATTERNS

Family home evening, family scripture study, and family prayer can be adjusted to meet the needs of your preschool-age child. Preschool-age children need mothers, fathers, and leaders who understand that it's not wise to punish their natural exuberance and inability to hold still. Little children can't be irreverent. They don't know enough. They need patience, love, and lots of opportunities to use their active bodies and minds. All of the materials mentioned in the following suggestions for involving preschoolers in family worship are available at the Church Distribution Center (1-800-537-5971) or online at www.ldscatalog.com.

To Involve Preschoolers in Family Home Evening

• Make sure your preschooler has lots of practice giving the prayer.

• Allow your child to select or lead a song from the *Children's Songbook.*

• Sing songs from *Hymns of The Church of Jesus Christ of Latter-day Saints* (available as a standard-size book with regular or spiral binding, as a pocket-size book, as a large-type book, as a set of 18 audiocassettes or as a set of 14 compact discs). Or use *Hymns Made Easy* or *Selected Hymns.*

• Make sure your preschooler has lots of opportunities to help with the lesson or choose the activity.

• Encourage your child to help select or make a treat.

• Play lots of games.

• Role play.

• Keep lessons short, interesting, and interactive.

• Use the *Gospel Art Kit* (the 160 pictures in this kit depict scripture or Church history stories, provide portraits of the Presidents of the Church, or illustrate gospel principles in action. The text on the back of each picture tells the stories or provides information about the picture and usually gives several scripture references for additional study).

• Use the *Family Home Evening Manual* and *Video Supplements I and II.*

• Use stories, activities, and recipes from the *Friend* magazine.

• Use *Visual Aids Cutouts,* individual sets that depict people, nature, domestic ani-mals, toys, wild animals, insects, people of the scriptures, pioneers, Christmas and Easter figures, foods, buildings, and homes.

• For additional ideas for family night activities consult *The Activity Book.*

To Involve Preschoolers in Family Scripture Study

• Purchase your child a sturdy, picture-filled, scripture storybook.

• Use the scripture storybooks, tapes, videos, and CD-ROM's published by the Church, including:

Book of Mormon Stories, available as a soft cover book; a set of two audio-cassettes; a set of two videocas-settes; or a CD-ROM.

Doctrine and Covenants Stories, available as a soft cover book; a set of three audiocassettes; or a set of two videocassettes.

Scripture Stories, available as a soft cover book.

Old Testament Stories, available as a soft cover book.

New Testament Stories, available as a soft cover book or a set of two audiocassettes.

Bible Stories for Children, Volume 1, available on videocassette.

Bible Stories for Children, Volume 2, available on videocassette.

Bible Stories for Children, Volume 3, available on videocassette.

• Concentrate on storytelling.

• Use lots of visual aids.

• Role play.

• Tell the scripture stories in your own words.

• Use the *Gospel Art Kit* (read the simpli-fied summaries at the back of each page or

> ### PRESCHOOLERS
>
> *Crayon masterpieces on the bedspread,*
> *Mud stuck all over his shoes.*
> *Peanut butter in the sofa*
> *Might have you singing the blues.*
> *But when the long days are over*
> *And all the monkeys and monsters are*
>   *gone,*
> *You'll long for just one more sticky bear*
>   *hug*
> *And one more silly Primary song.*

tell the scripture stories in your own words).

To Involve Preschoolers in Family Prayer

• Allow your preschooler to take her turn praying with the family during morning or evening prayers.

• Ask your child to take her turn offering the blessing on the food.

• Assist, prompt, or listen to your child saying her individual prayers at bedside.

• Teach your child to pray all during the day and night for special comfort, direction, and courage.

• Teach your child to pray when she's angry, sad, or lost; when she's excited, grateful, or happy; when she's scared, lonely, or bored.

• Allow your child to see you kneeling in prayer daily.

HOLDING ON AND LETTING GO

The day will come when your child can actually use the bathroom without yelling for a wipe, eat a meal without one spill, walk through the house without dropping 67 small sharp toys along the way and say, "Mommy, I love you. I'll never stop loving you." Suddenly you'll be a puddle of melted butter on the kitchen floor and you'll never want him to grow up. You'll want him to stay this age forever.

At the precise moment when you're thinking this, you'll realize that your child has just turned five and will be leaving for kindergarten in a few months. It's just not fair. It's like that again when they're teenagers. Right when your not-so-pleasant teenager finally turns into a normal human being capable of adult emotions and conversation, he leaves home. Life with children is not meant to be fair. So get over it. Life with children is meant to be gloriously unnerving and humbling. It's holding on that hurts—not letting go.

Preschool years pass so quickly. They might not seem that way while you're living through them with your children, but trust me, they will when you're looking back. Once your child enters school it will seem like time puts on its running shoes. You'll never again have those long hours at home to enjoy together without the worry of school, friends, homework, and outside schedules.

This makes the preschool years downright sacred. You will never have your child's undivided adoration again. There is something uncontaminated and pure about those early years. Spending these years with your child is worth any amount of sacrifice. There is no better season of life to share with your child, your whole, undivided, unhurried self.

DEALING WITH FEARS—YOURS AND YOUR CHILD'S

Many moms are surprised at how often they are asked to deal with fears. Because children are inexperienced in this thing we call life and don't have a large number of experiences on which to base new circumstances, they are naturally prone to feeling fearful. All children have fears. All adults have fears. You're just a little more secretive and quiet about yours and have learned over the years how to deal with them.

To help your child, you can try to reason with him about his fears or you can give him tools to deal with them.

Reasoning usually includes standard motherly lectures that include things like, "Now, honey, there aren't any monsters. That's just pretend. You don't need to be afraid—it's all in your imagination." Of course, your child knows you're a big liar at this point because he's as good as *seen* the monsters. In fact, they're under his bed right now. Either that, or they're hiding in his closet ready to get him as soon as you leave the room.

Giving your child tools to deal with his fears is usually more helpful. If your child has a fear of the dark you can give him a nightlight or a tiny flashlight next to his bed. If your child is afraid of monsters, give him something to kill them. My children have used monster spray, shadow chasers, and light sabers.

Multi-Generational Fears

Many fears are learned. So, if you're afraid of something, your child may be also. As I've prayed for counsel about how to love my children, I always felt impressed to change me and especially my thoughts. For instance I remember receiving the impression that if I truly wanted to help one particular child, I had to let go of all my fears. Those fears didn't just consist of spiders, public speaking, and death, but included fear of failure, of not being good enough or pretty enough or smart enough, of being rejected by those I love, or even that God could not possibly know me.

As I gradually discovered and let go of my fears, I watched my little girl find the strength to let go of hers. We even practiced deep breathing together. As I replaced my anxious thoughts with grateful ones, I watched my little girl blossom with greater freedom to become her true self and fulfill her potential. Today that same little girl who didn't dare leave the house alone because a grasshopper might jump on her is jumping on an airplane to attend a prestigious Ivy League school for a doctorate after a summer traveling through Europe and working at an archaeological site in Jordan.

Confronting your own fears and getting rid of them is one of the most challenging things about being a mother. Nobody likes to face their fears. Yet, if you are afraid, your children will sense it and be influenced by it. Most fears are a result of a basic lack of trust in our Heavenly Father. If something frightens you, don't let it stop you. Put your hand into the hand of God's and let him lead you to be the kind of mother He knows you can be.

YOUR SCHOOL-AGE CHILD

School-agers have a great reputation. Five- to 12-year-old children are just a lot more fun to be around than teenagers; they are easier to look after than babies; and they are far more tidy than toddlers and preschoolers. School-age children are industrious, willing to try new things, and eager to learn.

Take care to remember that while school-age children offer parents a relatively quiet span of years, they're actually growing and changing by leaps and bounds and should not be taken for granted. These are the years when you have the opportunity to form a bond with your child that is strong enough to get you both through the teenage years. These are the years when your child will be exposed to the world outside your home for the first time and reach the age of accountability.

School-age children are active and love games of all types. Boys this age learn what it means to be a boy and girls learn what it means to be a girl. They need the experience of making friends and resolving conflicts. Your school-age child needs you to listen and take personal time with him.

During these years, your child will enjoy much of his moral training at home and in Primary on Sunday. Formal education will come at elementary school. At the end of these years your child will be given the added blessings, responsibilities, and consequences of the priesthood or young womanhood. Think of these years as a great gift to you and an opportunity to introduce your child to the outside world with guidance and love.

ADVICE FOR A SCHOOL-AGER'S MOTHER

Your school-ager needs to be accepted for *who* she is, not *what* she is. She is a child of God with divine attributes and eternal possibilities. Your child is not a miniature version of you. She is a complete and unduplicated version of herself. She is your spirit sister. Your job is to love and lead *who* she is—not *what* you want her to be.

Don't fall into the trap of comparing your child to other children her age. Schools tend to continually compare and test children. Administrators and teachers may falsely assume all kinds of notions based on the results of those tests and comparisons. As your child's mother, never fall into the trap of assuming that your child's worth can be measured by a grade, an SAT score, or her ability to kick a soccer ball. Pray and ask your Father in Heaven to help you know your child and how best to help her reach her potential. Each child is blessed with gifts from God that need to be nurtured and valued.

Standardized tests measure your child's ability to take one particular test on one particular day—that's all. No exam has ever been written that can test for compassion, determination, creativity, or persistence— the very attributes your child will need most in life. Don't make your love and attention for your child a test that she has to keep taking.

Make sure that your school-ager receives *your* attention and learns from *you* the importance of developing character traits that really make a difference. Encourage enthusiasm, kindness, imagination, moral leadership, compassion, and courage.

PROVIDE YOUR UNDIVIDED ATTENTION

School-age children spend a lot of their day in a group, competing in the class-room. This means that they need some noncompetitive private time with you every day. Try to give your school-age child

some undivided attention each day. You can make this one-on-one time a part of the daily routine.

One-on-One Ideas for You and Your School-age Child

• Have family prayers or devotional time before anyone leaves home in the morning. Mention each child by name in your prayers.

• Kiss and hug your child good-bye every day. Whisper a word of encourage-ment in his ear, such as: "I think you're wonderful." "Make it a great day." "I'll be praying for you when you take your test today." "I'll love you forever." "I'm so glad I'm your mother."

• Develop a parting tradition, such as a wave from the window when they get on the bus or a family honk when you drop them off at school.

• If possible, be there when your child gets home from school.

• After school, enjoy a snack and some relaxed conversation about the day's events; you could also use this time to get some fresh air and exercise with your child.

• Establish and maintain a set time for parent-supervised homework or practice sessions before or after dinner.

• Establish and maintain a bedtime tra-dition, such as bathing, brushing teeth, reading books, bedside prayers, and tuck-ing in.

CHOOSE THE BEST TEACHERS FOR YOUR CHILD

Now that you'll be sending your child off to school, don't be afraid to help in the selection process of your child's teachers.

In elementary school, your child will spend long hours with this one person and deserves to have a teacher she can work well with. Talk to other parents who have had children in your child's school and your principal. Find out about the personality of each teacher. Then match your child with the teacher you think would best work with your child.

If your child is placed in a classroom where you can tell the teacher is not a good match for your child, don't be afraid to have your child moved. You are often the only true advocate your child has. Don't be intimidated by administrators and teachers. *They are your partners, not your bosses.*

Most of the time your school-ager will probably adore her teacher, for most teachers are drawn to the profession out of a love of children, not a love of money. This may be the first time you've had to share your child's adoration outside the family. Be grateful to have another adult in your child's life who cares about her. It's your job to surround your child with as many people who love her as possible. The more people in your child's life who love her and give her positive attention, the better. Think of your child's school and church teacher, uncles and aunts, grandparents and neighbors as your assistants in love and concern for your child, not your competition.

ENCOURAGE INDEPENDENCE

You're sending your child off to school now. That's a big step for him—and for you. But don't let this new, independent event be the only thing your child does on his own. Children this age need lots of practice making decisions. They can decide what to wear to school, how to

comb their hair, and how to arrange things in their rooms. Of course, you should still set bedtime, practice time, and homework time. Children this age can be expected to get themselves up, dressed, and ready for school with just a little help in the early years. Your child can be expected to pick up his bedroom, make his bed, and take care of his clothes.

If your child shows an interest in music, dance, or sports, consider lessons or signing him up for a team. The greatest danger lies in having too many outside activities, not too few. It helps to have you and your child select one or two (but don't do more than this) outside activities.

What Should I Wear?

Let your school-ager choose her own outfit for school, even if you think it's awful. Clothing that was popular when you were a child is not popular now. Don't insist that your child dress like you or act like you or think like you. Let your child discover her own likes and dislikes. Don't select her whole wardrobe and get stressed if she ruins it on the playground. Let her wear clothes that are functional, inexpensive, and comfortable.

ENJOY THE CALM BEFORE THE STORM

Think of the early school-age years as the great calm before the storm. You are given these less turbulent times to seal your love so tight that it will get you through the adolescent years ahead. Many parents largely ignore their children during these early school years because they aren't as demanding as preschoolers and haven't yet entered perturbing puberty. The trouble is, by the time you get around to spending quality and quantity time with your children, they will probably be more interested in their friends and the opposite sex.

Because you don't spend as much time together during these years, make sure the time you do spend together provides each of you something to look forward to every day. Remember, your child will soon be your adult friend. If you want an interesting adult friend later in life, try to give your child an interesting childhood. Take him places, talk to him, enrich his life, and share your values. Eat together, play together, work together, and just *be* together. A well-loved child is like a sponge. Love and learning go hand in hand. Give lots of praise and kisses and hugs. Love is a response, not an instinct. You can respond with love until it is instinctive. If you have to . . . fake it till you make it.

Things to Do with Your School-ager besides Telling Him to Clean His Room

- play ball
- go camping
- take trips
- hang out
- go shopping
- play board games
- cook dinner
- read books
- talk about the best/worst thing that happened that day
- sing songs
- dance to your or their favorite music
- do yard work
- ride bikes
- write in journals (make entries or notes in the other's written account)
- take pictures
- play video games
- go for a walk
- put a puzzle together
- go sledding
- create arts and crafts
- perform an experiment
- write a play, story, or poem

KNOW WHAT YOUR SCHOOL-AGER LIKES

Provide your school-ager with interesting learning tools, such as magnets, a magnifying glass or microscope, and a library card. Let her care for pets, do chores, and tend her younger brothers and sisters. School-agers need to feel useful. Enrich their minds, bodies, and spirits with your own daily excitement for learning, physical exercise, and reading the scriptures. Tell them you love them and that they're beautiful, marvelous, and fantastic several times a day.

MAKE MEALTIME SPECIAL

One of the best things you can do for your children is to eat dinner together every night as a family. Make sure dinnertime is positive and a time to reconnect with each other. You can ask your child something he learned that day or let him talk about the substitute teacher or the lunch menu. This is a good time to bring attention to the positive things he's doing. This is a good time to tell jokes, share news events, and read the scriptures together.

DEALING WITH CYCLING SICKNESS

The average school-age child will get about six to ten viral illnesses a year—most of them in the fall and winter while she's in school. So your best defense is a good offense.

Soap up. Most germs live a hand-to-mouth or -eye existence. Teach your child to wash her hands often. Bar or soft soap and water work well and so do no-water hand cleansers. Teach your child to sing a short song or count to thirty, so she scrubs long enough to get rid of germs.

Hands off. Teach your child to keep her hands off her face and out of her mouth as much as possible.

Get some fresh air. You can encourage your child to play outside. Your child can't "catch cold" from cold weather. Studies suggest that the traditional fall and winter illness season may result from people spending too much time indoors.

Get plenty of sleep. Research shows that sleep deprivation increases susceptibility to colds

Say no. When other sick children want to play with your child, just say no.
(See pages 161–167 for "A Primer on Childhood Illnesses and Ailments")

DON'T INTERFERE WITH PEER PROBLEMS

School-agers are learning the pains and pleasures of belonging to a group. These skills will help them as adults. Don't be too anxious to get involved with your school-ager's problems with other children unless abuse is involved. School children quarrel and have disagreements with other children their age on a regular basis. Then they get over it the next day or the next minute. When adults get involved, it just blows things out of proportion. If your child is having problems with friends at school, help him learn problem-solving relationship ideas. Abuse of any kind is another matter and should be dealt with by parents and teachers quickly and adequately.

MAKE LEARNING OF ALL KINDS IMPORTANT

Teach your child. Do so by example, in family settings, and one on one. Your child has lots to learn during these years, and the home is the ideal place to do that learning.

Read with Your Child

Take time to read to your school-ager, even if she can read to herself. You can take turns reading, or you can simply listen. Reading with your child speaks volumes about what you value. Remember, school-agers need your time and attention whether they insist on it or not.

Have your child read to you. This gives her practice and you opportunity to praise her.

If your child seems to have trouble

reading, don't be afraid to speak to her teacher, her pediatrician, or another specialist. Carefully enlist any help you can to help your child learn and love to read.

Teach manners

Don't be afraid to teach your child good manners. You don't do your child any favors by letting him get away with bad manners at home. An even, pleasant disposition and the knowledge of good manners will help your child later in life when you're not around. The best way to teach is to be a good example yourself.

Homework Help

You'll probably wonder about homework. Should you help your child? How much? During these elementary school years, you can decide on the appropriate use of homework for your child. Discuss your child's needs with her teacher and decide together how to complement and support work done in school at home. A child should be able to do her own homework without your constant supervision as she gets older, but you can still check her progress and monitor the level of difficulty.

Help your child with homework when necessary, but always allow your child to do her own work. If there is a problem with too much homework, talk to your child's teacher. You can decide on an appropriate amount of time that should be spent on homework and work together with your teacher.

Promote Good Hygiene

School-agers often go through several years when they simply don't want to take a bath anymore. They have more important things to do and they don't want to be bothered. You can make both of you miserable by insisting that your child take a bath every day or you can reach a compromise you can both live with. Don't worry, before long your child will be a teenager and you won't be able to get him out of the bathroom. Some children have extra dry skin and should be bathed only two or three times a week. School-agers can be taught to wash strategic parts of the body every day.

They should also be taught to brush and floss their teeth twice a day. Good dental care goes a long way towards preventing cavities. Encourage your child to brush for at least a few minutes each time, and provide him with a new brush every three months.

NURTURE YOUR CHILD

Don't waste any time wishing your child was anyone but who she is. Don't wish your child was less shy, more athletic, or smarter. Your child needs a number-one fan to help her through these years. Be that fan and cheer her on with all your heart and soul. No amount of nurturing is too much at this point.

Be Consistent

You can show your school-ager you love him by picking him up on time after school or at a friend's house. Let him count on you to be there when you say you will. You don't have to be perfect, just able to say you're sorry when you make a mistake or forget or miss an important event or pick-up time. If you have rules that you both have agreed on, stick to them with love and firmness.

A PUBERTY PRIMER

Prepare your pre-teen daughter for menstruation. Let her know that this is a physical change that comes with a lot of emotional baggage. Let her know it's normal to experience mood swings, tearfulness, and even pain or cramping just before and during a new menstrual cycle. Explain and demonstrate how to take care of personal hygiene. Decide together—and keep on hand—the most comfortable type of sanitary product for your daughter to use. You might even want to help her look forward to the day she begins menstruating as a day for celebrating womanhood.

Prepare your pre-teen boy for nocturnal emissions or "wet dreams," which occur when fluid and sperm fill the tubules and testes and are automatically released or ejaculated. This usually happens when a boy is asleep and is sometimes accompanied by an erotic dream. Boys should be told this is *not* masturbation but a normal part of puberty. Masturbation is when someone stimulates his own sex organs for the purpose of sexual arousal. Contrary to the world's teachings, masturbation is not necessary for either gender, and Latter-day Saints have been urged to avoid this practice.

Teach your pre-teen about the following physical changes that occur during puberty.

For Girls:
- hips widen
- breasts develop
- body hair grows under the arms and in the pubic area
- weight begins to increase some
- menstruation begins

For Boys:
- seminal fluid and sperm cell production begins
- shoulders broaden
- muscles expand
- voice deepens
- height increases, sometimes dramatically
- weight increases
- body hair grows under the arms, on the face, and in the pubic region

Give Your Head and Your Heart

School-agers need your head *and* your heart. If you make eye contact whenever she's talking to you, your school-age child is more likely to feel you value her and what she has to say. Children can tell if your heart or head is somewhere else. Some children like to talk about everything that happened at school and others need to be prodded.

Remember to ask for your school-ager's opinion. She'll learn to have one.

Please Do Touch

School-agers need to be touched with love. They might not be able to fit in your lap; but they still need the reassurance of physical affection. Don't be embarrassed to kiss and hug your school-ager good-bye before school and when he gets home. Tucking your child into bed at night is another good time for hugging and kissing. You can give your child a back rub or brush his hair while he lays his head in your lap.

Be a Volunteer

Consider volunteering to help in your child's school class. You don't have to be available every day or even every week. Even once a year communicates that you care.

PREPARING YOUR PRE-TEEN FOR PUBERTY

Every child needs to be prepared for the changes that come with puberty *before* the changes actually happen. Some children begin going through puberty as early as ten or eleven years of age. As your child nears puberty, take the time to talk about the hormones that will cause the body to change in ways that make procreation possible. Make sure your child knows that this changing process is good, clean, and part of God's plan. These changes are not something to be embarrassed about. Your children need to understand that they are capable of creating human life through sexual union after these changes.

Most elementary schools hold special maturation clinics for boys and girls to attend with their parents. Make sure you find out when this will happen at your child's school. Accompany your child to the meeting and spend as much time as he'd like answering questions and providing explanations.

Personal Hygiene

Before your children reach puberty, a bath probably isn't needed every day. Once puberty comes along, however, everything changes. Prepare your boys and girls for the chemical and hormonal changes of puberty that will cause their bodies to produce more oil and perspiration. Help your child to understand that he'll need to bathe more often and will need to start using deodorant. Be more than willing to help him pick out deodorant at the store and buy it for him.

YOUR SCHOOL-AGE CHILD AND THE GOSPEL

School-age children have a natural excitement and desire to spend time with their families and learn new things. When they reach the age of eight, they have the opportunity to be baptized and receive the gift of the Holy Ghost. School-age children will have distinct, recallable memories about their own spiritual awakenings as they pray privately, do kind things for their family members or friends, and study about the world and its people.

School-age children often feel tender and charitable feelings toward siblings, pets, and extended family members *if* they are allowed and encouraged to serve and minister. Now is a good time to hang pictures of the temple in their rooms, take them to the temple grounds, let them see pictures of the inside of the temple and explain what happens there. You can purchase *Temple Pictures*—a set that includes 53 11x17-inch pictures of temples—from the Distribution Center or buy prints individually.

ENCOURAGE PARTICIPATION IN PRIMARY

Primary offers your child the wonderful opportunity to present talks, scriptures, prayers, and testimonies in front of a group. When your school-age child is asked to participate, help her with preparation if she wants you to, but encourage your child to write her own talk if possible. Talks should be short and visual when your child is younger. As your child gets older, encourage her to tell stories from her own life, then apply these stories to gospel principles. You can sit in the back of the Primary room to offer support if you and your child want to. All this practice pays off when your child becomes a teen and, later, an adult.

Make sure your child has a chance to earn the Gospel in Action Award. If your child does not bring home the requirements for this award, request it from your Primary president. When your daughter turns eight, make sure she participates in Achievement Day activities. When your son turns eight, he will be included in the Cub Scout activities and advancement.

SPIRITUAL FAMILY PATTERNS

School-age children thrive on routines. If you've set the pattern early, no school-age child worth his salt will let you slip up on reading the scriptures, holding family home evening, and having twice-daily family prayer. With their added independence and confidence, school-age children often enjoy planning and carrying out family night activities. They can offer prayers without help. As their reading skills improve each year, they will enjoy showing off those new skills by reading the scriptures aloud. All of the materials mentioned in the following suggestions for involving school-age children in family worship are available at the Church Distribution Center (1-800-537-5971) or online at www.ldscatalog.com.

To Involve Your School-age Child in Family Home Evening

• Use the *Family Home Evening Manual.* It's a great resource for family night lesson ideas.

• Use *Family Home Evening Video Supplement I and II.*

• Develop and consistently add to a family home evening file with packets filled with pictures, lesson aids, activities, refreshment and activity ideas.

• Allow your school-age child to play the piano, lead the music, pray, give the lesson, and plan the activity and refreshments according to his ability and desire.

• Encourage your child to use the *Gospel Art Kit* (your child can read the simplified summaries provided at the back of many of the pictures as part of a family night lesson or for talks in Primary).

SPIRITUAL AWAKENINGS FOR YOUR SCHOOL-AGER AND YOU

- gaze at the stars
- make a snowman
- make a sandcastle
- tell made-up stories
- have family cookouts or bake-offs
- make holiday decorations
- clean up the house to music
- have a family talent night
- have a family awards night
- read the scriptures and other good books together
- start or add to a collection
- learn an instrument
- take pictures
- fly a kite
- watch birds

Give your school-age child the chance to visit local places of interest, such as:

- the library
- a greenhouse
- a museum
- a factory

- a fire station
- the post office
- the airport
- a bakery
- a fruit orchard
- the beach
- a river
- a lake
- a canyon
- an outdoor market
- a train station
- a newspaper office
- an artist's studio
- a television or radio station
- a park
- the police station
- a dairy farm
- a lumberyard

If possible, give your school-age child a chance to ride a:

- bus
- subway
- train
- boat
- airplane
- horse
- canoe

- Sing songs from the *Children's Songbook* and *Hymns of The Church of Jesus Christ of Latter-day Saints*.
- Purchase and use *Visual Aids Cutouts*. These full-color figures can be used in lessons. You can buy individual sets or the complete collection of sets 1 through 10. The sets include people, nature, domestic animals, toys, wild animals, insects, people of the scriptures, pioneers, Christmas and Easter figures, foods, buildings, and homes.
- If you don't own a piano, you can purchase an electronic music keyboard, along with a *Keyboard Course Kit* and *Conducting Course Kit* from the Church Distribution Center.
- Audio recordings of the *Hymns* can be used if no one in the family plays or has the desire to learn.

• If you run out of ideas for activities, consult *The Activity Book* for lots of ideas for family home evening.

• Purchase and use the *Primary Video Collection,* a videocassette that contains four segments that can encourage children to live the gospel, be baptized, and prepare to receive the priesthood.

To Involve Your School-age Child in Family Prayer

• Allow your school-age child to participate in family prayer without help or prompting.

• Allow your child to listen to you pray—and thus learn to pray herself.

• Encourage your child to take her turn saying blessings on the food.

• Hold family prayers morning and evening.

• Remind your child to say her personal prayers when you tuck her in each night.

• Teach your school-age child that divine guidance, peace, comfort, and help are only a prayer away.

To Involve Your School-age Child in Family Scripture Study

• Purchase your child an inexpensive set of the scriptures such as the *Economy Bible* and the *Economy Triple Combination.* Economy editions of the scriptures have bindings that are glued rather than sewn and come in regular and extra-large print.

• Purchase or make your child a scripture carrying case.

• School-age children are learning to read and are all at different stages and abilities in their reading skills. So let your school-age child take his turn reading straight from the standard works with as little or as much help as needed.

• Ask your school-age child questions, then read the scriptures to find the answer.

• Use audio recordings of the scriptures. These are available for the *Book of Mormon, Doctrine and Covenants and Pearl of Great Price, Old Testament,* and *New Testament* at the Distribution Center.

• Offer a dollar to any child who can answer a question based on what you just read in the scriptures.

• Use the *Gospel Art Kit* to add variety and interest to scripture study.

• Purchase and use:

Book of Mormon Stories, available as a soft cover book; a set of two audiocassettes; a set of two videocassettes; or a CD-ROM.

Doctrine and Covenants Stories, available as a soft cover book; a set of three audiocassettes; or a set of two videocassettes.

Scripture Stories, available as a soft cover book.

Old Testament Stories, available as a soft cover book.

New Testament Stories, available as a soft cover book or a set of two audiocassettes.

Bible Stories for Children, Volume 1, available on videocassette.

Bible Stories for Children, Volume 2, available on videocassette.

Bible Stories for Children, Volume 3, available on videocassette.

A PRIMER ON CHILDHOOD ILLNESSES AND AILMENTS

Your first child will probably see the doctor *much* more often than the rest of your children because you won't know when and how much to worry. My first child was premature and I was sure every time she got the sniffles that she was on the brink of death. Most moms start out believing that medical professionals know everything and they (the moms) know nothing. The fact is, most children survive childhood with or without a mother who knows how to handle every medical emergency. Motherhood is a very long medical training boot camp. You learn by trial and error.

You'll worry that you're not worrying enough. You'll worry that you're worrying too much. Mothers worry . . . that's your job and you're good at it. But don't let worry overwhelm you. Most of the time you just have to do the best you know how and then leave the rest in God's hands. Never hesitate to call your doctor when you have a question or when you feel something isn't right. Don't hesitate to ask for a second or third opinion if you're not satisfied with the first doctor's treatment options or outcomes.

Don't let anyone convince you that trying to comfort your crying baby (or your teenager for that matter) will spoil him. When you respond to your child's cry for help, you're teaching him that you can be trusted and he is safe with you. Children cry for a reason. There will be days when you will be able to figure out why your child is crying and remedy the situation and there will be times when you won't. Don't worry about giving your child too much attention when he is sick, especially your baby. Everyone deserves comfort and nurturing when something hurts. So rock your baby, sing to your toddler, hold your pre-schooler close and whisper in his ear, rub your teenager's back. Experiment with different ways to comfort. Offer your prayers, tenderness, and good home-cooked meals. Your husband or another worthy priesthood holder can give your child a blessing. It's hard to see your child in pain, even harder than experiencing pain yourself. But remember you'll need to keep yourself emotionally, spiritually, and physically healthy so you can help your child when he needs you most.

Upper Respiratory Infections

The common cold usually lasts from seven to fourteen days. Symptoms are congestion, mild cough, runny nose, and a low-grade fever. Antibiotics do not help a viral cold.

Check with your doctor about the use of antihistamines and decongestants for older children. Use a humidifier in your child's bedroom at night. Make sure they get adequate sleep, a nutritious diet, and lots of fluids. (See "What to Do if Baby Gets Sick" on pages 82–84 for information on upper respiratory infections in babies.)

continued on next page

Diarrhea

Diarrhea is a marked increase in the volume, frequency, and wateriness of your child's bowel movements. Apple juice, pear juice, grapes, soft drinks, dates, nuts, figs, honey, table sugar, milk products, chocolate, magnesium, and caffeine are common causes of diarrhea. A bacterial or viral infection can also cause sudden severe diarrhea in young infants. (See "What to Do if Baby Gets Sick" on pages 84–85 for information on babies and diarrhea.)

Dehydration is the most common danger of diarrhea. Symptoms of dehydration include dark urine, sunken eyes, a dry mouth, and the inability to tear up. To treat dehydration, you can give your child special drinks called oral rehydration solutions. They contain the right mix of salt, sugar, potassium, and other elements to help replace lost body fluids.

If your child responds well to that, you might want to start with bland food like bananas, rice, applesauce, toast, and unsweetened cereals. If these foods don't bother your child, then other foods can be added over the next few days. Most of the time normal eating habits can be resumed in about three days. If you suspect your child is dehydrated, call the doctor.

Constipation

Uncomfortable or infrequent bowel movements are a sign of constipation, which is commonly caused by a lack of physical activity, inadequate fiber and fluid intake, and stress or anxiety. Constipation can also be caused by an allergy, antibiotics, and yeast infections.

Keep in mind that the number of bowel movements your child has can vary considerably. Some children have a bowel movement several times a day and others have one every two or three days. (See "What to Do if Baby Gets Sick" on page 85 for information on babies and constipation.)

To treat constipation, try changing your child's diet to include more fluids and fiber. Exercise also helps. Some moms swear that prune juice or orange juice will do the trick. I've found that plain yogurt is helpful for stomach upsets of most any kind. Laxatives should be avoided. Enemas are seldom needed. Let nature work naturally.

Fiber-rich foods include unprocessed wheat bran, unrefined breakfast cereals, whole wheat flour, fresh fruits except bananas, whole grain breads, dried fruits—apricots, figs, and prunes—vegetables except potatoes, and beans of all kinds.

Sore Throats

Most sore throats are caused by viral infections and may be accompanied by a cold, cough, or low-grade fever. Common pain relievers, such as acetaminophen and ibuprofen, can be given to help with pain. Children over age six can suck on throat lozenges and gargle with a homemade solution of salt water or salt water mixed with hydrogen peroxide—just combine a few ounces of water with a pinch of salt and a tablespoon of hydrogen peroxide. Toddlers and younger children will do better with a Popsicle or other icy treat to temporarily numb the pain. Sipping warm broth is often soothing. A soft, liquid diet will be easier on any child's throat through the duration of the virus. If your child exhibits any of the following, you should call the doctor:

- sore throat pain is severe
- sore throat is accompanied by a widespread rash
- sore throat is accompanied by an earache or sinus pain
- an accompanying fever has lasted more than three days
- your child is under one year of age
- your child has been exposed to strep within the last seven days
- sores are present on your child's skin

Only 20 percent of sore throats are typically attributed to bacterial infections and thus need antibiotics. If your child also has a cough, hoarseness, or nasal congestion, that is the likely cause of the sore throat. Antibiotics won't be prescribed unless the doctor has run a laboratory test that confirms the infection is bacterial. Your doctor may also prescribe a soothing throat solution.

Nosebleeds

Nosebleeds are typically no cause for concern. They are usually caused by dryness inside the nose or vigorous blowing. To treat a nosebleed:

- Tilt head forward, pinch nose below the bone in the bridge of the nose, and hold for five minutes.
- If bleeding continues, blow the nose to clear passage. Pinch the nose again in the same spot.
- Do not blow the nose to clear the clotted blood once flow has stopped.
- Do not remove the blood clots for several hours.

If your child has any strange symptoms that accompany the nosebleed, call your doctor immediately. These include: bleeding that doesn't stop after applying continuous direct pressure for 20 minutes, bleeding that recurs 3 times in 24 hours even after applying direct pressure, skin bruises or bleeding gums that are not the result of an injury, or a large amount of blood loss.

Croup

Croup is caused by a viral infection of the airways, which in turn causes swelling of the lining of the airway and makes it hard to breathe. A child with croup sounds like a barking seal and has a hard time breathing, especially breathing in. Croup seems to hit children most often from six months to three years of age, but it can also affect older and younger children. (See "What to Do if Baby Gets Sick" on page 84 for more detailed information on treating croup, including what to do if symptoms are severe.)

continued on next page

Fevers

A fever is one way the body fights an illness. If your child has a low-grade fever, chances are it's because he's fighting an infection. Most doctors recommend giving medications such as acetaminophen and ibuprofen only if the fever is above 102° F. or if it's accompanied by pain. And then, give medication only to make your child comfortable. (Don't give your child asprin, however, because of its implications in Reye's Syndrome, a rare but severe brain disease.) Letting a fever run its course is actually quite beneficial. A fever above 104° F. is cause for concern and indicates that your child probably should be seen. Place a call to the doctor and tell the nurse about all of your child's symptoms.

When your child has a fever he may also have a loss of appetite, weight loss, fatigue, chills, and sweats. Cool and loose clothing should give added comfort. Talk to your doctor about sponging your child down to relieve fever.

Pinworms

Pinworms, like head lice, are not something most mothers want to think about, let alone deal with. A pinworm infection is a condition where a small, round worm grows and reproduces inside the intestines. Eggs are typically inhaled or swallowed. The worms then evidence themselves near the anus and subsequently rub off onto clothing, bedding, or toys. New eggs are then transferred by the fingers to the mouth of another child who swallows them. Children can reinfect themselves by transferring the eggs from the anus to their mouth.

If your child has pinworms, don't panic. This little parasite is extremely common and hardly ever causes any harm. Your child may display no symptoms or he may itch often around the anus. The skin around the anus can also become red and irritated.

The worms are white and hair-thin and can be seen wiggling around the child's anus after he has been put to bed. If your child complains that his anus is itching, take a flashlight and investigate the area. If you see a white, very thin, threadlike worm that is moving and is about a ¼-inch long, it's likely a pinworm. Your doctor can prescribe something that will cure this condition in most cases. All family members will have to take the medicine because the infection is easily spread. The doctor will also give you instructions for bathing your child, sanitizing his room and other areas, and taking special precautions to prevent the pinworms from spreading.

Head Lice

Head lice are spread by personal contact and by shared combs, brushes, hats, and other personal items. Head lice are common among all school-age children, no matter how clean you are. If your child has head lice, it will probably cause a lot of itching. If you suspect head lice, examine your child's hair for nits—shiny grayish-white eggs that can be seen as tiny globs stuck firmly to the hair shaft. Talk to your doctor about the best treatment, which may include medication applied as a cream, lotion, or shampoo. Usually just reading or thinking about lice makes your scalp crawl. Don't overreact. Most mothers have to deal with this problem sooner or later.

Sunburns

Sunburns are caused by an overexposure to ultraviolet B rays. Symptoms include red, swollen, and painful skin. Blisters may form and the skin may peel. The best way to prevent sunburns is to stay out of direct sunlight. Establish a lifelong habit of using sunscreen. Always apply a sunscreen to your child's skin when he is in the sun for long periods of time, even if it is cloudy outside. Apply sunscreen daily to kids during the summer. Sunscreens are rated by their sun-protection factor, the higher the SPF number, the greater the protection.

To treat sunburns, apply cool water immediately. You can use a cold, tap-water compresses or even a bag of frozen vegetables. Corticosteriods also reduce inflammation and pain. Some moms swear that a cool vinegar wash over the sunburn, followed by a cool wet towel or ice bag, is a good method of treating sunburns. Remember, suntans are not healthy.

Other Burns

Burns can also be caused by hot water, chemicals, electricity, or other heat sources. Minor burns should be immersed immediately in cool water. Severe burns require immediate care at a hospital equipped to treat burns.

Bumps

Most children get a number of minor and major bumps while they're growing up. Applying ice to the site of the bump for 20 minutes will ease swelling. Oftentimes, a bump on the head will result in a big goose egg. This is common. If your child has taken a fall and bumped his head, keep an eye on your child and allow him to rest as needed.

After a head injury, it's common for children to have a headache and feel nauseated and dizzy. Your child may also experience ringing in the ears, anxious or irritable feelings, and tiredness. Watch your child to see if she gets sleepy, pale, sweaty, or vomits. These are signs of concussion and indicate that a physician should examine your child. Trouble walking, drainage from the ears or nose, seizures, and weakness or numbness in the arms or legs imply a serious injury and require immediate attention.

Major head injuries result from a number of things: car accidents when seat belts aren't worn, bicycle wrecks, falls from windows, and stumbles around the house or off of playground equipment. After a bad fall such as this, your child might have to stay in the hospital to be watched. A doctor might even order a CAT-scan or MRI to test for damage to the brain or internal bleeding.

Scrapes and Cuts

Skinned knees and elbows mean your child is a normal child performing regular, childhood monkey

continued on next page

business. When your child runs screaming to you with a scrape or cut, take the time to reassure your child with hugs and kisses then get to work. First, apply direct pressure for ten minutes to stop the bleeding. Wash the area well with soap and water and/or with hydrogen peroxide. Don't let your child's screams keep you from getting the area thoroughly clean (it takes about five minutes to do a thorough cleaning). If the wound looks like it needs stitches, don't soak it in water. This will cause swelling to increase and make suturing more difficult. Dry the scrape with a tissue, apply antibiotic ointment, and cover it with a bandage. Children seem to feel much less pain if they can't actually see the cut or sore. Change the bandage daily.

Some mothers apply butterfly bandages themselves and others feel a doctor should decide if stitches are needed. Do what feels right with you. If your child will have to live with an unsightly scar in an obvious place for the rest of his life, get the best doctor you can to stitch up the cut. If the wound is gaping, you can see bones or tendons, the scrape is filled with debris that you can't get out, or the bleeding won't stop after ten minutes of direct pressure, go to the emergency room.

Watch any scrape or cut for a while to make sure that an infection doesn't start.

Ticks

Finding a fat, blood-filled tick on your child shouldn't be totally unnerving but it probably will be. Using a hot match or petroleum jelly to block the tick's breathing hole doesn't work. You just kill the tick, with his head stuck inside your child. You'll have more luck if you try to irritate the tick enough that it will let go by himself. Gently twist the tick until it lets go, then pull it out while making sure to keep the head intact. If your child gets a fever, swollen joints, or a rash and headache within three weeks of the bite, check with your doctor.

Choking

If your child is choking, he needs help fast. Check to see if your child can talk, cough, or breathe. If he can, place your child face down over your arm and hit him between the shoulder blades or encourage him to keep coughing to get the stuck object out. If he can't cough or breathe, try the Heimlich maneuver. Have someone call 911 while you're trying the Heimlich.

Broken Bones

Some children break bones after even a minor fall. Some children don't break any bones when all probability says they should. If you suspect your child has broken a bone, watch for sharp localized pain, blacking out, paleness, cold sweats, chills, vomiting, and double vision. If the bone is broken your child will need a doctor to set and immobilize it. Keep your child calm and warm as you drive to the nearest office or hospital. Ice packs will reduce swelling.

Hospital Stays

Surgeries or other medical procedures that require several days in the hospital will throw you for a loop because you'll probably have other children at home to take care of or a job to worry about or both. If your child requires a hospital stay, request that you stay with your child until she enters the operating room or is sedated. Most hospitals will let you stay with your child overnight. Hospitals and surgeries are scary and your child deserves your front and center attention.

Emergencies

Every mother faces medical emergencies while raising her children. Accept the inevitable, then find out where your nearest hospital is. Never be afraid to call and ask for expert advice. If you call your doctor first, he or she can help you give your child first aid or decide whether you need an office or hospital visit. Your doctor can also call an ambulance or tell you whether you can safely transport your child yourself. In addition, your doctor can call the emergency room while you are en route to alert them of your needs. Grab your purse because you'll need your insurance ID and a blank check.

For some reason, most medical emergencies seem to happen *after* doctor's office hours. In this case, find out where the nearest instant care or emergency room is located. A "better safe than sorry" rule of thumb is always best.

For your own peace of mind, receive professional training in mouth-to-mouth resuscitation. You'll need to learn this procedure and practice it before you'll feel competent to use it yourself during a medical emergency. Buy yourself a comprehensive basic medical reference book and use it.

Train yourself to deal with most minor problems on your own but equip yourself with a great professional backup team. You can spend your whole life worrying about what *might* happen or just deal with what actually happens one day at a time. You know more than you think you know. You can't always make it all better but you can help prevent many problems before they happen, aid the healing process after it does happen, and offer comfort and love after you've done all you know how to do.

Poison

If you think your child has been poisoned, call the Poison Control Center. This national toll-free number will connect you to your local poison control center: 1-800-222-1222.

Always keep your center's number close to the phone. Poison control will give you instructions on how to treat the child. You'll need to know if you should encourage your child to vomit or if you should take your child to the hospital. Always keep syrup of ipecac on hand.

THE TEENAGE YEARS

Teenagers often receive the same bad rap as toddlers—and for good reason. Toddlers and teenagers may not look at all alike; but they are both attempting to make a *major* move toward independence. Sometimes that's not easy for the child *or* the parent.

Your teenager will have to deal with a body that is transforming before her eyes. Usually noses, hands, and feet grow first—so teens often feel and look awkward. A combination of bacteria, oil, and hormones produces acne just when your teen is most self-conscious and least able to deal with anything negative that brings unwanted attention. This is not an easy time of life, and your teen needs a loving parent to help her through this important journey of becoming a woman or a man.

Your teen is discovering her identity and may become clumsy, silly, self-centered, or seem irresponsible. You can help by being supportive, encouraging, and accepting. Rules should be consistent and fair. Help your teen find something she enjoys doing and feels competent about. Encourage your teen to try new activities and interests. Avoid arguing, but be consistent in applying rules. Support your teen's activities and make your home a place where her friends want to be. Do whatever you can to make your home a haven during these challenging years. If home is a good place to be, that's where your child will turn if she's in trouble.

ADVICE FOR A TEENAGER'S MOTHER

DON'T FORGET TO TOUCH AND HUG

Even though they don't act like it, teenagers still want to be touched, hugged, and kissed. They won't ask for it, so don't wait until they do. Before they go to bed and when they leave or come home from school or work are great times to get in a hug without being too obvious. Some non-threatening forms of touch include back rubs and foot rubs. Most teenagers would appreciate a shoulder rub after a long day of sitting in classes or carrying around that humongous backpack. Lots of children this

---

THINGS TO DO WITH YOUR TEEN BESIDES WATCH TV

- Read your favorite book out loud.
- Play a card or board game.
- Go for a walk.
- Pack a lunch and ride bicycles.
- Work in the garden.
- Fix dinner.
- Make cookies for someone and deliver them.
- Visit a family member or friend.
- Go shopping.
- Attend a ward or stake activity.
- Write a letter to a missionary.
- Visit someone in a hospital or nursing home.
- Ride horses, four-wheelers, or motorcycles.
- Go camping or hiking.
- Play basketball, baseball, football, soccer, or run races.
- Climb a tree.
- Clean the car.
- Read the same book your teen is assigned in school, then have a discussion.
- Make music (singing, musical instruments, or listen to CDs and tapes) together.
- Practice dancing techniques.
- Sort, wash, fold, and iron laundry.

age like to wrestle with Dad on the floor and play contact sports outside.

EXPRESS YOUR LOVE OFTEN

One of the best ways for you to express your love for your teen is when you're having family prayer together. Call down divine help for your child. Be specific. Pray that Josh will do well on his chemistry test or that Amy will be able to memorize the piano piece she is learning or that Peter will have a good experience on his date Saturday night. There is nothing that will soften a heart quite as much as a teenager hearing his mother praying for him.

Focus on the Positive

Look for something positive to say about your teen every time you're together, even if the only thing you can think of is how she stands there on the floor and holds it down so well. Teens crave attention, and they'll get it in positive or negative ways. They need to hear every day that they're wonderful and that you love them, especially when they seem most unwonderful and unlovable.

Every time you hug your teenager good-bye, offer soft words of encouragement such as, "I think you're great." "I'm so glad you're my daughter." "Make it a great day." "You can do it." "I love you."

REMEMBER THE BASICS

One of the kindest, most overlooked, and most unappreciated things you can do for your teens is to fix them nutritious meals and make sure they get adequate rest. Eat at least one meal together a day as a family. With conflicting activities and part-time jobs it can be a real challenge to find a time when you can meet together; but it's worth any sacrifice. You need a daily way to connect with your child and find out what's going on in his life. If you meet and talk every day, little problems can be caught early and dealt with. Make family mealtimes relaxed, fun, and loving.

You should also set a good example of someone who takes good care of herself. Make sure you maintain a healthy diet, exercise, and get enough sleep.

Throw Out Your Scales

Try this easy trick to help your teen feel good about herself: throw out your scales and any other shallow measure of your physical body that focuses on appearance instead of fitness. Teens need to eat a healthy diet, they also need to exercise and get plenty of rest. Don't teach your teen to focus on her body weight, type, or appearance. Diets are not healthy and they don't work.

Stock your house with healthy food choices, provide opportunities for exercise, and organize your household so your teen gets plenty of rest. Teach her to see her body as a wonderful gift from God to be grateful for and not to compare with others.

LEARN TO TALK WITH YOUR TEEN

Many teens don't open up and spill their thoughts and feelings as the result of the direct-question method. They're more likely to open up when you're doing something side by side and carrying on a casual conversation.

For instance, if you ask your teen how his day went, he'll probably reply, "Fine." End of story; end of conversation.

If, on the other hand, you're peeling potatoes for supper, washing the car together, or going for a walk, the conversation will be less threatening, more natural, and you'll find out a lot more about what's going on in his life.

Use the time alone in the car when you're running your pre-driving teen somewhere as a time for one-on-one conversation. If your teenager sits in the same room as you for more than a few minutes, he probably wants to talk but doesn't know how to get things started. The tendency for mothers is always to talk too much and listen too little. Do some prompting to get him started, and then LISTEN.

Remember, if you want your children to be honest with you about their feelings, you have to be honest about yours and willing to share your thoughts as well. Your teen will be more likely to develop communication patterns that you model.

Affirm Your Teen's Feelings

Affirm and validate your child's feelings. Allow him to discuss his feelings without judgment. Communicate more empathy. Don't be afraid to be a "hands-on" parent. The authority in the family rests in your hands, not your child's. Help your teens find the feeling of happiness and peace that comes from serving other people. Make them part of the process when you mow a widow's lawn, donate your blood, and pay your tithing. Find ways to improve your community together.

PROMOTE WHOLESOME SOCIAL EXPERIENCES

During adolescence, most children enjoy associating with the opposite sex.

This is normal and natural. Make your home a place where your teenagers like to bring their friends. You and your teen should discuss rules about curfews and dating before sixteen. You can be honest and objective in your rules. Then hold your child responsible with the consequences that follow.

Discourage steady dating. Teach your teen that there is safety in numbers and more fun with group dates and activities. Discuss appropriate dancing positions and church standards on appropriate movies and activities. Remember that not every teen wants or has the opportunity to date. Don't push your teen to date or have a boy- or girlfriend. Encourage her to participate in appropriate activities with both sexes. These might include physical games, exercise, service, spiritual activities, firesides, dances, and educational experiences.

One of the main purposes of the Church organizations for youth is to provide wholesome activities for your teens. The Aaronic Priesthood and Young Women

programs can be a great support to you during these years. Work together with your youth leaders but don't expect them to replace you in your parental responsibility. You are the parent; they are there to assist you, not do your job for you. Don't support activities that require large amounts of money or time away from the family unit. Do support activities that promote developing talents and providing service. You are not required to support activities that take your teenager away from family responsibilities or outings.

BE PREPARED TO ANSWER TOUGH QUESTIONS

Teens can ask some tough questions; and all of them merit your respect and your honest answers. Teens need mothers—and fathers—who can talk openly about everything, including sexual relations before marriage, homosexual and lesbian activities, masturbation, and pornography in films, magazines, books, and on the Internet. They need mothers who aren't embarrassed to discuss anything of importance with them. Always define your own moral values as you discuss sensitive areas.

Make sure both you and your teen read and discuss all the topics included in the pamphlet *For the Strength of Youth*. In this pamphlet the standards of the Church are discussed in an easy-to-read and -understand format. Dating, dress, and appearance, friendshipping, honesty, and language are all discussed with clarity. Movies, television, radio, videocassettes, books, and magazines are also discussed and standards clarified. Sexual purity, including pre-marital sexual intimacy, homosexual and lesbian activities, and masturbation are also covered with discretion and openness. Sunday behavior, spiritual help, repentance, worthiness, and service are also topics in this wonderful resource for teens and their parents.

To Young Men Only is another helpful resource for teens and their parents. This pamphlet was originally given as an address at the priesthood session of general conference on 2 October 1976 by Boyd K. Packer. Elder Packer discusses the sacred life-giving "factory" that moves quietly into operation as a young boy matures and how young men can learn to control their sexual thoughts and actions as they move through the teen years.

Mothers and fathers should be both open and candid with their sons and daughters as they teach them to honor and control the life-giving power God has given them. *A Parent's Guide* is another resource for LDS parents who want to teach righteous intimacy and is a supplement for the information in the *Family Home Evening Resource Book.* This guidebook offers basic principles on the purposes of families and the teaching of children and suggestions on how to teach children righteous intimacy throughout all the stages of their childhood and adolescence.

Teach Sexual Purity

Teens may be tempted to have close, intimate relationships with members of the opposite sex before marriage. Both you and your husband are key in teaching your children about the sacred powers of procreation. Teens need to be taught that sexual intimacy should be reserved for marriage between a man and a woman. Teach your children that the physical relationship between married couples is beautiful, exciting, and ordained of God for the creation of children and deep expression of love, but only within the bounds the Lord has set. Obedience to these laws will bring eternal happiness and joy.

Teens need to learn from their parents that certain behaviors are forbidden and why. Discuss the Church's standards on homosexual and lesbian relationships. Explain what the terms necking and petting really mean. Help your children develop strategies for avoiding temptations and compromising situations. Discuss why they should avoid passionate kissing and explain in detail what is and is not appropriate affection and touch.

Along with teaching your children about what they shouldn't do, teach them what they can do in their formation of close relationships with others. Remind and instruct them about the healing power of repentance through the atonement of Jesus Christ. Help them live so that they have the constant companionship of the Holy Ghost.

Several publications can help and guide you as you work to teach your teenager the importance of sexual purity. *Of Souls, Symbols, and Sacraments*—available online at LDS.org by searching in the gospel library and in book, audio, and video form—is an excellent talk from Elder Jeffrey R. Holland that will help you and your teenager better understand the sacred nature of sexual intimacy and the power it possesses.

DEAL APPROPRIATELY WITH FAMILY PROBLEMS

If you and your husband are having problems that are not being dealt with, your teen will know. If you're not happy, your teen will know. If you have constant worries and fears, your teen will know. He may not be able to vocalize these feelings, but he knows deep inside when something is wrong with you or your marriage relationship.

Be honest. Teens can tell if you're living a lie. You don't have to bring your child into the center of your private difficulties with your spouse and expect him to solve the problems or carry the burden. But you can be honest about the fact that you and your spouse are having difficulties and that you are trying to resolve them. The best thing you can do for your teen is to forgive and love his father and be a happy and positive person.

Your teen may also have friends with major family problems. He'll need the reassurance that things are going well with you and your spouse for a sense of security. If things are not going well for you and your spouse, deal with your problems and make corrections and adjustments as needed.

You are the model for your teen about what a healthy marriage relationship should be. If there is abuse of any kind going on in your home, put a stop to it immediately. Protect your children. If you are the abuser, stop now and seek help. If your husband is the abuser, you are harming yourself and your child by failing to do anything to stop it. If you have a child who is abusive, put a stop to it immediately, seek help, and protect your other children as necessary.

NURTURE INDEPENDENCE WHILE TEACHING LIFE LESSONS

Your teen needs to be treated as an individual with a unique personality. Each of your children will experience the teenage years in his or her own way. Your job is to help your teen feel loved as you teach them skills that will help them live on their own one day in the too-soon future. If you continue doing for your child what he can do for himself, you will be teaching him to be dependent on you; and that's not healthy for either one of you.

Make Rules Clear

Insist on knowing where your child is going, who's he's with, and when he'll be home. Establish a curfew and enforce it. Provide mandatory, regular chores for your teen to do around the house and yard. Make it a priority to be home when your teen is.

Your Teen's Spending Money

You may want to encourage your child to earn his own spending money. You can provide basic food, clothing, and shelter. If your teen wants expensive brand-name clothing, fast food, and entertainment, let him know that he'll have to earn it himself. Teens learn a lot from a part-time job that they can't learn any other way. Part-time jobs often provide the motivation your child needs to get a good education so he doesn't have to spend the rest of his life in a dead-end, minimum wage job. Just make sure that your teen isn't overworked or that grades are affected. You'll also want to discuss with your child the importance of keeping a schedule, continually paying tithing, and what to do if he's asked to work on a Sunday.

Saving Money

A good way to motivate teens to save money for missions and college is to agree to match the amount of money they put aside themselves. Don't be afraid to let your child make a few mistakes with his spending. We all learn by trial and error. Open a savings account when your child is old enough to start saving. Open a checking account when your teen gets his first minimum-wage job. Teach your teens how to budget, save, and avoid debt. Show them how much they'll need to have saved for a mission and college and make a specific plan to reach savings goals and objectives. Discourage your teen from buying a car.

Car Privileges

Most parents of teens wonder about car privileges. Should your child pay for gas, for insurance, for upkeep? and how much? You can decide along with your teen and husband what you will and won't do. Some parents require their teens to buy their own cars and insurance. Others provide the car and insurance but ask the teen to pay for gas. Others provide car, insurance, and gas. Just remember, make your plans about car privileges based on what you think is *best for your child,* not on whether you can afford to do more.

Remind Teens to Pray

As your teen learns about life and the trials that come with it, she will need to be reminded that she has a loving Heavenly Father standing by and that she can trust Him. Teens who know that their Heavenly Father is approachable and understanding usually have earthly parents who are the same way. They've also been taught to pray over everything—the big and the small. Make sure your teen understands that she is part of a great plan of happiness and progression.

USE GOD'S HELP

Above all, remember, that *you* can call upon your mantle as your teen's parent to ask God for guidance. Once when I was praying about a certain child, I felt impressed to smile at him more often. You may feel impressed to take your child on your morning run or on a visit to the hospital with you. You have a constant source of inspiration when you keep the prayers going in your child's behalf.

YOUR TEENAGER AND THE GOSPEL

Teenagers are old enough to understand gospel principles on a deeper level and participate in religious observances with greater understanding and purpose. Joseph Smith was a young teen when he went to the Sacred Grove. Don't underestimate your teen's ability to feel deeply and question any superficial spirituality. Marinate your teen with experiences that give her a chance to feel the Spirit every day. Don't give up on having family prayer, scripture reading, and family home evening—even if your teen is less than enthusiastic and seemingly unavailable. A great time to read scriptures when you have teenagers in the house is between dinner and dessert.

SPIRITUAL FAMILY PATTERNS

When your child reaches the age of twelve, he or she leaves Primary and begins participation in the Young Men and

Young Women programs of the Church. Along with Sunday instruction, your teen will have a Church-sponsored activity on a set weekday evening once a week. Some of these activities will combine both young men and women and provide wholesome, spiritual, fun, and service-oriented opportunities that also build testimonies.

During these years you will be helping your teens prepare for the temple endowment, missions, temple marriage, and parenthood. Take the time to become familiar with the information in *Guidebook for Parents and Leaders of Youth*. Review *For the Strength of Youth* with your teen.

Become familiar with and review the

SPIRITUAL AWAKENINGS FOR YOUR TEEN *AND* YOU:

- Perform baptisms for the dead.
- Plan family service projects.
- Hike to the top of a mountain.
- Volunteer service at a local hospital, homeless shelter, humanitarian center, school, or rest home.
- Write your personal history.
- Read and discuss *The Family: A Proclamation to the World*.
- Read the *Testimony of the Apostles*.
- Obtain your patriarchal blessing.
- Fast with a purpose.
- Attend tithing settlement.
- Go to church.
- Plant and harvest a garden.
- Take a family history class.
- Write a song, poem, or story.
- Paint or draw a picture.
- Write secret notes of love and encouragement for family members.
- Memorize the sacrament prayers.
- Teach or learn a new skill.
- Prepare a talk.
- Participate in a play, speech, dance, or music performance.
- Write in your journal.
- Memorize your favorite hymn.
- Memorize the 13 Articles of Faith.
- Cook something delicious for someone you love.
- Repent.
- Learn to sew.
- Go on splits with the local missionaries.
- Collect favorite family recipes.

---

guidebooks *Aaronic Priesthood: Fulfilling Our Duty to God* for deacons, teachers, or priests with your sons. Become familiar with and review the *Young Women Personal Progress* guidebook with your daughters. Make it a priority to help your teens set and accomplish goals that will help them achieve the Duty to God award or the Young Womanhood Recognition award.

These achievement programs should provide your teen with growing experiences in the home, quorums, classes, and in Mutual activities. They are designed to teach your teen to follow the Savior's example and develop the traits of faith, love, obedience, unity, and sacrifice.

The greatest spiritual awakenings for your teen, however, will grow in the fertile soil of a relaxed and loving atmosphere in the home, where you model private and family spiritual practices for her to follow. If you make the time to read your scriptures, have personal prayer, and spend time with your family, your teen will be more likely to follow your example. If your outward spiritual practices are outward only, your teen will note the hypocrisy and be less likely to follow.

If you have set a pattern of regular family home evenings, scripture study, and prayer with your child from the time he is small, your teen will be more likely to continue with these practices and patterns when he is older. You can adjust your family home evenings, family prayer, and family scripture study to meet the needs of your teens. All of the materials mentioned in the following suggestions for involving teenagers in family worship are available at the Church Distribution Center (1-800-537-5971) or online at www.ldscatalog.com.

To Involve Teens in Family Home Evening

• Have a short lesson for the younger children first, then involve them in an activity while you have a discussion with your teens.

• Have your teen teach the younger children a lesson.

• Ask your teen to plan and prepare the refreshment or activity.

• Give your teen plenty of opportunities to play, lead, or sing music.

• Ask your teen to offer the opening or closing prayer.

• Plan lots of unifying family night activities with your teen.

• Have regular, private, personal interviews with your teen.

• Provide regular opportunities for testimony bearing.

• Provide lessons and activities geared to the needs and problems of your teen.

• Hold family council and calendar sessions to coordinate busy schedules.

• Encourage your teen to use the *Gospel Art Kit, Family Home Evening Manual,* and *Video Supplements,* or recent Church magazines when she takes her turn presenting the lesson.

• Sing songs from the *Children's Songbook* and *Hymns of The Church of Jesus Christ of Latter-day Saints* or other family favorites.

• Read the pamphlet *How to Talk to Your Teenager.*

• Teach from the manual *Achieving a Celestial Marriage,* which covers dating, courtship, and preparing for temple marriage.

• Use the booklet *The Holy Temple,* by Boyd K. Packer, when your teen is preparing to receive temple ordinances.

• Look through *The Activity Book* for ideas and suggestions for family activities.

• If you don't own a piano, you can purchase an electronic music keyboard, along

with a *Keyboard Course Kit* and *Conducting Course Kit,* from the Church Distribution Center.

• To help your teen learn to conduct, you can purchase the *Conducting Course Kit.*

• To help your teen learn to play the keyboard, you can purchase the *Keyboard Course Kit.*

• Purchase *New Era Poster Set A, B,* and *C* or the *New Era Postcard Set 1, 2, 3,* and *4* if you want to give your teen something that reinforces gospel principles taught at family home evening to hang on her wall or bulletin board, carry with her, or send to friends.

To Involve Teens in Family Scripture Study

• Purchase a *quality* set of scriptures and a scripture cover for your teen at an appropriate time, such as starting or graduating from seminary.

• Encourage your teen to participate in local seminary or institute classes.

• Motivate your teen to have personal scripture study each day by setting your own example.

• Hold family scripture study each day at a time when your teen will attend.

• Ask your teen to share a favorite scripture and talk about it during family scripture reading.

• Use the *Gospel Art Kit* for variety and added interest in family scripture study.

• Encourage your teen to select a hero from the scriptures.

• Purchase and encourage the use of *Scripture Audio Recordings.*

• Consider using the CES student manuals including: *Old Testament, Book of Mormon, The Pearl of Great Price* and *Doctrine and Covenants.*

• Consider using these videocassettes that teach principles from the scriptures:
Old Testament Video Presentations
New Testament Video Presentations
Book of Mormon Video Presentations
Doctrine and Covenants and Church History Video Presentations
Teachings from the Doctrine and Covenants and Church History

To Involve Teens in Family Prayer

• Include your teen in all family prayers, morning and night.

• Pray and fast together when your teen has a personal problem.

• Pray together at important times of decision and change.

• Pray before difficult tests and performances.

• Encourage your teen to have personal prayer every day.

• Give your teen a "prayer rock" to place on her pillow to remind her to say her personal prayers.

• Teach your teen to have silent prayers whenever she needs peace, answers, reassurance, a feeling of love, courage to resist temptation, and guidance.

WHEN I SEE YOU SLEEPING

*Sometimes when I'm washing your stinky
   socks
Or picking up your popcorn bowls and stuff,
I think I'll start charging you maid service
Or let you start living in the buff.
But late at night when I check on you sleeping
And see your sweet face dear and warm,
I wonder how that dear little princess
Could possibly do me any harm.
Sometimes when I'm picking up your wet
   towel
Or making your rumpled old bed,
I think I'll start charging for laundry duty*

*And that your rear end must be full of lead.
But late at night when I see you in moonlight
And kiss you on your forehead and ear,
I know I'm going to miss you
When you move somewhere far from here.
You might be a little work in the short run
But you'll always be my dear little girl.
And I'll always be your Mommy
Even after you've given life a whirl.
So stay here for just a little longer,
I won't mind picking up some of your things
If you promise to stay mine forever
Even after the fat lady sings.*

DISCIPLINE

The word *discipline* comes from the same root word as *disciple*. A disciple is someone who, by his own free will, chooses to follow another person because he respects them and knows he is loved. If you want your child to follow your lead, you need to love her and be worthy of her respect. Even then, your child has her agency and is always free to choose for herself. Truly learning to love someone and being worthy of respect is a lifelong quest, so don't get discouraged just thinking about it. Life is meant to be lived one day at a time—giving us plenty of time to repent and forgive.

Your children existed before they came to you. And though they may have forgotten their first estate, God will give you glimpses into their souls if you ask. The greatest truths you'll ever receive will come when you are looking into each of your child's eyes and praying for God to tell you who they are and how to love and lead them.

SHOW LOVE BY SETTING SAFE BOUNDARIES

Instead of thinking of discipline as a form of punishment, think of it as one important way you can show love for your child by setting safe boundaries. When children know that a self-mastered person who loves them is in charge, it gives them a sense of security in a very insecure world. Remember, you will be your child's model for normal human behavior. The best person to discipline is *you*.

DISCIPLINE DOS AND DON'TS

PRACTICE STRATEGIC PREVENTION

You'll probably discover that the more positive you are with yourself and your children, the less discouraged and rebellious you'll both feel. Effective discipline is never an afterthought—it's always planned ahead of time. Call it strategic prevention. Make sure you and your child get a healthy diet, adequate sleep, exercise, praise, and playtime. Everybody thrives on healthy routines. Children and adults who are hungry, tired, bored, ignored, or criticized feel and subsequently behave badly more often.

RESPECT YOUR CHILDREN

Remember that your children have deep feelings, just like you do. You never need to speak to them in an unkind or belittling way. When you're having a problem with your child and feel an angry outburst on its way from your mouth, stop and think: "Is this the way I would speak to another adult?" "Is this the way I would want someone to speak to me?" "Is this the way I would speak to my best friend?"

Children are not objects to dominate and control. They are your spirit brothers and sisters in little bodies who deserve to be treated with respect and patience. You can be firm and still be gentle and loving. Try to think of your child not only as he is this moment but also as who he was before birth and who he will become someday. Your child needs to hear your affirmations of his worth and goodness over and over again, especially when he's misbehaving.

If you have unkind words with your child, be the first to apologize and make up. That's what it means to be a mother . . . you are the *first* to love . . . the *first* to say you're sorry . . . the *first* to forgive . . . the *first* to praise . . . the *first* to encourage. You follow the pattern of your heavenly parents and the Savior, who loved you *first*, before you loved them.

REMOVE TEMPTATIONS

When children are very young it's better to remove a temptation than create a rule that will be broken over and over again. Young children are curious about everything. They have an inner drive that propels them to explore, manipulate, take

WHEN YOU FEEL THE TENSION RISING

If you feel tension building up inside you, count to a hundred, go for a walk, send yourself to your room, or send your child to hers before you do or say something that will hurt. You are the adult and it is up to you to keep control of yourself, no matter what your child says or does. No child ever deserves to be abused in any way. It is never your child's fault when you lose your temper. Losing your temper is a choice you make. When you lose your temper, apologize to your child then pray and ask for forgiveness. You too are God's child and He wants to help you.

Babies and young children don't cry or misbehave to annoy you. They're expressing their emotions and their budding independence. If your baby won't stop crying or your toddler or teenager won't quit misbehaving and you think you might hurt them, leave the room until you calm down. Never shake your baby or strike your child in anger. You risk not only causing great harm to his body but also to his spirit.

ruined or that can ruin her. Crawl around your house on your hands and knees to see what your child's world looks like from her perspective. Put childproof locks on any cupboard or drawer that contains potential for trouble.

REMEMBER THE AGE OF ACCOUNTABILITY

Remember that young children are not accountable for their actions from an adult point of view. Satan has no power to tempt little children until they reach the age of accountability. So it's more productive to spend time praising the good and ignoring the bad. Children crave attention, and they will get it from you any way they can. I also think it's important to spend at least a few minutes outdoors every day, even if you only stand on the other side of the front door for a few minutes with your child. There is something about being outside that helps calm frayed nerves and broaden broken perspectives.

apart, throw, bang, stuff up their nose, and taste everything around them with or without your support and blessing. Everything within your child's reach is fair game.

If you don't baby proof your house, your baby will. Everything that can be ruined, ingested, or torn apart will be, sooner or later. It's really not that much fun to sit in a room saying *"No!"* for several years. So don't drive each other crazy. You want your child to explore and learn; so put everything away that you don't want

SPANKING

Spanking has always been and will always be controversial. Some people think it's normal and necessary and some people think spanking is abuse. To be honest, there have been times when I've spanked my children, but I never felt good about it afterward. I never felt that I had done the right thing or chosen the best response. I always felt there was a better way to handle the situation and that I needed to repent. You have to decide what is the right action for you to take after asking for and receiving direction from God.

It's an hourly struggle to be true to the light that God gives you on a daily basis. When you're true to the light God gives you, you do what you feel in your heart is the right thing to do, even when it is difficult. You will make many mistakes; but in the process of learning to listen to your heart, you will learn, grow, and feel God's love, tenderness, and patience for you.

Motherhood will provide you with more opportunities to repent than anything else you'll ever do. When you view yourself as a child of God and know that he understands your childish mistakes as a mother much like you understand your own children's childish mistakes, you are better able to feel his love and forgiveness without paralyzing yourself in self-deception, doubt, and guilt.

is anything you do to help your child get his mind off himself. Young children don't misbehave to drive you crazy or make your life miserable. They don't know what misbehaving is. Children are constantly experimenting with cause and effect at your expense and they learn very quickly. So—and this is big—*give your children attention before they demand it.*

When babies and young children balk, scream, and fuss it's best to get their minds off themselves with gentle or silly invitations to put their thoughts elsewhere. You can change their surroundings, focus their attention elsewhere, or create a strategic diversion. Try whispering in your child's ear about something he really likes that is totally unconnected to what is going on and you'll be surprised how quickly he can be distracted from his grouch. As your baby grows older and can be reasoned with, you'll be more challenged to distract him from himself; but it still works. Giving your undivided attention to your child when he's not misbehaving is also a sure way to focus attention on something you really want to encourage.

PRACTICE THE ART OF DISTRACTION

The most important word to remember whenever you feel you need to discipline your young child is *distraction.* Distraction

TAKE TIME TO REALLY BE WITH YOUR CHILDREN

Children were not meant to compete with addictions, self-absorption, workaholism, and materialism. You can give your children positive attention when they're young and want to spend time with you or you can regret your decision big time later on when they no longer want to spend time with you and you have no control over their actions.

Children are smart. They do what works. They want your attention and they want it all the time. If crying, whining, or misbehaving is the only way to get your attention and get you to do something, your children will cry, whine, or misbehave a lot. If you give them your attention before they resort to misbehaving, both of you will be much happier in the long run.

IF YOU SAY NO TO ME, I'LL HAVE TO SAY NO TO YOU

Even children as young as three and four can understand the simple math of saying no. Try saying, "If you say no to me, that means I have to say no to you. If you say no to me two times that means I have to say no to you two times." For instance, tell your child, "If you say no to me when I ask you to brush your teeth, then I'll have to say no to you when you ask for a bedtime story." "When you say no to me when I ask you to go to the bathroom and get your pajamas on, then I have to say no to you when you ask me to tuck you in tonight." Then mean it.

TRANSFER RESPONSIBILITY TO YOUR CHILD

Your job is to gradually transfer the responsibility for life to the shoulders of your child. If you're ever in doubt about what you should or shouldn't do for your child, ask yourself, "Is this something she

can do for herself?" If it is, then don't do it for her even if she can't do it to your standards.

Mothering is a lot about letting your child learn from trial and error. It's hard to let your toddler feed herself when she makes a huge mess, but she has to learn somehow. It's hard to let your teenager drive a car for the first time, go on a date, or even start college; yet how can she become independent, get married, or obtain an education without taking risks and trying those things?

USE NATURAL *AND* IMPOSED CONSEQUENCES

Children learn *by* example and *through* experience. Part of their experience will be a growing knowledge of natural consequences and imposed consequences. Natural consequences are the best teachers; but sometimes they are not the best alternative. For instance, if your child runs in front of a moving truck, he'll be hit and might even die. That's a terrible way to learn about the consequences of not looking both ways. Naturally, a mother must simply *tell* her children about a number of natural consequences and then impose her own consequences in order to keep her children safe.

Other times, however, it's possible to allow natural consequences to tutor your young children.

I used to tell my children, "If you don't brush your teeth, you'll get cavities." This is a natural consequence. And I had one child who did not believe this statement and thus learned for herself the natural consequences. She used to wet her toothbrush and tell me she had brushed when

she hadn't. Sure enough, when she went for a checkup, she had cavities. She didn't tell me about this until she was in college. She told me that experience helped her pay better attention when I warned her of other consequences later in life.

In many circumstances, mothers have to take on the role of imposed consequence giver. Imposed consequences are the consequences you decide on. They go something like this: "If you don't brush your teeth and therefore get cavities, there will be no more candy." Or if the child is older, "If you don't brush your teeth and therefore get cavities, you'll pay for the dentist bill."

THERE'S NO SUCH THING AS CONSTRUCTIVE CRITICISM

No child is motivated by criticism. Did anyone ever motivate you to change by continually telling you what was wrong with you? Good relationships with children are like bank accounts. There have to be deposits before you can make withdrawals. *There is no such thing as constructive criticism; it leads to rebellion and stub-*

bornness. A better thing is called gentle guidance. Never underestimate the power of a positive mother.

For instance, you *can* say, "Brush your teeth you little brat or I'll spank you" and you might get the compliance you want for a little while. But do you really want your child to believe she is a brat? Do you really want a child who will do something only out of fear? Think positively about your child. Say positive things to your child all the time. You are creating a recording in her mind and heart that she will play back to herself over a lifetime. Tell your child what you love about her every day, and be specific.

STOP SAYING NO ALL THE TIME

Don't say no just to demonstrate that you're in control. If, for example, your child asks, "Can I have a piece of candy?" don't just reply, "No." Instead, try saying, "Yes, after you've had your dinner." If your child asks, "Can I use the car tonight?" don't just say, "No." Instead, try saying, "Yes, after all your homework is done and if you promise to be back by ten." Say yes as often as you can.

AVOID DIRECT CONFRONTATION

Direct confrontation seldom works with young children. For example, if you say, "Child, come over here and let me change your diaper," your quick-footed child will most likely dash off into the other room and wait to be chased down. If, instead, you sit in the middle of the floor where your child is playing and put the diaper over your head like a white tent hat, your child will probably run right over and try to

---

THE FIVE GIVES OF DISCIPLINE

So what do you do when your child is misbehaving? Smile with smoke shooting from your ears and twiddle your thumbs? No, have a plan of action in mind. I call these the five *gives* because they *give* you an alternative to overreacting in a heated moment.

Give the command. *For a younger child:* "No more throwing food at the table." *Older child:* "No more staying after school to hang out with your friends without letting me know where you are and what you're doing."

Give an explanation. *For a younger child:* "When you throw food at the dinner table it makes a big mess to clean up later." *Older child:* "When you don't come home from school at the expected time, I think something has happened and worry about you."

Give the consequences. *For a younger child:* "If you keep throwing your food, you'll have to stop eating and clean up your mess." *Older child:* "If you keep staying after school to hang out with your friends without getting permission from me first or letting me know, you won't be able to take the car to school anymore and you'll have to ride the bus."

Give an alternative. *For a younger child:* "Why don't you pretend you're a dinosaur and eat this broccoli tree." *Older child:* "You can bring your friends here after school if you want and hang out."

Give a follow-through. *For a younger child:* "It looks like you won't be eating any more food at this dinner. It's time for you to start cleaning up your mess." *Older child:* "It looks like you won't be taking the car to school anymore."

---

pull the diaper off. At that point your little bandit is snared and you can change the diaper as quickly as possible.

It's easy to get mad, punish, or bribe children; but those parental motivation strategies work only for so long. During the times you feel like "disciplining," you might find that you're responding to your child's behavior in a very "undisciplined" way yourself.

That's why parents are sometimes dumbfounded to find themselves screaming, "Don't you ever hit your brother again!" as they hit their child's behind—not exactly effective.

Children have a hard time modeling behavior they never see. So the next time you think your child needs some discipline, take a deep breath and ask yourself a few

questions like: "Am I calm? Am I confident? Am I in control? Am I connected? Am I compassionate? Or am I just mad?"

SET RULES

It's your job as a mother to educate, not just punish. Do you want your children to be sorry they were caught or wiser after your interaction with them? When you set limits with love, you have the ability to teach with power. Be very careful about setting rules, though. Too many rules about too many things is not fun for you or your child. Make sure that when you do set rules, you're also willing to enforce them consistently.

Loving and trusting your children are two totally different concepts and they aren't connected. It is possible to love a child and not trust him. Trust follows repetitive responsible behavior. Trust is earned as credibility is established. If you truly love someone you want to assist him in becoming responsible and worthy of trust.

DON'T BECOME TRAPPED BY A DESIRE TO CONTROL

The desire to control another person, even for her own good, is wrong. It is your opportunity to encourage your child to think for herself and assist her capacity for originality and growth. If you seek to rule and dominate, you risk killing your child's spirit. Children are full of life and liveliness. Jesus did not tell children to become like their parents, he told parents to become as their little children. If you come to realize how precious is the soul of a child, you will seek first to be taught, and then to teach.

Don't jeopardize your children's agency because you have become trapped by the desire that your family *appear* to be loving and happy. So many mothers want a righteous family and try to get one by forcing their children to look good and get along with and love each other. Once you truly open your heart to your child and seek *first* to love and understand instead of control and dominate, you will have your mind opened to your own weaknesses. God will tell you what changes you need to make in yourself. Then you will be at peace with whatever state your family happens to be in. If you delight in your children's individual agency instead of seeking new ways to control them, there will come a liberating light and love into your home. You will be blessed with understanding, judgment, and insight.

TIME-OUT

You may be the product of the "time-out" form of discipline, which consists of placing a child in a safe place away from Mom or the rest of the family while you both calm down. If your child is misbehaving, first approach him with the five gives . . . *command, explanation, consequences, alternative,* and *follow-through*. If that isn't effective, it might be a good idea to remove the child from the situation by placing him in his bedroom or another boring place until he is able to think things over and/or control himself. One minute for each year of age is about all it takes in time-out to give a child all the aloneness he can handle.

AFTER THE TIME-OUT

You don't want to give your child the idea that if she makes mistakes its means you don't want to be around her. Children need extra reassurance that they are loved, even when they make the mistake of misbehaving in a manner that warrants a time-out. To a young child, separation from loved ones can send a message of rejection. It needs to be followed by lots of hugs, kisses, and reassurance. When teens are mean and abusive and have to be asked to leave the room until they can control themselves, they also need and deserve the same reassurance after correction.

SIBLING QUARRELS

When siblings quarrel, they typically try to get Mom involved and taking sides. This is always dangerous business because you never really know what happened before you were brought into the argument.

It helps to simply escort quarreling siblings to a boring location, like the bathroom or an uncomfortable repentance bench, with the instructions that they are free to leave when they've reached a compromise they both feel good about *and* can tell you what *they* did wrong. They don't have to tell

you what the compromise is; but they both have to agree to it. All children can tell you what their sibling did wrong but they have a hard time owning up to the fact that they did something wrong.

Children who can articulate what they did to cause an argument and can then apologize and learn to compromise have a major advantage in the world when they leave home. They will learn effective problem-solving techniques when given the

opportunity to practice—especially without Mom getting in the middle of everything.

PROBLEM SOLVING IN RELATIONSHIPS

Children often model their parent's form of problem solving in relationships. If you and your husband give each other the silent treatment, yell, throw things, hit, or stomp out of the house when you disagree, you are teaching your children—who are always watching and learning—that those behaviors are acceptable ways to solve a problem. If you hide in your bedroom and never let your children hear you talking things over when you disagree, your children will have no model for conflict resolution. It's important, therefore, that you and your spouse know how to solve problems in a reasonable and loving way.

Ask yourself a few questions to discover your own conflict-resolution habits. Are you easily hurt and offended? Do you hold grudges? Do you back away from every disagreement because you think it will lead to a fight? Do you withhold physical affection when you're mad? Do you say mean or unloving things? Do you want your child's future marriage relationship to be like yours?

If you want your children to relate to people in positive and constructive ways you have to learn to relate to your spouse in positive and constructive ways, even when there is conflict or disagreement in your relationship. You are modeling behavior for your children every day, whether you realize it or not. Model behavior that you'd be proud to own up to. If you're not proud of it, change it.

AS A MOTHER THINKETH

Every mother has a train of thought that she rides on when she's alone. Make sure the ride is taking you where you want to go. If you pay attention to the running script in your mind you'll discover that many of the words running through your thoughts are things you've heard your parents—particularly your mother—say at one time or another. What you've been told about the world, other people, and yourself has unconsciously become the way you think about the world, other people, and yourself. Analyze those thoughts and figure out whether they are true. Can you think differently if they are false?

The way a mother thinks often becomes the way her children and her children's children think. If you take the time to cultivate loving, uplifting, forgiving thoughts, you can become the fertile field for your children's hearts to grow in. You can't control the elements of sun and storm but you can be their good earth. There are no secrets. As a mother thinketh, so goes the family and the world.

Mothers have great power to control the atmosphere of their homes and their children's hearts. You form your character and create your own happiness by controlling your thoughts. The world might teach you otherwise, but what goes on

---

SCRIPTURAL ADVICE ON DISCIPLINE

No power or influence can or ought to be maintained . . . only by persuasion, by long-suffering, by gentleness and meekness, and by love unfeigned; by kindness, and pure knowledge, which shall greatly enlarge the soul without hypocrisy and without guile—reproving betimes with sharpness, when moved upon by the Holy Ghost; and then showing forth afterwards an increase of love toward him whom thou hast reproved, lest he esteem thee to be his enemy; that he may know that thy faithfulness is stronger than the cords of death. Let thy bowels also be full of charity towards all men, and to the household of faith, and let virtue garnish thy thoughts unceasingly; then shall thy confidence wax strong in the presence of God; and the doctrine of the priesthood shall distil upon thy soul as the dews from heaven. The Holy Ghost shall be thy constant companion, and thy scepter an unchanging scepter of righteousness and truth; and thy dominion shall be an everlasting dominion, and without compulsory means it shall flow unto thee forever and ever.
—Doctrine and Covenants 121:41–46

---

inside your head is not private, personal, and something you have little control over. There is a direct connection between the way you think and your health, habits, ability to love, and motivation to take action. You have the power to weed out impure, critical, or fearful thoughts and choose to cultivate thoughts of forgiveness, unselfishness, and courage.

REPLACING THE OLD TAPES IN YOUR MIND

If you consistently pay attention to your thoughts and practice replacing the ones that are not bringing you joy or peace of mind, you will discover a transforming miracle. You don't always have control over what thought pops into your mind but you do have control over whether it stays there. If you can think only one thought at a time and you can control that thought, you have great power to change yourself from the inside out.

For instance, if you find yourself thinking, "I'm fat and ugly," replace that thought with, "I am an attractive and likeable human being. As a matter of fact, I'm a daughter of God! That makes me a royal princess!"

Or, if you think, "I can't do that. I'm not smart enough," replace that thought with, "I can do that. I might not be a rocket scientist but I can work hard and never give up."

Or, if you think, "I blew it. I can never be forgiven," replace it with, "I can make mistakes without being a mistake."

Or if you think, "Why don't they like me? There must be something wrong with me," replace it with, "I am loveable and there are healthy people waiting for my love."

SELF-PURIFICATION

Who you are before God—not how you appear to the world—will affect your children most profoundly. Your greatest influence will flow from who you are. You may have a library of books about the latest theories on child discipline, but they will have little effect if you have not first tried to purify yourself. Your ability to influence your child for good lies inside your soul and your desire to connect with him in loving ways. Purify yourself so that a great example of righteous will shine through your being and open your heart to feel unconditional love. When you feel that love, you will feel warmth, light, laughter, acceptance, spontaneity, joy, and human kindness.

If you are prayerful and listen carefully to the whisperings of the Spirit, you will be given direction when you most need it. Direction from the Spirit will teach you how to change yourself and then how to love your children. There will be no true love, order, or peace in your home until you have learned to love your husband and your children with all your heart and soul. As you attempt to change yourself to become a better model for your child, God will not leave you alone; for you too are his child and he knows and loves you completely. He will be there to strengthen and guide you, to provide you with a way to repent and have a true change of heart. At the core of all effective discipline is a loving mother's desire to purify herself before she seeks to influence her child.

HOUSEWORK

When it comes to housework, every mother has a different standard of what it means to keep a clean house. And that standard—whatever it is—inevitably becomes lower each time a new child is added to the family. This lowering of standards is very hard on some moms and rather easy for other moms to accept. Those who understand an important truth have the easiest time. Here is that truth: living with children is messy.

Trying to keep a house clean while raising a family is like trying to string beads without first tying a knot in the end of the string. You can work as hard and fast as you want, but when you look back at your handiwork to see how nice it looks, nothing's there. Please don't get caught up in thinking your house is a reflection of you. Hopefully your house will be a place where real, mess-making people are living and loving. Try to worry less about how your house *looks* and more about how your home *feels*.

If there's one thing you'll learn during your mothering career, it's that good housecleaning ideas don't last for long.

You simply can't keep the house perfectly clean unless you get rid of the children. If that's not an option, you don't have to give up but you do have to lower your standards. Your house will never be perfectly clean again. Get used to it.

Practice closing your children's bedroom doors without batting an eyelash. Walk past those muddy handprints in the hall like an art patron in a museum. Keep in mind that there will be days when the constant messes *really* do get to you. You'll feel so overwhelmed you'll either collapse in a crying heap, snap out grouchy orders like a brigadier general, or go on strike. These constant messes will bug you a lot more when you're feeling under the weather or pregnant and not quite up to running around all day picking up after the tornadoes who live with you. At these times, remind yourself that you are *not* the family maid. You are your children's teacher. Children won't learn what they don't do.

There will be days when you will feel all the housework piling up behind you. It will dawn on you that every article of clothing your family is wearing right down to the last pair of dirty socks, will soon require locating, sorting, washing, folding, and putting away. You will be cleaning up after breakfast five minutes before it's time to fix lunch. Then before you take a deep breath, it will be time to fix dinner

You'll feel dust bunnies multiplying under your bed and behind your

BASIC CLEANING SUPPLIES AND TIPS

Stock your cleaning shelf with these basic products and learn how to use them:

- ammonia
- baking soda
- cleanser
- cream of tartar
- dish soap
- fresh lemon
- laundry detergent
- lemon oil
- liquid bleach
- rubbing alcohol
- salt
- white vinegar

You'll be surprised at how many of these common household items have multiple uses. Read the labels to find cleaning uses and tricks. Here is a sampling of what some of these items can do:

Oven Cleaner. If something overflows and causes a messy spill in the oven, sprinkle water over the spill (while the oven is still warm), then sprinkle salt on it. After the oven has cooled down, scrape off the spill and wash it away.

Ceramic Tile Cleaner. Use lemon oil to clean the ceramic tile in your shower.

Drain Cleaner. Pour ½ cup baking soda down the drain. Add ½ cup white vinegar and cover the drain for five minutes. Pour a kettle of boiling water down the drain. This will break down the clogs and wash them away. (Don't use this method, however, if you've already tried a commercial drain opener, such as Drano, that might still be present in the drain.)

Aluminum Cookware Cleaner. This is great for shining up pots and pans and getting rid of burnt-on messes. Combine 2 tablespoons cream of tartar with 1 quart water. Place solution in your aluminum cookware, bring to a boil and simmer 10 minutes. Wash and dry as usual.

Brass Cleaner. Make a paste the consistency of toothpaste by combining lemon juice and baking soda. Rub onto brass with a soft, dry cloth. Rinse with water and dry.

Disposal Cleaner. Freeze vinegar in ice cube trays then grind in disposal once a week. This sharpens the blade *and* cleans the drain.

Stainless Steel Shiner. A cloth moistened with rubbing alcohol or white vinegar shines stainless steel very well.

Soap Scum Preventer. Dish soap works well to prevent a scummy ring from forming around your bathtub. Add a few drops to the bath water each time someone bathes.

refrigerator. You'll swear you can see microscopic dead fly wings, old toenail clippings, strands of hair, and dry skin flakes massing on top of every surface in your home. Candy wrappers, stubby pencils, chocolate chips, loose change, and Legos will peek out at you from cracks between the couch cushions. You'll feel like you're facing a massive invasion—a completely unarmed woman standing alone on a lifelong losing battlefield. This is a war you didn't sign up for—you were drafted!

HOUSEWORK AS A CIRCLE

So what's a mother to do? First, don't think of housework as a vertical list of things to do. Otherwise you'll never get to the end of the list and you'll always feel discouraged and depressed. Housework is a circle of things to do—there is no beginning and there is no end. Everything needs to be done all the time. This is not a defeatist attitude. This is reality. You'll find gobs of books that claim to have the secrets for housecleaning made easy or the perfect plan for an orderly home. Blacklist these books.

Any mother with experience knows that if you wash the sheets on Monday morning, Junior will get the stomach flu and fail to make it to the bathroom on Monday night. As soon as you clean your sliding glass door, all your children and a few of the neighbors' will immediately run over to the clean pane and mash their noses and lips on the glass. If you wash the kitchen countertop at 9:05 A.M. your two-year-old

will get an urge to fix himself a sandwich at 9:07 A.M. without your supervision.

What I'm getting to here is that most housecleaning advice would better serve you if someone condensed all of it to this: "If it's dirty, for goodness sake, don't clean it." You see, young children aren't interested in their toys until you've put them all neatly away. Schoolchildren don't want to go out and play in mud puddles unless you've just washed their jeans and tennis shoes. Nobody's hungry unless you've just cleaned up the kitchen. Children don't use their bed for trampolines unless you've just carefully made them. Husbands don't leave their morning-shadow pepper in the sink unless you've just disinfected the bathroom.

Housework is what you do that nobody notices until you *stop* doing it. Cleaning your house while your kids are still growing is like shoveling the walk before it stops snowing. And, as some of you may know, it's a lot easier to shovel a foot of snow if you started when there were just three inches of snow on the ground, then went out again after another three inches fell, then again . . . well, you get the picture.

TAKING A REAL LOOK AT SO-CALLED HELPFUL HOUSEWORK ADVICE

Be an Example for Your Children. Children *do* learn by example. But mother-depressing advice like this— "Children will learn to be tidy if their parents set a tidy example"—probably came from somebody who's never raised anything but petunias. Real, flesh-and-blood children use the entire bedroom floor as a giant, artistic collage for everything from old pizza crusts to late homework to day-old underwear. And they do this even if Mom is the neatest housekeeper on the block. The example part comes into play when your child grows up and has her own home to take care of—and her own children. So, do set an example. But don't get depressed if it isn't followed for 18 years or so.

De-junk Your House. De-junking your house is another suggestion that's really supposed to help. Because, according to housecleaning specialists, everyone has too much junk. The idea is, if you have less, you'll have less to clean up; your life will be smoother, and you will instantly have time to take long, hot bubble baths. Unfortunately, the advice doesn't consider that fact that your children will carry more *new* junk through the front door on any given day than you can possibly haul out the back door. So don't despair; just keep at it a little each day. De-junking really can be helpful. It's just not always the magical solution you thought it would be. If you're not using something, give it away, donate it to charity, or throw it away when the kids aren't looking. Don't let your things own you.

Make Cleanup Fun. Another popular cleaning-up suggestion for parents is to make pick-up time "fun." Recommendations in this category usually include using laundry bags that look like basketball hoops or creating a parent-child cleanup party. What you actually end up with, though, is a hamper full of basketballs and candy wrappers. Your parent/child teamwork party consists of one parent diligently picking up while one child is diligently waving from the sidelines.

If you keep the above in mind, though, you can use this advice to your advantage. Children, after all, generally like to throw things. Put their natural abilities to good use. Get yourself a large open container for each room in your house where you and the kids can toss in clutter at a moment's notice.

The "Your Stuff Is in Jail" Tactic. Another popular tactic desperate mothers try is the "if I have to pick it up, you have to pay to get it back" threat. This motherly action usually scares the dickens out of your children for about three minutes (the same amount of time it takes them to figure out that Mom can't possibly stand guard on her stash forever or remember what she put in there). Only make these kinds of wild claims when you are prepared to back them up like a prisoner of war camp commander.

So, How Do I Maintain at Least a Little Bit of Order? Now, don't get me wrong. All these ideas have merit and are worth trying. But rest assured that these "guaranteed to teach children to be tidy" ideas can quickly lose their shock value. Most kids will sooner or later resume their normal, casual living standard.

Do you give up and throw in the towel? No, just let go of your need for perfection or you'll drive you and your family crazy. Relaxing and enjoying a tidy but ofttimes cluttered house while attempting to train children to clean up after themselves is about all you can handle in one lifetime.

WHAT REALLY NEEDS TO BE DONE

While it's normal and acceptable for a house full of kids to be full of clutter, it's wise not to get too lazy. Some things just need to be done. Toilets need to be cleaned. Kitchen countertops need to be wiped down with bleach or another cleaner that disinfects and cleans germs. Dishes need to be washed—you *do* have to eat every day, after all. The oven, refrigerator, and other large appliances need thorough cleanings occasionally.

CREATE A BASIC CLEANING SCHEDULE

To help you wade through the enormous task of keeping a house presentable, it may help you to create a basic cleaning schedule. Keep in mind that this basic cleaning schedule has to be adaptable if you have children, because you can't plan on what

will happen at any moment. What you can plan on is this: if you don't work on cleaning your house a little every day, you'll sink. So get into a routine. For instance, if you're home in the morning, set a goal to get your housework done by a certain time early in the day. If you allow it, housecleaning can become life consuming and keep you from developing your talents and enjoying time better spent with your children.

After you've put in your set number of hours a day, don't forget to move on and reward yourself with something that feeds your spirit. Give yourself a few minutes to read your scriptures, listen to music, go for a walk, or meditate.

It might also help to develop your own daily, weekly, monthly, and yearly housework schedules to help you stay on top of things *before* they overwhelm you. Prepare, however, to have your schedule disrupted without falling to pieces.

Some Perspective for the Housework Weary

You can also do most housework chores on top of each other. Get a load of laundry going while you're doing the ironing and straightening up the house. If you fill your sink with hot soapy water while you're cooking, you can clean the refrigerator and mop the floor while you are preparing your meal. If you're gone during the workday, save housecleaning for later in the evening after the dinner hour and family time. Everybody will feel better about helping with housework if they are well fed and rested.

Also, it's perfectly all right to choose what you want to neglect. You can't always stay on top of everything. For instance, I choose to neglect my windows and blinds until I can't see out of them

APPROPRIATE HOUSEWORK SCHEDULES

The following housework schedules may seem overwhelming. And they are—if you have to cross off the lists all by yourself. Thankfully, children can make their own beds and clear their dishes from the table. You can assign the vacuuming to your 11-year-old, and Dad can mow the lawn. Do whatever works best for your family. And, remember, when you can't follow this type of a schedule, don't fall apart. Life will go on.

Daily Housework Schedule
- Fix breakfast, lunch, and dinner.
- Do breakfast, lunch, and dinner dishes.
- Make beds.
- Pick up and put away anything out of place on the floors.
- Vacuum, sweep, or mop floors—whatever is most needed that day.
- Dust.
- Collect and organize mail.
- Clean kitchen (sanitize countertops, wipe down the table, wipe fingerprints off the refrigerator and spills off the stove, etc.).

Weekly Housework Schedule
- Sort, wash, fold, and put away laundry.
- Gas up and wash car.
- Do basic yard work (mow lawn, weed yard and garden, water plants).
- Clean garage.
- Go grocery shopping.
- Check water softener.
- Empty garbages and take out trash.
- Clean bathroom(s).
- Water house plants.
- Wash walls (one room per week).

Monthly Housework Schedule
- Vacuum coils on refrigerator and freezer. Clear out any old food and wipe down shelves and other sticky spots.

very well. Yet I choose to carefully clean my bathrooms and kitchen every day because those are the rooms that spread the most germs. I choose to let my husband take responsibility for the messy, tool-filled garage. Yet I also choose to keep our joint bedroom a clean haven for both of us. You might even get to the point where your housecleaning schedule is one way to feed your spirit by changing the way you think and feel about housework. I used to hate doing dishes; but now I love to do the dishes. It is the only time and place where everybody pretty much leaves me alone and I have time to think. I love the warm feel of the soapy

- Clean any bad spills in the oven and any fixtures on the stovetop.
- Check and/or change heating and cooling system filters.
- Pay bills.
- Balance checkbook.
- Wash windows and blinds.
- Spray and fertilize outside plants.
- Clean pipes and drains.
- Purchase and organize items for food storage.

Semiyearly Housework Schedule
- Clear outside water lines for winter.
- Clean gutters.
- Shampoo carpets and upholstery.
- Seasonal plantings (fruit and vegetable gardens in the spring and bulbs in the fall).
- Seasonal harvesting (fruit and vegetables in the fall, flowers in the spring).
- Change oil in car.
- Remove or add extra blankets to beds.
- Place seasonal clothing in storage—or take out of storage.

Yearly Housework Schedule
- Trim and prune trees and shrubs.
- Paint or stain outside woodwork.
- Check roof for needed repairs.
- Caulk windows and doors.
- Check heating and cooling systems.
- Clean chimneys.
- Paint or stain inside walls and woodwork as needed.
- Can and freeze fruits and vegetables.
- Replace worn underwear, clothing, and bedding.

water in the winter and the cool feel in the summer. When I'm down on my hands and knees wiping up the kitchen floor, I always send a prayer heavenward. In the end, success at housework is like anything else in life. It boils down to having an attitude of gratitude and the willingness to work.

ENLIST HELP

The home you live in belongs to everyone in the family. And everyone—not just Mom—should learn to take care of the home. Do expect your children to help out. But don't expect them to do it right every time. Do start enlisting help right away. In

fact, it's wise to assign your children chores from a very young age: even two- and three-year-olds can pick up toys.

Getting Help from Your Younger Children

While you're attempting to teach your children to keep a clean house, always consider their age. Young children like job charts, checklists, rewards, structure, set schedules, and rules. At the same time, most young children are easily overwhelmed and will do better if you work along with them. Young children are also the most willing to help before they become legitimate help. It *will* take you longer to do the dishes, clean a room, or sort the clothes when young children help, but letting them help teaches them how to work and gives them a feeling of usefulness and competence. Experiment with family job charts, Saturday-morning house-cleaning chore races and giving out the "Hard Worker" award each week at family night.

Getting Help from Your Teenage Children

Teenagers, on the other hand, are much busier with outside-of-the-home school activities, church assignments, and possible part-time work. So you will need to be adaptable in your assignments and expectations. For instance, you can assign your teen to be responsible for a room in the house for a week or a month in addition to cleaning his own room and helping with meals, laundry, and dishes. Teens are fully capable of completing a housecleaning job on their own without your constant supervision. But don't always expect the job to be done the way you would do it. Teens tend to perform better when you don't bark out orders and set rigid time requirements. In other words, let your teenager know what you expect and widen the timeline of compliance.

Define What You Want

Many children and parents are at constant odds over housecleaning jobs because each parent and child has different expectations. So it helps to define what you want in the cleaning department. What a clean room means to you is different than what a clean room means to your child. For instance, a clean room to your child may mean throwing his bedspread up over his pillow and stuffing everything on the floor under his bed. You might consider coming up with several clean-room lists he can check off. For example:

A Clean Bedroom Checklist
- Pull up and smooth sheet.
- Pull up and smooth bedspread.
- Pull out everything from under the bed that doesn't belong there and put it away.
- Clear everything off the floor.
- Straighten and dust chest-of-drawers.
- Put toys in toy box.
- Put dirty clothes in hamper.
- Place books on the shelf.
- Throw garbage in trash can.
- Sweep, vacuum, or carpet sweep floor.

A Clean Bathroom Checklist

• Scrub toilet bowl inside and out with disinfectant.

• Scrub bathtub with disinfectant.

• Scrub sink and countertop with disinfectant.

• Sweep and mop floor.

• Clean and polish mirrors and fixtures.

• Check to see if the room needs more toilet paper, toothpaste, hand soap, or shampoo.

• Change towels.

Of course, checklists work only if your child knows how to do everything on the list. So . . . get with it and show your child how to use a toilet brush. Teach your child how to sweep or vacuum. Family night is a good time to demonstrate housecleaning skills for your children. They will probably whine and give you a hard time, but persevere. One day your children will actually thank you for teaching them how to take care of themselves and keep an orderly home.

THE VALUE OF HOUSEWORK

Although the sight of your child's bedroom floor may lead you to believe that he

hasn't learned a thing you've taught him, it's more than likely he has. Housework—work of any kind, really—does much more than lead to a tidy home. It teaches responsibility. It promotes a good work ethic. And it's an invaluable means for spending time together as a family.

REARING RESPONSIBLE CHILDREN

If you do for your child what he can do for himself, you're not doing him any favors. Children who learn responsibility at home have an easier time being responsible in school, at church, and on the job. Housework is a constant teaching opportunity. If your child uses a toilet, he should know how to clean it. If your child soils his clothes, he should know how to wash them. If your child eats food, he should know how to prepare it. Of course it takes time for children to learn how to do things. So get started—the sooner the better.

Housework is also a perfect opportunity to teach your child to feel responsible for someone besides himself. Allow your older children to care for and help their younger siblings clean up after themselves. Teach your children to perform small acts of kindness in secret for their brothers and sisters. You can assign an older child to a younger child. This older child can help get his sibling ready for church, clean him up after meals, and help him with his chores and homework.

PROMOTING A GOOD WORK ETHIC

Of course, the best way to teach your children to enjoy work is to enjoy work yourself. Check your attitude about hard

25 QUICK WAYS TO CLEAN UP AND ORGANIZE YOUR HOUSE

1. Place a large bucket or decorative basket in every room of the house for quick toy and mess pickups when your children are young.
2. Store small toys in labeled shoe boxes, fishing tackle boxes, vegetable bins, washtubs, laundry baskets, garbage cans, and restaurant supply jars.
3. Place half of your children's toys in storage every six months. This gives you fewer toys to clean up and makes your children think they have new things to play with.
4. Use your damp towel after you shower for quick dusting jobs around the house as you walk toward the washing machine.
5. Tie a plastic garbage bag to the handle of your upright vacuum cleaner to pick up clutter and transfer it to the right room as you go.
6. If something in your house is not serving a current useful purpose, give it to someone, throw it away, or donate it to charity. Beauty is a useful purpose.
7. Ask yourself if you've used it in the past year. If not, you probably won't and it's just taking up precious space. Throw it out.
8. Don't let paper overwhelm you. Open your mail over the garbage can or the shredder. Discard or recycle old magazines and newspapers quickly.
9. Use a binder for any of your children's schoolwork that you want to save.
10. Make a file folder for each child that contains important documents, such as his birth certificate, immunization records, and social security card.
11. Have one large, central scheduling calendar for the whole family in a central location.
12. Make a rule that everybody who eats, helps with the dishes. No one leaves the kitchen until everything is done.
13. Use a portion of family night for quick laundry folding and cleaning-job contests. Set a timer and give prizes.

work and make some changes if you need to. Make being a "good worker" the best way to get positive attention around your house. Notice when your child performs a chore especially well and make a big deal about it. When my mother-in-law died I was able to sit in on many hours of listening to her grown children as they remembered the good old days. Without exception, every child mentioned the long hot days working in the sugar beet fields in Lakeshore, Utah, on the family farm. The

whole family spent day after day thinning, weeding, and irrigating the family sugar beet crop.

Why did this hard work later become the Baadsgaard children's most pleasant memory? I believe it was because their mother worked right alongside her children and she tried to make work fun. She didn't send her children off to work, she went with them and brought along scrambled egg sandwiches and a good attitude. She spent those long hours

14. Plan a family outing for Saturday. Those who want to go must have their rooms clean and other chores completed beforehand.
15. Hang plastic netting over the shower faucet to store bath toys, then let your children play with them after they've been bathed. While they're playing in the bathtub, clean the bathroom sink, mirror, vanity, and toilet (just remember not to leave the bathroom to get anything—keep a close watch on the kids).
16. Hang a closet shoe organizer on the back of the bathroom door to organize beauty and hair care items.
17. Keep general cleaning supplies under the sink in your kitchen and each bathroom. This way you don't have to spend time trying to remember where you last used the cleanser or Windex.
18. Use shoe polish or matching crayons to cover small scratches on furniture.
19. Store plastic garbage bags in the bottom of the garbage can. When you lift the full one out, another new bag will be there to replace it.
20. Use comforters for easy bed making.
21. To save laundry on small children's bedding, try turning sheets head to foot before washing because they only soil the top half at a time.
22. Cover the mattress on your young child's bed with a plastic waterproof protector while they're still working on bladder control at night. Use a soft cotton mattress protector between the plastic cover and the bottom sheet.
23. Give your child an alarm to use to get himself up and ready for school without your help.
24. Set the clocks around your house five minutes fast if you want to make sure everyone gets to school and church on time.
25. Keep a bench, shoe rack, or other creative contraption at the doorway for your children to place their shoes on when they come in the house. This will keep down on all the mud, grass, and grime they track in and keep the shoes they would've left in the middle of the living room floor in a somewhat-organized place.

hoeing in the fields with her children singing songs, acting silly, and finding some treat when they were done.

THE PAYOFFS OF HARD WORK

With all the modern conveniences and increased incomes today it's easy to allow children to grow up without ever breaking a sweat. It takes a little more planning today to encourage your child to find meaningful and useful work. Every child should eventually learn how to wash the dishes, clean her clothes, make her bed, and pick up her room. Every child should know how to mow the lawn, fix meals, weed the garden, empty the garbage, and take care of younger siblings. Every child should learn how to fix a flat tire, change the oil, rake leaves, and paint the house.

Baby-sitting, mowing lawns, and delivering newspapers are good beginning part-time jobs for preteens. When your child

WHICH SOAP DO I USE WHERE?

Dishwasher Soap

Dishwasher soap comes in liquid gel and powder form. The liquid gel usually works best but is the most expensive. Store-brand powders are less expensive and work best if you turn on your sink water and run it until hot before starting your dishwasher (if the two are connected, of course). It's best to wash fine china and crystal by hand, not in the dishwasher.

Carpet Cleaners

The best way to keep your carpets clean is to vacuum each day and remove spills and dirt as soon as possible. You can rent or buy a carpet-cleaning machine. You can also hire a professional. Learn the content of your carpet pile and backing before selecting the type of cleaning method (steam or dry).

Hardwood Floor Cleaners

You can polish your wood floors yourself with a purchased or rented machine. You can also hire a professional. A polyurethane finish requires as little maintenance as most no-wax resistant flooring. Buy the hardwood floor cleaner that is designed for your type of flooring and follow directions carefully.

Wood Furniture Cleaners

Wood-surface furniture requires cleaning but seldom waxing. A soft, damp cloth is all that's required. Or if you prefer, a little furniture spray on a rag makes the rag pick up more dust than a dry cloth. Lemon oil also works well to bring out the wood's natural beauty and liven up a dull surface.

Upholstery Furniture Cleaners

Regular vacuuming is the best way to keep upholstered furniture clean. There are three ways to clean upholstery. You can use a cleaning product and apply it by hand. You can rent or buy a machine that cleans. You can call a professional. Try to spot clean spills before they become stains. Also, check to make sure your fabric can tolerate water-based cleaners.

Bathroom Cleaners

You can apply an all-purpose cleaner before mildew forms on tile and ceramic surfaces. Bleach applied with an old toothbrush can whiten the mildew stains between tiles. Remember that bleach is not a stain remover, but a color remover. Never mix chlorine bleach with ammonia or vinegar. Bathroom cleansers come in the liquid and powder form. Use the least abrasive type

becomes a teen and needs money for sports, choir tours, dances, and dates, it's time to encourage her to find a minimum-wage part-time job so she can begin the process of becoming a self-reliant adult. You can supply the basics in food, shelter, and clothing, but let your child earn the extras. Help your child set goals and start a savings plan for college, a mission, and a wedding.

Children need to know that their efforts and hard work matter most, more than grades, more than status, more than wealth, more than talent or fame. Children

that will do the job. Hard cleaning jobs will require a more abrasive cleaner. Finer surfaces will require a gentler product.

Drain Cleaners

To remove clogs you can push or pull with a plunger, a plumber's snake, or a drain auger. If you have a particularly stubborn clog you may have to apply pressure or air. Chemical drain cleaners are designed to eat and boil their way through the clog, so take special precautions when using.

Vacuum Cleaners

Before you purchase a vacuum, ask yourself what kind of surface you need to clean. Carpets can be cleaned with a good upright or canister with a power nozzle and motorized bushes. Canisters provide more attachments but can be awkward to use. The rotating brushes loosen and sweep up dirt in the carpet pile in an upright. The canister is designed for cleaning upholstery, stairs, and around furniture better.

Glass Cleaners

For light soil on glass, use plain water. Professionals use natural sponge applicators and rubber squeegees on windows. Paper towels usually work better than newspaper for drying. If you're interested in trying a homemade glass cleaner try these:

Lemon cleaner: 4 tablespoons of lemon juice mixed with one gallon of water (this is good for greasy handprints).

Heavy soil glass cleaner: ½ cup sudsy ammonia, one pint rubbing alcohol, 1 teaspoon dishwashing liquid, enough water to make mixture equal a gallon.

Oven Cleaners

Try to clean spills as soon as possible. Learn to use your self-cleaning oven features. Take caution when using commercial products. You'll need to take steps to protect yourself from the fumes and protect nearby surfaces. Don't use these products on self-cleaning ovens or bare metal.

Toilet Bowl Cleaners

The easiest way to keep the bowl clean is to brush frequently with a liquid, all-purpose cleaner. The automatic in-tank products are the easiest to use but don't usually take care of the whole job. You can use either liquid or powder cleaners. Liquid cleaners work better under the rim.

need to know that they are not measured against anyone else in the things that matter most. Hard work creates character. Character is who we are inside. Who we are inside is what matters. If we are impressed with and reward hard work, our children don't have to measure up to any standard other than the goals they've set for themselves.

Through the years I've observed my children taking piano lessons. Some seem to have such an easy time learning and performing while others have to really work and practice. In the end it hasn't

> ### HOMEMAKER'S LAMENT
>
> *To put it bluntly, this motherhood country*
> *Is not for the faint of heart.*
> *For you will find your days won't unwind*
> *And this will be your part:*
>
> *My breasts need a rest.*
> *My day's gone away.*
> *My son is undone.*
> *My teen split a spleen.*
> *My road is a load.*
> *My land needs a hand.*
> *My all is a wall.*
> *My name is a game.*
> *My dream's lost its steam.*
>
> *But soon you'll confess even in all of this*
>   *mess*
> *That you like this motherhood plan.*
> *Helping God bring to earth by you giving*
>   *birth*
> *To the souls of the family of man.*
>
> *So before you perish, please remember to*
>   *cherish*
> *Each child God gave you to mend.*
> *When you're over the hill and sitting very*
>   *still*
> *They might come home again.*
>
> *Of all worldly pleasures—even by the*
>   *strictest measure—*
> *Grandchildren are the sweetest rewards.*
> *So just keep on working and going*
>   *berserking*
> *And you'll never be lonely or bored.*

do the most good in life are just regular people with average ability who pay the price and work hard.

So don't be too eager to spare your child the very thing that will bring her the most satisfaction. Don't deny yourself or your child one of the greatest blessings in the world: the feeling of accomplishment and usefulness that follows a good day's work.

CREATING YOUR OWN PRIVATE WORLD

Through all of your endeavors to take care of the children, the housework, the laundry, the grocery shopping, and the ten million other things you are doing, try to keep an eternal perspective. Through the common tasks of everyday housework, you create your family's environment and set the mood and spirit in your home. Look at housework as an opportunity to create your own private world.

Above all, don't get discouraged. An elderly friend once told me, "Dirty sticky fingerprints all over your lower walls

been the most gifted who have used their talent to the fullest, but the children with average ability who are willing to pay the price and work hard. I think that scenario rings true in most areas of life. Those who

would soon be . . . dirty sticky fingerprints all over your upper walls. Children do grow up, you know."

Remember that your house is not you. Your clothes are not you. Your husband is not you. Your car is not you. Your children are not you. Your possessions are not you. Who are you? Find out.

There is something wonderful under this family mountain of mess and some- times you'll discover it when you least expect it. Under all those mounds of dishes and laundry, there's usually a giggling tod- dler begging to be hugged, a toothless school-age child waiting to be enjoyed, a terrified teenager trying to be understood, and a mellowing mother who sometimes realizes housework will always be there— but her children won't.

PREPARING MEALS

Fixing meals for a family is always a work in progress because everybody, it seems, is *always* hungry. Don't despair. Feeding the hungry sometimes seems a lonely job, but in reality, nothing you do brings so much immediate pleasure and serves such a basic necessity of life. Preparing family meals will not always feel like a joy but it will be easier if you organize your kitchen, enlist the help of other family members, keep the basics on hand, and approach cooking as a creative and soul-nourishing adventure. You don't have to be a gourmet cook to keep you and your family well fed.

FAMILY TIME/MEAL TIME

Find one time a day when the whole family can be together for a sit-down meal. For some, this is in the morning; for others, the evening. No matter the time, make it *the* hot meal of the day. If you can't find a time when the whole family can eat together, rearrange your life so you can.

Hunger is God's gift to you. Fixing and serving good food is often the only way you have to draw your family around you and reconnect. Every time you eat together, you renew your bodies *and* your relationships. It is very difficult to be angry with someone who has just given you something delicious to eat.

Food can become every mother's secret

A WELL-STOCKED KITCHEN

So, how do you stock the pantry, refrigerator, cupboards, and drawers with the items that will keep your family's kitchen up and running? Here are some ideas to get you started.

In the pantry you'll need:
- flour (white, wheat, oats, cornmeal, and barley)
- sugar
- salt
- powdered milk
- an assortment of spices
- rice
- pasta
- beans
- potatoes
- canned goods
- cereal
- vinegar
- syrup
- cooking oil
- baking ingredients, such as baking soda, baking powder, cocoa, vanilla, powdered sugar, brown sugar, and flavorings
- plastic and paper plates, cups and utensils
- salt and pepper shakers
- sandwich bags
- cookbooks and recipe file

In the refrigerator and freezer you'll need:
- meat
- milk
- juice
- fresh fruits and vegetables
- eggs
- butter or margarine
- yeast
- condiments: sandwich spreads, catsup, mustard, pickles, salad dressing
- bread
- jams and jellies
- water pitcher
- frozen food
- sauces and salad dressing

In the cupboards and drawers you'll need:
- a sturdy set of small, medium, and large saucepans
- a set of knives
- cooking and serving dishes and utensils
- a frying pan or skillet
- plastic wrap
- aluminum foil
- plates
- glasses
- cereal bowls
- silverware
- mixing bowls
- dish towels and washcloths
- hot pads
- a pizza pan
- cookie sheets
- cake pans
- pie tins
- muffin tins
- an electric mixer
- a blender
- a toaster
- a can opener
- a peeler
- a Crock-Pot or slow cooker
- a roasting pan
- baking dishes (glass and metal)
- measuring cups and spoons
- water pitcher
- a colander
- dish washing soap
- sink cleanser
- a broom
- a mop
- a garbage can

weapon. Think of your kitchen table as a sort of kindred altar or daily sacrament. The family meal is where you break bread, kneel to pray, and come to receive nourishment for your body *and* your soul. You and your children need a daily place of refreshment and celebration for the gifts of life and love.

KITCHEN ORGANIZATION

Most kitchens are overrun with gadgets that seldom get used. If you haven't used something stored in your kitchen for a year, you can safely give it away or throw it away. Organize your drawers and cupboards so that you don't have to search for something every time you need it.

Keep like items together. Mixing bowls, baking pans, and casseroles, for example, could be stacked inside of each other and put in the same cupboard.

Put the items you use to cook with in cupboards near the stove. For example, you may want to put your spices in a cupboard that you can reach while stirring something on the range. This way, you can keep stirring while you reach for some oregano to add to the sauce you're making. Stirring spoons, spatulas, and ladles should be in a drawer relatively near the stove.

Put glasses, plates, and bowls in cupboards near the sink or dishwasher to make cleaning up go more quickly.

USING RECIPES

Once you've spent a few years cooking meals for a family, you'll probably not need recipes very often, except for when baking. It's so much easier to cook with inexpensive food basics like potatoes, rice, pasta, and beans and then add in-season produce and a small amount of meat. Review the basics of making soup in a good cookbook and make up your own recipes by combining all your leftovers into a hot, nourishing meal. Your job is to make the same basic food "look" different with your own creative flair. Experiment. Chicken can be dressed up in dozens of ways—so can pasta, pork, rice, and beef. The worst that can happen is that you'll learn something new. (See "Cook from the Basics" on page 225 for more details.)

MAKE MEALTIME INTERESTING

Expect your children to learn good manners but don't make mealtime so stiff that nobody has fun. Talk about your day. Smile. Laugh. If your family has survived another day, with all of its ups and downs, come together and celebrate that fact. You don't have to wait for birthdays or holidays to be happy together. It doesn't matter that you're eating macaroni and cheese with mismatched forks. What does matter is that you make mealtime a relaxed and enjoyable time together.

Begin your meal with family prayer. This is a great way to invite a spirit of gratitude to your table. Grateful families are happy families. It's important to bring a cheerful attitude to the table. Your children will forgive you for the overcooked meatloaf as long as you don't forget to bring your sense of humor to the table.

Consider inviting guests occasionally, such as missionaries, neighbors, or friends to join you in a meal. Dinner guests tend to add a little spice to an otherwise routine event.

FOSTER MEALTIME CONVERSATIONS

Mealtime conversations can be lifelines used to reconnect busy families swimming in a sea of hectic and conflicting schedules. Families who eat together are more likely to take an interest in what all other family members are doing.

To achieve quality conversation time, eliminate as many distractions as possible before you sit down to eat. Blaring televisions, noisy stereos, and ringing telephones make it impossible to focus on the old-fashioned art of person-to-person conversation.

My husband and I have experimented over the years with many methods of steering dinnertime conversation, with varied amounts of success. We've found table talk a good time to teach our children, but always in an informal way. The most important thing we've learned is to keep mealtime *positive*. Family conflicts can be solved at a different time and place.

It's important for every family member to have a voice. This means you have to take turns. This is easier said than done because older or more assertive family members tend to monopolize the dinner-table conversation. Try taking turns by going around the circle relating one good or sad thing that happened to you during the day or sharing some interesting bit of new knowledge you've gained.

You might like to discuss and evaluate movies, books, world news, or what the children are learning in church or school or share a new joke you're learned. Try keeping the scriptures and other good books within arm's length of the table. Consider reading the scriptures between dinner and dessert. Use the dinner hour to plan for upcoming vacations and holidays.

Some of your best dinnertime conversations will take place after the meal while you're doing the dishes side by side with your spouse, son, or daughter. Remember, you're not simply getting the dishes done, you're building loving relationships.

VARY THE LOCATION

Try making creative alternatives to high-priced restaurant meals. Some of your most memorable family dinners will take place in unusual settings. Try tin-foil dinners in the mountains or your backyard. Spread a tablecloth on the family room floor. It doesn't really take more work or more money to alter the setting for meals—just a little creativity and playfulness.

START MEALTIME TRADITIONS

One loving tradition that I especially appreciate at the dinner table is a routine my husband began years ago. He walks around the table at dinnertime before he sits down and gently acknowledges each family member, from the youngest to the oldest, with a warm touch, pat, or kiss on the cheek—including me. Some families like to hold hands while they pray. Others make it a habit to put their arm around those sitting next to them. The important thing to remember is that all families need to show their affection daily for each other to remain close.

If you take the time to make your meals together more enjoyable by praying together, talking to each other, sharing loving mealtime traditions, reading from the scriptures, and showing your sincere affection and gratitude for each other, mealtime can be the highlight of your day.

DISH DUTY

Experiment with family dishwashing duty. In some families, if you help cook the meal you don't have to help with the dishes. In others, dish duty is assigned on a job chart where every family member takes his turn.

We've tried all kinds of dish-duty rules in our family and finally settled on the one that works best. In our family the rule is: If you eat, you help with the dishes until they're done. Cleaning up after a meal goes a lot faster if everybody helps.

LAUNDRY

If someone told you how much time you'd spend doing laundry after having children, you'd have laughed in total disbelief.

Life as a mother teaches you many things, and one of them is how to wash lots of incredibly dirty, smelly laundry. You can hate doing the laundry or enjoy it. Since you have to do it anyway, why not choose to love it?

Remember all the mothers in the world who have no source of clean water in their homes, let alone an automatic machine to do the work for them. Having access to a washing machine and a dryer is a true luxury that most mothers in the world don't enjoy. If you have that luxury, don't forget to be grateful for it.

TWO WAYS TO THINK OF CLEAN ENOUGH

There are basically two ways to face family laundry duty. The first way is to wash everything every time you wear it or use it. If you are a new mother you may choose to do this because it is possible. The second way is to wash things only when you absolutely have to. The second way is a lot better when you start adding family members to your roll. If you wash every towel or shirt every time you use it, you'll be better friends with your washer and dryer than your husband and children.

So, first decide what you can live with in the clean laundry department. You might like a clean towel every time you bathe, but can you live with clean towels once every week? You might like clean sheets every week, but can you live with clean sheets every few weeks instead? Everybody deserves clean socks and underwear daily, but can you live with outfits that get washed only when they look or smell like they need it? Here are some simple suggestions.

• Except for a change of socks and underwear, clothing doesn't need to be washed every time it's worn. Washing clothes—especially jeans and dark-colored clothing—wears them out.

• Put bibs on your babies so their spit-up, drool, and food stains make the bib dirty, not the entire outfit.

• Take shirts off your toddlers when they're learning to feed themselves.

• Set aside outside clothes for each child that can be worn for playing or working outside. Keep reusing those clothes until they demand to be washed.

• For extra reusability, buy black and dark blue pants or overalls that can be re-worn many times before they look and smell bad enough to need washing.

• Assign your teenagers to wash and iron their own clothes.

LAUNDRY HINTS AND HELPS

CUTTING ENERGY BILLS

Use your dryer for things you want to feel soft to the skin, such as socks, underwear, and towels. Otherwise you can hang and air-dry almost everything else. Your clothing will look better longer and your natural gas or electric bill will be lower. Bedding hung outside to dry keeps that fresh scent for days.

To further save on energy costs, set your washing machine to rinse in cold water for every type of load. You seldom need to wash clothes in hot water; warm or cold water will do fine. Try to limit or eliminate buying clothing that require ironing. Damp items can be tumbled in the dryer for a few minutes then hung on a hanger to finish drying if you want to eliminate ironing all together. When you do iron, wait until you have several items of clothing that need to be ironed to make heating up the iron cost efficient. A heavier—though more expensive—iron may also save you money in the long run because it will iron out wrinkles more quickly.

SORTING

The easiest way to sort colors is to put whites, lights, and darks in three separate loads. Dark colors tend to bleed and should be washed separately in cool water. Colorfast light colors and whites can be washed in warm water. If you want your whites to stay white, wash whites—and only whites—together in the same load.

SOAP

Experiment with different laundry soap until you find the least expensive one that works the best for you. If you have soft water, you'll need less soap. Treat stains before you put them through the wash because warm or hot water will set many stains for life. Stain removers that come in a solid stick form often work best for tough stains. The new, oxygenated powdered stain removers also work well.

FOLDING

Purchase a small laundry container or basket for each person in the family, then throw clean, dry clothes into them folded or unfolded—depending on your mood and the amount of time you want to spend. You or your family members can fold the clothes later as you place them in the drawers. If you find yourself wondering where all the sock mates go, someone once told me that missing socks are the larva form of wire coat hangers that get tangled up in the closet. Both remain a mystery even for the most learned.

LAUNDRY RESPONSIBILITIES

You may or may not want your children to help with the laundry. Some mothers prefer to have their children do their own laundry when they are old enough. I settle for the goal that every child should at least know how to wash his own clothes before he leaves home. When and how you want to teach your children is up to you. Some fathers take over laundry duty. Experiment. Do what works best for you and your family.

LAUNDRY PERSPECTIVE

Dirty clothes are the proof that some robust living and growing is going on around your house. A child in perfectly clean clothes is not normal. Children are experimenting and growing all the time and that requires lots of mess, dirt, and sticky stuff. As an aside, if you never get around to getting your young children dressed in the morning, relax. That means you won't have to get them into their pajamas at night and you save one whole outfit that needs to be washed.

Even putting clean laundry away can be a real discovery process. You'll learn more about what your growing children treasure while you put away their white socks than they'll ever tell you. You'll discover lost childhood treasures you'd otherwise miss. Somewhere stuffed between the underwear and socks you'll discover secret collections of Cub Scout bandana holders, candy wrappers, pocket-knives, baseball cards, shiny rocks, stubby pencils, spider rings, ball-point pen parts, scratch-and-sniff stickers, used blue chalk, dinosaur pins, old key chains with the keys, crudely cut magazine pictures of sports cars or pretty ladies, model airplane pieces, seashells, torn bookmarks, and plastic monster pencil toppers. Now, how would you know about all that without opening your child's dresser drawer to put away his clean clothing?

No, doing the family laundry isn't always easy; but there is something strangely rewarding about handling a pair of dirty jeans that recently slid triumphantly into home base. There is a little stardust in smelly tennis shoes that have raced with the wind, jumped over tall cardboard boxes in a single bound, and splashed through sixteen mud puddles all the way home. You'll begin to discover the meaning to the phrase, "Don't worry, it will all come out in the wash."

Doing the family laundry can be one of life's greatest metaphors. Look for connections where none seem to exist. Dirty clothes are the proof that some real, breathing human beings are living at your house.

YARD WORK

Like housework, yard work has its good points and a few not-so-good points. For the most part, however, there are not many things more rewarding than yard work. Yard work is yet another area that should involve the whole family. Mowing, watering, weeding, planting, pruning, sweeping, painting, cleaning, and generally keeping the place looking well kept is another of God's gifts to you as a mother. If it wasn't for yard work, most of us wouldn't have any direct connection with nature or the law of the harvest.

YARD WORK HINTS AND HELPS

WORKING WITH CHILDREN

Children of all ages can help with yard work. Don't make yard work gender specific. Both boys and girls should know how to mow the lawn, plant and care for landscaping, and keep a garden alive with adequate water, sunshine, and nutrients. Children are always more willing to help with yard work when they work alongside mom and dad. Children love to make secret places in their yards where they can hide or create secret gardens. Encourage your child in all of her outdoor adventures.

IF YOU DON'T HAVE A YARD

Of course, you may live somewhere that doesn't require any yard work. Whether you have a big yard or no yard, there is only one part of yard care you simply shouldn't miss when raising a family: a garden. If you don't have a yard, find a plot of ground near your house or apartment that can be made available for your use. Find out if your neighborhood has a community garden you can tend to regularly. No family should miss out on the experience of planting and harvesting a garden each growing season.

GARDENING

Growing a garden will put you back in touch with good-old basic dirt, sun, and water. You'll stay in touch with the seasons and have a built-in reason to think about the resurrection each spring.

• You can send away for seeds from a gardening catalog, visit on-line sites, or shop at a local greenhouse or store that carries seeds or bedding plants.

• Plant where there is at least four to six hours of direct sunlight.

• Your soil should drain well and have adequate water.

• If your soil needs help, improve it with fertilizer.

• Most seeds are planted at a depth three times the diameter of the seed.

• Straw, hay, and grass clippings are effective mulch.

• You can start a compost pile with organic matter from your garden and yard and any leftover food scraps.

THE FAMILY GARDEN PLOT

When the soil is dry enough to work and the warm sun spends a little longer hanging around each day, put on your work clothes then start the magic. It's more work and chaos if the whole family digs right in, but it's worth it. Before long, your whole crazy clan will be out stringing lines around each other's necks, hoeing crooked rows, planting onion bulbs upside down, and licking the pink poison off the corn seeds. But if you hang in there you will have the chance to relish not only the flavor of a juicy, red, ripe homegrown tomato but also the renewal of life and the law of the harvest.

You can plant in long straight rows or more densely in box-like areas. Some families prefer raised-bed gardening. Some families like to give each child a space of

earth to work and the choice of seeds to plant. That same child then becomes responsible for watering, weeding, and harvesting the crop. Other families like to decide on their garden plans together during family night then hoe, plant, water, weed, and harvest together. A garden, like owning pets, gives children something to love and care for that will die if they neglect it. No child should grow up without the magic of snitching baby vegetables or picking and sampling green fruit.

If you have the space, consider growing as many fruits trees as you can on your property. Fruit trees give you a colorful display of blossoms in the spring, shade in the summer, and a harvest in the fall. Fruit trees give your child a place to climb, build a clubhouse, or hang a rope swing. Train yourself and your children in the art of pruning, spraying for pests, watering, and picking/preserving fruit for the winter months. Grapes make a beautiful climbing fence.

A certain freedom comes from working the earth—the freedom to understand why you reap what you sow. People who grow living fruits and vegetables better understand their personal connection to the

---

GARDENS

I'm thinking of planting a garden.
I don't know what size or what shape.
I've never planted a garden before.
I don't know what depth or what space.

Have you seen the seeds of a carrot,
Like flecks of dust in my hand?
Can this tiny, crying baby
Really someday become a man?

I'm thinking of planting a garden.
I don't know the best time to sow.
Who will be the water and sunshine
So my tiny seedlings will grow?

Have you seen the seed of a woman
Like flecks of love in his hand?
Can you see the circle of families
As numerous as grains of sand?

I'm thinking of planting a garden
With stars, moon, and sun in my hand.
I will harvest the sons and daughters
Of the master gardener of man.

---

miraculous cycle of living, dying, and living again. People who know the feel of damp earth in the palms of their hands have a greater understanding and appreciation of the passing seasons.

Even if you have only one planter box on your porch, make it a habit to grow something *real* every year. You and your children shouldn't miss the wonder of watching something grow from a tiny seed. No one should walk through the growing season without relishing a harvest.

FAMILY FINANCES

It's a safe bet that most of us don't consider ourselves wealthy. Yet according to the United Nations, if you have a non-dirt floor in the place you live, you belong to the upper half of the world's most prosperous people. If you have a window, a door, and more than one room, you belong to the upper 20 percent of the world's richest people. Regardless of where you live, if you can read and you have a pair of shoes, a change of underwear, and can choose from two or more foods to eat, you belong to the top 10 percent of the world's most wealthy. Given that global perspective, we are all wealthy.

Mothers are in a perfect position to teach their children and exemplify the principles of wise stewardship over family resources. Mothers who are wise stewards create homes where a sense of order, abundance, and peace flourish and where gratitude, generosity, and service flower.

You need basic housing, food, clothing, and perhaps transportation. Needing money for resources to survive doesn't get you into trouble; but a preoccupation with money and resources can. Needing money for resources to live provides you with motivation to work. Work is an important part of a full and rewarding life. Every member of the family should have work to do—paid or unpaid—that is useful and appreciated. Be warned, however, that too much work done in order to buy too much stuff can be carried to the extreme and harm a healthy family life.

THE AFFLUENZA BUG

Have you ever fallen prey to the dreaded "affluenza" bug? The symptoms of this common human condition are overconsumption, overextended credit, and overwork to pay for it. Do you really need a bigger house, a newer car, more expensive clothing, furniture and food? Are you trading family time and loving relationships for more *stuff*?

OWNERSHIP AND STEWARDSHIP

Because you can be just as preoccupied with money or resources when you have too little as when you have too much, the challenge is to effectively manage your time, talents, knowledge, energy, and resources so that you have enough to meet your family's needs. When you have adequately met your family's needs, you are then free to share your excess.

It helps to understand the difference

between ownership and stewardship. Your home, lands, and possessions pass through your hands for a short time, but they are not yours. You have stewardship over your resources for a few short years but you do not own them. Everything you have is a gift from God. When you die everything you possess will pass into another's hands. The question to answer is not "How many possessions did you hoard in this life?" but, "How effectively did you use the resources that came into your hands to bless the lives of as many people as possible?"

THE PRINCIPLE OF ETERNAL INCREASE

The gospel of Jesus Christ provides you with the great principle of increase, or adding to what you already possess. Where much is given much is required. Any investment in winning the souls of children is worth a lifetime of effort. Children are the only assets you are allowed to keep after you die, and even then only if you've made wise use of your time on this earth and they are sealed to you in love. So be wise sooner rather than later and don't waste your precious time and energy acquiring more than the basic necessities of life.

A LASTING LEGACY

Focus on giving your children the best of everything money *can't* buy. Too often all this huge effort for acquisition is often at the expense of losing what is most important, loving relationships with your family. When you make wiser investments of time, energy, and love for your family, the dividends never end. Children grow up. Parents grow old. One generation dissolves into the next so quickly. Creating a loving family is the only lasting legacy. You don't have the time to sacrifice people who matter most for things that matter least.

Every investment you make in another human being contains your life's greatest meaning—every choice to love, your life's greatest wealth. Money can buy you a house but not a home, medicine but not health, amusement but not happiness. You don't need more money to be prosperous. You need only dream that what you always wished for is what you already have.

SACRED ACCOUNTABILITY

Wise stewardship includes a sacred accountability to acknowledge our blessings and a desire to share all we've been given, in trust from God, with others. Everything we've been given . . . our time, talents, families, energy, health, knowledge, and possessions are given to us in the sacred trust that we are willing to use them to bless more lives than our own.

That's what it means to build up the kingdom of God. When you use your resources only for yourself, you've limited your ability to bless others—and in that there is no increase or exaltation.

So, where do you start?

First, take an accounting of where you are today, at this moment. Take a new look at your blessings, whether they are money, talents, time, resources, or knowledge. How can you use your stewardship over these things to bless the lives of others? As a mother you can literally answer Christ's admonition to feed the hungry, clothe the naked, and care for the sick. That is your job description every day.

Look again, at *all* your resources, not just your income. Everything you are blessed with can be shared, whether it's a little or a lot. We're told that nothing is temporal to God and that all things are spiritual. The way you think about, earn, spend, and invest your money and resources is spiritual—for with it you have the ability to bless and increase or hoard and decrease.

Second, learn the difference between your wants and needs. You need nourishing food, adequate shelter, durable clothing, and perhaps reliable transportation. You may want expensive convenience food, a lavish home in the best neighborhood, designer clothing, and a new car. If you spend your life on these kinds of wants, you may bury your chance for eternal increase because you've squandered all you have on yourself.

Think about it long and hard and then decide what is enough. A modest home that you can afford to pay off quickly, a healthy diet, an adequate wardrobe, and reliable transportation are all worthy goals for a stable family life. When you move

beyond those basic needs into lavish earthly wants, you may find yourself on thin ice if your eternal perspective becomes clouded. The true wealth of a man is measured not in what he possesses but what he freely gives. If your desire is always for bigger, better, and newer for yourself, you will never arrive. *When* will what you have be enough? *When* will you be able to share? If not now, *when?*

Third, decide on a workable plan. Once you decide what is enough for your needs, find your excess and decide what you have to share. Some people call this a budget. Like using a map when you're going on a trip, a family financial budget is the map you follow to help in your goal to be self-sustaining and also allow you to use your excess to bless others.

Budgeting, simply put, is figuring out what your income is and then deciding how to use it most effectively. Developing and using a family budget means taking charge of your finances and becoming the owner of an official family spending *and* giving plan. Most of you will manage over a million dollars during the years you're in the work force. Sound stable families, like sound stable businesses, need some form of spending control, long-range planning, and sharing of ideas.

A SIMPLE BUDGET PLAN

The simplest budget plans include the following resolutions:

Pay your tithing first.

If you pay your tithes and offerings first from each paycheck, you will have God's help to wisely handle what's left. There is no better financial-aid plan. God's plan for sharing is simple. Whether you have a lot or a little, God requires an equal portion from all.

Pay yourself second.

Some people call this saving. Have the bank automatically withdraw a set amount from the checking account to deposit in a savings account. Savings should be divided into short-term, long-term, and retirement goals.

Pay for set bills.

Use checks or automatic withdrawals to pay for predetermined, life-sustaining items such as mortgage or rent, utilities, transportation, and insurance.

Withdraw a predetermined amount of cash for variable expenses.

Pay for everything else that's needed during the week or month with only the cash on hand. These items include variable spending for things like food and clothing. When the cash runs out, simply stop spending. Or, if you prefer, use your debit card up to a predetermined limit.

Always spend less than you earn.

If you spend less than you earn, you can save and invest a certain percentage of your income even on the tightest budget. You'll want a liquid savings account available for emergencies or to cover all your bills for at least three to six months. Always pay your taxes on time and honestly. Don't even consider bankruptcy except under the most unique and irreversible circumstances—and even then only if you've prayerfully thought through all the alternatives and consulted with church, legal, and financial advisors.

MONEY MANAGEMENT AS A PARTNERSHIP

Money management should be a partnership between you and your husband. Make sure both of you record each check when it is written and keep a running total of how much is left in the account. You may choose to have a joint account or separate accounts, but be sure both of you are fully aware of all money matters and have equal voice in all decisions concerning your family finances.

Be sure to balance the checkbook every month when the bank statement comes. If you bank online, look up your account balances regularly and be certain that they are accurate. Budgets should also take into account affordable recreation and allow for some spontaneity. Partners should each have some personal spending money that they need not account for to each other. Don't become a couple who

---

HOW TO GET OFF THE AFFLUENZA TREADMILL

Reduce your expectations and expenses.

Start by buying used items until you have enough money to purchase quality new items. Secondhand doesn't mean second-rate. A piece of really old secondhand furniture is called an antique. Little things add up. Do you really need more than basic phone service? Do you really need to eat several meals away from home a week? Do you really need another pair of shoes? Like finally getting around to fixing a leaky faucet in the bathroom, fix your leaky spending habits by keeping track of everything you spend for a month. You'll be amazed at how much you can save by making small changes in your spending habits.

Use your credit cards only for convenience and identification.

Always pay off the balance each month. Otherwise, pay cash. Credit card debt has soared in past years and families are paying the price with an all-time high level of bankruptcies. If you can't control yourself, cut up your cards and throw them away.

Make it a lifelong effort to increase your education and marketable skills.

You or your husband may need to change employment many times in your working life. Many communities offer low-cost or free classes on everything from car repair to computer processing. Evening classes at the local college or university are also good options for increasing your marketable skills.

Systematically accumulate basic food storage and fuel to last a year.

A prudent use of your resources is to plan ahead and store the things you need to survive in the case of an emergency. To improve your health, nutrition, and spiritual awareness, plant and harvest a garden each year. If you have the option and desire, consider raising animals.

Avoid debt.

Members of the Church have been counseled for years to avoid debt. With the possible exception of buying a home, paying for an education, or other vital investments, debt should be avoided. Money mastery is really self-mastery. Self-mastery is self-discipline. Debt, for instance, is really your unwillingness to discipline yourself and wait. Everybody hates to wait. Waiting is boring. Waiting is slow. But you need to remember, paying back money you borrow is also waiting big time. Paying off debt is boring. Paying off debt is slow. So there's waiting and boring stuff on both ends. You have to get used to waiting and being bored. That's life and it's good for you.

---

is so budget conscious that you never spend your money for unplanned diversions or for items that are part of joyful living.

Effective financial partnerships for couples include:

- shared financial responsibilities through open communication
- determining reasonable expectations and limits
- cooperating in the budgeting and saving process

• eliminating and avoiding debt

Couples *can* become free from the devastating trap of debt and enjoy greater peace of mind and harmony in their homes. Too many families are living from paycheck to paycheck just to keep current with their bills. Too many couples are working longer and longer hours at the expense of leisure and family time. Don't become one of them.

CREDIT CARD DEBT

In past years, credit card debt and the number of bankruptcies have steamrolled out of control in the United States. If you have a credit card balance of $3,900 and make only the minimum payment, which would be about $78 a month at 18 percent interest, it will take you *35 years* to pay off your debt. You will pay out more than $10,000 in interest before you are done.

RACCOON TRAPS/DEBT TRAPS

Raccoon traps work in much the same way as consumer debt. A raccoon trap has a small opening where a raccoon can reach into the trap to obtain a desirable piece of food or shiny object. Once the raccoon closes his fist over the desirable object, however, he can't pull it back through the small opening. All the raccoon has to do to free himself is drop the shiny object or food and pull his hand back out. But the animal always holds tight to the shiny object. And soon—when the trap setter comes for his due—the raccoon no longer has any freedom to act.

Debt, no matter how attractively packaged, is a huge trap. If you don't use your resources wisely, overspending will eventually rob you of money, time, health, family security, and peace of mind. Conflicts about money are a major cause of unhappiness and divorce. The money-management decisions couples make together have the potential to bring them happiness or despair, freedom or bondage. Church leaders have long counseled us to get out of debt, live within our means, and pay as we go.

Effective communication in financial matters includes a knowledge of income and expenses by *both* spouses. Problems arise when one spouse makes financial decisions without consulting the other. Because some attitudes and decisions about money stem from deep feelings associated with unmet needs, poor parental example regarding money management, or other influences, both spouses should examine their own feelings regarding money. If you fail to identify and resolve such fundamental issues, it can keep your family in financial chaos for many years.

PREPARING FOR HARD TIMES

Life will always be unpredictable, and hard times come to every family.

BECOMING DEBT FREE

If you want the freedom that comes from debt-free living, you have to be debt free. If you want to be debt free, you have to pay off all credit and stop paying interest—period. You don't have to pay some expert to find a new, improved, faster, less painful way to pay off all your credit. You just have to do it.

But the desire to be debt free and the belief that debt-free living is possible have to come first. Once you get the desire and believe you can do it, you can use these checkpoints to help on the rest of your journey to effective family financial management.

Checkpoint station #1 consists of three things. First, agree as a couple to live on less than you earn and to faithfully pay your tithes and offerings. Second, develop a detailed savings program. Third, come up with a detailed debt-elimination plan. Debt-elimination plans are simple. You must already budget a certain amount of your money for paying off your debts, so simply agree not to use that amount of money for any other purpose until *all* your debts are paid. Commit to focus on paying off the smallest debt first. When that debt is paid, apply that entire payment amount to the next largest debt, and so on.

Checkpoint station #2 includes the continuation of a controlled budget and the accumulation of a predetermined amount of savings, along with retirement reserves. At this point, your goal is to pay off all debt except the home mortgage.

Checkpoint station #3 continues the controlled budget and the saving/retirement plan. This checkpoint station also includes total debt elimination, including the home mortgage.

Checkpoint station #4 includes the continuation of a controlled budget with no new debt, and with an acceleration of your savings and retirement plan.

Unnecessary debt is a heavy burden to carry during times of economic decline. If you and your husband set reasonable financial goals early in marriage, you can avoid the pitfalls of being burdened by unnecessary debt.

For example, you can plan to budget carefully your husband's income, commit not to overextend yourselves in the purchase of an expensive home and furnishings, and agree to spend more time with your children and less money on things for them.

Where possible, agree to avoid debt that will force both of you to work outside the home. With the wisdom of long experience, many older couples—both those who have wisely avoided the debt trap and those who have learned from their past mistakes—often counsel young couples not to let money matter more than other things in life. They realize that commitment to the gospel of Jesus Christ and to loving family relationships yields life's greatest satisfaction.

LIVING ON ONE INCOME

If your circumstances permit, commit to living on one income even if you must decrease your standard of living. If there are two incomes, use the second income exclusively for savings or paying off debt. When your savings and retirement are adequate and all debt is paid off, prayerfully consider the best way to share your excess. Is there a missionary or college student in your family or your ward that could use some help? Is there an unemployed father who needs a job? Do you know a child who could use music lessons? Is there a worthy cause that needs volunteer help? Is there a single mother who needs free childcare? The possibilities are endless for a heart that is tuned in and ready to listen.

Whenever possible, it is the father—and therefore his income—that should provide the necessities of life for the family. Individual adaptation should always be made with serious thought and prayerful consideration by all family members.

Always remember that every family has financial difficulties. You can't control financial challenges that result from natural disasters, accidents, illness, unemployment, evil choices by others, weather, government leaders, or war. You *can* control your attitude and your ability to deal with financial problems or prosperity. You can control your pride, debt, envy, and selfishness. Trust your Father in Heaven and know that all things will work to your good when you're trying to keep the commandments.

CUTTING COSTS

One of the best ways to be a wise steward over the resources that come into your hands is to make sure each dollar you have is well used. Finding ways to save money on food, clothing, transportation, and housing can be great fun and provide huge rewards.

SAVING MONEY ON FOOD

My husband and I often have total strangers walk up to us in the supermarket, peer into our grocery cart, count our

13 gallons of milk, and say things like, "Boy, you folks ought to get a cow." When I go to the refrigerator searching for a little inspiration, what I usually find is wilted lettuce leaves, empty milk containers, iceless cube trays, and somebody's science fair project stinking up the whole joint.

Feeding a family is a thankless task. Let's face it, every time you cook something somebody eats it, and then you have to start all over. Nonetheless, even with all the bother of shopping for food, cooking the food, and then cleaning up after it, eating is one of the best ways to bring families together and make pleasant memories. It's well worth your effort to keep putting a meal on the table. And, with some creative thinking, you can save money while doing so.

BECOME MARKET SAVVY

Food manufacturers and retailers spend millions of dollars figuring out how to entice you into spending more money at the grocery store. Marketing studies have determined what forms of overhead music keep you in the store longer than others, what colors are better than others when it comes to packaging your food, and where to place high-profit products to increase sales. Marketers have you all figured out. Now, it's your turn to figure out the marketers. Train yourself to shop at your favorite neighborhood grocery store with new savvy, cunning, and skill. Here are a few tips:

• The highest profit items are placed at eye level in the store. The high and low shelves usually contain lower-priced items.

• You must check for unit pricing when looking for the best deal. Packaging can be deceiving and lead you to believe you're getting more for less, when you're really getting less for the same price—or, less for more.

• Be loyal to price, not brand names, and be willing to shop anywhere.

• Have a plan for your purchases. Buy the items on your list and then leave. The more time you spend in the store, the more money you spend.

USE GROCERY SHOPPING SMARTS

Entering a grocery store is much like going on a jungle safari. It's an adventure, and only the best prepared survive and thrive. The best hunters know their way around the grocery store. Ever wondered why you have to use a machete to cut through thousands of products before you can get a gallon of milk? Grocery stores are arranged in such a way as to force shoppers to hike through "willpower busters" (six candy bars for a dollar) in order to get to the basic and nutritious food at the end of the trail.

Before you leave home to go grocery shopping, glance through the Sunday newspaper or your favorite magazine for manufacturer's coupons, check the grocery chains' Web sites, and look at the local supermarkets fliers. You might find low prices at warehouse clubs like Costco or Sam's Club; but remember, they charge you each year for the privilege of shopping at their store. And if you have a small family, you may find it difficult to shop in bulk without something going to waste.

WATCH FOR
WILLPOWER BUSTERS

Willpower busters have less power over you when you make a list of what you need before you get to the store. Many times, willpower busters are not things you need. They just seem so tempting . . .

On the other hand, though, don't be so tied to your list that you neglect to take advantage of in-store specials on items you *regularly buy*. Look for sales on things you usually use and stock up.

Some people like to prepare their shopping list from a week's or month's worth of menus. I prefer to make a shopping list from the week's grocery ads and then figure out my menus from the best buys.

WATCH FOR SEASONAL DEALS

Be aware of seasonal deals. When food is in season and the supply is abundant, costs go down. You might consider cutting up, blanching, and freezing produce for later use—when it's not in season and nowhere near as inexpensive.

GROW AND PRESERVE
YOUR OWN GROCERIES

Grow all the food you can on your own property. Berries, grapes, fruit trees, and vegetable gardens are good for your body and your soul. If you don't have any ground available to you, use pots and planters or rent land nearby. Consider raising your own meat. Become as self-sustaining as possible. Ask yourself how long your family would survive if suddenly you couldn't go to the grocery store anymore.

For information on how to best grow food in your area contact local government or university sources. Learn the basics on how to preserve food. Drying, smoking or curing, salting, sugar preserving, canning or bottling, bin storage (spring houses, root cellars, cool dark rooms, or sand pits), cold storage, freezing, fermenting, and pickling are just some of the more common ways to store food for later use.

LIMIT PURCHASES OF
PREPACKAGED AND
CONVENIENCE FOODS

One of the best and least-known ways to cut back on the grocery bill is to cut back on pre-prepared foods and prepackaged meals. Packaging and processing adds to the cost of food. Rolled oats cost a fraction of the price of processed oat breakfast cereal. Fresh produce costs a fraction of the price of canned or frozen fruit. This is because each time someone handles the food item, a profit must be made. Therefore, every time an item of food goes through one more processing step, it adds to the final cost. This is why a whole turkey costs much less per pound than turkey steak.

You have to decide if the convenience of pre-prepared or pre-cut or pre-anything food is worth the extra cost.

At the same time, though, some convenience foods cost less than home-prepared items and save time. Day-old bread at the bakery thrift store, for example, is cheaper to buy than bread made at home.

CUT BACK ON TRIPS TO THE STORE

Each time you run to the store for a gallon of milk, you usually buy the milk and a lot of other things you don't really need. The fewer trips you make to the grocery store, the less you'll spend. If your local grocery stores are located near each other, it may be worth your time to shop the specials at each store. Yet, if you pay more than you save for the gas to chase around, then it doesn't make sense. It really helps the family food budget to limit major grocery shopping trips to once or twice a month, with small, in-between trips to buy milk and fresh produce.

SHOP SOLO

Try to shop solo when shopping for groceries. Sometimes husbands and children try to fill the basket with impulse items. Shop during off hours during the middle of the week or even late at night when one spouse can be home to tend the children. Remember to eat before you shop and stay on the lookout for unusual or discount food stores.

WHAT AND HOW TO BUY

When you see an item you normally buy on sale, buy enough of it to stock up for a few months or a year. Some stores will include an additional, reduced case lot price for items bought in bulk. When you buy in bulk you don't have to pay full price for an item and you can wait until it goes on sale again to purchase it.

Day-old bread and pastry stores, along with warehouse stores that sell perishable past- or near-code foods, can also save you money. (Remember to buy bread by weight and meat by the price per pound.)

BE CAREFUL ABOUT FOOD EATEN AWAY FROM HOME

Consider the *real* cost of any meal eaten away from home, including the tip, the gas used to get there and back, and the babysitter. Most meals eaten out will typically cost *four times* the amount the same meal would cost if prepared at home. Most families are better off limiting restaurant meals to special events like holidays and birthdays. Eating good food in a nice atmosphere with someone else doing the work or frequenting fast food establishments is one of life's pleasures, but doing so on a regular basis represents a choice between this pleasure and using that money for something else more important or lasting.

Many families lose sight of the dollars spent on fast food, such as hamburgers, malts, pizza, soft drinks, hot dogs, tacos, and other food eaten away from home. It all adds up quickly. Picnic basket candlelight dinners in the park, barbecues in the backyard, and bike-ride sack lunches are creative, inexpensive alternatives to more expensive restaurant meals.

If you are not satisfied with a restaurant meal, tell the management. Most of the time they won't make you pay for it. Also don't be afraid to ask for special deals for birthdays or group discounts.

FOOD STORAGE BASICS

Basic food items (based on a 2,300-calories-a-day diet) needed for one year for the average adult include:
- grains: 400 pounds (wheat, flour, rice, corn, oatmeal, pasta, barley, millet)
- powdered milk: 16 pounds
- sugars: 60 pounds (granulated sugar or honey)
- salt: 8 pounds
- cooking oil: 10 quarts (vegetable oil or shortening)
- dried legumes: 60 pounds (beans, split peas, or lentils)
- garden seeds or multivitamins (especially A and C)

Alternative Live storage includes:
- fresh taro
- sweet potatoes
- pigs
- chickens
- fish

All storage should include water
- a two-week supply of water is 14 gallons per person

Expanded food storage, for variety, taste, and nutrition, might include:
- meats (canned, freeze-dried, or frozen)
- cheese (canned, bottled, freeze-dried, or frozen)
- fruits (frozen, freeze-dried, canned, or dehydrated)
- vegetables (canned, bottled, frozen, or freeze-dried)
- yeast (baking soda, baking powder)
- vinegar
- spices
- soups

Other useful tips:
- Acquire a wheat grinder and a manual can opener to keep with your stored foods.
- If you store frozen foods, keep in mind that a long-term power outage could wipe out your entire deep-freeze reserve. Don't open the freezer during power outages. This will keep the cold in. Refer to your freezer's manual for advice on what to do if the power's been out too long to maintain a healthy, frozen temperature for your food.
- The method you use to store your food is not nearly as important as remembering to *use* your stored food. Rotate it on a regular basis. Eat from it regularly. Replenish it as needed. There's nothing worse than ten tubs of vegetable shortening that have all gone rancid.
- Get a copy of *Essentials of Home Production and Storage*. This great booklet is produced by the Church and includes ideas for personal and family preparedness; gardening; home food production, preservation, and storage; production of nonfood items; water storage; first-aid supplies; fuel and light; buying and selling storage items; inventory methods; and recipes.

A WORD ABOUT GENERIC BRANDS, COUPONS, AND FOOD CO-OPS

Most generic brands are as good as national brands. If in doubt, taste test a generic brand before buying a large quantity. Many stores also have an in-house brand that sells for substantial savings.

Keep in mind that coupons are a good deal only when they are for items you normally buy. Some stores will double or triple coupons while others offer their own in-store coupons. Many stores will match a competitor's price on the same item if you bring in the ad.

Consider joining a food co-op, where you can buy food for wholesale or reduced group rates. A food co-op is a group of people who join together to buy food in bulk at wholesale prices then split the food between the group members.

COOK FROM THE BASICS

Another great way to save money on the family food budget is to cook from basics. Think of inexpensive yet nutritious foods like beans, rice, pasta, and potatoes as your core meals. Keep these basics on hand for year-round use. Then add perishable food, such as meat and fresh produce, to complete your meal.

If you select meat and produce that's on sale or in season, you can create nutritious yet inexpensive meals year-round. If you buy meat in bulk—such as a roast or a turkey—you can cook the meat once at the first of the week and use what's left over the rest of the week disguised in other dishes. Look for a good price *per pound* for meat.

Rice, pasta, beans, potatoes, or other staples topped with leftover meat and inexpensive in-season produce provide great nutritional value for the dollar. Any leftover food at the end of the week will combine together to make great soup.

It's fun to make a family favorite dish like pizza or lasagna for a Friday night dinner. Weekends are also good times for cooking breakfast foods for supper because they're quick and easy. Cooked cereal, pancakes, waffles, muffins, or French toast along with eggs, milk, and fruit make quick and easy weekend dinners.

Here's an example of how this basic plan can work:

• Sunday: prepare a bulk meat meal (save leftover meat for the rest of the week).

• Monday: prepare a potato meal. Leftover chicken mixed with potatoes, fresh or frozen vegetables, and canned soup, for example.

• Tuesday: prepare a pasta meal. Leftover chicken tossed with herbs, garlic, some tomatoes, and farfalle pasta, for example.

• Wednesday: prepare a rice meal. Leftover chicken stir-fried with vegetables and served over rice, for example.

• Thursday: prepare a soup or bean meal. Use leftover chicken to make a noodle soup.

• Friday: prepare a favorite family meal.

• Saturday: prepare a breakfast meal.

You seldom need to use recipes for basic family meals unless it's for baked goods. Saving money on food includes learning to cook using basic ingredients with a little flair and creativity. On the other hand, some prepared foods such as frozen French fries, orange juice, and fish sticks save precious time and may be worth the money for the convenience they offer. Weigh the costs and benefits of saving money versus saving time.

FOOD STORAGE

A year's supply of food is great security for times of need or disaster; but it is also a great hedge against inflation. Most families can't afford to buy or find the place to store all the food their family would *normally* consume in one year. But most families, if motivated, can buy a year's supply of basic *life-sustaining* food for one year.

Accumulating a year's supply of food is a smart way to save money. When you buy food items in bulk and on sale for your home storage, you save money two ways. First, you buy in bulk at today's sale prices, and second, you have a huge hedge against inflation, because you'll be eating food tomorrow at yesterday's prices.

Buy basic food items that store reasonably well for long periods, such as grains, dried milk, legumes, sugar, salt, fat, and water. It's also wise to store a year's supply of garden seeds or multiple vitamins to supplement the diet. If you don't have the space to store a whole year's supply, store as much as you can. If you don't have the money to acquire a year's supply, then start your storage by obtaining supplies to last for a few weeks, then a month, then a few months, then a year. It is our obedience to this commandment that will bring blessings. And you are being obedient if you are setting money aside and purchasing food for storage—even if you can't afford to do it all at once.

SAVING MONEY ON CLOTHING

Clothes are protection from the elements and covering for your naked body.

They keep you warm in the winter and cool and comfortable in the summer. Forget the illusion that the clothes you wear will make you better looking or more admired. Why even bother buying clothes to impress your friends or your children's friends? It never works. People like you or your children for how they feel about *themselves* when they're around you. So get the focus off you and your need to impress. If you want to feel important and valued, try loving and caring about the people around you instead. Of course, this doesn't mean you can send your husband to work in sweatpants and a T-shirt. It's also important to dress appropriately for the setting and the occasion and to keep your clothes clean and well pressed, especially if you or your spouse must meet with clients, coworkers, or others during a business day.

Now that you're convinced that spending tons of money on clothes is really a foolish and insecure vanity, how do you stretch the dollars you *do* need to spend on clothes? For starters, quit buying clothes, at least for a while. If you put your mind to it, I'll bet you and your children can actually survive on the clothes you already have for quite some time.

CHECK THE LABELS

Next, always check the label for washing instructions before you buy. If you really want to stretch your clothing dollar, dry-clean–only clothes are not worth it. It's wiser to buy a few durable, timeless clothes that coordinate well with each other than to have the latest, trendy clothing that is continually redesigned to keep you spending. It usually takes years to acquire clothing shopping savvy, so be patient with your mistakes and learn from them.

PLAN AHEAD

The family wardrobe is an expense more easily managed by planning ahead so that you can get what you need for less money or get better clothes for the same amount of money. If you wait to shop until you need something, you'll have to pay the peak-of-the season price, and that's always higher. So buy summer clothes at the end of the summer and winter clothes at the end of winter to take advantage of clearance prices.

A MOTHER'S BASIC WARDROBE

While you're raising children it doesn't aways pay to buy clothing that soils easily and needs dry cleaning. Buy sturdy, practical, machine-washable clothing that can stand the test of dirt, spit up, and leaky diapers and still come out of the wash looking good. (Of course, it's always nice to have a few "fancier" outfits for formal occasions or dates. An outfit you look smashing in can do wonders for a stressed-out and overtired mom.)

It pays to shop in unusual places like secondhand and discount stores and to take advantage of extended family and friends who have good used clothing they want to get rid of. You can organize clothes-swapping organizations with your family, friends, or Relief Society units.

Buy clothing that is timeless in color and style. Neutral colors go with everything and can be mixed and matched. Pay attention to your husband's wardrobe. Men generally wear the same clothes year after year and decade after decade because men's clothing is less trendy and more functional. You don't have to keep up with the latest style. Create your own style. Your clothing should work for you, *not* make your life more expensive and stressful.

SEWING

The trick to saving money by sewing your own clothes at home is in knowing when to bother. If you realistically figure the costs and find you save money and love to sew, it may be worth it; but if you usually lose money and hate sewing, it's not worth it. If you're good at it, making prom dresses or a suit can save hundreds of dollars. If you're not good at it, making a prom dress or suit can cost hundreds of dollars because nobody will wear them. Sewing window treatments, recovering chair cushions, and cutting and hemming worn pants into shorts are some of the

quickest and easiest ways to save money by sewing.

Look at old or worn items of clothing with your creative eyes. For instance, when your children outgrow their jeans or get a hole in the knee, think of ways you can reuse the *unworn* fabric on that pair of pants. Worn or outgrown jeans can be cut into squares, pieced together, and used to make a variety of things like quilts, carry bags, pillow covers, or window toppers. When chair cushions wear out you can recover them to look like new with upholstery scraps. Most areas have several discount fabric and upholstery stores where you can buy material for a fraction of the retail price.

Large, flat sheets can also be made into clothing, drapery, blankets, bed ruffles, and pillowcases. Worn and flat king-sized pillows can be folded over, recovered, and made into throw pillows. You can make memory quilts for your children from squares cut from their worn or outgrown clothing. Wedding dresses can be remade into blessing dresses or baptism gowns.

DISCOUNT STORES

Discount department stores like T.J. Maxx, Marshalls, and Ross offer you first-quality overstock clothing from companies who have gone bankrupt and irregular goods.

Discounters such as Kmart, Target, and Wal-Mart are options for lower prices on clothing. Look for fabric that is durable and machine washable. Turn the clothing inside out to check for construction quality.

Remember to check out warehouse clubs like Costco and Sam's Club. What they lack in service and selection they often make up for in price. Remember, you won't have the luxury of dressing rooms.

Don't discount the values you may find at regular department stores. They usually have great clearance sales at the end of summer and after Christmas. Department stores usually offer superior service and guarantee satisfaction. Don't forget to check hybrid stores like Sears®.

Factory outlet stores offer name brand clothing for much less money than you'd find at your local department store. Many areas have an entire mall filled with a variety of factory outlet stores. Many clothing manufacturers have a factory outlet store near the sewing plant or warehouse where they sell seconds and irregulars along with wholesale samples.

Be sure to check for clothing purchases on-line at your favorite store for another way to stretch your clothing dollars.

THRIFT STORE SHOPPING

Young children grow so quickly that buying expensive, trendy clothes for tots and active grade-school children is a waste of money. Become a fan of thrift shops such as Deseret Industries. Donate any clothing you don't need and buy clothing there when you do need it.

When you spend only a few dollars for your children's clothes, you don't have to waste time worrying about holes and stains. Thrift stores like Deseret Industries also wash and sanitize everything they sell, so you have the added advantage of knowing what an article of clothing looks like after it's been washed.

There is an art to secondhand clothing shopping. You have to be willing to spend additional time sorting through outdated or worn pieces to find good quality used clothing. It helps to walk through the local mall and study the clothing displays for ideas on up-to-date looks you can duplicate at thrift-store prices. Classic cuts and neutral colors are always in style. Many articles of clothing are mis-sized or mislabeled—so check all departments. Leave the tags on clothing you may need to return.

DRESSING YOUNG CHILDREN FOR LESS

Many parents dress their young children to suit their own taste and show off the family income level. This is dumb. Young children should be allowed to wear inexpensive clothing they can soil and destroy as they work at the difficult task of growing up. Young children should never be taught to be clothing conscious when it comes to name brands and trendy styles. Shop clearance sales, take advantage of hand-me-downs, and be sure to check the thrift stores when buying children's clothing. Remember, dark colors hide stains.

Decide when enough is enough. A child's basic wardrobe includes underwear to last a week, a half dozen play outfits, one Sunday best outfit, a sweater or jacket, play shoes, and dress shoes, two pair of pajamas, and cold weather clothing like a coat, hat, boots, and gloves.

TEEN CLOTHING DOLLARS

Saving money on clothing when your children are teenagers requires a whole new strategy. Teens generally become more clothing conscious and want to look like and impress their peers. You might be asked to provide expensive name brand clothing or trendy clothes. If your child is old enough to ask for trendy name brand clothing, he's old enough to pay for *all* or *part* of the price.

Before your child is old enough for a minimum wage job, he can baby-sit, mow lawns, deliver newspapers, and do a host of other odd jobs to help with his own clothing budget. Teens have a way of adjusting their taste in clothes when they are required to earn all or part of the cost. Try to teach your teen by your own example that there are wiser ways to spend money than filling an already crowded closet with one more outfit or pair of shoes.

CLOTHING STORAGE

Keep a year's supply of durable new or used clothing in your storage program to meet your family's needs for at least a year. You'll want to remember seasonal needs and changing sizes. If possible, store quilts, blankets, sheets, and sleeping bags. Also include fabric, patterns, needles, and thread in your supplies. If possible, have a sewing machine available.

Remember to check the Internet for great clothing shopping experiences without leaving home.

SAVING MONEY ON TRANSPORTATION

One of the biggest roadblocks to debt-free living for the average family is the purchase of a newer and more expensive car than you need. Cars are never a good value for your money. Many of us buy cars to show off and get attention. Yet the best way to save money on a car is not to own one. If walking or taking public transportation is not an option, you can do the next best thing—drive an old car. If you drive two cars, you can consider selling one. The point is, the less money you sink into your cars, the better off you'll be.

If you have to buy a car, then it's important to remind yourself that a car is not a reflection of your success, personality, or self-worth. A car is not a legitimate way to boost your ego. A car is a swirling black vacuum that sucks up your money. It will not make you instantly popular to drive an expensive car—except with the car dealer.

A car is a form of transportation. A car takes you from point A to point B. The truth is, the cost of owning and operating a

motor vehicle is a nightmare if you consider payments, interest, depreciation, insurance, taxes, gasoline, oil, maintenance, repairs, tires, parking, tolls, license fees, registration, and all the other stuff that comes with car ownership. The average annual cost of owning and operating a vehicle eats up a major portion of your disposable income.

SHOPPING FOR INSURANCE

The initial price of the car is just the beginning. Insuring the car never ends. Insurance rates for the same coverage can vary by hundreds of dollars, so it pays to take time to shop around. Ask friends, check the Yellow Pages, call the state insurance department, check consumer guides, and call insurance companies and agents. This will give you an idea of price ranges and tell you which companies or agents have the lowest prices. Consider simple liability insurance for older cars.

The insurer you select should offer both fair prices and great service. It's smart to talk to a number of insurers and get a feeling for the quality of their service and ask them what they would do to lower your costs. You can check the company's financial rating and get price quotes.

To lower the rate you pay, ask for the highest deductible you can afford and consider dropping expensive comprehensive and collision insurance when the car gets old. The purpose of insurance is to protect against big losses, not against the things you can afford to pay on your own. The deductible is the amount of money you pay before you make a claim. By requesting higher deductibles on collision and comprehensive coverage, you can lower your costs substantially.

The blue book available at dealers and banks can tell you how much the car is worth. Also, if you have adequate health insurance, you may be paying for duplicate medical coverage in your auto policy. In some states, eliminating this coverage could lower your personal injury protection cost a lot.

Before you buy a new or used car, it makes sense to check into insurance costs. Cars that are expensive to repair or that are favorite targets for thieves have much higher insurance premiums. Costs tend to be lowest in rural communities and highest in central cities where there is more traffic congestion. Some companies offer discounts to motorists who drive fewer than a predetermined number of miles a year. Others offer discounts for automatic seat belts or air bags. Some insurers offer discounts for having more than one car, for not having any accidents in three years, for drivers over 50 years of age, for taking driver training courses, for having anti-theft devices, for having anti-lock brakes, and for having teenagers who get good grades.

NEW OR USED?

It usually doesn't make financial sense to buy a new car—they simply depreciate in value too quickly. A good used car is usually a better deal. Before looking at used cars, it helps to evaluate your family needs in terms of size, body, style, and how much money you're willing to spend.

When buying a car from an individual, it's better to deal with someone you know, because friends are less likely to lie about why they are selling the car. As a general rule, people don't sell cars that are running well, so that's the risk you take when you buy a used car. It helps to be cautious. Rental car companies sell late-model cars that are generally well maintained and driven primarily on the highway. Car dealers can also be a good source, but you usually have to pay more. Choose someone who has a good reputation and who has been in business for several years. You can contact the Better Business Bureau to find out about complaints against the dealer. If possible, get the name of the previous owner of the car and talk to him.

The U.S. Customs Service sells seized automobiles, and the U.S. General Services Agency sells surplus property. Other sources include the IRS, the Department of Defense, and local financial institutions and police departments. When considering a used car, it helps to check *Consumer Reports* annual Buying Guide in the April Car Issue and other such sources.

Rely on a Trusted Mechanic

After you've checked the used car yourself for obvious problems, it's wise to have a trusted mechanic check out the car you are considering and have him tell you about any problems. Mechanical problems don't need to prevent you from buying a car, but you should know how much it will cost to repair and figure that in as you consider the purchase price.

If you hope to negotiate a good price, you need to be prepared to walk away from the deal even if you fall in love with the car. And remember that the purchase price is only one of several factors to consider. Depreciation, gas mileage, repair costs, and insurance rates should also affect the cost.

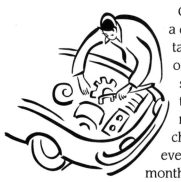Once you buy a car, it pays to take good care of it. You really should read the owner's manual, change the oil every three months or three thousand miles, have hoses and belts replaced regularly, and rotate the tires at recommended intervals:

TAKE CARE OF WHAT YOU HAVE

Most women don't take the time to understand how to take good care of the car they drive until something goes wrong. This is dumb. If you drive it, you should know how to take care of it. It really pays to read your owner's manual for an overview of general maintenance for your individual car. General car maintenance includes checking things like fluids, oils, tire pressure, and filters.

• Fluids of a car include power steering fluid, brake fluid, windshield washer fluid, and coolant. Power steering fluid helps your car steer easily. Brake fluid prevents excessive brake wear. Washer fluid helps keep the driver's view clear. Coolant keeps your engine from overheating. Coolant should be half antifreeze and half water. The rest of the fluids can be poured in straight. Fluids are vital for engine performance and vehicle safety.

• For best engine performance, it's recommended that you change your oil every 3,000 miles. As you operate your engine, heat, friction, and gases from combustion break down the lubricating properties of the oil. Changing your oil gets rid of contaminants and maintains optimum lubrication. The inexpensive cost of an oil change is cheap insurance that prevents the failure of an expensive engine.

• Tire pressure should be checked once or twice a month because tires are not totally sealed. Proper tire pressure is imperative for safe driving. To know how much pressure your tires need, look on the sidewall of a tire and it should give the pressure needed for that tire. When your tire pressure is low, your gas mileage goes down, unnecessary tire wear occurs, and the ride of the car will not be as smooth.

• Filters help keep an engine clean and efficient. They also extend the life of an engine. The main filters on a car are the fuel filter, air filter, and oil filter. If you use oxygenated fuel, check your air filter once a year. Your oil filter is changed with every oil change. When a filter is clogged or dirty, your engine will not run efficiently because it will not be able to breathe.

If you don't want to mess with any of this stuff, you can go to a quickie shop that will do all this for you. Keep records of what is done for future reference. Remember, if you take care of your car, it will take care of you.

SAVING MONEY ON HOUSING

You don't have to have a big fancy house, town house, apartment, or condo to be an absolutely wonderful person. The type of house you live in will not make you happy, healthy, or wise. Your house or apartment keeps the rain off, gives you a

place to get warm, affords a little privacy, and provides a setting for family gatherings, meals, play, and memory making. It is this last part that really makes a house (or an apartment) a home, and what is most important. After all, what attracts people to a house is not the brickwork, but the people who live there.

Some of your best memories will be made in the most humble living arrangements with the most meager resources. Early married living arrangements certainly give you a better appreciation for anything that comes later. Housing doesn't have to be first rate to offer some first-rate memories. On the other hand, where you live is probably the biggest financial decision you'll ever make, after your choice of occupation. If you spend too much or too little on your housing, it's possible to put a huge dent in quality family life. Even though housing generally takes the biggest bite from your budget, it's easy to ignore sound decision making. Housing decisions have to be made with your heart and your head.

RENT OR BUY?

The decision between renting and owning boils down to a financial choice and a lifestyle choice. Any analysis of buying a home solely on financial grounds is going to fall short because the value of home ownership cannot be found in money alone. Neighborhood pride, living space control,

privacy, building equity, tax write-offs, and building up a community are advantages that mean a great deal to some people. Renting, on the other hand, offers the advantage of fixed payments for housing, no accountability for breakdowns, fix-ups or repairs, freedom from yard work, and the ability to pick up and move at a moment's notice.

Saving Money on Rent

To save money on rent, consider helping the landlord with management, yard work, maintenance, or cleaning in return for a reduction of your monthly payment. Many landlords are happy to deduct any improvements you make to the property from your rent. Consider any skill you have as barter for all or part of your payment.

Some young couples choose to live with a senior citizen who needs help with medicine, meals, and cleaning in exchange for rent. Some couples buy a house and rent out the basement, thereby enabling them to make two house payments a month. Other older couples buy a second home, townhouse, or condo and make the mortgage payment by renting it to younger couples or their adult children. If you're creative, adaptable, and willing to work for what you get, you can find ways to save money on housing.

BUYING A HOUSE

If you decide the time is right to buy a house, the best shopping strategy is not to start with the house. Better housing decisions are made when you take the time to look at yourself and your family first. A home should suit you in design, cost, appearance, size, and type. It helps to take a good look at your living patterns, then decide what is important to you and your

family and what is not. For instance, if privacy is important, you need to look for a secluded location. If you like to party with family and friends, you should look for a home with a large kitchen and family room. If your children lead separate lives, you need to look for a house with ample bedroom space that will keep them from disrupting each other. If you hate home repairs, you should look for a newer home.

Location

Once you understand your needs, it's better to focus first on location then later on the actual house. As you look for a good location, keep in mind how long it will take you to get to work and other places you frequently visit. It pays to become aware of zoning ordinances, building codes, local property tax ranges, and the availability and price of utilities. It's wise to pay attention to the neighbors, local schools, shopping areas, fire and police protection, libraries, parks, post office, banks, hospitals, churches, and services like water, sewage, and garbage collection. The yard is another important location consideration. People who love yard work should look for big lots or yards and people who hate yard work should look for small lots or plan to hire a gardener.

Affordability

After you consider the location, the next important question to answer is how affordable is the house. When you talk to your realtor or banker about a mortgage, he'll tell you how much money you qualify to borrow, based on your income. These figures give you limited information, because realistically you may or may not be able to afford a house in that price range. These figures give the lender and agent an idea of whether you are qualified to get a loan, but they don't really tell *you* if you can afford the house. These figures don't take into account the number of children you have, the stability of your income, the amount you give to charity, or the amount you regularly need to save. A good way to be house poor is to borrow right up to your credit limit.

Most experts say the purchase price should either not exceed 2½ times your annual income or monthly payments should approximate weekly income. After you consider what the experts say, it's time to sit down, be realistic, and settle on a reasonable amount that won't strap you down. There are always unexpected expenses that come out of nowhere. There really aren't many bargains out there in the real estate market. The law of supply and demand works pretty well. If a buyer pays less initially, he'll most likely make up the difference through higher maintenance costs or declining resale price as the house ages.

Because houses wear out, looking for a new home and looking for an older home require two different strategies. There is not as much room to bargain on the price of a new home as there is on an older home. Quality of material and workmanship are important to a new home. How well these materials have stood the test of time is important when considering an older home. When the IRS allows landlords of rented houses a depreciation allowance, it is based on the assumption that a building will wear out in 40 years.

It's important to find out about the person from whom you will be buying the house. Do all you can to make sure the seller has not misrepresented the condition of the house. Be sure to obtain clear title to the property. When selling a home you can cut realtor costs by negotiating for a lower commission, using a discount broker, or selling the home on your own.

Building

Before hiring a builder, it's wise to check with the local office of the National Association of Home Builders and the Better Business Bureau to see if they have had any complaints. Ask your builder for the name of his bank, then visit the bank and talk with one of the commercial officers about the builder. Ask the builder for his business or home number and the names of a few people he has built houses for. Then call and see what they think about the quality of his work.

Mortgage

Most of this home-buying business will finish up with a mortgage. A mortgage is money you borrow, then hand over to buy property at the same time the property becomes security for the loan—which you pay off over a long period of time with interest in regular installments. Obtaining the mortgage and buying the property are two separate transactions, even though they take place at the same time at a single sitting called a closing. At the closing you receive title to the property; that is, you become the actual owner with all of an owner's legal rights and obligations. If you fail to repay the loan, the lender can take possession of the property and foreclose or sell the house to repay the debt. The lender has a lien on the property until it's paid for. A lien is a creditor's legal claim on a property for the satisfaction of a debt.

Tax Deductible Interest

Mortgages are usually the least expensive loans, and the interest is tax deductible. While the interest rate on mortgages is comparatively low, the total dollar amount of interest you pay on a home mortgage is huge. Most homeowners pay two or three times more in interest than the house sold for in the first place.

If you don't plan to keep the house until the mortgage is paid off, it's a good idea to figure out the costs and benefits of the different kinds of mortgages over the period of time you plan to stay. The longer you plan to stay in the house, the more valuable the shorter mortgage.

How Long Should I Hold on to My Home?

Most experts recommend that you hold on to your property for five to seven years to make purchasing a house or condominium worthwhile. Owning property for three years or less virtually guarantees that you will lose money because buying a home can cost you as much as 6 percent in closing costs, including 1 percent of the loan amount for every point on your mortgage loan plus other fees. Probably no more than 40 percent of your gross income should go toward paying off debt.

THE PARABLE OF ENOUGH

Keep reminding yourself that you have enough, you do enough, and you are enough. If you are listening with gratitude, you will discover that your life is blessed and brimming over with every good thing. Open your heart to the wonder of your life and thank God for the privilege of being alive one more day.

Perhaps the most underrated way to be happy is to learn to appreciate what you already have. If you have a grateful heart for everything you already possess . . . you will always be rich and always have enough. When you're having a bad day and feeling down because you feel you don't have enough, read this story out loud to yourself.

Once there was a young girl who lived in a small house in a small town. Except for having to do the dishes, make her bed, and clean her room, the young girl had a pretty good life.

"When I grow up," the girl said to herself one day, "I will live in a large white house out in the country and I will have a small, quiet family. I will be wise, rich, and famous. I will hire a maid to cook and clean. My husband will cherish me and my children will honor me. When I am grown up enough, then I will be happy."

The girl got into her pajamas, brushed her teeth, and went to bed. Then she woke up in the morning, went to school, and soon she was grown up. After she graduated from high school, the girl dreamed of going to the university, but her parents didn't have enough money.

"There is never enough," the girl said to herself. "When I have enough money to go to the university, then I will be happy."

So the girl took three jobs, one at the library, one cleaning apartments for her landlord, and one cooking at the diner. After three years of working three jobs and studying at the university, the young girl was tired and lonely.

"When I don't have to work and someone loves me enough, then I will be happy," the girl said.

Later, a young man asked the girl to marry him. She said yes, quit her three jobs and school and went to live with the young man in a tiny apartment without windows. Soon the girl was lonely again because now her husband was working three jobs and studying at the university.

"When I have enough children to keep me company, then I will be happy," the girl said.

The girl had two babies before her second wedding anniversary.

"I never have enough sleep," the girl said. "When I have enough sleep, then I will be happy."

One day the girl sat down at the kitchen table covered with spilled milk and said, "There is not enough money to finish my degree at the university. When I have enough money to finish my degree, then I will be happy."

So the girl saved her money, then went back to school to finish her degree. After many papers and late-night study sessions while rocking her fussy babies and studying for exams, the girl graduated from the university.

Then one day the girl said, "There is not enough room in this house. I have too many children and they are too noisy. When I have a large house in the country, then I will be happy."

So the girl saved her money. Then she found out she was going to have another baby. She was not expecting this news.

"I have too many babies," the girl said. "I don't have a big enough house or enough strength. I will be happy when I stop having babies."

Finally, after many years, the girl and her family bought a large house in the country.

"I don't have enough energy to keep up this large house and clean up after the children," the girl said. "When the children are raised and I can move back to a small house, then I will be happy." The years went by, the children were growing up, and the girl was still waiting. Her husband didn't always cherish her. Sometimes he ignored her and watched basketball on the television.

"You don't give me enough attention," the girl told her husband. "You love basketball more than you love me."

"But I keep the car filled with gas and make waffles every Saturday," her husband answered.

The girl was not listening.

The girl's children didn't always honor her. Sometimes they said mean things and came home after curfew.

"You children don't obey me enough or keep your rooms clean enough," the girl said to her children.

"But we are growing up and soon we will be gone and you will miss us," the children answered.

The girl was not listening

"I don't have enough help around the house," the girl said one day as she sorted the socks. "I still have to cook my own meals and clean my own house. My children are noisy, not quiet, and I live in a red brick house, not white."

The socks did not answer. The girl went to a therapist because she was talking to socks. The therapist told the girl that her family did not understand or appreciate her enough. The therapist said that the girl must go home and go to bed and not get out until she was appreciated and understood. The girl was glad. She did not want to get up because her family was too big and too noisy and they did not love her enough.

The girl stayed in bed for a long time. She had lots of time for thinking.

"Why didn't you make me wise or rich or famous?" the girl said to God one night. "Why didn't you give me a husband and children who would honor and cherish me? Why do I have to work so hard? Why don't I ever have enough?"

"You've always had enough," God said. "But you weren't listening."

The girl thought for a long, long while.

That night, the girl dreamed a new dream. She dreamed that what she always wanted was a red brick house, a husband who made waffles on Saturday, and many noisy children to keep her company.

The next day, the girl got out of bed. She did not go back to the therapist. The girl found her husband watching a basketball game on television. She sat on his lap and kissed him. She found her children yelling in the family room. She hugged them, one by one. Then she walked downstairs to the laundry room and talked to the dirty socks. The socks answered her because the woman was listening.

TO PAY OFF YOUR MORTGAGE EARLY

- Check with your bank or lending institution about your contract first, then consider variations in your payment pattern. Anything you pay above the minimum payment should go straight to principal.
- Make one extra principal payment each year.
- Pay every two weeks instead of once a month.
- Apply all the second wage-earner's income toward the house loan.
- Use tax-free retirement funds to pay off your mortgage.
- Ask your parents to give you your inheritance early.
- Refinance for a lower interest rate and/or a shorter payback period.

Saving for a Down Payment

If you're wondering how much to save before buying, experts suggest having between 3 and 10 percent of a house's sale price in cash to cover the down payment and closing costs. Also, just because you can afford to rent in an area doesn't mean you can afford to buy there. If the monthly cost of buying would be about the same as for renting and you intend to stay in the area, you're better off buying.

Home Equity Loans

It's tempting to borrow money against your home for consumer goods by adding a home-equity loan to the mortgage; but please beware, it makes no sense to borrow *more* money when your house is on the line. Owning a home free and clear gives you a sense of security that money can't buy. Even if hard times come, you will at least have a roof over your head.

GENERAL HAGGLING ADVICE FOR ANY PURCHASE

- Always ask for a discount. What have you got to lose?
- Say something like "Oh, that much?" then wait for the salesman to answer. They may offer less.
- Don't forget to check the Internet to come up with rival stores' offers. Go shopping with those offers in hand.
- Look for flaws in the merchandize. Then say, "I don't want to pay full price for something that's defective."
- Before handing over your card or cash, ask the salesman to throw in something extra for goodwill.
- Tell the salesman how much you are willing to spend, especially if it's less than the ticketed price.
- Be nice to the salesman. They often reciprocate with a better deal.
- Ask for a discount when you pay cash up front.
- If buying a large quantity, ask for a quantity discount.
- Ask to speak to the manager when negotiating for a discount. Minimum-wage sales clerks often do not have the power to cut any deal.

FITNESS AND BEAUTY

A physical fitness program for a mother does *not* include jumping to conclusions, flying off the handle, and running up the electric bill. A physical fitness program for mothers should be more like the oft-quoted saying by Michelangelo: "I saw the angel in the marble and I just chiseled till I set him free." A mother needs to remember the beautiful spirit inside her body and set it free.

Take time to exercise, eat a healthy diet, and get adequate sleep to preserve your physical and spiritual health. You should also take the time to keep yourself looking your best and feeling good by maintaining a simple beauty routine. Remember, though, a beauty routine is what you do to keep yourself clean and attractive and feeling good. A *preoccupation* with your physical appearance to the neglect of more important or eternal mat-

ters is called vanity. And vanity is most often a symptom of inner insecurity or a woman's lack of ability to find herself beautiful in the natural state.

Clothing, hairstyles, and makeup need not consume too much of your thoughts or time. Choose a simple hairstyle, comfortable clothing, and a beauty routine that's quick and easy. Then forget about yourself and focus on others. When you focus on others, you feel beautiful inside and radiate a kind of loveliness that can't be bought for any price. That kind of beauty never fades with time or diminishes with age.

LOVE YOUR BODY

Women as a general rule tend to dislike or be dissatisfied with their bodies and their appearance. Maybe it's simply a lack of eternal perspective. Maybe you compare yourself with others, or perhaps you forget to be grateful for your unique gifts.

You *can* live joyously with the body you've been given. Your body is the crowning achievement of all God's creations. Don't focus on what you don't like about your body and fail to remember that you are eternally blessed simply to have one. Taking good care of your body is really a way of honoring God's gift to you and the earthly home for your spirit. There was a time when you shouted for joy to have the chance to obtain your body and come to earth. You were not teasing.

COUNT YOUR BLESSINGS

The best cure-all for the "I hate my body" blues is a good blessing-counting session. Here are some ideas to get you started. Be grateful that you can use your body—and its large number of parts—to:

- run
- walk
- hold a crying baby on your hip all day long
- play tag with your five-year-old
- make silly faces that send your one-year-old into fits of laughter
- smile reassuringly at your 16-year-old daughter as she runs to answer the door on her first date
- crawl around the floor with your baby in search of adventure
- swing at the park with your ten-year-old
- carry out your favorite hobby: cooking, playing the piano, singing, gardening, writing, reading
- wink at your husband when he walks into the room
- cheer your heart out at a football game

WHY IS PHYSICAL FITNESS IMPORTANT?

Being physically fit isn't something you do so you can look good. It's something you do so you can feel good. And even though it may seem impossible to find time to stay in shape, it's well worth the effort. Even if you have to get Dad or a baby-sitter to watch the kids for a while so you can work out, you

shouldn't feel guilty for taking the time to improve and maintain your health. The Surgeon General's office of the United States has determined that regular exercise will:

- reduce your risk of dying from coronary heart disease
- reduce your risk of developing high blood pressure, colon cancer, and diabetes
- keep your bones, muscles, and joints healthy
- help you control your weight while building lean muscles and reducing body fat
- help control joint swelling and pain associated with arthritis
- reduce symptoms of anxiety and depression
- promote improvement in mood and general feelings of well-being
- reduce blood pressure in some women with hypertension

Certainly, your family wants a healthy and happy mom. Let them know of your desire to stay in shape and ask them to help you find the time.

HOW MUCH EXERCISE DO I NEED?

The United States Department of Health and Human Services issues a variety of

---

12 WAYS FOR BUSY MOMS TO FIND TIME FOR EXERCISE

1. Get up ten minutes earlier and do some stretching or strength training in the morning.
2. Turn on some fun tunes and dance with small children for a half hour. You can play the hokey pokey, make up other musical activities, or just dance around in circles.
3. When the weather's nice, take the kids on a walk every day. Pushing a stroller will add resistance and strengthen your muscles.
4. Tell your husband that this is important to you and make an agreement that he'll watch the kids while you spend an hour exercising three times a week.
5. Find a few other moms in your ward or neighborhood who want to get in shape—or stay in shape—and start a baby-sitting/exercise co-op with them.
6. Take a community-education fitness class. Sign your children up for one too.
7. Garden.
8. Count heavy housework, such as vacuuming, mopping, and sweeping, as exercise.
9. Go on a family bike ride several times a week.
10. Play with your kids: jump rope, hopscotch, kick a ball around, play tag.
11. Find three times during the day that you can exercise for 10 minutes: run up and down the stairs, do squats and leg lifts, do push-ups and crunches.
12. Ask the Young Women president in your ward if one of the girls needs to complete a service project for the personal progress program. Suggest that one of the girls volunteer to watch your kids for 45 minutes three times a week while you work out at home, at the park, or at the gym.

---

recommendations for staying healthy. Among those is the recommendation that adults get at least 30 minutes of physical activity every day. Children and teenagers should get 60 minutes of physical activity every day.

Your 30 minutes can be broken into two 15-minute sessions and can be as simple as going for a walk or as planned out as going to the gym. Simply put: break a sweat every day. In addition to 30 minutes of physical activity, you should also incorporate some strength training and endurance exercises, such as squats, crunches, leg lifts, or weight training.

MAKE TIME TO STAY FIT

Regular, consistent exercise is a must for your physical, emotional, and spiritual health; but actually making the time to exercise is a lifelong challenge. Finding and making time to exercise when you're a mother is *never* easy. If you're pregnant

10 TIPS FOR LOOKING PUT-TOGETHER

1. Find a simple hairstyle. You don't have to go along with the latest craze in hairstyles. Find a classic style that looks good on you, not the latest model. Look at your hair and see what it has to offer. If your hair is fine and straight, find a style that looks great straight or blown dry with a round brush. If your hair is curly, find a style that lets you shampoo, comb, and run. Every woman knows what a bad hair day is and most would rather feel put-together. So make the best of what God gave you. One of the best investments you can make is a good hair stylist. A good simple haircut can save you time, money, and a lot of aggravation.

2. Allow yourself to age gracefully. You don't have to color your hair to look good. Coloring your hair is time-consuming and can be expensive. Consider allowing your hair to age gracefully. As your hair grays with age, it complements your skin tone changes and gives you a mature and wise look. Growing older is not something to be ashamed of or to hide. As the years pass, heredity takes its toll. Learn to love your new body shape, hair color, and skin changes. (Of course, if you color your hair because some blonde highlights make you look good or because color thickens your otherwise limp hair, or because you just love red, that's great. A little fun color is often just the ticket to complete your look.)

Look at your wardrobe. If you haven't purchased any new clothing for a while, go shopping. Every wardrobe needs some updating every decade or so. Your life changes constantly and your wardrobe should change with it. When you have young children you need wash-and-wear clothing in colors that hide stains. As you and your children age, dress to suit your own fancy. If you've always wanted to wear purple, go for it.

3. Apply makeup sparingly and well. Seek out help if you want to learn how to apply makeup. You may want to attend a class during Relief Society enrichment night or go for a free makeover at the local department store. Most professionals tell you to choose makeup that is good for your skin and matches your skin tones and type (oily, normal, dry, or combination.) Accentuate your eyes and lips with colors that closely resemble natural shades. Makeup should accentuate your natural beauty, not make you look made up and false.

you're cautioned about high-impact exercise. If you're nursing you're tied to a feeding schedule so tight you can't break away for long. If you have preschoolers they tend to whine for a hug whenever you start moving too quickly. Life with children is always hectic and busy, but if mom doesn't take care of herself, who will?

When you take appropriate care of your physical body, you're doing something for yourself *and* your family. You don't have to look like a movie star. Throw out your scales, forget about dieting, and focus on eating a healthy diet, drinking plenty of water, getting adequate sleep, and maintaining some kind of exercise program.

4. Select clothing that looks best on your figure type. Solid colors and long lines make you appear thinner and taller. Any horizontal line in your clothing will cut you in half and draw attention to that part of your body. Select clothing that isn't too tight or trendy. Go shopping for clothing by yourself and take your time. Try on many different types of clothing and select what makes you feel great. You don't have to spend a lot of money to look great. Buy clothing that is well made and that highlights the part of your body you want to draw attention to. Select a hemline length that looks best on your legs. For instance, if you have large calf muscles you might look best in knee- or-ankle length skirts and dresses and not in ones that hit you in the middle of your calf.

5. Be true to your personality and taste. Don't dress or wear your hair to please someone else. Decide what *you* like. If you have an outdoor personality, find a look that serves your rugged life. If you are feminine and romantic, don't be afraid to dress dramatically with all the lace and ribbon you desire. Notice menswear. It doesn't go out of fashion. Select clothing and hairstyles that are functional and don't come and go with the changing seasons.

6. Go for neutral colors. Neutral colors are colors that go with everything. Colors like navy blue, tan, white, and black will go with everything in your closet. A basic wardrobe will go further if you stock it with neutral colors. A dress, skirt, blazer, blouse, pants, and shoes in neutral colors can be combined with any color clothing.

7. Keep exercising. Exercise helps you look and feel great. Your muscles, bones, and skin all need the benefit of regular, consistent exercise. When you feel better, you look better, naturally.

8. Don't wear peek-a-boo socks. Match your stockings to your clothing or shoes or both. That means if you're wearing black shoes and slacks, white socks will stand out like a traffic light on your ankles.

9. Find out what colors you look good in. There are lots of fads for discovering your "season" or the spectrum of colors that you look best in. Most of the time, you know what these colors are because when you wear them, you always receive the most compliments.

10. Stay clean. It takes some extra time, but keep your body, hair, clothing, shoes, and coats in good repair and clean.

BEAUTY ROUTINES

Although we should all be cautious about letting the way we look control the way we feel, there is some truth to the statement "you've got to look good to feel good." Sometimes all it takes to get you feeling better is a little lipstick or a new haircut. Being stuck in the middle of an endless parade of messy diapers, baby spit-up, and toddler messes can make a mom feel quite frazzled. So frazzled that it may be tempting to give into the stress and

give up your own needs: a shower, makeup, a hairbrush. Some days this will even be necessary; getting dressed, let alone showering, will seem impossible. On other days, make the effort to shower, put on some makeup, and fix your hair. When you look put together, it's a little bit easier to actually start putting other things together—like the kitchen, the playroom, the bathroom . . .

Make your beauty routine simple. If it takes you more than 45 minutes to get ready to go somewhere, you do *not* have a simple beauty routine. If it takes you *less* than 30 seconds, you might want to give your appearance a little more thought. Your beauty routine starts when you step into the shower and ends when you're dressed and out the door. This does not include the time it takes you to eat breakfast, feed the kids, and get them ready to leave the house—that could be hours! A sample beauty routine would likely include the following:

- shower/bathe
- shave armpits and legs
- apply moisturizer
- apply deodorant
- blow dry and style hair
- apply makeup
- brush teeth
- get dressed

EXERCISER'S LAMENT

My two-year-old just ate some ants
Before he tipped over four houseplants.
My mate says, "Hon, how 'bout a date?"
I'm sorry, Dear, I'm running late.
Bishop says, "We need more work."
But I'm already half berserk.
My doctor says to exercise;
Where'd that fat come from on my thighs?
Can't get my visiting teaching done
My car's a wreck and so's my son.
Sometimes I wonder what I'll do,
That's when I always get the flu.

THINGS I WISH MY MOTHER HAD TOLD ME

♥ Everybody has two chances to have a happy childhood. The first is when you're growing up, and the second is when your children are growing up.

♥ All of us can do our work, however hard, for one day.

♥ Most unhappy people haven't discovered what work they want to do.

♥ Nothing is really work unless you'd rather be doing something else.

♥ In the end, satisfaction comes from a job well done, not from money and things.

♥ You don't have to be great to start but you do have to start to be great.

♥ Your house is not you. Your clothes are not you. Your husband is not you. Your car is not you. Your children are not you. Your possessions are not you. Your job is not you. Your volunteer work is not you. Who are you? Find out.

♥ The only people who care what your house looks like don't make good friends anyway.

♥ Dry-clean–only clothes are not worth it.

♥ The whole family can vaporize at the exact moment when it's time to do the dishes. Everybody wants to save the world but nobody wants to help Mom with the dishes.

♥ You will never be through with housework. So just put in your hours, then be done with it for the day. Homemaking, however, takes a lifetime—work at it constantly.

♥ Your family will not remember the color of the food you fixed for supper 20 minutes after they've eaten it. So don't spend your life in the kitchen.

♥ Children always wet the bed, throw up, or get a nosebleed right after you change their sheets.

♥ If you never get around to getting your children dressed, you won't have to get them into their pajamas at night.

♥ Eat, drink, and be merry, for soon it will be time to do the dishes.

♥ Don't worry about how your children look. Be concerned with how they feel.

♥ If you miss the joy in the growing season, you miss it all.

♥ When you take your child's hand, you hold a piece of heaven.

♥ The best "toys" you can give your child are rocks, sticks, clouds, trees, water, earth, and sunshine.

♥ Each moment with your child will never come again.

♥ Teach your child to relish and savor the changing seasons inside and outside himself.

♥ If you don't do it . . . who will?

♥ With a child, anything is possible.

UNDERSTANDING THE BASICS END NOTES

There will be many times when you'll wonder about your choice to be a mother. It may be late at night when your baby won't stop crying or when you're waiting up for a teenager who has lost his way. You will be exhausted physically, emotionally, mentally, and spiritually. In moments of doubt like these, try to remember that by small and simple things—like mothers who never stop loving God, themselves, and their children—great things are brought to pass. Believe. The love you feel will sustain you through the dark nights.

You, who cannot make a simple raindrop or grain of sand, have been privileged to work in partnership with your husband and God to create and nurture totally unique, one-of-a-kind human beings. There is nothing more important or challenging, nothing more Godlike, nothing more exhausting, nothing more humbling, nothing else worth the work and worry—nothing, absolutely nothing. No amount of money, possessions, or notoriety comes close. Loving and leading a child is the most important work you will ever do.

Motherhood is a hard and often thankless job. You're popped on, puked on, spit on, chewed on, peed on, kicked, and pinched. You're screamed at, have food thrown at you and insults hurled at you. You eat cold meals, wear stained clothes, and never get any sleep. When the day finally comes that your child is capable of being a pleasant, mature, adult friend, he *leaves* . . . for a mission, work, college, or to get married.

There will be dark hours and days when you'll doubt your ability to be the kind of mother God wants you to be, when you find yourself racked with guilt for your weaknesses past and present. If you approach God with a broken heart and a contrite spirit, he will affirm to you that you're loved as you are and that your efforts are appreciated and valued. He will forgive and strengthen you. He will give you the will to go on. He will whisper to your soul that what you are doing is worth it—no matter how hard it is or how many times you've messed up.

Please don't worry about measuring up to some ideal standard in your mothering. There are no perfect mothers. There are no perfect children. We're all in the same boat, rowing as fast as we can. I've never met a mother who thought she did it right. So if you doubt yourself, you have a lot of company.

You don't have to measure your success as a mother by the way your children turn out or compare yourself or

your children to anyone else. You don't have to handle everything with dignity, bravery, nobility, and wisdom at all times. You have to simply be yourself and offer your love. The greatest treasure you have to give your children is *you*.

We never obtain anything of real worth unless we're willing to pay the price. Becoming a righteous mother who loves, leads, and creates an eternal family comes with a price—that price is your own life. As you offer yourself, you will discover what *real* loving is all about. It doesn't matter if anyone else, including your own family, thinks what you do is important or appreciates you, for God does. Open yourself up to the potential of what you are beginning. You are laying the foundation of your future kingdom.

Motherhood will teach you to savor the commonness of your life and link your heart to generations past and those yet to come. Motherhood will teach you to love someone more than yourself and give a

dimension of sacredness to everything you do. Never trade this opportunity for a mess of pottage.

Keep listening to your heart. After years and years of nurturing, encouraging, feeding, hugging, reading, and cleaning, you will be given what you desire most: the ability to love and be loved. Your heart will open to the sweet essence of another human being in ways you now don't understand. You will be transformed as you transcend yourself. Your love can become your children's semblance of the Savior's love.

So on those good days *and* those bad days, choose motherhood again with even greater tenderness, awe, and joy. By small and simple things, like making dinner, washing dishes, and rocking babies, great things are brought to pass. Believe. I absolutely promise you that every sacrifice you make for your family will contain your life's greatest meaning, every choice to love, your life's greatest purpose.

NOTES

IMPORTANT INFORMATION, FAVORITE WEB SITES, AND GOOD BOOKS ABOUT UNDERSTANDING THE BASICS

CREATING CELEBRATIONS

CELEBRATIONS

Family life would soon become merely one day fading into the next without the occasional celebration—a great reason to stop right in your tracks and give significance to the day. Holidays and important events give you the opportunity to pause and notice the passing days, weeks, months, and years, reminding you of the time hurrying past unappreciated and the reverence and wonder you should lend to each priceless day.

A celebration can be a more traditional holiday happening or it can be a mind-set of gratitude for your abundant gifts of life and love. You can celebrate both large and small occasions, involving props and people or focusing solely on a deep feeling of inner thankfulness. If you celebrate every day as if it were your last, heaven will be a simple extension of the life you're living now.

As a mother, you will often be admonished to remember the firsts with your children—the first tooth, the first Christmas, the first step, the first ride on a two-wheeler. Firsts are easy to notice. My advice to you is to look for and remember more of the lasts.

There will be a last time that your little bursting boy runs through the house scattering trucks and mud. "This is the last time I'm going to tell you to clean up this mess!" you will hear yourself lecture. Then tomorrow it *is* the last time, and your little boy is a young man, too mature for trucks and mud. Children refuse to stay small. Lasts don't cry out to be remembered. You find yourself wondering, "When did he quit throwing his pudgy arms around my neck and kissing me good night? When did she put her dolls away and start having her own babies instead?"

There is not nearly as much time as you think. Time flutters past like a leaf in the wind, here one minute and gone on the next breeze. Try to capture the joy in today. Take time to celebrate the special days on the calendar as well as the daily gift of life itself, and you will truly rejoice in all the firsts and the lasts.

BIRTHDAYS

Birthdays give you a once-a-year opportunity to celebrate the life of someone you love. Take the time to make birthdays something distinct and memorable for each child every year. Try to select family traditions for birthdays that help each child feel loved and honored for the day. Traditions don't need to be elaborate, but they should create positive feelings and fun memories.

The tradition of birthday cake, candles, and a few presents always works well, but feel free to select any unique variation that you and your child agree on. You may want to make small adaptations like allowing your child to select the cake and frosting flavor and decide how he wants to decorate the cake. My children have chosen everything from lighted sparklers to giant gummy worms to decorate their annual birthday cakes. Or you may want to make major adaptations to your birthday plans, like a once-a-year mini trip or a day on the town with Mom and Dad, a campout in the back yard, or a stay at the beach.

Think about the birthday traditions you've experienced or observed, then decide which ones you want to use or eliminate. For instance, as a child I hated the birthday spanking tradition, so when I became a mother I decided to replace it with another tradition for my children. While we're eating the birthday cake and

---

THE NEW BABY

Your child's first true birthday is, of course, the day he is born. Mark this moment by beginning a memory book, box, or file that includes the following:
- front page of the local newspaper the day your child was born
- birth certificate
- immunization record
- social security card
- personal account of the birth by mom and dad in text, audio, or video form
- pictures of the newborn
- pictures of parents, brothers, sisters, grandma, and grandpa holding the baby
- blessing outfit or dress
- picture of the current First Presidency in the Church
- copy of father's infant blessing

You might consider opening a bank account in the exact amount of the child's birth weight. Then each year add to the account the birth weight multiplied by the number of years the child is old. For instance, if your child is two years old and weighed 7 pounds, 12 ounces at birth, round the weight up to 8 and multiply by 2. Sixteen dollars would go in the account.

You might also consider making the blessing dress or suit from your wedding dress.

ice cream, we go around the table and have each family member and guest say what they love about the birthday person. I have heard more tender expressions of love and gratitude around the table at birthdays than at any other time during the year. Every person deserves to hear kind and positive things said about him at least once a year.

If you don't like the traditions you've tried in years past, don't be afraid to change or adapt them as you see fit while your children grow older. Start the new tradition process by asking your child this simple question, "How would you like to celebrate your birthday this year?"

FIRST BIRTHDAY

The traditional first birthday is when your child turns one year old. Your child won't remember or care how you handle his birthday at the time, but you will, and the pictures you take will help your child

feel loved for years to come. Consider letting your one-year-old star "have at it" with the cake. You can expect to see him with both hands and face covered with cake and frosting, but it makes great pictures for the memory book. You can make a small cake for baby and another for the rest of the guests if you actually want to eat some yourself.

If you invite guests to your child's birthday party, let them know you don't expect expensive presents and the gift of their presence is always enough. You can teach your child early that birthdays aren't about getting lots of gifts but about celebrating life with the people you love.

TODDLERS

Your toddler will be delighted with whatever you furnish in the way of a birthday party with close family. You can invite perhaps one young friend who is accustomed to spending time at your home, but any more will usually be trouble. Toddlers need a few more years to develop social skills and independence before they can really enjoy being dropped off at a birthday party.

Consider taping balloons to the mailbox on your child's birthday and letting her discover a present inside. You can make your child the star of the week on the family bulletin board by placing her picture in a prominent place. Write in your child's journal on her birthday or act as a scribe as she "writes" or tells you what to say.

PRESCHOOL AND SCHOOL-AGE CHILDREN

Consider asking your child to choose between having a party with friends and doing something special with Mom and Dad, such as going out to dinner. Most of our children have chosen to go out to

dinner the majority of the time. Each child had a few parties with friends during their growing-up years, but not every year.

Because preschool and school-age children are often invited to so many birthday parties, keep several small, wrapped presents on hand. Many invitations don't give you much warning or enough time to shop. Don't go overboard in the expense department—a birthday present that costs a few dollars will do.

When you give your child a party with friends, make sure he is in on the planning. With supervision, he can make invitations and decide which games to play. Birthday parties with friends work best if you plan ahead. Allow your child to invite as many children as he is old. For instance, a five-year-old can invite five children. Don't let your party last more than two hours; drive the guests home yourself if you want the party to end on time.

Consider baking a money cake. Boil coins until they are sterile and then stir them into the batter. Children love finding money in their slice of cake (be sure to warn them in advance so they don't swallow any coins). School-age children also love being relieved of all household duties on their birthdays. Your child might enjoy picking out what he wants for breakfast or supper. Remember to write an entry in your child's journal and encourage him to do the same.

TEENS

When your child gets older, let her choose between gifts selected by mom and dad or a certain amount of cash for her birthday. Many teenagers seem to enjoy a solo shopping trip with both parents where they can spend their birthday money. They also enjoy going out to dinner or on some other outing with Mom and Dad.

Consider retelling your child's birth story on her birthday so she knows what a joy she's been to you right from the start. Recall and share some of your favorite memories with her from before she can remember. I love to tell my children what they were like as babies, toddlers, and preschoolers so they can grow up with a story of themselves retold by someone who adores them.

ANY AGE

Birthdays are a great time to document the year for individual and family histories. Take pictures of the birthday boy out in the backyard or in his bedroom. Videotape him speaking about the past year. Have him include accomplishments and talk about what he is interested in. Ask questions that inspire a unique response: "What was one of your happiest moments this past year?" "What was an embarrassing moment?" "What trips did you go on?" "What is your favorite subject at school and why?"

Consider asking your child to perform on a musical instrument, show a piece of artwork, or read a poem or story he wrote while you record or videotape him. You might want to show the details of your child's bedroom, such as bedding, favorite toys, pictures, and a host of childhood and teenage possessions that will bring back sweet memories some day.

Birthdays can be a good time of year to make sure you're caught up on all the things that need to be done for each child each year. Check the immunization record and annual doctor visits and make sure you have a nice yearly portrait taken. This is also a good time to write a letter to your child or make an entry in his journal.

You can make birthdays a time for parents to take a better look into the heart of their child and ask God what they can do to better love and lead him in the coming year. Each child has gifts, talents, skills, and attributes that need to be nurtured and appreciated. A birthday can be a day of prayer as well as celebration as you center your thoughts on this particular child and what you can do to bless his life. You may want to consider offering your child a father's blessing each year on his birthday. Love letters written by his mother or father for each year of his life will become treasures for your child to read and reread when he leaves home.

Remember the worth of a soul by yearly celebrating the birth of each individual child. Birthdays are an opportunity for us to set a pattern of blessing our children one by one. Each child is a gift from God and deserves to be the family star at least one day a year.

HOLIDAYS

EASTER

Every year at Easter time, spring will bring you the perfect backdrop for a meaningful family celebration of the resurrection. Create Easter traditions that help you and your family think about and appreciate the miracle of the Savior's resurrection and the rebirth of nature all around you.

Find stories, pictures, and readings from the scriptures or other good books to help your child understand the true significance of Easter and the connection between nature and the life and resurrection of the Savior.

EASTER CELEBRATIONS

Easter traditions that include the Savior will bring a sense of reverence to this holiday. You may consider celebrating the Easter bunny tradition on the Saturday before Easter Sunday so your children can separate the religious and secular traditions.

Christ-Centered Easter Traditions

Here are some ideas for making your Easter celebration more meaningful:

• Watch the sunrise as a family. Talk about the miracle of each new day. Teach your children that the Savior is the light of the world. Like the sun, the Savior's love and atonement bathe the earth with light, hope, and warmth. Liken the start of a new day to the new heart that follows personal repentance and forgiveness.

• Have a family gathering where you bear your testimony about the Savior, His birth, life, death, atonement, and resurrection. Testify of the reality and importance of Jesus Christ in your life. Give every family member the same opportunity to share their testimony or feelings about the Savior.

• Watch the video *The Lamb of God* or *Special Witnesses of Christ* with your family. After listening to the First Presidency and Quorum of the Twelve Apostles, bear your own testimony and tell your children what the Savior means to you.

• Invite your young children to look at pictures of the Savior surrounded by little children. Tell them the stories of Christ's dealings with little children in both the new and the old world.

• Celebrate the real Christmas on April sixth with an outside sunrise or sunset service and testimony meeting. Sing Christmas hymns and give small gifts.

• Read from the scriptures about the Resurrection.

• Present your children with an article of new clothing. Teach them that new clothes symbolize new life and new beginnings, or casting off the old and starting fresh. New clothes can symbolize the new person we become with repentance through

NEW LIFE EASTER TRADITIONS

• Organize an Easter egg hunt in your backyard, neighborhood, ward, or city.

• Visit the newest baby in your extended family, ward, or branch. Bring along a gift for the mother and father and thank them for helping to bring a new soul to earth.

• Go to a local nursery and let each child select a flower seedling to plant and care for in your yard or in a pot outside your door.

• Visit the newest baptized member of the Church in your extended family, ward, or branch and ask them to share their testimony with you.

• Go to a local farm where new animals are born. Let your children see and touch the new mothers and babies. Talk about the miracle of new life.

• Take a walk through your yard or neighborhood looking for the first signs of spring. Ask your child to discover any clue that spring is coming. Take a picture of the clue, go home and draw it, write a poem, or make up a song about it.

• Go for a picnic on the first warm day of spring. Spread a blanket and enjoy lunch. Watch for birds, new grass, flowers, and leaves on the trees.

• Deliver Easter baskets to the families you home teach or visit teach.

• Watch the sunrise and have a breakfast of orange juice and sweet bread.

the atonement of Jesus Christ. New clothes can also symbolize Christ's resurrection.

• Ask family members to secretly sacrifice to bring happiness to other family members during the week preceding or following Easter Sunday.

Spring Celebrations

For your secular Easter bunny celebrations, choose family traditions that lead your child to appreciate the miracle of new life and the changes the seasons bring. Celebrate the end of winter and the beginning of spring with traditional Easter egg hunts. Every family should try dying Easter eggs at least once.

Be sure to warn your child that if you go somewhere to roll Easter eggs down a hill the eggs will be smashed. Most young children don't understand this and will be upset at such an unexpected outcome. An easier tradition is hiding eggs and treats around different rooms of the house or in the yard, depending on the weather. Have your child find and collect the eggs and treats in an Easter basket or any other container that is handy.

MEMORIAL DAY

Holidays like Memorial Day, while often overlooked, are opportunities to relearn for ourselves and teach our children how precious and fleeting life really is. Most of us don't like to think or talk about death, but the reality that we all die is what gives life its urgency and wonder.

Visits to cemeteries are an important part of teaching children about the plan of salvation and the need for earthly life and death. Cemeteries remind us that when we die, we can't take anything with us but what we have learned and eternal loving relationships.

Any holiday that helps you slow down and remember those who have died is a perfect opportunity to celebrate life. When you remember and honor a loved one with a trip to the cemetery or a similar family tradition, children learn firsthand that people are precious and families matter, even beyond the grave. The plan of salvation can be taught in a simple and profound way when you contemplate the end of your second estate. The eternal nature of families is taught as you love and honor those who came before you.

Picnics, barbecues, and other wholesome recreational family activities are wonderful, but be sure to include some sort of remembering as part of your memorial celebration.

By choosing any simple tradition that suits your family you can make a neglected holiday into a wonderful opportunity to teach eternal truths and have family fun at the same time. Holidays like Memorial Day remind you that family relationships are the most important things, that life is precious, and that any day could be your last. An annual trip to the cemetery will do wonders for your eternal perspective. So on Memorial Day, remember to teach your children that life is too short to leave any

MEMORIAL DAY CELEBRATION IDEAS

- Offer a simple prayer at the family barbecue or picnic thanking God for the gift of life and mentioning past loved ones.
- Tell a story about a relative who has died.
- Take a walk through the crosses at the cemetery representing all the fallen soldiers in war. Talk about the men and women who have given their lives so that you can enjoy the life you have today.
- Organize a private family memorial service of prayer, song, and tribute at a gravesite or in the backyard.
- Take your child to visit a town veteran or aging relative.
- Plant a tree in honor of someone you love.
- Attend a memorial service for veterans at your local cemetery.

loving undone, any appreciation unfelt, or any joy unembraced.

My young son once hugged his freshly bathed newborn baby sister and said, "Boy, I sure do like to sniff her, 'cause she smells so good." You can take sweet-smelling flowers to the cemetery on Memorial Day, but it might be even better to find someone in your own family circle who is still alive and would enjoy those flowers even more. For newborns and roses are meant to be sniffed and enjoyed today. Memorial Day should be

a time to remember and honor the gift we sometimes take most for granted—life.

PIONEER DAY

Pioneer Day celebrations should not depend on whether you live in Utah or whether you had ancestors that made the trek west. Don't let your child miss out on commemorating the day the pioneers entered the Salt Lake Valley.

Every member of The Church of Jesus Christ of Latter-day Saints becomes a member of the Church family at baptism. The pioneer legacy lives on in your life and the lives of your children as you live the gospel and honor your legacy. In a very real sense the Utah pioneers are kin to us all. They who froze, starved, and lost husbands, wives, and children made all our present lives possible.

Pioneers were surely heroic, but they were also real, vulnerable human beings who got tired and irritable as well as lived and died for what they believed in. We become pioneers every time we have the courage to make a difficult decision, become the first in our family to heal a wound, forgive a debt, or right a wrong. We are pioneers every time we leave our homes and possessions to become representatives of Christ on missions or even when we agree to teach the Sunbeams in church. We are pioneers whenever we choose to do something that takes personal courage and sacrifice.

Children in Primary learn the words to a pioneer song: "Pioneer children sang as they walked and walked and walked and walked." I used to think the lyric writer of that song had a rather limited vocabulary.

PIONEER DAY TRADITIONS

- Discuss around the dinner table what it means to be a pioneer. Talk about courage, hardship, sacrifice, conviction, faith, and testimony. Ask what challenges your family faces and how you can be pioneers.
- Consider celebrating Pioneer Day with your immediate family, extended family, ward, or branch. Fix Dutch oven meals and sing around the campfire. Wear pioneer clothing and have a square dance.
- Organize a Pioneer Day Primary parade in your ward, neighborhood, or family. Young children love dressing up for a parade. Have your children dress like pioneers and reenact the handcart or covered wagon trek. Plan horse, wagon, or buggy rides. Sing Primary pioneer songs. Eat campfire food.
- Organize a reenactment of the pioneer trek with the families in your ward. Plan a hike where each family carries their own food and belongings to a distant destination.
- Go for a family hay ride and sing campfire songs along the way.
- Go camping and tell true campfire stories about real pioneers in your family.
- Assign each child and parent one ancestor to research and learn about. Have them present their findings in family home evening, in full costume as if they were the ancestor.
- Find out who was the first member of your family to accept the gospel. Host a party in his or her honor on Pioneer Day.

But now I think Elizabeth Fetzer Bates caught the vision of what it means to be a pioneer. Pioneers are simply people who dust themselves off when the way is rough and keep putting one foot in front of the other. So when the way gets rough for us we need to remember the pioneers and keep on walking.

Help your child remember the pioneers. Tell her stories about them. Consider making costumes and acting out events that happened during the trek west to Utah. Every child should know about the history of the Church and the courage and sacrifice of the Mormon pioneers.

If possible, plan a trip to Salt Lake City and let her visit Temple Square and Church headquarters. If you have pioneers in your family, read their life stories and let your child get to know them. Consider hanging pictures of your ancestors on your walls and teaching your child how to fill in her family tree, pedigree chart, and family group sheets. Teach her how to use the Church's Family Search program on the Internet.

Find out who were the first members of your family to join the Church and make this holiday a time to honor them and their courage to be baptized. Perhaps you and your family are pioneers in a variety of ways even today. Help your child discover what it means to be the first to do something, the first to make a change in her home and in her heart. Help her discover what it means to be true to her faith and courageous in her actions.

HALLOWEEN

You don't have to be one of those mothers who go all out for Halloween to enjoy this holiday. You know the ones I mean. They sit on the front row in the gymnasium during the kindergarten Halloween assembly with a video camera, taking pictures of Melvin in his homemade, green satin stegosaurus costume complete with stuffed spikes and a six-foot tail. When my children ask for help with their costumes, I tell them to tape a raisin to their belly buttons and go as cookies. Find the level of involvement you're comfortable with, then relax and let your children lead you through the day.

HALLOWEEN FROM YOUR CHILD'S POINT OF VIEW

Children love to dress up, pretend they are someone else, and eat candy. Think of Halloween from your child's point of view. Most of the year your mother is trying to keep you out of the cookies and candy in the cupboards and suddenly she approves of you going door to door begging for that

stuff. Not only does your own mother suddenly approve but every other adult actually hands out candy for free with a smile. Wow!

Relax and enjoy this holiday with your children. Dress yourself up and decorate your house if you feel like it, have a party if you're so inclined, but don't stress out about your child having the perfect homemade costume. He'll be excited to do anything out of the ordinary, and chances are the weather will be so cold that he will have to wear a coat over his costume anyway.

Toddler and Preschooler Costumes

Halloween is simple when you have a toddler or preschooler. You simply get her ready for bed in her usual pink or yellow blanket sleeper, paint a couple of whiskers under her nose with an eyebrow pencil, and tell her she's a bunny (or whatever animal she prefers). Then you drag her around enough blocks to get a stash of candy big enough to make you and your husband hyperactive for a week.

School-age Children's Costumes

After your children start school, they are seldom satisfied with the old blanket sleeper trick anymore. You now have the impossible job of figuring out what your child wants to be for Halloween when he changes his mind every seven minutes. This is definitely not the time to spend a lot of time sewing costumes and paying top dollar at the retail store, because as soon as you get his costume ready, your child will change his mind again and refuse to wear it. So what's a mother to do?

Now's the time to start your own collection of dress-up items to create costumes from. Grandma's house and secondhand

COSTUME BOXES

To make your own costume box, collect the following:
- hats (all types and sizes)
- weird shoes and boots
- wigs
- purses
- military uniforms
- vintage dresses and suits
- old scrubs from hospitals
- small pillows for stuffing rear ends and tummies
- face makeup
- sports uniforms
- worn sheets
- old dance costumes
- prom dresses
- outrageous sleepwear
- cloth and felt scraps
- crowns
- cowboy, pioneer, and Native American clothing
- hobo rags
- fake glasses
- wire for wings and halos
- princess and ballerina outfits
- swords, sabers, and helmets
- old Christmas tree trimmings
- gaudy jewelry
- clothing from a foreign country
- fake noses, teeth, and mustaches
- clown accessories
- movie character outfits
- shawls and canes
- old swimming suits and tights
- plain colored T-shirts
- old balls of yarn

Now let your child decide how to use what you have on hand to create his own costume. Add a few pieces to your dress-up collection each year and before you know it, your grandchildren will be enjoying your costume collection too.

stores like Deseret Industries are good places to begin your search. This private collection of dress-ups can be used all year 'round.

Trunk or Treat

You might want to start a ward or branch "trunk or treat" if you worry about your children trick-or-treating in your neighborhood. For a "trunk or treat," each family in the ward or branch comes to the church parking lot on Halloween with their car trunk decorated inside and filled with candy. The Primary children go from car to car "trunk-or-treating" among people you know and trust.

Halloween Parties

Some moms like to plan a Halloween party for the neighborhood or at the local elementary school to replace the traditional trick-or-treating. These parties often include apple bobbing, fish ponds, cake-walks, games, face painting, dinner, costume parades, spook alleys, games, and contests. If you'd rather your child went to a Halloween party than trick-or-treating, consider planning and carrying out one of these parties.

Halloween Service

As your children get older, you might consider going trick-or-treating in reverse.

As a family you can dress up and take treats to members of your extended family or ward that could especially use a visit any day on or near Halloween. Consider taking treats to share at a rest home or a hospital.

Decorating Pumpkins

If you choose to decorate a pumpkin, don't carve it too soon or it will get soft and rot before Halloween. Painting a face on the pumpkin will last longer and is safer. If you don't grow your own pumpkins, consider a visit to a local pumpkin patch where your child can pick out her own orange friend and take it home. Some pumpkin patches offer hay hides and visits with farm animals as well.

Handling the Candy

There are ways to handle the sugar overload that comes after an evening of successful trick-or-treating. When your child gets home, have him choose his favorite candy and eat it that night. Then he can put the rest of his candy in the cupboard and select two or three pieces to eat after supper each night until it is gone. When children are young they don't seem to mind dumping their stash in a big bowl and sharing it with everybody in the family. When they get older they like to be in charge of their own candy. But they can still be encouraged to share a piece with each family member after supper until the candy is gone.

Answering the Door

Staying home to answer the door on Halloween can be a lot of fun. You stay close to the front door for hours, answering the doorbell for little children who sometimes aren't quite sure what they're supposed to do. If the children are accompanied by an adult, don't be afraid to invite them inside to chat for a minute or two. Whatever you do, remember that Halloween is for children and for the child in all of us, so get a little scared and have a little fun.

THANKSGIVING

You will be more thankful for Thanksgiving Day if you keep your celebration simple. Many young children are a bit disappointed about Thanksgiving because to them it's just a larger-than-usual meal they have to wait longer than usual to eat . . . and then it's over. So consider making Thanksgiving your official family thankfulness day. Start or continue family traditions that promote an attitude of gratitude.

GRATITUDE JOURNALS

A family gratitude journal is a great tradition for Thanksgiving. Purchase a large bound journal and have family members write a list of what they're grateful for during the Thanksgiving holidays. Have them sign and date their entries. Adults can act as scribes for young children before they learn to write.

THANK-YOU LETTERS

You may want to present a letter of gratitude to each of your children and your spouse each year on Thanksgiving. You might even give your family members the inspiration to write their own. Write letters to family members who live far away from you. Tell them why you are grateful for them.

GRATEFUL CONTESTS

Have everyone in the family write a list of what they are grateful for. The person with the longest list wins a prize or gets to be served first at Thanksgiving dinner.

TAKE A FAMILY PICTURE

Thanksgiving is a good time to get the whole family together and take a picture. The picture can be used for Christmas gifts later. Don't forget to take pictures of extended family members at your get-togethers.

REACHING OUTSIDE THE FAMILY

If you don't have extended family close by, consider ways to reach outside your immediate family with your celebrations.

Invite single members of the ward or branch over for dinner and games. Write letters of thanks to grandparents, aunts, uncles, and cousins. Help with dinner at a local hospital or homeless shelter as a family.

EXTENDED FAMILY IDEAS

If you get together with extended family, try exchanging favorite family recipes, retelling family stories, taking pictures, playing board or card games, singing songs, going for walks, playing sports, or sitting in a circle while you catch up on the latest news from each family.

When extended families get too big to make eating at one home possible, consider using the local church. You might consider eating in your individual homes on Thanksgiving and then getting together sometime during the holiday weekend with other extended family members just to visit and perhaps share favorite desserts.

Whatever you do, plan menus that are simple. Your holiday should be restful and a break of pace, not a frantic gathering and extra work for Mom.

CHRISTMAS

Christmas when you are a mother is even better than Christmas when you are a child. You not only get to feel the wonder and magic but you also get to create some of it for those you love. Yet most mothers try to do far too much during the holiday season, believing they're in charge of the ultimate failure or success of Christmas at their home. But the true Christmas has already happened, and it was a complete success. Now you get to celebrate what

CHRIST-CENTERED CHRISTMAS TRADITIONS

- Set a place for Jesus at the table when you eat your Christmas dinner. Arrange his picture on the empty place setting and sing happy birthday before the blessing on the food.
- Act out the nativity story from the Bible using props, costumes, and a narrator.
- Have each family member select a piece of the family nativity set. Turn off the lights and light a candle. Have each member of the family take turns placing his piece of the nativity back around the stable while he tells the rest of the family what gift he would like to give to Jesus that year.
- Have family members choose their favorite Christmas song from the hymn book and sing each song together.
- Have family members write a promise to Jesus and put it inside a chest to be opened the next Christmas Eve and read silently by each person before dinner.
- Have a family testimony meeting on Christmas Eve or Christmas Day.
- Read the Book of Mormon account of the Savior's birth.
- Watch a video on the life of Christ.
- Listen to favorite Christmas songs while sitting around the Christmas tree with only the lights from the tree illuminated.
- Buy inexpensive nativity sets to place around the house for young children to play with.
- Make a manger, complete with straw and a baby Jesus, to place in an honored place in the house.
- Create a miniature village complete with houses, animals, and people that resemble those in the Holy Land at the time of Christ.
- Visit the grounds of the temple closest to you.
- On the first family home evening in December draw family names from a hat. Do nice things for that person during the week anonymously. Draw new names each week until Christmas.
- On the first family home evening in December set a manger next to a pile of straw in a prominent place in your home. Tell your children that each time they choose to do something kind for a member of the family, they can put a piece of straw in the manger. On Christmas Eve you will place baby Jesus on their bed of kindness.
- Select a favorite poem or story that invites you and your child to turn your thoughts to the Savior and his life and mission.

that sacred birth long ago means and share the good news with your family.

It is easy to focus on cooking, shopping, presents, decorating, and parties to the exclusion of deep heartfelt appreciation for the birth of the Savior of the world—God's greatest gift—and the glorious promises his birth represents. Mothers can lead their families to Christ by forming traditions that help their children discover their Savior.

Christmas can be a time of joy and celebration, even for Mom, if you remember that the greatest gift you have to offer your children at this time of year is your love of the Savior and a home that invites His presence.

HOMEMADE GIFTS FROM YOUR CHILDREN

Receiving homemade gifts from your children will be one of the sweetest dilemmas you'll face as a mother at Christmas. What do you do with all the wonderful, creative handmade gifts you receive from your children? The older I get the more I wish I'd saved them all. Now I realize those child-made gifts were the truest presents I've ever received. Pencil holders made from potato-chip cans, laminated bookmarks made with school pictures, construction-paper Christmas trees, and clothespin tree ornaments are among the gifts that I remember. But what do you do with a zillion tiny paper snowflakes?

One year, my nine-year-old daughter presented me with a homemade snow scene she'd made from a pint-sized mason jar filled with tap water and zillions of tiny pieces of paper she'd cut into microscopic snowflakes.

Grinning, my daughter shook the bottle back and forth and said, "Look, Mom, a snow scene just like those ones you like in the fancy stores."

I glanced from my young daughter's beaming face to the mason jar, and suddenly it was even more exquisite than the glass figurines in the fancy stores.

You, too, will be given gifts from your children that will open your eyes and your heart, for the best gifts seldom come from expected places. Consider making a file or a box for each of your children and keeping their homemade gifts in a safe place. One day you can look at them and remember with fondness that the truest gifts are a toothless grin, two chubby arms wrapped tightly around your neck, and a zillion tiny pieces of white paper in a mason jar.

CELEBRATING WITH SANTA

Whether you choose to include Santa or other legends or cultural traditions into your Christmas celebration is up to you. Children can be taught that anyone who secretly does kind things for another person is a Santa Claus. When my children asked me if there was a Santa Claus, I always answered, "What do you think?" Then my child would tell me what he thought—which was usually what he wanted and needed to believe at that time.

Christmas Mayhem

One of the most marvelous messes in the world is the chaos created in the family room after a family has just opened Christmas presents—a wrapping paper, cardboard box, orange peel, and gooey ribbon candy land of delicious disorder. It should not be cleaned too quickly.

You'll probably develop several annoying habits as a mother, one of which is noticing messes, cleaning messes, or demanding that messes be cleaned everywhere you go. Try to learn that there are important messes and unimportant messes. The problem is that after several kids, one mess will start to look pretty much like any other. But if you don't take the time to really look, you might miss your child's childhood.

Whatever Christmas traditions you choose to include in your celebration, don't forget that celebrating Christmas while you have children in your home is a joyous time to treasure and enjoy. Don't forget to savor the frantic ripping of paper, the slurping of wet tongues on peppermint, and the fresh scent of oranges losing their skins. Christmas with children is loud, confusing, messy, and wonderful. So take a deep breath, scratch a few things off your "to do" list, and enjoy these fleeting years before they're gone.

THE CHRISTMAS TREE

Whether you use a fresh-cut tree or an artificial tree is up to you. Fresh trees are messy and hard to keep from drying out, but they offer such a great scent to fill your house. Fresh trees drop needles faster than you can keep them cleaned up and tend to fall over more often because tree stands are seldom stable. My husband usually resorted to nailing the tree to the floor.

If you prefer fresh cut, look around for a Christmas tree farm or canyon in your area and cut your own or go to a local tree lot and make your choice. Going as a family and choosing or cutting down your own tree will be a real memory maker. When

you get home, make a fresh cut across the trunk of the tree and let it soak in a bucket of water before you bring it inside and set it in a water-filled basin tree stand.

If you prefer an artificial tree, you'll have less mess and better stability but you'll miss picking out a tree and enjoying that great pine scent in the house. Artificial trees cost less in the long run and look pretty real these days.

Decorating the tree should be a family affair. If you have any breakable ornaments, they will be broken sooner or later no matter how careful you are or how high you put them on the tree. So try to collect ornaments children can handle. Look for ornaments made of wood, yarn, felt, beads, cloth, ribbon, and raffia. If you're dead set on having a fancy, breakable ornament-covered tree to impress the neighbors, then consider adopting your children out for the season or buying a second tree for your children to decorate.

Consider Christmas tree ornament traditions such as buying or allowing each child to pick out his own ornament each year, making your own ornaments, or creating a memory tree with dated ornaments from each year of your marriage. Hand down ornaments from one generation to the next or make all your Christmas tree ornaments edible using candy, cookies, popcorn, and cranberries.

CHRISTMAS ACTIVITY TRADITIONS

Choose a few family activities that you want to include in your holiday celebration. You might decide to make a family trip to see the light displays or parades in your area. Sleigh riding, tubing, caroling, providing Christmas for a needy family, or baking cookies for the neighbors are ideas for Christmas activities you might want to make a family tradition each year. Try making green pancakes topped with red strawberry syrup. Children also enjoy advent calendars.

You might also want to plan some activities for the days after Christmas before your children head back to school. Consider writing thank-you cards for gifts received or writing to family members living far away. Attend a movie, shop the after-Christmas sales, go out to dinner, check out the Christmas displays around town, or visit with relatives. After Christmas is also a good time to go through your closets and remove old toys and clothes that can be donated to local thrift stores like Deseret Industries.

OVERSPENDING

You will be tempted to overspend at Christmastime. Hold firm and remember that persuasive advertising will make it seem like lasting Christmas memories will come only if you buy expensive toys. The opposite is always true. Your best memories of Christmas will come from close, warm family relationships, not material things. One day you will look back and relish the days when money was tight but your children were plentiful.

Some families find that exchanging only handmade gifts or limiting the amount of money spent on presents enhances the spirit of the Christmas season in their home. Your gifts will be more personal and less expensive if you use what you love and have on hand for gift giving, such as your children's artwork, a favorite seashell, or perhaps a heartfelt love letter.

Large families can choose to draw names for sibling gift giving. You might want to exchange a sample of your favorite homemade Christmas food along with the recipe. Consider giving gift certificates from your child's favorite store along with a coupon for a shopping trip and lunch. Then the magic of Christmas lasts a bit longer than one day.

Christmas is a good time to add to your library. Well-chosen books are inexpensive gifts that last a lifetime. Families low on cash can give the gift of their time by making coupons to be redeemed for a favorite service like a backrub, an extra turn at the dishes, cleaning the garage, painting a room, or a walk in the park.

Consider giving your child the gift of helping someone else at Christmastime. Spend a day at a children's hospital or homeless shelter. Take part in a community fund-raiser or Christmas play. Participate in the ward Christmas program or choir. Select a family in the ward or community to help.

To stretch your dollar and find unusual gifts, consider thrift stores and garage sales when Christmas shopping. Be on the lookout all year for items or supplies that will delight, teach, and motivate your child. Most children own many more toys than they need for their growth and development. One more toy won't mean as much as a once-in-a-lifetime moonlight walk with Mom.

Your children won't remember many gifts you give them, but they will remember the things you did together and the feelings that they felt at this time of year. When you are tempted to overspend, ask yourself if you are giving your children all the things that money can't buy: your unhurried time, a favorite well-read Christmas story, unique family traditions, hugs, kisses and smiles, homemade cinnamon rolls, adventure and whimsy and a happy mother who loves the magic of gift giving and receiving.

REMEMBERING CHRISTMAS WITHOUT CHILDREN

Someday, somewhere back in the far recesses of your mind you will remember a Christmas as a married couple before you were a mother. You will remember when you actually slept in on Christmas morning. You will remember having a Christmas tree in the front room that no one had pulled over and ornaments no one had tugged off, sucked on, licked, or squished.

You will remember actually being alone in the house and peacefully listening to Christmas carols on the stereo. Your carpet was not decorated with juice stains and your sliding glass door was not adorned with dozens of fingerprints. Wrapping paper was not flying through the air or working its way through your baby's digestive system.

Later, when you walk into the kitchen for breakfast you will remember when the cabinets were not locked or even tied together. You'll remember eating a leisurely breakfast when no one in the entire family threw food on the floor, flipped food across the table with a fork, or oozed food out between their teeth in a spray. You'll remember doing such spontaneous things as running outside and playing in the snow with your husband without first finding and tugging on boots and gloves, zipping and snapping little coats, or positioning tiny hats and scarves.

You will remember visiting family and friends without having to take along a huge suitcase of diapers and supplies. You will remember driving in a small sedan with no one fist-fighting in the backseat. You will remember reading the story of the famous family in Luke, without anyone arguing over who gets to be Mary.

You will remember when there were no stockings lined up in a row, no giggling, ripping, taping, and frantic wrapping of presents for Mom and Dad behind locked doors. You will remember when no one begged you to read "The Night before Christmas" or to sing a duet with them when you play "Jingle

Bells" or "Silent Night" on the piano. You will remember when there were no grade school Christmas programs to make costumes for, no junior high chorus concerts to attend, and no piano recitals to clap at.

Frankly, you will wonder how you ever stood it. Talk about boring! You had no idea what you were missing. Thank heaven for the chaotic, child-filled Christmas you relish now. Christmas with children has its own special magic and is truly a time of life to savor and enjoy.

VALENTINE'S DAY

Valentine's Day is not just for children. You will enjoy this holiday more as a mother if you celebrate by giving valentines to your spouse and children. They can be simple, funny, or a lasting tribute of your love.

REMEMBERING YOUR VALENTINE

Becoming a parent makes romance a little more difficult and complicated but not impossible. You'll find that after a few years of marriage and children, your love for your spouse will have a way of surfacing at uncommon and unexpected times.

Where you used to love him for the way he looked in his sports uniform, now you love him for the way he looks in his striped flannels after being up with a sick baby all night so you can get some rest. Where you used to love him for taking you out to expensive restaurants, now you love him for making you cinnamon toast to eat while you watch the ten o' clock news.

Where you used to admire your husband's latest intellectual recital from his vast store of knowledge, now you admire him most when he's crawling on all fours and acting like a goon to get your baby to laugh. There's something downright heart-melting about the way he attentively listens to your preschoolers tell knock-knock jokes without punch lines, helps your

---

RELATIONSHIP REFRESHERS FOR COUPLES

Consider putting into practice one relationship refresher each year, starting on Valentine's Day.

- Focus on the first few minutes after you wake up in the morning, the first few minutes when you greet each other at the end of the day, and the last few minutes just before going to bed. Use this time to express affection and reconnect.
- Surprise your partner with a small treat, gift, favor, kiss, or hug every day.
- Get out of the house alone together at least once a week for a date, even if it's only for a short time. Keep the courtship going.
- Make long-term goals for the future while you're alone together.
- Make all your hellos and good-byes more tender and sincere.
- Be the last one to break up a good hug or kiss.

A MOTHER'S VALENTINE TO HER CHILDREN

Dear Child,

You are the best decision I ever made. I thought I was happy sleeping in on Sunday, eating peaceful meals, and wearing unstained clothing, but I was living only for myself. I had no idea how much motherhood would change my life forever. It just seemed like a good idea at the time. Young and newly married, I had no idea how much I'd grow to love you.

You are a living, breathing miracle, a completely unique human being, never to be duplicated. You have given me my greatest joys and deepest challenges. I've discovered through you that anything truly worth having comes with a price. I don't want to regret not loving you enough, not enjoying your growing years enough, but I know I will someday, as all mothers do. So take time becoming you. Be patient. I'm still growing too.

Cold and afraid, you cried out to me when you were born. I could comfort you and keep you safe. You needed me. Though I didn't know it at the time, I needed you more. I don't live my life through you, but I've discovered life through you. In your exhilaration and your spontaneous delight with living, I've learned to truly feel again, to reawaken the child within. You are my most important teacher. You've taught me that love will fail me only when I fail to give it. You've taught me to keep my heart in wonder at the daily miracles all around me.

When I chose to become your mother, I didn't know you. I chose first to be the mother of the hope of you. If I had the decision to make over again, knowing you as I do now, the choice would be the same, only I would make it with even greater relish. I had no idea that motherhood would be so difficult and life altering. At the same time, I had no idea motherhood would be so fulfilling and soul expanding.

As I've fumbled about trying to meet your needs, I've discovered that a truly meaningful life is about big people helping little people. It's about healthy people helping sick people. It's about young people helping old people. It's about old people helping young people. It's about caring for someone more than for yourself.

In giving you birth, I've made the sweet connection to life even after death. For life goes on. Soon, you'll be grown. And then, if you're lucky, you will be rocking your child, who someday will rock his child.

Someday you may look back and wonder why I didn't do something more noteworthy with my life, why I decided to have you and all your brothers and sisters. I became your mother because I decided some time ago that nothing was more important than giving others life, learning to love them, and helping them grow and reach their potential. Maybe I haven't made a big difference in the world, but I hope I've made a little difference in your world. I love you, more than you know.

And that is why I chose to be your mother.

Love,
Mom

FUN FAMILY TRADITIONS FOR
VALENTINE'S DAY

- Make heart-shaped pancakes, biscuits,
  cookies, or cakes.
- Purchase and exchange small, inexpensive gifts such as porcelain figures, decorated boxes, single flowers, or jewelry.
- Select a lonely person in your ward and
  deliver Valentine's Day goodies to
  them.
- Place a decorated box in the center of
  your table a week before Valentine's
  Day. Keep a pad of paper and a pencil
  nearby. Instruct members of your family
  to write love notes to each other after
  supper each night. Read the notes after
  dinner on Valentine's Day.
- Serve a pink, red, and white supper on
  Valentine's Day. Red hot candy will
  color drinks and sauces.
- Place a single red rose in the center of
  the table on Valentine's Day. Take turns
  telling each family member why you
  love them.
- Tie red, pink, and white balloons to
  your mailbox, your child's bedroom
  door, or your husband's office door
  with a personal love note.
- Give your husband and children red-
  hot kisses and hugs (the candy kind)
  followed up with the real thing.

teenagers with algebra, or reads bedtime stories on the loveseat.

Where you used to admire your husband's courage to travel to exotic foreign lands, now you admire his courage to stay home, get up, go to work and come back to a sticky kitchen chair, a teenager with a learner's permit, and last-minute peanut butter and jam dinners.

You will love your husband for the way he spends his free time fixing flat bicycle tires, holes in the plasterboard, leaking faucets, washing machines, hair dryers, squeaky doors, remote control cars, beheaded dolls, and runny noses. You will love him for building dollhouses, model airplanes, clubhouses, and your children's childhood memories.

True parental romance is a lot of work and effort, but it's so much deeper than the Hollywood illusions. And that is really worth celebrating on Valentine's Day. Take the time to write your husband a valentine letter each year expressing your love, which will only grow deeper and richer and live on inside your children and grandchildren forever.

SCHOOL-AGE CHILDREN AND VALENTINES

Your children probably won't notice Valentine's Day until they start school, unless they have older brothers and sisters at home. When your child is in school, you'll probably get a note from the teacher listing the name of each of your child's classmates and describing how Valentine's Day will be celebrated during the school day. You can buy your child valentines or give him materials to make his own. Just make sure that he has a valentine for every member of his class so no one gets left out. Some mothers like to buy candy to put inside the envelopes with the valentines. You and your child can decide together how you want to handle the annual classroom Valentine's Day party.

IMPORTANT EVENTS

INFANT BLESSINGS

Celebrating the dawn of life gives reverence and importance to earthly existence. Every time a new child is born, it is time to celebrate the greatest of all miracles—life.

An infant blessing is a father's blessing generally given by the child's father in front of the ward or branch or in the home of the infant. If the father is unable or unwilling to name and bless the baby, another close family member or friend who holds the Melchizedek Priesthood can perform this ordinance. If you want to have your baby blessed in your home, contact the bishop and have a member of the bishopric in attendance.

"Every member of the church of Christ having children is to bring them unto the elders before the church, who are to lay their hands upon them in the name of Jesus Christ, and bless them in his name" (D&C 20:70).

The ordinance of the blessing of children is customarily performed in fast meetings a few weeks or months after the birth of the child. This is the time when the child is officially given a name and Church records are made so the necessary genealogical data will be preserved. The blessing of children, like the dedication of a grave, is not an ordinance of salvation but is done for the comfort and encouragement of the Saints.

To preserve this celebration, you might choose to save the blessing outfit and booties in a frame or a box. The father's blessing can be recorded and typed for the child to read later. A newborn bonnet can be made from a handkerchief that can be

---

PREPARING CHILDREN FOR THE BABY'S BLESSING

- Discuss the meaning of the name of each child in the family and tell why it was chosen.
- Tell the older children when, where, and why you will be naming and blessing the new baby.
- Explain how the blessing of your new baby is like the blessing that Jesus gave to little children. Discuss why little children are so precious in the eyes of God.
- Share your feelings of gratitude and joy about the new baby.
- Show all your children their blessing certificates if you have them. Explain that the ward clerk will send in all the information about this new child so that she will officially be on the membership records of the Church.
- Show the blessing clothing of older children in the family and review that special day by looking at pictures in memory books.
- Talk about who will be invited to the blessing and who will be in the circle.
- Allow older siblings to describe their feelings for the new baby and record them in a notebook or journal.

used later at the baptism and the wedding. Don't forget to take pictures of your baby with her parents, and if possible include grandparents, brothers and sisters, and any other guests.

Some parents like to mark the day with a ring to fit the tiny finger, followed by a ring at baptism and a ring at marriage. Others like to compose a song, read a poem, or write a love letter to their new-born on her blessing day.

Think ahead and decide how you want to celebrate your newborn's blessing day.

FIRST/LAST DAY OF SCHOOL

The beginning of a new school year is another opportunity to mark the passing years with a celebration, photographs, and written accounts. Don't forget to take pictures of your child with his teacher, bus driver, and in front of the school with his best friends on the first day of school. Write dates and names on the back of the pictures.

On the last day of school, consider showing up unexpectedly at your child's school to take pictures, present flowers, grant a homemade diploma, bring treats for his last class, or take him somewhere special to celebrate. Plan an end-of-the-year party at your house with your child's friends, your immediate family, or the whole neigh-borhood. Take time to cele-brate with your

child the successful completion of another year of learning and growth.

WEDDINGS

Wedding celebra-tions honor the moment when a man and a woman come before God in love to create a new family. Each member of the wedding party experiences major life and relationship changes. With the healthy formation of a new family, previous relationships have to adapt, and sometimes transition is chal-lenging. At first all that growing can be like licking honey off a thorn—both painful and sweet.

When a bride and groom leave their families of origin to make their own home, it means fathers and mothers, brothers and sisters now become the extended family and take on different roles. Parents have to step back into a position of advising only on request. Close brothers and sisters see far less of each other because the day-to-day contact is gone. So a wedding is a mixed bag of emotions for everyone involved. Weddings are a time of endings and beginnings. The birth of each new family is always something to honor and celebrate with thanksgiving.

CHANGING RELATIONSHIPS

The bride and groom will inevitably feel tender or anxious about the nuclear family they're leaving, especially in the weeks before the big day. I'd always imagined that the night before my own wedding day would be spent sitting out under a star-filled sky with my fiancé, sharing a private, quiet, romantic moment. Yet on my wedding eve, my intended was miles away getting a good night's sleep before our bright and early 8:00 A.M. wedding in the Salt Lake Temple the next morning. I ended up sleeping outside in the backyard with my twin sisters because I couldn't get into the bathroom with all the visiting relatives staying at my house.

The night before our first daughter got married, she spent the evening going from bedroom to bedroom to privately express her love for each family member. Our son spent the night before his wedding doing cartwheels in the living room and singing, "I'm getting married in the morning!"

Those tender moments never get into the photo album, but they need to be noticed and recorded. The best wedding memories have little to do with the images that develop in the posed pictures. The sweetest memories come when family members take the time to express their love in private one-on-one golden moments during this important time of endings and new beginnings.

MOTHER OF THE BRIDE OR GROOM

Being the mother of the bride or groom gives a wedding a whole new perspective. You become the hostess of a celebration that should enhance, not detract, from this important day while you're adjusting to all the major changes taking place in your parent/child relationship.

After you've spent decades serving, loving, and living with someone, it takes a while to get used to the idea that she has grown up and is ready to get married. You might find yourself pulling out photographs or watching old videos with misty eyes. It will not seem like you've had enough time together. Don't worry too much if you find yourself with an immense longing to stop time in its tracks. The nature of a wedding is that the celebration sometimes gets in the way of truly understanding or expressing the mixture of joy and sadness you feel when your child leaves home to start her own family.

There will be moments on your child's wedding day when you can't even swallow or breathe. You'll feel full and empty, overjoyed and despondent. Weddings are a whirl of pictures, flowers, parties, food, and faces. Then late that night, long after the ceremony, wedding breakfast, and reception, you'll drag the last sagging section of wedding cake, gift boxes, and flower arrangements into your house just before you collapse on the couch, so exhausted you can hardly move.

Then you or your husband will wonder or express this thought:

"When did she grow up? Wasn't I there? You spend all this time loving them and raising them so they can just leave?"

What you won't realize at that moment is that your child will come back home many, many times, and she'll bring along your new son-in-law and grandchildren to add to your family, your experience, and your love. What you think you're losing will never really be lost, only transformed and increased.

PREPARING FOR
THE TEMPLE SEALING

Many engaged couples and their parents forget to prepare for the most important event of the wedding day, the sealing of a man and wife in the temple and the creation of an eternal family.

Interviews with the
Bishop and Stake President

Before your child can enter the temple to receive her endowment and be sealed, she will need to have an interview with the bishop and stake president. Tell her what to expect in the temple recommend interview. The bishop and stake president will ask searching questions that need to be answered openly and honestly. She will be asked if she is morally clean and if she keeps the word of wisdom. She must be a full tithe payer, live in harmony with the teachings of the Church, and not have any affiliations with apostate groups.

If your child has any problems with these things she will be asked to demonstrate true repentance before she can be issued a recommend. Tell her that her interview with the bishop and stake president will be in strict confidence and that she should not wait to be asked before

volunteering information on any important worthiness issue.

PREPARING YOUR CHILD
FOR TEMPLE ORDINANCES

Make talks, booklets, and books on the temple available to your children so they can learn as much as possible before they enter. *Temples of The Church of Jesus Christ of Latter-day Saints* is an excellent resource. What happens in the temple is not so much secret as sacred.

Keep pictures of temples around your house and talk about the temple each time you attend with your husband. Show your children your temple clothing and express the feelings you have when you're in the temple. Visit the temple grounds as a family and talk about your sealing. Encourage your children to do baptisms for the dead with your ward youth group or with your immediate family. Make temple attendance a part of your family life and discussions.

PREPARING FOR
THE ENDOWMENT

Both the bride and groom will need to have received their endowments prior to the sealing. Temple workers recommend that individuals wait until about a week before the wedding day to go to the temple unless they have previously received their endowments. Some couples combine the endowment and the sealing on the same day.

Take the time to teach your son or daughter that the temple endowment includes instruction on the significance of past dispensations. The endowment reviews the story of the Creation and explains the purpose of life, the mission and Atonement of Jesus Christ, and Heavenly Father's plan for his children. During the endowment session we are presented with obligations to live by a strict law of virtue and chastity. We covenant to be charitable and pure and to devote our talents, time, and material means to building up the kingdom of God.

The Work Done in Temples

In the temple your son or daughter will be taught, make covenants, and in turn receive promised blessings. Temple ordinances include baptisms for the dead, endowments, and sealings. Each temple is dedicated as a house of the Lord, a place of holiness and peace apart from the outside world. Some people view the temple as a bridge from this world to the next. Temple work is all about families, both earthly and heavenly. Marriage partners and children who are sealed have the opportunity to be joined after death if they are true to their covenants.

Tell your children that after they are washed, anointed, instructed, endowed, and sealed, they will return to the temple to do these things by proxy for others. Every living soul will have the opportunity to hear the gospel and accept or reject what the temple has to offer. Temple readiness includes faith, repentance, baptism, confirmation, worthiness, and maturity. Let your son or daughter know that teaching in temples is done in a symbolic fashion and instruction is offered in spiritual matters.

Calling the Temple

Have your child contact the temple closest to you and ask for help and instructions on how to prepare. When your child goes to the temple for the first time, she will need to bring along a pair of garments to wear home. Ceremonial temple clothing can be purchased and brought to the temple or rented at the temple. She should dress in her Sunday best and should not wear too much jewelry or makeup.

Dressing in Temple Clothing

Tell your child that she will exchange her street clothes for white temple clothing in a private locker room. This white clothing will help her experience a oneness and equality with everyone around her and is also a symbol of purity. Most temples have a special bride's room where mothers and brides can change into their white temple clothing. Brides need to know that their wedding gowns should be modest and cover their garments respectfully.

THE SEALING ORDINANCE

Though the sealing ordinance can't be quoted, your son or daughter should be told that the sealing room will be beautiful, quiet, and sacred. After the bride, groom, and other family and friends are assembled in the sealing room, the temple officiator will offer the couple some counsel. Then he will perform the sealing ordinance.

WEARING THE HOLY GARMENT

Teach your child that the temple garment is a reminder of the sacred covenants he makes in the temple, a protective covering for the body, and a symbol of modesty in dress and living. Wearing the garment is like taking the temple with him when he leaves, or putting on the armor of God against a world filled with darkness, evil, and sin. The garment will strengthen him to resist temptation to the degree that he honors his temple covenants with God. The garment should be worn both day and night.

CIVIL CEREMONIES

If your child is not able or does not desire to go to the temple, he can ask your bishop to perform a civil ceremony. You can focus on making the wedding a happy time to remember, and the couple will know they can always count on you to love and support them. Your love, happiness, and acceptance of your child shouldn't be conditional. Couples who are not able to go to the temple when they are first married can prepare, with the guidance of their bishop, to be sealed in the temple later. Couples should go to the temple when they are ready and prepared to make and keep sacred covenants.

RECEPTIONS AND FAMILY DINNERS

Preparing for a wedding involves more than invitations, dresses, tuxedos, flowers, decorations, and food. If you're the mother of the bride or groom, don't get so caught up on the party details that you forget to open your heart to all the feelings you're experiencing.

How little or how much you are involved in the wedding party plans should be up to your child who is getting married. Don't take over. Ask what he wants you to do and try to do it with as little stress as possible. You needn't be extravagant and spend a lot of money for a wedding celebration. Consider letting your son choose between having a reception and/or family dinner and having the amount of cash you'd expect to spend to host those events.

Receptions or wedding parties of the past served the useful function of having family, community, or ward members get together to help a new couple obtain the basics they need to set up housekeeping. But these days more and more parents are overspending on receptions and dinners to impress their family and friends. It may be difficult to buck the trend, but remember that bigger is not always better. Simple receptions or wedding dinners don't need to cost a lot of money to be enjoyable and create good memories.

My husband and I served a casual wedding supper in our backyard for both families when our son got married. We ate Dutch oven turkey my husband had marinated and potatoes he had peeled along with a large mix of fruit and garden salads—several brought by helpful sisters and friends. We used loaner tables and chairs from the local church building. For our daughter's reception we served her favorite fudge brownies with ice cream and soda.

Consider having receptions at family homes or in churches that don't charge for use. Food can be homemade and simple. Photographers don't have to be professional to take good pictures. Decorations can be simple and still be beautiful. Honeymoons need not be exotic or extravagant.

At any wedding celebration, consider displaying a memory book, picture collection, or video about the bride and groom.

Whatever form your celebration takes, don't forget to allow family members to express their love for the bride or groom. Allow the bride and groom time to express their love and appreciation to their parents and siblings. Let the bride and groom have the floor with the instructions to tell their "story": how they met, their courtship, why they love each other, and their future plans and dreams.

In all this celebration keep a sense of humor, perspective, and reverence. What is taking place is sacred and a bit overwhelming. Show up, smile, and enjoy. Anything that doesn't go as planned will make great stories to tell later on.

ANNIVERSARIES

How you choose to celebrate your wedding anniversary is up to you. Don't be afraid to try something new or start a simple tradition you can maintain through the years.

As children come along it becomes harder to get away for an anniversary celebration, but a once-a-year getaway may be just what a harried mom and dad need. There's something about getting away together that helps you remember why you got married in the first place and helps you see your spouse as your sweetheart. If you can't afford a hotel room, get grandma to baby-sit and go camping. If it's too cold outside, switch houses with your parents for a night. Make the health of your marriage your number one priority.

ANNIVERSARY PRESENTS

Do anniversary presents your way. You may consider exchanging love letters, singing each other a silly or romantic song, dancing to candlelight, or revisiting special places that mean something to both of you. Remember that a present is something given of your own free will that you think will bring the other person pleasure or joy. If exchanging presents makes you both feel pressured, think of another way to surprise or delight each other.

Anniversary presents are gifts both tangible and intangible. If you'd rather buy an experience than just another possession, do something together that you both enjoy and that creates warm memories. The best present to give your spouse on your anniversary will always be the gift of your time, attention, forgiveness, and love.

Imagine your marriage over a lifetime. See how the choices you're making today send you on a path to tomorrow. What path are you on? Is it taking you where you want to go? The truest security you can give your children is a mother and father who love each other. Your love, marriage, and anniversary are meaningful enough for both of you to enjoy and celebrate them.

WRITE YOUR LOVE STORY

Consider writing a preview of your own fiftieth wedding anniversary now, no matter how long you've been married. How do you want your love story to read in years to come? Here's an example:

Richard and Karen are celebrating their anniversary today. Fifty years ago, they were young and had big dreams. Richard was going to be a famous novelist and tell all the important untold stories. Karen was gong to be a portrait artist of world renown. They were going to have their dream house, a two-story white frame nestled in the privacy of oak and pine.

But Richard was in school and Karen soon became pregnant. Years followed with tiny, cramped apartments, tuition to pay, and diapers to change. And Karen was pregnant again. After graduation, Richard found a job teaching English at the local junior college and Karen was pregnant again. He told funny stories to the children. She crayoned pictures with the children on the kitchen table. They saved for a down payment.

Their first home was not a two-story white frame nestled in aging pines and oaks. It was a small, one-level frame, and there was no landscaping at all. They planted trees and fixed and painted. And Karen was pregnant again. He wished he could find time to write in his journal. She wished she could find time to paint portraits of her children because they were growing up and changing so fast.

With their family population explosion, Richard decided he'd better add on to the house. He spent his workday hours teaching students to write essays and research papers. She spent her workday hours scrubbing her children's portraits off the living room walls.

Soon there were recitals and school plays, football games and proms, worn-out vans and bathrooms. Before long there were graduations, weddings, and grandchildren. Now Richard is ready to retire and Karen has all the children married off.

"Maybe now, I'll have time to write," he says. "But it will just have to wait until we get back from our trip to see Jamie get baptized, and Karen and I have always talked about going on a mission together."

"Maybe now I'll have time to paint," she says. "But it will have to wait until I get my lesson prepared for Relief Society and get a couple of sessions in at the temple."

Now they are on the way home to spend a quiet evening together for their anniversary. They are holding hands as they walk up the sidewalk to their home. When they look up, it seems to them that they are seeing their old home for the first time. The addition he built has made the house into a two-story. The trees they planted long ago are tall and aging. There is a banner across the front porch saying, "Happy Anniversary, Mom and Dad," in big bright red letters on butcher paper. Their children and grandchildren surprise them when they step inside the door.

As Richard and Karen watch their loved ones crowd around them, Richard suddenly realizes he was the author who began each of his children's life stories. Karen suddenly realizes the children are her greatest masterpieces.

Richard and Karen are seventy-two years young. He's still writing his life's story and she's still completing her masterpiece in the two-story white frame house nestled in the privacy of oak and pine.

FUNERALS

Funerals are seldom thought of as celebrations, especially when the death involves someone you love. Yet a funeral for members of The Church of Jesus Christ of Latter-day Saints can be an inner celebration of faith in the miracle of the resurrection and an outward celebration of your love for a singular, precious life. Birth and death mark our entrance and exit from this life, and both deserve to be honored and hallowed occasions celebrated with love.

When one of your loved ones leaves this life, it is time to review and renew your faith and belief in life after death. A funeral draws extended family members together like no other life event and is a perfect time to review the plan of salvation and the miracle of the resurrection. The questions we all have about the meaning of life and death can't be dismissed when someone we love dies. It's only fitting that family and friends instinctively gather to support and comfort each other.

When someone in your family dies suddenly, unexpectedly, or while they're still young, funerals can be traumatic and tragic. Yet at that same time there is a celebration or homecoming on the other side. Experiencing the death of someone you love is something no one wants to go through, but there is no way to avoid death either for yourselves or your loved ones.

WHEN SOMEONE DIES

If you have a loved one die at home, be aware that the death must be pronounced by someone who is authorized to do so, usually a licensed doctor. The cause and circumstances of that death must be certified. Each area of the world has specific requirements in this area. So, if a family member dies at home, call the police or another public official.

If you are in a hospital or hospice, notifying officials will probably be taken care of for you. The funeral home director or medical examiner will then be called. You will need several copies of the death certificate to be used later for making insurance claims, getting access to financial accounts, and settling the estate.

RECONSTRUCTING YOUR LIFE AFTER THE DEATH OF A LOVED ONE

Trying to reconstruct your life after a death depends on your relationship with the one who died, the age of your loved one, the way that the death occurred, and the emotional, financial, and spiritual reserves you have. People don't really "get over" the death of a close loved one—they just learn to go on with life in spite of it.

When you are the one who has just lost a mother, father, spouse, child, or grandchild, you're still in a state of shock when the funeral takes place. Close friends, neighbors, and extended family members can step up and help make the funeral experience as comforting as possible.

People who experience the death of a close family member have to face the shock of death, prepare an obituary for the newspaper, choose a casket and vault, select flowers, buy a burial plot, and plan a funeral while they are still in deep mourning. Add all these death-related responsibilities to all the normal cares of living, and life after death can be overwhelming for the grieving family.

HELPING THE GRIEVING FAMILY

If you're not in the immediate family of the person who died, you can do many things that will make the funeral and all the days before and after easier to bear. Consider organizing or assisting with a luncheon to be served after the funeral or graveside service. Help family members or friends organize pictures for display at the viewing or funeral. Set out blank memory book pages for guests to write on and later collect them into a book to be presented to the grieving family.

Write a letter recalling memorable experiences and character traits you admired about the person who passed away. Offer to take care of the flowers in any way the bereaved desires. You can deliver excess funeral flowers to local hospitals, rest homes, or extended family and friends. Offer to return dishes to people who have brought food. Offer to clean the house or wash the clothes. Offer childcare or a listening ear. Offer to pay bills or run errands. Offer your home as a place for visiting family to stay.

THE GLOVE DEMONSTRATION

To help your child understand death, tell him to pretend that your hand is a spirit *(hold up your hand)*. Tell him that all of us used to live with our Heavenly Father before we came to earth *(wiggle your fingers)* and that this spirit could move and live by itself in heaven. Tell your child that this glove *(hold up a glove)* is like his body. Until the spirit *(wiggle your hand)* enters the body, the body has no life. Tell your child that when he came to earth, his spirit entered his body *(put your hand inside the glove)*. Then his body became alive *(wiggle your hand inside the glove)*. His spirit will stay in his body until he dies. When he dies, his spirit and body will be separated *(take your hand from the glove)*. His body will be *buried (place the glove on the ground)* and his spirit will return to the spirit world *(hold your hand up high)*. Tell your child that when we die our spirits are separated from our bodies. Even though a body is dead, the person, or the spirit, is not dead. (See Boyd K. Packer, *Teach Ye Diligently* [Salt Lake City: Deseret Book, 1975], 273–81.)

Most people are glad to help the bereaved for the first few weeks after a death. But soon the letters, phone calls, and visits stop and people go on with their lives. Be the person who calls and comes over when everyone else has gone home. Be the person who will sit and listen.

HELPING CHILDREN COPE WITH DEATH

Most children don't face the death of a parent or sibling in their young years, but some do. Many will face the death of their grandparents or great-grandparents. As a mother you'll need to be sensitive to your child's needs at the time of a death. Young children don't comprehend death and need easy-to-understand explanations about what happens when someone dies. This is a good time to explain the difference between the spirit and the body and how they separate at death.

HELPING CHILDREN COPE WITH THE VIEWING AND FUNERAL

Forcing young children to see, touch, or kiss a dead relative is never a good idea. Always give your children the opportunity and option of viewing the loved one who has passed away, but prepare your child beforehand. Your loved one's body will not look like it did before death. The skin will feel cold and hard to the touch. The funeral director will apply makeup to help with the body's appearance. Some adults and children are comfortable touching the dead body and others prefer not to.

HELPING PREPARE THE BODY FOR BURIAL

You may consider helping dress and prepare your loved one's body for the viewing and funeral in any number of ways. Most funeral home directors will allow you to clothe, fix hair, and apply makeup if you so desire. You may want to bring burial clothing and perhaps ceremonial temple clothing to the mortuary for your loved one. You may choose to leave the preparation and dressing of the body to the morticians.

Most states have laws about cremation and embalming. You will want to be informed about the laws where you live. For instance, your state may require that you bury a body in the first 24 hours if you choose to forgo embalming. After a body is embalmed, it will be preserved for weeks so there is no rush to plan and host the viewing and funeral. You will have ample time to assemble family members.

FAMILY TRADITIONS AT THE TIME OF DEATH

You might want to consider beginning a family tradition at the time of death, such as planting a tree or starting a scholarship fund. Making gifts of the loved one's possessions or asking that money for flowers be spent on a favorite charity are also possibilities. The way you choose to honor a family member at death should be as individual as you are. I know one family that lined their father's usual jogging route with yellow ribbons.

You might sing or compose a song, write a poem or love letter, make a memory book, light a candle, or create your own private memorial. When someone passes from this life to the next, you can choose to celebrate your loved one's life in ways that bring you comfort, peace, and closure.

BAPTISMS

PREPARING YOUR CHILD FOR BAPTISM

When your child reaches the age of eight years, she is considered accountable for her actions and can choose to accept the ordinance of baptism. Baptism by immersion (going completely under the water) by one having authority from Jesus Christ is the way to become a member of The Church of Jesus Christ of Latter-day Saints.

Many children worry about sinning after baptism and should be taught that they can be cleansed and forgiven by repenting and recommitting themselves to their baptismal covenants when they partake of the sacrament every week.

Teach your child that with baptism she

witnesses to the world and to God that she is willing to follow Jesus. She covenants (promises) to serve Jesus, keep his commandments, and always remember him.

After your child is baptized, she will receive the gift of the Holy Ghost by the laying on of hands by one who has authority from Jesus Christ. Teach her that the Holy Ghost is a member of the Godhead who can be a constant companion as long as she lives righteously. The Holy Ghost does not have a body and can offer comfort, protection, and help in choosing between right and wrong. Everyone who repents of his sins, is baptized as a member of the Church, and tries to live worthily can have the constant influence of the Holy Ghost.

Teach your child to recognize the Holy Ghost as a still small voice or a feeling of love and peace. It is through the Holy Ghost that people gain a testimony of Jesus Christ. The Holy Ghost may warn your child of danger, offer comfort in time of need, help her understand sacred things, and testify of truth.

Practice Baptism

You may want to have your husband or another priesthood leader "practice" baptism with your child so he is less nervous and knows what to expect. Show him how to bend his knees and hold his nose when he goes under the water.

BAPTISM DAY

Children can be baptized in any body of water, but your child will most likely be baptized in a baptismal font at the closest stake meetinghouse in your area. Your child and anyone attending the baptism should wear Sunday-best clothing to the baptism. Many baptisms are held on a stake-wide basis with each ward taking turns to provide the music and talks before the baptism. Or you may need to provide the music and talks yourself. You can bring your own white clothing for your child or use the clothing provided by the stake meetinghouse.

Your child and the person performing the baptism will change into white clothing in separate men's and women's dressing rooms. After the baptism, your child and the person who performed the ordinance will change back into dry clothes. Later your child will be confirmed and receive the gift of the Holy Ghost.

You can help your child in the dressing room before and after the baptism. Be sure to bring towels, dry underclothing, a bag for wet clothes, and hair drying and styling equipment with you. You won't be allowed to take pictures during the actual baptism but you can take pictures before and after the baptism. You can host a family meal or refreshments if that will add to your joy on your child's baptism day.

Be sure to write about the day in your journal and encourage your child to do the same. Make a special place of honor in your child's memory book for his baptism certificate and photographs of everyone who attended. You might also consider giving your child a small present such as a set of scriptures.

TURNING EIGHT

Turning eight not only means your child can be baptized but it also begins new involvement in a Church-sponsored activity program. When your daughter turns eight, she becomes involved in the Achievement Day program. When your son turns eight,

---

YOUNG WOMEN PROGRAM

To honor a daughter entering the Young Women's program, consider the following ideas.

• Hold a special family home evening explaining the Young Women's program to the family. Explain the details of the program and decide on ways the family can support the daughter who has turned twelve.

• Assign the daughter who is entering the Young Women's program to explain to the family all the goals and values of the program and what she intends to work on for the following year.

• Hold a family dinner or another special family activity chosen by your daughter.

PRIESTHOOD ORDINATIONS

To honor a son who will be ordained to an office in the Aaronic priesthood, consider the following ideas.

• Hold a special family home evening in honor of the family member who will be ordained. Give a lesson on the priesthood to all family members. Explain that God gives his power to worthy men here on earth so they can bless themselves, their families, and the whole world. Explain the many duties and functions of the priesthood.

• Assign the person who is being ordained to explain to the family all the duties of the office to which he will be ordained. Have him tell ways he would like to use his priesthood to bless the lives of others.

• Tell family members about the ordination and invite every family member to attend.

• Hold a family dinner or another special family activity chosen by the one being ordained.

---

he becomes involved in Cub Scouts. Your child will later appreciate having photographs of their leaders, activities, and friends in the ward. You can celebrate this time in your child's life by participating in her activities and supporting her goals.

TURNING TWELVE

Turning twelve is a major milestone for both boys and girls. Young men have the opportunity to be ordained to the Aaronic priesthood. Young women begin

participation in the Young Women program. Each advancement in the priesthood and the Young Women program offers you a great opportunity to take a picture of your child with his parents, siblings, and peers. Also consider taking a picture of your child with his youth leader and members of the bishopric. Memory book pages can be put together that include priesthood ordination certificates, goals completed, and service activities completed as a family or in the youth group.

GRADUATIONS

Graduations mark the end of one era of schooling and the beginning of another. Whether your child is graduating from preschool, junior high, high school, or a university, don't let the moment pass without a little pomp and circumstance.

Encourage your child to wear the cap and gown, march in the procession, sing the school song, and listen to the long speeches and fanfare. Gather with friends and family for good food, fun, and some great pictures. Celebrate the accomplishment of a goal, the end of an era, and the beginning of the next. Celebrate the opportunity to receive a formal education, the joy of learning, and the potential of the human mind and spirit.

I finished my college degree after my first six children were born. I knew I wouldn't be a very good example for my sons and daughters later in life if I didn't. I took evening classes after my husband got home from work. Later, when I received the outstanding student award, we went as a family to purchase a new dining room set with the award money. That set contained a chair for each family member as a life-long remembrance of the support they each gave to me in accomplishing my dream of becoming a college graduate.

I still display the graduation picture of myself surrounded by my family so that my children will know that in our home we finish what we start. I want them to know that the pursuit of education and knowledge is important to their mother. Yet that picture and graduation wouldn't mean much if I didn't continue day by day to demonstrate a love of learning.

Mothers are their children's first and greatest teachers. You can teach your children to value the opportunity to learn. Teach them by your example that a true education is a lifelong pursuit worth any work and sacrifice.

LEAVING HOME

When a child leaves home to marry, work, go on a mission, leave for college, or simply move out on her own, think about having some kind of celebration or send-off party. This celebration can be as simple as writing your child a letter expressing your love and confidence in her ability to make a difference in the world. Or your celebration might entail a flying leap where you both click your heels together in the

air and give each other a high five. You might want to find a sentimental or corny song of parting that you sing to each other. At the very least, take your child's face in your hands, kiss her, and say, "I love you and I'm going to miss you."

When your child cleans out her bedroom and boxes up or throws away her childhood menagerie, give yourself something ceremonial to do so you won't feel like you're coming apart at the seams. You might want to assemble a memory box where you keep things that remind you of your child as she was growing up. Change is hard for both of you. You might find you're getting on each other's nerves or snapping at each other. The emotions that come from parting are confusing.

You can help your child go through her childhood belongings or stay as far away as possible so you won't start blubbering on her old paper dolls. But don't be afraid to show her how much she means to you. Tears are not something to be ashamed of. Tears cleanse the soul and hallow an occasion.

When your child leaves home, mark the occasion with something positive that builds your relationship. Take your child out to dinner, go for a long walk and say everything you've been meaning to say, or

kneel side-by-side and pray together. Whatever you do, by all means say good-bye with love and tenderness.

LEAVING ON A MISSION

For a mother, a mission farewell is a mixed bag of emotions. You spend your whole life hoping your child will want to serve a mission and be worthy to do so, but when the time comes to actually say good-bye, it's always more difficult than you think.

Getting a child ready to leave on a mission is a wonderful and heart-wrenching process. You'll worry about your child's spiritual, financial, social, and emotional preparation. You'll regret all the things you've left undone. You'll worry that your missionary might get hurt or sick and you won't be able to help. You'll worry that your child might be one of those few who are injured or killed while serving. You'll worry about not teaching your child to wash his clothes, fix his meals, or clean up after himself well enough. You'll wish you had more time to do all the things you thought mothers were supposed to do before their child leaves home.

You'll be right there as your child fills out his papers and gets home from bishop and stake president's interviews. You'll wait anxiously for that large white envelope from the Office of the First Presidency. You'll be accompanying him to the temple for the first time and helping him pick out garments. You'll be shopping together for white shirts, ties, and suits. You'll be dropping him off at the airport or the

IDEAS FOR FAMILIES WITH PROSPECTIVE MISSIONARIES

- Before your missionary leaves home, have a special family dinner with centerpieces made from flags or other articles from the place where your missionary will be serving. Invite extended family members, friends, or people who have served in your child's mission before.
- Prepare the missionary's favorite meal or a typical meal from the place where he will be serving.
- At a special family meal or meeting, ask each family member to come prepared to share a piece of information about the area where the missionary will be serving. Also ask your missionary to share information he has about the area.
- At a family home evening, special meal, or meeting ask each family member to share several experiences they have had with the future missionary or tell several reasons why they love him.
- Have a special family testimony meeting where all members are encouraged to share what the gospel means in their life.
- Assign family members to share a conversion story about an ancestor during a family home evening or a special meal.
- Ask your husband (or another worthy priesthood holder) to give your missionary a blessing.
- Ask each family member (friends, teachers, and leaders) to write a short letter to the missionary expressing their love and confidence.
- Give small, useful gifts to the missionary such as favorite recipes, a small first aid kit, a sewing kit, a family picture, or a map of the area where the missionary will be serving.
- Present your missionary with personalized copies of the Book of Mormon with family testimonies written inside ready to be given to investigators on his mission.
- Place a large map of the area where your missionary will be serving on the family bulletin board or another prominent place in the house. Ask your missionary to send home the name of his first area along with a picture of his living arrangements and his companion. The missionary could also send home pictures of local members or people they are teaching. Place a flag or pin on the map with pictures in the corner for all family members to see. Each time your missionary is transferred, ask for the same things. Then every family member can keep up with the latest events in the life of your missionary.

missionary training center. You'll be happy and sad, nervous and relieved, scared and full of joy. And you'll probably cry a lot.

You will miss your child more than you thought you would. You will be much kinder to anyone who knocks on your door. You will anxiously await those weekly letters. You will put your child in God's hands and pray like you've never prayed before.

You will also have compensating blessings that you didn't expect. One of those will be your missionary's letters home that express love and appreciation for everything you did for him as he was growing up. You will see spiritual growth and development and heartache and disappointment change your boy or girl into a man or a woman. You will see the effect your missionary's service is having on his brothers and sisters. You will feel the spirit of missionary work inside your home and heart like you never have before. You will think more deeply about all the thousands of missionaries out there and all their parents and brothers and sisters, and you will feel connected to a work that will astound you.

Write your missionary every week and save his letters home. A mission is a two-year-long celebration of ups and downs that will change hearts, enlarge minds, and give your family back more than you gave.

THE GREAT OUTDOORS

Nature is good for your body, your soul, and your sense of gratitude. Whether you're gazing at a fabulous sunrise, strolling barefoot along a peaceful shoreline, or taking a brisk jog around the block, you can improve your physical, mental, and spiritual health by including a daily outside adventure. A regular celebration of the great outdoors is a healthy way for families to live. You will feel better inside and out when you make it a habit to go outside at least once a day and enjoy some kind of contact with plants, animals, fresh air, and sky. Scientists are discovering what most of us instinctively know—nature heals.

With any outdoor celebration or outing, make sure you tell someone where you are going and when to expect your return. Dress appropriately, pack a first aid kit, plenty of food and water, a good map, and lots of common sense. Insect repellant, sunscreen, wet wipes, and a port-a-potty are also great additions to your adventure. Don't take any unnecessary risks. Start with small and manageable outings. Dress in clothes you can play and sleep in and have fun getting dirt in your teeth, wind in your hair, and a blush on your cheeks.

WALKS

Going for a walk is perhaps the simplest way to let nature heal you, your relationship with your child, and your marriage. If you take a walk by yourself, you allow yourself the time to think about your day and your life. You give yourself the time and space to pray and meditate. As you separate yourself from the routine of your life for a few minutes, you present yourself with the gift of distance, perspective, and objectivity. The exercise gets your heart beating and your digestive system moving and energizes you with new enthusiasm. You feel somehow closer to the divine. For walking, like other forms of exercise, refreshes and rejuvenates the body, mind, and spirit.

If you go for a walk with your husband, you give your relationship time away from the telephone, children, television, and other commitments. You can focus on each other and enjoy being together without distractions. The exercise will help keep you both healthy and able to control weight gain. Your conversations can be restoring and help reconnect you after a hectic day. Going for a walk together with your spouse is intimate and invigorating.

Going for a walk with your children at any age is always a good way to spend time together. If your child is still very young, you can push a stroller and often she'll fall asleep and give you a needed break. If she's a little older, you get to share your own love of the earth, wind, and sky with your eager, active child and get her a little more worn out so she'll take a good nap. If your child is school-age, walking is often the best way to get her to really talk. There's something about walking that brings on the conversations you struggle for at home. Going for a walk with your teen is often the easiest way to stay in touch with each other. Walking and talking with your teen may be just what the doctor ordered.

You don't have to be rich to go for a walk. You don't have to have lots of time to go for a walk. You don't have to pay for fancy equipment or a gym to exercise. You don't have to pay a counselor to get your children to talk to you. You don't have to deal with health problems from sedentary lifestyles. You feel better, look better, and keep your relationships strong.

PLAYGROUNDS

All children love playgrounds. Take the time to search out and locate every playground near your home. Better yet, create a playground in your own backyard. A playground for a child can consist of the typical swings, slide, and jungle gym equipment found in a city park or many other settings. A playground for a child is anywhere you go with the grand intention of playing. Any large open area with grassy hills to run up and roll down is a playground. Any large dirt, gravel, or sandpile is a playground. Clumps of trees are playgrounds. Any ditch, canal, river, stream, or lake is a playground. Wide open fields, junkyards, ponds, and weed patches are playgrounds. Try to remember the way you once viewed the world as a child. The whole world is one very large, interesting playground if you see properly.

CAMPING

Camping has been reported to be the most common recreation of healthy, happy families. Now if you don't think that's a funny piece of information, you haven't been camping with children lately.

Camping means many different things to different people. Some people set up camp in their backyard with a tent. Some sleep out under the stars in the mountains. Some take trailers to the sand dunes. Others find a lonely beach and sleep on the sand. Camping simply means sleeping outside somewhere, with or without the shelter of a tent or trailer.

All camping experiences with children

start out with sappy sentimentalism, but the hodgepodge of scary business that happens while you're actually camping will give you gray hair. You dream of sitting around the campfire swapping spooky stories, sharing perfectly toasted marshmallows, and bonding. What you get never quite fits that ideal image.

Camping experiences with children are always very educational. You and your children may learn:

• how to try and fail to start a campfire for two hours in a windstorm

• how to touch poison ivy without really trying

• how to hike for two yards before breaking down and blurting, "I'm hungry! I'm tired! I have to go to the bathroom!"

• how to invite the nearest bumblebee into your pants

• how to dry wet jeans over the fire on used marshmallow sticks before you drop them into the flames

• how to get lost in the woods when no one's looking

While you're camping, you'll likely have one child come down with a fever and another have an accident in his sleeping bag. But there is nothing quite like a burned piece of bacon cooked over a gas grill on a sticky fly-infested picnic table. There's nothing like Boy Scout pepper in your tinfoil dinner (if you remember to bring the ketchup). There's nothing quite like ticks hiding out on all the private parts of your body.

Getting the kids to go to sleep will be your favorite part of your little family outing. This may sound easy, but let me tell you, pushing several smelly, black, sootcovered, sunburned, insect-bitten children into a tiny enclosed area is like lighting a short fuse.

You'll likely hear such memorable children-in-tent-after-dark comments as

"Your toes are touching me."

"Get off my face!"

"What stinks around here?"

"Would you guys shut up. I'm trying to go to sleep."

"What's that scratching sound?" "Are there bears in the forest?"

"I have to go to the bathroom."

"Well go then."

"I'm not going out there in THE DARK by myself."

"All right then. Hold it all night."

"You guys better quit throwing your underwear or I'm telling."

"Quit twitching, will ya."

"Are there bears in the forest?"

"I still have to go to the bathroom."

The fact that experts have reported that camping is the most common activity of happy families will never cease to amaze you. Why? After two days in the hills with your children, you realize home never looked so good.

If you do want to give camping a try, you don't have to have all the equipment on hand. You can borrow or rent many items before you decide if you want to buy them for yourself.

HOW TO MAKE ALUMINUM FOIL MEALS

Fold foil to double thickness. Place the food you want to cook on the foil. Fold the foil over the food and make a tight package. After the fire burns down and there are hot coals, place the foil dinner on the coals to cook. Turn several times during cooking. After the food is cooked, carefully open the foil and enjoy. Try a quarter pound of

CAMPING EQUIPMENT

- tent
- plastic tarp
- rope
- sleeping bags (and foam rubber pads)
- compass
- cooler
- gas stove (optional)
- fishing pole (optional)
- hatchet
- lantern
- canteen
- map
- blankets
- towels and washcloths
- wet wipes or a bar of soap
- toothbrush
- toilet paper
- comb
- change of clothing
- insect repellant
- sunscreen
- first-aid kit
- flashlight
- candles
- frying pan, saucepan, or aluminum foil
- oven rack (for cooking over the fire)
- fork and spatula with long handles
- knife
- can opener
- disposable plates, bowls, and flatware
- large plastic bowl
- plastic trash bag
- non-perishable food
- salt and pepper
- entertainment for rainy days (games, books, musical instruments)
- entertainment for sunny days (balls, Frisbee, binoculars, magnifying glass)

If you take a baby, be sure to bring along a portable playpen or a stroller. Be sure to wear good hiking shoes or boots and a sweatshirt with a hood for cool nights and mornings.

BACKPACKING

Backpacking means you pack everything you need on your back and hike to where you camp or sleep out. It generally requires good planning because you will probably hike too far from civilization to turn back for the toilet paper.

Consider taking along the following items:

- two-man lightweight tent
- plastic tarp
- sleeping bag
- canteen
- individual stove
- mess kit
- rope
- trash bag
- flashlight
- first-aid kit
- toothbrush and toothpaste
- soap
- insect repellant
- sunscreen
- chlorine tablets or water purifier
- raincoat
- matches
- toilet paper
- change of clothing
- extra pair of socks
- towel and washcloth
- food (powdered milk, dried fruit and vegetables, soup mixes, drink mixes, and water)

hamburger or a piece of chicken combined with potatoes, carrots, onions, or other vegetables for a great hot meal. Cut up little bits of butter over the vegetables, add salt and pepper, or sprinkle with your favorite seasoning to enhance the flavors.

TO MAKE A FIRE

Find a safe place to build a fire. Rock, gravel, or an area of dirt away from dry grass or leaves is best.

Place paper or tinder (anything that lights easily) in the center.

Place kindling (small sticks or dead wood) on top of the tinder to make the fire stronger.

Place fuel (larger pieces of wood or dead branches about one foot long) on top of the kindling to keep the fire burning in a teepee fashion.

For cooking, remember to keep your back to the wind. Let the fire burn down from large flames to smoldering sticks and coals. Roasting marshmallows on sticks is one of the highlights that should not be missed. Smashing melted marshmallows and chocolate chips between two graham crackers is another favorite.

CHOOSING A CAMPSITE

A good campsite should be clear of most trees and bushes. Look for a place where there are trees to the west and north of your site. That should let the morning sunlight through in the morning and protect you from strong winds. The site should also be higher than the area around it. Don't camp too close to the edge of water. Water levels can change quickly and water also invites mosquitoes. Find a place with fresh water

BEACHING

Anything you do at a beach is called beaching. This includes hunting for seashells, making sand castles, playing or swimming in the water, fishing, clam baking, or simply lying around on the sand enjoying the sun.

Consider bringing along these things:
- beach blanket
- towels
- tennis shoes
- bathing suit
- extra outfit
- umbrella
- sweatshirt
- life jacket
- sunscreen
- pail and shovel
- food and drink

close by and bring along a water purification system.

HIKING

Hiking is taking the basic walk to a higher level and making an outing or excursion out of it. I think my husband has hiked our family up every major mountain in Utah. Hiking to the top of a mountain is hard work, but it gives children and parents a sense of accomplishment after reaching a lofty goal. It's also amazing how your sense of perspective changes when you get up high and look down below to the world you thought you knew. If you can hike to the top of a mountain even when you don't think you'll make it, you can conquer other mountains or obstacles in your life as well.

Bring along a hiker's snack in self-sealing plastic bags. Hiker's snacks can include things like raisins, nuts, dried fruit, chocolate chips, and cereal. Always bring water and sip from it frequently; it's easy to get dehydrated when you're hiking.

Teach your children to follow a trail. Stones placed on top of each other and notched trees often mark trails.

Always bring along a map or plan and a compass. Keep your toes pointed straight ahead or slightly inward, then lean forward a little. Push off with your toes and let your heel down lightly. Watch where you're walking so you won't slip and fall. Watch for animal tracks. See if you can identify what animal passed by recently by the footprints left behind.

OTHER "-INGS"

DESERTING

Deserting is anything you do in the desert, including rock hunting, hiking, riding motorcycles and four-wheelers, and rolling down sand dunes. When you spend time in the desert, remember to bring along plenty of water, wide-brimmed hats, a good map, and lots of sunscreen.

MOUNTAINING

Mountaining is anything you do in the mountains, including hiking, camping, riding horses or motor vehicles, fishing, hunting, and basically hanging out with the trees and wildlife. When you spend time in the mountains be sure to remember that the weather and temperature can change quickly and you need to be prepared for storms and unexpected injuries.

SNOWING

Snowing is anything you do in the snow to have fun, including cross-country skiing, downhill skiing, making snowmen, building forts, having snowball fights, making angels, and snowmobiling. When you spend time in the snow you need to dress properly to keep yourself warm and prepare for basic survival if you get lost.

BACKYARDING

Backyarding is anything you do in the backyard for fun, including throwing balls, running through the sprinklers, swinging, digging, jumping, rolling, and sleeping out. Backyards are great places to make a trial run with your outdoor equipment. Remember your insect repellant and sunscreen.

FAMILY VACATIONS

Any parent knows that family vacations are not vacations at all for mom and dad. They are hard work and great opportunities to practice patience and perseverance.

If you want to take a true vacation complete with rest and relaxation, get away with your husband and leave the children home. Despite the difficulties, however, a family vacation gives you and your child an important celebration of change. Everyone needs to get out of the rut of everyday living and go somewhere else. Family vacations put you together in unique places and create the most vivid memories because each experience is new and fresh. So it's worth it to be your best self on vacation—relax and have fun. The point is to enjoy each other while you're experiencing new things. Even if things don't go according to plan, a vacation will give you, if nothing else, a new appreciation for home.

A family vacation creates lasting memories—some good, some funny, and some not so funny. The experiences that are not so funny while they are happening always turn out to be the very experiences that you laugh about the most as the years go by. So muster up your courage, decide to take your family somewhere—anywhere—and let the games begin.

GETTING THERE

Most family vacations are actually fun—once you get there. Traveling can be another story. A family road trip is like ushering your entire household one by one into your cramped bedroom closet with these instructions: "Please behave yourselves and enjoy the ride." For a toddler or infant who can't see out of car windows, there really is about as much scenery to look at as there is in a dark closet.

Cars are simply not designed for families. There is no soundproof window to separate the parents from the kids, and things always tend to get a little out of hand. What can you expect when you put several healthy, hostile siblings in an enclosure where their skin touches? All in the name of creating happy family memories, moms and dads are also asked to hog-tie our wiggly little offspring into child straightjackets called car seats. There's no doubt about it, seatbelts and car seats save lives. They just don't do a very good job of saving a parent's sanity.

One of the toughest things about taking a baby on a trip is the inevitable hour when all the bottles, snacks, toys, and silly faces won't entertain your little less-than-happy bundle anymore. If you take your child out of her car seat, you'll be endangering her life and breaking the law. If you don't, you endanger your mental health. Great choice, huh? Now you have the privilege of listening to your screaming maniac for the remainder of the drive. If you stop the car and give baby the needed hug, you run the risk of being quickly flattened by a passing motorist. If you don't stop the car and give baby the needed hug, you run the risk of losing your hearing.

When you finally reach your vacation destination, some fellow traveler might ask, "Are you all one big happy family?"

"We were *before* we came on this trip," you'll feel like answering.

Family travel always looks better in retrospect. You start flipping through all the old vacation photos and get all sentimental and mushy because you've forgotten all the hard parts. Then you find yourself doing the whole thing over again next year.

SHOULD YOU TAKE A VACATION THIS YEAR?

Every family of every income can plan a yearly vacation that meets the budget. If you don't have much money, you just need

---

FUN FAMILY VACATIONS

Close-to-Home Mini Adventures

Close-to-home mini adventures are trips you can take in one day. Check with your local travel bureau. Many people ignore the fabulous places to visit close by their own homes.

Exotic Excursions

Exotic excursions include foreign vacations and trips that expose your children to other cultures and people.

Outdoor Living

Outdoor living vacations include any outdoor destination or basic camping.

Visiting Relatives

The main purpose of visiting a relative is to reconnect with family members who live far away. Planning things to do while you're there is also part of the fun.

Historical/Learning Experiences

Historical vacations include destinations nearby or far away that have historical significance. Learning experiences include any place that is new to you or your child. Learning experiences can also include youth summer camps and conferences.

Theme Parks

Theme park vacations include places like Disneyland, Epcot Center, and local amusement parks.

---

out, and pack a cooler stocked at the local grocery store. You can stay at a cabin or a beach house, switch homes with someone, or stay at your Great Aunt Martha's house. The point of a family vacation is to make memories, build relationships, and have fun.

HOW TO SAVE MONEY ON VACATION PACKAGES

To save money on lodging expenses, consider joining a hospitality club where you stay in member's homes for free and they stay in yours. You might enjoy being a caretaker or host at a farm, ranch, canyon, or park for a few weeks or a few years in the United States or abroad. If you're good at enlisting friends and family to go on a trip, you can often get your ticket free, along with a good group rate.

Many airlines, trains, and buses offer group rates and huge discounts if you meet their requirements. Check the Internet or your local travel agent regularly for good deals on cruises, vacation packages, and work/play opportunities. Students can find great deals in every area of travel.

to be more creative. Children often have more fun going camping than going to Europe. If you have the money, you can fly, stay in hotels, and eat at restaurants. If you're short on cash, you can drive, camp

ENTERTAINING CHILDREN

To keep children busy on long road trips, try the following ideas:

- **Play navigator**. Assign a child (preferably an older child who can read maps) one hour to be the navigator. Give the child a map and let him tell you where to go.

- **Write or draw in a journal**. Give your children notebooks to take on your trip. Tell them to write, draw pictures, or take photographs about the places you visit.

- **Tell family stories**. Tell your children about your childhood, parents, brothers and sisters, courtship, wedding day, or any other family story. If you're going to a Church history site, tell your children about an ancestor who might have lived there.

- **Play the alphabet game**. Look for the letters of the alphabet in succession from A to Z on license plates, billboards, and street signs. The first one to Z wins.

- **Play scavenger hunt**. Give each child a list of common things they might see along the road. The first child to spot every item on the list wins.

- **Play the counting game**. Have your children count items easily seen along the road. The first one to reach a predetermined number wins. You can count red cars, motorcycles, green trees, or road mileage markers.

- **Play the "guess how far we've gone" game**. Tell your children to say when they think you've gone a predetermined number of miles. For example, have them call out five, ten, or twenty miles when they think you've covered that distance. Have the driver watch the odometer, and the child with the closest guess wins.

- **Play "categories."** Have someone in the family select a category such as movies, fruits, colors, or candy bars. Go around the family and have each member think of an item in that category until someone runs out of ideas. The first one to run out of ideas drops out of the game. The last family member in the game wins.

- **Take along a travel bag**. Give each member of the family a travel bag filled with treats, notebook, maps, and grooming supplies. Each child can save souvenirs in this bag also.

- **Sing songs as you drive**. Choose old family favorites, hymns, or Primary songs to sing as you drive. Be careful not to teach any particularly annoying song that you don't want to hear over and over.

- **Play the license plate game**. Try to find license plates from all 50 states as you drive.

CELEBRATING DAILY LIFE

GIFTING

The giving and receiving of gifts doesn't have to be a chore or an obligation. Giving a gift at times other than the culturally assigned holidays and birthdays is what true gifting is. Gifting is offering gifts for no special reason except love and generosity. Gifting is offering someone something that you believe will bring them joy or lighten their load. These gifts usually can't be bought with money but are more likely to be your time, knowledge, resources, meals, conversation, and friendship. When you learn the art of gifting, you make any day a celebration with your love.

MEMORY BOOKS OR QUILTS

A memory book (also called a baby book or photo album) is a visual celebration of your child's life. Memory books can take on any form you're comfortable with. The simplest form is a three-ring binder filled with pages of pictures of your child as he grows up. You can also include such items as hand drawn pictures, awards, pictures of classmates, certificates, report cards, written accounts of important events, and any number of other documents, memorabilia, and pictures you want to save.

When your child leaves home, you'll have to decide if you'll send the book with him or keep it yourself. If you don't want to be faced with that choice, keep two memory books—one for you and one for your child. Scrapbooking is a multi-million dollar industry now, so you'll have no trouble finding supplies.

Memory quilts are wall hangings or blankets made from scraps of well-worn or outgrown clothing your child has worn while growing up. Most clothes, no matter how old, have a spot or two of fabric that is still in good shape. Cut old clothes into squares of the same size and save the assorted collection of fabric until you have enough to piece together a quilt top. You can also use old sheets and blankets.

Another way to make a memory quilt is to ask important people in your child's life to help you make a square or two to include. You give the person a square or two of cloth and ask her to decorate it any

COLLECTING

Collecting is creating and saving large or small groups of just about anything you think is beautiful or interesting—a celebration in miniature of what you love most. To a small child, a shiny rock looks like a nugget of pure gold. You and your children can collect anything you find beautiful, including:

- rocks
- insects
- leaves
- flowers
- foreign money
- trading cards
- paper dolls
- coins
- stamps
- antique furniture
- toys
- dishes
- dolls
- cups
- spoons
- doodads
- costumes
- jewelry
- bottles
- glassware
- vintage clothing
- hats
- seashells
- bones
- fine art
- books
- holiday decorations
- miniatures

way she desires. You can ask her to write her name on the square or include a picture. These squares can be decorated with embroidery, iron-on letters, scanned pictures, or appliqué.

KEEPING CONNECTED

As families grow and change it becomes more difficult to keep in touch with each other, but the extra effort is always worth it. Consider ways to keep your family connected when not everyone lives at home.

SUNDAY OR MONDAY FAMILY DINNERS

Some extended families like to get together once a week for Sunday dinner or once a month for family night. Extended family dinners can be potluck so grandma and grandpa aren't overwhelmed. Birthdays for the week or month can be celebrated at these gatherings so all family members can attend.

PERSONAL LETTERS/E-MAILS

Write or call often if you are far away from each other. Write to family missionaries. Whether living at home or somewhere else, children always love a personal note written just for them. Take the time to write to your children through snail mail or e-mail.

FAMILY NEWSLETTERS/E-MAILS

Whether sent by e-mail or in paper form, family newsletters are a great way for all the members of the family to stay updated on what is happening in the lives of all the other members. An easy way to begin a newsletter is for one person to write a page about the news from his family. He then sends the page to another family member, who in turn writes her own page and sends the two pages on to the next person. The pages stay in circulation until they come back to the first person, who takes out his old page, adds a new one, and keeps the bundle of pages in circulation.

HISTORIES

Your family history is happening right now. The characters in your story are all around you, and key events are happening every day. Go to family reunions, funerals, weddings, and graduations. Take photographs and keep records of traditions and

---

DAILY OR WEEKLY CELEBRATION RITUALS:

Celebrations need not be fancy. You can develop family rituals that serve as everyday mini celebrations for your family.

- wave good-bye or blow a kiss at the front room window every morning.
- bring home Friday night treats and pizza every weekend.
- make every Monday night a family night.
- tell bedtime stories every night.
- read scriptures at the dinner table.
- say a family prayer every morning.
- kiss and hug each other good night, good-bye, and welcome home.
- have dinner between five and six o'clock every weeknight.
- make Sunday dinners special or traditional.
- tuck your child in bed at night with a ritual only the two of you know about.

---

celebrations. Visit grandparents, aunts, uncles, and cousins and share stories about relatives, both living and dead. As you go along, write the story of your own life. Your personal and family history is one of the most important things you will ever write, and it will be the best way for family to feel connected to you after you die.

THINGS I WISH MY MOTHER HAD TOLD ME

- *Your children are not you. The childhood they are experiencing is something very different from the childhood you think they are having. Don't worry, they'll tell you about it when they grow up.*
- *You don't have to do big, glorious, important things to have a great life. Just do small things with big, glorious, important love.*
- *Anything that can keep your children quiet and entertained for an hour can't be all bad.*
- *You are an attractive and likeable human being—especially when you smile.*
- *Add years to your life and life to your years by preventing a hardening of the attitudes.*
- *Joy comes when you are paying attention to all the things you're grateful for instead of all the things you're miserable about.*
- *You were not joking when you shouted for joy the day you found out you got to come to earth, get a body, and have your life.*
- *Surround yourself with people who help you see the good in yourself and in your life.*
- *Time is the gift we are all given equally.*
- *Always make important decisions with your heart. Make little decisions with your heart too.*
- *Give your children your unhurried time. Children know that their parents give their time to what they love most.*
- *Time invested in children will give you a posterity that will never end.*
- *Good marriages take a lot of mutual toleration, patience, work, and forgiveness.*
- *Children grow up and parents grow old. Be glad you're the middle of God's sandwich.*
- *Don't take anything for granted. Everything can be taken away.*
- *This day is as good as it gets. Have the best time of your life today or you'll never get to have it. Yesterday's gone. Tomorrow's a dream. Today is your present.*
- *Keep your heart in wonder at the daily miracles of your life.*
- *It's not easy to find happiness in yourself, but it is impossible to find it anywhere else.*
- *Sure, heaven will be wonderful, but so is life right now. There is more joy and wonderment in your life than you are willing or able to enjoy. Loosen up and celebrate. You're not in control of anything or anybody except yourself and your attitude.*
- *The joy of life is the ride.*
- *Laughter is the jest medicine.*
- *Don't take life too seriously; you'll never get out alive.*
- *Treasure your positive friends and family like rare jewels.*
- *If you're not grateful for your blessings, who will be?*
- *Whenever you feel blue, down, grouchy, or rotten, try completing this thought: "I am so grateful for . . ."*

301

CREATING CELEBRATIONS END NOTES

Celebrating holidays, special occasions, and other important events with your family helps children feel like exceptional, extraordinary individuals who deserve to be honored with a party, send-off, salute, or blessing. Creating moments to make merry and reasons to raise the roof is not only fun but vital for an abundant and joyful life. Celebrations give you and your child a brighter, more grateful way of living and an excuse to relax, kick back, and relish the present moment.

Every day can be a celebration. You can celebrate the day your child first sleeps through the night or uses the potty. You can celebrate the first snowfall or spring flower. You can celebrate the last night your child sleeps in his bed in your home or the day his college acceptance letter comes in the mail. Celebrations mark moments in the constantly flowing stream of life. You can't dam the flow and stop the river, but you can picnic at the side of the stream for a few moments before you move on. You can

even celebrate the end of life and your hope of a glorious resurrection.

Life is good, rich, and full if you are awake to all your blessings. Whether in times of sorrow or joy, celebrations send a message to God that we are pleased with his plan and in wonder at our place in it. Celebrations are thank-you cards to the Creator.

One evening soon after my husband and I moved into our first new home, we seeded our front yard with grass. The next morning my husband told me it was important to keep the dirt wet or the grass seeds wouldn't sprout. Then he kissed me on the cheek and left for work. Since it was the middle of a hot July, this wet-dirt assignment was a full-time job. On top of that, I was pregnant and had two baby daughters to care for. I remember standing out on the front porch feeling light-headed and nauseated, squirting the dirt for hours while my one- and two-year-old daughters tumbled down the steps, threw their shoes in the ditch, and stuffed tiny rocks up their noses. After days and days of constant watering, our front yard began growing the biggest, greenest weeds in the whole neighborhood.

"This is my life," I remember thinking as I sprayed the dirt. "All I do is water weeds. I feed one end of the girls and clean up the other. Nothing I do really matters. All I do is water weeds."

A few days later I began having serious complications with my pregnancy, and late one night I began hemorrhaging. My husband quickly called a neighbor to watch our children and raced me to the emergency room of the nearest hospital. After the doctor arrived at the hospital and slowed the bleeding, he told us that our baby had died.

Leaving the hospital that night with empty arms was one of the hardest things I've ever done. When we arrived home, we found our two baby daughters asleep on our bed. I had always loved my daughters but never quite as much as I did at that moment.

"Thank you, God," I whispered. "They are alive. It is such a miracle to have a child who is alive."

Several days later when I went out to check on our front lawn of weeds, I found something I hope I will never forget. When I got down on my hands and knees and took out a magnifying glass, I could see tiny green blades of grass so fine they looked like green sewing thread. All my watering was starting to pay off.

It occurred to me that perhaps all the work involved in caring for a family was like our newly seeded lawn. It seems to be all work and water at first. It's hard to see the tender seedlings or take joy in the growing. But in time children, like the lawn, will not require constant care, and our mutual growing season in my home will have passed all too quickly.

So celebrating is really all about not putting off living, loving, and laughing today. The joy of life is in the ride. So stop waiting. Eat more ice cream, go barefoot, watch more sunsets, laugh more, cry less, let out a few screams, and get into the adventure. Quit viewing life as a long, hard, uphill ride to the ultimate destination of heaven. Heaven will be wonderful, but so is life right now.

Just think, all this and heaven too! Now that's worth celebrating!

NOTES

IMPORTANT INFORMATION, FAVORITE WEB SITES, AND GOOD BOOKS ABOUT CREATING CELEBRATIONS

ENCOURAGING EXPRESSION

EXPRESSION

At the heart of all nurturing is the ability of the nurturer to see the other person as separate and *real*—a unique, living soul with limitless potential and abilities. Each child comes into the world with her own dreams, personality, talents, and needs. Learn who your child is. Delight in her individuality, personality, and agency. Encourage her to express herself, whether it is through dance, drama, music, the written word, or the artist's palette. As your child expresses herself and develops her talents, she will be given the tools she needs to become who she already is and who she has always been.

As you nurture your child and provide opportunities for learning, expression, creation, and growth, you will be forever changed by the essence of your child.

Remember that you will influence your child most by the woman you are before God. If you focus on being open, compassionate, vulnerable, kind, playful, and forgiving, you will find that you've lost your desire for status, power, or wealth.

You will also lose your desire to manipulate or dominate. You will be able to set your child free to be herself.

Your personality, character, and ability to love will affect forever the opportunities and happiness of your children, grandchildren, and great-grandchildren. Loving your husband and each of your children will be the most important work you will do with your life. If you choose to profoundly know and love your husband and each of your children *first*, before they know and love you, you will discover, in time, that you have been transformed.

Help your children find a means of creative expression—a way to respond to the beauty and truth that surrounds them. Doing so is an excellent way for you to nurture yourself and your child and demonstrate your love for God and your fellowman. The gospel of Jesus Christ opens you up to the wonder, beauty, love, and truth that surrounds you every day and fills you with a longing to respond in gratitude. So, choose a way to respond, whether it is with your whole body, voice, hands, mind, words, music, art, or even the way you decorate your home. Nurture and express the best that is in you and open the endless possibilities to your child.

THE THINGS IN YOUR HOUSE

The framework, walls, doors, and windows of a house are not what make it a home. It's the people inside and the love they share. The way you decorate your home, however, does go a long way toward making your children feel comfortable, happy, and at ease expressing themselves in all the best ways. Make your child's bedroom a place where reading, playing, studying, singing, praying, and rocking to sleep are everyday activities. Consider creating a play area or room in your house. Provide your children with toys, art supplies, books, music, and other items that will teach, inspire, and offer hours of fun.

CHILD-FRIENDLY DECORATING

When you're a mother, you can have a child-friendly house or you can have a child-unfriendly house. A child-friendly house is a place where children are wel-comed and enjoyed. Don't decorate your house to impress the neighbors. Decorate your house to create a nurturing and stimulating place for children. When you run out of your own children in your home, fill it with grandchildren or neighborhood children. If you're longing for the day when you can have fancy breakable house décor because all the children are gone, think again. If you are particularly blessed, your children will come back in the form of your grandchildren. Never forget, children make a house a home.

You cannot have a perfectly clean and uncluttered house when you are raising children unless you become obsessive or compulsive and drive yourself and your children crazy. Do you want your house to be a place where your children like to be or do you want to impress potential visitors?

Select floor coverings that are easy to clean and furniture that hides stains and dirt. Teach your children to respect and take good care of family possessions but don't buy things that are easily ruined or broken. Buy sturdy furniture that's made to last. Everything you own will be put through an endurance test if you have children.

If you let them, your children will teach you not to prize possessions too highly. Your house will be cluttered and dinged, scratched and dented. All your corners will all be nicked and your glass broken. But you will know your house has become a home when children want to be there.

Work on developing skills in quick clutter control. Keep bins and baskets in every room so you and your children can quickly throw clutter inside. Buy a carpet and upholstery cleaner. Make sure your kitchen and bathroom floors can be easily cleaned. Light colored carpets are difficult to keep clean with small children. Plaid upholstery, multicolored carpet, and medium-colored linoleum all hide stains well.

Consider what your child looks at in his bedroom when he goes to sleep at night. You might want to paint tiny fairies in hidden corners of the house or place glow-in-the-dark stars on the ceiling. Every object in your house becomes magical to your child, from the pattern on your kitchen floor to the articles on the fireplace mantel. Place things around your house that delight and engage your children's imaginations.

A child-friendly house may not have a baby grand piano, but it may have a modest console and many children who know how to play it with gusto. A child-friendly house may not have a lavish library, but it will have many, many dog-eared books that have been devoured by children of all ages. A child-friendly house always has something good to eat, lots of good books to read, and a pile of games to play. A child-friendly house has stools for reaching high places; cupboards full of interesting, touchable, and reachable objects; and a toy chest full of wonders. But most important, a child-friendly house has a mother or grandmother who loves children and welcomes them into her home and heart.

YOUR CHILD'S BEDROOM

The Nursery

Your child's first real look at the world will likely be a small space at the side of

your bed. During those first few weeks both you and your baby will be pretty sleepy. It's nice to have your newborn close at hand where you can pick her up easily and quickly. Some mothers make a bed on the floor at the side of their beds, while others use a dresser drawer or a bassinet. Be cautious about having your baby sleep in the same bed with you and your husband. Babies can fall off the bed, get stuck in the crack between the bed and the wall/headboard, or get smothered under pillows or parents.

Your baby's next bedroom will probably be the nursery where she'll sleep in a crib. You can make her first bedroom as engaging and interesting as you'd like. Study your child. Learn her likes and dislikes. Most experts say babies respond best to rich colors and high-contrast designs. Experiment and see what your child responds to. It's nice for the room to have a comfortable rocking chair and a small, soft light to use for middle-of-the-night feedings and other soothing sessions.

Consider a chest of drawers for baby's clothes, a changing table for diaper changes, and shelves for toys, blankets, and books. You can consider hanging mobiles from the crib and colorful pictures or murals on the walls and ceiling; but remember, a fluttering curtain in your baby's sunlit window will be just as spectacular as the most expensive decorating scheme. It's also nice to have a CD player or other small sound system in the room. Soothing music close at hand will calm your baby and you as the two of you rock away the hours.

Your Toddler and Preschooler's Adventure Castle

Toddlers will move to a regular bed about the time they don't fit in the crib anymore. Make sure your child's bed is built low to the floor because he might fall out of bed many times before he gets the hang of sleeping in a regular bed without bars to restrict his movement.

Because you want to teach independence, make your toddler and preschooler's bedroom child friendly. Supply low shelves for toys, books, and clothes so your child can put them away himself. If this isn't possible, supply your child with a small step stool and teach him how to use it. Adjust the closet so your child can reach his own clothes and learn to dress himself. He can also be expected to put his clothes away.

Consider a small table and chairs for all his projects and perhaps simple play house furniture. It also helps to have blinds on the window so you can block out the light when you want him to nap or go to sleep at night. Some children this age like a nightlight or a flashlight by their bed for when they wake up at night.

Consider placing the alphabet or numbers on the walls for your child to look at and play games with when you're putting him to bed. Give your toddler something soft and comforting to hold at night. Run a fan on low while your child naps or until he goes to sleep at night. Fans supply

"white noise" and block out other household noises so your little one can settle down and go to sleep. A comfortable chair for reading is also nice.

Your School-ager's Adobe

Your school-age child will want to have more say in the way her bedroom is decorated; but you can still exert your guidance by offering options. Let your school-age child help with decorating decisions and the placement of bedroom furniture. School-age children like tents, secret places to crawl inside, and the companionship of pets. They like learning and watching how things grow and how things work. So consider allowing your school-age child to use her bedroom for all the experiments she wants to learn about.

Many school-age children have a collection of some kind and pictures or posters they want hung on the walls. Give your child a place to display her "treasures," whether they are rocks, dolls, or toy cars. Consider a large bulletin board for changing décor tastes and displaying quality school and artwork.

You can expect your school-age child to clean her own room but don't expect her to keep it the way you would. Consider supplying your school-age child with a calendar for planning ahead and a desk for organization and homework space. A comfy chair for reading is also nice. It's

best to keep the computer in an open area in another part of the house. Televisions in the bedroom are not a good idea for your school-age child.

Your Teenager's Haven

Most teenage children like their bedrooms to be a private place for listening to music, reading, and sleeping late. Many teens have trouble keeping their bedroom tidy because they simply have other, more important priorities. They also tend to plaster their walls with a menagerie of posters or school dance pictures.

If you don't have a separate room for each child in your family, don't worry. Your children will learn how to share, adapt, and develop character. If your teen is sharing his bedroom with other siblings, plan on the inevitable turf wars and bedroom and bathroom partner complaints. A child who learns to get along and share living space with a variety of siblings is much further ahead when it comes time to get along and share living space with a missionary companion, roommate, or a future spouse. Unless actual abuse is involved, let them settle their own disagreements to their mutual satisfaction.

Consider supplying your teen with a picture of the Savior, a local temple, and a family picture for his bedroom. A desk and a good reading light for homework is also helpful. Consider closet organizers to make it easier to take care of clothing and shoes, along with an in-bedroom clothes hamper for soiled clothing.

Let your teen be in charge of how he decorates his bedroom. I know that is a scary thought; but your teen craves freedom, self-expression, and fun. Let him

experiment and try new things with your support and blessing.

Your teenager is old enough to keep his bedroom clean without being told. But choose your battles carefully. Sometimes it's better to close your teen's bedroom door when you walk past. There are more important issues to focus on during these years with your child. Some children are naturally tidy and some are not. Remember, you are not the family maid or drill sergeant. Think of yourself as the family teacher instead.

Teach your child the blessings that come from living in a comfortable, organized home in the rest of the house, then let him practice his agency on his private bedroom space. The easiest way to get most children to clean their rooms is to announce a fun family activity on Monday or Saturday after everyone gets their bedrooms cleaned up.

The Playroom

Your child's bedroom may double as her playroom if you don't have the space. If you do have the space in your house, a playroom is wonderful. Young children love cozy nooks and crannies, along with open spaces for rough and tumble play. You can make a playroom from any part of another room by positioning your furniture in creative ways. Playrooms should be designed for children, not impressing the neighbors.

COMFORT CORNERS

Every home should have comfort corners or particular places where family members can go to be alone or to be with someone who loves them. Your teenage daughter's comfort corner may be an over-stuffed rocking chair next to a stereo, window, or bookshelf. Your five-year-old's comfort corner may be a spot next to the heat vent on cold winter mornings or a soft place in your lap while you sing to him or read him a bedtime story. Your eleven-year-old daughter's comfort corner may be a hidden place in your yard where she can hide from everybody when she feels like running away. Your husband's comfort corner may be a flower garden with a rock path and a swing. Your comfort corner may be your bathroom with a locked door and a long, hot bubble bath.

Comfort corners are places where mothers, fathers, and children go to renew their spirits.

You can help your child create and use comfort corners every day. Take the time to be still, meditate, read, listen, and think. Comfort yourself and your child with the soothing, read-aloud melody of well-written words or the swell of emotions you feel from listening to fine classical music or viewing beautiful visual images on your walls. Find a corner to display family pictures, fresh flowers, or something good to

PLAYROOM PARAPHERNALIA

Consider including these items in your playroom:
- comfortable, easy-to-clean furniture
- a tape or CD player for recording and listening to music and story tapes
- an easel for painting pictures
- a child-sized table and chairs
- various simple musical instruments
- an assortment of toys
- a housekeeping corner
- building blocks
- dress-up clothes
- books
- puzzles
- computer
- a quiet, comfortable area for reading books and assembling puzzles
- an open space for tumbling, jumping, dancing, and climbing
- an assortment of art supplies
- blankets for making tents

eat. Make your physical home nourishing and comforting. Make your spirit and personality comforting and warm. You may be the best comfort corner of all.

Invite your child to lay his head in your lap. Stroke his brow or brush his hair. Invite your child to sit with you in the garden or under a shady tree as you listen for the sounds of nature. Invite yourself into your child's tree house. Waltz with your husband by candlelight after all the children have gone to bed. Bake cinnamon rolls or burn scented candles. Go for long, leisurely walks and plant flowers next to your front door.

Comforting is perhaps one of the sweetest, calming parts of nurturing, for when you truly comfort someone, you are comforted in return.

MEMORY CHESTS

Hope chests of the past were often wooden cedar chests purchased for young women to be filled with all the finery of future homemaking. Today a hope chest can be converted to a memory chest filled with anything and everything that re-creates the bits and pieces that make a childhood. Consider giving your child boxes or chests for Christmas and birthday gifts where she can store her life's treasures.

You can start by filling the chest with a lock of her hair, her first pair of shoes, or her blessing dress. You can fill the chest or box with a favorite toy, a favorite book or blanket. You might consider filling the box with tapes of your child's voice or a video of special events from your child's life. Tuck away original artwork, journals, and family pictures. Perhaps grandma or grandpa might want to add a special gift or memento to be remembered by.

As your child gets older, she might want to tuck away a favorite piece of music, a dance uniform, a school award, or a dance picture. Perhaps she will include a collection of seashells, toy cars, or dolls.

Memory chests are treasure chests filled with the menagerie of a child's life— bits and pieces of memory that are too easily tossed aside and forgotten. If you treasure your child's life, she will think of herself as a treasure. If you think her experiences matter, she will believe her life matters.

TOYS

BABY TOYS

Think of your baby's toys as her tools to learn about the world and delight herself at the same time. Your baby's toys should be fun; they should also challenge the mind, encourage creative thought, and enhance coordination.

You can buy your child toys twice a year—at Christmas and at her birthday. I promise you that you'll accumulate far too many before long, so restrain yourself. Friends, siblings, and grandparents speed up this process. After you get a big stash of toys, you might want to store half of the toys at any given time and switch them occasionally to keep your child's interest. Here are a few pointers on choosing toys for baby:

• Purchase toys that are not toxic or flammable.

• Even though you'll regret it later, purchase toys that make noise. Babies love to shake, rattle, and push buttons that make incessantly annoying noises all day long. You will, in fact, become so annoyed with your child's noisy toys at times that you'll vow to never buy another one again. Of course, you'll never live to keep that promise.

• Buy toys that are washable.

• Buy toys that are minus any sharp edges. Also, don't buy toys with small parts. Babies put everything in their mouths and they can choke on small pieces—even pieces that look as if they'd never come off the toy.

• Buy toys that appeal to your child's senses: things to nibble on, look at, touch, and shake.

• Consider buying a mobile. Or make one yourself by stringing or dangling anything bright, noisy, or interesting above your baby's changing table or crib.

• Consider rattles, shiny things, and a few soft stuffed animals to hug.

• Don't forget to include sturdy board books for your baby to handle and nibble on when you read together.

TODDLER AND PRESCHOOLER TOYS

Toddlers and preschoolers enjoy toys that can be manipulated creatively each time they use them. Look for toys that have stood the test of time, such as blocks, balls, dolls, games, and any sort of pretend-play toy. You'll also want toys that are well made and durable. Toddlers are known for hurling toys across the room on an almost-hourly basis. Watch your child carefully so you will recognize the type of toys he seems to prefer. Every child has a unique preference for toys. You may have one child who would rather play with balls than anything else and another who spends long hours with art supplies or playing house with dolls. Keep the following in mind when collecting toys for your toddler or preschooler:

• Toddlers like to empty everything. Make your lower kitchen drawers child friendly. During these years, your kitchen drawers will be more interesting than your toy box. Put a basket or plastic tub in every room for a while to toss toys into and eliminate clutter quickly.

• Most toddlers will enjoy having a doll—to cuddle or to propel into the universe and beyond, depending on their personality.

• Toddlers and preschoolers love interesting bath toys.

• Look for puzzles, push and pull toys, and something to carry things in, such as a doll carriage, wheelbarrow, play shopping cart, or wagon.

• Supply an assortment of books to read by going to the library regularly or starting your own home library.

• Preschoolers love blocks of all sizes. They also make great use of old cardboard boxes and other stacking things.

• All children love anything that makes music they can dance to, sing to, or just sit and listen to.

• Preschoolers love creating things. Try keeping a stack of old magazines on hand and a pair of child scissors for your preschooler to use as he cuts out pictures and learns manual dexterity.

• Keep clay, paste, markers, crayons,

stickers, paper, paint, and brushes in a plastic tote, so everything he needs to be creative is readily available—and easy to put away afterward.

• Consider suplying your preschooler with a sand box and outside play equipment.

• Collect dress-up clothes and pretend aids.

• Consider a tape or CD player for music and an assortment of dolls, stuffed animals, and bean bags.

• Most preschoolers love a wheel toy they can ride on and the chance to blow bubbles, shape clay, and cut and paste.

TOYS FOR SCHOOL-AGERS

School-age children are introduced to new, faddish toys all the time. So be prepared for your nine-year-old or seven-year-old to regularly hit you up for the latest thing. And, it's probably okay to buy a few faddish toys for your child so she won't feel totally left out, but don't buy too many. Fads come and go about as easily as your child's interest in them. Here are some ideas for more classic toys that your school-ager might enjoy:

• School-age children do well with an assortment of art supplies and lots of board or card games.

• Consider purchasing your school-ager's first bicycle, roller skates, or scooter.

• Don't forget kites, pogo sticks, marbles, hopscotch, and jacks—all classic toys that schoolboys and girls love to revisit.

• When looking for good books, watch for winners of the Caldecott and Newbery medals; but don't stop there. Ask your librarian for favorites and let your child pick out her own books as often as possible. Many school-age children love a magazine subscription all their own about something they are particularly interested in.

School-age children don't have as much time at home as preschoolers, but they still need interesting things to do when they are home. Your school-age child will probably be taking lessons of some type by this time. Gifts that help her improve at what she's learning are always welcome. If your child is taking piano lessons, take her to the music store and let her pick out a favorite piece of sheet music. If your child is taking dance lessons, take her to a dance performance or concert. If your child is on a sports team, take her to a professional game of the same.

A computer is perhaps one of the best toys or tools for your school-age child. Computer games that help your child in an area she struggles with at school may be a perfect gift. Teach your school-age child how to safely surf the Internet as a great research tool and how to send and receive e-mails from teachers, family members, and friends.

It's at this stage that you'll have to start thinking of toys as *tools* or *experiences.* You can buy your child "toys," or you can give her the "tools" she'll need to have fun and learn new things.

TEENAGE "TOYS"

Teenagers don't necessarily play with toys; but that doesn't mean they don't want to acquire more tools to help them have fun and explore the world. Take a

look at your teen's talents, hobbies, and sports activities, and encourage him to choose "toys" that will help him excel in these areas. Consider sparking your teen's interest with a microscope, camera, art supplies, private lessons, summer camps, or wilderness experiences. You or your spouse might also want to try four-wheeling, motorcycling, boating, canoeing, fishing, or collecting with your teen. Encourage your teen to choose good books, movies, and music. For some teenagers, the best toy might just be the keys to your car on a Friday night. And remember, you can buy *things* or *experiences* for your teen. Both serve a function and should be selected carefully as a way to help your teen develop his talents, knowledge, and experience.

HAVING FUN IN YOUR OWN BACKYARD

Your backyard is the second new world your child experiences. The first world is the environment inside your home. For many children, the backyard is a whole new planet to explore, a novel world perfect for restoring and renewing the child in all of us.

The following items are all appropriate for your backyard and may be just what your family would pick to create a home away from home in the great outdoors:

- a shed for storing yard care equipment, bicycles, trucks, and wagons
- a playhouse or clubhouse
- a sandbox
- a wading pool
- shade
- playground equipment in a shady area (swings, slides, monkey bars, rings, racks, gliders)

- ground cover (small wood chips or smooth pea gravel under play equipment)
- something to climb on (old telephone poles, railroad ties, or trees)
- a picnic area with table
- a fireplace or fire pit
- a treehouse
- gardens (flower, vegetable)
- a cement or pavement square (bicycle pad, basketball hoop)
- a baseball diamond or kickball field (if you have an enormous yard)
- a grassy area (for a volleyball or badminton net)
- pet homes (rabbit hutch, chicken coop, dog run, pigeon roost)

ART

The desire to create, the yearning to learn, the need to experience—these things manifest themselves early in life. An alert infant fills all her waking hours with endless curiosity and observation. The toddler expresses her strong will with "Me do it!" Allowing your children to create through a variety of art media can be an extension of these desires.

Art doesn't have to become just some pretty pictures and fancy statues that someone else makes. You can approach art with your children as a way to challenge them to reconstruct what they see and how they feel inside. You can use art to help them see their surroundings with different, more sensitive eyes.

Art can be one positive means for your child to explore and experience the world and thus discover herself. Through art, your child can discover her own way of learning. Boldness, for example, may exhibit itself as part of your child's personality when she works with finger paints. Determination and the ability to see things through to completion may start to become part of her personality as she works long and hard at detailed drawings.

The courage to try new experiences may emerge and become part of a healthy personality when she works with clay.

HOW DO YOU TEACH A CHILD ART?

How do you take your eager child and launch their rocket of energy into art? There are better ways than giving them crayons and coloring books. Sometime around the fourth or fifth grade, most people tell themselves they are not artists because they become dissatisfied with their drawings. Look for ways to keep your child's heart open to the possibility that he is and will always be a creator. You do this by helping him think in terms of *process,* not *product.*

The *process* of creating something is more important than the finished *product* because the creator learns something new each time he makes an attempt. In other words, tell your child to start making some wood chips, draw till the cows come home, and pound that clay to smithereens. The business of creation is full of work *and* fun, experimentation *and* initiative. A person who thinks creatively is better at solving problems, sees situations in a different light, and is able to respond to people and events with a more sensitive heart. Every child is born an artist.

So, don't think that you have to "teach" your child art. Instead, understand that you will be allowing your child to have experiences. The teaching will be a natural result of the experience. Art can promote a child's ability to think because it teaches him how to solve problems for himself. Art can give him a sense of security because he finds that he can do something meaningful all by himself. He doesn't need to rely on outside praise to feel good about himself. Art can help him be more perceptive as his senses come alive. Art can help him learn to appreciate beauty.

START YOUNG

Infants and young children are absorbed in exploring their world through senses and movements. From the day a child is born, give her something to reach out for, something interesting to look at. The more your child sees, touches, feels, and hears, the more she will want to see, touch, feel, and hear.

Art is rooted in everyday experiences. Surround your child with color, from her bed sheets to her mobile. Dangle objects in front of her eyes and constantly move her tiny body around the house with you. Talk to her, imitate her sounds, let her hear different noises and music. You can let her experience new sensations in tasting and smelling.

As your child grows, continue to create conditions that encourage her exploration of the exciting world she lives in. Promote and value her creative efforts. Encourage your child to be original, not copy the ideas of others, by valuing her attempts and giving audience to her efforts.

PROVIDE A CREATIVE ENVIRONMENT

Ideally, we would all have a room with a scrubbable floor and whole walls of shelves just waiting for art supplies. But most people don't have this kind of space in their homes. Don't worry. You probably have a kitchen and a drawer. Try to secure one area that can be reserved for art supplies and activities. It should be a place where cleanliness is not a major concern and where cleanup is easy. A patio works well in the warm months of the year, and a corner of the kitchen or low table in the playroom or bedroom works well during the cold months.

Buy the best materials you can afford and keep them in good condition. Dried clay is not very stimulating, and scissors that won't cut are more apt to frustrate than provide a creative experience.

If you can't afford to buy anything right now, look at common household garbage as your new artistic treasures. Art objects can be made from any kind of material. For instance, junk mail includes lots of free paper and envelopes. Start collecting art supplies at art and craft stores or in the school supply section of your favorite variety store. Talk to local artists and schoolteachers for good places to get supplies or shop on-line.

TEACH THAT THERE ARE NO RIGHTS AND WRONGS

Almost from the very beginning, most of us find ourselves telling our children all the don'ts—"Don't touch that!" "Don't do this!" Children naturally want to please us. But in art, they should get the pleasure

ART SUPPLIES

This list is full of items you can use to make art projects:

baby-food jars
balloons
balls
beads
blocks
blotters
bolts
bones
bottles
boxes

buckles
buttons
candles
canvas
cardboard
carpet
cartons
cellophane
chains
clocks
cloth
coins
combs
cones
confetti
contact paper
corncobs
cotton

cups
drapery samples
driftwood
feathers
felt
fishnet
flour
flowers
foam rubber
foil
fossils
fur
greeting cards
hair clips
keys
leather
magazines
marbles
matchsticks
mirrors
nails
newspapers
nuts
paint

paper towels
pebbles
plastic or paper bags
plywood
Q-tips
reeds
ribbons
rope
rubber
rugs
salt
sandpaper
seashells

sponges
spools
sticks
straight pins
straws
tar paper
tile
tins
toothbrushes
toothpicks
trays
tree bark
wallpaper
wax
weeds
wire
yarn

themselves from the experience. There is no right way to draw a tree, and no right color to paint a sky. Your children need the freedom to explore.

If your child always draws blue skies, you might point out all the beautiful colors a sky can be while you're watching a sunset together. You can help your child observe the movement and shading of the clouds, or sit with him in the evening and see how many shades the sky turns after the sun has gone down.

Children don't need to paint or draw or mold specific items in order to make a beautiful picture or object. Often they enjoy working with lines and colors and shapes. In art, a child is finished when he loses interest in the project or when the experience is complete for him. Some children destroy their picture or objects when they've finished them, and that is all right too.

MOVE BEYOND THE COLORING BOOK

Each child is unique. Each one has her own way of doing things. Providing coloring books can be a classic example of one way you may unknowingly pervert and destroy a child's own way. A coloring book is full of someone else's pictures. A professional artist's depiction of people and places and things can give a child an

inferiority complex. She soon begins to think that she can't produce anything as good, so she learns to content herself with filling in the spaces and saying it's her picture. Coloring pictures in a coloring book is easy; it is a mindless activity in which a child invests minimum risks and gets a maximum result.

You may say, "But my child spends hours coloring in her coloring books." Well, many of us spend hours watching poor television programs too. The problem with coloring books and paint-by-number illustrations is that they teach children they can't draw. Then children become dependent and lose confidence in their abilities. They don't receive the same satisfaction that comes from creating their own work.

USE EXPERIENCE AS THE CATALYST

Children need to draw from a variety of experiences. They also need to have something to say. Your child's most rewarding art experiences will be the direct result of doing something interesting. Drawing flowers, trees, and rocks after an afternoon walk where your child discovers and becomes acquainted with nature is a natural extension of experience.

PROVIDE YOUR CHILD WITH INTERESTING EXPERIENCES

Direct experiences. These include something your child actually does. He picks a flower, plants a seed, or builds a castle of sand.

Indirect experiences. These are things your child does indirectly, or something he observes. He may watch a construction worker hammering nails, a florist arranging flowers, or a neighbor washing his window. Remember, almost *everything* is new to a child. A trip to observe the local mechanic at work in a garage may prove as exciting as a trip to Disneyland.

Pretending. Take your child on a fantasy flight by suggesting that he pretend he is something or someone else. Ask him what it would be like to be a flower, for instance. Discuss the details of breaking through the soil as a seed and have him think about what it would feel like to be rained on and have the wind blow him back and forth. Or have him imagine how it feels to have a bumblebee buzzing around his face.

Unusual experiences. Help your child look at something from an usual point of view. If you've ever been on an airplane, you know what a difference perspective can do to the size of a house or cars or mountains. Looking through a microscope, observing the valley from a mountaintop, and similar broadening experiences can give your child a new way of seeing things.

Group activities. Working together with others to build a snow castle, or even clean a room, lets your child see how other people do things. Through group activities, children learn that cooperation and mutual respect help us to accomplish great things.

PRAISE YOUR CHILD

When children are young, they don't usually try to reproduce what they see. They paint or draw or mold just to paint or draw or mold. When they are very young, any resemblance in their artwork to specific objects is usually coincidental. We can encourage their efforts but we should try not to impose our standards on their work or be fanatical about neatness.

Judging and praising children's artwork requires sensitivity and even caution. Excessive praise may be damaging because if they see that you are completely thrilled over every picture, they may doubt your good judgment or try to duplicate what they think you like.

Children need support for their artwork by talking about what they have produced. You might say things like, "Tell me about your picture," instead of "What's that?" Ask yourself whether your recognition is strengthening or demeaning to your children, then you'll know if your comments are helping or harming their creativity.

For children, art is an ongoing activity, not a finished product. It is a process of discovery through which they see and understand their world better. They can live through a whole series of experiences as they paint or model.

PROVIDE LOTS OF SUPPLIES AND FUN ACTIVITIES

Crayons

Buy crayons for young children that are sturdy and well made. Quality is more important than a wide range of colors. The quality of the crayon can be tested by scraping a patch of crayoned paper. Cheap crayons will flake off the paper and leave only light colors, while crayons of good quality will have rich tones even after scraping. Most art supply stores carry good-quality crayons that are sturdy enough for young children to use.

Remember, after a crayon is peeled, it has more than one surface; there is the sharp point, the flat end, and the round or square side. A crayon can be used from any angle.

Chalk

Chalk is a great art medium for children of all ages. Chalk can decorate a blackboard or the front porch. Chalk can be used for experiments in blending by placing one chalk color on top of another, then rubbing with your finger to blend the colors together.

You can make bright pictures with chalk by first wetting the paper. Let the extra water drip off, then draw on the wet paper with the colored chalk. You can spray chalk pictures with a fixative, like hairspray, to keep them from smearing.

Felt Markers

Most children love the bright colors of felt markers to create drawings. If you don't want to ruin all your child's clothes, walls, and furniture, buy felt markers that wash out with water.

Pens and Pencils

Buy a collection of pens and pencils for your child to use while creating original artwork. There are pens for writing on dark paper and pens for writing on white paper. Colored pencils come in every price range, quality, and color of the rainbow. Encourage your child to create his own drawings.

Finger Paints

Finger painting is great fun for children of all ages. Put a smock over yourself and your child then wet some paper and spread it smoothly over newspaper placed on washable flooring. Spoon some paint on the paper. Use fingers to make the pictures. Let it air dry. Finger painted paper makes great wrapping paper for later use.

Also consider using any glossy surface for finger painting, including: Formica, porcelain, plastic tabletops, aluminum cookie sheets, shiny shelf paper, glazed butcher paper, and gift wrapping paper. Finger paint can be purchased or made at home. You can even make it from buttermilk or instant pudding.

Poster Paints

Art teachers consider poster paint to be the best all-around medium for young children's painting. Watercolor and oil paints can be difficult to work with, while the commercial paint sets that

GETTING CREATIVE WITH CRAYONS

There are many ways to use crayons. Here are a few ideas:

Crayons on Cloth

Crayons can be used on many kinds of cloth. After the crayon design is on the cloth, stamp it with a hot iron. To do so, turn the fabric—crayon-side down—onto a piece of newspaper. Iron the fabric on the wrong side. (You may want to use a pressing cloth to protect your iron.) A crayon design can also be put on cloth and later dipped in dye for an unusual look. Reverse designs can be made by putting the design on one piece of cloth and then pressing it onto another piece of cloth. Just put the right sides of the fabric together and iron.

Crayons on Wood

Crayons can be used to decorate boxes or anything else made from wood. A coat of shellac will add a final touch.

Crayons and Water

After making a thick, bright crayon drawing on paper, brush the paper with a light wash of colored water. (Use water colors, poster paints, or food coloring to dye the water.) This idea can be used in numerous ways. Remember, crayons contain wax, and wax won't mix with water.

Crayon Etching

Crayon etching involves scraping designs from richly built-up crayon surfaces. Mark off sections of paper and apply a thick coat with light-colored crayons. Then cover the entire area with a dark crayon. With a sharp instrument, such as a fingernail file or paper clip, scratch through the darker crayon to the lighter color underneath. You can scratch out a specific object or an artistic design.

Gift Wrap and Stencils

You can use crayons on gift wrap and stencils. Crayons can be used on a variety of surfaces, including paper, cloth, wood, and stone. Let your child experiment with all these surfaces.

Furniture Repair

Okay, so this one is for you, not your child. Crayons can be used to fill in scratches on furniture surfaces. Just match the color of the crayon to the color on the damaged surface.

have hard squares of color set in cups are often frustrating for young children to use.

Poster paint can be purchased in powdered or liquid form; the liquid usually has richer color. Prepare the powder by following directions on the package. One suggestion: place the powder in the container

FINGER PAINT RECIPES

COOKED FINGER PAINT

2 cups flour
2 teaspoons salt
3 cups cold water
2 cups hot water
Food coloring

Combine flour and salt. Pour in cold water and beat mixture until smooth. Put mixture in a large saucepan. Add hot water. Boil until glossy. Beat until smooth. Mix in coloring until you reach the color you'd like.

SOAP FLAKE FINGER PAINT

Soap flakes
Water
Food coloring or powder paint

Stir flakes into a small amount of water until mixture reaches the consistency of whipped cream. Add color and mix.

LIQUID STARCH FINGER PAINT

1 cup liquid laundry starch
4 teaspoons tempera paint or other water-soluble powdered paint

Mix ingredients in a small plastic bowl until blended. Or, pour liquid starch onto dry paper and put tempera paint in a large-holed salt shaker. Have your child shake the powdered paint over the starch and spread the concoction with her fingers to create neat designs all over the paper. (You can also make this into a washable finger paint by combining 2 tablespoons liquid tempera paint to the laundry starch and 1 tablespoon powdered detergent soap.)

PUDDING PAINT

Instant pudding of any kind and flavor
Milk, as called for on pudding box

Follow instructions for making instant pudding. Put pudding on your child's high chair tray or a large piece of butcher paper, and let her loose. Your child will love eating the paint, too.

SUPER EASY FINGER PAINT

1 cup flour
¼ cup salt
1 cup, minus 2 tablespoons cold water
Few drops food coloring

Combine all ingredients.

LAUNDRY STARCH PAINT

½ cup powdered laundry starch
1 cup cold water
4 cups boiling water
¼ cup soap flakes
Food coloring or powdered poster paint

Dissolve powdered laundry starch in cold water; stir until mixture is the consistency of thick cream. Bring 4 cups water to a boil over medium heat. Gradually add starch mixture, stirring constantly. Remove from heat. Add soap flakes and a few drops of food coloring or powdered poster paint. Cool.

CORNSTARCH PAINT

2 heaping tablespoons cornstarch
¼ cup cold water
2 cups water
1 tablespoon soap flakes
Food coloring or powdered poster paint

In a heavy pan, combine cornstarch and ¼ cup cold water. Stir until smooth. Add 2 cups water, and stir well. Bring to a boil over medium heat. Remove from heat and beat soap flakes into the mixture. Cool. Add food coloring or powdered poster paint.

PASTE AND GLUE

Most children enjoy pasting or gluing things together. You don't need to invest in expensive products at the variety store. For example, inexpensive wallpaper paste can be put in squeeze bottles for children to use. An advantage of this product is that it will wash out of clothing.

Here are some recipes and ideas for making your own paste or glue at home.

Thin White Glue

Combine water with ½ cup commercial glue. Put mixture in a clean squeeze bottle.

Flour Paste

In a saucepan combine 1 cup flour, 1 teaspoon salt, and 2 cups water. Place over medium heat and stir until mixture is bubbly and thick. Cool. Store in covered containers in the refrigerator.

Homemade Paste

In the top of a double boiler, combine 1½ cups flour and 1¼ cups cold water; stir until smooth. Stir in 2¾ cups boiling water. Cook over boiling water until lumps disappear. Cool. Stir in 1 teaspoon oil of wintergreen and 1 teaspoon powdered alum. Store in covered containers in the refrigerator.

Roll-on Paste or Glue

Pry off the ball on the top of an empty roll-on deodorant bottle. Rinse the bottle and the ball well and let them air dry. Fill the bottle with glue or paste. Push the ball back in the bottle.

and shades can be made by combining these. Select brushes that are fairly stiff and from one-half inch to one and one-fourth inch wide. If possible, have a brush and a container for each color. Muffin tins make good paint holders. Paint can be stored in small jars, such as baby-food jars.

Almost any kind of paper can be used to paint on, including newsprint, butcher paper, or poster paper. Use a work surface that is washable and work in an area with a washable floor. You can improvise an easel by using an overturned chair set on a table or desk or table. An inexpensive and washable smock will protect your child's clothing.

Basic Painting

Your children can paint pictures with anything that puts marks on paper. You can use a paintbrush, an old toothbrush, sponges, rags, fingers, cut vegetables, or any other instrument you feel like using. Experiment and have fun.

Papier-mâché

Children enjoy making papier-mâché–covered balloons for a variety of holiday projects: Easter eggs, Christmas ornaments, Halloween ghosts, or Thanksgiving turkeys.

An inexpensive, easy-to-make papier-mâché paste can be made by combining in a saucepan: 3½ cups water, 1 cup flour, and 1½ tablespoons sugar. Cook over medium heat, stirring constantly, until mixture becomes translucent. Cool. (An alternative is to use wallpaper paste, mixed according to instructions on the package, or watered-down commercial glue.)

Soak strips of newspaper in the paste. Then

first, then stir in water. Paint should have the consistency of thick cream.

Basic colors to start with are red, yellow, blue, black, and white. Other colors

MISCELLANEOUS ART ACTIVITIES

The following are art-related activities for your children:

- Visit an art museum or gallery. Some museums have special exhibits of particular interest to children. Some communities even have children's museums with exhibits that the children can touch and handle.
- Visit an artist's studio. Have the artist explain how he gets his ideas and how he creates with various media, such as watercolors, oils, clay, or stone.
- Set aside an area in the home where children's artwork and collections can be displayed.
- Attach a tree branch or limb to a sturdy base. Decorate the branch with the children's homemade decorations. Use the branch for seasonal displays or holidays, such as Valentine's Day, Easter, Independence Day, Halloween, Thanksgiving, and Christmas, as well as spring and fall.
- Help your children start a file or collection of interesting photographs and artwork, such as posters or illustrations cut from magazines.
- Mount, frame, and hang your children's pictures for more permanent display in your home.
- Let your child pose as a model for your other child to paint.
- Help your child prepare and perform a puppet show. Good books are available in libraries and bookstores with instructions on how to make puppets and puppet stages.
- Make a wall mural. Let each child do a section of the mural. Newsprint roll ends from a printer or butcher paper from the local grocery-store meat department can be used to make the mural as long as you wish.
- Paint to music. Play various kinds of music and let your child use his imagination to illustrate what the music brings to mind.

lace the soaked strips over an inflated balloon or a wire form. Smooth the paper and let it air dry completely before painting. Use poster paint to make the shape into whatever object is desired.

Printing

Another activity that children—even young ones—enjoy is printing. Three items are needed:

- **A color pad:** An absorbent piece of material or a sponge. Saturate it with poster paint, vegetable coloring, or watercolor paint.
- **A stamper:** Use a spool, sponge, cork, carrot, potato, block, cookie cutter, pebble, leaf, stick, comb, brush, straw, or anything else with a raised design, including commercial stamps.
- **An absorbent surface:** You can stamp on a sheet of paper or a piece of cloth for starters.

Simply press the stamper on the color pad and then on the absorbent surface. Complete books have been written on various ways to print. Check with your local library or craft store if you want to take this idea further. Most children are content to just stamp on whatever they'd like for as long as they'd like.

Collages

Children can let their imaginations soar when they create collages. The only materials needed are a board or sheet of paper, some paste, and various items to paste.

Most children enjoy collecting items that can be used to create the collage. These might include pieces of paper, felt, cotton, lace, gift-wrap, or wallpaper and envelopes. Items that have interesting shapes might include bottle caps; buttons; beans; confetti; pieces of yarn, string, wire, and ribbon; toothpicks; straw; and twigs. Items with interesting textures include sandpaper, bark, leather, burlap, shells, cardboard, velvet, Styrofoam, and cork.

To make the collage, simply glue the items on the board or paper in any manner or design you wish.

COOKING WITH KIDS

All children love to cook, especially in the early years. If you wait until they can do it without making a mess, they may lose their desire. You can start your child cooking with simple fare, such as lemonade, gelatin, ice cream cones, cake, sandwiches, hot dogs, salads, beans, potatoes, eggs, toast, and popcorn. Consider allowing your child to try making noodles, oatmeal, French toast, and pancakes. Let her stir, scoop, and pour as you make breakfast or dinner. Children are always much more excited about eating what they have helped prepare.

SIMPLE RECIPES

As you teach your child to cook, start out with some of these very simple recipes:

LEMONADE

2 tablespoons lemon juice

2 tablespoons sugar

1 glass of water

Let your child pour the juice and sugar into a glass of water and stir.

GELATIN

1 small package of flavored gelatin

1 cup of hot water

1 cup of cold water

1 dish or mold

Let your child dump the gelatin into a bowl. You should pour in the hot water to prevent burning. Let your child stir for three minutes or so to dissolve the gelatin. Have her pour in the cold water and stir again. Then help her pour the gelatin into a mold or dish and put it in the refrigerator to set up.

SANDWICHES

Two slices of bread
Sandwich spread
Meat
Pickles/vegetables

Give your child a butter knife and let her spread the bread with mayonnaise or some other sandwich spread. Have her add meat, pickles, lettuce, tomatoes, whatever she likes, then stack the second slice of bread on top.

FRUIT SALAD

Fruit, cut up

Chop a few pieces of fruit for your child. Let her combine it in a bowl.

BOILED EGGS

1 egg
Water

Let your child place an egg in a saucepan filled with enough water to cover the egg. You should then let her watch as you turn on the stove to medium heat. Bring the water to a boil. Boil the egg for 2 to 20 minutes, depending on desired hardness.

MAKE COOKING FUN

As you teach your child how to cook, give him a few simple instructions, such as how to measure ingredients in measuring cups and measuring spoons. Many cooking experiences for young children don't need to include recipes. You can work with what you have on hand and experiment a little. Very young children can stir and dump in ingredients. They also like to arrange things on the plate. Most children love working with their own wad of dough while you bake bread, rolls, or cookies.

USE FINGER FOODS

Sometimes you might try eating a whole meal with only finger food. Carrots, cheese, chips, fruit, and bread are foods that can be eaten with fingers. Children like to help with the preparation as well as the digestion. Eating with their fingers also helps adults remember what it is like to be small and to enjoy again the sense of taste and touch as a new experience.

EAT "OUT"

It's fun to have an occasional eating-out-at-home meal with candlelight, a tablecloth, and the best dishes. While you pretend to be eating out, your children can assume roles, such as waiters, cooks, cashiers, or patrons. This is a good way for them to practice table manners. Even small children can help set the table and provide a centerpiece of their own choosing. Many children enjoy selecting the dishes and deciding what else they want to use to make their table interesting.

EAT FOREIGN FOOD

Children can be introduced to other cultures by helping to prepare a special meal from a different country. You can spend

time reading about the country and learning about the customs, cooking, and manner of dress. Some families even like to wear clothing from the country of choice or use special utensils and decorations from that area.

CELEBRATE WITH FOOD

One of the most enjoyable experiences of many holidays is preparing, eating, and sharing food—with your children's help. With a little imagination, you can put excitement into your holiday food preparation. For example, on Halloween you might make treats for the children to take to special neighbors and friends instead of sending them out to beg for treats. A special birthday cake might replace the traditional Christmas fruitcake. Children can celebrate the harvest by helping to carve pumpkins, string popcorn, or make creative vegetable people from garden produce such as squashes, cucumbers, and peppers. It doesn't really matter what traditions you have as long as you continue them for as long as they bring your family a sense of joy and belonging.

BE CREATIVE

Cakes can be cut into rabbits, hearts, or Christmas tree shapes. Pancakes can be made into various shapes as you pour the batter or cut them up after they are cooked. Cookie cutters can be used to cut cheese or bread slices into interesting shapes for sandwiches. Pears, peaches, cottage cheese, lettuce, raisins, and other foods can be made into people or animals for salads. Gelatin can be molded into a variety of shapes. Orange peels and radishes can be made into roses. Unusual ways of making and arranging ordinary food can make eating a creative visual experience.

EXPERIMENT WITH FOOD

Growing mold in the refrigerator may be an experiment instead of an accident. Children can be a big help when you preserve foods that are canned or dried. When you clean out the refrigerator, the leftovers can become a creative combination meal. Children find imaginative ways to combine different things to eat, such as putting peanut butter in the celery or cereal in yogurt.

Children also like to make things from food. Necklaces can be made from macaroni. A peach half can become a sailboat in a bowl of milk. Dried beans can be glued on a paper to make a picture.

COOK TOGETHER

The following recipes are perfect for cooking together and are among my children's favorite things to make with Mom.

FREEZER JAM

4 cups of berries (grow your own for even more fun)

¼ cup sugar

1 package pectin

2 cups sugar

Crush berries with a potato masher or fork. Combine the ¼ cup sugar and pectin in a small bowl; stir into crushed berries. Let berries stand 30 minutes. Stir in the 2 cups of sugar until sugar dissolves. Fill jars or plastic containers with jam and freeze. Refrigerate after opening.

MYSTERY DESSERT

1 cup sugar
1 cup flour
1 teaspoon baking soda
1 teaspoon salt
1 egg
1 can fruit cocktail or other "mystery" fruit
1 teaspoon vanilla
½ cup brown sugar (to sprinkle on top)

Combine all ingredients, except brown sugar, in a baking dish. Level and top with brown sugar. Bake at 325° F. for 45 minutes. Tastes great topped with ice cream.

APPLESAUCE COOKIES

2 cups flour
½ teaspoon salt
½ teaspoon cinnamon
½ teaspoon nutmeg
½ teaspoon cloves
½ cup shortening
1 cup sugar
1 egg
1 teaspoon baking soda
1 cup applesauce
1 12-ounce bag chocolate chips

Combine all ingredients in a large bowl. Drop by spoonfuls onto ungreased cookie sheets and bake at 350° F. for 10 to 15 minutes, until just golden brown.

QUICK CINNAMON ROLLS

3½ cups warm water
1 cup oil
½ cup sugar
5½ tablespoons yeast
1 teaspoon salt
3 eggs
10½ cups flour

Combine water, oil, sugar, and yeast in a large bowl and let sit for 15 minutes. Add salt, eggs, and flour. Mix well. Knead until dough holds together. Split dough in half and roll each half into a rectangle. Spread with butter and top with a cinnamon and sugar mixture. Roll up and slice. Place rolls in a greased or sprayed pan. Let rolls rise until they reach a desired size. Bake at 350° F. for 15 minutes.

ZUCCHINI BREAD

3 eggs, beaten
1 cup salad oil
2 cups sugar
2 cups zucchini, grated
3 teaspoons vanilla
3 cups flour
1 teaspoon salt
¼ teaspoon baking powder
1 teaspoon baking soda
1 teaspoon nutmeg
1 cup nuts (optional)

Combine all ingredients and pour into 2 standard-sized greased and floured loaf pans. Bake 1 hour at 325° F. or until a toothpick comes out of the center clean.

CABBAGE SALAD

1 head cabbage
5 green onions, chopped
½ cup slivered almonds
1 or 2 cans chicken (or fresh cooked)

2 tablespoons sugar

½ cup oil

3 tablespoons vinegar

½ teaspoon salt

½ teaspoon pepper

½ package uncooked ramen noodles, crushed

Chop head of cabbage into a large bowl. Toss with onions, almonds, and chicken. To make a dressing: combine sugar, oil, vinegar, salt, and pepper in a small bowl. Pour over salad to coat. Stir in crushed ramen noodles just before serving.

DINNER ROLLS

3 tablespoons yeast

1 cup warm water

3 cups milk

1 tablespoon salt

1 cup shortening

1 cup sugar

6 eggs

8 to 10 cups flour

Soften yeast in water in a small bowl; set aside. In a large bowl, combine milk, salt, shortening, sugar, and eggs. Stir in softened yeast. Gradually stir in flour until you have a soft, pliable dough. Cover bowl and let dough rise in a warm place until double in size. Punch dough down, then shape rolls as you desire and place on greased cookie sheets or muffin tins. Let rise again until rolls are the size you desire. To save time, you can simply shape the dough after kneading and let rolls rise once to desired size. Bake at 350° F. for 20 minutes. Makes 4 to 5 dozen rolls.

CHIP/VEGETABLE DIP

8 ounces cream cheese, softened

1 cup sour cream

1 cup grated cheese

1 16-ounce package frozen broccoli

1 package Italian dressing mix

Combine all ingredients in a medium-sized baking dish and bake at 350° F. for 15 to 20 minutes.

WHOLE WHEAT BREAD

4 cups hot water

⅔ cup oil

⅔ cup molasses or honey

3 tablespoons yeast

2 tablespoons salt

10 to 12 cups whole wheat flour or
    white/wheat combo

Combine water, oil, and molasses or honey in a large bowl. Sprinkle yeast over top and let soften for about 5 minutes. Stir in salt and enough of the flour to make a soft dough. Knead in remaining flour and let rise until doubled. Punch down and shape. Place in standard-sized greased bread pans and let rise until desired size. Bake at 350° F. for 30 minutes.

FRENCH BREAD

2½ cups warm water

2 tablespoons sugar

2 tablespoons yeast

1 tablespoon salt

3 tablespoons oil

6 cups flour

Combine water, sugar, yeast, and salt in a large bowl; set aside for 10 minutes. Stir in oil and half the flour. Stir in remaining flour. Raise 10 minutes or more. Knead in a small amount of shortening until dough is smooth.

Shape into loaves, place each loaf on a greased cookie sheet and score top of loaves with a knife in a crisscross shape. Let rise until double in size. Bake at 400° F. for 30 minutes. Makes 2 loaves.

EASY WHITE BREAD

6 tablespoons shortening
1½ cups dried milk
9 tablespoons sugar
3 tablespoons salt
6 cups hot water
3 tablespoons yeast
12 cups flour

Dissolve shortening, dried milk, sugar, and salt in hot water; cool. Add yeast and let sit 5 minutes. Stir in flour. Knead dough until it holds its shape and can be handled easily. Let rise for one hour. Punch down, then divide dough and shape into desired number of loaves. Place in standard-sized greased loaf pans. Bake at 400° F. for 20 to 30 minutes.

BANANA BREAD

1¾ cups flour
1½ cups sugar
1 teaspoon baking soda
½ teaspoon salt
2 eggs
2 ripe bananas, mashed
½ cup vegetable oil
¼ cup buttermilk
1 teaspoon vanilla
1 cup nuts (optional)

Combine all ingredients in a large bowl using an electric mixer. Pour batter into 2 standard-sized greased loaf pans. Bake at 325° F. for 1 hour and 20 minutes.

FOOLPROOF FUDGE

3 cups chocolate chips
1 14-ounce can sweetened condensed milk
Dash salt

1½ teaspoons vanilla

Cook and stir chocolate chips and condensed milk over low heat until chocolate is melted. Stir in salt and vanilla. Pour into an 8x8-inch baking pan. Chill 2 hours.

CARAMEL CORN

1 can sweetened condensed milk
1 cup Karo syrup
1 1-pound package brown sugar
½ cup butter
1 large bowl popped corn

Combine all ingredients in a heavy saucepan and cook and stir over medium heat until mixture reaches the soft ball stage. Pour over popped corn.

BASIC MUFFINS

2 cups flour
½ teaspoon salt
2 teaspoons baking powder
1 egg
1 cup milk
2 tablespoons oil
2 tablespoons honey

Combine all ingredients just until moistened. Spoon batter into greased muffin tins. Bake at 400° F. for 20 to 25 minutes. Makes 1 dozen muffins.

GINGERSNAPS

¾ cup margarine or butter
1 cup sugar
1 egg

¼ cup molasses
2 teaspoons baking soda
2 cups flour
¼ teaspoon salt
1 teaspoon cinnamon
1 teaspoon cloves
1 teaspoon ginger

Cream butter and sugar until light and fluffy. Mix in egg and molasses. Stir in dry ingredients. Shape dough into small balls and place on greased cookie sheets. Bake at 375° F. for 10 to 12 minutes.

GINGERBREAD

½ cup sugar
½ cup butter or margarine
1 egg
1 cup molasses
½ teaspoon salt
2½ cups flour
1½ teaspoons baking powder
1 teaspoon cinnamon
1 teaspoon ginger
½ teaspoon cloves
1 cup very hot water

Cream sugar and butter together in a large mixing bowl. Beat in egg and molasses. Add dry ingredients and mix well. Beat in hot water. Place in a greased 9x13-inch pan. Bake at 350° F. for 40 minutes.

CORN BREAD

¼ cup vegetable oil
1 cup cornmeal
1 cup flour
2 to 4 tablespoons sugar
4 teaspoons baking powder
½ teaspoon salt
1 cup milk
1 egg

Combine all ingredients in a large bowl. Pour into a greased 9x13-inch cake pan and bake at 400° F. for 20 to 30 minutes. You can also fry corn bread in a skillet if you'd like to try something different.

FRESH SALSA

10 fresh tomatoes, chopped
1 cucumber, chopped
1 white onion, chopped
¾ cup cilantro, chopped
3 tablespoons lime juice
¼ cup vinegar
2 teaspoons cumin
3 bell peppers (1 red, 1 yellow, 1 green), seeded and chopped
2 jalapeño peppers (optional), seeded and chopped
Salt and pepper to taste

Combine all ingredients in a large mixing bowl and refrigerate until serving.

QUICK FRUIT DESSERT

1 can crushed pineapple, undrained
1 can apple pie filling
1 package yellow cake mix
Nuts (optional)
¾ cup margarine, melted

Grease and flour a 9x13-inch pan. Layer pineapple and pie filling on bottom. Layer dry cake mix over top. Sprinkle with nuts. Drizzle melted butter over top. Bake in oven according to cake mix directions.

MACARONI SALAD

1 16-ounce package macaroni noodles, cooked and drained
3 medium tomatoes, chopped
3 small zucchini, chopped
1 large cucumber, diced
1 medium green pepper, diced
1 medium red pepper, diced
1 8-ounce bottle Italian dressing
2 tablespoons parmesan cheese, grated
½ teaspoon paprika
¼ teaspoon celery seed
⅛ teaspoon garlic powder

Combine all ingredients and refrigerate 2 hours before serving.

HOT APPLESAUCE CAKE

4 cups flour
3 teaspoons baking soda
1¼ teaspoon salt
2 teaspoons cinnamon
½ teaspoon nutmeg
½ teaspoon gorund cloves
2 teaspoons cocoa
1 cup oil
2 cups sugar
3 cups applesauce

Combine all ingredients in a large bowl. Pour into a 9x13-inch, greased and floured cake pan. Bake at 400° F. for 15 minutes. Turn temperature down to 375° F. and bake for another 15 minutes.

STRAWBERRY SALAD

1 8-ounce tub Cool Whip®, thawed
1 16-ounce carton cottage cheese
1 small package strawberry gelatin
1 20-ounce can crushed pineapple, drained
Fresh strawberries, sliced

Combine all ingredients. Chill until ready to serve.

FRUIT DIP

1 large jar marshmallow crème topping
1 8-ounce package cream cheese, softened
Combine and chill until served.

PIZZA DOUGH

2 to 3 cups flour
1 package yeast
1 egg
1 teaspoon salt
2 tablespoons butter or margarine, softened
1 cup lukewarm milk

Combine all ingredients. Mix well. Knead until dough holds together well. Let rise until ready to form pizza rounds. Top with sauce, toppings, and cheese. Bake at 400° F. for 10 to 15 minutes.

PANCAKES

1¼ cups flour
1 tablespoon baking powder
1 tablespoon sugar
1 teaspoon salt
1 egg
1 cup milk
2 tablespoons oil

Combine all ingredients. Pour batter onto hot griddle. Cook until bubbly; flip.

BAKED BEANS

4 slices bacon, cooked and crumbled
½ cup onion, chopped
2 cans pork and beans
2 tablespoons brown sugar
¼ cup catsup

Combine all ingredients in a large casserole dish. Bake at 325° F. for 1½ hours.

APPLE CRISP

6 apples, peeled and sliced
½ cup sugar
2 tablespoons water
4 tablespoons butter or margarine

1 cup quick rolled oats
½ cup brown sugar
½ teaspoon cinnamon
½ cup nuts
1 teaspoon grated lemon peel

Coat apples with ½ cup sugar and 2 tablespoons water. Place in large baking dish. Cut butter into oats, brown sugar, cinnamon, nuts, and lemon peel. Spread mixture over apples. Bake at 350° F. for 45 minutes

MAGIC MIX

4 cups instant (2⅓ cups non-instant) dry milk
1 cup flour or ½ cup cornstarch
1 cup margarine

Combine dry milk, flour, and margarine in large bowl. Mix until it looks like cornmeal. Keep mix tightly covered in refrigerator. Use magic mix in the recipes that follow. Makes 5 cups.

CREAM SOUP

4 cups water
2 cups magic mix (see provided recipe)
1 cube bouillon
Carrots
Potatoes
Onion
Leftover meat

Place water in a large pot and stir in magic mix. Cook and stir over medium heat until combined. Add bouillon, vegetables, and leftover meat; heat until bubbly. Reduce heat and simmer until vegetables reach desired tenderness.

WHITE SAUCE

½ cup magic mix (see provided recipe)
1 cup water

Combine mix and water in a small saucepan and cook over medium heat, stirring often, until thick and bubbly.

MACARONI AND CHEESE

1 cup white sauce from magic mix (see provided recipe)
1 cup uncooked macaroni noodles
4 to 5 ounces grated cheese (about one cup)
1 teaspoon salt

Cook noodles according to package directions. Meanwhile, add grated cheese to white sauce and heat until bubbling. Drain noodles. Pour cheese sauce and salt over noodles and stir well.

CHOCOLATE PUDDING

½ cup sugar
1 cup magic mix (see provided recipe)
1 teaspoon vanilla
2 to 3 tablespoons cocoa
2 cups water

Combine dry ingredients in a medium saucepan. Stir in water and cook and stir until mixture is thick and bubbly. Cool before serving.

FUDGESICLES

1 pudding recipe (see above)
½ cup milk

Combine pudding with milk and pour mixture into ice cube trays or plastic cups. Insert plastic spoon and freeze.

CRAFTS

All children love to make things. And, left to their own devices, they will make things—usually messy things—with or without your blessing. But the *process* of creating something opens your child's mind to new experiences and lots of fun. Let your child experiment with clay and dough, encourage her to create her own dolls and make homemade Christmas ornaments together. Following are some easy instructions for crafting with your child.

MAKING DOLLS

Give your child the opportunity to make an assortment of dolls. Dolls are a universal and timeless toy that have been made by and played with by children—boys and girls—all over the world through all the ages.

SOCK DOLLS

Old, clean socks
Batting, cotton, paper towels, or toilet paper
    (anything that will stuff)
Needle and thread
Odds and ends from your sewing basket: buttons, yarn, etc.

1. Stuff an old sock with batting, cotton, paper towels, or toilet paper.
2. Use thread to tie off a neck.
3. Cut other socks into smaller pieces to stuff and sew onto the large sock for arms and legs.
4. Sew on buttons for eyes.

5. Glue on yarn for hair.
6. Rickrack, lace, thread, beads, raffia, and any number of other things can be glued or sewn on to socks to make personalized dolls.

YARN DOLLS

1 thick 5x8-inch or 6x9-inch book
Yarn

1. Wrap yarn vertically around a fat book about 90 to 100 times. You can count out loud with your child to help her get it right.
2. Slip a 5- or 6-inch piece of yarn underneath one end of the book and tie a loose knot to secure the strands as you pull the book out of the looped yarn.
3. Tie a knot around the yarn about 3 or 4 inches from the top to make a head.
4. Now wrap yarn around the width of the book about 40 or 50 times. This will be for the arms.
5. Slip the book out of the yarn.
6. Tie both ends to make hands.
7. Slip the arms through the strands under the head.
8. Use a short piece of yarn underneath the arms to secure them. This will make a waist.
9. You can either cut the ends of the yarn at the bottom and separate the strands to create a doll with pants, or leave the ends looped so the doll is wearing a dress.

PAPER DOLLS

Paper
Pencils
Crayons, markers, or colored pencils
Glue sticks
Scissors

1. Have your child draw a person with a body, arms, legs, and a head.

2. Trace around that body to create clothes of the right size for the body.

3. Draw small square tabs on each side of every shirt, skirt, pants, dress, or other object of clothing.

4. Color the clothes and the face and hair of the person.

5. Mount the person on cardboard with a glue stick.

6. Cut out the person and the clothes, making sure not to cut off the tabs.

APPLE DOLLS

Peeled apples
Popsicle sticks
Soda bottles
Fabric
Ribbon

This one works best in the dry months because it takes a long time for the apple to dry, and moisture might cause the apple to get moldy.

1. Peel and core an apple.

2. Poke holes in the apple where eyes would be.

3. Carve out a crescent shape for the mouth.

4. Fashion a nose by cutting away some of the apple from around the place where a nose should be.

5. Insert the Popsicle stick in the bottom of the apple and place the stick in a soda bottle, with the apple on top, for the apple to dry.

6. Dry for nearly two months, then remold the face a bit.

7. Dry for another 2 weeks.

8. Secure fabric at the top of the Popsicle stick to make a dress for your doll.

9. Tie a ribbon around the neck.

YARN PICTURES

Yarn or thread pictures are great fun for kids who are eager to do "grown-up" things. Try one of these easy ideas to keep your child busy for quite some time. If you use a large needle that doesn't have a very sharp point, even children as young as three can make yarn pictures.

CLOTH PICTURES

Scrap of fabric
Yarn or thread
Needle
Fabric marker

1. Draw a simple picture on a piece of cloth.

2. Thread a needle with yarn or thread.

3. Sew along the lines of the picture. Your child can choose to make his stitches any length, and may want to try switching colors in the middle.

CUTOUT PICTURES

Paper
Pens or markers
Scissors
Fabric scrap
Yarn or thread
Needle

1. Draw shapes, such as houses, trees, and animals, on paper with markers or pens.

2. Cut out shapes.

3. Pin the pieces to the fabric scrap.

4. Sew around the pieces.

CARDBOARD SEWING CARDS

Cardboard
Pens or markers
Scissors
Hole punch
Yarn
Needle

1. Draw and color pictures on cardboard.

2. Cut out pictures, but not right on the lines. The lines should be visible after cutting.

3. Punch holes ½-inch to 1 inch apart all along the outside line of the drawing.

4. Use the yarn and a needle to make stitches all around the cardboard pictures.

CLAY

There is nothing quite like the feel of clay or dough in your hands. Every child should have the chance to make things with clay or dough. Let your child experiment with making a ball or log. Then move to making animals, people, and shapes, such as bowls and cups.

CRAFT CLAY

1 cup cornstarch
1¼ cups salt
2 cups baking soda
1 tablespoon oil

Combine all ingredients in a medium saucepan. Cook over medium heat until thickened. Knead. Keep soft in a plastic bag. Dough can be painted when dry.

PLAY DOUGH

2 cups flour
1 cup salt
1 tablespoon oil
¾ cup water (can be colored with food coloring)

Mix dry ingredients. Add water and oil. Add

CREATIVE CRAFT PROJECTS

Look through your drawers and cupboards at home and find things to help your kids make the following craft projects:

- tin can stilts
- paper airplanes
- button necklaces
- paper pinwheels
- bookmarks
- card table/blanket tents
- cardboard dollhouses
- potato prints
- hanger mobiles
- carved soap figures
- wooden boats and cars
- homemade puzzles
- place mats
- paper chains
- decorated bottles, cans, and boxes
- paper, wooden stick, or straw houses

more water if dry or flour if sticky. The oil preserves the dough and keeps it soft. Store in a plastic bag in the refrigerator.

MODELING CLAY

2 cups salt
⅔ cup water
1 cup cornstarch
½ cup cold water

Combine salt and the ⅔ cup of water in a saucepan and stir over medium heat for five minutes. Remove from heat. Add cornstarch and cold water. Stir until smooth. Cook again until thick. Store in plastic bag.

BAKED CLAY IMPRESSIONS

4 cups flour
¾ cup water
1 cup salt

Combine all ingredients. Press out dough onto a cookie sheet or other baking pan. Use dough to make hand or foot impressions. Then bake at 325° F. for an hour.

SALT DOUGH

2 cups flour
2 cups salt
1 cup water

Combine all ingredients to make a stiff mixture. Knead for 10 minutes.

CORNSTARCH CLAY DOUGH FIGURES

2 cups cornstarch
2 cups baking soda
1¼ cups cold water

Combine cornstarch and baking soda. Add water until mixture is smooth. Heat, stirring constantly until mixture reaches a moist, mashed-potato consistency. Turn onto plate, cover with a damp towel. Knead dough when cool enough to handle. Mold clay into a figure or roll dough about ¼-inch thick on a floured board and cut out figures. Bake on a flat cookie sheet at 225° F. for 2 or 3 hours. Turn figures over to keep them from curling. Paint when finished.

COMPUTERS

Computers give you and your child privileges, opportunities, and, unfortunately, dangers unsurpassed in previous generations. Most children today are taught to use computers, including simple word processing programs, before they leave elementary school. If you don't have a computer in your home, consider buying one. It will prove to be a wonderful learning, creating, and communicating tool for your family. As your children get older, recognize that the majority of their homework and assignments will be done on the computer.

Learn now how to use a computer so that you will be the one teaching your

child what he can do with technology and "where" he can go on the Internet. You'll be amazed at what even young children can do on a computer: create artwork, make cards, keep a journal, play educational games, conduct research, send e-mails, listen to music, and participate in a host of other entertaining and educational activities.

After your child starts school, the Internet will prove useful for keeping in touch with his teachers and checking on his attendance, homework, and grades. Your child can research and write assigned papers. You can keep in touch with family members who live far away. You can read the newspaper, make calendars, buy transportation tickets, find directions to any address, scan family pictures for posterity, play games, write, draw, create CDs, listen to music, record music, talk to people all over the world, download clip art, prepare lessons, find a recipe, and shop for anything under the sun if you have the Internet.

There are literally millions of educational, commercial, and governmental Web sites. The Church also runs a wonderful Web site full of magazine articles, conference talks, teaching helps, genealogical research, and other valuable data.

FAMILY RULES FOR INTERNET USE

Your computer will introduce you and your child to amazing and wonderful things. The Internet is a great resource, research, and idea tool; but it can also be a dangerous place. Carefully consider what rules you and your family should follow for protection from these dangers.

• Leave your computer in an open area

of the house to lessen the chance any family member will use the computer in ways that might be inappropriate.

• Warn your child about chat rooms and the availability of inappropriate viewing material. Let your child know you will be checking regularly for sites visited on your computer.

• Use an Internet service provider that screens out objectionable material so you and your child will not be exposed to offensive material.

• Make sure that one parent is home whenever the Internet is used.

• Set time limits for Internet use.

• Instruct your children to never reveal information about themselves on the Internet. If someone asks for their name, address, phone number, or a credit card number, instruct your child to leave the site immediately and tell you what happened.

• Teach your child what to do if she accidentally comes upon a Web site with pornographic material. Many objectionable Web sites will automatically begin linking your child to other Web sites, making it difficult for her to exit. If this happens to your child, tell her to immediately turn off the computer and tell you what happened.

DANCE

Dance, or creative movement, is an important part of any child's experience. It is a direct, personal means of communication and expression. Most other forms of self-expression require a medium or instrument, such as a pen, a brush, clay, a violin, or piano. But with dance, the body becomes the instrument. The whole person is the form of expression. The dance and the dancer become one.

I remember the first warm spring day after a long, cold winter when I was a small child. I'd been locked up in the house for months, waiting like a caged animal to play outside again. I still remember the sun rising over the mountains that morning and the excitement I felt inside. As if on cue, I tore off my flannel pajamas and slid into my prettiest, frilliest petticoat. Then I darted from the door into the morning's first rays of sunlight with vapor still rising from the new green grass. I twirled and leaped on our front lawn and made a dandelion-chain necklace for my hair. I became part of the birds in the air, the blossoms on the tress, and all the new life around me. Leaping and twirling through the crisp air was the most perfect means I had to express my sheer joy.

Of course, all the average adults who passed my house that morning were probably thinking, "What's that little girl doing outside, dancing in her underwear?"

DANCE THROUGH THE AGES

BABYHOOD

Your baby's body is a wonder, a miracle in motion. Any type of movement will be a new and creative form of expression for your little one. Hold him. Rock him. Sway back and forth with your little angel in your arms. Your baby will find comfort in the warmth of skin contact and suckling. In fact, physical affection is just as important to an infant as food.

Watch as your baby discovers his body and first discovers that he is not simply an extension of his parents, but a separate and complete human being. Soon he'll find his hands; for hours he'll be absorbed and fascinated with those wonders at the end of his arms. He'll watch and observe and study the motions he is making and suddenly discover he has power or control over those movements. He'll kick with his legs and arch his back. He'll lift his head and then his belly from the floor. Soon he will be crawling, walking, then running. Discovering what his body can do will be a wonder to him. Let it be a wonder to you, as well. The human body is God's finest piece of workmanship. Helping your child discover his marvelous body is a great way to help him feel important and to retain his innate sense of wonder.

TODDLERS AND PRESCHOOLERS

Toddlers need the opportunity to discover each unique part of their bodies. This is the perfect time to start playing "Head, Shoulders, Knees, and Toes" or "I'm All Made of Hinges." Try playing other movement games with them. Here is a fun one:

"What's this?" (It's a head.)

"What can a head do?" (a head can nod, droop, shake, tilt, or bend.)

"Can you nod your head?"

"Can you make your head droop?"

"Can you shake your head?" and so on.

Children will develop better feelings about themselves when they learn to control their bodies. The way a child moves tells us a lot about how she feels and the attitude she has about herself.

Once, one of my young daughters was undressing to take her bath. She tossed her clothes in the air and flew down the hallway kicking up her heels and shaking her head. She stretched and twirled.

"I like to wear clothes sometimes," she said, smiling at me. "But sometimes it's nice to have them off for a while. It makes me feel free, like one of those wild horses."

Another young daughter had tried and tried to learn how to skip, but had been able to develop nothing more than a gallop. One day out on the front lawn, with the wind in her face, and the sun at her back, she kept practicing until finally that little hop step came and she started to skip. She was so delighted with herself that

she almost shook. She pulled me away from the sink and demonstrated her latest body mastery. After that, she skipped to bed, to the bathroom, and everywhere she went.

Encourage your toddler to learn how to run, skip, jump, hop, twirl, and spin. Dance in circles with your toddlers and preschoolers. Help them feel free to release their emotions through creative, energetic movement.

Instead of zeroing in on one specific activity, expose your child to lots of different forms of creative movement—dance, tumbling, soccer, and so on—then sit back and watch. Don't be in a big rush to enroll your preschooler in a premier ballet program in an attempt to make her a star. Take your time, and let your child take her time growing up and trying lots of different things. And in the meantime, turn up the music and dance to the beat.

SCHOOL-AGERS

Do you remember how you felt the first time you realized your parent had let go of your two-wheeled bike and you were on your own? Do you remember learning to tie your shoes or roller skate? Do you remember when you learned how to swim or do a cartwheel? There is a kind of sheer ecstasy that comes after trying and finally mastering a skill with your body. Think of all these "masteries" and other sports-oriented activities as a form of dance.

When a child becomes aware of his body and learns to control it, a feeling of freedom emerges. Through movement a child can say what he can't express any other way. Children can move or dance out hidden emotions and even dreams. Most children love to dance and do so unless you try to restrain them. Even severely handicapped children love to shake their heads to a beat. In a few years, if you aren't careful, that natural dancer will turn into an awkward adolescent who will move self-consciously and even be embarrassed by his own body.

Right now is the time to introduce your child to the possibilities of coordinated movement. To start with, you might have them take off their shoes and socks and wear comfortable clothing that promotes body movement. Next, help them become aware of each separate body part and what each part can do. The child can lie down and close his eyes, then move just his toes or just his fingers. Next he can move that part fast or slow; then he can let each part of his body dance separately—a foot dance

or an arm dance, for example. Now he can move the dancing hand, foot, or head through the air. Then he can try walking, skipping, leaping, sliding, crawling, hopping, and running.

There are basically three elements of dance or movement: *time, space,* and *energy.* You can help your children become aware of these elements through carefully observing things around them. Watch a leaf fall from a tree. Does it fall quickly? (time) Does it drop straight down or wave through the air? (space) Is the leaf light or heavy? How does that affect the way it falls? (energy).

At home you can help your child become aware of time by having them run fast or walk slow. You can help them become aware of space by having them lift their legs or reach to the ceiling or bend sideways. You can help them become aware of energy by having them move like an elephant or a mouse or having them pretend to be lifting something heavy or something light.

Once these basic movements are natural to them, they might start combining simple movements, such as crawling, then sitting, then hopping; skipping, then falling, then rolling over; twirling, then jumping, then rolling up in a ball. These can be done to simple accompaniment. Many children will make up their own accompaniment by humming or clapping.

Ask your child if he wants to enroll in a gymnastics, dance, or individual or team sport program. Allow him to select and try several options before he zeros in on one choice. Think of activities such as ballet, football, baseball, swimming, gymnastics, tap, and track as a form of dance. Any time

DANCE MOVES TO LEARN WITH YOUR PRESCHOOLER OR SCHOOL-AGER

Try some of these "creative movements" with your young child and teach him how to express himself.

- *Transportation:* Have your child pretend to be a car, bus, or airplane.
- *Slow motion:* Have your child move in slow motion.
- *Statue:* Have one child gently fling another child around and tell the other child to hold the position he lands in.
- *Sculpture:* Have one child bend and shape another child into a certain position of his choosing.
- *Occupation:* Have your child pretend he is a doctor, teacher, baker, truck driver, and so forth and go through the different physical movements of these jobs.

- *Facial emotions:* Say such words as happy, sad, scared, and tired. Then ask your child to move his face or body to respond to those emotions.
- *Copycat:* Have your child imitate your movements.
- *Dancing motions:* Have your child express in dance things that go up and down, spin, go in and out, or things that are soft or hard or heavy (merry-go-rounds, umbrellas, hammers, and so on.)
- *Dancing objects:* Have your child express, through dance, objects in the house, like a computer, a can opener, a CD player, or television set.
- *Dancing color:* Have your child express in dance how a color makes him feel.
- *Life cycles:* Have your child dance the life cycle of a flower or a butterfly.
- *Weather:* Have your child dance to a suggested weather condition, such as rain, snow, wind, or sunshine.
- *Poetry dancing:* Have your child dance or move while you read a poem or nursery rhyme.
- *Name dancing:* Have your child dance or clap out names.
- *Touch dancing:* Have your child close his eyes and then touch something like velvet or sandpaper. Then have him move to express through movement how it feels.
- *Animals:* Have your child pretend to be an animal and move like that animal.
- *Stories:* Have your child express the actions of a story while you read.
- *Sounds:* Have your child move to sounds, such as a toaster popping or a car starting.

you use your body for expression—using time, energy, and space—you are "dancing" to the beat of your own drummer.

TEENAGERS

If your teen is interested, she may choose to continue or begin school, private, or community dance classes or sports programs. Any kind of movement, dance, sports, or exercise plan will help your teen feel healthy inside and out. A personal movement program such as aerobics, walking, jogging, or bicycling may be another wise option. Your teen might enjoy clogging, gymnastics, ballet, country dancing, swimming, or team and individual sports programs. Help your child learn to choose carefully and not stretch herself too thin during her teen years.

Most teens are interested in learning social dance so they know what to do at all the school, church, and community-sponsored dances they attend. When the opposite sex starts looking interesting to them, even previously reluctant children are suddenly motivated to learn.

Teach your teen that her body is a precious gift. Every child should learn to love her body and all the wonderful things it can do. Remind your teen not to compare herself with her peers, for there will always be someone who can do everything better or worse than she . . . but help your teen reverence the body she has and enjoy all the wonderful forms of movement and expression open to her.

THE JOY OF DANCE

In the early years, movement for the pure joy of it is your goal. There is no right or wrong way for a child to move or dance, only his way. The success is in the trying, not the result. So give your child plenty of opportunities to use his body in fun ways that bring him satisfaction and a feeling of competence and joy.

The only physical way some children have of relating to each other is by hitting or attacking or teasing. But a child who knows and respects his own body and what it can do is less likely to relate to others in an abusive manner. Sports programs give children a constructive way to compete with each other and learn body mastery skills. So don't think of dance as just a sissy thing for kids in tights. Dance is body movement in any form.

The purpose of dance is to teach your child to love and respect his individual body and master movements that bring him joy. Whether your child is swinging a bat or doing a pirouette, the point is the same: creative expression with his body for the joy of it.

When was the last time you skipped down the sidewalk or took off your shoes to wiggle your toes in the grass? How do you view your body? Before you put one more load of laundry in the washing machine tonight, ask your sweetheart for a dance. Then turn out the lights and try a waltz.

DRAMA

Drama is the art of pretending. And who doesn't love pretending every once in a while? Encourage your child in the healthy expression of drama and pretend play. The following will offer a number of ways to bring out the "actor" in every child.

ENCOURAGING YOUR PRESCHOOL PRODIGY

PLAYING DRESS UP

Perhaps the first dramatic performance your child participates in will be when she dons Dad's shoes and begins walking around the house pretending to be someone else. Dressing up is a classic childhood pastime. Supply your children with a collection of unique clothing for dress-up and pretend adventures. Deseret Industries and local thrift stores are invaluable when putting together a dress-up wardrobe for your children. Look for dance costumes, vintage clothing, capes, hats, feathery boas, furry scarves, long silk gloves. Save your old prom dresses and your husband's old tux. Keep everything in a big tote or box with a mirror nearby, then let your child loose to dream up amazing adventures.

PLAYING HOUSE

Another early experience in drama is playing house. Whenever a child plays at being a mom or dad, he is playing house. Miniature stoves, sinks, and refrigerators, along with cupboards, tables, and chairs make great props, but children can play house with what you have on hand inside or outside your home. Dolls for babies and pretend food make playing house even more fun.

PLAYING STORE

Playing store is a great way for children to imitate the adults in their life. Using shopping carts, cash registers, and money even teaches simple math concepts.

PLAY ACTING

Children learn by imitating. After your children go to church, they come home and play church. After they go to the doctor, they come home and play doctor. After they watch you care for their baby brother or sister and prepare a meal, they play house. All this may seem like play to you, but for a child it is his work. Every time he explores something new, he learns and grows from experience.

DRAMATIC IDEAS FOR SCHOOL KIDS

MAKING NEWS

Encourage your children to duplicate the evening news or variety shows on television with their own make-believe news casts or talent shows. Use the video camera to record and play back their presentations. If you're really into it, invite grandparents and aunts and uncles over to cheer on your kids as they create their own variety show.

PLAYING CHARADES

Charades is a great dramatic game for family members of almost any age. Get the gang together and "act out" the name of a movie, book, television show, or any other subject you pick and agree on as a family. The family member who is "on" must act out the information without using his voice.

PLAY WRITING

Older children might want to try their hand at writing a play. Given a few simple instructions, children can write their own imaginative plays (a story acted out in front of an audience). All a play script really needs are characters and a story line. A familiar fairy tale or a simple story from the Bible can be acted out with original dialogue.

Very young children will need a scribe, or someone to write down their ideas and story line. Older children may want to do their own writing with some assistance. Let your children "write" the script in their minds or on paper.

If you want, help your child to make the play script look official by putting it in a simple binder or folder.

Once the play is written or the story decided on, let the fun begin. Encourage your children to learn their parts and complete the play with props, costumes, rehearsals, and a final performance. Agree to be a character in the play or the adoring audience.

RADIO-PLAYWRITING

Writing a play intended only to be heard and not seen opens up new possibilities of presenting ideas and stories. In a radio play only the voice and sound effects are heard. This makes for great fun for the whole family as children learn to produce their own sound effects and directions to go along with stories or advertisements.

Stories can be simple or complex, depending on the age of the child. Have each family member take a speaking part, narrate a part, or produce sound effects. Sometimes your very timid child might want to share a little time in the spotlight if he knows he'll be reading behind a sheet or speaking into a tape recorder.

STORY TAPES

Your children might also enjoy taking a familiar story and reading it onto a tape. They can add music, sound effects, or other commentary as they like. Many children love listening to tapes like this over and over again. Even grandparents who live far away can participate by recording on tape some of the grandchildren's favorite stories and sending the tape as a gift.

COMMUNITY, SCHOOL, OR CHURCH-SPONSORED THEATER

Most communities, schools, and church units give children, teens, and adults a chance to take part in amateur theater. Take advantage of this opportunity if you are so inclined. You don't have to be an actor to enjoy drama. Theatrical productions need people who can create a cos-

tume, run the lights and sound system, design the set, direct the production, and teach any number of skills from dancing and singing to choreography and acting.

PUPPET SHOWS

I've never met a child or an adult who wasn't captivated, or at least entertained, with puppets. Whether you use old socks, buy or make a marionette, or put your old gardening gloves to another use, don't forget to make puppets part of your child's growing up experience and exposure to the delightful world of drama.

Let your child choose a story and act out the story with puppets. Hide behind a couch or use a home-made theater for your puppet shows.

MAKING MASKS

Papier-mâché Masks
8 sheets of newspaper, cut into strips
1 cup wallpaper paste
1 balloon
Tear paper into strips and soak in paste for a few minutes. Drape strips over one half-inflated balloon. Make strips into eyes, nose, mouth, and ears, hold in place for facial features. Wait two days to dry. Paint with poster paints.

Easy Homemade Puppets

From stick puppets to marionettes to wall-shadow puppets, this is an art everyone in the family will love. Here are some simple instructions for making your own puppets at home.

STICK PUPPETS

1. Cut out magazine pictures of people standing.
2. Paste those pictures on cardboard then cut them out.
3. Tape each picture standing up to a strip of wood, a frozen treat stick, or an old ruler.
4. Use a box or table for a stage.
5. Hang a cloth over the stage to hide the puppeteer.

FINGER PUPPETS

1. Draw a body (a head and torso) without legs.
2. Glue this body to the back of an old glove above the second finger.

3. Cut off the second and third finger of the glove.

4. Place the glove over your hand and use your exposed fingers for the legs.

HAND PUPPETS

1. Make a fist with your thumb tucked inside your fingers. That fist will be your puppet's head. Your thumb will become your puppet's mouth.

2. Use makeup or colored markers to paint eyes and lips on your hand and thumb to create a face.

3. Wrap a piece of cloth around the rest of your hand.

4. Move your thumb up and down and talk for your puppet.

PAPER BAG PUPPETS

1. Lay a brown paper bag flat with the bottom away from you.

2. Draw a face on the upper half of the bag.

3. Cut holes in the sides of the bag for your fingers to fit through. Your fingers will become the arms of the puppet.

PAPER PLATE PUPPETS

1. Draw a face on a paper plate.

2. Use your hand or a stick to move your puppet.

SOCK PUPPETS

1. Paint a face on the foot section of an old sock.

2. Add hair or ears as desired.

3. Place your hand inside the sock and form a mouth for the puppet with your fingers.

4. Move your fingers to make the puppet talk.

SAWDUST PUPPETS

1. Add a cup of sawdust to enough water to make it pack like wet sand.

2. Add paste to the mixture until it has the consistency of clay.

3. Wrap a scrap of old cloth around a vase or pop bottle.

4. Stick a lump of sawdust clay over the cloth on the neck of the vase or bottle and mold it into a head.

5. Let it dry.

6. Take it off the vase or bottle and smooth it with sandpaper.

7. Paint the head with paints or markers and cover it with varnish or shellac.

8. Fashion a body with cloth, wood, or a glove.

STYROFOAM PUPPETS

1. Styrofoam balls can be used for puppet heads. Punch a finger hole in the bottom of the ball.

2. Push a piece of an old cardboard roll into the ball for a neck.

3. Paste on yarn for hair and pin facial features on the ball for a face.

MARIONETTE PUPPETS

1. Marionette puppets can be made from cardboard figures with separate movable arms and legs attached to a string and tied to your fingers.

2. Other marionette puppets can be made with papier-mâché heads and bodies. Movable arms and legs can be made with wood, cardboard, or yarn pieces.

3. Papier-mâché over balloons also makes great puppet parts. You can tie puppet strings to a pencil, an ice-cream stick, or a small piece of wood.

AT THE MOVIES

The most popular commercial use of drama these days is movies. Yet it's getting harder and harder to find good movies the whole family can enjoy these days. Fortunately, there are still some oldies but goodies out there. Most older versions of the same title are better than the newer adaptation; but there are still a few good remakes today. Always view a video before you let your child see it. The following are movies that families can enjoy together, although some of them are better for families with older children and others for families with younger children:

An American Tail (1986)
Anne of Avonlea (1987)
Anne of Green Gables (1985)
Annie (1982)
Arsenic and Old Lace (1944)
Awakenings (1991)
Ben Hur (1959)
Bambi (1942)
Beauty and the Beast (1991)
Bedknobs and Broomsticks (1971)
Bishop's Wife, The (1947)
Black Stallion, The (1979)

Born Free (1965)
Brian's Song (1971)
Captains Courageous (1937)
Chariots of Fire (1981)
Cheaper by the Dozen (1950)
Charlotte's Web (1973)
Christmas Carol, A (1984)
Chosen, The (1982)
Diary of Anne Frank, The (1959)
David Copperfield (1935 or 1999)
Dead Poet's Society (1989)
Dumbo (1941)
El Cid (1961)
Elephant Man, The (1980)
Enchanted April (1992)
Enchanted Cottage, The (1945)
Ever After (1998)
Faerie Tale Theatre (TV series, 1982–1987)
Fiddler on the Roof (1971)
Friendly Persuasion (1956)
Fourth Wise Man, The (1985)
Frog and Toad Together (1993)
Gandhi (1982)
Ghost and Mrs. Muir, The (1947)
Goodbye, Mr. Chips (1969)
Go Toward the Light (1988)
Great Escape, The (1963)
Hans Christian Andersen (1952)
Heaven Knows, Mr. Allison (1957)
Heidi (1937)
High Noon (1952)
Hoosiers (1987)
How Green Was My Valley (1941)
How the Grinch Stole Christmas (1966)
Inn of the Sixth Happiness, The (1958)
I Remember Mama (1948)
It's a Wonderful Life (1946)
Jane Eyre (1944)
Jesus of Nazareth (1977)
Joan of Arc (1948)

Jungle Book, The (1967)

King and I, The (1956)

Lady and the Tramp (1955)

Les Miserables (1935, 1978–TV)

Life Is Beautiful (1998)

Life with Father (1947)

Lion, the Witch and the Wardrobe, The (1988)

Little Lord Fauntleroy (1980)

Little Mermaid, The (1989)

Little Princess, The (1939 or 1995)

Little Women (1933, 1994)

Lost Horizon (1937)

Lost in Yonkers (1993)

Magnificent Obsession (1954)

Man Called Peter, A (1955)

Man for All Seasons, A (1966)

Mary Poppins (1964)

Meet John Doe (1941)

Miracle on 34th Street (1947)

Miracle Worker, The (1962)

Mission, The (1986)

Mr. Smith Goes to Washington (1939)

Mr. Holland's Opus (1995)

Mrs. Miniver (1942)

Music Man, The (1962)

Mutiny on the Bounty (1935 or 1962)

National Velvet (1945)

NeverEnding Story, The (1984)

Night Crossing (1982)

Old Yeller (1957)

Oliver! (1968)

Other Side of Heaven, The (2001)

Peter Pan (1953)

Picture of Dorian Gray, The (1945)

Pinocchio (1940)

Pollyanna (1960)

Pride and Prejudice (1940 or 1996)

Pride of the Yankees, The (1942)

Prince of Egypt, The (1998)

Princess Bride, The (1987)

Rainmaker, The (1956)

Red Balloon, The (1955)

Robe, The (1953)

Road Home, The (1999)

Rookie, The (2002)

Rudolph the Red-Nosed Reindeer (1964)

Rudy (1993)

Russians Are Coming, the Russians Are Coming, The (1966)

Sarah, Plain and Tall (1990)

Scarlet and the Black, The (1983)

Scarlet Pimpernel, The (1982)

Secret Garden, The (1993)

Secret of NIMH, The (1982)

Sense and Sensibility (1995)

Shadowlands (1993)

Singin' in the Rain (1952)

Skylark (1993)

Sleeping Beauty (1959)

Tales of Beatrix Potter (1971)

Snowman, The (1982)

Sound of Music, The (1965)

Spirit of St. Louis, The (1957)

Swiss Family Robinson (1960)

Tale of Two Cities, A (1935)

Ten Commandments, The (1956)

Tender Mercies (1983)

To Kill a Mockingbird (1962)

Tom Sawyer (1973)

To Sir, with Love (1966)

Toy Story and Toy Story II (1995 and 1999)

Treasure Island (1950)

Ugly Duckling, The (1931)

Wind in the Willows, The (TV series, 1984)

With Six You Get Eggroll (1968)

Wizard of Oz, The (1939)

Yearling, The (1946)

WALL SHADOW PUPPETS

1. Use your hand to shape shadow creatures on the wall.

2. Shine a bright light at the wall and put your hand puppet in front of the light beam.

3. Move your fingers to open and close your creature's mouth, move wings, or wiggle ears.

A Puppet Stage

Any number of items can be used to make a puppet stage.

Turn a card table on its side and kneel behind the table, with the puppets dangling over the top.

Tack an old curtain, tablecloth, or other piece of fabric across the bottom half of a doorway. Hide behind the fabric and have the puppets pop up above the top of the curtain.

Cut a window in a large cardboard box and have the puppets appear in the window while you hide behind the sides of the box.

MUSIC

Childhood is a magical, musical time. A tiny infant responds to your voice even in the womb. After birth, your baby becomes quiet when she hears a lullaby or a reassuring voice. Long before speech, your child delights in trying out new sounds. A toddler is a natural percussionist. Banging lids, kicking doors, dropping toys, she listens and plays a musical game of sorts. School children, year after year and generation after generation, repeat jingles, rhymes, and rhythms to accompany their play. They like to drag sticks along the sidewalk or a fence, open and slam doors, run, skip, hop, and dance. Then there are those bright moments when a child becomes the lead singer in the musical production of her own life and breaks into song without even being cued.

PROVIDING MUSICAL EXPERIENCES

What becomes of your child's interest and feeling for rhythm and harmony? Most of us usually do one of two things. We either tell the child to be quiet or we give him music lessons. With the former he may be cut off from a joyful spontaneous part of his life. With the latter, he may be forced to change his spontaneous delight into memorizing scales.

Most music educators recommend that children be able to read well and know some basic math principles before they begin to take formal music lessons. And lessons certainly may be the answer for some children, but not for all. If you aren't careful, the adventure may be lost or your child may be turned off.

Before your child is ready for lessons, help him discover and keep the magic of music. Even if your child never develops a talent for playing an instrument, he can develop a more sensitive ear and the ability to really enjoy music.

Music is not just for the gifted or talented. Musical training is always worthwhile. We don't reserve training in reading, writing, and math for only those who are gifted. Like those subjects, music is a basic human need and experience. Musical training should be as much a part of your child's education as skills in reading or writing. It isn't essential that these skills turn into performing sills. Music training can simply lead a person to a more joyful and sensitive life. It can provide children with beauty, variety, inspiration, and comfort. How do you create for your child an atmosphere in which his natural instincts and feelings for music can flower and be given expression?

Sing, listen to recorded and live music, train the ear, make simple instruments, and play musical games. All of these things will introduce the magic of music to your children.

SINGING

Music can become an important part of a child's life from earliest infancy. Babies love the delight and comfort of being sung to. It doesn't matter what kind or quality of voice you have. Children respond to the feeling of the music. If you spontaneously sing or hum or whistle around the house, at work and at play, your child will soon learn that music is something that expresses good feelings and brings pleasure to both the performer and the listener. Children love to sing. It's only after parents or teachers call attention to their loudness or tendency to sing off key that they begin to feel inhibited by their singing voices.

Teaching children songs in the family circle is a natural way to help them appreciate music. Families can sing before or after a meal, during an evening at home together, around the piano or fireplace before bedtime, or when someone is in a bad mood. If singing is accepted naturally in your home, you may find your child singing in bed, in the bath, while playing, eating, traveling, and just about any place and any time they feel like it.

Singing can also influence a person's attitude and disposition. Try singing your next reprimand, instruction, or question to your child. It's difficult to keep a straight face. Even if you consider yourself unmusical, you probably know dozens of familiar melodies. Any song that gives you pleasure is a good song for your child.

Children enjoy songs with patterns and repetitive phrases or words that suggest actions. They also like to hear their names put into the words of songs: "How I love my pretty Annie, sweet and precious little Annie," or "Oh, where oh where has my

CHILDHOOD SONGS

Here are the words to a few fun songs that no young child should miss. Use any hand actions that the words inspire. Whisper some of the words, shout out others; just let the feeling of the songs guide you:

Five Little Monkeys Jumping on the Bed

Five little monkeys jumping on the bed.
One fell off and bumped his head.
Mommy called the doctor and the doctor said,
"No more monkeys jumping on the bed."
(repeat with dwindling numbers)

Five Little Monkeys Swinging in a Tree

Five little monkeys swinging
    in a tree
Teasing Mr. Alligator,
    "Can't catch me! You
    can't catch me."
Along comes Mr. Alligator
    quiet as can be . . .
And snatches that monkey right
    out of that tree.
(repeat with dwindling numbers)

Five Little Ducks Went Out to Play

Five little ducks went out to play
Over the hill and far away
When the mommy duck said, "Quack, quack, quack,"
Four little ducks came waddling back.
(repeat with dwindling numbers until no little ducks come waddling back)
Sad mother duck went out one day
Over the hill and far away
When sad mother duck said, "Quack, quack, quack,"
Five little ducks came waddling back.

Five Bears in the Bed

Five bears in the bed and the little one said,
"I'm crowded—roll over."
So they all rolled over and one fell out
Four bears in the bed and the little one said . . .
(Repeat with dwindling numbers until all the bears but one fall out)
and the little one says,
"I'm lonely."

Here's a Ball for Baby

(do actions with your hands)
Here's a ball for baby—big and soft and round.
Here's the baby's hammer—see how he can pound.
Here's the baby's trumpet—toot, toot, toot, toot, toot.
Here's the way the baby plays "peek-a-boo."
Here's the big umbrella—keeps the baby dry.
Here's the baby's cradle—rock a baby, bye.
Here's the baby's music—clapping, clapping so.
Here's the baby's soldiers—marching in a row.

The Wheels on the Bus

The wheels on the bus go round and round,
    round and round, round and round
The wheels on the bus go round and round,
    all through the town.

The people on the bus go up and down . . .
(repeat, following pattern in first stanza)

The babies on the bus go wah, wah, wah
(repeat, following pattern in first stanza)

The mommies on the bus go shh, shh, shh
(repeat, following pattern in first stanza)

The wipers on the bus go swish, swish, swish
(repeat, following pattern in first stanza)

The horn on the bus goes beep, beep, beep,
(repeat, following pattern in first stanza)

The driver on the bus says, "Move on back,"
(repeat, following pattern in first stanza)

I Had a Little Turtle

(use hands for actions)

I have a little turtle, his name is Tiny Tim.
I put him in the bathtub to see if he could
    swim.
He ate up all the water—he
    ate up all the soap.
And now he's
    sick in bed, with
    a bubble in his
    throat.
Bubble, bubble,
    bubble, bub-
    ble, bubble
    bubble
Now he's sick in bed with a
    bubble in his throat.
It got bigger and bigger and bigger, POP!

Where Is Thumbkin?

(use fingers for actions)

Where is Thumbkin, where is Thumbkin?
Here I am, Here I am
How are you today, sir?
Very well, I thank you.
Run away, run away.
(repeat, substituting these other finger people:
    pointer, tall man, ring man, pinky)

Rainbow Song

Red and yellow and pink and green
Purple and orange and blue.
I can sing a rainbow, sing a rainbow, sing a
    rainbow tune.
Listen with your eyes, listen with your eyes
And sing everything you see.
You can sing a rainbow, sing a rainbow
Sing along with me.

Sleep Tight

Sleep tight, sandman's a comin'
And he'll be here mighty, mighty soon.

So if you don't cry, he'll be comin' by
With a great big lollipop moon.

How I love my little (fill in your child's name),
Sweet and precious little (fill in your child's
    name).
How I love my little (fill in your child's name).
Honest to goodness I do.
(repeat both verses many, many times)

Crazy

Boom, boom ain't it great to be crazy.
Boom, boom ain't it great to be nuts.
Giddy and happy all day long.
Boom, boom ain't it great to be crazy.

Up, Up in the Sky

Up, up in the sky,
Where the little birds fly.
Down, down in their nests
Where the little birds rest.
With a wing on the left and a wing on the right
The little birds sleep all the long night.
When the round sun comes up
And the dew floats away,
"Good morning, good morning," the little
    birds say.

Aulie, Baulie, Bee

Aulie, baulie, aulie, baulie, bee
Sitting on my Mommy's knee.
Pinein' for a wee bobbie
To buy some Colter's candy.
Living's very hard to do,
Your father's sighted on the brew.
But your mommy's got a penny for you
To buy some Colter's candy.

Bumblebee

I'm bringing home my baby bumblebee,
Won't my mommy be so proud of me?
I'm bringing home my baby bumblebee.
"Ouch! It stung me."

continued on next page

I'm squishing up my baby bumblebee,
Won't my mommy be so proud of me?
I'm squishing up my baby bumblebee,
"Eww! It's all over me"

I'm wiping off my baby bumblebee.
Won't my mommy be so proud of me?
I'm wiping off my baby bumblebee.
(repeat and add any actions you'd like,
    continue for as long as desired)

Pokey Bear

"Pokey bear, pokey bear, Why are you so
    slow?"
"I don't know. I don't know. I, I, I don't
    know."
"Run, run, run. Run, run, run. It is so much
    fun"
"No, no, no. No, no, no. I like to go slow."

Bear Hunt

We're going on a bear hunt.
We're not scared.
What a beautiful day.

Uh-oh! Long grass, wavy grass.
We can't go over it.
We can't go under it.
Oh no! We have to go through it.
Swishy, swashy, swishy, swashy, swishy,
    swashy.

(Repeat, following the same pattern with
    these obstacles:
A river, a deep cold river; splash, splash
Mud, thick oozy mud; squish, squish
Snowstorm, a swirling whirling snowstorm;
    woo, hoo
Forest, a deep dark forest; stumble,
    trip
A cave, a narrow gloomy cave; tip, toe.
Then continue with the following)

What's that?
One wet shiny nose,
Two big googly eyes
Two big furry ears.
It's a BEAR.
(go through everything backwards till you
    end up in bed)
We're not going on a bear hunt ever
    again.

Other Fun Songs Include:

Eensy Weensy Spider
BINGO
Head, Shoulders, Knees, and Toes
Do As I'm Doing
Follow the Leader
If You're Happy and You Know It
This Little Piggy Went to Market
Do Your Ears Hang Low?

John gone? Oh, where oh where can he be?"

Small children like songs in which they can do the actions along with you even before they can say the words or sing the melody.

When singing with your children, improvise with melodies and change the words to apply to what you're doing, such as singing "Here we go to the grocery store" to the tune of "Over the River and through the Woods, to Grandmother's House We Go." Children will soon learn the idea and start improvising their own new sets of words. Even small children who can't remember the words to a song will often join in a simple repeated ending or verse. Preschoolers also love songs where words or phrases are added to the previous list.

You can teach your child singing games by tapping on her back the rhythm of a familiar melody and letting her guess what song it is. Another version of "Name That Tune" involves playing or singing the first few notes of a song and letting your child guess what song it is.

Singing has the most marvelous effect on a tired parent or child. Singing to and with children is such a simple thing to do. If you sing to your children, they will be much more likely to develop good feelings about music. They might even learn a little about rhythm and pitch. Twenty years from now they may not be in the Mormon Tabernacle Choir, but they will think of music as something positive.

LISTENING TO MUSIC

Hearing music being played on the radio or stereo is another way for our children to make music a natural part of their lives. Of course, a radio or CD player that is left on all day will teach them to be insensitive to music, because even the best music is abused if it is merely background noise.

Children can learn how to listen actively and responsively when music is a special activity. The kind of music selected and how long to listen to it depend on the individual. But each child should have

some experience with music as a special experience, a delight in and of itself.

If you regularly listen to music in the home, your children will probably want to listen also. An opportunity for quiet sharing and some very informal instruction may present itself. But there should be formal instruction only if the young child asks questions. If they become curious about what made that sound, for instance, you could answer or find out together.

I have a friend whose father was a professional musician. He forced his children to listen to what he considered beautiful classical music until they grew to hate it. Their music experiences were forced on them by a well-meaning father who wanted them to love what he loved even if he had to make them do so. It didn't work.

It's a good idea to get your child his own tape or CD player when he's old enough to take good care of it. There is no substitute for being able to control your own music.

LIVE MUSIC

Listening to recorded music is good; but there is no substitute for live music. Many children like to see and touch real instruments. It helps children understand how music is made when they see the real people who play the instruments. Once children are past the "I won't hold still for a second" stage, they might be ready to enjoy grown-up concerts that are well chosen. A two- or three-hour program is probably too long for a young child, but a program that lasts an hour or less with a choir might be a good experience.

Whenever you plan to take young children to programs of live music, it's helpful to prepare them before leaving. Tell them what will be expected of them. You can give them background information about the music and perhaps go to a library to check out some of the selections that will be heard.

DEVELOPING AN EAR FOR MUSIC

Before children can respond to music, they must be able to hear it. That might sound facetious because most of us think that hearing is a natural trait, but sometimes even so-called natural traits must be learned. Most of us have become used to constant noise. Much of the time our senses are dulled and we've learned to tune it out. But if you take the time to teach your children to really listen, they may even be able to pick out the separate instruments in an orchestra. Here are some games that will help children listen more sensitively:

• Have your child sit very quietly and tell you what she hears. Next have her close her eyes and listen very quietly; then let her tell you what she hears.

• Have your child sit very still and close her eyes. Now make noises for her and have her tell you what those noises are. Young children respond very well to animal noises, for example.

• Close your eyes and have the child make noises while you tell her what you hear.

• Practice your own listening abilities by concentrating on what your child says to you. Look her right in the eye and respond appropriately. Children who are listened to are more likely to listen in return.

MAKING INSTRUMENTS

Many children like to explore musical sound. Instead of getting angry when toddlers bang on a pan, try showing them how different beaters make different sounds. A spoon or stick or a whisk beaten against a pan each produces a unique sound. Believe it or not, most of the time children aren't just trying to be noisy and drive you nuts—they are experimenting. It is natural for them to tap, shake, hit, or bang things together. From these simple things they can start to make their own percussion instruments:

• A small box or tin filled with beans or rice makes a shaker.

• Bones that are washed and dried make good clatter sounds.

• Walnut shells clapped together sound like castanets.

• Pie plates or pot covers banged together produce a muffled cymbal effect.

• Forks suspended on a string and struck with another fork give a delicate, triangle-like note.

• Ordinary drinking glasses offer an experience in music making for children. At the end of the meal, line up the glasses, pour consecutively more and more punch or water in each glass, then tap them and make music. Or you can wet your finger and rub the rim of the glass until it starts to hum a sound of vibration.

• Possibilities for makeshift drums are endless—a wooden salad bowl with a cloth tacked over the top, a shortening can with a "lid" of heavy wrapping paper secured by a rubber band, and so forth. Almost anything that a child can hit with something to make a sound is a drum.

• From percussion, children can move

to woodwinds, where sound is produced by blowing. They can blow through different lengths of paper or plastic straws, or across wax paper held over a comb, or softly across the top of an empty bottle.

• Stringed instruments are a little more difficult to improvise, but with rubber bands and boxes and twigs, it is possible to demonstrate how sounds result from plucking or strumming. For example, loop a rubber band between your teeth and two fingers of one hand; then pluck very gently with the fingers of your other hand. A wishbone or slingshot with one or more rubber bands stretched across the Y makes a tiny harp.

These kinds of activities are more than just play. Children can develop a true musical sense and a natural instinct for free, creative adventure in all fields related to music.

In addition to making their own musical instruments, it is nice if children also have experience with real instruments. Such instruments as drums, rhythm sticks, wood blocks, rattles, and bells are best bought at

MUSICAL GAMES

♪ Ask your child to imitate common sounds around the house, like a knock at the door or a phone ringing. Have him use percussion instruments to imitate the sounds.
♪ Beat a pattern on a drum and have the child repeat it.
♪ Ask the child to use an instrument to describe the weather.
♪ Have the children follow someone who is beating a drum. If he beats hard, have them stomp. If he beats soft, have them tiptoe.

---

a music store, not a toy counter. We can do a lot more with these things than have a rhythm band. In addition to showing children how to beat, bang, or shake to the rhythms of a familiar piece of music, we can encourage them to add to it or enrich it at appropriate places in the piece.

You can ask your child what kind of voice his instrument has. Does it make a crashing sound? What instrument makes a ringing sound? After he knows what each instrument can do, he can accompany songs with them.

TAKING LESSONS

After your child is reading well and understands simple math concepts, you might consider providing music lessons for her. Training in music is always valuable and worth the expense and time. If you can't afford lessons, consider trading services in your field of expertise or making arrangements for your child to earn the lessons in exchange for something of value to your teacher. Your child might mow the lawn, baby-sit, or help with younger music students. You might exchange one of your abilities like housecleaning, a haircut, or reading tutoring.

Perhaps you will want to teach your child yourself; but many children don't progress well with a parent teacher. Try your options and don't be afraid to switch teachers, including yourself, if things are not working well.

When choosing a teacher for your child, look for a good match. You don't want a teacher who is too lenient or too strict.

Look for a teacher who provides plenty of non-stressful times for your child to play in front of others. Look for a teacher who can motivate your child with interesting and varied incentive programs.

Help your child develop a schedule for practicing times and experiment with your own incentive programs. Taking a child out for an ice cream sundae when she learns six hymns might work for one child, while taking your child to a ballgame after he memorizes a recital piece might work for another. Musical training brings a lifetime of enjoyment.

PHOTOGRAPHY

A camera may seem like a big investment when parents consider buying a present for a child; but a simple one can be purchased for the same price as many toys. Even a young child can learn how to take pictures. As he gets older, your child may or may not want to pursue photography as a hobby or take classes; but even if he simply learns to take good quality pictures for himself, the effort to teach him how to use a camera will pay off in the long run. Photography is an art form that can bring years of enjoyment to the amateur as well as the professional.

Conventional Cameras. When teaching a child to use a camera, start with very simple instructions. (Most stores that sell photography equipment have employees who will take the time to teach you how to operate the equipment.) Show your child where to look to find his subject and how to hold the camera. Let him practice with an unloaded camera while he is learning.

Video Recorders. With the inexpensive video cameras on the market today, you might want to consider buying a camcorder for your family and allowing your child to learn how to use it. Children can put together their own movies, commercials, documentaries, family histories, tributes, wedding day records, clay-mation, magic, or talent shows.

Digital Cameras. You or your child can take pictures, download them on your computer, and never have to use film. You can send these pictures to loved ones anywhere in the world over the Internet. You can add pictures to family history texts. The possibilities are endless. You can store all your priceless family pictures on a CD and keep them in a safe, fireproof place.

READING

If you want your child to develop a love of reading, let her catch *you* reading for pleasure and read to her every day. The child is fortunate who can associate both pleasure and parental attention with the raw materials of a book: words. Seeing their parents read for pleasure and reading out loud in the family can provide children with some of the most pleasant, lifelong memories. Families who send children out into the world knowing and appreciating good books have given them a lifelong source of strength and enjoyment. Books aren't a substitute for living, but they can do much to add to life's richness. When you become absorbed with living fully, good books serve to intimately enhance your life experience.

Reading is a natural extension of thinking and speaking. So along with reading to your child, talk to her, listen to her, tell her what's on your mind, play games with her, share hobbies, discuss the news and television programs.

Along with your everyday use of language through conversations and discussions, you can supply your child with books, writing supplies or equipment, and a special place for reading and studying. You can keep routines around your home for meals, bedtime, and homework. You can monitor the amount of time your child spends watching television and at after-school jobs. You set the stage for learning with daily conversation, household routines, attention to school matters, and an affectionate concern for your child's growth.

INTRODUCE YOUR CHILD TO A WORLD OF GOOD BOOKS

Children learn to understand themselves better as they meet literary characters with similar problems. They broaden their horizons as they read of places they may never visit personally. Books stimulate hungry minds, provide information, and give immeasurable pleasure. But the riches that books offer are left as buried treasure unless we help children desire to begin the hunt.

Books are one generation's greatest gift to the next. Through books we have access to all the thoughts, ideas, questions, and answers of everyone who took the time to write. Even God in his omniscience chose to have his words given to us in the form of a book.

At our convenience, we can pursue a subject, find information, be entertained, and transport ourselves into another man's heart and circumstances. We can find ourselves and face fears through carefully portrayed characters. The majesty of good books elevates us, inspires us, educates, entertains, and befriends us. Eager readers gain an early advantage in finding out about things they have never seen, experiences outside their own, and empathy for other people. Eager minds grow used to organized thought. Characters of strength and softness can become welcome friends.

Storytelling or reading aloud to small children is a powerful way to bring children to books. A well-told or well-read story can also fill the gap between what a young child can read himself and what he would like to read. Reading poetry aloud is another effective way to share with children the pleasant sounds of words. Small children love the rhymes and rhythms of favorite verses.

SELECT GOOD BOOKS FOR CHILDREN

How do you select good books for your children? First you need to know the child by really taking the time to understand his unique gifts and interests. Observe your child and take note of his special abilities and needs. Wise mothers will expose their young children to a wide variety of books, such as Mother Goose rhymes, ballads, folk tales, fables, myths, epics, humor, poetry, animal stories, adventure tales, historical fiction, biographies, informational books, religious books, modern fiction, and fantasy.

Children's needs are very personal at a young age. Good literature has the potential to help them fulfill some of these needs: the need for physical well-being, the need to love and be loved, the need to belong, the need to achieve, the need to change, the need to know, and the need for beauty and order. As your children get older, they will be able to select the books that most interest them.

You can select quality books more wisely by observing such things as:

- setting
- style and language
- point of view
- character development
- plot
- theme
- tone

- illustrations
- mood
- pacing
- design
- layout
- accuracy

Basically, a book is a good book for your child if he enjoys it. It can be as simple as that. Even if the book has been labeled a classic by experts and literary critics, it isn't a good book for your child if he does not enjoy it.

You can help your children learn to understand what the author is saying by asking *why, how,* and *what* questions. Stories can be acted out by children or pantomimed. Many children enjoy drawing a picture about a favorite part of a story. Flannel board figures or puppets can also be used to illustrate stories. What matters most is that you let books stir each child's imagination and help him find ways to express what he sees and feels.

MAKE READING TIME FUN

Every year there's another study that reveals all the benefits of reading to your children. Reading to your children is supposed to increase your child's vocabulary, widen her experience, expand her listening and comprehension skills, and foster quality parent-child relationships. Reading to children may increase their vocabulary, but that isn't what you should be concerned about. Enjoying this time together should be your first consideration.

Reading to wiggling youngsters can be a challenge. Some of my reading experiences with my children, especially when I've tried to read to them all at once, have turned into a real circus. For one thing, I

have only two sides and one lap and I have more than three children.

To make reading time more fun, try to do the following:

Make Reading Time Snuggle Time

Sit close together and put your arm around your child. Reading with your child is a wonderful gift of your precious time. Children who feel you have time for them will be more likely to think they are valuable and worthy of that gift. In the time you could be scrubbing the floor or reading the newspaper, you have chosen to be with your child. A child will know what you value most by how much of your time you are willing to give.

Mix Up the Plot

Mixing up the plot is a sure way to discover if your children are listening. This works best when the stories are familiar ones that they have heard over and over again. My husband loves to do this. Sometimes he will take characters from one story and put them in another, or he will change the details or the order of the events in the story. He always has as much fun as the children do.

Look at Picture-Only Books

Books without any words offer another reading delight because you or your child must make up the words. After looking at the pictures with your children, make up stories to go with them. Help the children make up their own stories.

Anticipate the Story

Read the first page of the book and then have your child make up a story ending. Children often tell us a great deal about themselves in their own stories. Then read the story and see if you are close.

Put Some Drama into Your Reading

Become the wicked witch with a shrill voice, or the baby bear with an innocent-sounding high-pitched voice. Be frightened at scary parts and sad at sad parts of a story. Grumble like an angry grandfather or babble like a brook. Some words, such as bump, crash, and flutter, can be expressed by the voice to sound like the actual meaning. Reading to and with children is more enjoyable if you get down on their level for a while and giggle, laugh, and make faces.

Explore a Subject in Depth

If you and your child want to learn more about trees, gather all the information you can find on the subject and then study the subject together. The study period can last for an hour or a day or a week. Other possible subjects might include learning more about a holiday's origin, how babies are born, how to care for a family pet, your family tree/family histories, and a foreign country (including foods you might learn to cook together). If you're planning a family vacation, read all the information you can find on the areas you'll be visiting.

Involve the Children

Ask questions. Point out interesting details in illustrations. Let your children make the animal sounds or be the train's whistle. Let them repeat familiar phrases.

MAKE READING TIME QUALITY TIME

Whenever possible, make reading time a special time for each child. Reading time with my two-year-old is very different from reading time with my eleven-year-old. When your children are babies, share books with bright, colorful pictures that have familiar objects in them. Make up your own text and try to gear it to what your child is interested in. At about a year or so children enjoy very simple short stories with lots of pictures. As they get older, the story can get a little longer, and fewer pictures will be required to keep their interest.

Habits are hard to break, so try to make daily reading a habit. Try reading to your preschoolers after lunch. It makes them sleepy and ready for a nap. Try reading with your school-age children as soon as they return from school. Try reading a classic around the table after dinner with your teens. Go to the library and local bookstore regularly. It would be impossible for many parents to accumulate a library varied enough for their child, but public libraries or bookmobiles can fill that need. Watch for books that your child checks out more than once when considering what books to buy for them later.

A NOTE ON EARLY READING LESSONS

I've never tried to teach my children to read before kindergarten. In their eagerness to unlock the treasure between the covers, some of them have taught themselves. Your job is not to push, but to delight. Never teach your child to read for your pleasure or pride. Give your child the opportunity to become familiar with letters and sounds by teaching the alphabet, but don't push.

ACQUIRING BOOKS

One of the best places to put your money is in a good home library. If you can't afford to buy many books, frequent the library or buy at thrift stores. Libraries today are exciting places. They have magazines, puzzles, tapes, CD's, movies, flannel board stories, art prints, and patterns. Take advantage of story time or reading incentive programs.

Good books always make excellent gifts for children. Low-cost books can be purchased at thrift stores and yard sales. But even the retail prices for books are a bargain, for good books are a possession that children can keep all their lives and pass on to their own children and grandchildren. Good books are always a great investment.

As you select good books to read, look for books that may have won an award. Keep in mind, though, that some of the book awards—including the National Book Award, the Nobel Prize, the Pulitzer Prize, and the Faulkner Award—are given to books that have very adult themes and contain language and scenes that are not appropriate for children of any age. Review any book before giving it to your child to read.

The National Book Award

The National Book Award is given annually by the National Book Foundation, a consortium of book publishing groups, for the best books of the previous year.

BUILDING YOUR OWN LIBRARY

As your children grow up, make the effort to collect books and build your own, wonderfully rich home library. Select books from all genres, including these:
- Baby/board books
- Mother Goose and other nursery rhymes
- Hans Christian Andersen fairy tales
- Grimm Brothers fairy tales
- *A Child's Garden of Verses* or other poetry collections
- Alphabet and ABC books
- Numbers and counting books
- Concept books
- Wordless books
- Pattern or predictable books
- Holiday books
- Folk tales
- Tall tales
- Fables
- Myths
- Epics, ballads, and legends
- Religious storybooks
- Winnie-the-Pooh tales
- Informational books
- Biographies
- Beginning reader books
- Literary classics

This is one of the nation's preeminent literary prizes.

The Nobel Prize for Literature

The Nobel Prize is awarded annually to individuals who have made valuable contributions to the good of humanity in the fields of physics, chemistry, medicine, literature, and peace. The award is named after Swedish chemist and industrialist Alfred Bernhard Nobel. The Nobel Prize was first awarded in 1901 and remains the most honored prize in the world.

PEN/Faulkner Award

The PEN/Faulkner Award is a national prize honoring the best published works of fiction by American citizens in a calendar year. It is named after William Faulkner, a Nobel Prize-winning author, and is affiliated with PEN, Poets, Playwrights, Editors, Essayists, and Novelists.

The Pulitzer Prize

The Pulitzer Prize was established by Joseph Pulitzer, an American newspaper publisher. The award is given yearly by the Columbia University School of Journalism, which Pulitzer's money founded.

Boston Globe-Horn Book Award

This annual award is co-sponsored by *The Boston Globe* and *The Horn Book* magazine. The award recognizes outstanding children's and young adult books in these categories: picture book, fiction book, and nonfiction book.

The Caldecott Award

The Caldecott Award is presented annually by the American Library Association to the illustrator of the most distinguished children's picture book. They also award honor books.

The Newbery Award

The Newbery Award is given annually by the American Library Association to the author of the most distinguished contribution to children's literature published in the United States. They also award honor books.

Other Awards

The Edgar Award is presented annually by the Mystery Writers of America. The Golden Spur award is given annually by the Western Writers of America for distinguished writing about the American West. The Rita is awarded annually by the Romance Writers of America for the best romance writing. The Hugo Award, also known as the Science Fiction Achievement Award, is given annually by the World Science Fiction Society for various categories of the genre. The Nebula Award is presented annually by the Science Fiction Writers of America to acknowledge excellence in science fiction writing.

Individual states also have their own book awards each year to watch for. If you live outside the United States, your country

also awards national book awards that you can watch for.

RECOMMENDED READING LISTS

The purpose of a reading list is not to limit your choices but to give you a starting place when you're looking for a good book to read for your child or yourself. Take the time to develop your own favorite book list as you read. A book is perhaps the best bargain for the money today, outside necessary food for your body, for books are necessary food for the soul.

Picture Books (ages 2 to 7)

Alexander and the Terrible, Horrible, No Good, Very Bad Day, by Judith Viorst and Ray Cruz (illustrator)

All the Places to Love, by Patricia MacLachlan, and Mike Wimmer (illustrator)

Always Room for One More, by Nonny Hogrigian

Amelia Bedelia series, Peggy Parish

Anansi and the Moss-Covered Rock, by Eric A. Kimmel and Janet Stevens (illustrator)

Animals Should Definitely Not Wear Clothing, by Judi Barrett and Ron Barrett (illustrator)

Babushka, by Sandra Ann Horn and Sophie Fatus (illustrator)

Barnyard Lullaby, by Frank Asch

Bedtime for Frances, by Russell Hoban and Garth Williams (illustrator)

Bread and Jam for Frances, by Russell Hoban and Lillian Hoban (illustrator)

Brown Bear, Brown Bear, What Do You See? by Bill Martin Jr. and Eric Carle (illustrator)

Chair for My Mother, A, by Vera B. Williams

Chester's Way, by Kevin Henkes

Chicka Chicka Boom Boom, by Bill Martin Jr., John Archambault, and Lois Ehlert (illustrator)

Chicken Soup with Rice, by Maurice Sendak

Chicken Sunday, by Patricia Polacco and Edward Miller (illustrator)

Chrysanthemum, by Kevin Henkes

Come Along, Daisy! by Jane Simmons

Curious George, by H. A. Rey

Dark, Dark Tale, A, by Ruth Brown

Day Jimmy's Boa Ate the Wash, The, by Trinka Hakes Noble and Steven Kellogg (illustrator)

Fanny's Dream, by Caralyn Buehner and Mark Buehner (illustrator)

Fortune-Tellers, The, by Lloyd Alexander and Trina Schart Hyman (illustrator)

Freight Train, by Donald Crews

Frog and Toad Together, by Arnold Lobel

Funny Little Woman, The, by Arlene Mosel and Blair Lent (illustrator)

Girl Who Loved Wild Horses, The, by Paul Goble

Gates of the Wind, The, by Kathryn Lasky and Janet Stevens (illustrator)

Giving Tree, The, by Shel Silverstein

Good Night, Gorilla, by Peggy Rathmann

Goodnight Moon, by Margaret Wise Brown and Clement Hurd (illustrator)

Grandfather's Journey, by Allen Say

Guess How Much I Love You, by Sam McBratney and Anita Jeram (illustrator)

Happy Birthday, Moon, By Frank Asch

Harriet's Recital, by Nancy L. Carlson

Harold and the Purple Crayon, by Crockett Johnson

Heckedy Peg, by Audrey Wood and Don Wood (illustrator)

Hole Is to Dig, A, by Ruth Krauss and Maurice Sendak (illustrator)

Horton Hatches the Egg, by Dr. Seuss

How Much Is a Million? by David M. Schwartz

I Like Me, by Nancy L. Carlson

I Know an Old Lady Who Swallowed a Fly, by Simms Taback

If You Give a Mouse a Cookie, by Laura Joffe Numeroff and Felecia Bond (illustrator)

Imogene's Antlers, by David Small

Incredible Painting of Felix Clousseau, The, by Jon Agee

It Could Always Be Worse: a Yiddish Folk Tale, by Margot Zemach

Joseph Had a Little Overcoat, by Simms Taback

Julius, the Baby of the World, by Kevin Henkes

Jumanji, by Chris Van Allsburg

King Bidgood's in the Bathtub, Audrey Wood and Don Wood (illustrator)

Koala Lou, by Mem Fox and Pamela Lofts (illustrator)

Legend of the Indian Paintbrush, The, by Tomie dePaola

Lilly's Purple Plastic Purse, by Kevin Henkes

Little Bear, by Elsa Holmelund Minarik and Maurice Sendack (illustrator)

Little Engine That Could, The, by Watty Piper

Little House, The, by Virginia Lee Burton

Little Mouse, the Red Ripe Strawberry, and the Big Hungry Bear, The, by Audrey Wood and Don Wood (illustrator)

Little Old Lady Who Was Not Afraid of Anything, The, by Linda Williams and Megan Lloyd (illustrator)

Madeline (series), by Ludwig Bemelmans

Magic Paintbrush, The, by Laurence Yep

Many Moons, by James Thurber and Louis Slobodkin (illustrator)

Max's First Word, by Rosemary Wells

Mike Mulligan and His Steam Shovel, by Virginia Lee Burton

Miss Nelson Is Missing, by Harry G. Allard and James Marshall (illustrator)

Miss Rumphius, by Barbara Cooney

Monster at the End of This Book, The, by John Stone and Michael Smollin

Musicians of the Sun, by Gerald McDermott

My Great-Aunt Arizona, by Gloria Houston and Susan Condie Lamb (illustrator)

Mysteries of Harris Burdick, The, by Chris Van Allsburg

Napping House, The, by Audrey Wood and Don Wood (illustrator)

No, David, by David Shannon

Officer Buckle and Gloria, by Peggy Rathmann

Olivia, by Ian Falconer

Owen, by Kevin Henkes

Owl Moon, by Jane Yolen and John Schoenherr (illustrator)

Ox-Cart Man, by Donald Hall and Barbara Cooney (illustrator)

Papa, Please Get the Moon for Me, by Eric Carle

Pigsty, by Mark Teague

Polar Express, The, by Chris Van Allsburg

Rainbabies, The, by Laura Krauss Melmed and Jim Lamarche (illustrator)

Red Balloon, by Albert Lamorisse

Relatives Came, The, by Cynthia Rylant and Stephen Gammell (illustrator)

Rosie's Walk, by Pat Hutchins

Rapunzel, Jacob W. Grimm and Paul O. Zelinsky (illustrator)

Runaway Bunny, The, by Margaret Wise Brown and Clement Hurd (illustrator)

Saint George and the Dragon, by Margaret Hodges and Trina Schart Hyman (illustrator)

Seven Blind Mice, by Ed Young

Seven Silly Eaters, The, by Mary Ann Hoberman and Marla Frazee (illustrator)

Snowman, The, by Raymond Briggs

Snowy Day, by Ezra Jack Keats

Song and Dance Man, by Karen Ackerman and Stephen Gammell (illustrator)

Stellaluna, by Janell Cannon

Stinky Cheeseman and Other Fairly Stupid Tales, The, by Jon Scieszka and Lane Smith (illustrator)

Stone Soup, by Marcia Brown

Story of Babar, the Little Elephant, The, by Jean de Brunhoff

Story about Ping, The, by Marjorie Flack and Kurt Wiese (illustrator)

Strega Nona, by Tomie dePaola

Sylvester and the Magic Pebble, by William Steig

Tale of Peter Rabbit, The, by Beatrix Potter

Ten, Nine, Eight, by Molly Garrett Bang

There's a Nightmare in My Closet, by Mercer Mayer

Three Billy Goats Gruff, The, by Stephen Carpenter (illustrator)

Tikki Tikki Tembo, by Arlene Mosel and Blair Lent (illustrator)

Time Flies, by Eric Rohmann

Tops and Bottoms, by Janet Stevens

True Story of the Three Little Pigs, The, by Jon Scieszka and Lane Smith (illustrator)

Tuesday, by David Wiesner

Velveteen Rabbit, The, by Margery Williams

Verdi, by Janell Cannon

Very Hungry Caterpillar, The, by Eric Carle

Water Dance, by Thomas Locker

We're Going on a Bear Hunt, by Michael Rosen and Helen Oxenbury

When I Was Young in the Mountains, by Cynthia Rylant and Diane Goode (illustrator)

Where the Wild Things Are, by Maurice Sendak

Wheels on the Bus, Paul O. Zelinsky (illustrator)

Where's Spot? by Eric Hill

Where the Sidewalk Ends, by Shel Silverstein

Why Mosquitoes Buzz in People's Ears, by Verna Aardema and Leo Dillon (illustrator)

Wing Shop, The, by Elvira Woodruff and Stephen Gammell (illustrator)

You Are Special, by Max Lucado and Sergio Martinez (illustrator)

Middle Readers (ages 8 to 12)

Across Five Aprils, by Irene Hunt

Adventures of Pinocchio, The, by Carlo Collodi

Adventures of Tom Sawyer, The, by Mark Twain

Alice's Adventures in Wonderland, by Lewis Carrol

Anne of Green Gables, by Lucy Maud Montgomery

Babe: The Gallant Pig, by Dick King-Smith

Bambi, by Felix Salten

Behind the Attic Wall, by Sylvia Cassedy

Bet You Can't: Science Impossibilities to Fool You, by Vicki Cobb and Kathy Darling

Black Beauty, by Anna Sewell

Black Stallion, The, by Walter Farley

Borrowers, The, by Mary Norton

Bridge to Terabithia, by Katherine Paterson

Bronze Bow, The, by Mary Norton

Bunnicula, by Deborah and James Howe

Caddie Woodlawn, by Carol Ryrie Brink

Call of the Wild, The, by Jack London

Call It Courage, by Armstrong Sperry

Charles Dickens: The Man Who Had Great Expectations, by Diane Stanley

Charlotte's Web, by E. B. White

Cheaper by the Dozen, by Frank B. Gilbreth Jr. and Ernestine Gilbreth Carey

Chocolate Fever, by Robert Kimmel Smith

Chocolate Touch, The, by Patrick Skene Catling

Columbus and the World Around Him, by Milton Meltzer

Cricket in Times Square, The, by George Selden

Danny, the Champion of the World, by Roald Dahl

Dark Is Rising, The (series), by Susan Cooper

Day No Pigs Would Die, A, by Robert Newton Peck

Diamond in the Window, The (The Hall Family Chronicles), by Jane Langton

Devil's Arithmetic, The, by Jane Rolen

Dollhouse Murders, The, by Betty Ren Wright

Egypt Game, The, by Zilpha Keatley Snyder

Ella Enchanted, by Gail Carson Levine

Family under the Bridge, The, by Natalie Savage Carlson

Fantastic Mr. Fox, by Roald Dahl

Fighting Ground, The, by Avi

Forgotten Door, The, by Alexander Key

Freckle Juice, by Judy Blume

Frindle, by Andrew Clements

From the Mixed-up Files of Mrs. Basil E. Frankweiler, by E. L. Konigsburg

Great Brain, The, by John D. Fitzgerald

Great Gilly Hopkins, The, by Katherine Paterson

Harry Potter series, by J. K. Rowling

Hatchet, by Gary Paulsen

Heidi, by Johanna Spyri

Holes, by Louis Sachar

Homer Price, by Robert McCloskey

House with a Clock in Its Walls, The, by John Bellairs

How to Eat Fried Worms, by Thomas Rockwell

Hundred Dresses, The, by Eleanor Estes and Louis Slobodkin (illustrator)

Incredible Journey, by Sheila Burnford

Indian in the Cupboard, The, by Lynne Reid Banks

Iron Ring, The, by Lloyd Alexander

Island of the Blue Dolphins, by Scott O'Dell

Jacob Have I Loved, by Katherine Paterson

James and the Giant Peach, by Roald Dahl

Julie of the Wolves, by Jean Craighead George

King Author and His Knights, by Thomas Morte D'Arthur Malory

Lassie Come-Home, by Eric Knight

Lincoln: a Photobiography, by Russell Freedman

Lion, the Witch and the Wardrobe, The, by C. S. Lewis

Little House in the Big Woods, by Laura Ingalls Wilder

Little Princess, A, by France Hodgson Burnett

Maniac Magee, by Jerry Spinelli

Mary Poppins, by P. L. Travers

Matilda, by Roald Dahl

Moffats, The, by Eleanor Estes

Mouse and His Child, The, by Russell Hoban

Mouse and the Motorcycle, The, by Beverly Cleary

Mr. Popper's Penguins, by Richard and Florence Atwater

Mrs. Frisby and the Rats of NIMH, by Robert C. O'Brien

My Side of the Mountain, by Jean Craighead George

Old Yeller, by Fred Gipson

Peppermints in the Parlor, by Barbara Brooks Wallace

Phantom Tollbooth, The, by Norton Juster

Prairie Songs, by Pam Conrad

Ramona the Pest, by Beverly Cleary

Riddle of the Rosetta Stone, The, by James Cross Giblin

Roll of Thunder, Hear My Cry, by Mildred D. Taylor

Roller Skates, by Ruth Sawyer

Sarah, Plain and Tall, by Patricia MacLachlan

Secret Garden, The, by Frances Hodgson Burnett

Short Walk around the Pyramids and through the World of Art, A, by Philip M. Isaacson

Skinnybones, by Barbara Park

Slave Dancer, The, by Paula Fox

Snowdrops for Cousin Ruth, by Susan Katz

Sounder, by William H. Armstrong

Stonewords: A Ghost Story, by Pam Conrad

Story of Doctor Dolittle, The, by Hugh Lofting

Tales of a Fourth Grade Nothing, by Judy Blume

Treasure Island, by Robert Louis Stevenson

True Confessions of Charlotte Doyle, The, by Avi

Tuck Everlasting, by Natalie Babbitt

Tulip Touch, The, by Anne Fine

Up a Road Slowly, by Irene Hunt

Way Things Work, The, by David Macaulay

Where the Lilies Bloom, by Vera Cleaver

Where the Red Fern Grows, by Wilson Rawls

Wind in the Willows, The, by Kenneth Grahame

White Mountains, The, by John Christopher

Witch of Blackbird Pond, The, by Elizabeth George Speare

Wonderful Wizard of Oz, The, by L. Frank Baum

Wrinkle in Time, A, by Madeleine L'Engle

Young Adult and Adult Readers

84 Charing Cross Road, by Helene Hanff

Adventures of Huckleberry Finn, The, by Mark Twain

Adventures of Sherlock Holmes, The, by Arthur Conan Doyle

Anna Karenina, by Leo Tolstoy

Anne Frank: The Diary of a Young Girl, by Anne Frank

As a Man Thinketh, by James Allen
Autobiography of Benjamin Franklin, The, by Benjamin Franklin
Book of Mormon, The
Breathing Lessons, by Anne Tyler
Canterbury Tales, The, by Geoffrey Chaucer
Chosen, The, by Chaim Potok
Complete Works of Shakespeare, The, by William Shakespeare
Crime and Punishment, by Fyodor Dostoevsky
Crucible, The, by Arthur Miller
David Copperfield, by Charles Dickens
Death of a Salesman, by Arthur Miller
Divine Comedy, The, by Dante Alighieri
Doctrine and Covenants, The
Don Quixote, by Miguel de Cervantes Saavedra
East of Eden, by John Steinbeck
Eleni, by Nicholas Gage
Emma, by Jane Austen
Enchanted April, The, by Elizabeth von Arnin
Essay on Man, by Alexander Pope
Ethan Frome, by Edith Wharton
Fahrenheit 451, by Ray Bradbury
Far from the Madding Crowd, by Thomas Hardy
Frankenstein, by Mary Shelley
Gift from the Sea, by Anne Morrow Lindbergh
Giver, The, by Lois Lowry
Glass Menagerie, The, by Tennessee Williams
Gone with the Wind, by Margaret Mitchell
Grapes of Wrath, The, by John Steinbeck
Great Expectations, by Charles Dickens
Great Gatsby, The, by F. Scott Fitzgerald
Gulliver's Travels, by Jonathon Swift
Hiding Place, The, by Corrie Ten Boom
Hobbit, The, by J. R. R. Tolkein
Holy Bible, The

How to Win Friends and Influence People, by Dale Carnegie
Hunchback of Notre Dame, The, by Victor Hugo
Iliad, The, by Homer
Jane Eyre, by Charlotte Bronte
Jude the Obscure, by Thomas Hardy
Jungle Book, The, by Rudyard Kipling
Koran, The
Leaves of Grass, by Walt Whitman
Les Misérables, by Victor Hugo
Little Women, by Louisa May Alcott
Look Homeward, Angel, by Thomas Wolf
Lord of the Rings, The, J. R. R. Tolkien
Madame Bovary, by Gustave Flaubert
Man's Search for Meaning, by Viktor E. Frankl
Mayor of Casterbridge, The, by Thomas Hardy
Mere Christianity, by C. S. Lewis
Mice and Men, Of, by John Steinbeck
Midwife's Apprentice, The, by Karen Cushman
Moby-Dick, by Herman Melville
My Ántonia, by Willa Cather
O Pioneers! by Willa Cather
Odyssey, The, by Homer
Old Man and the Sea, The, by Ernest Hemingway
Origin of the Species, The, by Charles Darwin
Paradise Lost, by John Milton
Pearl of Great Price, The
Picture of Dorian Gray, The, by Oscar Wilde
Pilgrim's Progress, The, by John Bunyan
Poetry of Emily Dickinson, by Emily Dickinson
Pride and Prejudice, by Jane Austen
Prophet, The, by Kahlil Gibran
Pygmalion, by George Bernard Shaw
Raisin in the Sun, A, by Lorraine Hansberry
Rebecca, by Daphne du Maurier

Red Badge of Courage, The, by Stephen Crane
Rescuers, The, by Cecilia Maria Hilliard
Robert Frost Poems, by Robert Frost
Robinson Crusoe, by Daniel Defoe
Roots, by Alex Haley
Scarlet Letter, The, by Nathaniel Hawthorne
Screwtape Letters, The, by C. S. Lewis
Sense and Sensibility, by Jane Austen
Separate Peace, A, by John Knowles
Sign of the Beaver, The, by Elizabeth George Speare

Story of My Life, The, by Helen Keller
Summer to Die, A, Lois Lowry
Tale of Two Cities, A, by Charles Dickens
Talmud, The
Tess of the D'urbervilles, by Thomas Hardy
To Kill a Mockingbird, by Harper Lee
Tree Grows in Brooklyn, A, by Betty Smith
Uncle Tom's Cabin, by Harriet Beecher Stowe
Walden, by Henry David Thoreau
War and Peace, by Leo Tolstoy
Wuthering Heights, by Emily Bronte

SCIENCE AND MATH

Don't wait till your child gets into school to introduce her to the wonders of the natural world. Science is definitely *not* limited to a bunch of smart guys in white coats. From the beginning, encourage your child to explore, manipulate, and experiment with everything in her environment. If you're afraid of something, get over it and don't pass your fear down to your child. Cultivate your child's natural curiosity. Explain the microscopic world she can not see. Spark her imagination and natural curiosity in the universe. In general, show her the world with gladness—and let her make a mess.

YOUR CHILD AND THE WORLD AROUND HER

Science is all about asking questions and contemplating possibilities. Science literally plays a part in everything you and your child do.

Gardening can teach your child the elementary principles of botany. Pets can introduce him to biology. Blocks can help him learn simple laws of physics. Cooking can bring out the chemist in him.

When you introduce your child to science, you teach him all about wondering

SCIENCE ACTIVITIES FOR CHILDREN

• Perform various weather experiments and moisture measurements.
• Create insect, rock, or leaf collections.
• Play answer-the-question games, such as: What is a sunbeam? Why is the sky blue? Why do stars twinkle? Where does rain come from? What is wind? How far is the moon? What are rocks made of? What is thunder and lightning? Why do we have seasons? Why do some trees stay green all winter?
• Study the human body on the outside and the inside (bones, muscles, organs, blood, nerves, digestive system, and skin).
• Learn about human development from conception to birth.
• Take things apart: doorknobs, stereos, radios, watches, and engines.
• Experiment with a magnifying glass, binoculars, microscope, camera, pulleys, wheels, and axles.
• Explore all the branches of science, including: math and logic; physical sciences such as astronomy, chemistry, geology, meteorology, and physics; biological sciences, including botany, zoology, and paleontology; and the social sciences, including anthropology, economics, geography, linguistics, political science, and sociology.

and pondering, making careful observations, standing in awe, speculating, experimenting, and deep thinking. Who wouldn't want her child to do all of these things. So let your young child dig in the dirt, chase butterflies, experiment with water, take apart his toys, dismantle his bed, and put together odd pieces of junk. Encourage your older children to take demanding science classes in school and perform experiments and studies about whatever they find fascinating.

And don't worry, you don't have to be a genius to teach your child to be curious. You teach your child naturally every day through daily conversation, household routines, paying attention to school matters, and displaying an affectionate concern for your child's progress in any area of life.

Provide books, supplies, and a special place for your child to study. Enlist other adults who are willing to mentor your child. Take your child places and let him experience many different environments and cultures. You and you alone can provide a mother who is excited about all forms of learning. You can provide a mother who is curious and enthralled with everything. My child who always wanted to reconstruct the Thanksgiving turkey bones and dig for buried treasure in the backyard is now a professional archaeologist.

KEEPING THE SCIENTIST IN YOUR CHILD ALIVE

How do you keep your child-sized scientist excited about discovering and analyzing the world around him? Try some of the following:

• Invite your child to use the scientific method for solving everyday problems, such as sibling quarrels. The scientific method includes five steps: (1) stating the problem, (2) forming a hypothesis, (3) observing and experimenting,

(4) interpreting the data, and (5) drawing conclusions.

• Encourage your child to help you in the garage and the yard. Let her become familiar with tools.

• Take your child to the library. Let her select books about any subject of interest to her. Help her learn how to use the catalogs and computers to find any information she wants to acquire.

• Ask your child to interview someone who works in a field that involves problem solving and research. Have your child ask that person how he or she prepared for his or her present employment.

MATH

Math is one of those subjects that can lead parents to do pretty silly things as they push their children into genius-hood. Some parents become so obsessed with numbers and formulas that they equip their one-year-olds with flash cards and make quizzing a part of playtime. In reality, children *do* need to learn math; but they need it so they can make sense of the world, not so they can rehearse complicated equations and formulas in front of a critical audience. Math is a useful measure we apply to time, money, objects, space, buildings, roads, volume, area, memory, thought, work, nature, animals, and people.

Your young children will learn to count and even understand the nature of fractions just so they can make sure that brother or sister doesn't get a bigger piece of pie or more presents from Santa. Children learn to understand the useful measure called money when they

earn their own and spend it at the store. Paying tithing teaches them about percentages and subtraction. Hanging a calendar in your preschooler's room and showing him what day it is every time he wakes up will teach him a few concepts about time. Watching the sun come up and then set again in the afternoon is great fun for kids and demonstrates important laws of nature. Children know that it gets dark outside and light outside but they don't understand why. Show your child the sunset and explain why it gets dark. Help him learn the answers to his questions about time and math: How do you know that the earth is a sphere that revolves around the sun? How do you know that the moon revolves around the earth? Why don't we fly off? Why can't we return to yesterday?

Many simple and fun games will teach your children the basic principles of counting, addition, and telling time. Make your child's learning fun, relaxed, and natural. Use play money and food to set up a store with your child. Read books about numbers and time. Play board games that involve counting and numbers. The best way to introduce your children to math is to make it useful for everyday life.

Once your child is a bit older and has started to learn addition, subtraction, multiplication, and division in school, you can help him practice his skills in a number of ways. Here are some ideas:

• Teach your child the principle of tithing and what it means to give 10 percent to the Lord.

• Help your child compare the price of different brands of any item while grocery shopping.

• Help your child compare the price of items on your grocery list at different stores.

• Help your child watch for different prices at different gas stations in your neighborhood.

• Open a savings account for your child.

• Help your child make deposits to the account.

• Ask your child to keep a record of how many miles you travel on a family vacation.

• When you go to a restaurant as a family, let your child check to see if the bill is correct. Let him figure the sales tax. Let him figure out how much to pay for a tip. After you pay, ask your child to count the money and make sure you received the correct change.

• Help your child fill out a catalog or Internet order. Let him figure the sales tax and shipping costs.

• Take your child with you when you go car shopping. Let him compare the price for an identical car at several locations.

• Let your child take part in bill paying. Let him see the energy bill for gas or electricity. Ask him to divide the monthly price

by the number of days in the billing period and figure out how much on average you pay for that utility.

• Include your child in figuring out how many gallons of water you actually used during the billing period for the water bill.

• Let your child assist you when you pay your telephone bill. Let him figure out how much you pay for long distance. Ask him to compare rates with other companies and decide if you should switch.

• Let your child call a travel agent or browse Internet sites and compare different airline prices for a family vacation.

• Let your child figure out an approximate bill from the items in your shopping cart. Ask him to figure out about how much sales tax he will owe.

• Take your child to a fabric store. Select something you want to sew and have your child figure out how much fabric he will need for the project.

• Encourage your child to read the daily newspaper by asking him to select a favorite professional sports team. Have him figure out the average number of points they scored all season.

• Bring your child to an open house. Let him fill out a piece of paper with important facts, like square footage, price, average monthly utility bills, real estate taxes, etc. After going to several houses, ask your child to decide which house was the best house for the price.

• Let your child figure out how much it would cost your family to go on a vacation. Help him figure out how much gas, lodging, meals, and entrance fees would cost. Compare these prices with other vacation destinations.

• Ask your child to find the cheapest way to transport your whole family to another city or state. Let him find out about using a bus, train, plane, family car, or any other means of transportation.

• Take your child to the post office when you go. Let your child help you make a decision on how much different rates would cost you to send a package.

• Ask your child to research the price per person for certain entertainment activities in your town. Compare the prices of bowling, skating, going to a movie, and attending a sporting event.

• Encourage your child to go through the newspaper and cut out coupons for any item he wants to buy. Ask him to figure out how much he will save.

• Encourage your child to read and compare sports figure statistics.

• Ask your child to compare the price of having the oil changed in your car with how much it costs to change it yourself.

• Ask your child to compare insurance rates with three different companies.

• Encourage your child to cook with you in the kitchen. Let him double or triple a recipe. Let him learn from measuring spoons and cups.

• Ask your child to call and compare the different prices for season tickets to cultural, sports, or popular entertainment in your area.

• Ask your child to compare the price for an annual subscription to any magazine he is interested in reading. Compare that price to the newsstand price.

• Teach your child how to write out a check. Show him how to write it correctly and how to subtract the amount of the check from the running total in your checkbook.

• Encourage your child to understand the value of money from several different countries. Ask him to convert that into your country's money standard.

• Encourage your child to read the newspaper or watch the news to find out about weather. Your child can compare temperatures in different parts of the country or chart storms.

• Ask your child to select a CD he wants to buy. Have him compare the price for that CD at three different stores including one CD exchange store.

WRITING

Writing lets you look at the world through your own words. Your child can write long before she ever starts school; she just needs *you* to give her the opportunity. All children have something to say if someone is listening. And there are many ways to introduce young children to writing before they can construct a perfect sentence or remember their pronouns and proper punctuation. During the preschool years, introduce your child to the world of words. Let your child scribble stories (pretend she is writing). Then ask her to "read" the scribble back to you. Act as your child's scribe while she dictates what she has on her mind. Encourage your child to write (with you as her scribe) in her journal. Let her draw pictures and scribble the story beneath the picture. A child who feels she can use written language to express her feelings has a great advantage all through life.

observe the world inside and outside himself in an effort to prepare to write. Brainstorming can include thinking, imagining, listening to music, and talking about ideas. During this part of the writing process, the writer mentally and physically collects information and ideas. The writer is constantly on the lookout for beauty and conflict in nature and people. He listens to dialogue, his own feelings, and the real stories in his neighbor's life. Prewriting and brainstorming involve paying close attention to your life.

TEACH WRITING AS A PROCESS

No matter what age your child is, you can help him with his writing by remembering that writing is a *process*. The writing process includes at least four steps: brainstorming, composing, revising, and editing.

BRAINSTORMING/PREWRITING

Prewriting can include anything a writer does to perceive, question, and

COMPOSING/FIRST DRAFT

Composing is better known as writing a first draft. While writing the first draft, it is helpful to reserve evaluating content or correcting mistakes for later. Composing may also include free writing (nonstop writing) while listening to music or typing on a blank computer screen so the writer will not block his flow of ideas. The purpose of the first draft is to get something down on paper, not to compose a perfectly written piece of writing.

REVISING/REWRITING

Revising or rewriting happens after the writer has allowed a period of time to pass and returns to a piece of writing with a different set of eyes. The revising part of the writing process requires the writer to look for ways to improve the writing. The writer can also ask family, friends, or teachers for suggestions.

While revising or rewriting, the writer checks his organization, ideas, voice, and transitions. As your child's teacher at any age you can comment on the creativity and organization or ask your child questions that are not answered clearly in the work. The writer should be encouraged to consider the feedback and decide how or if to use it on the next draft. The art of writing well is really rewriting.

EDITING/FINAL DRAFT

The editing process includes a final correction of the writing for such things as spelling, grammar, and punctuation. Editing is detail oriented and requires the writer to look carefully for mistakes. If this part of the process is used too early in the writing, the writer will be blocked from producing his best work.

For very young children, brainstorming and writing the first draft is enough. As your child grows older, he can learn to revise and edit for a purpose . . . that purpose is so someone can read and understand what he has written. It helps to give your child an audience that points out his strengths.

TEACHING YOUR CHILD TO ASSESS HIS OWN WRITING

As your child gets older, you might find it helpful to teach your older child to assess his own writing by using these six different ways to evaluate his work:

Ideas and Content. Ask, "Is my writing fuzzy, sketchy, without apparent logic or seem to have no purpose? Or is my writing clear, thoughtful, focused, and in control? Do I have something interesting to say?"

Organization. Ask, "Does my writing have a weak opener? Do I have a conclusion? Does my writing ramble? Does my work have natural patterns where the ideas are linked? Do I have a solid introduction and conclusion?"

Voice. Ask, "Is my writing flat or boring? Is my work honest and believable? Does my writing have a quality that uniquely identifies me as the writer?"

Word Choice. Ask, "Is my choice of words inaccurate, forced, repetitive, or vague? Is my writing accurate and precise? Does my work include rich imagery? Do I use action verbs? Is my writing forced? Am I trying too hard to impress?

Sentence Structure. Ask, "Are my sentences awkward or confusing? Are my sentences wordy? Does my writing sound natural?"

Writing Conventions. Ask, "Does my writing have many errors in grammar, capitalization, punctuation, spelling, paragraphing, and readability? Is my paper easy to read with no glaring errors?"

JOURNAL WRITING

Many events happen in your child's life before she is able to record it. A personal journal for each child is a good way to introduce children to writing. Purchase a journal for each child as soon as you learn that she is expected. In it record your feelings for the unborn child and something about your family circumstances.

When the child is born, write about the events surrounding her birth. Periodically during the first year or two, record the child's firsts, such as birthdays, blessings, and holidays. Include what she looks like at each age and stage, describe the child's personality, and include some amusing experiences or heartwarming happenings.

By the age of two or so, many children will be speaking well enough to start dictating to a scribe. You will be your child's scribe. Before long your child will want to try her own hand at writing. Don't be surprised if you're asked letter by letter how to spell word after word.

Before long, your child will be able to take over writing her own journal. By this time, she might be a little self-conscious or tend to record things that make you seriously question her priorities. But don't worry. Somewhere along the line your child might even discover who she is and what makes her unique.

Writing in a journal is an excellent way for your child to learn to express herself and also record the events of her life. Journal writing is a healthy way for children to learn to reproduce their thoughts in a way that they and others can understand. Making a record of their lives gives children a sense that their life is worth recording.

MAKING CARDS

For some reason most of us allow a total stranger at a faraway greeting-card company to decide how to express our sympathy or our feelings of appreciation. You don't write the letter or draw the picture; you buy a card. Why? Maybe you think you're too busy. Maybe because it's easier to let someone else do it. Maybe because it's easier to pay the cashier than it is to dig up your own emotions and try to sort through them and express them. This is such a terrible waste of feelings and expressions. Writing about your feelings forces you to think them through and make them specific.

If a child feels that he can produce his own cards of thankfulness, greeting, or celebration with original pictures and written thoughts, he will be less likely to go through life unable to express his love and appreciation later on. He will be more likely to stay in touch with his feelings toward others. Sending cards shouldn't be a mindless ritual of carbon-copy lives. Children can make their own birthday party invitations and cards for holidays and special occasions. This is an excellent way to use both written work and artwork in one nice venture.

LETTER WRITING AND E-MAILING

Most children have relatives who live some distance away. But even if most of your relatives live in the same town, letter writing via snail mail or e-mail is a nice habit to start at a young age. Phone calls can bring a familiar voice to you in a matter of minutes; but phones can never take the place of written expression.

If you've ever lived far away from loved ones, you know how precious a letter can be. You can touch a letter or an e-mail that has been printed. You can re-read it and enjoy the message over and over again. It becomes a tangible object. With a letter or an e-mail you can take time to really think through your life and what you want to say. You can express feelings you may not be able to say verbally.

Even before a child can write, you can still encourage him to express his ideas as you record them. Your child can write letters to thank someone for a gift or send an e-mail to Grandma, keeping her up with the latest school achievement.

POETRY WRITING

Children have such a fresh way of looking at things. Listen to them describe their world . . . then view those descriptions as poetry. Perhaps, for instance, your daughter will describe lightning during a rainstorm as "fire scribbles" in the sky. Children are natural poets and they enjoy expressing what they see and feel. Poetry writing is a natural extension of journal writing. When your child becomes comfortable with expressing herself and you teach your child to share that expression, you have a poem. Listen to your child as she learns to talk. Write down her verbal expressions into written form.

For example:

The whole world is wonderful
The world has oceans and trees
and little streams
that can float little boats.
(age five)

I used to kiss
Loud,
but now
I kiss
soft.
(age four)

I like to go outside
on the patio
sometimes
when other kids
aren't with me.
I like to go
out there
and listen
to the birds.
They make music
and it
makes me relax
in the chair.
(age six)

When my dad
comes home from work
he'll burst us
up in the air.
(age three)

As your children get older, encourage poetry or any other form of writing as a form of self-therapy. Poetry is the proof of deep thinking. Before you can write a poem, essay, or story you have to think about life and feel it. Before you can write anything you have to have something to say that longs for expression. Teaching your child to write a poem, story, or essay becomes an excellent way for her to learn that she has something unique to say.

MAKING BOOKS

All children love to make books. So let your child be the author and illustrator of his own creation. When your children are young, you can write down their stories or any words as they dictate to you. Older children want to do their own writing. Encourage your child to draw his own illustrations for the story or book idea.

Making a book is as simple as stapling a few pages together. As children grow older, they usually become increasingly sophisticated with their book making. The most important part of book making is imagination. All children can imagine, all children can create a book.

Books can be made very simply and bound by folding paper in half and punching holes in the pages, then tying with

yarn, stapling, or joining pages together with rings. Plastic or cardboard three-ring binders also work well. You can have the finished product laminated or make a special cover to display the name or picture of your youthful author.

Books can be about the child and what he likes or dislikes, about his family or home, about shapes or colors or the alphabet or numbers, or anything else that interests him. You can use a tape recorder and later transcribe what your child says so he can rattle off his story as fast as he can think it.

STORYTELLING GAMES

Storytelling games are also fun. Start a story and let your child continue it. Take turns adding to it. Or give your child a "what should or would you do" situation. Help him think through story ideas and solutions. Many children enjoy solving a problem or mystery in a story that someone else starts. Record your storytelling sessions on tape, then key them into the computer. Your child can illustrate the text and make a book from the game.

MEMORY BOOKS

Another way to introduce the making of books is through memory books. Purchase a three-ring binder filled with good-quality paper and plastic page protectors for your child. Fill the book with photographs and written accounts of events from your child's life. You can photocopy your child's handprint periodically and add that to a page that includes artwork done by your child. Have your child scribble or write descriptions of the people or events in the pictures. Be your child's willing scribe until she can write for herself.

THE JOY OF WRITING

Words and writing are two of the great things about being human. Exposing your children to the magic of self-expression in written form at a young age will increase the likelihood that they'll be hungry for what words can do for them the rest of their lives.

There are many Web sites that help children find and connect with pen pals in a foreign country. You might want to check out or involve your child in writing to another child in a foreign country.

Every child should grow up knowing he can express himself, his beliefs, feelings, fears, joys, sorrows, embarrassments, and boredom. When your child believes he has something valuable to say simply because he is himself, he can heal himself and change the world.

FAMILY FUN AND DYNAMICS

TALENTS, GIFTS, AND ABILITIES

All children have talents, gifts, or abilities that are unique to them. Every human being has an area of human performance where they shine. Watch your child for clues about her capacities. When you notice strengths in your child, make positive comments about her abilities. Imagine a productive and happy future for your child.

Think of yourself as a detective who is solving the mystery of who your child is and who she can become. Notice your child's preferences. All her skills translate into unique abilities and aptitudes for certain occupations, parenting, and volunteer

work later in life. Your child will likely be happiest doing what she does best. Allow your child to carefully pull back the layers of herself and become who she is and who she always has been with your careful observation, insight, and positive attitude.

Your child will likely have a unique way of processing information. Some children absorb information best when they see something (visual learner). Other children absorb information best when they hear something (auditory learner). Many children learn best when they have a hands-on experience (kinesthetic learner). Your child may also be a combination of these different learning styles. When you are trying to teach your child, notice when the lights come on inside her head. Your child will teach you how she learns best if you are observant. There are no dumb children, but there are many uninformed teachers.

Talents and gifts take on many forms, including:

Mechanical: Does your child love to take things apart and put them back together? Is he interested in machines and how things work?

Social: Does your child talk to strangers with ease? Is she a good negotiator? Is your child often voted into leadership positions?

Body: Is your child physically active and coordinated? Does your child enjoy team and individual sports?

Words: Does your child love to read, write, and tell stories? Does your child talk a lot and enjoy word games? Does your child memorize words easily?

Emotional: Does your child enjoy hobbies and spending time alone? Does your child write or talk about her feelings easily?

Spiritual: Is your child interested in spiritual things? Does she have empathy and a desire to help other people?

Visual: Does your child like to draw? Is your child creative? Does your child enjoy geometry more than algebra?

Logical: Does your child enjoy chemistry sets, puzzles, and math? Does your child watch science and nature shows on television?

Musical: Does your child love to sing or listen to music? Does your child play a musical instrument?

These are just a few of the many talents, gifts, and abilities your child may have. Talk to a counselor at school for further information and to learn more about interest and aptitude tests your child can take. Encourage your child to shadow people in the community who may have similar interests and gifts. Let your child volunteer or perhaps work a summer or part-time job that exposes her to occupations and volunteer work that use her unique talents, gifts, and abilities.

TALENT NIGHTS

Children who have opportunities to perform often in their own homes are usually less frightened when they start to perform outside the family. At family talent night, each child might perform individually or as a group. Singing, dancing, or playing an instrument aren't the only talents to share and display. Consider storytelling, poetry reading, and displaying paintings, needlework, or handicraft. One family member might want to display his talent for making people laugh with jokes or magic tricks.

A SENSE OF BELONGING

A sense of belonging and a need for individuality are two seemingly contradictory needs. In reality, they actually complement each other and are best served within the family circle. Lucky is the child who can say, "I belong to a family who loves me. And even though I am different from each of my brothers and sisters, I am a necessary and contributing part of the family. Without me, we wouldn't be the family that we are."

Families really are the most important organizations we will ever belong to. Unfortunately, however, it is often the family organization to which we give the least attention. In our fast-paced, modern world, most of us will change homes and jobs several times during our lifetime. A number of things compete endlessly for our attention—computers, employment, church service, television, outside activities, clubs, and sports. As we deal with the changes life brings and try to keep up with the long list of things that need our attention, many of us find ourselves drifting farther and farther apart as a family.

Real family unity takes effort and time. Every effort you make to foster close, meaningful relationships in your own family will help your home become a sanctuary, a source of strength to each member.

Sometimes brothers and sisters seem to have little more in common than their set of parents. Many have the idea that everyone in a family should get along well all the time because they all think alike and enjoy the same things. In fact, one of the greatest enrichments that families offer each other is the fact that very different people with different needs, personalities, and temperaments can learn to live with each other, get along, and have fun together.

Your home is a place where you don't have to think the same, act the same, or even have similar interests as others in the group, and yet you can still be an integral and necessary part of the whole. Families teach that you can live together and work together with others who you may not even like at times. If you learn to get along in your family circle, you will likely have an easier time getting along with those outside family.

Families can share experiences, talents, and abilities to the advantage of each individual family member. If you really try to do things together as a family in meaningful, positive ways, you will give your children a strong sense of belonging that will sustain them all their lives.

IDENTIFYING FAMILY TIME STEALERS

Modern life seems to require that mothers become masters at organizing their family's hectic schedules. They are asked to effectively juggle a dozen or more different activities every day. Some mothers even begin believing that having a "good" family means being completely involved in a myriad of activities by signing up their children—and themselves—for every good thing under the sun. Then, as they try to do everything and be everything, they wonder why they wish for a much simpler life with more time to spend together as a family.

If you find yourself feeling this way, try to stop and look objectively at your life. Ask yourself the following questions:

• What, specifically, are you and your children doing with your time?

• What activities are stealing the time you could be spending with your family doing simple things like playing board games, cleaning out the garage together, talking, serving, and so on?

• Are these things that are replacing your family together time really worth your time and the time they take away from your family?

It may come as a shock to you to realize that many of the so-called family activities in the community are actually thieves of family togetherness. It is all right to pass up some good and wholesome activities. It's all right not to be constantly busy with volunteer work, clubs, sports teams, employment, or any of the other 101 things you want to do. Cut back until you have only a few quality activities. When you and your children are overbooked it adds too much pressure on the whole family.

SPENDING PERSONAL TIME WITH YOUR CHILD

Spending unhurried time with your children will help them develop a healthy communication system with you. It will give them the idea that you think they are important and worthwhile. Children need to feel they are unique and loved simply for being themselves. You can help your child feel more loved by providing her with personal parental attention. Here are some suggestions for specific ways to do this:

• Use eye-to-eye contact when talking with or listening to each of your children.

• Pray for guidance on the best ways to meet your children's needs.

• Take each child out alone for a ride in the car, a trip on a bus, or a walk.

• Get rid of a few toys, turn off the TV set, and spend more time playing with your child.

• Talk to each child before bedtime. End the day with words of affirmation whispered into her ears.

• Set aside time to talk to each child alone.

• Remember that happy children are more

important than a clean house or a fat paycheck.

- Give your children back rubs or foot rubs or leisurely brush their hair.
- Allow one child at a time to prepare dinner with you.
- Take one child at a time shopping.
- Occasionally allow one child to stay up for a little longer than the others.
- Take one child to a movie or to buy an ice cream cone.
- Read with one child at a time.
- Plan a special trip to town with one child.
- Let one child go to work with Dad or Mom for a day.
- Let each child plan a date of her own choosing alone with either Mom or Dad.
- Mention each individual child in family prayers.
- Lie or sit next to each child for a few moments at bedtime.
- Give each child a hug and kiss and a smile every morning.
- Get a treasure box for each child where she can keep her own individual keepsakes.
- Help each child keep her own journal.
- Take plenty of individual pictures of each child, and save some for the child to keep.
- Honor one child at a time at meals with a special plate and a card explaining why she is special.
- Leave little love notes around the house for each child, mentioning specific things you love about her.
- Make "I love you" badges for each child.
- Make individualized gifts for each child.
- Make up and sing songs about each child.

- Have personal parent-child interviews.
- Make or purchase a special pillowcase, blanket, or quilt for each child.

DEVELOPING FAMILY UNITY

Many people wear hats or T-shirts displaying the name of a team or an organization they admire. Some families have found that their children feel more pride in being part of the family when they adopt similar symbols.

Here are a few ideas to increase feelings of family unity:

- Wear a family T-shirt.
- Write a family song.
- Select a family flower.
- Write in a family journal.
- Create a family flag, motto, or mission statement.
- Compile a family memory book.
- Have family prayers.
- Prepare and circulate a family newsletter.
- Develop family traditions for holidays.
- Quilt or tie a family quilt.
- Work on the family tree.
- Have a special family award night.
- Plant and harvest a garden together.
- Create a family Web page.
- Visit extended family members.
- Attend family reunions.

FAMILY COUNCIL

Most organizations find it next to impossible to succeed without regularly holding planned meetings. Yet most of us "ad-lib" our family organization; in other words, we just go about what we have to do and hope everything will turn out all right.

Many families have found that if they hold a council meeting regularly once a week, it's easier for them to work together and feel close. In these weekly planning sessions, you might decide on family goals, fill in the calendar for the coming week, make sure you support each other, discuss family finances and budget, brainstorm for solutions to problems, and plan vacations or outings.

Find a place to mount a large wall calendar and jot down each appointment or activity of each family member for the week. You might use a different color for each family member. Coordinate rides and baby-sitting and be sure to set priorities when there are conflicts. A weekly date for Mom and Dad, along with a well-planned family home evening lesson and activity, should take first priority.

DEVELOPING FAMILY HOBBIES AND SKILLS

Consider helping your family develop new skills and hobbies by taking the time to try new things. Take the time to teach your children how to:
- sew
- change a tire or the oil in the car
- sing
- garden
- hike
- swim
- jog

EVERYDAY ADVENTURES

All work and no play makes for a very dull family, so your family might enjoy planning an activity once a week where you can enjoy one another's company in a relaxing way. Turn simple, everyday happenings into everyday family adventures:

- Camp out in the backyard or a nearby campground.
- Watch a thunder and lightning storm together.
- Spend 30 minutes stargazing.
- Make a snowman.
- Build a sandcastle in the sandbox or at the beach.
- Make up stories together.
- Have family cookouts or bake-offs.
- Create holiday decorations.
- Make wall hangings and arrangements.
- Have a family award night.
- Host a family talent night.
- Clean up the house together with loud or dramatic music in the background.
- Cook something to take to someone else.
- Repair something around the house.
- Bake bread.
- Hold a read-a-thon.
- Work on merit badges.
- Sing together.
- Learn to iron.
- Dance together.
- Exercise together.
- Write a family history.

- bowl
- start a private collection
- read
- write a personal history
- enjoy museums
- collect art objects
- play a musical instrument
- learn a language
- take photographs
- operate a video camera
- create a personal Web page
- cook
- paint or draw
- boat
- play football, basketball, or baseball
- roller or ice skate
- ride a horse
- take care of animals

Some families like to develop their talents together. A family music hobby may lead to a family singing group or band. Photography can be an engrossing family hobby as members create their own darkroom and facilities for processing photos.

CELEBRATE YOUR CULTURAL HERITAGE

Families can grow closer together by learning about the heritage their ancestors have left them. With a little work, most families can find out where their ancestors came from, how they lived, and what their lifestyle and occupations were like. Answers might be found in family records, histories, and journals.

Libraries are good places to find out about the music, art, dance, literature, food

| SIMPLE FAMILY GAMES |

Remember the good, old games you played as a child. Get them out and play them again with your children:
- Blindfold
- Spin the bottle
- Charades
- Kick the can
- Run, sheepy, run
- Kickball
- Hopscotch
- Marbles
- Jacks
- Chess
- Checkers
- Card games
- Board games
- Jump rope
- Dodgeball
- Musical chairs
- Red Rover
- Tag
- Duck, duck, goose

customs, and recreation of your progenitors. Books, magazines, tapes, and films from the country of your ancestors can teach your children about the customs of the people on your family tree.

After some preliminary work, you might try one or more of these activities:

- Have a heritage dinner with food from your ancestors' homeland. Make place mats, centerpieces, flower arrangements, or flags to go along with the meals.

• Make flannel board figures and use them to tell stories from family journals and histories.

• Decorate your home with items from your ancestors' homelands.

• Find out about the talents and interests of your ancestors and consider carrying on some of those talents and interests in your present family; or start traditions of your own.

• Invite a grandparent or the eldest member of your family to your home for a special evening. Tell the guest to bring old photographs, journals, diaries, and letters and to be prepared to share experiences about the family's past.

• Spend an evening filling out a pedigree chart for each family member. Help the children write their own names on line 1. Now help each family member fill the other spaces with family names: lines 2 and 3 for the child's parents; lines 4 and 5 for paternal grandparents; lines 6 and 7 for maternal grandparents' names, and so on.

• Purchase and present to each family member a personal book of remembrance binder in which pedigree charts, family group sheets, and other important documents and records may be kept. Each family member who is able to do so should write his own personal history and put it in the binder.

FRIENDS FOREVER

Don't forget to create relaxing times for your family. Take walks around your neighborhood, play at the park, or read a book. If you cut out even one TV show you have an extra thirty minutes to spend doing things together. If you involve your children in your everyday work, like sorting laundry or doing the dishes, you will encourage conversation and connection. If you set a fixed bedtime it will keep you and your children more rested.

Your children will not always be small. You won't always have them with you. They won't always be so excited about spending time with you. One day they will grow up and you will grow old. If you have taken the time to be together, you will find that you have become friends as well as family members. Taking the time to enjoy your children is perhaps your greatest assignment *and* blessing.

SNUGGLE TIME

Every child needs to spend time snuggling with his mother. Rocking, singing, patting, stroking, rubdowns, tummy blowing, and baby toe kissing are as important as food. Your child never outgrows his need for snuggling. Everybody needs to be hugged several times a day. Take time to say goodbye in the morning with a hug, kiss, and a kind word. Take time in the evening to kiss your child good night, hug him, and say a kind word. When you sit next to your child, put your arm around him.

Take your child's hand or tickle his arm.

Give your child a foot rub or a back rub. Most children like to wrestle with Dad on the floor. Let your child crawl all over you. Dance your child to sleep in your arms as you play your favorite music. Sing to your child in the rocking chair. Lie next to your child in bed for a moment and talk. Tousle or stroke your child's hair. Appropriate loving touch is necessary for your child to feel loved and connected. You can schedule snuggle time right along with teeth brushing and homework time.

NURTURING YOURSELF

Mothers are famous for placing themselves last on their priority lists. If you don't nurture yourself, you won't be able to nurture your child. You need to see yourself as real . . . a unique soul with limitless possibilities and potential. If you haven't neglected yourself for too long, you know what you love doing and what brings you joy. Every mother needs time to develop her own talents and fill her inner need to grow, learn, and develop. If you don't have a passion for something, keep trying things until you find something to be passionate about. Try to remember what you loved doing as a child.

Your children will move through your life. They are in your home for a short time and then they leave. You need to keep creating your life as you go along and continue to fill it with work, joy, pleasure, fun, and usefulness. Then when your children leave, you will continue a pattern of living that is fulfilling and meaningful.

Many mothers feel a certain amount of guilt whenever they do something for themselves because they believe they are being selfish. The truth is, when you develop yourself as an individual and nourish your spirit, you bring your child a whole and healthy mother who has the inner reserve to share and uplift. It is not selfish to take time to nurture and develop yourself; it is vital for your spiritual, emotional, and physical health.

HOW DO YOU NURTURE YOURSELF?

Make sure you have female friends to talk to. Most women *need* to talk like they need to eat. Get to know your female neighbors, co-workers, and ward members. Attend Enrichment night each month and find a new circle of female friends.

Women share the same hormones and have similar problems, stress, and needs. Talking to your female friends can relieve your stress because you realize everyone has challenges and frustrations just like you. Good female friends are a place of retreat and refreshment and an opportunity to have good, old-fashioned fun. Don't rely solely on your husband as your only communication buddy.

Have a place in the house that you can call your own. Set aside a private spot in your house, no matter how small, just for you. It can be a corner of a room, a place in the basement, attic, or even an entire room. This is the place where you go to regain your sense of self and establish an important personal boundary. Retreat to your place regularly. When you find yourself feeling overwhelmed, tell your children and your husband that you need to regroup and recharge.

Ideally this place will have a nice lock on the door. Retreat and refresh regularly . . . think, sew, read a book, listen to music, pursue a talent, talk on the phone, or enjoy a special treat. (If your children are small you may have to stay up late or get up early to actually have some solitude in your private space.)

Find a saying or motto that can keep you going when the going gets tough. Post this favorite motto or saying on the refrigerator, hang it on your bedroom wall, or place it strategically in your bathroom. Find something meaningful to you such as:

"I Am Doing God's Work."

"Families Are Forever . . . If I Can Survive Today."

"We Are All Enlisted Till the Conflict Is Over."

"I Am Enough, Do Enough, and Have Enough."

"I Am Loved."

"When the Going Gets Tough, the Tough Go Shopping."

"Everyone Wants to Save the Planet, but Nobody Wants to Help Mom Do the Dishes."

Nurture someone outside your family circle. Select a woman outside your family circle to befriend. This person may be a woman on your visiting teaching list or anyone else you choose. Don't limit yourself to women in your same age group. Younger or older women are good for your soul. Take your friend flowers, write thank-you and I-love-you notes, bring over treats, or simply set aside regular times to visit. When you get out of the house and place your mind on someone else, you develop a better perspective on your own personal problems.

Take time every day to play. Everyone needs to relax and unwind. Make play as important as scripture reading and prayer. Swing in the swings, jump on the trampoline, play a board game, dress up, dance around the house, growl and chase your children like a bear, eat on the floor, or make funny faces. Use your children as models for how to enjoy your day. Making time for play helps you keep your sense of humor, perspective, and gratitude.

Find you time. Every mother deserves a period of time each day and on weekends where she can do anything she wants to do or go anywhere she desires. If you neglect yourself long enough, you'll forget what you like to do. You'll forget what makes you you. You can read the Sunday paper in bed while you munch on strawberries with a dead bolt lock on your door. You can take a bubble bath or attend concerts and plays. You can shop, go to the beach, or just take a nap. During *you* time you can read a novel at the library *alone,* exercise, or take lessons or a class. You can learn to play an instrument or join a book club. Your time is as individual as you. Just make sure you do it.

Learn to love your body. Having children tends to add on a few pounds and inches and you may spend way too much time wishing you were back to the size you were before you had children. Adjust to your new shape. Love your new body. Perhaps you are a little softer around the edges and nicer to hug. Look at your body as the wonder it is. If you have gone through pregnancy, childbirth, and motherhood and you're still *alive,* count yourself as a pretty tough lady. If you can do that, you can do anything. (See pages 239–244 for more ideas on learning to love your body while staying healthy and fit.)

Don't be afraid to ask for help. Many mothers think they should *be* everything and *do* everything well, but that just isn't possible. You can't do everything. You can't be everything. You can't go everywhere. Take a deep breath and let go of your need for perfection in yourself, your surroundings, and in your family members.

Most husbands simply do not notice what needs to be done unless you tell them and ask for help. Learn to negotiate on the dozens of items that need to be done in your home each day. Don't keep gender roles so rigid that you can't mix and match up the chores to every person who lives in your house. Maybe it's easier for your husband to go grocery shopping on his way home from work and easier for you to empty the garbage.

Your children can do much more than you realize if you insist on their help and lower your standards. Children may not do chores the way you would but you can learn to live with their imperfect abilities. Don't be a martyr . . . be a leader, teacher, and guide.

Make the time to pray, read your scriptures, and meditate. You will need the spiritual nourishment that regular scripture reading, prayer, and meditation offer. It's easy to let your personal worship habits take second place to your children's needs. You may forget that your children need a mother who can communicate with God, find answers to life's problems, and have a peaceful spirit. Set aside a time every day to pray, read, and think about eternal matters. Open your heart to the nurturing of your heavenly parents.

Don't become a clean freak. Your house will never be perfectly clean once you start having children. Get used to a certain degree of disarray and learn to live with a certain amount of disorder. Focus on creating a home where love and dust co-exist. Relax your standards for the health of your whole family. You can actually learn to enjoy your somewhat cluttered house because your living space is a learning center, not a sterile operating room.

Your housecleaning abilities will not be an admission test to get into the celestial kingdom. Family life is dirty business. Children and clean do not go together. *Do* have one place in your house that you can keep just as you want to even if it is only your underwear drawer. This place will become your comfort corner amidst the clutter and chaos.

If you can afford housecleaning help, don't be afraid to use it. Organize your husband and children to help more often. Remember, humor and bribery work better than barking out orders and sulking. House cleaning can be totally life consuming. Decide when enough is enough and learn to let some things go. It's more important to spend quality time together with your husband and children than to have a sparkling kitchen or bathroom. (For more ideas on managing your house and motherhood, see pages 189–203.)

Run away every once in a while. Occasionally spend a weekend with your sister or go visit your mother alone. Sometimes your children and husband don't appreciate everything you do until you're *not* there doing it every day. You deserve a break every once in a while.

Motherhood simply does not give you much downtime. You have company in the bathroom, screaming in the back seat of the car, and demanding big and little people following you everywhere you go. It's vital to get away by yourself every once in a while so you can remember who you are and recharge your batteries.

Depend on yourself. Of course it's nice if you have your family's support while you nurture yourself, but don't depend on it. Depend on yourself to nurture you. Don't ever stop nurturing your soul and enjoying life, learning, and growing. You are your child's model. Do you want your daughter to live like you do when she's your age? Your children deserve a mother who knows how to love herself, enjoy life, and reach her potential. The greatest gift you have to offer your children is a happy you.

GRANDMAHOOD

Becoming a "grand" mother gives you a second chance to nurture as you are nurtured. Grandchildren are the fountain of youth as you age and the best reward for not killing your own children when they were teenagers. By the time you become a grandmother, you're old enough to have raised a child from infancy to adulthood. You've learned a few things along the way that help you appreciate and treasure children of all ages.

I became a new mother and a new grandmother so close together it left me panting. My oldest daughter and I were in the hospital having our babies at the same time. Experiencing pregnancy, childbirth, and new motherhood along with my daughter felt like a mystical linking of generations one moment and a science fair project gone mad the next. My daughter and I raced each other for the bathroom, craved the same frozen yogurt, and kept each other company waiting for appointments at the obstetrician's office. Talk about a crazy way to bond.

Yet the moment I saw my grandson

enter the world I knew the cycle of life, love, and family had come full circle. My baby was having her baby. There in that labor room as I stroked my daughter's moist forehead, I realized in the most profound sort of way that everything I'd done as a mother for the past twenty-five years was worth it . . . absolutely *everything*. Every single common, everyday moment I'd chosen to serve and love my child was more important than anything else I'd determined to do with my life.

As I watched my first grandchild enter life, I knew my part in the creation and development of his mother was my life's most important work. My grandson's birth also gave new meaning and direction to the remainder of my life. I understood for the first time that the whole purpose of the world was bringing down children from God and helping them find their way back to him. Before that moment I simply could not begin to comprehend the significance of my own motherhood and the limitless life- and love-giving potential it offered.

It occurred to me that a thousand years hence, my babies will still be having their babies and the miracle of the life and love I'd begun would go on forever. I also understood that taking part in the creation and development of another human being was the greatest way to give birth to my own best life. I'd never even imagined I could feel so much joy and love inside.

Your soulful quest to bring down children from God will someday give you the blessing of grandmahood and great-grandmahood. If you are faithful, your motherhood will go on and on forever. As you welcome your first grandchild or great-grandchild into the world, you will be able to continue loving and nurturing with even

> MOTHER, LOOK INTO MY EYES
>
> *Mother,*
> *Look*
> *Into my eyes.*
> *See*
> *Me*
> *As I am*
> *Today.*
> *Don't deny*
> *My hopes and dreams,*
> *My reality.*
> *By God's grace,*
> *In bonds of love,*
> *Be mine.*
> *Refuse*
> *All power*
> *Over me.*
> *Bond yourself*
> *To me*
> *For all eternity.*
> *Look*
> *Into my eyes,*
> *Mother*
> *And see.*
> *Look*
> *Into my eyes*
> *And*
> *See*
> *Me*
> *As I will be*
> *Someday.*

greater tenderness, awe, and joy. When you are a grandma you'll know for yourself that every sacrifice you make for your child contains your life's greatest meaning and every choice to love, your greatest purpose.

THINGS I WISH MY MOTHER HAD TOLD ME

♥ The greatest gift you can give your children is your unconditional love. Your unconditional love will liberate your children and give them the courage to succeed.

♥ When you truly love someone you are able to see them in small measure as God does—and that is a miracle.

♥ Start a gratitude journal.

♥ Play with your child every day.

♥ You don't have to irrigate the whole field; a small garden will do. You can't water anything from an empty cup.

♥ Learn what fills your reserve of peace and strength and don't feel guilty when you are alone replenishing your supply. Even mothers need time out.

♥ Every mother has a train of thought that she rides on when she's alone. Make sure the ride is taking you where you want to go.

♥ Laugh at yourself at least once a day. You're a lot funnier than you realize. If you don't believe me, ask your children.

♥ Don't worry so much about how your children turn out. Be more concerned with your ability to inspire your children and love them.

♥ You can't control your children. You can only control yourself.

♥ Possessions are really just things you keep and guard for fear you might need them someday. By the time you're willing to let go of most of them your children won't have room in their homes to accept them. If you see someone who could use your possession more than you, give it to them before you die. Then your possessions will bless many more lives than your own and you'll be around to see it.

♥ Develop a deep and sincere desire to truly understand your children, yourself, and your husband.

♥ Take God's hand and rest your heart a while. Remember you are his child and he knows you better than you know yourself.

♥ Your greatest challenges and rewards in this life will come from mastering yourself and loving and serving your family.

♥ Each child comes into the world with his own personality, talents, and needs.

♥ Never forget: children make a house a home.

♥ Create comfort corners in your home and your heart.

♥ The child is fortunate who can associate both pleasure and parental attention with the raw material of a book: words.

ENCOURAGING EXPRESSION END NOTES

Every child needs a safe place to call home where he is free to be himself. After establishing that safe haven, the greatest gift you have to offer your child is a healthy, happy, nurturing mother. For home is not really a place of residence but the knowledge that you have a secure place in someone's heart. Every child needs to be loved just as he is. Every child needs to know that he has infinite worth, that his feelings matter, and that someone really cares about him. You can be that person for your child.

Give your child more opportunities to nourish his soul and express his gratitude to God by writing, telling stories, drawing, cooking, making music, pretending, meditating, going barefoot, and playing. Life is more than getting, spending, or even being good at something. Life is also about continual growth, taking risks, challenging yourself, and expressing your own vision. Rediscover the sacred craft of person-making and respond to the beauty and truth that surrounds you in your own unique way.

Encourage and revitalize creativity and individuality in your home. Your job is not to judge but to bless. Your job is not to control but to set free. Your job is not to close possibilities or inhibit energy but to open potentialities and advocate initiative.

One of the biggest problems you will face as an LDS mother is unproductive guilt or the feeling that you must keep up with some ideal image. You may believe that to be a good Mormon mother means all your kids have to be well behaved in church and excel in sports, academics, or the arts. You may think you're supposed to bake bread, tend a perfect garden, and read the scriptures every morning at dawn. You may be unable to relax and enjoy life unless your house is perfectly clean, you've brought dinner to the neighbors, and hold weekly spiritual family home evenings. You may feel that you must stay attractive for your spouse, research your ancestors, and get your visiting teaching done—all by *last* week.

Then your children grow up and perhaps they make decisions that bring both of you great pain. The guilt and second-guessing can be consuming and debilitating. Yet being an LDS mother doesn't have to be totally overwhelming or guilt inducing.

The gospel of Jesus Christ is actually simplifying—if you listen to your heart. The only thing that is truly essential is that you *do* what you *feel* in your heart is the right thing to do at any given moment, that you are true to the light God gives you. No one but you knows what insights and direction God has given you. This is private and personal between you and your Maker.

Finding out what God's will is for you and trying your best to do it doesn't guarantee that you won't make mistakes, but it does guarantee that you can repent from those mistakes and experience a change of heart and a new way of thinking and feeling. It does guarantee that you will open your heart and let God nurture you.

Remember, you are his child—and your children are his, too. When you become overwhelmed by the conflicting commitments you feel to your husband, children, extended family, church, work, and community, come home to that place in your heart where God nurtures . . . and you will be comforted.

NOTES

IMPORTANT INFORMATION, FAVORITE WEB SITES, AND GOOD BOOKS ABOUT ENCOURAGING EXPRESSION

RENEWING THE SPIRIT

YOUR FAMILY
AND THE CHURCH

The family is the most important unit in time and eternity. The Church was established to exalt families, temples are built so families can be together forever, and God formed families to allow children and parents to learn correct principles in a loving atmosphere in preparation for eternal life. It is in families that we have the greatest potential for happiness.

The home is the first, the best, and the most crucial laboratory for teaching and living the gospel of Jesus Christ. No other organization in society can fill the function of a righteous family. Marriage and family are the central components of the plan of progression, which leads to exaltation—the continuation of the family through eternity.

You, your spouse, and your children need to be your first and most sacred priority—your most important Church calling. Worry less about how you appear to those outside your home and

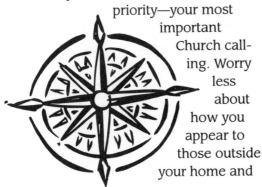

more about how completely you love and serve each member of your family individually, including yourself.

The purpose of the Church is to bless and strengthen you and your family. All church organizations and programs fall under priesthood authority and are created to help you work toward the goal of exaltation. Programs are designed to serve people, not people to serve programs. Participate in activities outside your home after taking counsel from your Heavenly Father, listening to your heart, and being observant about your family's needs. Many of your choices will not be between good and bad but between good and better. Over-participation in the programs of the Church to the neglect of your family can actually harm your relationships at home. Remember that extracurricular church activities are optional.

No church meeting, assignment, or activity is more important than your family. No program, procedure, or misplaced desire to impress others is more important than the worth of each individual soul entrusted to your care, including your own. So ask your Father in Heaven often and listen carefully as you make choices about where you should be and what you should be doing every day. The only "church calling" from which you will never be released is that of wife, mother, and daughter of God.

As you participate in Church activities and programs, take care to remember one other thing: the gospel is not about appearances. If you and your family are simply going through the motions of Church activity—having family home evening, participating in meetings, and so on—so that it appears you are living the gospel, you are on a dangerous path. Take care to really *live* the gospel of Jesus Christ every day, by loving, serving, caring for, and forgiving each other. Let the light of the gospel change your heart, and teach your children how to seek that same conversion.

This final section of the book will help you to remember the purpose of your family and the Church in this earthly life and the life to come. That purpose is to come unto Christ. As a mother, wife, and daughter of God, you have a crucial role in furthering the kingdom of God and helping your family to fulfill the three goals that make up the mission of the Church: perfecting the Saints, proclaiming the gospel, and redeeming the dead. And although this section is full of advice for teaching, sustaining, and renewing the spiritual self, the main message is simple: Stay close to the Lord, stay close to your husband and children, and continually do things that will lift you and your children spiritually. These things will outweigh everything else you do or have done as a mother, from diapering to discipline, from toilet training to driver's ed training.

PERFECTING THE SAINTS

A GOSPEL STUDY PLAN

No expert can give a step-by-step guide for teaching the gospel in your home because you, your spouse, and your children are individuals with singular needs and experiences that change every day. The only true guides are the scriptures, personal direction from church leaders, and personal revelation from God.

There is nothing fluffy about the gospel of Jesus Christ. The answer to every difficult problem, large or small, in your family can be found in living the gospel of Jesus Christ and applying his infinite atonement. There is no pain or sorrow he cannot help you endure, no trouble or tempest he cannot still, no sin he cannot forgive. All you need to offer is a broken heart and a contrite spirit. Because of Jesus Christ you can forgive and be forgiven and you—and those you love—will live after death.

Keep looking for the answers God will send you if you ask. Contemplate your relationship with Heavenly Father, Jesus Christ, your spouse, and each of your children individually. Study, pray, fast, read the scriptures, ponder, ask, meditate, repent, and forgive. You are fully capable of deciding what direction you should take at any given time in leading your family to Christ. Give your will to God. Lean on the great mediator, Jesus Christ. You are stronger than you realize and you are never alone.

WHAT TO TEACH YOUR CHILD BEFORE THE AGE OF EIGHT

Before your child reaches the age of eight, you are given the wonderful responsibility to teach him basic gospel principles before he is exposed to the influence of Satan. Church meetings, classes, and activities can supplement you in this responsibility, but not replace you. No one can effectively teach principles they don't understand or live. So study, ponder, and pray, then ask God how to best exemplify and teach these basic principles to your individual child after you have considered his unique needs.

FAITH

Faith, the first principle of the gospel, is a belief in things that aren't seen but are true. Faith must be centered in Jesus Christ. You can't have faith in Jesus Christ without also having faith in your Heavenly Father. If you have faith in them, you will also have faith in the Holy Ghost. Faith is a gift from God. You can pray and ask for faith and then increase it through study, practice, and work. Faith is knowing that you can trust God completely as you strive to find his will and do it.

To teach your child about faith, you must first acquire it yourself. Do you have faith in God the Father, Jesus Christ, and the Holy Ghost? Does your child know that? Do all you can to increase your own faith, and your child will see your example and begin to learn the importance of faith.

A simple way to teach a young child about faith is to plant a seed together. Explain to your child that the things you do to nourish the seed, such as watering it and giving it soil and sunlight and patience, will help it to grow and become a plant. Faith is like a seed. If your child will nourish her faith by attending church meetings, reading the scriptures, praying, and obeying the commandments, her faith will grow.

Helping your child to plant and nourish seeds also teaches her to demonstrate faith by taking action to bring about an end result that she can't yet see. Just as a strong plant is the result of patience, diligence, and work, so is a strong, unshakeable testimony of Jesus Christ.

REPENTANCE

Everyone sins and needs to change and repent. Sin is knowing what is good and choosing not to do it. Repentance is the way to become free from the effects of sin and to receive forgiveness—a necessary step because sin blocks spiritual progression. Children under the age of eight are not accountable for their sins, but they can learn about the importance of repentance and forgiveness and gain a positive attitude toward repentance that will help them throughout their lives.

To teach your child to repent, repent yourself. Say you're sorry when you've done something wrong. Let your child see you forgive others when you have been hurt or offended. Ask for your child's forgiveness when you have acted or spoken unkindly. Teach him to forgive his siblings and friends.

Make sure your child understands that  repentance is a positive thing—a gift from God—and not something to be feared or avoided. A good way to demonstrate that repentance brings happiness is to fill a backpack with rocks or other heavy objects and have your child put it on his back. Ask him if he'd like to carry it around all day long, everywhere he goes. Tell him that each rock represents a sin and that repentance lets him remove the rocks, or erase his sins, one by one. When you have removed all the rocks, tell him that repentance lightens our heavy load and makes us happier.

The backpack demonstration is also a good way to teach older children about the steps of repentance. Each rock could represent one of the five steps: recognizing the sin, confessing, making restitution if possible, forsaking the sin, and obeying the commandments of Jesus Christ. As you remove each rock, explain the step of repentance and give examples that your child can understand. Explain that the repentance process is not easy and it must be done prayerfully and sincerely, but when it is done properly it takes away our heavy sins and brings us closer to Jesus Christ.

To teach your child that his worth in the sight of God does not diminish when he sins, show him an increase of love when he makes a mistake. Help him understand that everyone makes mistakes, but Jesus Christ made it possible for us to repent so that God will not remember our sins.

BAPTISM

When your child reaches the age of eight, she is considered accountable for her own actions and can choose to accept the ordinance of baptism. Baptism is the introductory ordinance of the gospel. Your child becomes a member of the Church of Jesus Christ when she is baptized by immersion by one who has authority.

Teach your child that baptism is showing God and the world that she is willing to follow the Savior. She makes a promise with God that she will keep his commandments and serve him. God promises her that he will give her the Holy Ghost and that she can one day return to his presence.

Share with your child the scriptural account of Jesus being baptized by John the Baptist. Teach her that Jesus set the example for us all to follow. When she is baptized she will be clean and pure, and if she will remember the promises she made at baptism, repent when she makes mistakes, and take the sacrament each week, she will stay clean and worthy to return to Heavenly Father some day.

Baptism may be a good time to decide with your child that she is now old enough to stop bringing treats and toys to church, carry her own set of scriptures, and start fasting on Fast Sunday.

CONFIRMATION AND THE GIFT OF THE HOLY GHOST

After your child's baptism, he will be confirmed a member of The Church of Jesus Christ of Latter-day Saints and will receive the gift of the Holy Ghost.

Teach your child that he may hear or feel the influence of the Holy Ghost in many different ways: as a still, small voice, a feeling, or a sense of peace. The Holy Ghost will help him know right from wrong, give him strength to live righteously, warn him of danger, send comfort, and help him understand sacred things.

Help your child understand that the Holy Ghost is a member of the Godhead and a personage of spirit, not flesh and bones. Your child can gain a testimony of Jesus Christ with the help of the Holy Ghost. The gift of the Holy Ghost will allow him to receive added light, knowledge, companionship, and guidance if he is worthy.

PRAYER

Children can learn at a very young age that prayer is the way to talk to their

INVITING THE SPIRIT

Help your child learn that she can invite the Spirit into her life in the following ways:
- by praying
- by reading the scriptures
- by bearing her testimony
- by listening to uplifting music
- by expressing gratitude
- by sharing spiritual experiences when prompted
- by asking for priesthood blessings

Heavenly Father. Teach your child that Heavenly Father wants to hear from her and to bless her. He has promised that he will always listen to every prayer. She can thank him for her blessings and ask him for the help she needs. She can pray whenever she wants and know that her Heavenly Father loves her and is listening.

The best way to teach your child to pray is by example. Make your house a house of prayer. Pray for your child as well as with your child. Pray at the dinner table before each meal. Hold family prayer every morning and evening. Pray before a trip, a performance, or a big test. Pray in gratitude, giving sincere thanks for the blessings you have received as a family. Pray at times of sickness and decision. Pray for world and Church leaders. Pray to feel God's love. Pray with your child at any time and for any reason, and she will quickly

TEACH YOUR CHILD TO PRAY

Help your child learn these simple guidelines and she'll soon be able to fill in the blanks with her own thoughts and feelings.

- Begin with "Our Father in Heaven . . ."
- Thank Heavenly Father for everything: "I thank thee . . ."
- Ask Heavenly Father for help, guidance, or blessings: "I ask thee . . ."
- Close with "In the name of Jesus Christ, amen."

understand the importance of prayer and learn to rely on it throughout her life.

Individual Prayers

Teach your child how to say his individual prayers by praying with him. Kneel next to him and have him repeat one phrase at a time. Allow him to say his own prayer when he is ready and willing.

Family Prayers

When families pray together, they learn to listen to the Holy Ghost and become closer as a family. They learn to love each other and to serve each other. Teach your child about the importance of family prayer by holding family prayers each day. Have the whole family kneel together. The

head of the family should pray or ask someone to pray. Everyone in the family should be given regular opportunities to say the family prayer. Small children can take their turn with one parent assisting them.

Blessings on the Food

Regular blessings on the food teach children humility and gratitude, reminding them that Heavenly Father gives them all of their blessings. Teach your child to thank Heavenly Father for the food and to ask him to bless it before the family eats. Each child should be given an equal chance to say the blessing on the food.

Special Prayers

Teach your child to pray at any time and place. Whenever possible, he should kneel, fold his arms, and close his eyes, but he can offer a prayer in any position and in any location. Teach him to express his love and gratitude to Heavenly Father and ask for help and guidance whenever he needs to during the day.

THE SACRAMENT

Family home evening is a good time to teach your child about the significance of the sacrament. She should understand that the sacrament is a priesthood ordinance that helps us think about Jesus and the Atonement. The bread and water help us remember the body and the blood of Christ that were offered as a sacrifice for everyone. Talk about things your child can do during the administration of the sacrament to stay reverent and think about Jesus Christ.

The ordinance of the sacrament is an opportunity to renew baptismal covenants each week. Although children under the age of eight have not yet been baptized, they can still be taught to sit quietly and think about Jesus while the sacrament is being passed. They can also freely participate in the ritual of taking the bread and the water. If your child has a hard time sitting still or being quiet, consider bringing to church some picture books or scripture stories that will help her think of Jesus. When she approaches the age of eight you can teach her about baptismal covenants and renewing them each week when she takes the sacrament.

FASTING

Fasting alone is just going hungry. Fasting coupled with prayer and meditation feeds your spirit and gives you the blessings of a true fast. Though you abstain from eating and drinking for two meals, true fasting increases your spirituality and love for God. It strengthens your faith, encourages humility, and teaches you to understand more deeply your dependence on Father in Heaven.

Though a child under the age of eight may have difficulty understanding the purpose of fasting, you can begin to teach him through your example. Explain to him what Fast Sunday is and let him observe you fasting, studying the scriptures, and praying. Be aware of your actions and attitudes on Fast Sunday, and remember that he will form his opinion of fasting based on what he observes while growing up. Teach him about the blessings fasting brings and then encourage him to fast when he is old enough to understand what

he is doing and why. You might suggest that he begin by skipping just one meal until he feels ready to skip two.

Consider meeting as a family before the beginning of a fast and discussing a reason for the fast, such as a desired blessing or an answer you are seeking. Begin and end the fast with both family and personal prayer. This is also a good time to discuss the purpose of fast offerings. Let your child know what you are contributing as a family and how it will be used. Explain that at baptism you agreed to help others who cannot help themselves.

If you provide a good example for your child, he will grow up with a correct understanding of fasting and fast offerings and be more likely to follow your example.

SABBATH DAY OBSERVANCE

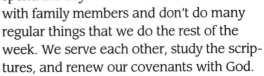

Teach your child that Sunday is a day that is different from all the other days. It is a special day when we rest from our work and remember God. We go to church on the Sabbath to worship Heavenly Father and learn more about his plan for us. We spend the day with family members and don't do many regular things that we do the rest of the week. We serve each other, study the scriptures, and renew our covenants with God.

SCRIPTURE STUDY

Explain to your child that Heavenly Father asked prophets to keep records. These records are called scriptures. Scriptures teach us how to return to Father in Heaven. If we read the scriptures we will be blessed with knowledge, wisdom, and guidance. We will learn the solution to many of life's problems and receive comfort and reassurance of God's love.

Teach your child the importance of reading the scriptures by providing family scripture time each day. Tell her stories from the scriptures. (Bedtime can be an ideal time to tell such classic stories as Daniel and the den of lions, Jonah and the whale, David and Goliath, and so on.) Help her become familiar with ancient prophets and stories before she's old enough to read about them herself. Let her see you reading the scriptures. Take your scriptures to church. Make sure your child has her own set of scriptures when she is old enough to read, and help her locate familiar chapters to read on her own.

THE WORD OF WISDOM

Your child should learn that his body is a great blessing from God. Father in

KEEPING THE SABBATH DAY HOLY

The following are a few ideas for helping your family keep the Sabbath:
- attend church
- read the scriptures and other good books
- visit relatives
- visit the sick and lonely
- listen to uplifting music
- sing hymns
- pray
- perform service
- work on family history
- write letters
- fast with a purpose
- spend time with family
- watch homemade family videos
- make Sunday a family day with no outside friends
- write in a journal
- prepare lessons
- simplify meal preparation, cook ahead, and use paper plates
- limit television
- plan family home evening or have a lesson
- read *Friend*, *New Era*, or *Ensign* articles
- meditate
- take a nap

Heaven wants him to take good care of his body. The Word of Wisdom is a commandment God has given us to help us stay healthy and take care of our precious bodies.

Teach your child that there are certain things he should not take into his body, such as coffee, tea, alcohol, tobacco, and harmful drugs. There are also good things that were created to make his body healthy and strong, such as fruits, vegetables, herbs, and grains. He should take care to eat healthy foods, get enough sleep, and not do anything that would harm his body. If he keeps the Word of Wisdom, God has promised to bless him with wisdom and health. He will also be better able to hear the promptings of the Holy Ghost.

Practice healthy eating, exercising, and sleeping habits in your home. Provide your child with a good role model. Emphasize health over body size, type, and weight. Teach your child to love his body as a great gift from God. Read Doctrine and Covenants section 89 together and discuss with your child the good things he should do and the things he's been asked not to do.

TITHES AND FAST OFFERINGS

Explain to your child that tithing is a voluntary payment to the bishop of one-tenth of your increase. A fast offering is another voluntary payment to the bishop to provide food, shelter, clothing, and medical care to those in need. Tithes and offerings are used for missionary work, to build chapels and temples, to educate young people, to print and distribute lesson materials, to help in family history

work, and to help those who cannot help themselves. God has promised that those who pay their tithes and offerings will be blessed.

Teach your child about tithing and fast offerings by your example. Let her accompany you to tithing settlement. Teach her to pay tithing on her first earned income. Show her how to fill out the tithing slip and give her tithing to the bishop. Talk about the blessings you have received from paying your tithing. Also, let her observe you paying fast offerings and explain where the money will go.

THE CREATION

Explain to your child how this beautiful world came to exist. Under the direction of our Father in Heaven, Jesus Christ created the earth. Tell him the story of the seven days of creation, discussing the different parts of the earth that were created on each day. Teach him that this world was prepared as a place where we could receive bodies, learn about the gospel, and be obedient.

To teach your child to enjoy the

ARTFUL GOSPEL STUDY

When the brain learns something via writing, music, art, dance, or drama, it retains, recalls, and comprehends the new information at a higher level. As you teach your children to love the scriptures, consider teaching them through the arts. Here are some ideas:

Writing

- After reading the scriptures, have each family member write in his or her journal and make personal applications from the scriptures.
- Invite your child to write a poem, song, nursery rhyme, or ballad about a scripture story or character.
- Invite your child to write a character sketch of a prophet or scripture hero, including what made them great.
- As a family, record the principles learned in the scriptures then note the parallel promises.

Dance

- Try dancing a scripture story to spoken narration.
- Experiment with ballroom dancing to hymns and Primary songs.
- Exercise to hymns and Primary songs.
- Play scripture charades by dancing or pantomiming a scripture hero or story to bring it to life.

Art

- Make simple, homemade scripture storybooks by drawing pictures accompanied by simple text.
- Draw or paint pictures of scriptures heroes.
- Display pictures of Jesus, temples, and the prophets around your home.
- Use the *Gospel Art Kit* as you study the scriptures together.

Music

- Memorize scriptures, the Articles of Faith, or other sacred text by setting the words to music.
- Write a song about a scripture story or character.
- Read the scriptures to music and candlelight.
- Pick a song from the hymn-book or *Children's Songbook* and read the scriptural passages noted at the bottom of the selected song.

Drama

- Act out scripture stories with costumes.
- Act out famous speeches by scripture heroes.
- Make puppets of scriptures heroes and act out stories.

creations of God, take him on outside adventures often. Show him the stars at night, plant gardens, go for hikes, work in the yard, paint pictures, and write poetry about the wonders of creation. Teach him to be observant and grateful for the changing of the seasons. Teach him to see himself and other people as the highest and most beautiful of all of God's creations.

THREE ESSENTIALS OF GOSPEL LEARNING

There are several important ways to pass down a legacy of testimony to your children and thus perfect the "saints" in your own home. First, *teach* the truths of the gospel. Family home evening, family prayer, and family scripture study are perfect times to do this. These are what we could call the three essential things a family must do to further gospel knowledge and strengthen the spirit. As you practice these three things, you must also *testify* that what you have taught is true. Finally—and this is the most important— you must *live* so your child will see that your actions agree with what you have said is true. When you do these things, you open the door for the Holy Ghost to testify to your child of the truthfulness of your teachings.

Personally living a Christlike life is the best way to lead each of your children to the Savior. Loving your children with the pure love of Christ will bring the good news of the gospel into your home and into your children's hearts. Applying the Atonement every day by forgiving and repenting brings meaning to all of life's experiences, including joy and suffering.

The gospel is simplifying, restoring, renewing, and full of hope because of the atonement of Jesus Christ. But remember that, unlike factual knowledge that is usually built upon by each succeeding generation, spiritual knowledge must be relearned by each generation and each soul by the use of individual agency. In other words, being a righteous mother doesn't guarantee that you will have righteous children. You can do only so much and the rest is up to your child.

FAMILY PRAYER

Among the most important things you can do in your home to help your children in their eternal progression is holding regular family prayer. Of course, we all know how difficult this can be once a few children of varying ages, a busy spouse, and a demanding schedule are thrown into the mix. Holding regular family prayer will never be an easy thing to do, but it will always be worth the effort. Decide to hold

---

SINCERE PRAYER

The following are some simple principles of sincere prayer that you can teach your children by example:
- Be humble when praying.
- Kneel.
- Pray with sincerity and faith.
- Ponder.
- Listen for answers.
- Use the power of fasting.
- Confess your sins.
- Live worthily so you can receive and recognize answers.

---

family prayer every day, preferably in the morning and the evening. Families with children of different ages and schedules might need to have more than one prayer in the morning—an early prayer for the older children and one later on for the younger children. You could have your evening prayer around the dinner table or just before the family starts to go to bed.

Though holding family prayer is obviously a priority, it is easy to give up trying when family schedules are hectic or some family members don't want to cooperate. But no excuse can keep you from holding family prayers if you decide in your heart that doing so will bless your children beyond measure.

Where to Hold Family Prayer

You can hold family prayer kneeling around your bed, at the dinner table before a meal, or in a circle in the family room. You can hold family prayer outside in the backyard, in the car, or at your child's bedside. Decide which location works best for your family.

How to Hold Family Prayer

When the father is present, he presides over family prayer and calls on a family member to pray. Mother presides when no father is present. Allow each family member a turn to pray. Consider taking time before family prayer to ask if there is anything that a family member would like to express thanks for or something they would like to ask Heavenly Father for. You can remind your children to pray for Church leaders, missionaries, and family members living away from home or friends that may need extra help.

You can use family prayer as a time to teach your children about expressing gratitude, seeking direction, and being concerned with helping and serving other people. You can mention each child by name as you pray and let your children know of your love and concern. Speak with sincerity when you pray and try to really communicate instead of just saying words. Children will learn to pray by listening to the way you pray.

When to Pray

You can hold a family prayer any time you feel the need. Say a prayer together before you leave for vacation. Have a special family prayer before a big event for one family member, such as a speech or a test. Pray with your family in times of stress and trouble. Offer a prayer of gratitude in times of happiness and joy. Don't limit your family prayers to only mornings and evenings.

For ideas on how to involve toddlers, preschoolers, school-age children, and teens in family prayer, refer to pages 133, 148, 160, and 177.

FAMILY SCRIPTURE STUDY

Set aside a time to study the scriptures as a family every day. Scripture study has so many benefits that bless and enrich a family. Families who regularly and consistently read the scriptures together are more likely to gain personal testimonies of Jesus Christ and the Atonement. Children will better learn how to pray, exercise faith, repent, and resolve problems. Children will acquire values and learn how to apply them in their personal lives.

Reading the scriptures together opens the door for families to receive direction from God and creates family worship time. It turns scripture characters into family heroes and helps the values of one generation to be passed down to the next.

How to Read the Scriptures

There are many different methods for reading the scriptures together as a family. How you actually go about scripture study is your decision. You may choose to start with prayer. You may want each member of the family to take turns reading. You may want to study a few verses at a time or a whole chapter. You may want to stop and ask questions after a few verses. You can read the standard works together from cover to cover or you can select a topic and look up all the scriptures on that subject.

To check your child's comprehension, you can ask a variety of questions. Ask him about basic facts, ask how certain scriptures make him feel, or ask how the scripture can be likened to his time and life. You can add personal experiences, bear your testimony, and use the topical guide, footnotes, and dictionary. You can cross-reference or talk about what the most important thing was you learned that day. You can sing a hymn or Primary song.

SCRIPTURE TIME ACTIVITIES

- Keep a notebook for recording impressions, goals, or questions as you do your personal reading. Then use family scripture time to discuss what you've written down.
- Mix in a variety of devotional readings to give family scripture reading a little more interest.
- Have each family member share something challenging that happened to them recently. Discuss ways you can support or help each family member.
- Read a letter from a missionary.
- Read a conference talk.
- Read articles from the *Ensign, New Era,* or *Friend.*

Consider asking family members to share a favorite scripture from their personal reading. You may choose to have a closing prayer. Don't feel you need to read a certain amount each day. Perhaps you'd prefer to read just a few verses and then seek understanding, feeling, and application. You might consider holding a scripture chase or assigning one family member to prepare a talk on a favorite scripture.

Many families have discovered that their young children have actually learned to read by following along during family scripture study. Young children can also draw pictures of scripture stories. You may choose to memorize special scriptures that relate to a coming special occasion in your family. If it works better with your family's schedule, plan to hold scripture reading at a certain time during the week and at different times on weekends.

For more ideas on how to involve toddlers, preschoolers, school-age children,

> ### SAMPLE FAMILY
> ### HOME EVENING OUTLINE
>
> - opening song
> - opening prayer
> - scripture, thought, poem, or short story
> - lesson
> - activity
> - closing prayer

and teens in family scripture reading, refer to pages 132–33, 147, 160, and 177.

FAMILY HOME EVENING

Families will be blessed when parents make it a habit to hold a weekly family home evening to teach, strengthen, and have fun with their families. Family home evening may include family prayer, gospel instruction, hymns and Primary songs, and family activities. The Church produces lessons and other materials for families to use in their family home evenings. Church magazines are also helpful resources.

Hold family home evening every week, preferably on Monday evenings, even if it only lasts a few minutes. You may prefer to have a lesson on Sunday evening and an activity on Monday evening. Church leaders have asked us to keep Monday evenings free from all activities so families can use this time to be together.

If the father is present in the home, he presides at family home evening. If no father is in the home, the mother presides. Both parents conduct family home evening or assign another family

LESSON MATERIALS

The following are materials you can use to create family home evening lessons:

- the scriptures
- personal experiences
- personal testimonies
- *Gospel Principles*
- *Gospel Fundamentals*
- Church magazines, especially issues of the *Ensign* containing general conference messages
- *Family Home Evening Resource Book*
- *The Family: A Proclamation to the World*
- *The Living Christ: The Testimony of the Apostles*
- *Duties and Blessings of the Priesthood,* Parts A and B
- *The Latter-day Saint Woman,* Parts A and B
- *Our Heritage: A Brief History of The Church of Jesus Christ of Latter-day Saints*
- *Family Guidebook*
- *A Member's Guide to Temple and Family History Work*
- *Gospel Art Kit*
- *Hymns of The Church of Jesus Christ of Latter-day Saints*
- *Home Spun Fun* (FHE CD-ROM vols. 1 and 2)

Copies of these and other materials may be purchased through Church distribution centers, service centers, and on the Church's Web site. The assistant ward clerk over materials can also help members order these items.

Be sure to make many of your lessons center on the life, teachings, and atonement of the Savior by reading the scriptures and discussing gospel topics. Always offer an abundance of attention and love.

---

member to do so. Every family member should be able to participate. For instance, parents and older children may give the lesson while younger children lead the music, sing, play games, answer questions, hold pictures, pray, or pass out and eat refreshments. Keep your lesson simple and short.

Ideas for Family Home Evening Lessons

The following are some ideas to help you create family home evening lessons:

- Take turns presenting lessons from the manual.
- Read and discuss the scriptures.

• Invite the missionaries over.

• Write in journals.

• Make a list of goals and the steps needed to accomplish them.

• Read a book together.

• Record a tape or make a video for family history.

• Read and discuss a Church magazine article.

• Research a gospel question.

• Read and discuss patriarchal blessings.

• Write letters, send e-mails, or call members of the extended family.

• Work on genealogy.

• Write to missionaries.

• Learn about self-sufficiency in such areas as auto repair, cooking, decorating, yard work, food storage, and home maintenance.

• Read and discuss the First Presidency message, visiting teaching message, conference talks, or next week's Sunday School lesson.

• Write a tribute to an ancestor to be read at the next family reunion.

• Work on family memory books.

• Create a library of lessons, talks, books, or other resources.

• Invite a nonmember family to your home one evening.

• Select one problem area for your family that causes conflict and search the scriptures and other good resources for solutions.

• Ask what aspect of life is most challenging to your spouse and children and discuss ways you can be more supportive.

• Ask your spouse and children what makes them feel loved. Actively search for ways to express your love in the ways they most appreciate.

Effective Family Discussions

Because many enjoyable family home evenings involve a discussion of some kind, it may be helpful to review the elements that contribute to an interesting and worthwhile discussion:

• Begin with prayer.

• Establish a good atmosphere.

• Decide on a topic or take turns presenting a topic.

• Be sincerely interested in others' points of view.

• Apply what you're discussing to your personal life.

• Listen.

• Share ideas.

• Ask questions.

• Answer questions.

• Don't monopolize the time.

• Allow all family members to have their own point of view.

• Avoid contention.

• Remember the purpose of the discussion is to draw you closer as a family and learn more about the gospel of Jesus Christ.

• Summarize.

• Help reach a conclusion.

• Evaluate the discussion.

Activity Ideas for Family Home Evening

Well-chosen activities that bring your family closer, strengthen your love, and help you feel closer to Heavenly Father are always appropriate for family home evening. The following are some ideas for worthwhile activities:

• Visit temple grounds.

- Paint a room.
- Go on splits with the missionaries.
- Wash windows.
- Watch a movie.
- Plan a vacation.
- Sing.
- Visit the library.
- Go for a walk.
- Ride bicycles.
- Hold a combined family home evening with extended family.
- Visit a museum.
- Wash the car.
- Refinish furniture.
- Share family home evening with another family.
- Dance to golden oldies.
- Plant, weed, or harvest a garden.
- Bake goodies for the neighbors.
- Play a game.
- Fly a kite.
- Watch a sunset.
- Develop a family hobby.
- Put a puzzle together.
- Attend a cultural activity.
- Perform a service project.
- Donate blood.
- Clean up local roadways, parks, beaches, and community centers.

- Go on a flip-the-coin hike (heads we go right, tails we go left).
- Make a family quilt.
- Hold a family talent show.
- Put together a family puppet show.
- Make and wear family T-shirts.
- Keep a family journal up-to-date.
- Tell an around-the-family-circle story.
- Keep little hands busy with cutting or clay while holding a discussion with older children.
- Go on a picnic.
- Go camping.
- Clean the yard.
- Go swimming.

Locations for Family Home Evening

To make family home evening interesting, try holding it in the following locations:

- outside on the lawn
- around the table
- in a circle on the floor
- in one child's room
- on Mom and Dad's bed
- at the park
- at the library
- at the temple

For additional ideas on how to involve toddlers, preschoolers, school-age children, and teens in family home evening refer to pages 133–34, 147, 157–60, and 176–77.

Family Councils

Parents can call family members together for a family council at any time and any place. Family councils can be used to set goals, resolve problems, discuss finances, make plans, and give support and strength to each other. Family councils can be used for scheduling family commitments and activities for the coming week. Family councils can be held in connection with family home evening or at other times.

SPIRITUAL FAMILY LIVING

Of all the work you do in an effort to help "perfect the saints," none is more important than the work you do in your individual home. A family working toward spiritual wellness begins with a spiritually healthy couple. A loving, happy marriage doesn't just happen; it takes work, mutual toleration, time exclusively dedicated to each other, and lots and lots of unconditional love. It takes mutual goals, frequent kind words, the ability to be humble and grateful, continued courting, and a desire to forgive and bless each other by keeping covenants made with God.

The family is pivotal in God's plan for the destiny of his children. A family seeking to connect with heaven and fulfill God's plan will welcome children into the world, work to provide those children with the basics that sustain life, find regular reasons to celebrate, encourage creative expression, dedicate time for each other, and teach and live the gospel.

THE SAFE HARBOR CALLED HOME

A spiritually centered family life includes time for solitude and meditation for each family member. There is an art to selecting uplifting music, wholesome recreation, welcoming nature's healing and finding refreshment in quiet reverent places in the home and in the heart. Seek for simplicity and find ways to untangle your family from too many lessons, too many extracurricular activities, too much materialism, and too many commitments. Let go of the world and listen to your heart. Find time to let nature nurture your soul. Eat, pray, and play together. Talk, touch, and take time for each other. Support, harbor, and comfort each other.

Spirituality is not reserved for the three-hour block of meetings at church on Sunday. Spirituality is the connecting of your physical and spiritual self. Spirituality is about *who* you are, not *what* you are. *Who* you are before God, stripped of all titles, roles, and responsibilities, is what you bring to your home and your children.

REMEMBERING YOUR SENSE OF HUMOR

A spiritually centered family life also includes time for laughter and silliness. A sense of humor is perhaps your most important sense. After all, you don't experience true joy on a smooth celestial highway. To experience joy, you have to experience its opposite. Without opposition, sorrow, and pain, there are no hills to ascend, no thrills to anticipate, no rewards to work for, and no true joy to experience.

Humor is an effective way to manage the daily stress of family life and prevent mother burnout. Stress is actually caused by our perception of events, not the events themselves. You can't control what happens to you; but with a healthy dose of humor, you can control your *perception* of what happens to you.

Research has shown that people who laugh frequently decrease the stress hormones in their body and increase the body's ability to defend against diseases. People who are sour and gloomy exacerbate their illnesses and shorten their life spans. Mothers striving for spiritual wellness in their families should look at stress as a challenge or opportunity for growth rather than a negative event.

Changing Your Attitude

It isn't always easy to reverse a bad mood, dark thoughts, or the evil choices of others. But you can change the way you feel by changing the way you think. Grateful people are healthy people. Happy people are spiritual people. Joy comes when you're paying greater attention to all the things you're grateful for instead of all your problems.

One major complaint of children today is that their mothers are boring. Children long for playfulness and almost always resent a bad case of "hardened attitude."

WHAT IF I RISK IT ALL?

What if
I risk it all,
Give my love
And
It's not returned?
Should I hold back,
Measure my love,
Take inventory
Of my heart,
Tally and measure,
Calculate
How much love
To give
By
How much love
Comes back?
Shall I cling to remnants
Of what used to be
So I won't fall
Into the darkness
Where
There is nothing to cling to,
No map to follow
Home?

Fall.
Leap
Into the darkness.
Don't be afraid.
Love
With all your heart and soul.
Don't look back
Without outstretched arms.
Fly.
Find the light.
Face the mystery.
Loving hands
Will
Guide you home.

Look into your children's eyes and be touched by them. See what wonderful individuals they are. Open your heart to them, be vulnerable, learn what they have to teach you, and laugh with them.

Every season of family life is filled with good times and bad times. You get to live each time only once before it's gone. Whether you're a new parent coping with an insomniac infant or a hearing-impaired parent of a stereo-blasting teen, each season cries out for your attention, regard, and appreciation.

Sure, heaven will be wonderful, but so is life right now. There is more joy and wonderment in your life right now than you are willing or able to enjoy. Loosen up; you're not in control of anything or anybody except you and your attitude. The joy of life is the ride. Refuse to be intimidated by reality. It is with gratitude that you get a God's-eye view of your life.

ALLOWING YOUR CHILD TO LEAD YOU

In a spiritually healthy home, mothers let their children become their teachers. After all, children live in the present and take spontaneous delight in today. Watch a small child for an hour and count how many times he laughs, cries, or giggles. When Christ told you to become as a little child, I think that included emulating their obvious delight and enjoyment of life and their spontaneous ability to find a good laugh or cry in almost every situation.

As a mother you will too often live life in the driver's seat by continually gazing in the rearview mirror. The space and time you see in that mirror has already been traveled through. You need to glance into the past occasionally, but you'll crash if you leave your eyes there.

A spiritually healthy family has a mother who really believes that all things will work together for her good, even the awful things. Sincerely believe that common everyday events are out there to do you good, to add to your experience and ultimate joy.

OPPORTUNITIES TO BLESS AND BE BLESSED

NEIGHBORLINESS

As you and your family work and grow together, you will find innumerable opportunities to bless others and receive blessings yourself. This is one of the great benefits of service in the family and the Church,  and is something no family should miss out on.

You can start by simply being neighborly. Being neighborly means treating each person in the world with the same love and respect you give yourself. Teach your children to think of each other as neighbors. Family members are neighbors who must figure out how to live with, love, and forgive those with whom they spend the most time. Of course, neighborliness also includes a sustained effort to know and care about the people who live next to you. It is the awareness that all of us on this planet are brothers and sisters.

Children learn warmth, friendliness, and humanity from parents who live with love—for themselves, for each other, for their own family, and for all of God's children. Teach your child to be the first to be friendly. Encourage her to look out for the new student at school. Give her opportunities to learn to know and love a wide variety of people from all different backgrounds.

Encourage your child to travel and see the world and study about other cultures and countries. Encourage her to take foreign language classes and study about other religions.

VISITING TEACHING

Visiting teaching is one way mothers in the Church can help the Savior administer to the needs of God's children, especially his daughters. You are invited to love, teach, and serve your assigned sisters by visiting them at least once a month. You are instructed to seek the Spirit and teach doctrine from the scriptures and church leaders. But what does this have to do with being a mother? The way you go about your visiting teaching will become a model for your child on how to serve and love strangers.

The way you perform as a visiting

teacher will teach your child how you feel about serving people when you have nothing to gain for yourself. Get your children involved as you serve the sisters who are assigned to you. Make friends with their families and provide opportunities for your children to play together. Your children can help you prepare meals for the sisters you visit teach. They can deliver notes of love, they can drop off cookies or play with the children of those you visit teach while you care for them in your home.

Visiting teaching gives you the chance to practice loving your neighbor as yourself whether you feel like it or not. Perhaps we are given this assignment of neighborliness because most of us don't do it very well without an assignment. But in time, if you do it right, you'll be able to be loving and friendly spontaneously and your children will catch the vision.

As you go about your duties as a visiting teacher, don't gripe. Have a positive attitude. Let your children see your excitement. Let them hear you pray for your sisters. Show them that visiting teaching is a priority by going every month to every sister.

PRIESTHOOD BLESSINGS

Members of the Church have the opportunity to receive special priesthood blessings throughout their life. These blessings include your baby blessing, blessings given when you are sick or troubled, your patriarchal blessing, and the blessings you receive when you are ordained and set apart to serve the Lord in a church calling.

Work with your husband (or, if you are single, with a home teacher or bishop) to teach your children about the miracles, strength, and healing that come from priesthood blessings. Explain to your children that the priesthood is given to righteous men on earth and is the power to act in the name of God. When we receive priesthood blessings, it is as if God himself is administering to us.

Encourage your children to seek for blessings when they are sick. Teach them that consecrated oil is pure olive oil that has been dedicated and set apart for the purpose of anointing those who are ill. Let them witness an anointing and sealing, where a Melchizedek Priesthood holder places a small amount of consecrated oil on the top of a sick person's head and anoints the oil with a short prayer. Then two or more Melchizedek Priesthood holders lay their hands on the person's head and seal the anointing, offering blessings of healing and counsel to the sick.

Let your children witness other special blessings, such as father's blessings, baby blessings, blessings given at ordinations, and blessings given for peace and understanding. Teach them that the person who is blessed must exercise faith in the power of Heavenly Father and Jesus Christ. Not everyone is healed after a priesthood blessing because God knows what's best. Sometimes blessings work to bring comfort and remind individuals of how much Heavenly Father loves them. Children of all ages need to witness, take part in, and receive blessings throughout their lives.

PATRIARCHAL BLESSINGS

A patriarchal blessing is a priesthood blessing that a patriarch gives to worthy members of the Church. This inspired blessing declares your lineage and gives you counsel and insight about your life. When your child is mature enough to understand what a patriarchal blessing is, and when he desires to receive his, he may schedule an interview with the bishop to receive a recommend. Then he will contact the patriarch for an appointment. He may wish to fast and pray in preparation for his blessing. Mothers and fathers or other immediate family members are usually allowed to be present.

Explain to your child that blessings usually have several parts. The Lord, through the patriarch, will tell him from which tribe of Israel he is descended. He will talk to him about his life mission and give other blessings, advice, and precautions. A blessing will not answer all the questions he may have about future events.

Patriarchal blessings are sacred and personal. Explain to your child that he should talk about his blessing only at special times or when prompted by the Holy Ghost. Family members can discuss their blessings with each other. Make sure your child knows that the fulfillment of the blessings is conditional on his keeping the commandments and being true to the covenants he has made. A patriarchal blessing is a personalized gift from the Lord that should be read and pondered often.

THE BLESSINGS OF PRIESTHOOD POWER

The priesthood can be a great comfort and blessing to mothers in the Church. Although women do not hold the priesthood themselves, the priesthood presents women with the opportunity to be endowed with power from on high, to be sealed eternally to their spouses, to have their children eternally sealed to them, and to receive all the blessings and promises associated with celestial glory and exaltation.

The ordinances of the priesthood bless people of all ages. Prepare your children for them and for partaking of the great blessings that come from obedience to the Lord and membership in his church. Teach your children about the ordinances of the gospel, which include baptism, confirmation, administering and partaking of the sacrament, ordination to the priesthood, the endowment, and temple sealings. Explain that these ordinances must be authorized by a presiding authority—the bishop or stake president—and performed by a worthy and ordained Melchizedek Priesthood holder. (The blessing of a baby and the dedication of a grave are not saving ordinances but are done for the comfort, blessing, and uplift of Church members. They must be authorized by the presiding authority.)

CORE FAMILY VALUES

Every mother has a vital role to play in training the minds and hearts of her children toward good. You will be the one to assist your child in forming worthy habits. Yet it is mighty difficult to effectively teach anything you don't practice yourself. Ah, there's the rub—that's why motherhood is so humbling. You can't teach your child not to hit by spanking him. You can't teach your child to be honest if he hears you lie. You can't teach your child to have courage when you are controlled by your fears. You can't teach your child to work when you're idle. You can't teach your child to persevere when you give up when the going gets tough. You can't teach your child to forgive when he has never experienced forgiveness from you.

But—and here's the good part so you don't have to give up and get totally discouraged—you can effectively teach values you are *practicing* yourself.

All values are learned by *practice* and *example.* As you teach the gospel in your home, teach other core values as well. Being honest, working hard, accepting responsibility for actions, maintaining courage, persevering, and forgiving others are among the most important values a mother can teach. Others include developing gratitude, being hopeful and helpful, and educating yourself.

No matter the values you teach, however, don't ever forget that your children will ultimately learn to value the same things you do. Your child knows what you value most by where you spend your time. If you preach that you value one thing but your actions demonstrate that you value something else, your child will see the dishonesty and hypocrisy. It's impossible to live one value and preach another.

HONESTY

Teach your child to be honest and be honest in all your dealings with your child and others. English poet Alexander Pope wrote, "An honest man's the noblest work of God." Teach your children that part of their noble heritage and royal future depends on their honesty. Help your child understand that honesty means more than simply telling the truth. It means being true to themselves and honest about their motivations and effort; it means telling the whole truth and staying

away from things that are deceitful and dangerous.

Teach your child to put in an honest day's work, to refrain from being idle and wasting time. Remind your child that many of the rewards of honesty come much later in life and come in the form of a clean and clear conscience, not money, fame, or success.

WORK

Work is sustained physical, mental, or spiritual effort and the source of happiness, self-worth, and prosperity. Accomplishment in a particular activity is more often dependent on hard work and self-discipline than innate ability. Teach your children this principle early on in life. As she begins school, for example, and you feel tempted to reward good grades with money or achievements with material things, remind yourself of the value of hard work. Help your child understand that the work she does in school will be rewarded with greater understanding, with the ability to learn more, and with skills that will help her succeed later in life.

Happiness follows useful activity, whether it is physical or mental. Mothers are in a great position to help their children find and enjoy work. Work brings joy and fulfillment. Heavenly Father said *everyone* should work. When you work you feel useful and needed. The ability to work is a blessing.

Not everyone can be a genius. Few will ever have world-class talent. Yet there's one area where everyone can shine. After applying a heavy dose of elbow grease, everyone can reap the blessings that come from hard work. People who aren't afraid of hard work are the healthiest and happiest. So what's a mother to do when even the hint of hard work sends her children into hiding? Here are some ideas:

• If you want to teach your children to work, work with them and make work fun. Encourage and appreciate their efforts.

• Emphasize hard work over grades, popularity, money, or status.

• Find joy in work yourself. Do your household chores cheerfully.

• Give your children responsibilities that match their abilities.

• Do what you have to do cheerfully and with pride. Your child will pick up on your attitude.

• While you're working with your children, sing, play word games, tell stories, and whistle. The attitude you have toward work will affect your children's attitude toward work.

• Teach your children not to compare themselves to others and worry about how they measure up.

• Encourage your child to set goals for herself, work hard, and then measure her progress with God on an individual basis.

• Make the "Hard Worker Award" the most esteemed family honor. If you do not need to work for the necessities of life, then work to help those who cannot help themselves.

• Don't be too eager to spare your child the very things that will bring her the most satisfaction: the feeling of accomplishment and usefulness that follows a good day's work, even if it's hard work. (For more details on inspiring your children to work, see pages 195–202.)

RESPONSIBILITY

A responsible person takes responsibility for her own thoughts, words, and actions. She doesn't blame others for her mistakes, and she understands that her choices are creating the circumstances of her life. When something goes wrong, a responsible person responds by holding herself accountable— even when it is easier to excuse herself and blame someone else.

Exemplify this principle. Teach your

child to learn responsibility by giving him chores, allowing him to care for a pet, setting aside regular time for homework, encouraging him to participate in extracurricular activities, helping him find an after-school job, and performing volunteer work with him.

Hold your child responsible for his words and actions after making a mistake by showing him how to respond after the misdeed. Teach your child the law of the harvest. Plan for childhood experiences that teach your child how work and effort in the beginning bring desired results and accomplishment in the end.

COURAGE

Having courage doesn't mean you're never afraid. Being courageous is doing what you feel is right even when you are afraid. Courage is the will to press forward in difficult circumstances. Courage is choosing to keep commandments and covenants when you are tempted to break them. Courage is the power to act according to the light you've been given and speak when it is easier to remain silent.

Teach your child courage by providing regular new experiences for her. Let your child see you do things that scare you. Praise your child for her efforts, not for the outcome. Give your child the opportunity to do difficult things like climb a mountain, give a talk in church, or learn to ride a bicycle. Give your child lessons in useful lifesaving skills. Give your child lessons in performance. Help your child develop her physical strength by regular family physical exercise.

Teach your child to have the courage to keep commandments and covenants by your example. Teach her to speak up for truth by your example. Teach her to face life's challenges by the way you face yours. Teach her to do the right thing even when she is scared and alone.

PERSEVERANCE

Persistence is the key to accomplishing anything that matters. Perseverance is the ability to continue working for something even though it may be difficult or even impossible. All important things are accomplished by regular people who don't give up.

Stand with and behind your child when he attempts something difficult or new. Videotape your child each year to show him how much progress he's made in long-term ventures, such as learning to play a musical instrument or understand a new language. Show your child what happens when you don't give up by attempting something that is difficult for you and sticking with it.

Set and work toward worthy goals all

your life. Show your child that great things can be accomplished by small and simple means. Keep plugging along every day with a heart that never gives up on you or your child.

FORGIVENESS

Genuine and loving family relationships always require forgiveness. Forgiveness means you no longer carry bitter, angry, or resentful feelings about another person who has hurt you. Forgiveness means that you let these feelings go through a process that occurs over time with much prayer and personal introspection. Forgiveness is not a dramatic event that happens in one day.

Likewise, forgiveness is not connected to the offenders' repentance. Forgiveness means that *you* accept responsibility for how *you* feel, act, and respond and that you no longer desire to remain a victim. You allow yourself to heal regardless of the location or the attitude of the offender.

When you truly forgive you no longer give the offender the power to invade your thoughts and actions. You choose to stop caring about the offense and no longer use it as an excuse for your own poor behavior.

You don't have the authority to excuse the offender from repenting. You do have the power to name the offense, experience the healing that follows, and prevent the offense from happening again. When you are injured you can't demand or impose consequences on the offender any more than you can repent for the offender's actions. You can embark on the journey of forgiveness that brings peace of mind and joy. Here are a few things that can help you teach your children the principle of forgiveness:

• Set a good example by practicing forgiveness yourself. Forgive your children. Ask them to forgive you.

• Have a "repentance and forgiveness room," or even a small bench, where family members go to resolve small differences before they become large problems. When you hear your children having a heated argument about something, invite them into this work-it-out room with these instructions, "When you both feel satisfied about the resolution to this difference of opinion, you can come out." Use the bathroom or any other boring room where children who are fighting can't do much but attend to the resolution business at hand. It usually takes a while, but eventually both children will come out smiling.

• Most adult family members also have arguments. Unfortunately no one is there to send them into the bathroom until they both feel satisfied with the resolution. As a result, many families are plagued with multi-generational resentments, estrangements, and bitterness. Make the bitterness stop. Forgive your husband, parents, brothers and sisters, neighbors, and ward members. If your children are aware of the problem—and most are—let them know

that you were wrong to hold a grudge and that you love others enough to let go of your resentment and love anyway.

• Teach your children that when someone takes something from you (such as your pride, peace, possession, innocence, or health) and doesn't give it back or attempt to make restitution, you have three choices: (1) You can spend your life tending to the unpaid debt and dreaming about all the things you'd do if the debt were paid; (2) You can use the debt as an excuse and feel justified about carrying around resentful feelings; or (3) you can write off the loan, absorb the loss, and get on with the business of today.

• Teach your child that if she forgives the debt, she frees herself, not the debtor.

• Teach your child that when she forgives the debt, she does not send the debtor the message that she somehow is off the hook. She frees herself from the burden of keeping track of the debt. She no longer gives the debtor power to invade her thoughts and actions. She is free to act, not react, and live her life without resentment and bitterness.

• Teach your child that forgiveness doesn't mean the forgiver merely *pretends* the relationship with the offender is normal or even that a relationship exits at all. Forgiveness changes the forgiver's heart, thoughts, and behavior.

• Teach your child that no one ever has the right to do wrong to another human being, even when wrong has been done to him.

• Teach your child that when you say, "I forgive," it means, "I let it go." Forgiveness allows healing regardless of the location or the attitude of the offender.

PROCLAIMING THE GOSPEL

TRAINING FUTURE MISSIONARIES

Every member of the Church has been asked to take the restored gospel to every nation, kindred, tongue, and people in the world. Missionary work gives all people an opportunity to hear and accept or reject the gospel. Yet effective missionaries don't appear out of nowhere. They have to be trained—preferably at home.

TEACH YOUR CHILD HOW TO LOVE PEOPLE

Perhaps the best way to prepare your child to be a missionary is to teach him to love people. Learning to love family members is an excellent training ground. Look for ways to help your child feel and demonstrate love for his parents and siblings. Encourage secret acts of service. Point out good qualities in each of your children.

Another way to teach your child to love people is to discuss the differences and similarities of all people around the world. Do away with bias or prejudice you may have against any race or group of people. Never judge a large group of people or a country by the actions of a few.

Help your child overcome shyness and learn to be friendly. Give him opportunities to serve other people. Consider inviting nonmembers to activities and meetings in your family or ward. Encourage family members to fulfill their responsibilities as home or visiting teachers.

TEACH YOUR CHILD CHURCH HISTORY AND DOCTRINE

Your child needs to learn about Church history, organization, and doctrine.

Encourage your child's attendance at church, but don't neglect parental teaching at home during family home evening and the normal course of the day. Study all the scriptures as a family with a student guide to provide added insight into the historical events surrounding the revelations.

Encourage your child to attend seminary and discuss what she is learning at home. Become a student of Church history and doctrine to learn for yourself and to set a good example for your child.

ENCOURAGE THE BEARING OF TESTIMONY

Make it family practice to share testimonies. If your child has the chance to hear and practice bearing her testimony in the small, intimate circle of your family, she will be better able to bear testimony to strangers or large groups of people. Ask your child how she feels about Jesus. Consider holding family testimony meetings in special places when you travel. Teach your child to close her talks with her personal testimony.

ENCOURAGE PERSONAL AND FAMILY SCRIPTURE READING

Another way to train a future missionary is to encourage personal and family scripture reading. Set an example for your child to follow. Make sure each child has his own set of scriptures. You might consider getting a list of scriptures that missionaries memorize and learn them as a family. Scripture study might consist of presenting a problem and then having family members look to the scriptures for a solution.

INVITE THE MISSIONARIES OVER

Children will be inspired by the examples of full-time missionaries. Invite returned missionaries into your home and have them share their experiences at a family home evening. Have the local missionaries over for dinner. Go on splits with the missionaries.

TEACH THE SKILLS
USED ON PREPARATION DAY

Help your child learn to organize his time, get up early, and work hard. Teach him how to be independent. When he is a missionary he will need to know how to wash and iron his own clothing, shine his shoes, shop for and prepare food, and clean his place of residence.

ENCOURAGE AND
PRACTICE PUBLIC SPEAKING

Help your child to prepare and practice giving talks at home and at church meetings. When possible, encourage her to take a public speaking class in school. Help her learn how to explain the gospel to other people by assigning her to give lessons in family home evening.

INITIATE A MISSIONARY
SAVINGS PLAN

Open and contribute to a missionary fund. Encourage your child to earn as much of the money to support himself on a mission as possible. As a family, you could choose to help support a missionary in your ward or in your extended family.

ENCOURAGE PARTICIPATION
IN TEMPLE WORK

Encourage your child to participate in temple work by performing baptisms for the dead at the nearest temple. Prepare her to receive her endowment by explaining the significance of the covenants she will be making with God and the promises God makes in return.

ENCOURAGE YOUR CHILD TO
TAKE A FOREIGN LANGUAGE
CLASS AT SCHOOL

Any language training your child receives will help him if he is called to a foreign mission. Even if your child is not called to a foreign mission, a second language will be a great benefit to him all his life.

VIEW VIDEOS, READ BOOKS, AND ATTEND CLASSES THE CHURCH PROVIDES

The Church makes available many good books, videos, and classes for missionary preparation. Make yourself aware of the opportunities currently available to your family and take advantage of them.

INVITE YOUR CHILD TO BE FAMILIAR WITH PRIESTHOOD BLESSINGS

Make priesthood blessings available in your home. Let your child see and participate in blessings given to the sick and father's blessings when she starts school, leaves home, experiences a major change, or has a difficult decision to make.

REDEEMING THE DEAD

Each child born into the world has a place in history. Each child has a mother and a father. Each of those parents has a mother and father, and so on and so on. It doesn't matter if your child's history is particularly noteworthy because, good or bad, that history is uniquely his. From the moment he is born, your child enters this world with ties to the past. His life will constitute his own unique link to the future. As a mother you have the responsibility to teach your child about his own history, to encourage him to live worthy of his ancestors' names, and to help him develop a desire to serve his ancestors through family history and temple work.

A FAMILY HISTORY

YOUR PERSONAL HISTORY

You may not ever do anything that will mean more to your child than leaving an honest, open account of your life for her to read. Take the time to record the events of your life in a short history or journal. So many memories are lost when mothers don't take the time to write them down.

Be as open and honest as you can possibly be. Your weaknesses and struggles will endear you to your child, for she, too, will face her own struggles. Your inner thoughts, dreams, and wishes will help her bond with you beyond the grave.

You can leave a video of yourself speaking, along with pictures and tours of your childhood home. You can take pictures of schools and siblings and leave a treasure box filled with old keepsakes.

Take the time to record your testimony of the gospel of Jesus Christ in written, audio, or video form.

Stories are a timeless means of communicating and carrying on a legacy. Don't forget to tell your life story for your posterity. Though you may consider yourself uninteresting, you are an original for those who will follow. Your life is their personal link to the past, their gift to build upon.

YOUR EXTENDED FAMILY

Children are better able to develop a sense of individuality when they know where they come from. Every family tradition your child participates in, every family recipe he eats, every word he hears pronounced uniquely becomes part of his sense of family and identity.

Your child will have a richer childhood if you live near relatives. Every family has quaint or bizarre members. Every family has cousins that you love and those who are a bit more difficult to appreciate. Yet every family reunion gives your child a sense of who he is and where he came from. Don't impoverish your child with a family-less childhood. When aging siblings get together, they talk about the good old days. Children love to hear what their parents were like when they were small.

Healthy extended family members give your child a support system or cheering section. Your child deserves grandparents, aunts, uncles, and cousins who mill around in the background of the special events in his life. On the other hand, every family has black sheep and shameful experiences. Don't feel you have to protect your child from the truth. Protect your child from hidden resentments, lies, and multi-generational problems by throwing open the family truth door, no matter how painful, and letting in the light of understanding and forgiveness.

Encourage your child to love and forgive flawed family members even if they are annoying, difficult, or strange. If you are not able to have an ongoing relationship with your extended family because of continuing abuse, you can still teach your child to forgive and love those family members.

YOUR CHILD'S HISTORY

How much of your child's history do you really want to leave to memory? If you think your memory could use a little help, then try starting a personal history for your child. If all you can see when you hear the words "personal history" are stacks of empty diary pages and boxes of old unorganized certificates, then the following list might be what you need to get going.

• **Keep a written journal for your child.** Even before your child is born, you can purchase a journal and begin the entries. Write about your feelings, your pregnancy, and your circumstances. After the baby arrives, write about her birth, her firsts, holidays, and birthdays. This journal can be given as a gift to your child when you feel it is time that she can continue it on her own.

• **Start a memory quilt.** An unusual but comfortable way of remembering, a memory quilt can be either put together with scrap pieces from your child's old clothing or embroidered with names, dates, and pictures of important times for your child.

• **Keep a memory box.** Get a trunk or special box of some kind in which to keep christening outfits, toys, quilts, booties, or anything that is important to your child. This is a good place for gifts or keepsakes from grandparents.

• **Create a "This is Your Life" presentation.** Use audio and video recorders to record your feelings for your unborn child as well as the child's first cry, laugh, party, or prayer. As your child grows older, interview her teachers, friends, church leaders, siblings, and parents. Ask them to make positive or humorous comments about your child and relate experiences they have had together.

• **Make a memory book.** Take lots of pictures of everything. When creating a memory book, include pictures of your child as well as of yourself, grandparents, friends, and brothers and sisters. Write names and dates under each picture. You can keep your child's memory book when she is small. When your child gets old enough, let her take over making her own memory book.

• **Use your own talents.** Embroider, paint, write a song, create a model of your child's hand, or use any other variety of your talents to prepare a unique remembrance of your child's history. Think of something you can do and like to do. Don't try to do everything. Pick one idea that is best suited for you and then keep with it.

TEMPLE BLESSINGS

Teach your child that he can receive sacred ordinances and enter into covenants with God when he makes himself worthy to attend the temple. These ordinances and covenants are necessary for him to be exalted in the celestial kingdom. They are, in fact, necessary for every person who desires exaltation in the highest kingdom of God.

Your child should be encouraged to participate in the worthy endeavor of redeeming his dead. Teach him how to research family names and

important dates, such as birth, marriage, death, and burial dates. Contact your ward's family history specialist to learn how to use your membership record number and a password provided through your ward clerk to get online and view your family's ordinance history.

When your child turns 12, accompany him to the temple to perform baptisms for the dead. Teach your child about the temple and the ordinances performed there. See pages 275–277 for more information on preparing your child for temple attendance.

Temple work also includes keeping your personal and family records. Keep written records about you and your family. Save certificates of blessing, baptisms, ordinations, marriages and death in a secure place. Encourage your children to keep their own records when they are old enough.

THE BALANCING ACT OF FAMILY LIFE

An important purpose of the Church is to provide you and your family with opportunities to serve and be served as you work together to further the mission of the Church. Your calling in the ward, no matter what it is, will help you grow, learn, and receive blessings over and over again. For instance, while you are teaching your fellow sisters in Relief Society, other ward members are blessing your family by teaching your children in Primary, taking your sons on Scout camps, and providing service opportunities for your teenage daughter. Others are busy planning and hosting meaningful activities for your whole family to attend on a ward, stake, or regional basis.

Not only do you grow from accepting and magnifying the callings you receive, but other families in the ward are also

blessed and strengthened. Magnifying your callings gives you a chance to bless and uplift other ward members as they in turn bless and uplift you. Every family needs help, and every family needs to give help.

Of course, all of this may sometimes seem overwhelming. Balancing family and church activities takes patience, prayer, and prioritizing.

Don't forget to look for ways to involve your husband and children in your calling so they, too, will be blessed with experience in serving. While you should take care to fulfill your calling to the best of your ability, don't be afraid to suggest that planning meetings be held judiciously or during early-morning or late-night hours so they won't interfere with the precious few hours your family has to spend together. If your participation in your church calling is not serving your family well, counsel with your spouse and Father in Heaven and decide what you can do to improve the situation. Your bishop will appreciate you counseling with him as well.

TAKE ADVANTAGE OF CHURCH-SPONSORED TEACHING

The Church provides many opportunities for gospel instruction for your family members on a regular basis. Effective teachers and class discussions help you and your children learn and apply gospel principles if you're humble and teachable. Take the time to read lessons before you attend so you can be a better help and support for your teacher and a better student for yourself.

SUNDAY SCHOOL

In Gospel Doctrine, the weekly Sunday School class for adults, the Church offers curriculum based on one of the four standard works each year. Other adult Sunday School classes, such as Marriage and Family Relations, are also offered periodically. Teens also attend weekly Sunday School classes in their own age groups and follow a curriculum similar to that of the adults. You can initiate family discussions based on what you and your children learn each week in Sunday School.

RELIEF SOCIETY

The purpose of Relief Society is to assist priesthood leaders in carrying out the mission of the Church by helping sisters and families come unto Christ. The Relief Society helps sisters and their families receive all essential priesthood ordinances,

---

THE PURPOSE OF THE RELIEF SOCIETY

The Relief Society exists for the following reasons:

- to build faith in the Lord Jesus Christ and teach the doctrines of the kingdom of God
- to emphasize the divine worth of each sister
- to exercise charity and nurture those in need
- to strengthen and protect families
- to serve and support each sister
- to help sisters become full participants in the blessings of the priesthood

OFFICES IN THE PRIESTHOOD

Deacon

A baptized boy who is worthy may be ordained to the office of a deacon when he is 12. Deacons are assigned to pass the sacrament, act as ushers, keep church buildings and grounds clean, and collect fast offerings.

Teacher

A baptized and worthy boy of 14 can be ordained a teacher. Teachers have all the duties of the deacon as well as additional duties. Teachers usually serve as home teachers. Teachers also prepare the bread and water for the sacrament.

Priest

At the age of 16, worthy boys may be ordained to be priests. Priests have all the rights and duties of deacons and teachers as well as additional duties. A priest may baptize. He may also administer the sacrament. He can ordain other priests, teachers, and deacons. A priest may take charge of a meeting when no Melchizedek Priesthood holder is there.

Elder

All Melchizedek Priesthood holders are elders. They have the right to confirm baptized members to receive the gift of the Holy Ghost. Elders may conduct meetings, administer to the sick, give names and blessings to babies, and perform priesthood blessings for their family members and others who request it.

High Priest

A worthy Melchizedek Priesthood holder may be ordained to be a high priest when he is called to a bishopric, stake presidency, or high council. Older men who are faithful can also be ordained high priests without having one of the callings just mentioned. A high priest has the right to officiate in the Church and direct spiritual matters. The stake president leads the high priests quorum, with a leader assigned to each group of high priests in a ward.

keep the associated covenants, and qualify for exaltation and eternal life. Relief Society is for all women ages 18 and older and for women younger than 18 who are married.

The Relief Society offers Sunday lessons that are designed to draw you closer to the Savior and strengthen your faith in him. Lessons should also help you learn the gospel and apply its principles in your life.

Share your experiences and testimony during lessons. Make new friends and enjoy the feelings of unity and sisterhood.

On the first Sunday of the month the lesson is taught by a member of the ward Relief Society presidency. This lesson is geared to the immediate and individual needs of the sisters in the area. On the second and third Sundays of the month,

Seventy

A seventy is a worthy high priest who has a specific call to preach the gospel. Seventies help to administer the affairs of the Church throughout the world.

Members of the five Quorums of the Seventy serve under the First Presidency and the Quorum of the Twelve Apostles. Some are temple presidents or area presidents. Some are full-time servants of the Lord who have been asked to leave their professions and serve the Church. Others keep their jobs and serve in their own areas for three to five years under the direction of an area president.

Patriarch

Patriarchs are high priests who have been ordained on a stake level to give special patriarchal blessings to members of the Church. These blessings give members greater understanding of their unique gifts, their personal challenges, and their individual course through life. Patriarchal blessings declare lineage and are the word of God to individual members. A patriarch is called to serve for life.

Apostle

An apostle is a special witness of Jesus Christ to the whole world. Apostles administer the affairs of the Church. Those who are ordained to this office are usually set apart as members of the Council of Twelve. Each apostle is given the keys of the kingdom of God on earth, but only the senior apostle, who is president of the Church, actively exercises all keys.

Prophet

The prophet is the only man on the earth who is authorized to exercise all of the keys of the priesthood. When the prophet cannot function fully, his counselors carry on the work of the First Presidency. No decision comes from the First Presidency and the Quorum of the Twelve without total unanimity.

One man at a time is appointed to be the prophet and president of the Church. The prophet is God's mouthpiece and the one who acts in God's stead. The prophet receives the keys, or authority, from Jesus Christ and gives them to other members of the Church to baptize, preach the gospel, lay hands on the sick, preside, and teach. He gives others the authority to officiate in the ordinances of the temple and perform temple sealings.

Only the prophet has the right to declare new doctrine and receive revelations for the Church. The head of the Church is not the prophet, however. The head of the Church is Jesus Christ.

lessons are taught from the writings of the modern prophets. The lesson on the fourth Sunday is taken from recent general conference talks. It is helpful to have your own lesson schedule, lesson manual, and set of scriptures so you can read the lesson ahead of time and prepare to participate during class and then apply the principles discussed.

PRIMARY

Primary offers weekly classes on Sunday geared to young children ages three to 12. Nursery is provided for children ages 18 months to three years. Parents take their babies with them to other adult meetings until the children are eighteen months old. Children in Primary participate in music instruction, sharing time, and individual class instruction in separate age groups. Primary children have the opportunity to offer prayers, recite scriptures, and give talks in front of the group. They have the chance to bear testimony and participate in gospel-centered learning activities.

YOUNG WOMEN

The Young Women organization offers girls ages 12 to 18 Sunday class instruction during the same time as Relief Society and priesthood quorum instruction. The Young Women hold individual classes grouped by age.

YOUNG WOMEN VALUES

• faith
• divine nature
• individual worth
• knowledge
• choice and accountability
• good works
• integrity

In addition to Sunday lessons, young women have the opportunity to learn and grow through participation in a Personal Progress program. The Personal Progress program is designed to help your daughter learn and apply the teachings of Jesus Christ in her life, to prepare her to make and keep sacred temple covenants, and to arm her with the skills needed to strengthen her family.

The program uses seven values to help your daughter understand who she is, why she is here on earth, and what she should be doing to prepare to enter the temple. The program teaches her to make commitments and goals, follow through with them, and then report to a parent or leader.

When young women complete the Personal Progress program, they are eligible to receive the Young Womanhood Recognition award. To receive the award your daughter must:

• Live the standards in *For the Strength of Youth.*

• Complete six value experiences and one value project for each of the seven values.

• Keep a personal journal.

• Record her testimony of the Savior Jesus Christ.

As a mother, it is your privilege to work closely with your daughter to help her achieve her goals. Always remember that you are her principal teacher and leader, not the Young Women leader or adviser. You should work closely with your daughter and encourage her to make and complete worthy goals based on the seven values. Be available to discuss the goals and sign them off as she completes them. If she doesn't approach you first, approach her about Personal Progress and help her to become excited about this unique program.

PRIESTHOOD QUORUMS

Priesthood quorums offer Sunday instruction for males ages 12 and older. Young men holding the Aaronic Priesthood attend the class for deacons (ages 12 to 14), teachers (ages 14 to 16), or priests (ages 16 to 18). Men who are 18 years or older attend Melchizedek Priesthood quorums, either elders or high priests.

The priesthood gives worthy boys and men the authority to act for God and do his work on the earth. Worthy male members who hold the Aaronic Priesthood have the authority to administer the outward ordinances of faith, repentance, and baptism. Those holding the Melchizedek Priesthood have the power and authority to lead the Church and direct the preaching of the gospel in the world. They are in charge of the spiritual work of the Church. They direct the work done in temples and preside over wards, stakes, and missions.

Every priesthood holder belongs to a quorum. If the quorum is functioning well, all the members will be blessed, encouraged, fellowshipped, and taught the gospel by one another. Membership in a quorum of the priesthood continues for a lifetime.

Duty to God Award

As part of the Aaronic Priesthood program, your son will be asked to set worthy goals and standards in the Duty to God program. The Duty to God program is designed to help your son's personal growth in four areas:

- spiritual development
- physical development
- citizenship and social development
- educational, personal, and career development

Deacons, teachers, and priests can earn a Duty to God certificate during the two years they spend in each of the three quorums. After earning all three certificates, they earn the Duty to God award. To receive each certificate, your son must:

- regularly keep the priesthood duties and standards, which include: having daily personal prayer, living the standards in *For the Strength of Youth,* reading the scriptures, attending all church meetings, paying a full tithe, and participating actively in the priesthood responsibilities associated with his quorum (for example, passing the sacrament as a deacon, preparing it as a teacher, blessing it as a priest)
- complete a set number of family activities as detailed in the guidebook for his quorum
- complete a set number of quorum activities as detailed in the guidebook for his quorum
- complete eight or more personal goals in each of the four areas described earlier
- complete a Duty to God service project
- keep a personal journal

Work closely with your son as he sets goals and directs his efforts toward receiving the Duty to God award. Be willing to sign off goals and projects as he completes them. Read the guidebooks he will be given as he enters a new quorum on his 12th, 14th, and 16th birthdays. If he doesn't approach you first, approach him and help him get started in this valiant effort.

Encourage him to set goals that will bless his life and the life of others—goals that will lead him to the temple and service in the mission field. Help him apply the goals he sets as a Duty to God toward the Scouting program, as well. Encourage him to live the Scout oath, law, motto, and slogan.

GETTING YOUR HERD TO CHURCH

Most Mormon mothers have been crowned with the glorious opportunity of orchestrating the frantic race to get to church on time. And, no matter what time that is, this can be very difficult.

If you have the early schedule, you're required to get up with the chickens and fly as you drag your sleepy-eyed children out of bed and try to get them to hurry. (By the way, children have no idea what "hurry" means.)

If you get the middle schedule, you spend your time trying to decide if you should feed the kids lunch at 10 A.M. so you can make it to church at 11 or whether to wait until you get home at 2. Of course, the first alternative means the kids won't eat because they're not hungry, and the latter alternative means your young children will turn into raving monsters during sacrament meeting.

If you get the late schedule, forget about naps. You get to shake your child awake, then drag this delightful companion with you to church and spend three hours keeping him quiet.

And, despite all of this, it's inevitable that you will still make it to church one way or the other. That's what moms do after all. To make it a bit easier on yourself, try a few of these ideas:

- Get up earlier than your children to make sure that you are ready to go before they wake up. This will be tiring, but well worth the effort. It may also give you some quiet time to study the scriptures or begin your fast with a meaningful and uninterrupted prayer.
- Always bathe the children the night before.
- Assist your children in picking out their Sunday clothes and shoes—including things like ties, socks, tights, slips, etc.—on Saturday night so they know exactly what they're wearing beforehand.
- Assign an older child the task of getting a younger child ready.
- Make a schedule with your children of what has to happen and at what time. Post the schedule on the back of the bedroom door.
- If your children struggle to get up early, you may want to purchase an alarm clock to help them wake up. Preschoolers may think it's fun and important to have an alarm clock "just like Mom and Dad."
- Make sure the family gets to bed early on Saturday night.
- Pack "the bag" the night before. Include board books, crayons, coloring books, quiet activities, diapering items for the baby, and a few simple and relatively mess-free snacks.
- If you have the early schedule, make sure that breakfast is simple. Have some juice boxes or premade orange juice on hand. Give your kids breakfast bars or muffins or a bagel to eat so you don't have to take a lot of time to prepare breakfast. These items all make good 10 A.M. snacks to help stave off hunger if you have the 11 A.M. schedule.

Once you know when your meeting is supposed to start, your next challenge is to get there. Why do mothers with young children look as if they've just been through a war when they walk through the doors of the chapel? Because they have. And getting to church is only part of the problem. Keeping the kids quiet once you get there is another interesting part of keeping the Sabbath day holy.

Coping with Noisy Children

Going to church with young children is a workout. Try to remember, though, that little children *can't* be irreverent; they don't know enough. Little children are supposed to be noisy and wiggle a lot. They aren't trying to drive you crazy. It is their job to explore this big, wide, wonderful world. Your job is to keep them from killing themselves.

Being the creator of noisy, restless children is bound to teach you great humility. That humility will be perhaps the greatest attribute you gain in those early parenting years while you're struggling to make it to church on time and keep your little ones quiet so they won't disturb the worship service of others. You may not be able to hear many of the sermons or lessons given in church for a while. But you are learning something of great importance . . . you are learning the worth of a child . . . your own.

When all your children have grown and you're done wrestling with your own little ones, never *ever* forget that parents with young children at church need love, acceptance, and help. Remember what Jesus Christ said about little children, then look at those who are wrestling with their little ones as the greatest unheralded heroes of your ward.

The following are suggestions for keeping your children quiet during sacrament meeting:
* Sit together as a family.
* Sit close to the front row.
* Feed your children a snack and ask them to use the bathroom before leaving home.
* When you need to take children out during a meeting, take them to a boring place without toys or distractions.
* Ask an older couple to sit next to you and help if your husband has to sit on the stand or doesn't attend church with you.
* Focus on making church meetings a positive experience for your child. Do whatever you think is appropriate to keep your child entertained and quiet.

Quiet Toys

The following toys are quiet enough to not disturb others but interesting enough keep your young child occupied:
* magnets or magnetic paper dolls
* pipe cleaners
* crayons and paper
* *The Friend* magazine
* magic slate (like an Etch-a-Sketch® or a Magna Doodle®)
* old jewelry
* small flannel boards
* quiet books
* board books

SEMINARY

The Church's seminary program offers weekday classes for high school students from the ninth through the twelfth grades. Your sons and daughters will learn about all of the four standard works during the four years they attend classes. In some areas, high schools allow Latter-day Saint students released time from public school to attend seminary during the school day. Other areas hold seminary in the early morning hours before school begins.

INSTITUTE

Institute offers weekday classes on various religious topics of choice for students attending colleges and universities or working full time. Latter-day Saint young adults are encouraged to attend institute classes wherever they live to receive gospel instruction and attend social activities with other Latter-day Saints their own age.

PARTICIPATE WISELY IN CHURCH-SPONSORED SOCIAL ACTIVITIES

The Church provides members with a variety of worthwhile and wholesome activities to attend during the week. Look carefully at the needs of your individual family members when deciding which activities to attend.

Relief Society Activities. Home, Family, and Personal Enrichment Night is held once a month for all Relief Society sisters. These evenings include lessons and activities that provide instruction on principles of the gospel, skills for strengthening marriage, advice on parenting, and helpful ideas for homemaking and nurturing. Principles of spiritual, emotional, physical, and mental well-being are also taught, along with skills in provident living, self-reliance, and personal, family, and emergency preparedness.

Mutual. Aaronic Priesthood quorums and Young Women groups have weekly activities and service projects for boys and girls between the ages of 12 and 18. These activities are called Mutual. Some weeks the Young Women and Young Men meet separately, other weeks they meet together. Every week they should hold a combined opening exercise before the Mutual activity that provides a spiritual thought, a scripture, and a prayer to begin the planned event.

When the Young Men meet separately, the Mutual activity may also count as the Scouting activity for the week.

Children's Activities. The Primary offers quarterly activities for all children between the ages of three and 12. Girls and boys from eight to 12 years of age also participate in regularly scheduled Achievement Day and Cub Scout activities.

ATTEND CHURCH-SPONSORED MEETINGS OR GATHERINGS

SACRAMENT MEETING

Sacrament meeting is the most important meeting held outside your home during the week. Do everything you can to attend, no matter how hard it is to make it there. Sacrament meeting gives you the chance to renew your baptismal covenants by partaking of the sacrament, to worship through prayer and song, and to receive instruction. On the days when your efforts seem like too much work without any payoff, you might begin to wonder if you should even try to keep going to sacrament meeting. But don't give up! You and your family will be blessed by your attendance.

LEADERSHIP MEETINGS

Leadership meetings are typically held twice a year to teach ward leaders their duties, increase their abilities, and build their faith. Leadership training meetings are also held in connection with stake conference.

Priesthood holders attend a general priesthood session on the Saturday evening during general conference. The Relief Society and Young Women organizations also hold a meeting once a year.

Leadership meetings function to help Church members seek the Spirit and consider ways they might better apply gospel principles and organization objectives in their callings. Presidencies in all the auxiliaries also meet regularly to plan and seek the Spirit to bless those they lead.

If you are involved in leadership meetings of any kind, apply what you are learning to your leadership in the home as a mother. Listen carefully to counsel and decide to change one behavior or habit that is not working for you. Use every leadership meeting to give you insight into your own leadership abilities as a mother.

FIRESIDES AND DEVOTIONALS

Firesides and devotionals can be held on a family, branch, ward, stake, or regional level. These meetings are intended to enhance family life and encourage Christlike living. Firesides and devotionals are held to give you instruction, encouragement, and added motivation to keep the commandments.

Involve your children in firesides and devotionals when you feel it would add to the spirit in your home. If your children are too young to attend, apply the principles you learn there to help you be a better mother.

CONFERENCES

Adult and youth organizations in the Church offer the added resources of annual or semi-annual conferences for Church members. These include youth conference, super activity days for young men and young women, special gatherings for Relief Society sisters, and any other event that brings groups together for more than a couple of hours to focus on serving and learning. If you have concerns in your family life that you would like help with, let your leaders know so they can plan conferences that are more helpful. Your ward can plan family preparedness fairs, employment fairs, skills expositions, parenting workshops, or any number of other events.

Stake conference, regional conferences, and general conference are annual and semi-annual meetings that Church members attend in place of the normal three-hour block on Sundays. These meetings should be approached with prayerfulness and an open heart, for they are times to receive answers, guidance, and counsel from the Lord's anointed. Don't be tempted to make times such as general conference weekend a vacation for your family. Instead, teach your children to look forward to hearing from the prophet and learning what it is specifically that your family can do to serve the Lord in the next six months.

SPIRITUAL GROWTH FOR MOM

DON'T NEGLECT YOUR OWN GROWTH

Mothers often face a number of challenges when it comes to their own spiritual growth. Sick children often cut down on church attendance. Pregnancy and nursing frequently preclude fasting. Small children can make church attendance grueling and leave the mother little chance to listen to or participate in meetings. And with little ones in the home, time and privacy are at a premium, making personal scripture study, prayer, or meditation difficult.

The following are some potential challenges and what can be done to help:

SPORADIC CHURCH ATTENDANCE BECAUSE OF SICKNESS

Try not to put the responsibility for your spiritual growth solely on church attendance. When you need to stay home

because of illness (yours or your children's), continue to make Sunday a day to feed your spirit. Read and study the lesson—along with your scriptures—you would have heard in Sunday School and Relief Society. Listen to uplifting music. You might want to wear your Sunday clothing. Ponder your baptismal covenants and mentally review your blessings. Ask your spouse or older child to take notes of or tape record all the speakers. Pray more sincerely. The Aaronic priesthood in your ward may be willing to come to your home with the sacrament if you're down for a long time due to bed rest or a chronic illness.

NOT BEING ABLE TO FAST BECAUSE OF PREGNANCY AND NURSING

Going without food is not the only way to fast. When you can't fast for medical reasons, determine to keep food preparation to a minimum. Eat only simple foods that take no preparation, such as milk, bread, and cheese. Make an effort to open and close your fast day with purpose and prayer. Pay your fast offering. Sing or listen to the hymns. Pay particular attention to the sacrament songs. Prayerfully determine

a purpose to your "fast." Don't feel guilty for not "fasting" in every sense of the word. Remember that your body is nourishing and protecting a child of God, which is a sacrifice worthy of many blessings.

SERVING IN THE PRIMARY OR YOUNG WOMEN

If you miss attending Relief Society because of a calling in the Primary or Young Women, read and study the lessons you miss or ask the Relief Society presidency to tape record the lessons for you to listen to later. Attend enrichment night even if you don't attend Sunday lessons. And keep in mind that once you're able to attend Relief Society again you may just find yourself longing to go to Primary or Young Women classes.

FINDING TIME FOR PERSONAL MEDITATION

When your children are young, use naptime and their bedtime for your own personal "work." Read the Church magazines or your scriptures. Study for your Sunday lessons. Occasionally sit in the rocking chair, gaze out the window, and

SIMPLIFY

There are so many things I want to do
And not enough time in the day.
Maybe I could put life on hold
So I could stop and play.
But summer's almost over
And the leaves are turning brown.
It seems like yesterday I was dressed
In my wedding gown.
Now my life's a whirl of needs—
I feel like I'm running in a race.
But I can't see the finish line,
I feel like I might break.
Where do you search for answers?
Where do you find peace of mind?
What is truly treasure,
Where is the diamond mine?
He said, consider the lilies
Neither do they toil or do they spin.
Yet Solomon in all his glory
Can't compare to this floral hymn.
I think I've found the diamond mine
Right in my own backyard.
Help me, Lord, to simplify
Before I cross the bar.

meditate. Forget about rushing around the house picking up toys, washing dishes, and dusting. Instead, feel refreshed and ready to handle the demands of life with small children the rest of the day by feeding and giving rest to your soul.

No matter what age your children are, you still need the time to think, ponder, and pray. Go for a walk or a drive alone. Take the time to write in your journal or work on family history. Give yourself the gift of solitude, even if for only a few minutes a day.

Learn what fills your reserve of strength and don't feel guilty when you are alone replenishing your supply. Even mothers need time out. You are re-filling yourself so you have something to draw from when you return. You don't have to irrigate the whole field; a small garden will do. You can't water anything from an empty cup.

FINDING TIME TO PRAY

You may be holding family prayer every morning and night in addition to mealtime blessings and couple prayer. You may be helping your children with their personal prayers and praying before scriptures and family home evening, but if you forget your personal prayers, you will feel that something is missing in your life.

You can set aside a special time in the morning or evening for personal prayer, but don't forget that you can pray any time you want to. Pray while washing the dishes, changing a diaper, or taking a shower. Pray in the car, in the bedroom, or in the backyard. Pray as if your life depended on it. It does. Pray as if you needed help all the time. You do.

FINDING TIME TO ATTEND THE TEMPLE

Make a commitment to go to the temple as often as possible. Many couples try to attend once a month. Do whatever works best for your family. Swap baby-sitting services with another couple in the ward or call on young women in your ward to tend. If you can't afford a baby-sitter, ask the ward Young Women president for the name of a girl who will be willing to donate her services while you attend the temple. If possible, purchase your own temple clothing. Don't let anything keep you from the enlightenment and blessings that come from attending the temple.

Remember, however, that there are seasons in life that will make temple attendance more difficult. When you find yourself in one of these seasons, don't feel guilty about your priorities. Many moms, for example, find it hard to attend the temple as regularly as they'd like during the months when they're nursing a baby around the clock. Other moms live hours away from a temple and can't regularly leave their very small children with sitters for longer periods of time. Eventually the season will change and you will be able to devote more time to temple attendance; so save your guilt for something else and look forward to the time when your situation changes—as it inevitably will—and you can spend hours and hours in the temple every week.

FINDING TIME TO READ THE SCRIPTURES AND CONFERENCE TALKS

Try placing your scriptures and church magazines in the bathroom for quick readings. Place your scriptures next to the side of your bed and read before you go to sleep. Carry a set of scriptures or the conference talks in your purse. When you are waiting in the doctor's office or in line at the bank, read a few verses or a talk or two.

THE TOO-TOO-BUSY-BUG

As you add more and more children and commitments to your life, you will often long for a simpler life. Most mothers long for a sense of peace in their busy lives. Give yourself official permission to let go of the need to do more and instead learn to do *less with more love.*

When I have to play the piano or organ in church, I can miss a few notes with my left hand and no one notices, as long as I keep the melody going with my right hand. Being a mother is like that. The real trick is to learn what notes are the melody in family life and what notes can be selectively dropped without losing the beauty of the song. Family life can't really be balanced, for true balance is impossible from moment to moment. If you learn what is necessary for love—the melody—you can find true harmony.

Think about feeding your spirit by simplifying your life in three ways.

First try to remember to simplify your outward life by shedding. This includes continually cleaning out your garage, storage rooms, or closet and getting rid of everything that is not your friend. Shed possessions. Keep a simple hairstyle and wardrobe. Shed relationships that aren't healthy. Shed the need to keep your house and yard tidy at the price of spending time with your children. Shed unnecessary debt, work, busy-ness, and ambition.

Second, simplify your inward life. Give yourself quiet time alone for contemplation without interruption. Go for walks and pay attention to the beauties all around you or look up at the stars at night. Let prayer become a running dialogue with your maker. Read scriptures and good books and study to learn something new. Be playful. Work in the yard, do the dishes, fix a meal, or sort the laundry with a simplicity of heart that comes from gratitude. See homemaking and soul caring as the greatest of all art.

Simplifying your inward life includes continually thinking of all the things you're grateful for. Become an inverse paranoid by truly believing that every life event and every person you deal with is out there to do you some profound good.

Third, simplify your spiritual life. Try to remember that there are no perfect lives, there are no perfect people, and there are no perfect families. The word *gospel* means "good news," not guilt trip. The good news is that if you make a mistake or someone you love makes a mistake, you can repent and be forgiven. If you die or if someone you love dies, you don't stay dead. What else is there to worry about? What better news is there? If you truly believe that the Savior atoned for your sins then you will allow yourself to feel the acceptance of your heavenly parents and be filled with their unconditional love.

Ask yourself: "What is most important at this moment? Where is the love? How do I want it to feel in my heart and in my home?" The answers to those questions reveal the real melody of life. You don't have to do big, glorious, important things to have a great life, only small things with big, glorious, important love.

UNPRODUCTIVE GUILT

Most mothers feel guilty about a lot of things. It goes with the job description. For your own spiritual well-being, learn the difference between unproductive and productive guilt. Guilt is not always bad if it leads to desired change. Unproductive guilt, on the other hand, is always a loser because you feel guilty about things you have no control over.

For instance, you may feel guilty whenever your child has problems or makes unwise choices. In fact, your child has his agency and a separate destiny to fulfill. There will be times when your child feels pain or sorrow that you will want to take away. Doing so, however, is impossible. What you *can* do is offer support and love.

You may feel guilty about all the hundreds of worthwhile activities you don't get around to. Face it. You can't do everything. But you can do what is essential. Figure out what is most important and put your time and energy there.

You may feel guilty about past mistakes. But you can't change the past. You can't go back and undo anything. You have only the present. So repent today, focus on what you've learned, and get busy doing the things that are important *now*. Living in the past or the future is the surest way to miss the whole point of life . . . the beauty and power of the present moment and your ability to choose your actions and thoughts right now.

You may feel guilty about your decision to work inside or outside the home. Prayerfully decide what is best for you and your family and be flexible about options. Don't compare yourself to others or let their comments influence your feelings about your decision. Have the courage to act on the light God gives you and don't look to others for approval or praise.

Unproductive guilt will make you physically and spiritually sick. The next time you feel guilty, listen. Then ask yourself, "Is this something I can do something about?" If so, do it. If not, let it go and focus on what you can actually do something about. Learn to love yourself *with* your shortcomings and limitations and make small achievable goals to improve. In the end it boils down to mostly this: Take care of yourself and do your best. Love yourself, your children and your husband. Count your blessings.

NOT UNDERSTANDING SPIRITUALITY

Don't be fooled into thinking that leading a spiritual life is like cruising along on a long celestial highway with no potholes, rough turns, washed-out bridges, or traffic jams. Spirituality is more of a lifelong journey to self-purification and the humility to let go of things you have no true control over.

True spirituality provides you with an inner reserve that gives you the strength to trust God and know that your life has purpose and meaning, even amidst all your problems. Leading a spiritual life gives you a feeling of wholeness and connectedness with God and the universe. At the same time, it enables you to experience a feeling of incredible smallness, humility, and eternal gratitude. Spirituality means you can be gentle with yourself and others because you know that no matter how many mistakes you make, *you* are not a mistake and your divine worth never diminishes.

Everyone has difficult times of life. Like the long winter months, sometimes we just have to hold on and keep hoping for spring. The ultimate goal of life is the spiritual growth of the individual. Spiritual growth seems a solitary journey but is really a partnership with God. That celestial journey begins one step at a time.

THE SUPER-MOM SYNDROME

Many Latter-day Saint mothers believe they have to be a "super-mom" to be acceptable to God, the Church, their husbands, their children, and themselves. This leads to a tendency to confuse goals with perfection. A self-defeating loop often develops when "super-moms" discover perfection is not possible. If you have the super-mom syndrome, your most likely symptom is a belief that perfection *is* possible and *you* are simply failing to achieve it.

This leads to depression, which is an even more serious problem. Fortunately, there are healthy ways to treat this syndrome:

• Once a day, take the pressure off yourself to be perfect by understanding that perfection is not possible in this life.

• Tell yourself three times a day, especially at mealtime, "I do not have to be super-mom."

• Remind yourself each night before retiring that you are not just a bundle of labels or roles, such as mother and wife. You are a child of God and a unique beautiful woman with a separate destiny to fulfill.

• Take a healthy dose of diversification. Love yourself and your family enough to diversify your life by having interests other than your husband and children.

• Prescribe yourself the healing medicine of time. Take an hour a day to do something just for yourself.

• Practice soul aerobics by learning to pace yourself. You can't do everything. Do less, much less with more love.

• Make friends with other women. Develop close friendships. Don't expect your husband to supply all your emotional needs.

You will know you are recovering from super-mom syndrome when you develop symptoms of inner peace. When you have inner peace you will observe the following things happening to you:

• You will find yourself thinking and acting in the present rather than the past. You will display an undeniable ability to enjoy the present moment.

• You will lose your desire to judge yourself and others.

• You will lose all interest in conflict and contention.

• You will feel frequent, overwhelming feelings of gratitude and awe.

• You will often find yourself feeling a deep connection to other people and nature.

• You will often feel the susceptibility to receive love from others and give it without keeping score.

• You will find yourself *letting* things happen around you and losing the desire to *make* things happen.

• You will lose interest in interpreting other's actions and start accepting people just as they are.

DEALING WITH PROBLEMS IN LIFE

Your attitude about what happens to you is the only thing you have control over. You *can't* control the events and people in your life. You *can* control your thoughts and your ability to look for the positive in every situation. You *always* have a choice. Most mothers have a suffering Sheba and a Grateful Gert vying for supremacy inside their heads. Suffering Sheba and Grateful Gert are the attitude toads. Let me illustrate with their latest barnyard adventure.

Sheba and Gert were hopping through the barn croaking to each other one day and forgot to look where they were going.

Wouldn't you know it, they both hopped right in to a big vat of milk . . . kerplunk.

Now, Suffering Sheba was a very realistic frog who prided herself in looking at life with a seasoned, mature eye. She took one look at her situation and sighed, "Big vat of milk. No way out. Gert, why did you distract me like that?! This is all your fault! I hate you and never want to speak to you again! Why are bad things always happening to me? I haven't done anything to deserve this. Why didn't God stop this from happening? It's not fair. It's no use."

So Suffering Sheba became very depressed for quite a while and finally drowned in the large vat of milk.

Now, Grateful Gert, on the other hand, took a look around her and said, "Big vat of milk, no way out. Well, let's see . . . why, I haven't had time for my daily cardiovascular workout. This is the perfect opportunity."

So Gert backstroked herself around the vat several times, all the while singing her favorite tune. When she got tired, she stopped, dog paddled for a few moments, then took a refreshing milk shake break. Then she dove, twirled and even tried a few difficult swimming stunts she'd never tried before.

After a while the milk seemed to be getting thicker and harder for Gert to swim in. This was a new problem for Gert, and she reasoned that she must be getting a little winded. So she floated on her back, rested, and whistled. When she felt her energy come back she zippity-do-dahed herself back and forth through the milk then zigzagged, whirled, and hooted.

Gert was in the vat of milk for a long time. Because she wanted to make good use of her time, she also mentally prepared her next Sunday School lesson and planned next year's family vacation. Before Gert knew what had hit her, that big vat of milk suddenly turned into sweet butter. It was thick enough that she could climb up and hop right out.

"What an adventure," Gert exclaimed. "Boy is this going to make a good story for the grandkids someday."

Mothers are given a choice each time they are presented with a problem. Like Gert and Sheba, you can feel sorry for yourself, get depressed, blame other people, curse God, and give up. Or you can solve the problem. You may even discover that your problem is really the means of your rescue. I once heard someone say she used to have motherhood pity parties for herself almost every day until she discovered she was the only person who attended and there were never any refreshments served.

Between the time you are presented with a problem and the time you respond there is a space of power and freedom in which you choose your response. In that space of choice lies your potential for growth and happiness. Each problem that comes your way is asking you for a response, not just a knee-jerk reaction.

We all have the tendency to avoid problems and the emotional pain that comes with them. It's human to avoid pain. Yet pain is the pathway to growth. Most of us want to avoid guilt. Yet guilt is the opportunity to change. Everybody wants to avoid death. Yet death is the incentive to take responsible action now. Those who choose to have a grateful heart are also those who accept problems as life's gifts waiting to be discovered.

You can't solve your problems by avoiding them. You have to solve problems by solving them. A meaningful life is full of joy *and* pain. If you can't feel acute pain, you can't feel transcendent joy. That is the deal. You can't have one without the other. Ask any new mother when she is holding her newborn if the pain she just went through is worth the reward and I know what her answer will be.

There is a truth in life that whispers to you if you're listening. Spring always follows winter. The sun always rises after the darkest night. Pain is inevitable, but suffering is optional. The next time Suffering Sheba and Grateful Gert are vying for control, choose wisely.

SCORING YOURSELF TOO EARLY IN THE GAME OF MOTHERHOOD

How do you know if you're winning or losing the motherhood game? Watching my son play football in high school helped me find the answer. When my 16-year-old son decided he wanted to play football he was a junior. He soon found out that everyone on the team had been playing football for years. He felt uncomfortable and embarrassed because he didn't know what was going on during practice.

Being a mother is like that. One happy day after deciding you want to play motherhood, you find yourself holding a brand new human being in your arms and the game begins. It feels like everyone around you has been playing this game for years and you are the only "rookie."

During football season, my son made it a habit to study the offensive and defensive plays from his coach's notebook in the evenings. He also watched college and professional teams with a new eye to learn and improve. He often asked his dad to videotape his games so he could watch replays and critique himself. He continually devised new plans to improve. He asked for and took advice from his father and worked hard at every practice.

My son beamed after the successful completions of some plays but worked on ways to improve his game plan after the less than successful completion of others. He definitely felt discouraged at times, but he never wanted to quit. He believed that if he worked hard and kept trying he'd improve. He made sure he ate nutritious food, slept eight hours a night, and exercised every day. He also ached in a thousand places he didn't even know existed before football season. His ultimate goal was to play on the  varsity team and earn a letterman's jacket.

The rewards for motherhood aren't quite as tangible or immediate as playing on the varsity mother's squad or earning a wonder woman's jacket. It's even hard to know if the family game is won or lost at the end of the day or even at the end of a lifetime.

Motherhood is a lot like playing football. If you want to improve you have to ask for advice from your Father through honest prayer and thoughtful scripture study. It also helps to study your coach's offensive and defensive playbook by listening to the prophet and other priesthood leaders. Improvement is slow but sure when you take good care of your physical body and make sure you have a nutritious diet and get plenty of exercise and adequate rest. You can make a specific plan to improve each week through sincere repentance and taking the sacrament.

My son's football team had a losing season. Yet even at the end of all his games, banged up, bruised and swollen, he was making plans for what he could do better next year.

"I've learned some great stuff this year, Mom," my son said. "Even if my team didn't win much, I think I got a little better each game and I really want to keep trying."

All mothers realize—some sooner, some later—that they don't have total control over whether their team wins or loses each year. Real families are full of victories and failure, joy and sorrow. Children who are loved and protected sometimes grow up to be strong, well-adjusted, and loving adults, and sometimes they don't.

There is no direct correlation between the quality of the mothering and the outcome of the child. Every single member of the family team has an important role to play and contributes to the outcome of the game. Yet there is a direct correlation between the quality of mothering and the individual growth of the woman who does that mothering.

So while you're working hard at the sacred craft of soul caring . . . don't give up. There is no clear and easy path through the overwhelming and conflicting commitments you have to your husband, children, extended family, friends, church, and community. Mothers need the hope that no matter what the statistics are at the end of the game, there will always be another season to be played.

DEALING WITH TOUGH PROBLEMS

Mothers face a myriad of challenges, trials, and heartache in rearing and teaching their children. Latter-day Saint mothers, however, have the revealed gospel of Jesus Christ and access to the power of the priesthood to aid them in this often-treacherous endeavor. Many Latter-day Saint moms pull their families through financial trouble, toddler troubles, and teenage troubles and never face some of

454 Renewing the Spirit

the uglier evils in the world. Unfortunately, some wickedness still takes place in homes where righteous mothers and daughters of God are doing the best they can: children are abused, teens are lured into drug use, and spouses deal with addictions or other destructive behavior.

What follows is not meant to be a comprehensive look at the worldly problems that can sneak into Latter-day Saint homes. Dealing with problems such as child abuse, drug addiction, and pornography requires reading from much more detailed material written by expert psychologists, medical doctors, counselors, and Church leaders. It also requires immediate intervention by specialists who can get your loved ones the help they need. If you suspect that any of these problems exist in your home, talk to your bishop. He will help you make the first step in dealing with these destructive issues.

ABUSE

Child abuse is evil and invalidates the very soul of a child. It destroys, deceives, confuses, controls, diminishes, and discourages. Mothers should never abuse their children in any way. Failure to protect children from the mistreatment of others, including your spouse and other siblings, is just as serious as the abuse itself.

Your relationship with your child, especially in his early years, will have a profound effect on the rest of his life. If abuse exists in your family's past, open the windows of your home to the light and love of the Savior and end that cycle. Promote healing, laughter, spontaneity, joy, service, and human empathy.

As your child's mother, it is vital that you recognize all forms of abuse and protect your child at all costs. Never forget that you are profoundly influencing the formation of your child's soul. The following information briefly outlines three different forms of abuse and the behaviors from which they are comprised.

Physical abuse includes, but is not limited to, slapping, shaking, scratching, squeezing, hitting, beating, throwing, pushing, whipping, shoving, or overworking. Physical neglect includes withholding healthy and appropriate physical affection. Not providing adequate protection from the elements, necessary nutrition, or needed medical care is also a form of physical neglect.

Sexual abuse includes, but is not limited to, inappropriate touching, leering, and sexual punishments like enemas. Sexual abuse includes any sexual contact between parent and child. Exposing your child to inappropriate movies, jokes, language, magazines, or Internet material can also be a form of sexual abuse. Not teaching children about sex, puberty, menstruation, and nocturnal emissions is neglectful behavior.

Emotional abuse includes, but is not limited to, threatening, name calling, put downs, belittling comments, the silent treatment, constant criticism, yelling, angry outbursts, expecting children to meet parent's emotional needs, letting children into marital arguments, perfectionism, inability to express feelings, sending double messages, withdrawing affection, and manipulation. Emotional abuse is also the refusal to provide adequate praise, encouragement, interest, and time for your child. Neglect, abandonment, and insufficient supervision or discipline are also forms of emotional abuse.

SEEKING HELP FOR ABUSIVE BEHAVIOR

If you or your spouse need help in understanding and changing abusive behavior, turn to your bishop. He will counsel you and may recommend counselors in LDS Family Services or other community or private resources that provide help consistent with the standards of the Church. Children never deserve to be abused. Children need love, kindness, affection, time, love, and nurturing. Never use your power over your child to abuse him in any way.

Abuse often runs in families and is kept secret from those outside the family circle. Have the courage to name the abuse and be the person to stop the cycle. Secrets can destroy families if voluntary confession, repentance, and the cleansing power of the atonement of Jesus Christ is never used.

Your family's ultimate survival will hinge on your ability to change yourself. Your dedication to reality and truth is worth every effort.

You are a player in the ultimate battle of good versus evil. Jesus Christ already won the battle over sin and death. The final battle, over individual men's souls, is still raging. God gave you your agency and never uses his power to force or harm you. God's work and glory is to bring to pass the immortality and eternal life of man. He wants to bless and lift you as much as you will let him.

ADDICTIONS

Church members are not immune to devastating addictions. Maintaining a righteous, obedient, and pure lifestyle takes work. Satan is constantly at the door, hoping you and your children will let him into your homes and your life. Although we may do all we can to rear righteous children and help our spouses keep their covenants, we can't control another's agency. If a loved one seems to be facing a

particular problem or addiction, do the best you can to help and understand. If that addiction is harming others in the family or making your home a residence for evil, you may have to make difficult decisions about removing that person from the home or moving others in the home to a safe location.

At the heart of all addictions are personal feelings of loneliness, sadness, fear, anger, shame, rejection, or guilt. The addiction is a symptom of a larger problem that needs to be dealt with. Never hesitate to seek help from your bishop and competent professionals who work within the standards of the Church.

You may be surprised at all the things in the world that lead to addictions. They include alcohol, caffeine, cults, danger, drugs, exercise, food, gambling, illegal drugs, nicotine, nonprescription drugs, pornography, power, prescription drugs, reading, relationships, sex, spending, stress, television, and work.

UNDERSTANDING BASIC HUMAN NEEDS

If you suspect that you, your child, or your spouse has an addiction, get professional help. Pray for understanding and guidance. Educate yourself about the addiction and its symptoms and root causes.

Make sure you have an understanding of basic human needs. Those needs include unconditional acceptance, security, love, structure, stimulation, and spiritual guidance. If you have supplied these needs for your child—after accepting responsibility for your own actions, fulfilling your own spiritual needs, and acquiring the self-discipline

needed to delay your own gratification—you have likely done everything you can to help your child.

You can turn to the Lord and those who have been trained to treat and heal children and adults with addictions. Trust in the Lord; rely on the promises granted to all parents who live worthy and honor the covenants they have made in the temple. And don't forget that blessings are often a long time in coming.

TROUBLED PARENTS AND CHILDREN

TROUBLED PARENTS

Many women struggle with the role of motherhood because they drag around a ball and chain that was affixed in their own family of origin. Don't feel alone if you are the victim of past abuse.

If you lack the blessing of coming from a healthy, functional family, you should not feel doomed to repeat the same unhealthy behavior with your own children. You may not have received the nurturing you needed as a child, but you can still give that needed nurturing to your children with God's guidance.

You may need to get help to heal yourself first. Talk to a bishop, a trusted friend, your spouse, or your doctor about ways to face your problems. Sometimes you can heal yourself and change your behavior through concerted effort, study, prayer, and meditation. President Boyd K. Packer said, "True doctrine, understood, changes attitudes and behavior. The study of the doctrines of the gospel will improve behavior quicker than a study of behavior will improve behavior" (*Ensign,* November 1986, 17). Some women, however, may need professional counseling or prescription medicines to overcome the devastation caused by abuse or the chemical imbalances that cause depression and darkness to seep into their lives. Always remember that healing yourself will help your child because you will be able to give him a whole and healthy mother who has the capacity to love and be loved.

Now that you are an adult, you can choose to allow the love of God and Jesus Christ to heal and nurture you. You can provide for yourself those things you missed as a child. Because of the atonement of Jesus Christ, you can be free of the effects of your past life. The Atonement not only helps you to repent but also gives you the ability to forgive.

TROUBLED CHILDREN

Your success as a mother does not rest solely on how your children turn out. Don't assume it is your fault if your child makes unwise or dangerous choices. Undeserved maternal guilt doesn't accomplish much. Could it be possible that God gave this particular child to you because He knew He could trust you to love that child no matter what? Our Father and Mother in Heaven are perfect parents; yet many of their children make unwise choices every day.

Never give up hope for you or your child. Honest and moral mothers don't always raise honest and moral children. Some children who are loved and cherished grow up well adjusted and strong, but some don't. Some well-meaning parents have children who struggle with unwise choices all their lives. There are no perfect families or individuals. All families and individuals are diverse and complex.

One of the most difficult things in life is to love someone who continues to make destructive choices. Sin *doesn't* diminish the worth of a soul. Sin blocks personal progression. So keep trying. Don't get discouraged. Hang in there. The race is not over yet. God is not through with you or your child. Keep putting one foot in front of the other. You and your child are the work and the glory of God. He is not through loving and blessing you or your child—not ever.

REALITY

Real mothers, contrary to many Sunday School Mother's Day tributes, are not

always heroic and strong. Real mothers are not perfect examples of human virtue. Real mothers burn the toast, lose their patience, and fail to meet their children's needs. Real mothers sometimes lose their marbles and their minds. Real mothers sometimes feel overwhelmed and get discouraged. No matter how imperfect you may be, however, you can still choose to love.

You will have days of deep discouragement. The vast majority of parents will have a child who chooses to abandon their rules and values for a time. There is no certainty in this motherhood business. In the majority of cases, good parenting produces relatively stable, trouble-free adults,

but there are no guarantees. Even in the best cases, most of the rewards of mothering are long in coming. In the worst cases, the rewards don't seem to come at all. But I do believe all your effort, loving, and caring do count—if not for the child, then unknowingly for yourself.

Mothers with troubled children always seem to change from people who know all the answers to people asking the important questions. They become searching, nonjudgmental human beings. Hopefully they can see what God sees: a beautiful woman who has never given up looking for ways to love and bless her child. A successful mother has loved, served, sacrificed, taught and lead her child. If your child is still wayward, you are still a successful mother.

In time, your child will come to his own understanding of life and loss. Yet your child may require many difficult experiences before he can grow into who he is meant to be. In the end, all roads lead back home. Make sure there is always a home in your heart to return to. No matter how far he strays, be patient, be loving, be forgiving, be still, and trust God.

THINGS I WISH MY MOTHER HAD TOLD ME

- Problems are always happening because you are still alive.
- Your problems are ordinary. You, however, are extraordinary.
- If you can't change the situation, change yourself.
- You can accept what life hands to you. Without pain and death, life would not be complete.
- When you forgive, you accept pain as part of life but you choose not to suffer.
- Forgiveness empowers the injured. There is no way to genuinely forgive without experiencing a great deal of personal growth.
- When you say, "I forgive," it means "I let it go." Forgiveness allows healing regardless of the location or the attitude of the offender.
- There is no escape from problems by avoidance. They always have a way of catching up to you no matter how fast you run.
- Don't assume it is your fault every time your child makes an unwise choice with his life. Maternal guilt doesn't accomplish much.
- Be gentle with yourself. No matter how many mistakes you make, you are never a mistake.
- Take time to pray every day. Take time for friends. Take time for work. Take time to think, read, laugh, love, dream, play, and worship.
- The greatest purpose in life is serving and helping others.
- Pain is an opportunity for growth. Guilt is the opportunity to change. Death is the incentive to take responsible action now.
- We are all given the same amount of time in an hour, day, week, or year. The only variable is that we don't know how much time we have before we die.
- Whatever doesn't kill you will make you stronger. You will know from your own personal experience that you can survive at least that one.
- Don't complain about getting older. The only alternative is dying young.
- If you learn to love what you have to do, you don't have to do it anymore—you get to do it.
- You want your child to be wiser after your guidance—not just sorry he got caught.
- You will never regret the time you sacrificed for your child.
- Self-worth is a byproduct of a life wisely lived.

RENEWING THE SPIRIT END NOTES

The spiritual education of your child concerns the person your child becomes on the inside. As your child's first example and teacher, your opportunity and responsibility is to find loving ways to invite your child to make choices that are kind and wise, choices that will eventually lead him to make and keep sacred covenants in the house of the Lord.

As you and your spouse focus on the mission of the Church—which is to come unto Christ—you will discover that the same mission applies to your own children and family. Following it will lead your family through life and onto the path of eternal progression. Work together, right in your own home, to perfect the Saints, proclaim the gospel, and redeem the dead. Teach your children to pray, study the scriptures, and understand the important doctrines of the gospel. As you do, you will be building your child's character and instilling a sense of self-worth that comes from an inner belief that he is a child of God and an integral part of your family circle.

Children are spiritually broken when their mothers don't feel and demonstrate true love for them. If you do nothing else for your child, love him—love him unconditionally with all your heart and soul.

Love him deeply and sincerely. Always remember that you won't become a better mother by changing your child, but by changing yourself. You can't force your child into heaven. But you can use persuasion, gentleness, meekness, and long-suffering—as well as good humor,
playfulness, and fun—to draw your child to Christ.

Your mother love is sacred and will always be needed to provide nourishment and life. Like fresh bread, it must be made new each day. The most sacred place on earth should be your home, where eternal, loving relationships are being formed. Work to create a spiritually health family.

In a spiritually healthy family, children experience Christlike love and gentle guidance, parents are more concerned about truth and reality than appearances and hiding flaws, and family members apply the atonement of Jesus Christ every day through personal repentance and forgiveness. In spiritually healthy families, children have the opportunity to be individuals while still contributing to the good of the family as a whole. They learn to put others' needs ahead of their own while still retaining a sense of wholeness and individual completeness because their mothers personally demonstrate these attributes every day.

Spiritually healthy families are about joy, even in sadness. They find ways to

make time sacred by sharing unconditional love that is rich, distinct, and extraordinary. Whether they are eating meals, working in the yard, or playing ball, spiritually healthy families try to find something to appreciate and enjoy in every family member every day.

Unhurried time together shelters families. Good cooking takes time. Regular mealtimes require time. Touching, lively conversations, hugs, good-bye kisses, reading aloud—all these things done with love take time and make everyday family life holy, for all things are spiritual to God.

Creating a loving family will be your most enduring legacy. The most profound speech I ever heard at a funeral was given by a young man who stood at the pulpit and wept for a long time before he could compose himself enough to say these words, "She loved me." That was all he said before he sat down. If someone can say those words about you when you die, you will have lived a life that truly mattered. Your life can be irreplaceable by living and loving so that your husband and children become heart of your heart and soul of your soul. That may not get you on a magazine cover, but it will get you back to your heavenly parents sealed to your loved ones. Heaven will be the continuation of a loving family and exaltation will be eternal increase forever.

Your children need your time, affection, attention, and spiritual guidance. Offer it. Stop waiting for your children to be perfect and delight in their agency. Stop waiting to feel up to the task and jump in with both feet. Make your home a sanctuary from the world by offering your child one place in the world where he is loved simply because he is himself.

One important caution: your child will be scarred by a mother who lives with personal worthiness issues or emotional problems but refuses to acknowledge them or deal with them. Much of the craziness in families comes when members run away from painful personal truths. Unresolved sin can destroy families.

Truth heals. Applying the atonement of Jesus Christ is the answer for all family problems and pain. Through Jesus Christ, all individuals and families can be forgiven and made whole. If there is anything in your past or present life that is not in harmony with the teachings of Jesus Christ, decide to rid yourself and your family of that burden of sin. Release yourself and future generations from the effects of sin by sincere repentance. Let the Savior make you new again and heal your heart. Let Jesus Christ be your personal Savior and free your posterity.

Life eventually teaches you what is most important, and what is most important is . . . family. That's it. Any other career is a means to a life, but it isn't a life. The love and service you offer your family are the most important labors you will ever perform. So surround yourself with work that really matters. The radiant transformation motherhood offers you is that your life becomes irreplaceable as you choose to give it away without thought of return, reward, or recognition.

Your greatest challenges and rewards in this life will come from mastering yourself and loving and serving your family. God bless you, my dear friend, in this your most perilous, joyous, and meaningful journey.

NOTES

IMPORTANT INFORMATION, FAVORITE WEB SITES, AND GOOD BOOKS FOR RENEWING THE SPIRIT

INDEX